8.99

THE NEW CAMBRIDGE SHAKESPEARE

GENERAL E
Brian Gibbo

ASSOCIATE
A. R. Braun

From the pu
Shakespeare
Robin Hood
General Edi

THE TRA

For this upc
section on r
account of S
the play; a d
Jay Halio
question of i
quarto and t
from Shakes
seventeenth
the differenc
means of a s
annotated pa

THE NEW CAMBRIDGE SHAKESPEARE

All's Well That Ends Well, edited by Russell Fraser
Antony and Cleopatra, edited by David Bevington
As You Like It, edited by Michael Hattaway
The Comedy of Errors, edited by T. S. Dorsch
Coriolanus, edited by Lee Bliss
Cymbeline, edited by Martin Butler
Hamlet, edited by Philip Edwards
Julius Caesar, edited by Marvin Spevack
King Edward III, edited by Giorgio Melchiori
The First Part of King Henry IV, edited by Herbert Weil and Judith Weil
The Second Part of King Henry IV, edited by Giorgio Melchiori
King Henry V, edited by Andrew Gurr
The First Part of King Henry VI, edited by Michael Hattaway
The Second Part of King Henry VI, edited by Michael Hattaway
The Third Part of King Henry VI, edited by Michael Hattaway
King Henry VIII, edited by John Margeson
King John, edited by L. A. Beaurline
The Tragedy of King Lear, edited by Jay L. Halio
King Richard II, edited by Andrew Gurr
King Richard III, edited by Janis Lull
Love's Labour's Lost, edited by William C. Carroll
Macbeth, edited by A. R. Braunmuller
Measure for Measure, edited by Brian Gibbons
The Merchant of Venice, edited by M. M. Mahood
The Merry Wives of Windsor, edited by David Crane
A Midsummer Night's Dream, edited by R. A. Foakes
Much Ado About Nothing, edited by F. H. Mares
Othello, edited by Norman Sanders
Pericles, edited by Doreen DelVecchio and Antony Hammond
The Poems, edited by John Roe
Romeo and Juliet, edited by G. Blakemore Evans
The Sonnets, edited by G. Blakemore Evans
The Taming of the Shrew, edited by Ann Thompson
The Tempest, edited by David Lindley
Timon of Athens, edited by Karl Klein
Titus Andronicus, edited by Alan Hughes
Troilus and Cressida, edited by Anthony B. Dawson
Twelfth Night, edited by Elizabeth Story Donno
The Two Gentlemen of Verona, edited by Kurt Schlueter
The Two Noble Kinsmen, edited by Robert Kean Turner and Patricia Tatspaugh
The Winter's Tale, edited by Susan Snyder and Deborah T. Curren-Aquino

THE EARLY QUARTOS

The First Quarto of Hamlet, edited by Kathleen O. Irace
The First Quarto of King Henry V, edited by Andrew Gurr
The First Quarto of King Lear, edited by Jay L. Halio
The First Quarto of King Richard III, edited by Peter Davison
The First Quarto of Othello, edited by Scott McMillin
The First Quarto of Romeo and Juliet, edited by Lukas Erne
The Taming of a Shrew: The 1594 Quarto, edited by Stephen Roy Miller

THE TRAGEDY OF KING LEAR

Updated edition

Edited by
JAY L. HALIO
Emeritus Professor of English, University of Delaware

CAMBRIDGE
UNIVERSITY PRESS

CAMBRIDGE UNIVERSITY PRESS
Cambridge, New York, Melbourne, Madrid, Cape Town,
Singapore, São Paulo, Delhi, Tokyo, Mexico City

Cambridge University Press
The Edinburgh Building, Cambridge CB2 2RU, UK

Published in the United States of America by Cambridge University Press, New York

www.cambridge.org
Information on this title: www.cambridge.org/9780521612630

© Cambridge University Press 1992, 2005

First published 1992
Twelfth printing 2004
Updated edition 2005
4th printing 2012

Printed in the United Kingdom at the University Press, Cambridge

A catalogue record for this book is available from the British Library

ISBN-13 978-0-521-84791-9 Hardback
ISBN-13 978-0-521-61263-0 Paperback

IN MEMORIAM
PHILIP BROCKBANK, 1922–1989

CONTENTS

ILLUSTRATIONS

Illustrations 1 and 2 are reproduced by permission of the Syndics of Cambridge University Library; illustrations 5, 8, 9, 10, 11 and 14 by permission of the Shakespeare Centre Library, Stratford-upon-Avon; illustrations 12 and 13 by permission of Joe Cocks Studio; illustration 16 by permission of the Estate of Tennessee Williams and the University of Delaware Library; illustration 17 by permission of New Directions Publishing Corporation and Martin Secker and Warburg Ltd; and illustration 15 by the Shakespeare Theatre.

PREFACE

For over two hundred years editors of *King Lear* have based their work on the theory that the two early texts of the play, the first quarto of 1608 and the Folio of 1623, represent incomplete and faulty approximations of the play as Shakespeare originally wrote it. This single-text theory, so-called, is in the judgement of many scholars today no longer viable. In their view, an alternative theory – that Q and F (as they are known) represent different versions of the play – must replace it. These scholars believe that the quarto, poorly printed by Nicholas Okes's compositors in the winter of 1607–8, derives from an early manuscript copy in Shakespeare's hand, and that the Folio derives from a considerably altered and revised version, one more closely approximating the play as the author visualised it in performance, or as the King's Men actually staged it in the period between its first performances and the third decade of the seventeenth century.

The implications of the alternative, or revision, hypothesis are significant for a modern editor, who must now decide which version to follow as his copy-text. The advocates of a quarto-based edition have strong arguments to support them; so do those who advocate a Folio-based edition. Final choice will depend upon one's preference for an early manuscript version, as reflected in the first printed edition, however corrupt or incomplete, or for a revised version of the play which, though in many respects offering a better text, involves problems of its own. Among those problems is the vexed question of revision and the issue of authenticity or legitimacy that revision, including authorial revision, raises.

Recently revision and the issue of intentionality it involves have also come under renewed scrutiny by theoretical and practical critics alike. If years have passed between the original composition and the revision (in the case of *King Lear*, perhaps more than five years), may it not be argued that the original creative impulse and sense of design have long since vanished, that the author can no longer be sure what he intended? My colleague, Hershel Parker, has asked just such questions and provided answers to them in his stimulating enquiry, *Flawed Texts and Verbal Icons* (1984). Using examples from American fiction, he maintains that authors may be subjected to pressures and motives having to do with commercial viability or public taste or other matters that are irrelevant to the composition at hand and which are extrinsic to the creative process. Much of his argument is of course applicable to other forms of literature, perhaps even – or especially – to plays, which are above all forms of literature highly susceptible to the pressures of production, box-office concerns, shifts in taste or decorum (not to mention morality), and so forth. But it is precisely here that plays also differ from novels or poems in that they are, by their very nature, collaborative undertakings. A play by Shakespeare, no less than one by Tennessee Williams, Tom Stoppard, or Eugène Ionesco, is seldom the same on the boards as in the playwright's study. And it may change from production to production, revival to revival, raising questions about the nature of the play as well as its interpretation.[1] In the quarto and the Folio, *King Lear* presents two significantly different versions of Shakespeare's play, one closer to the composition as he originally conceived it (Q), the other closer to an actual staged production after revision (F). The two versions involve a host of variant readings in addition to unique passages, alternative speech assignments, missing stage directions, and other divergences, besides numerous printer's errors. Editors have hitherto thought that by conflating, or splicing, the two versions they could approach what they assumed to be the 'ideal' form of the play, apparently lost; but this belief violates theatrical tradition and otherwise has little to support it.

Establishing the definitive text of such a fluid enterprise as a play is in its evolution from conception through performance under a variety of exigencies becomes impossible, unless one arbitrarily decides (as past scholars usually have done) that the last published version in the author's lifetime in which the author had a hand is 'definitive'. Questions about the soundness of this procedure aside, what if the author had no hand in the publication of the work? Shakespeare was dead before half of his plays were published, and it is uncertain what role, if any, he played in the publication of any of the others, including *King Lear* in 1608. Although he oversaw the printing of his long poems, *Venus and Adonis* and *The Rape of Lucrece*, dedicated to his patron Southampton, he apparently cared much less about the publication of his dramatic works, leaving to generations of scholars the fascinating problems of establishing an authentic, if not definitive, edition of his plays. An authentic, not definitive, edition of *King Lear* is the goal of this one. Founded on a fresh examination of the texts as well as on the best available scholarship and criticism regarding the text, the total historical context (including theatrical data), and the study of extant sources, this edition tries to provide a clear, up-to-date, readable, and reliable version based on the Folio text of Shakespeare's *King Lear*. Throughout, the emphasis is upon the play *as a play*, not just a literary document, though it is that too, of course, and the Commentary accordingly ignores neither aspect of the work.

Modern editors of Shakespeare owe enormous debts to the countless scholars, editors, critics, and theatre professionals who have preceded them. Wherever possible, I have tried to record specific debts in footnotes or Commentary, but more generalised and personal debts must be acknowledged here. Many friends and scholars have lent assistance by reviewing various parts of the typescript in preparation and making invaluable suggestions and often corrections of error or misunderstanding. Donald Foster, Trevor Howard-Hill, and Gary Taylor all read the Textual Analysis in its original form; it appears here much changed as a result of their suggestions and those of Philip Brockbank who, until his death, served as General Editor of the New Cambridge Shakespeare. Thomas Clayton, Richard Knowles, and George Walton Williams read the original *and* the revised versions of that analysis – a service well beyond the call of collegiality and friendship. Indeed, Thomas Clayton read all of the Introduction, except

---

[1] So, too, poems may change from one printing to another, in new editions or new anthologies, as the texts of Robert Lowell's early poetry attest. See Hugh Staples, *Robert Lowell: The First Twenty Years*, 1962.

the stage history, which Marvin Rosenberg read in an earlier form. Philip Brockbank also vetted the original version of the section on dates and sources, which (like the Textual Analysis) has been entirely reorganised and revised according to his recommendations. I am sure, had he lived, he would have made further recommendations concerning other sections of the Introduction, which then would have profited from his advice and counsel. Since his death, Brian Gibbons, who has succeeded him as General Editor, has been of great assistance, offering many suggestions and not a few corrections of detail. It was, in fact, his suggestion to follow the example of John Hazel Smith's edition of *Bussy D'Ambois*, and include a sampling of parallel passages from quarto and Folio to highlight the kinds of changes that occur between them. The Associate General Editors, Robin Hood and A. R. Braunmuller, have also been most helpful in making suggestions and corrections. Sarah Stanton has advised me on various aspects of format and procedure, and Paul Chipchase's copy-editing has been both thorough and acutely perceptive. To all of these dedicated professionals, I express my gratitude and exempt them from any errors or infelicities that remain. They are of my own making and my own responsibility.

Several scholars have generously permitted me to see their work in typescript or in proof. Among them are J. Leeds Barroll, Peter Blayney, Frank Brownlow, G. Blakemore Evans, F. D. Hoeniger, Arthur King, Alexander Leggatt, and Stanley Wells. Others have kindly sent me offprints or pre-prints of articles or have answered queries concerning some aspect of *King Lear*. These scholars have demonstrated once again that Shakespearean – indeed, all – scholarship at its best is always a collaborative venture.

I must also express gratitude to the following libraries and their staffs, who have been unfailingly co-operative and helpful: the University of Delaware Library, the Folger Shakespeare Library, the British Library, the Shakespeare Centre Library, and the Library of Congress. Several graduate students and secretarial staff have assisted in various aspects of research or preparation: Kate Rodowsky, Patience Philips, Susan Savini, Suzanne Potts, and Victoria Gray cheerfully carried out duties that must often have seemed at least tedious. To the Trustees of the University of Delaware, I owe thanks for awarding me a sabbatical leave in the autumn term of 1987 and for a research grant in the summer of 1988. Such assistance has greatly facilitated work on this edition.

J. L. H.

ABBREVIATIONS AND CONVENTIONS

Shakespeare's plays, when cited in this edition, are abbreviated in a style modified slightly from that used in the *Harvard Concordance to Shakespeare*. Other editions of Shakespeare are abbreviated under the editor's surname (Theobald, Duthie) unless they are the work of more than one editor. In such cases, an abbreviated series title is used (Cam.). When more than one edition by the same editor is cited, later editions are discriminated with a raised figure (Rowe²). All quotations from Shakespeare, except those from *King Lear*, use the text and lineation of *The Riverside Shakespeare*, under the general editorship of G. Blakemore Evans.

1. Shakespeare's plays

Ado	*Much Ado About Nothing*
Ant.	*Antony and Cleopatra*
AWW	*All's Well That Ends Well*
AYLI	*As You Like It*
Cor.	*Coriolanus*
Cym.	*Cymbeline*
Err.	*The Comedy of Errors*
Ham.	*Hamlet*
1H4	*The First Part of King Henry the Fourth*
2H4	*The Second Part of King Henry the Fourth*
H5	*King Henry the Fifth*
1H6	*The First Part of King Henry the Sixth*
2H6	*The Second Part of King Henry the Sixth*
3H6	*The Third Part of King Henry the Sixth*
H8	*King Henry the Eighth*
JC	*Julius Caesar*
John	*King John*
LLL	*Love's Labour's Lost*
Lear	*King Lear*
Mac.	*Macbeth*
MM	*Measure for Measure*
MND	*A Midsummer Night's Dream*
MV	*The Merchant of Venice*
Oth.	*Othello*
Per.	*Pericles*
R2	*King Richard the Second*
R3	*King Richard the Third*
Rom.	*Romeo and Juliet*
Shr.	*The Taming of the Shrew*
STM	*Sir Thomas More*
Temp.	*The Tempest*
TGV	*The Two Gentlemen of Verona*

Tim.	*Timon of Athens*
Tit.	*Titus Andronicus*
TN	*Twelfth Night*
TNK	*The Two Noble Kinsmen*
Tro.	*Troilus and Cressida*
Wiv.	*The Merry Wives of Windsor*
WT	*The Winter's Tale*

2. Other works cited and general references

Abbott	E. A. Abbott, *A Shakespearian Grammar*, 1894
Berlin	Normand Berlin, *The Secret Cause: A Discussion of Tragedy*, 1981
Bevington	*King Lear*, ed. David Bevington, 1988 (Bantam)
Blayney	Peter W. M. Blayney, *The Texts of 'King Lear' and Their Origins*, 2 vols., I (1982)
Booth	Stephen Booth, *'King Lear', 'Macbeth', Indefinition, and Tragedy*, 1983
Bradley	A. C. Bradley, *Shakespearean Tragedy*, 2nd edn, 1905
Bratton	*King Lear*, ed. J. S. Bratton, 1987 (Plays in Performance)
Brockbank	Philip Brockbank, *'Upon Such Sacrifices'*, The British Academy Shakespeare Lecture, 1976
Bullough	*Narrative and Dramatic Sources of Shakespeare*, ed. Geoffrey Bullough, 8 vols., 1957–75, VII (1973)
Cam.	*The Works of William Shakespeare*, ed. W. G. Clark, J. Glover, and W. A. Wright, 1863–6 (Cambridge Shakespeare)
Capell	*Mr William Shakespeare his Comedies, Histories, and Tragedies*, ed. Edward Capell, 10 vols., 1767–8, IX
Cavell	Stanley Cavell, *Must We Mean What We Say?*, 1969
Cercignani	Fausto Cercignani, *Shakespeare's Works and Elizabethan Pronunciation*, 1981
Chambers	E. K. Chambers, *William Shakespeare: A Study of Facts and Problems*, 2 vols., 1930
Clayton	Thomas Clayton, ' "Is this the promis'd end?": revision in the role of the king', in *Division*, pp. 121–41
Colie	Rosalie Colie, 'The energies of endurance: biblical echo in *King Lear*', in *Some Facets*, pp. 117–44
Colman	E. A. M. Colman, *The Dramatic Use of Bawdy in Shakespeare*, 1974
conj.	conjecture
corr.	corrected
Cotgrave	Randall Cotgrave, *A Dictionarie of the French and English Tongues*, 1611
Danby	John F. Danby, *Shakespeare's Doctrine of Nature*, 1948, reprinted 1961
Davenport	A. Davenport, 'Notes on *King Lear*', *N&Q*, n.s., 98 (1953), 20–2
Dent	R. W. Dent, *Shakespeare's Proverbial Language: An Index*, 1981
Division	Gary Taylor and Michael Warren (eds.), *The Division of the Kingdoms: Shakespeare's Two Versions of 'King Lear'*, 1983

Doran	Madeleine Doran, *The Text of 'King Lear'*, 1931, reprinted 1967
Duthie	*King Lear: A Critical Edition*, ed. George Ian Duthie, 1949
ELR	*English Literary Renaissance*
Elton	William Elton, *'King Lear' and the Gods*, 1966
F	*Mr William Shakespeares Comedies, Histories, and Tragedies*, 1623 (First Folio)
F2	*Mr William Shakespeares Comedies, Histories, and Tragedies*, 1632 (Second Folio)
F3	*Mr William Shakespeares Comedies, Histories, and Tragedies*, 1663–4 (Third Folio)
F4	*Mr William Shakespeares Comedies, Histories, and Tragedies*, 1685 (Fourth Folio)
FQ	Edmond Spenser, *The Faerie Queene*, 1596
Furness	*King Lear*, ed. Horace Howard Furness, 1880 (New Variorum)
Globe	*The Globe Shakespeare*, ed. W. G. Clark and W. A. Wright, 1864
Goldring	Beth Goldring, 'Cor.'s rescue of Kent', in *Division*, pp. 143–51
Granville-Barker	Harley Granville-Barker, *Prefaces to Shakespeare*, 2 vols., 1946, 1
Greg, *Editorial Problem*	W. W. Greg, *The Editorial Problem in Shakespeare*, 1942, 2nd edn, 1951
Greg, *SFF*	W. W. Greg, *The Shakespeare First Folio*, 1955
Greg, *Variants*	W. W. Greg, *The Variants in the First Quarto of 'King Lear'*, 1940
Halio	*King Lear*, ed. Jay L. Halio, 1973 (Fountainwell)
Hanmer	*The Works of Shakespear*, ed. Thomas Hanmer, 1743–4
Harbage	*King Lear*, ed. Alfred Harbage, 1958 (Penguin)
Harsnett	Samuel Harsnett, *A Declaration of Egregious Popish Impostures*, 1603
Heilman	Robert Heilman, *This Great Stage: Image and Structure in 'King Lear'*, 1948, reprinted 1963
Hinman	Charlton K. Hinman, *The Printing and Proofreading of the First Folio of Shakespeare*, 2 vols., 1963
Hoeniger	F. D. Hoeniger, *Medicine and Shakespeare in the English Renaissance*, 1992
Holland	Norman N. Holland, *The Shakespearean Imagination*, 1964
Hunter	*King Lear*, ed. G. K. Hunter, 1972 (New Penguin)
Jackson	MacDonald P. Jackson, 'Fluctuating variation: author, annotator, or actor', in *Division*, pp. 313–49
Jennens	*King Lear*, ed. Charles Jennens, 1770
Johnson	*The Plays of William Shakespeare*, ed. Samuel Johnson, 8 vols., 1765, VI
Joseph	Sister Miriam Joseph, *Shakespeare's Use of the Arts of Language*, 1947
Kerrigan	John Kerrigan, 'Revision, adaptation, and the Fool in *King Lear*', in *Division*, pp. 195–245
King	Arthur King, *Materials for the Study of 'King Lear'* (in preparation)
King Leir	*The History of King Leir* (1605) (Malone Society Reprints), 1907

Kittredge   *King Lear*, ed. George Lyman Kittredge, 1940
Kökeritz   Helge Kökeritz, *Shakespeare's Pronunciation*, 1953
Mack   Maynard Mack, *'King Lear' in Our Time*, 1965
McLeod   Randall McLeod, '*Gon*. No more, the text is foolish', in *Division*,
                  pp. 153–93
Malone   *The Plays and Poems of William Shakespeare*, ed. Edmond
                  Malone, 10 vols., 1790, VIII
Meagher   John C. Meagher, 'Vanity, Lear's feather, and the pathology of
                  editorial annotation', in Clifford Leech and J. M. R. Margeson
                  (eds.), *Shakespeare 1971*, Toronto, 1972, pp. 244–59
MLR   *Modern Language Review*
Montaigne   *The Essayes of Michael Lord of Montaigne*, trans. John Florio,
                  6 vols., 1897 (Temple Classics)
MP   *Modern Philology*
Muir   *King Lear*, ed. Kenneth Muir, 1963 (Arden)
N&Q   *Notes and Queries*
Noble   Richmond Noble, *Shakespeare's Biblical Knowledge*, 1935
NS   *King Lear*, ed. George Ian Duthie and John Dover Wilson, 1960,
                  1968 (New Shakespeare)
OED   *Oxford English Dictionary*
Onions   C. T. Onions, *A Shakespeare Glossary*, enlarged and revised,
                  Robert D. Eagleson, 1986
Oxford   *William Shakespeare: The Complete Works*, gen. eds. Stanley
                  Wells and Gary Taylor, 1986
Partridge   Eric Partridge, *Shakespeare's Bawdy*, 3rd edn, 1969
PBSA   *Papers of the Bibliographical Society of America*
Peat   Derek Peat, ' "And that's true too": *King Lear* and the tension of
                  uncertainty', *S.Sur.*, 33 (1980), 43–53
Perrett   Wilfrid Perrett, *The King Lear Story from Geoffrey of Monmouth
                  to Shakespeare*, Berlin, 1904
Pope   *The Works of Shakespear*, ed. Alexander Pope, 1723–5
Q   *M. William Shake-speare: HIS True Chronicle Historie of the life
                  and death of King Lear and his three Daughters*, 1608 (first quarto)
Q2   *M. William Shake-speare, HIS True Chronicle Historie of the life
                  and death of King Lear, and his three Daughters* [1619] (second
                  quarto)
Qq   quartos
Reibetanz   John Reibetanz, *The Lear World*, Toronto, 1977
RES   *Review of English Studies*
Riverside   *The Riverside Shakespeare*, gen. ed. G. Blakemore Evans, 1974
Rosenberg   Marvin Rosenberg, *The Masks of 'King Lear'*, 1972
Rowe   *The Works of Mr William Shakespeare*, ed. Nicholas Rowe, 6 vols.,
                  1709, V
Rowe²   *The Works of Mr William Shakespeare*, ed. Nicholas Rowe, 2nd
                  edn, 8 vols., 1714
Rubenstein   Frankie Rubenstein, *A Dictionary of Shakespeare's Sexual Puns
                  and Their Significance*, 1984
Salingar   Leo Salingar, *Dramatic Form in Shakespeare and the Jacobeans*,
                  1986

SB	*Studies in Bibliography*
Schmidt	Alexander Schmidt, *A Shakespeare-Lexicon*, 3rd edn, Breslau, 1901
Schmidt 1879	*King Lear*, ed. Alexander Schmidt, Berlin, 1879
SD	stage direction
SFNL	*Shakespeare on Film Newsletter*
SH	speech heading
Shaheen	Naseeb Shaheen, *Biblical References in Shakespeare's Tragedies*, 1987
Sisson	C. J. Sisson, *New Readings in Shakespeare*, 2 vols., 1956, II
Some Facets	Rosalie L. Colie and F. T. Flahiff (eds.), *Some Facets of 'King Lear': Essays in Prismatic Criticism*, 1974
SP	*Studies in Philology*
Spurgeon	Caroline Spurgeon, *Shakespeare's Imagery and What It Tells Us*, 1935
SQ	*Shakespeare Quarterly*
S.St.	*Shakespeare Studies*
S.Sur.	*Shakespeare Survey*
Stampfer	Judah Stampfer, 'The catharsis of *King Lear*', *S.Sur.* 13 (1960), 1–10
Staunton	*The Plays of Shakespeare*, ed. H. Staunton, 1858–60
Steevens	*The Plays of William Shakespeare*, ed. Samuel Johnson and George Steevens, 15 vols., 1793, XIV
Stone	P. W. K. Stone, *The Textual History of 'King Lear'*, 1980
subst.	substantively
Taylor, 'Censorship'	Gary Taylor, 'Monopolies, show trials, disaster, and invasion: *King Lear* and censorship', in *Division*, pp. 75–119
Taylor, 'Date and authorship'	Gary Taylor, '*King Lear*: the date and authorship of the Folio version', in *Division*, pp. 351–468
Taylor, 'New source'	Gary Taylor, 'A new source and an old date for *King Lear*', *RES* 132 (1982), 396–413
Taylor, 'War'	Gary Taylor, 'The war in *King Lear*', *S.Sur.* 33 (1980), 27–34
Textual Companion	Stanley Wells and Gary Taylor, with John Jowett and William Montgomery, *William Shakespeare: A Textual Companion*, 1987
Theobald	*The Works of Shakespeare*, ed. Lewis Theobald, 7 vols., 1733, V
uncorr.	uncorrected
Urkowitz	Steven Urkowitz, *Shakespeare's Revision of 'King Lear'*, 1980
Urkowitz, 'Editorial tradition'	Steven Urkowitz, 'The base shall to th'legitimate: the growth of an editorial tradition', in *Division*, pp. 23–43
Warburton	*The Works of Shakespeare*, ed. William Warburton, 1747, 8 vols., VI
Warren, 'Albany and Edgar'	Michael Warren, 'Quarto and Folio *King Lear* and the interpretation of Albany and Edgar', in David Bevington and Jay L. Halio (eds.), *Shakespeare: Pattern of Excelling Nature*, 1978, pp. 95–107
Warren, 'Diminution'	Michael Warren, 'The diminution of Kent', in *Division*, pp. 59–73
Warren, R.	Roger Warren, 'The Folio omission of the mock trial: motives and consequences', in *Division*, pp. 45–57

Werstine	Paul Werstine, 'Folio editors, Folio compositors, and the Folio text of *King Lear*', in *Division*, pp. 247–312
Wiles	David Wiles, *Shakespeare's Clown*, 1987
Wittreich	Joseph Wittreich, *'Image of that Horror': History, Prophecy, and Apocalypse in 'King Lear'*, 1984

Biblical quotations are taken from the Geneva Bible, 1560

THE
True Chronicle Hi.

ftory of King LEIR, and his three
daughters, *Gonorill, Ragan,*
and *Cordella.*

As it hath bene diuers and fundry
times lately acted.

LONDON,

Printed by Simon Stafford for Iohn
Wright, and are to bee fold at his fhop at
Chriftes Church dore, next Newgate
Market. 1 6 0 5.

1 The title page of the 1605 quarto of *King Leir*

INTRODUCTION

Date and sources of Shakespeare's *King Lear*

KING LEAR: DATE OF COMPOSITION AND FIRST PERFORMANCE

Although *King Lear* was probably performed earlier at the Globe, the first recorded performance of the play was at the court of King James I on St Stephen's Day during the Christmas holidays in 1606, as indicated in the Stationers' Register (26 November 1607) and proclaimed on the title page of the first quarto (1608). Both the king and the playwright must have brought to the performance a keen sense of occasion.[1] Shakespeare was a leading member of the company of actors honoured by royal patronage, the King's Men, and he knew that his play touched on a number of sensitive issues. In his first parliament, James had declared his intention of uniting the kingdoms of Scotland and England as one realm, Great Britain, restoring the ancient title and unity to the land. While he received considerable support from the lords and judges, the commons were hesitant and did not jump to ratify the proposal. Against this background of political activity, Lear's speech, 'Know, that we have divided / In three our kingdom', must have been startling indeed.[2] James was in a position to see, however, that similar material had attracted theatrical attention as early as Sackville and Norton's *Gorboduc* (1561) and *Locrine* (c. 1585) as well as *King Leir* (c. 1590); moreover, he would quickly have recognised that Shakespeare's play vividly dramatised the tragic consequences of dividing the kingdom, as opposed to unifying it.

Composition of *King Lear* had begun by spring or summer 1605, possibly sooner. Gloucester's references to 'These late eclipses in the sun and moon' (1.2.91) may allude to actual eclipses in September and October 1605. The anonymous play, 'The moste famous Chronicle historye of Leire kinge of England and His Three Daughters', first entered in the Stationers' Register on 14 May 1594 but performed earlier, was again entered (as 'the Tragecall historie') on 8 May 1605 and published, presumably for the first time, later that year. If Shakespeare's play was responsible for the revival of interest in the old play, whose title page proclaims that it was 'diuers and sundry times lately

---

[1] In the Christian calendar, St Stephen's Day (26 December) was the first of four festivals ending on New Year's Day that stressed man's folly and worldliness. Biblical readings on St Stephen's Day urged patience in adversity and the festival was celebrated by granting hospitality, especially to the poor. For these and other reasons, *King Lear* was thus an appropriate choice for the evening. See R. Chris Hassel, Jr, *Renaissance Drama and the English Church Year*, 1979, pp. 22–30, and Leah Marcus, *Puzzling Shakespeare*, 1988, pp. 148–59. In his recent edition of Harsnett's *Declaration of Egregious Popish Impostures*, Frank Brownlow speculates that Samuel Harsnett, then Bishop of Chichester, Vice-Chancellor of Cambridge University, and Master of Pembroke College, might also have been in the audience. On Shakespeare's debt to Harsnett, see below.

[2] Compare Annabel Patterson, *Censorship and Interpretation*, 1984, pp. 64–73, and Glynne Wickham, 'From tragedy to tragi-comedy: "King Lear" as prologue', *S.Sur.* 26 (1973), 33–48, who notes that the two sons of James I were at this time Duke of Cornwall and Duke of Albany. See also Wittreich, pp. 17–24.

acted', then *King Lear* must have been on the boards by early 1605.[1] On the other hand, revival of *King Leir* may have been otherwise occasioned, and composition of Shakespeare's play, clearly indebted to it, may have begun afterwards. It could not have been written before 1603, the date of Samuel Harsnett's *A Declaration of Egregious Popish Impostures*, since much of Tom o'Bedlam's language derives from that document.[2] And if *Eastward Ho* inspired several passages, then composition occurred after April 1605.[3]

THE PLAYWRIGHT'S READING

The great variety of sources of *King Lear* becomes coherent when we recall the use to which the play puts the material. Although *The Chronicle History of King Leir* was Shakespeare's principal source, the Lear story goes back as far as Geoffrey of Monmouth's *Historia Regum Brittaniae* (*c.* 1135). Shakespeare may have read this in the original Latin (no Elizabethan translation exists) or, as Bullough suggests (p. 273), he may have taken details from more recent writers who were themselves directly or indirectly indebted to the *Historia*. Geoffrey was as interested in the political implications of his *Historia* as in the social narrative; therefore, he focuses as much upon the consequence of Leir's action in dividing the kingdom between his two older daughters, as upon the initial love contest. The division eventually leads to insurrection as the two dukes, his daughters' husbands, rise up against the old king and strip him of his rights and dignities. Leir flees to France, is reunited with a forgiving Cordeilla, and finally restored to his kingdom. When he dies three years later, Cordeilla succeeds to his throne.

But the story as Geoffrey tells it is not yet over. The dissension that was Geoffrey's leitmotiv from the reign of Brut onwards continues, as Margan and Cunedag, the sons of Cordeilla's sisters, rebel against their aunt and imprison her. Overcome with despair, Cordeilla commits suicide. Further tragedy lies in store for England, as Margan and Cunedag fall out with each other, civil war ensues, and after much of the land has been laid waste, Margan is finally killed. Only then is peace restored to Britain for a prolonged period during Cunedag's reign.

Many of the later accounts of Leir and his three daughters include the episode of Cordeilla's suicide; it is told, for example, in Holinshed's *Chronicles*, Higgins's *Mirour for Magistrates*, and Spenser's *The Faerie Queene* (II.x.27–33), all of which Shakespeare knew. It may be from Cordeilla's death in these accounts that Shakespeare got the suggestion for turning the old *Chronicle History* from a tragicomedy into tragedy, although his sub-plot, borrowed from Sidney's *Arcadia*, may also have influenced him.[4] From the old play he got the basic outlines of his fable and adapted it to his own purposes, which were quite different from those of the anonymous author.

---

[1] W. W. Greg, 'The date of *King Lear* and Shakespeare's use of earlier versions of the story', *The Library*, 4th ser., 20 (1939–40), 377–400.
[2] Chambers, I, 467–70; Bullough, VII, 269–70.
[3] Taylor, 'New source', pp. 396–413.
[4] Fitzroy Pyle, '*Twelfth Night, King Lear*, and *Arcadia*', *MLR* 43 (1948), 449–55.

THE TRUE CHRONICLE HISTORY

The old play called itself a 'true chronicle history', meeting a taste for the retelling of 'true' stories from the past with often overt didactic intentions. Holinshed's *Chronicles* incorporates a span of reigns from Geoffrey of Monmouth (including Cymbeline as well as Locrine and Gorboduc), and Shakespeare was clearly interested in this early phase of British history, besides the events of the fifteenth century which he dramatised earlier in the Henriad. Unlike the anonymous *King Leir*, which is thoroughly infused with Christian pieties, Shakespeare's play is neither wholly pagan nor wholly Christian, although at certain points Lear speaks with and for the thunder as if he were indeed the thunder god himself.

Other differences between Shakespeare's play and his principal source are significant. While keeping to the main outlines of the Lear story, Shakespeare not only introduced a major second plot, inspired by the misadventures of the Paphlagonian King in Sidney's *Arcadia*; he also introduced several new characters and episodes that *King Leir* lacks, such as Lear's madness, the storm, Oswald, and the Fool (who may, however, have been suggested by the Gallian King's jesting companion, Mumford, in *King Leir*). The rather low comic relief provided by the scenes of the Watch in the anonymous play is omitted, as are several melodramatic incidents, such as Gonorill and Ragan's murder plot[1] against their father, and Perillus's offer to let a starving Leir have his arm to eat. The Gallian King has a substantial role in the old play, but Shakespeare limited him to the first scene and eliminated the Gallian Ambassador, sent to invite Leir to France, although the Ambassador's fruitless wanderings from France to Cornwall and Cambria resemble the journeys in Shakespeare's second act. In sum, Shakespeare both condensed and expanded his source to exploit its tragic potential, broaden its range, and, as F. D. Hoeniger has shown, explore the primitive aspects of the legend 'in all its depths and terror'.[2]

Perhaps the most significant alteration Shakespeare made in the Lear story is the ending. Unlike all previous accounts, *King Lear* concludes not with the old king restored to his throne, but with Cordelia and Lear dead.[3] Though France in *King Leir* invades Britain victoriously, no one dies in that play – all three sisters are spared. The wicked ones and their husbands become fugitives and are absent from the final scene, which includes no reference to the later fate of Cordella. Unlike his counterpart, Kent, Perillus is not banished, and at the end Leir rewards him for his loyalty. Departing widely from the contours of the old tragicomedy, Shakespeare thus seems intent on stripping away every possible consolation from the action to present it with the starkest reality.[4]

---

[1] In Shakespeare's play, Gloucester twice refers to such a plot (3.4.147, 3.6.45), but it is not developed.
[2] 'The artist exploring the primitive', in *Some Facets*, p. 98.
[3] In *King Lear*, Harvester New Critical Introductions to Shakespeare, 1988, pp. 6–7, Alexander Leggatt argues that Shakespeare actually compressed his sources, which include Cordelia's later death in prison, and that the happy conclusion of *King Leir* was new.
[4] For more detailed analysis of *King Leir* and *King Lear*, see Bullough, pp. 277 ff.; Muir, pp. xxvi ff.; Dorothy Nameri, *Three Versions of the Story of King Lear*, 1976, 1, 26–121; Stephen J. Lynch, 'Sin, suffering, and redemption in *Leir* and *Lear*', *S.St.* 18 (1986), 161–74.

FOOLISH FOND OLD MAN: FATHERS AND DAUGHTERS

King Lear is not only about a monarch and his divided realm, but also about a father, his property, and his three daughters. Several contemporary analogues exist, of which the most important are the events surrounding Sir Brian Annesley and his daughters, the youngest of whom was named Cordell.[1] An old servant of Queen Elizabeth, Sir Brian held an estate of some value in Kent. In October 1603 his eldest daughter, Lady Grace Wildgoose, or Wildgose, attempted to have her father certified as incompetent so that she and her husband, Sir John Wildgoose, could take over the management of his affairs. The part played by his second daughter, Christian, is unknown, but Cordell opposed the plan, successfully it appears, by appealing to Sir Robert Cecil. She argued that, given his loyalty and long service, her father deserved better than to be judged lunatic in his old age. Sir Brian died in July 1604, and the Wildgooses contested his will, since in it he left most of his property and possessions to Cordell. One of the executors was Sir William Harvey, third husband of the dowager Countess of Southampton, the mother of Shakespeare's early patron. The will was upheld, and after the countess died in 1607, Harvey married Cordell Annesley. It may be that the Annesley case was responsible, at least in part, for the revival of interest in *The True Chronicle* or for Shakespeare's rewriting it (Bullough, pp. 270–1).

FOOLISH FOND OLD MAN: FATHERS AND SONS

Shakespeare took his second plot from Sidney's *Arcadia*. Sidney's romance suggested not only a chivalric colouring, as in the duel between Edgar and Edmond, but a more epic sweep than that of the old play and its analogues. Furthermore, through the parallel story of the Earl of Gloucester, modelled on that of the Paphlagonian King, Shakespeare universalised his theme and raised it to 'cosmic' proportions: 'Lear's world becomes the entire world, and it becomes clear that Lear's fate may be the fate of any man.'[2]

Book II, chapter 10, of the *Arcadia* (1590) describes the encounter of the princes Pyrocles and Musidorus with an old blind man led by his son, Leonatus. The old man is the deposed King of Paphlagonia, dethroned and blinded by his wicked bastard son, Plexirtus, who persuaded his father first to dislike and finally to seek to destroy his elder, legitimate son. Having accomplished that, Plexirtus systematically took over control of the kingdom so that his father left himself (like Lear) 'nothing but the name of a King'.[3] Still not satiated, Plexirtus took the title, too, put out his father's eyes,

---

[1] C. J. Sisson, *Shakespeare's Tragic Justice*, 1963, pp. 80–3. G. M. Young, in 'Shakespeare and the Termers', *Today and Yesterday*, 1948, is usually credited with this discovery; but Charlotte C. Stopes quotes Cordell Annesley's letter to Lord Cecil dated 18 October 1603 in *The Life of Henry, Third Earl of Southampton, Shakespeare's Patron*, 1922, p. 274. Compare also G. P. V. Akrigg, *Shakespeare and the Earl of Southampton*, 1968, pp. 257–8.

[2] Irving Ribner, 'Sidney's *Arcadia* and the structure of *King Lear*', *Studia Neophilologica* 24 (1952), 67; but compare S. L. Goldberg, *An Essay on 'King Lear'*, 1974, p. 79. In 'The very pompes of the divell – popular and folk elements in Elizabethan and Jacobean drama', *RES* 25 (1949), 10–23, Douglas Hewitt shows how Shakespeare universalises his theme in other ways, e.g. through analogous representation of folk ceremonies, such as banishing the scapegoat, a ceremony still practised in Shakespeare's time. See esp. his pp. 18–20.

[3] Quotations are from Bullough's extracts, pp. 402–14; references are to the facsimile edition published by Kent State University Press, 1970.

THE
COVNTESSE
OF PEMBROKES
ARCADIA,

WRITTEN BY SIR PHILIPPE
SIDNEI.

LONDON
Printed for William Ponſonbie.
Anno Domini, 1590.

2   The title page of Sir Philip Sidney's *Arcadia* (1590)

and cast him off to feel his misery, 'full of wretchednes, fuller of disgrace, and fullest of guiltines'. Shunned by his countrymen, the king is reduced to seeking alms until Leonatus discovers him and leads him on his way, refusing only to help him commit suicide by jumping off a cliff.

The parallels so far to the Gloucester–Edgar–Edmond plot in *King Lear* are evident, but the differences, too, are important. Edgar conceals his identity from Gloucester during almost all of their journey together; Edmond shares Plexirtus's ambition and informs on his father but is not present at the blinding; Edgar assumes the identity of Tom o'Bedlam, feigning madness, a recourse that Leonatus does not seek. As Sidney's chapter continues, Plexirtus attempts to hunt his brother down and kill him, but he and his troops are repulsed by Pyrocles, Musidorus, and their allies. Eventually, Plexirtus is defeated, Leonatus is placed on his father's throne, and the old king dies, 'his hart broken with unkindnes and affliction, stretched so farre beyond his limits with this excesse of comfort, as it were no longer to keep safe his roial spirits'. A seemingly penitent Plexirtus, with a rope around his neck, surrenders to Leonatus who, ever loving and kind, forgives him on the promise of an amended life.

Other incidents from Sidney's epic romance influenced Shakespeare's play. Queen Andromana's lust for both Pyrocles and Musidorus in chapter 20 is the mirror image of Gonerill's and Regan's lust for Edmond; her death by stabbing herself after her son Palladius is killed may have suggested Gonerill's suicide after Edmond's defeat. The mortal combat ending in mutual forgiveness between Plexirtus's allies, Tydeus and Tylenor, in chapter 22 resembles the duel between Edgar and Edmond, just as the vivid descriptions of the storm in chapter 7 may have suggested Lear's experience in Act 3. From the story of Plangus, King of Iberia, in chapter 15 Shakespeare may have got the idea for Edmond's deception of Gloucester, and in chapter 12 the verse of Basilius and Plangus anticipates Gloucester's despairing thoughts and attitude.[1] But these parallels and several verbal echoes apart, Shakespeare's greatest debt to Sidney is the hint he found in the *Arcadia* for the kind of mould in which he could shape his tragedy.

THE THEATRE OF FOLLY

Apart from the altered ending and the parallel plot, Shakespeare's introduction of the Fool is his most important contribution to the Lear story. In addition, he conspicuously extends the king's own foolishness into madness ('folly' in its extremest degree) when, exposed to rain and cold, Lear calls upon divine power. The development of King and Fool in the play derives partly from the long tradition of the court fool, but Shakespeare's handling of both character and theme is unique.

As Enid Welsford has shown in her classic study, *The Fool: His Social and Literary History* (1935), the court fool can be traced back to ancient times. By the late Middle Ages, the jester was a familiar figure, and in the Renaissance the fool had become a domestic servant in the homes of many aristocrats, in Britain as well as on the continent. The motley coat, eared hood, bells and *marotte*, or bauble, were traditional, but fools might also be dressed like other household servants. Regarded as pets or mascots, they

---

[1] Muir, pp. xxxix–xli.

served not simply to amuse, but to criticise their masters and mistresses and their guests; Queen Elizabeth is said to have rebuked one of her fools for not being severe enough with her. On the other hand, they might be whipped for excessive behaviour, as Lear threatens to punish his Fool. Mentally deficient and/or physically deformed, they were 'exceptional' in almost every respect, requiring the protection of powerful patrons to avoid social ostracism or abuse.

Distinctions can be, and were, made between the 'natural fool' and the 'artificial' or professional fool, as well as between the fool and the clown (the rustic, or country bumpkin), but the principal feature that is relevant here is the fool's privileged status in a royal or noble household. While his folly could be disregarded as the raving of a madman, it could also be seen as divinely inspired: the natural fool was 'touched' by God (or 'tetched', in American dialect). Lear's 'all-licensed fool' enjoys a privileged status, much to Gonerill's annoyance (1.4.160), and his characteristic idiom suggests he is a 'natural' fool, not an 'artificial' one, though his perceptiveness and wit show that he is far from being an idiot or a moron, however 'touched' he may otherwise be.

Fools or jesters had appeared occasionally but not often in Elizabethan drama, as in Greene's *Friar Bacon and Friar Bungay* and *James IV*. With the advent of Robert Armin, who replaced Will Kempe in the King's Men and made a speciality of fools (as distinguished from Kempe's clowns), the character became more popular on the stage between 1598 and 1605. Armin successfully undertook the roles not only of Touchstone, Feste, and Lavatch in Shakespeare's comedies, but of Carlo Buffone in Jonson's *Every Man Out of His Humour* and Passarello in Marston's *The Malcontent*.[1] Whether or not he himself played Lear's fool (see p. 32 below) is less important than the fact that by 1605 the character had become both a popular and a significant one in plays performed by the King's Men. Shakespeare then developed the role and extended it in *King Lear* so that folly became a dominant theme in his tragedy.

Lear's folly – his foolishness in giving away everything to two daughters and banishing the third – is the Fool's persistent early refrain. This foolishness turns into madness and leads directly to the commentary in Act 4 upon 'this great stage of fools', which Lear delivers to Gloucester, his counterpart in the second plot (4.5.174 ff.). If Shakespeare derived his use of 'fool', as William Empson and others claim,[2] from a rather generalised memory of Erasmus's *Praise of Folly*, he developed it in ways only glimpsed or implied by Erasmus. The ironic inversions of folly and wisdom that abound throughout the play cast darker shadows. Shakespeare had experimented with bitter fools in *Troilus and Cressida* (Thersites) and *All's Well That Ends Well* (Lavatch), but the Fool in *King Lear* is a more complex creation than these bitter fools – more affecting in his vulnerability and his closeness to Lear, yet with a perception of the horror of the situation which drives him to a relentless goading of his master.

Enid Welsford relates the central scenes of Acts 3 and 4 to the culminating moments in the *sottie*, a type of comedy especially popular in Europe from the end of the fifteenth

---

[1] Enid Welsford, *The Fool: His Social and Literary History*, 1935, reprinted 1961, pp. 245–6; Wiles, pp. 144–58.

[2] *The Structure of Complex Words*, [1951], p. 124. Compare Leo Salingar, *Shakespeare and the Traditions of Comedy*, 1974, pp. 246–7, and Walter Kaiser, *Praisers of Folly*, 1963, pp. 21–2, 99.

century to the beginning of the seventeenth. The theme of the *sottie* is the universal sway of Mother Folly, and it ends with the reduction of every class of person to 'the man in cap and bells'.[1] *The Praise of Folly* is a derivative of the *sottie*, which flourished more on the continent than in Britain, although it influenced Sir David Lindsay's *Satire of the Three Estates* (Welsford, p. 233). Whether Shakespeare consciously contrived his tragedy according to the vision of the *sottie*, we cannot know, and in any case we must guard against believing that there must be a specifically identifiable source for everything. The topsy-turvy world is implicit in the opening scene (from which the Fool is notably absent), proceeding inexorably from Lear's actions and reaching a climax in Acts 3–4. After 3.6 the Fool disappears, and after 4.1 Edgar drops his pretence of madness, leaving the stage of folly to Lear and, less obviously, to others.

THE THEATRE OF EXORCISM

All of the Fool's efforts prove incapable of preventing Lear's descent into madness, which accelerates after he meets Edgar in disguise as Tom o'Bedlam in Act 3. The purgation, or exorcism, that Lear requires is highlighted by the assumed madness of Edgar, who screams that he is possessed by devils. Exorcism had become a form of popular theatre, as priests gathered audiences to watch demonstrations of their power over evil spirits. The Anglican church vigorously opposed such demonstrations, and Samuel Harsnett exposed the practice as fraudulent in a treatise usually referred to by its shortened title, *A Declaration of Egregious Popish Impostures*.[2]

Harsnett was chaplain to the Bishop of London and part of his job was reading and licensing books, including plays. His *Declaration* followed enquiries begun in 1598 into a series of exorcisms in 1585–6 practised by Father William Weston *alias* Edmonds and performed in the household of Sir Edward Peckham. Harsnett's *Declaration* characterised exorcism as a stage play 'fashioned by cunning clerical dramatists and performed by actors skilled in improvisation'.[3] It thereby attempted to expose what Harsnett saw as its falsity and emptiness. Nevertheless, the illusion was gripping, as Shakespeare doubtless realised when he borrowed from Harsnett's exposé much of the language of possession for Edgar's masquerade as Poor Tom.[4] At the same time, he appears to support Harsnett's position in the *Declaration*, that evil is of this world, not a nether world of devils and demons, as Catholic priests like Father Weston believed.[5]

---

[1] Welsford, *The Fool*, p. 220.

[2] *A Declaration of egregious Popish Impostures, to with-draw the harts of her Maiesties Subiects from their allegeance, and from the truth of Christian Religion professed in England, under the pretence of casting out deuils. Practiced by Edmvnds, alias Weston a Iesuit, and diuers Romish Priests his wicked associates. . . . At London Printed by Iames Roberts . . . 1603.*

[3] Stephen Greenblatt, 'Shakespeare and the exorcists', in *Shakespeare and the Question of Theory*, ed. Patricia Parker and Geoffrey Hartman, 1985, p. 169.

[4] See Kenneth Muir, 'Samuel Harsnett and *King Lear*', *RES* 2 (1951), 11–21, and Bullough, pp. 299 ff. In his forthcoming edition, Brownlow argues that the *Declaration* does not represent a 'source' for *King Lear* in the ordinary sense; rather, the play is the result of an encounter with that text, a kind of dialogue between cleric and poet, in which Shakespeare delivers a 'massive reply'. Its effect was to undo Harsnett's book and reopen matters the cleric had meant finally to close.

[5] Greenblatt, 'Shakespeare and the exorcists', p. 177.

The effect of Shakespeare's use of Harsnett in *King Lear* is yet more complicated, Greenblatt says, in so far as Harsnett's position seems there to be reversed. Since scepticism, an instrument of seekers after truth, is expressed through the villainous Cornwall, Gonerill, and especially Edmond, whilst possession and exorcism, regarded as fraudulent practices of the wicked, are given to the legitimate Edgar, Harsnett's arguments against exorcism are curiously 'alienated' from themselves. 'In Shakespeare, the realization that demonic possession is a theatrical imposture leads not to a clarification – the clear-eyed satisfaction of the man who refuses to be gulled – but to a deeper uncertainty, a loss of moorings, in the face of evil.'[1] We are not comforted by the knowledge that Edgar's performance is precisely that – a performance – any more than we can find comfort in the fact that Lear's prayers, like his curses, remain unanswered throughout the play. In any event, his exorcism, or purgation, such as it is, comes not at the hands of a priest, but through the ministrations of Cordelia, unassisted by either a 'Doctor' or by music in the Folio revision; and Gloucester's is effected by his son Edgar. Both are extraordinarily, though differently, dramatic.

THE THEATRE OF THE BLIND

When Edgar in his disguise takes his father to Dover, he means to perform a kind of exorcism, telling Gloucester, for example, that there stood behind him on the cliff 'some fiend' from whom he has miraculously escaped (4.5.66–74). The old man's resistance, here and later, after his 'fall', is confused because he has lost his eyes. The blind figure is taken from Sidney's *Arcadia*, but Shakespeare develops and dramatises his source not only in the mimed 'leap', but later in the confrontation between the unseeing old man and the mad king. Their meeting becomes the climactic spectacle in the play's theatre of folly, to which Montaigne also was a major contributor. It was in Florio's translation of Montaigne that Shakespeare found that a dog could be 'obeyed in office' (4.5.151) and that a man could see with no eyes (144–5). Similarly, Montaigne several times refers to unrighteous judges (146–8), and elsewhere Shakespeare seems indebted to the French essayist not only for phrases and ideas but for the sceptical attitudes that pervade the play.[2]

SALT AND CINDERELLA

Folklorists towards the end of the nineteenth century noticed the connection between the old Leir story and some versions of the Cinderella tale. Although Shakespeare makes no direct use of these versions, Geoffrey of Monmouth in his *Historia* must have drawn upon a related body of folklore and folktales for which no record any longer exists.[3] The affinity between the story of Leir and his three daughters and the ancient Cinderella tale, moreover, has recently aroused much interest among anthropologists

---

[1] *Ibid.*, p. 179. John J. Murphy comes to an opposite conclusion in *Darkness and Devils: Exorcism and 'King Lear'*, 1984, pp. 200–1. Compare Brownlow, cited above.
[2] See Muir, pp. 249–53, and Salingar, pp. 107–39.
[3] See Alan R. Young, 'The written and oral sources of *King Lear* and the problem of justice in the play', *SEL: Studies in English Literature* 15 (1975), 309–19.

and psychoanalytically oriented literary critics, who focus upon the incest motif latent in the tales and in Shakespeare's tragedy.[1]

Briefly, the love contest with which *King Lear* opens and which appears, *mutatis mutandis*, in all of the analogues, closely parallels the folktale tradition of the rich man or king who asks his daughters to tell him how much they love him. The two eldest daughters respond much as Gonerill and Regan do, but the youngest replies that she loves her father as fresh meat loves salt, or words to that effect.[2] The father, enraged, disowns his youngest daughter, who then follows her Cinderella-like adventures until, married to her prince, she invites her father to the wedding feast. There he is served food without salt, learns at last the meaning of his daughter's words, and is reconciled. Folklorists refer to this motif in the tales alternatively as 'Love like salt' and 'The King Lear judgement' and group the tales under the Cinderella type.[3]

The folk paradigm is therefore always auspicious for the Cordelia figure, and when Nahum Tate in the Restoration gave Shakespeare's play a happy ending, he was reverting to that type (see p. 34 below). On the other hand, as Katherine Stockholder notes, 'The conventional fairytale would have the two sisters either dead or repentant . . . by the time Cordelia achieved her happiness [marriage to France]. As it is, the fairy tale ends when the play has scarcely begun, and leaves the play with the task of resolving in a more realistic mode issues put forth in fairy tale starkness and absoluteness.'[4] The long-delayed scenes of reconciliation between Lear and Cordelia in Acts 4 and 5 have a 'lyric separateness' from the rest of the action, suitable for a fairytale ending, but their reconciliation cannot reshape the world Lear has created by banishing his daughter.[5]

THE TRAGEDY OF KING LEAR

Although called a 'True Chronicle Historie' in the 1608 quarto, the Folio title is 'The Tragedy of King Lear', which sets up expectations about the form and outcome of the play. While linked with the Cinderella story, it diverges from that story's familiar course and recalls, rather, the ancient biblical story of Jephthah and his daughter, as well as a number of dramas in which a daughter is sacrificed, such as those dealing with

---

[1] The seminal paper is Sigmund Freud's 'The theme of the three caskets', *The Standard Edition of the Complete Psychological Works of Sigmund Freud*, trans. James Strachey, 1958, XII, 291–301. Compare John Donnelly, 'Incest, ingratitude and insanity: aspects of the psychopathology of King Lear', *Psychoanalytic Review* 40 (1953), 149–55, and especially Alan Dundes, ' "To love my father all": a psychoanalytic study of the folktale source of *King Lear*', in *Cinderella: A Casebook*, ed. Alan Dundes, 1983, pp. 229–44.

[2] Perrett comments on the two dozen or so most pertinent folktales (among the 345 tabulated and arranged by M. R. Cox, *Cinderella*, 1893). He notes the essential features that connect them with the Lear story: the love test and the outcast heroine. While Geoffrey includes nothing about salt, this is a literary narrative, Perrett says, and sophistication is likely – sophistication so subtle that the real significance of Cordeilla's cryptic and jesting reply (*quantum habes, tantum vales, tantumque le diligo*) has eluded commentators. It can be roughly translated as 'As much as you have, so much do you value, and so much do I love you.'

[3] Stith Thompson, *Motif-Index of Folk-Literature*, Bloomington, 1956, III, 432: Motif H592.1, *Love like salt*; V, 29: Motif M21, *King Lear judgement*. See also Antti Aarne, *The Types of the Folktale: A Classification and Bibliography*, trans. and enlarged by Stith Thompson, Helsinki, 1961, p. 175: Tale type 510; and 'Cap o' Rushes' in Katherine M. Briggs, *A Dictionary of British Folk-Tales in the English Language*, 1970, Part A, II, 387–90. Briggs includes a tale-type index in I, 35–77.

[4] 'The multiple genres of *King Lear*: breaking the archetypes', *Bucknell Review* 16 (1968), 45.

[5] *Ibid.*, p. 60.

Agamemnon and Iphigeneia. Similarly, *King Lear* borrows from but alters the form of the Morality play and stories from the romance tradition.

In *'King Lear' in Our Time* (1965) Maynard Mack cites many parallels from the old Morality plays and from scripture. The Morality play tradition, of course, extends down to plays as late as Marlowe's *Dr Faustus*, and Shakespeare's dialogue is full of allusions to it. Characters like Edmond have a sharp affinity with the Vice of these old plays, as Gloucester does with Mankind or Everyman. From the romance tradition, stories like those of King Robert of Sicily provide important analogues in the theme of the Abasement of the Proud King. Thomas Lodge's prose romance, *The Famous true and historicall life of Robert second Duke of Normandy, surnamed for his monstrous birth and behavior, Robin the Diuell* (1591), besides recounting Robert's humbling and penitence, prefigures many incidents in *King Lear*, such as Robert's sheltering in a homely cottage during a storm, his growing compassion for fellow sufferers, and a trial by combat.[1] But although heavily indebted to Sidney's *Arcadia*, Shakespeare saw in it the possibilities for transforming his fable into tragedy. The Folio revision, moreover – specifically by its omission of the scene in Act 4 (see p. 271 below), as well as Shakespeare's alteration of the traditional ending of the Lear story – suggests a further hardening of this anti-romantic impulse without, however, altogether abandoning the tantalising positive possibilities still inherent in the later scenes of the play.

FRAGMENTARY RECOLLECTIONS

Consciously or otherwise, Shakespeare drew upon other materials as well. Numerous parallels with *Gorboduc* exist, not only in the language, political implications, and plots of the two plays, but in their symbolism and treatment of nature.[2] The play *Selimus* also bears close resemblances to the plot structure of *King Lear*,[3] and Shakespeare may have borrowed from *Eastward Ho*, a play by Chapman, Jonson, and Marston, performed and then banned in 1605.[4] Classical mythology plays its part, too: in the specific allusions to centaurs and Lear's 'wheel of fire' (4.6.44), as well as the overall structure and development of the play, the influence of the myth of Ixion may be recognised.[5] Similarly, the political and philosophic thought found in William Jones's translation of Iustus Lipsius's *Six Bookes of Politickes or Ciuill Doctrine* (1594) appears pervasive in *King Lear*.[6]

The biblical parable of the Prodigal Son probably influenced Shakespeare's handling of situation, theme, and imagery in both the Lear and Gloucester plots.[7] The frequent references to nakedness and raggedness in the heath scenes apparently derive from

[1] Donna Hamilton, 'Some romance sources for *King Lear*', *SP* 71 (1974), 173–92.
[2] Barbara Heliodora Carneiro de Mendonça, 'The influence of *Gorboduc* on *King Lear*', *S.Sur.* 13 (1960), 41–8.
[3] Inga-Stina Ewbank, '*King Lear* and *Selimus*', *N&Q*, n.s., 4 (1957), 193–4.
[4] Taylor, 'New source', pp. 396–413.
[5] O. B. Hardison, 'Myth and history in *King Lear*', *SQ* 26 (1975), 227–42. Compare Jonathan Bate, 'Ovid and the mature tragedies: metamorphosis in *Othello* and *King Lear*', *S.Sur.* 41 (1989), 133–44.
[6] Arthur F. Kinney, 'Some conjectures on the composition of *King Lear*', *S.Sur.* 33 (1980), 13–25.
[7] Susan Snyder, '*King Lear* and the Prodigal Son', *SQ* 17 (1966), 361–9.

Shakespeare's conception of the Prodigal. That Lear and Gloucester are old men and the Prodigal is a young one signifies only that Shakespeare inverted the biblical story to produce a parable of Prodigal Fathers.

THE THEATRE OF THE BIBLE

In *The Story of the Night* John Holloway shows that the movement of *King Lear*, especially from Act 4 to the end, parallels the movement of the Book of Job. The action of the play is prolonged, he says, by the same ironic conception that informs the biblical narrative of Job's ordeal: whenever we (or the characters) are made to think that release from suffering is imminent, the suffering is renewed; the 'bitter reversal of events comes again and again'.[1] Holloway also draws parallels between apocalyptic prophecy in the New Testament and specific references to Doomsday in the play, evidence that Shakespeare shared with many of his contemporaries a preoccupation with the end of days.[2] Joseph Wittreich has argued at length that Shakespeare was directly influenced not only by James I's interest in the Book of Revelation, but also by the 'secular millennianism' that dates back to the fifteenth century in England and became more pronounced from 1550 onwards.[3]

Marshalling considerable scholarship, Wittreich argues that the apocalypse is a radical metaphor in *King Lear*, 'a mind-transforming event that culminates in a king's redemption'.[4] After a close reading of all of the available evidence, he concludes, however, that while apocalypse is an essential element in the play, its function is ambiguous, 'so much so that it may be construed as lending all degrees of darkness to the play or, conversely, as shattering that darkness by letting in the light, however scattered, of Revelation itself'.[5] As many critics have said, Kent's and Edgar's lines at the end explicitly invoke Doomsday: 'Is this the promised end?' 'Or image of that horror?' But the analogy does not proclaim the play Christian, even though it provides, in Wittreich's view, an important clue to interpretation.[6] For Doomsday is not yet: Shakespeare's strategy 'is to use apocalypse against itself, not to deny it as a possibility but to advance the consummation of history into the future'.[7] Although redemption is not proclaimed, it is held out as a possibility for both individuals and nations; errors of the past are, after all, reparable.[8] The burden of the play's ending, therefore, is not simply pessimistic or optimistic, but a complex of possibilities, complicated further, as Wittreich fails to note, by divergences between the quarto and Folio texts (see Commentary at 5.3.286).

[1] Holloway, *The Story of the Night*, 1961, p. 89.
[2] In '*King Lear* and Doomsday', *S.Sur.* 26 (1973), 69–79, Mary Lascelles discusses the existence in Shakespeare's time of wall paintings in many churches, including Stratford's Holy Trinity Church, that depicted Judgement Day, and connects these thematically with imagery and incidents in *King Lear*.
[3] Wittreich, p. 26. Like most scholars until very recently, Wittreich bases his study on a conflated text (Muir's Arden edition). Except as regards 'Merlin's Prophecy' at the end of 3.2, he fails to distinguish between alternative versions of the play in the quarto and Folio.
[4] Wittreich, p. 33.
[5] *Ibid.*, p. 90
[6] *Ibid.*, p. 123.
[7] *Ibid.*, p. 32.
[8] *Ibid.*, p. 79.

Wittreich's analysis focuses for us the long controversy regarding Shakespeare's handling of biblical material. He raises the vexed question of *King Lear* and its Christian framework, and the religious milieu in which the play was composed and performed. Religious allusion, however dense, does not imply that the experience of the play can be contained within the parameters of a single religious interpretation. The attempts of those who try to do this prove the effort misguided because they reach opposite conclusions. Clearly they are working to too narrow a base. As elsewhere in Shakespeare, most notably in *Hamlet*, much of the evidence in the play is contradictory or at best inconsistent. By sorting through the evidence selectively, one could conclude that the 'constant association of Cordelia with Christian doctrine' is a 'foreshadowing' of Christ.[1] Cordelia's remark, 'O dear father, / It is thy business that I go about' (4.3.23–4) closely paraphrases Luke 2.49, 'knewe ye not that I must go about my fathers business?', and the Gentleman's comment at 4.5.196–7 echoes the Christian belief that Jesus redeemed fallen humanity from the general curse. Other associations also enforce this symbolic role of Cordelia. But at the other extreme are those who, like William R. Elton, similarly working with a conflated text, argue that despite its Christian references, *King Lear* is by no means 'an optimistically Christian drama'.[2] Scriptural echoes are adapted to the pagan context of the play, and in any case the 'business' that Cordelia serves has an unhappy outcome.[3] Rather than an analogue to Christ, Cordelia (like Pamela in Sidney's *Arcadia*) represents the pagan *prisca theologia*, or 'virtuous-heathen' view, embodying virtues and pieties derived from natural, not Christian, beliefs. As such, the virtues approach the Christian ideal but are not identical with it.[4] Elton attempts to demonstrate, moreover, that the play does not show Lear saved, redeemed, or regenerate, and that a benevolent providence does not preside over the action; therefore, he concludes, the optimistic Christian interpretation of *King Lear* is 'invalid'.[5]

Complementing this view, Thomas P. Roche argues that although he is convinced that Shakespeare was a Christian writer, *King Lear* is not a Christian play. Rather, it depicts 'the plight of man before the Christian era, that is, before the salvation of man by Christ's sacrifice was available'.[6] Shakespeare altered the story as it appeared in *King Leir* precisely to emphasise this fact. (Paradoxically, this emphasis, I believe, would seem to make his play more Christian, not less, than the pietistic old play.) In bringing to bear a host of biblical allusions from both the Old and New Testaments, Shakespeare drew upon such language, Rosalie L. Colie maintains, 'to remind us both of man's predicament and of the options he has within that predicament'.[7] But her conclusion

---

[1] S. L. Bethell, *Shakespeare and the Popular Dramatic Tradition*, 1944, p. 68.
[2] Elton, p. 3.
[3] *Ibid.*, pp. 83–4, 292.
[4] *Ibid.*, pp. 38–42.
[5] *Ibid.*, p. 336.
[6] Roche, ' "Nothing almost sees miracles": tragic knowledge in *King Lear*', in *On 'King Lear'*, ed. Lawrence Danson, 1981, p. 149.
[7] Colie, p. 121.

differs from both Wittreich's guarded optimism and Roche's frank pessimism:[1] the play demonstrates the necessity for endurance, the need for men to 'test and make their own values',[2] in so far as no transcendent morality is available. 'The use of biblical echo to suggest a morality past ordinary hopes', she says, 'allows us to work through the complicated paradoxes of the play to accept the essential, inevitable, unalterable limitations of human life.'[3] For her, as for John Holloway, the parallels to the Book of Job are compelling.

The truth surely is that biblical allusions and parallels operate in *King Lear* not to assert particular Christian or non-Christian points of view, but to suggest a wider dimension of experience than either approach provides. Or, as Philip Brockbank perceptively says, 'the experience of both the Reformation and the Renaissance in England made possible, through a fuller and more direct access to the Bible, a recovery of the imaginative inheritance of Hebraic and Christian literature as distinct from its institutional, doctrinal, and ritual inheritance'. If in the Middle Ages the movement was from imaginative truth towards doctrine, in the Renaissance the movement went in the opposite direction.[4] *King Lear* thus offers a powerful, imaginative rendering of conflicting and sometimes complementary attitudes and beliefs. If none dominates the action, our final impression of the play must remain what A. C. Bradley called a 'mystery we cannot fathom'.[5] Here, as elsewhere in his tragedies, Shakespeare appears intent on exploring the possibilities of human experience, religious and secular. If his thrust is 'inquisitive rather than affirmative',[6] the relentlessness of his searching endows the plays with enormous energy.

The play

Lear's failure to see is wilful in the extreme. It is not only that he lacks foresight and cannot see people clearly or assess their motives accurately; he *will* not. Both Cordelia and Kent try to correct his vision. Kent cries out in vain, 'See better, Lear, and let me still remain / The true blank of thine eye' (1.1.152–3). The disasters that follow are thus the direct result of wilful blindness; unlike Hamlet's or even Othello's, the tragic situation is of Lear's own making. Although their experiences run parallel and eventually intersect, in this regard Lear is also unlike Gloucester, manipulated by his bastard son, Edmond, who scoffs at his father's belief in 'planetary influence' or 'spherical predominance' (1.2.108–10) and holds with the Renaissance belief that man is the measure of all things. If the gods are invoked, as they are by Lear, Gloucester,

---

[1] 'The ending of *Lear* is as bleak and unrewarding as man can reach outside the gates of hell', Roche, ' "Nothing almost sees miracles" ', p. 156.

[2] Colie, p. 141.

[3] *Ibid.*, p. 140.

[4] Brockbank, p. 17.

[5] Bradley, p. 279. Compare Wittreich, p. 122: 'The play quarrels with all perspectives it countenances, questions a universe that never seems to answer back, and finds its essential meaning therefore in silences, which is to suggest that even if the work is not meaningless its mysteries are beyond man's comprehension.'

[6] René Fortin, 'Shakespearean tragedy and the problem of transcendence', *S.St.* 7 (1974), 323.

and others, their presence is nowhere found or felt.[1] The cause of thunder remains unknown, and no one can tell Lear what there is in nature that makes hearts hard.

Meaning in *King Lear* is not *a priori*, and absurdities result mainly because of human, not divine or supernatural, acts. Positive meanings in the world of *King Lear* come from human activity, deliberate choices, such as Kent's decision to serve his king despite the decree of banishment, or the Fool's decision *not* to turn knave and run away, leaving his master alone in the storm. But where good sense yields to appetite, or (in Hamlet's phrase) 'reason panders will', human behaviour moves further and further to extremes.[2] Truth and rationality are violated *ad libitum*, and the result is a world turned upside down; but it is a world formed and determined by the people who inhabit it.

ACT I, SCENE I AND ITS AFTERMATH

Almost from the outset, the play propels us into a complex of irrationalities. Having already divided up his kingdom and assigned the parts to his heirs (as we learn from the opening dialogue between Gloucester and Kent), Lear asks his daughters to engage in a contest that will decide who shall get what. Gonerill and Regan play along: as they later reveal (1.1.280–92), they know Lear's capriciousness and his dotage. Cordelia knows, too, yet she refuses the gambit. To Lear's question, 'What can you say to draw / A third more opulent than your sisters?' she answers, 'Nothing' (1.1.82). In the most literal sense (the sense commonly ignored by critics intent upon the larger implications), she understands the question perfectly and answers it correctly. Since the division has been made and her sisters have already received their shares, nothing she *can* say now can give her anything more than what is left. She can get less, in fact nothing; for nothing may come of 'Nothing'; and it does.

Cordelia's refusal is thus a refusal to participate not only in a show trial, but in the unreasonable behaviour that Lear demands, insists upon. Although his daughter, tied to him by bonds of filial devotion – and more, much more (as the play ultimately reveals) – she is no partner to his foolishness here. Or if she is, she shows it by also being insistent, demanding. Her logic nevertheless is irrefutable. 'Why have my sisters husbands, if they say / They love you all?' (1.1.94–5). But Lear, in open court, is in no mood for truth or logic, and Cordelia's irony stings. Despite his abdication, he means (again, irrationally) to continue exercising control over the world as he knows it – that is, the world as he has shaped it and intends to keep on shaping it. He has been told he is 'everything'; only later does he realise that he has been lied to, that he is not even 'ague-proof' (4.5.101). But by then the absurdities he has set in motion are moving to their inexorable conclusion: 'Why should a dog, a horse, a rat have life, / And thou no breath at all?' (5.3.280–1).[3]

---

[1] Compare George Walton Williams, 'Petitionary prayer in *King Lear*', *South Atlantic Quarterly* 85 (1986), 363: 'There are no supernatural responses in *King Lear*; there are only natural ones.' But Williams goes on to argue that human agents fulfil the will of the gods in *Lear* as elsewhere in Shakespeare's plays.

[2] G. Wilson Knight, '*King Lear* and the comedy of the grotesque', *The Wheel of Fire*, 5th revised edn, 1957, p. 168: 'The core of the play is an absurdity, an indignity, an incongruity.'

[3] For an alternative explanation of Lear's motivation in 1.1 and Cordelia's, see Cavell, pp. 285–94. To summarise: Cavell's argument is that Lear does not really want love but the avoidance of it through flattery.

Cordelia is not the only one who challenges Lear to desist from his reckless behaviour. Kent also tries to get Lear to confront reality and reject the fantasy his irrationality creates – including the fantasy that by dividing up his kingdom he will prevent future strife. Forsaking polite courtier talk, he resorts to direct confrontation: 'Be Kent unmannerly / When Lear is mad. What wouldst thou do, old man?' (1.1.139–40). His monosyllables are emphatic. Earnestly, he asks Lear to check his 'hideous rashness', keep his kingdom intact, and recognise what Lear himself well knows – that his youngest daughter does not love him least. But Lear is by now fully committed. He has sworn; he is firm; and Kent is banished.

Yet the scene is not without its positive aspect. Struck by the sudden turnabout in affairs, Burgundy and France have their choices also to make. Conventional Burgundy cannot deal with the situation; he will accept not less than the dowry originally offered. France is more perceptive as well as more humane. Only some aberration of Cordelia's, an offence of such 'unnatural degree' that nothing but a miracle could make any rational-minded individual accept it, can make him change his opinion of her. The play is notably free of any sort of miracles, except the miracle of love, such as France demonstrates here. In a speech studded with oxymorons, he concludes with the paradox:

> Gods, gods! 'Tis strange, that from their cold'st neglect
> My love should kindle to inflamed respect.   (1.1.249–50)

Making Cordelia 'queen of us, of ours, and our fair France', he sees what only Kent has been willing or able to see, that Cordelia is 'herself a dowry' (236).

Swiftly (nothing in this play moves slowly),[1] the consequences of Lear's action follow. Various forces combine to drive the king over the edge into madness: his elder daughters' ingratitude; guilt over his treatment of Cordelia (compounded later by guilt over the 'poor naked wretches' that populate his kingdom); the Fool's relentless taunting; loss of his hundred knights and increasing awareness that his world is now drastically altered; dread of impotence and disabling illness (*hysterica passio*); the stubborn indifference of the elements. But the culminating event is meeting Tom o'Bedlam. As Kenneth Muir says, 'Edgar, in acting madness, precipitates Lear's'; for as a raving madman, Poor Tom is what Lear has most feared he will become.[2] The scene in Act 3 where the Fool, Edgar, and Lear all act out their various forms of madness represents a *terminus ad quem* for the action that the main plot has dramatised.

THE GLOUCESTER PLOT

Meanwhile, the play has introduced a parallel though not identical strand of action in the second plot. 'This is the excellent foppery of the world', Edmond comments upon hearing his father's troubled and confused reaction to recent events. Edmond's view is the modern scientific one that regards 'planetary influence' as foolish and belief in it a

---

Cordelia 'threatens to expose both his plan for returning false love with no love, and . . . the necessity for that plan – [Lear's] terror of being loved, of needing love' (p. 290).
[1] Compare Reibetanz, p. 16.
[2] 'Madness in *King Lear*', *S.Sur.* 13 (1960), 35.

commonplace kind of absurdity.[1] The 'nature' Edmond worships (1.2.1 ff.) is the nature that frees him as an active intelligence from all arbitrary bonds, including 'the curiosity of nations' – social *mores* and conventions – as well as superstitious adherence to an outworn creed. But anything carried to an extreme will result in absurdity, precisely the *reductio ad absurdum* that not only philosophers but poets and dramatists – Shakespeare as well as Marlowe – recognised, for example, in their portraits of 'overreachers'. Hence, Edmond errs in carrying his convictions to extremes. In a way not unlike Lear, impelled by a powerful will that lets him believe he can shape the world to his own purposes, he pursues and extends his goals to excessive lengths. Eventually, it will be not only 'legitimate' Edgar's lands that he seeks, but the entire kingdom of Britain. He almost succeeds, but he seriously underestimates the counter-forces in nature and society that finally combine to confound his efforts.

His success at first is astonishing in its quickness and completeness. 'A credulous father and a brother noble' (1.2.151) are easy victims, almost willing ones, to Edmond's Machiavellian 'practices'. Gloucester is tricked into believing something that initially he finds unthinkable, let alone credible: 'My son Edgar, had he a hand to write this? a heart and brain to breed it in?' he asks of the letter Edmond has shown him (1.2.53–4). Then his anxiety undoes him: 'He cannot be such a monster . . . I would unstate myself to be in a due resolution' (1.2.85–8), he says to Edmond, giving him *carte blanche* to resolve the situation. Whereupon Edmond manoeuvres both Edgar and Gloucester into suspecting – and believing – the worst of each other, without their ever exchanging so much as a word or a glance.

For a while, Gloucester's behaviour follows this pattern of complicity and compliance with experience as others shape it for him, until – at the crucial point in Act 3 – he begins to see the moral disasters that will result unless he alters his course. Regarding Cornwall as his 'worthy arch and patron', he does acquiesce, however, reluctantly, in the stocking of Kent and later tries to smooth things out between Cornwall, Regan, and the outraged king. His actions seem in line with the advice the Fool gives Kent, to let go of the wheel that goes down a hill and cling to the 'great one that goes upward' (2.4.67).[2] Eventually, he gives up temporising and takes a dangerous, morally more courageous stance. He begins to move against his patron in favour of the abused and much wronged king. But he errs in confiding his position to Edmond, whom he still believes is his loyal, loving son. The confidence is immediately betrayed, and Gloucester pays with his eyes for his bravery and his misplaced trust. In a stunning instant, Edmond's true nature is revealed to him. This further insight, ironically, does not deter Gloucester later from behaviour, such as his attempted suicide, even more naïve than that into which his overcredulous acceptance of Edmond's 'practices' led him (see pp. 21–2 below).

Edgar's credulity and too-ready compliance also combine to propel him, like his father, into accepting the manipulations of his brother. His passive submission is the reverse of Lear's refusal to tolerate anyone else's participation in the determination of events; both extremes of behaviour lead to disaster. Forced to flee as the result of

---

[1] Danby, p. 38.
[2] Compare Helen Gardner, *King Lear*, 1967, p. 14.

Edmond's stratagem, Edgar in disguise as Tom o'Bedlam becomes the image of that *reductio ad absurdum* to which everything in both plots tends. If 'Robes and furred gowns hide all' (4.5.157), paradoxically Edgar chooses 'the thing itself' – 'unaccommodated man' – for his disguise (3.4.95–6). With 'presented nakedness' he will 'outface / The winds and persecutions of the sky' (2.3.11–12), anticipating Lear's experience in the storm. An earl's son, one who is so 'noble, / Whose nature is so far from doing harms / That he suspects none' (1.2.151–3), Edgar is reduced to emulating 'Poor Turlygod! Poor Tom', a crazed servingman who claims to have committed all manner of evil. Thus he finds his place in a world turned upside down; but for him, now, 'That's something yet' (2.3.21).

THE MAD SCENES IN ACT 3

Edgar survives by submerging himself in the destructive elements that threaten him. In the central episodes of the play, Shakespeare uses him and the Fool to function partly as Lear's shadows. As Lear goes mad, first the Fool and then Edgar as Tom o'Bedlam become superfluous and drop out of the picture. If the Fool's role is 'to heal the gaping wound of the mind's incongruous knowledge by the unifying, healing release of laughter',[1] then he fails, as perhaps he realises; in any case, he is upstaged and finally silenced by Edgar as Poor Tom.[2]

Edgar's wild imaginings outdo the Fool's and unleash Lear's. The compassion Lear had begun to feel for his 'Poor fool and knave' (3.2.70), and for the 'Poor naked wretches' (3.4.28) out in the storm with him, gives way for the moment to self-pity and projected fantasy. Immediately the sight and sounds of the Bedlamite arouse a self-centred sympathy: 'Didst thou give all to thy daughters? And art thou come to this?' (3.4.47–8); 'What, has his daughters brought him to this pass? / Couldst thou save nothing? Wouldst thou give 'em all?' (59–60). Kent's intercession – 'He hath no daughters, sir' – brings a furious rejection:

> Death, traitor! Nothing could have subdued nature
> To such a lowness but his unkind daughters.
> Is it the fashion that discarded fathers
> Should have thus little mercy on their flesh?
> Judicious punishment; 'twas this flesh begot
> Those pelican daughters.   (65–70)

Lear's comments and questions, provoked by his self-preoccupation and the vision of Poor Tom, get a quizzical response from Edgar. To the query, 'Didst thou give all to thy daughters?' Edgar replies, 'Who gives anything to Poor Tom'; reference to Lear's 'pelican daughters' evokes the bawdy verse, 'Pillicock sat on Pillicock Hill', followed by what sounds like a cockcrow or halloo. To all this the Fool aptly responds: 'This cold night will turn us all to fools and madmen' (3.4.72). Though it has failed to attract notice from commentators, Edgar's absence from Act 1, Scene 1 is curious: Edmond is there, but not his elder brother. Moreover, during Edgar's three brief appearances

---

[1] Knight, *The Wheel of Fire*, p. 165.
[2] Compare Kerrigan, pp. 226–9.

3   Act 3, Scene 4: Edgar as Tom o'Bedlam: 'Away, the foul fiend follows me. Through the sharp hawthorn blow the winds . . .' A possible staging by C. Walter Hodges

before this scene, nothing is said of Lear's situation. Is it possible that Edgar has no knowledge and only now learns of it? His father's remark, 'Our flesh and blood, my lord, is grown so vile, / That it doth hate what gets it', moves Edgar to whimper merely, 'Poor Tom's a-cold' (3.4.129–31). But the full irony of Gloucester's comment will not be revealed until several scenes later.

His father's appearance in 3.4 subdues for a while Edgar's rant. Perhaps he does not hear Gloucester's subsequent comments on the daughters' plot against Lear's life or his expression of grief over Edgar's supposed plot (147–52), for Lear has taken his 'philosopher' aside to speak 'one word in private' (144). But the counterpointing of Lear's mounting insanity and Edgar's feigned madness remains for the audience, and in their next scene together Edgar resumes his mad act. The Folio version of the play abbreviates 3.6, deleting the mock trial and with it much of Edgar's rant as well as his commentary *in propria persona* at the end of the scene.[1] One effect of the cut is to reserve the extended display of Lear's madness until 4.5; another, more immediate effect is to juxtapose more swiftly the madness of Lear, the Fool, and Tom with the barbarity of Gloucester's trial in the scene that follows.

Act 3, Scene 7 develops vividly the irrational behaviour of Lear's enemies. From here onwards the vicious lusts underlying their cool but superficial rationalism stand

[1] See below, pp. 270–1.

revealed and control their every action. Gonerill and Regan show their passion (here, their lust for cruelty) in unhesitating reaction to Gloucester's 'treason':[1]

> REGAN Hang him instantly.
> GONERILL Pluck out his eyes.   (3.7.4–5)

Cornwall spells out precisely the nature of the proceedings he will undertake:

> Though well we may not pass upon his life
> Without the form of justice, yet our power
> Shall do a curtsy to our wrath, which men
> May blame but not control.   (3.7.24–7)

Cornwall will pay with his life for the enormity of his conviction when a nameless servant, one who has served him all his life, revolts against the maiming Cornwall inflicts upon his host. Gonerill and Regan suffer later for their lusts, which by then include a deadly competition for Edmond. In this respect, in so far as they mean to enforce their wills in order to realise their purposes and desires without regard for the interests and claims of others, Gonerill and Regan show themselves to be truly Lear's daughters.

GLOUCESTER'S DESPAIR AND EDGAR'S MINISTRY

As Act 4 opens, Edgar attempts with stoic counsel to find consolation for his miserable condition and fortify himself against it, but he is shocked by a sight that mocks every consolation.

> O gods! Who is't can say 'I am at the worst'?
> I am worse than e'er I was.   (4.1.25–6)

Yet the sight of his blinded father is not without its redeeming aspects. Admittedly the servant who intervenes to prevent further outrage is killed without achieving his object, and the Folio omits the kindness to Gloucester that the remaining servants intend at the end of 3.7. Yet the Old Man's loyalty to his master and concern for him are retained. Evil is not omnipotent or completely pervasive, after all. Edgar's ministrations to his father and then Cordelia's to hers demonstrate this fact more fully, although the end of the play leaves unanswered, or answered ambiguously, questions about the effectiveness of their ministry. For the moment, at the beginning of Act 4, other questions arise. For example, why doesn't Edgar reveal himself at once to his father, whose plea is clear and direct?

> Oh, dear son Edgar,
> The food of thy abusèd father's wrath:
> Might I but live to see thee in my touch,
> I'd say I had eyes again.   (21–4)

As the scene progresses, Edgar is nearly overcome with grief watching and listening to his father; but all he says is that he must continue in his disguise. No explanation here is

---

[1] Reibetanz, p. 87, notes a significant change in their style of speech: here, they speak directly from the heart.

offered. Perhaps, as Leo Kirschbaum argues, Edgar is not a 'dramatic unity' but only a 'dramatic device', contributing not to a 'rich psychological unity but to Shakespeare's poetic purposes'.[1] Thus the scene ends with the mad leading the blind, a fit emblem for the Lear world as it has evolved to this point.

The explanation, such as it is, for Edgar's continued disguise comes in the scene at Dover. Gloucester has asked Poor Tom to bring him to the edge of a cliff so that he may commit suicide. Edgar pretends to comply, and the episode is one of the most grotesque in a play noted for grotesquerie. Some critics have argued that Shakespeare intended his audience as well as Gloucester to be taken in by Edgar's descriptions, since they are like those used elsewhere to evoke scenery on the bare platform stage. Jan Kott, for example, says: 'The non-existent cliff is not meant just to deceive the blind man. For a short while we, too, [believe] in this landscape and in the mime.'[2] We do and we don't. In so far as we sympathise or identify with Gloucester, we do; Edgar's sharply detailed verse deludes us into imagining the dizzying verge just as it does his father. At the same time, we are aware that Gloucester's doubts are well founded: the uphill 'labour' is all pretence; Edgar's voice has changed; the ground is both 'even' (the Globe stage: see illustration 4) and 'Horrible steep' (4.5.3). The trick Edgar plays on his father's imagination is also the trick Shakespeare plays on ours – except that here he means us to be conscious of everything that is happening, including the way in which our imagination is being made to work.[3]

This heightened awareness alerts us to other incongruities, such as those in Gloucester's prayer (4.5.34–40), that make a further mockery of his leap. Were he truly patient, Gloucester would not try to shake off his 'great affliction'; and if he really believes the gods' wills are 'opposeless', would he attempt suicide?[4] Gloucester's leap is not a leap into death, as he thinks, or even into the 'abyss', unless that abyss is the abyss of utter meaninglessness, as in a sense it is. And it is everywhere.[5] Edgar realises some of the dangers and risk: 'trifling' with his father's despair in order to cure it, he recognises the power of illusion, particularly an illusion willingly embraced, and does not know 'how conceit may rob / The treasury of life, when life itself / Yields to the theft' (4.5.42–4).

'Thy life's a miracle', Edgar tells his father (4.5.55), and in one sense, of course, it is. But if a kind of 'fiend' led him to the edge, to suicide, it was not the 'clearest gods' who preserved him.[6] It was his unrecognised son, now in the role of a man of Kent, who will perform still other services in still other disguises to protect his father before the

---

[1] Leo Kirschbaum, 'Banquo and Edgar: character or function?', in *Character and Characterization in Shakespeare*, 1962, p. 61.

[2] *Shakespeare Our Contemporary*, Doubleday Anchor Books, 1966, p. 145. Compare William Matchett, 'Some dramatic techniques in *King Lear*', in Philip C. McGuire and David A. Samuelson (eds.), *Shakespeare: The Theatrical Dimension*, 1979, pp. 190–4.

[3] Compare Booth, p. 33: 'Over and over again . . . throughout *King Lear*, an audience thinks in multiple dimensions – entertains two or more precise understandings at once, understandings that might, but do not, clash in the mind.'

[4] Compare Virgil Whitaker, *The Mirror up to Nature: The Technique of Shakespeare's Tragedies*, 1965, p. 221.

[5] Kott, *Shakespeare Our Contemporary*, p. 146.

[6] Harry Levin says that unless Edgar's presence is taken as providential, the so-called miracle here is 'more truly a pious fraud'; see 'The heights and the depths: a scene from "King Lear" ', in John Garrett (ed.), *More Talking of Shakespeare*, 1959, p. 98.

4 Act 4, Scene 5: Gloucester's 'suicide' leap: 'Now, fellow, fare thee well.' A possible staging by C. Walter Hodges

play is over – much in the manner of a Morality play figure, or guardian angel.[1] For the moment, Edgar's stratagem works: Gloucester exchanges despair for stoic resignation: 'Henceforth I'll bear / Affliction till it do cry out itself / "Enough, enough", and die' (4.5.75–7). But before he can long entertain 'free and patient thoughts', Lear enters, dressed fantastically and raving that he is 'the king himself'.

[1] Compare Alan Dessen, 'Two falls and a trap: Shakespeare and the spectacle of realism', *ELR* 5 (1975), 306: 'The true miracle is not Gloucester's survival from an illusory fall, but rather Edgar's meaningful assertion of the bond between child and father, a bond rejected by the blind parent but upheld by a loving son.'

KING LEAR AND GLOUCESTER AT DOVER

What follows is the most powerful and most disturbing episode in the play. Earlier, Lear was astonished by 'unaccommodated man' and sought to become like him; here, he *is* unaccommodated, not physically but mentally, as Edgar remarks (81–2). Paradoxically, his wits turned inside out, Lear sees more clearly and speaks truths more profound than ever before. Having dropped his disguise as Poor Tom, Edgar now recedes into the background, as the true madman and the truly blind confront each other at the play's climax.

For in Gloucester Lear sees and recognises a reflection of himself, literal blindness reflecting the mental blindness that led him to give away his kingdom, banish Cordelia, and trust his two elder daughters. In the lunatic king, Gloucester recognises a 'ruined piece of nature' (130), the mirror image of his own behaviour in believing his bastard son Edmond and precipitately outlawing Edgar.[1] When Lear hands him a 'challenge', ordering him to read it and 'mark but the penning of it' (134), Gloucester must again painfully confront his initial lack of perception in 1.2 and its result.[2] Earlier Lear wounds him in proclaiming that 'Gloucester's bastard son / Was kinder to his father than my daughters / Got 'tween the lawful sheets' (110–12). But the cruelty is self-reflexive. Through Gloucester, Lear berates himself, inflicts punishment for his own imperceptiveness and rash behaviour. His imagination has become diseased, and he knows it. But the disease is purgative. Just as 'a man may see how this world goes with no eyes', a madman can see through the camouflage of convention: 'See how yon justice rails upon yon simple thief. Hark in thine ear: change places, and handy-dandy, which is the justice, which is the thief?' (145–7).

Throughout this episode, 'unaccommodated' Lear removes the accretions of custom, propelling his hearers to recognition of essences, not forms. He knows he is not 'everything' (101), that he lacks soldiers (113). Though he insists he is 'every inch a king' (103) and issues royal commands, he is aware that he is merely mortal, a man sharing common human frailties, and that he is performing on 'a great stage of fools' (175). These insights might provide the basis for an eventual recovery, as some interpret the play, noting Lear's ability (in Cavell's terms) not only to recognise, but to allow himself to be recognised for what he truly is. This dual recognition will occur in his meeting with Cordelia in the next scene, when he awakens from a deep, healing sleep, dressed (again) in different clothes – both the awakening and the new dress signalling significant change. But not yet. When the Gentleman and attendants appear, Lear, fearing discovery, runs away.[3]

REVELATION, RECONCILIATION, AND DEATH

Lear and Gloucester never meet again. Thanks to Edgar, Gloucester survives Oswald's attempted murder and later a relapse into despair, but his conflicting emotions when

---

[1] Compare Cavell, p. 280: 'Gloucester has by now become not just a figure "parallel" to Lear, but Lear's double; he does not merely represent Lear, but is psychically identical with him.'

[2] *Ibid.*, p. 279.

[3] In a scene that F omits, Kent explains that 'burning shame' makes Lear avoid Cordelia (see Appendix, pp. 305–6 below, xx, 40–5).

5 'Hark in thine ear' (4.5.146): Paul Scofield as King Lear and Alan Webb as Gloucester in the production directed by Peter Brook (1962)

his son finally reveals himself are too much for the old man to bear. If one strand in the play's action is to show the need for genuine and deep feeling, especially a feeling for others,[1] then it is at least ironic that when one of the characters most deserving and needing this feeling at last experiences it, it kills him. Hearing Edgar's story of their 'pilgrimage', Gloucester feels both joy and grief – joy at his son's safety and charity, grief at the misery he has caused him. For his father's death, Edgar assumes responsibility, recognising too late his 'fault' in not revealing himself sooner. He reveals himself then only because he wants his father's blessing before going into combat against Edmond. Blessing Edgar, Gloucester dies.

This off-stage event, however, is but a prelude to the more catastrophic one that follows: the death of Cordelia. Many critics echo the sentiments of Samuel Johnson, who was so shocked by Cordelia's death that he could not bear to reread the final scenes of the play until he undertook to revise them as editor.[2] The reason for his reaction is that he found her death not only disappointed expectation but violated our 'natural ideas of justice'. Cordelia's death *is* a violation of that kind, and being so, it is the final

---

[1] Compare Leggatt, *King Lear*, pp. 26–7.
[2] Compare, for example, Booth, p. 5, who cites Johnson's remarks verbatim.

crushing experience in the play. By comparison, Lear's death is a welcome release, as
Kent says:

> O, let him pass. He hates him
> That would upon the rack of this tough world
> Stretch him out longer.   (5.3.287–9)

Why must Cordelia die as she does? The question has often been posed; evidently
from the later seventeenth century to the mid nineteenth no satisfactory answer could
be found, and the happy ending in Nahum Tate's redaction of the play was preferred.
Twentieth-century critics, perhaps more in tune with attitudes and experiences that
the early Jacobean stage reflected, have not objected, however deeply disturbing they
have found it. It is not simply that our age has grown more pessimistic than previous
ages were, or that our understanding of human nature is more profound than theirs.
More likely, Holocaust and Hiroshima have prepared us so that we know Cordelia's
fate corresponds to a truth of experience, not to 'natural ideas of justice'.[1]

Shakespeare puts the matter differently – more clearly and inescapably – in Lear's
anguished question:

> Why should a dog, a horse, a rat have life,
> And thou no breath at all?   (280–1)

Perhaps there is no answer after all to such a question, and the absence of an answer
compels us to feel the absurdity of existence, as so much else in the play does. If Lear's
death is a welcome release, it is nevertheless ironic that he should die (like Gloucester)
just as he has finally come to know himself and others. Some knowledge still eludes
him: he never identifies Kent with his servant Caius and, as at the beginning, he is
oblivious to other claims upon his daughter's love – her husband's – as he dreams of
having her to himself alone. But in the Folio version of the play, Lear's gaze is no longer
merely self-regarding. If he still engages in fantasy, it is a more generous-spirited one,
filled with hope, and directed outward: 'Look on her!' he says, 'Look, her lips. / Look
there, look there.' The world of *King Lear* is one still pervaded by outrageous and
preposterous extremities, but it is not without redeeming elements that may rescue us
from despair.

SHAKESPEARE'S EVOLVING VISION

In revising *King Lear* from its early form in the 1608 quarto to the later Folio version,
Shakespeare did not weaken the nihilistic energies in his play; he heightened them.
For example, to Lear's 'We'll go to supper i'th'morning', the Fool adds, 'And I'll go to
bed at noon' (3.6.40–1). References to a French invasion are almost all cut in the Folio
so that Cordelia's appearance in Act 4 seems more like an attempt to restore rightful
authority and forestall an inevitable and overwhelming anarchy than mere political
aggrandisement, though on an international scale.[2] 'Merlin's Prophecy', long suspected

---

[1] Compare Mack, p. 25; Whitaker, *Mirror up to Nature*, p. 237.
[2] Compare Taylor, 'War', p. 31.

6   Lear and Cordelia: 'Is this the promised end?' A painting by Maciek Swieszewski

of being a spurious addition (see below, pp. 281–2), fully captures the absurdist attitude of the play:

> When every case in law is right;
> No squire in debt nor no poor knight;
> When slanders do not live in tongues,

Nor cutpurses come not to throngs;
When usurers tell their gold i'th'field,
And bawds and whores do churches build,
Then comes the time, who lives to see't,
That going shall be used with feet.   (3.2.85–92)

If Shakespeare did not write these lines, then whoever did certainly understood the perversions that lie at the heart of the drama.

More extensive than the revision of his own play was Shakespeare's revision of his sources. He reconstructed the familiar story of old King Leir and his daughters so that the ending is far from what his audience expected or, in Shakespeare's sequence of events, from what any audience might reasonably expect. Edgar's experience at the beginning of Act 4 thus becomes a paradigm for the audience's experience. He consoles himself that his situation, bad as it is, cannot get worse:

Yet better thus, and known to be condemned,
Than still condemned and flattered. To be worst,
The low'st and most dejected thing of fortune,
Stands still in esperance, lives not in fear.
The lamentable change is from the best;
The worst returns to laughter.   (4.1.1–6)

Edgar of course is mistaken, as he learns almost immediately when he sees his father, blood oozing from empty eye-sockets, led by an old man. As Tom o'Bedlam, he has not yet hit bottom and realises that awareness of one's misfortunes provides no insurance against further misfortune: 'Who is't can say "I am at the worst"? / I am worse than e'er I was' (25–6).

With these lines Shakespeare prepares us for what we should expect – should, but probably do not. For just as the 'low'st and most dejected thing of fortune' lives still in hope, anticipating an end to misfortune or at least some alleviation of it, so do most of the rest of us. Shakespeare's audience, moreover, from what they knew of the Lear story, would also expect something quite different from the catastrophes that end the play. Certainly the story as it was told from Geoffrey of Monmouth's *Historia* down through the centuries to Elizabethan accounts in Higgins's *Mirour for Magistrates*, Holinshed's *Chronicles*, Spenser's *The Faerie Queene*, and the old play of *King Leir* would prepare a literate audience for something other than the image of the end that Shakespeare offers.[1] If we add to these literary renderings the fairytale structure and motifs that lie behind them, then the anticipation of a happier outcome is further strengthened.[2] And for much of the play, especially in Acts 4 and 5, *King Lear* also seems to be following, if not building upon, those deeply-rooted expectations.

PROMISED AND DISAPPOINTED ENDINGS

As early as Act 2, we discover that the disguised Kent has been in communication with Cordelia in France, and by Act 3 movement to rescue the old king and restore

---

[1] Cordelia's death by suicide, included in some accounts, is actually a separate story. See above, p. 2.
[2] See p. 10 above, and compare Young, 'Written and oral sources', pp. 309–19, esp. p. 317.

his authority has begun. In *Macbeth*, where Shakespeare more closely followed his sources, the reaction against Macbeth's tyranny similarly begins to gather and gain strength well before the climactic scenes in which evil is finally overthrown and the rightful heir ascends the throne. In *King Lear*, as the resistance to tyranny and anarchy gathers, the forces of evil do also, but with this difference: jealousies, rivalries, and suspicions begin to appear, revealing cracks in what should be (and in the sources are) a firmly united front against the enemy, especially an enemy from abroad. Although Albany remains willing to fight off the invaders, he has grave doubts about the justice of his cause, having seen what his wife and Regan have done and are.

In addition, the wicked sisters, for all their apparent cleverness and control, have begun making mistakes. Regan admits that 'It was great ignorance, Gloucester's eyes being out, / To let him live' (4.4.11–12). Wherever the old earl goes, she says, he arouses feeling against them among the people. It was a mistake in the first instance to mutilate Gloucester so brutally, motivating Cornwall's servant – loyal since childhood – to attack his master and fatally wound him. And, moving back in time still further, we may infer that it was similarly a tactical as well as a moral error, having stripped him of his dignity and his knights, to allow Lear to run off into the storm with only the Fool as company. These errors by Lear's enemies might seem to promise his happy restoration.

As against these actions, both cruel and foolish, other events occur that encourage hope for a happy outcome. Lear is safely brought to Dover, where he is eventually reunited with Cordelia. As she prepares to minister to the father who cast her out, so the other outcast child, Edgar, ministers to his father, saving him from despair and the suicide he intends. If Edgar errs in not revealing himself to Gloucester sooner (5.3.183), Cordelia does not make the same mistake; her gentle ministrations to her father succeed. Although Lear requires some 'further settling' of his wits, he has come a long way:

> You must bear with me. Pray you now, forget
> And forgive. I am old and foolish. (4.6.81–2)

In the Folio, 4.6 ends here, a deeply moving scene of reconciliation and forgiveness between Lear and Cordelia. A dozen lines of dialogue in the quarto between Kent and the Gentleman are omitted. Some of the information they contain is distracting, such as the news about Cornwall's death, and the Gentleman's reference to Edgar in Germany with Kent is a red herring. More to the point is the concern shared by both speakers about the impending battle. The end is not yet, but the Folio tends to soften that fact by removing the concluding, ominous remarks:

> KENT 'Tis time to look about; the powers of the kingdom approach apace.
> GENTLEMAN The arbitrement is like to be bloody. Fare you well, sir. [*Exit*]
> KENT My point and period will be throughly wrought,
>   Or well or ill, as this day's battle's fought. *Exit*

Without these lines, and with the gradual but consistent upturn of events in Act 4, the outcome in Act 5 appears more promising. Both the traditional narrative and its underlying folktale structure seem to imply a happy ending.

That we are disappointed in this expectation has aroused a good deal of critical comment. Susan Snyder, for example, says of Lear's awakening in Act 4, Scene 6: 'The scene is so charged and so satisfying that the unknowing audience could easily forget that Edmond, Goneril, and Regan are still at large, and feel that here was the end of the story.'[1] Citing many instances, John Kerrigan remarks that the play 'constantly provokes its audience to predict a return from "the worst", only to disappoint'. Stephen Greenblatt compares *King Lear* to what the Italians called a *tragedia di fin lieto*, a play wherein villains absorb calamity and the good are marvellously spared. Shakespeare in effect invokes the conventions of this genre, only to overturn them in the end.[2] And Stephen Booth says, commenting on Lear's entrance with Cordelia in his arms: 'Shakespeare has already presented an action that is serious, of an undoubted magnitude, *and complete*; he thereupon continues that action beyond the limits of the one category that no audience can expect to see challenged: Shakespeare presents the culminating events of his *story* after his *play* is over.'[3]

The play indeed seems to end several times before it is over. When Edgar presents Gonerill's intercepted letter to Albany in 5.1, we know that whatever else happens, her mischief will end, as of course it does, though in a way that – like much else in the final scene – comes as a surprise. Even before Edgar enters in disguise to deliver the letter, the dialogue among the British leaders is hardly auspicious for victory on their part. The rivalry between Gonerill and Regan for Edmond's favour is by now intense, and Albany openly proclaims his sympathy for Lear and his supporters. Determined to oppose the French invaders, he is equally determined to see justice done to the old king when the battle is over.

It is startling, then, in the short scene that follows, to see Lear and Cordelia carried off to prison. But the dismay that Cordelia feels – and with her, the audience – is immediately and heavily qualified by Lear's reaction. Nothing daunted by losing the battle, in his eloquent speech, 'Come, let's away to prison' (5.3.8 ff.), Lear focuses on what to him is most important: reunion with his beloved daughter. This lyric moment, like the earlier scene of reconciliation, conveys a beauty and harmony that are appropriate to the conclusion of a fairytale. But the world that Lear brought into being when he banished Cordelia still exists,[4] and its worst manifestations are still to come. For the moment, however, Lear is utterly oblivious of it, and like him, so may the audience be, forgetting that the earthly paradise Lear imagines will be a prison cell.[5]

Ensuing events further encourage optimism, particularly the downfall of Gonerill, Regan, and Edmond. All the forces of evil now appear to be vanquished once and for all. It only remains to bring Lear and Cordelia back on the stage for the happy conclusion of the main plot, as in the old play of *King Leir* and its many antecedents. But Kent's reminder to rescue the prisoners comes too late.[6] When Lear enters, he carries Cordelia

---

[1] *The Comic Matrix of Shakespeare's Tragedies*, 1979, p. 154.
[2] Kerrigan, p. 225; Greenblatt, 'Shakespeare and the exorcists', p. 180.
[3] Booth, p. 11.
[4] Stockholder, 'Multiple genres', p. 60. Stockholder otherwise argues that *King Lear* violates fairytale structure and therefore expectations from the first scene onwards. See *ibid.*, pp. 44 ff.
[5] Snyder, *The Comic Matrix*, p. 155.
[6] Compare Booth, p. 9: '. . . Kent enters, and a finished chapter continues. Kent's first sentence violently aborts the ceremony of theatrical conclusion that began when Albany called the herald to supervise the

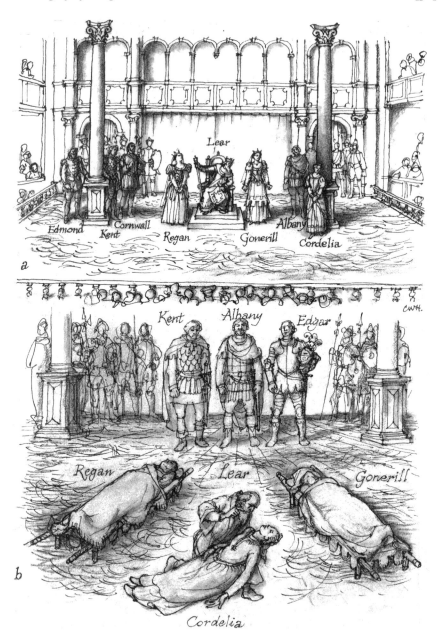

7   Lear and his daughters: *a* Act 1, Scene 1; *b* Act 5, Scene 3. Possible stagings by C. Walter Hodges

in his arms. They emerge as a kind of inverted *pietà*, and Albany, Kent, and Edgar stand aghast at the spectacle. This is not what any of the survivors – including the audience – had expected or wanted. As Ruth Nevo has said, Lear is taken 'out of the grave' in 4.6 to suffer a still greater loss. And it is this loss that precipitates Shakespeare's 'most unmitigated and quintessential tragic outcome, pitched as it is against an opposing pull toward restoration in the plot itself'.[1]

CONCLUSION

Early in *The Sense of an Ending* (1967), Frank Kermode discusses the differences between myth and fiction as he defines them, and the way that popular stories stick close to established conventions, while major novels tend to vary them more and more. 'The story that proceeded very simply to its obviously predestined end', he says, 'would be nearer myth than the novel or drama.' Peripeteia, or tragic reversal, is important in sophisticated fictions; it is equivalent in narrative to irony in rhetoric. Furthermore, it depends on our confidence of the end: 'it is a disconfirmation followed by a consonance; the interest of having our expectations falsified is obviously related to our wish to reach the discovery or recognition by an unexpected or instructive route'. He continues:

The more daring the peripeteia, the more we may feel that the work respects our sense of reality; and the more certainly we shall feel that the fiction under consideration is one of those which, by upsetting the ordinary balance of our naive expectations, is finding something out for us, something *real*. The falsification of an expectation can be terrible, as in the death of Cordelia; it is a way of finding something out that we should, on our more conventional way to the end, have closed our eyes to. Obviously it could not work if there were not a certain rigidity in the set of our expectations.   (p. 18)

As the episodes cited indicate, and as Kermode rightly assumes, the expectations *King Lear* arouses are, with cause, very strong if not rigid. The reality that the ending reveals is so powerful and, to many, unbearable, that we may understand why during the Restoration and for a hundred and fifty years afterwards it was not presented on the stage as Shakespeare wrote it. Shakespeare shocks us out of complacency, and as though Gloucester's off-stage death were not sufficient, he gives us Lear's which, as Kermode later comments, is terribly delayed. 'Beyond the apparent worse there is a worse suffering, and when it comes it is not only more appalling than anything expected, but a mere image of that horror, not the thing itself' (p. 82).

Recent productions of *King Lear*, certainly since Peter Brook's landmark staging in 1962 for the Royal Shakespeare Company (see p. 47 below), rarely shun the tough reality that the play reveals; if anything, they tend to highlight it. With Lear, we are stretched out on the rack of this tough world as long as possible. Not satisfied with Shakespeare's exceptional version of the story, Edward Bond has devised his own *Lear*, which is more violent still. But perhaps there is a point beyond which we cannot taste the actual horrors of the thing itself, and only the image will serve. Shakespeare seems to

formal combat between Edgar and Edmund . . . For the audience, the smooth ceremony of conclusion presumably collapses only moments before Kent ends it for the characters.'
[1] *Tragic Form in Shakespeare*, 1972, p. 301.

understand this, and disturbing as his flouting of our expectations may be, he does not venture beyond the pale, modifying the harsher quarto ending of the play accordingly (see p. 25 above, and Textual Analysis, pp. 80–1 below). If, as Kermode says, everything in *King Lear* tends to a conclusion that does not occur – that is, a reunion with Cordelia that endures and includes restoration as well as redemption – it is sufficient for a true fiction. Drawing upon myth, Shakespeare transforms it and presents us instead with 'something real'.

King Lear on stage and screen

Although *King Lear* is a difficult play, it is not difficult to stage, notwithstanding Charles Lamb's famous demurrer – that only the imagination can encompass it. Few props are needed, and except possibly for the scene in Act 2 where Edgar descends from his hiding-place (see Commentary 2.1.19), no elaborate stage set, no upper acting level is necessary. The play thus eminently suited the bare apron stage of the Globe, where it was probably performed in 1605, although the first record of any performance is at court on 26 December 1606 (see p. 1 above). The first play produced at court for the holiday season, it was also the first play performed by any company since the plague had broken out again in London in July.[1] It is possible that the plague, which continued for much of the decade after James I's accession, severely curtailed performances at the Globe; little is known of *King Lear*'s early stage history. Except for a production in 1610 at Gowthwaite Hall in Yorkshire by a provincial company under the protection of Sir Richard Cholmeley,[2] no records exist of any other seventeenth-century performances until after the Restoration. Perhaps the play never became popular, but the revisions reflected in the Folio text suggest attempts to revive it, at least in the decade immediately after its first production.

Though the cast of characters is large, it was not beyond the resources of the King's Men.[3] With doubling of some roles, only fifteen players were required.[4] Burbage, as the company's leading actor, played Lear. Scholars have long believed that Armin played the Fool, but William Ringler has argued[5] that he probably played Edgar instead, since Armin was adept at shifting roles within a single play, as Edgar does.[6] The boy actor who

---

[1] J. Leeds Barroll, 'Shakespeare and the plague', in *Shakespeare's Art from a Comparative Perspective*, ed. Wendell M. Aycock, 1981, pp. 22–7. See Barroll, *Politics, Plague, and Shakespeare's Theater*, 1991, pp. 217–26, for a compilation of plague statistics.

[2] C. J. Sisson, 'Shakespeare's quartos as prompt-copies, with some account of Cholmeley's players and a new Shakespeare allusion', *RES* 18 (1942), 129–43; John J. Murphy, *Darkness and Devils*, 1984, p. 106.

[3] For the composition of the King's Men at this time, see William A. Ringler, Jr, 'Shakespeare and his actors: some remarks on *King Lear*', in *Shakespeare's Art*, ed. Aycock, p. 193, n. 2. Compare Chambers, 1, 79–80; Bernard Beckerman, *Shakespeare at the Globe, 1599–1609*, 1962, p. 133.

[4] As few as thirteen could perform the quarto version, according to Kent Cartwright, 'Casting the quarto *King Lear*', Shakespeare Association of America seminar paper (April 1989); compare John Meagher, 'Economy and recognition: thirteen Shakespearean puzzles', *SQ* 35 (1984), 7–21. In another SAA paper, Skiles Howard found fifteen required for the Q version and still more for F, including two musicians and enough mutes to carry the dead bodies off at the end.

[5] Ringler, 'Shakespeare and his actors', pp. 187–93.

[6] On the other hand, would Armin's small size suit Edgar, especially as the champion against Edmond in 5.3? See Wiles, pp. 136–63.

played Cordelia also played the Fool, Ringler and others have maintained.[1] Doubling would be feasible, since Cordelia leaves the action before the Fool enters in 1.4 and returns only after the Fool's final exit in 3.6.[2] The lines introducing the Fool (1.4.60–3) and the ambiguous reference in 'my poor fool is hanged' (5.3.279) provide thematic or conceptual linking of the two roles, which some critics reject as modern thinking, not Shakespearean. But as Giorgio Melchiori has shown, doubling for effect was practised in dramatic representations before Shakespeare, who developed the usage further as 'a way of suggesting parallelisms in the roles played by different characters'.[3]

FINDING THE TEXT: *KING LEAR* FROM THE RESTORATION
TO THE NINETEENTH CENTURY

Whatever its success, or lack of it, under the Stuarts, *King Lear* underwent a sea-change in the Restoration. Officially closed in 1642, theatres did not reopen until after the monarchy was restored in 1660 and the court returned from exile in France, bringing with it much French influence. Public theatres were now enclosed, proscenium staging became the norm, movable painted flats provided scenic effects, and actresses took women's parts. Above all, the stage was ruled by a new decorum, which led to the transformation of Shakespeare's texts to suit newly refined tastes. Two companies were licensed, one under Thomas Killigrew (the King's Company), the other under William Davenant (the Duke's Company), both at first using converted tennis courts as theatres. Davenant's company won the right to perform *King Lear* among others of Shakespeare's plays, and performances are recorded in January 1664 at Lincoln's Inn Fields, and on 25 June 1675 at the new Dorset Garden Theatre built in 1671 by Christopher Wren.[4] Although the casts are unknown, Thomas Betterton as the company's leading actor no doubt played Lear.[5]

The text of *King Lear* used in these Restoration performances is not known either, but among the Smock Alley prompt-books that have survived (from the Theatre Royal in Smock Alley, Dublin) is one of *King Lear*. This prompt-book, now at the Folger Shakespeare Library, contains annotated pages from a copy of the Third Folio (1664), marked with entrance warnings, emended readings, deleted lines, calls for props, and so forth. Because of the number of hands involved in marking it up, and because some emendations in the margins appear to anticipate, if they do not derive from, eighteenth-century editions, such as those by Pope and Hanmer, it is difficult to date

[1] See Booth, pp. 129–55.
[2] In 'The double casting of Cordelia and Lear's Fool: a theatrical view', *Texas Studies in Literature and Language* 27 (1985), 354–68, Richard Abrams accepts doubling but rejects Ringler's argument for the boy actor in both roles.
[3] 'Peter, Balthasar, and Shakespeare's art of doubling', *MLR* 78 (1983), 790. Note that Edgar's absence in 1.1 may be explained by the need for the actor to play the King of France. Similarly, whoever played Edmond could have doubled as the Duke of Burgundy (if Edmond exits with Gloucester at 1.1.30), making for a nice symmetry. But since the roles of Burgundy and Oswald could be doubled instead, Edmond could remain on stage throughout most of 1.1.
[4] *The London Stage, 1660–1800: Part I, 1660–1700*, ed. William Van Lennep, 1965, pp. 22, 75, 234.
[5] In 'The Stage History of *King Lear*', University of Texas dissertation, 1940, pp. 40–2, Leland Eugene Derrick speculates that Henry Harris played Edgar; James Nokes, the Fool; Thomas Lovell, Gloucester; John Richards, Kent; Samuel Sandford, Edmond; Cave Underhill, Oswald; Mrs Saunderson, Cordelia.

the *Lear* prompt-book, which may have gone through several stages of adaptation. On the other hand, as James McManaway once suggested, the relationship of the stage to the study may have then been close enough for the emendations of eighteenth-century editors to reflect or perpetuate those of stage tradition.[1]

Whatever the truth may be, available evidence does not point to *Lear* as a frequently performed play. The theme of fallen royalty and the absence of a love story may explain its lack of popularity.[2] The situation changed after 1681, when Nahum Tate rewrote it to suit contemporary taste. Consulting both quarto and Folio texts,[3] Tate not only overhauled Shakespeare's language, he drastically altered the structure of the play and its plot, changed several characters, introduced a new one (Arante, Cordelia's confidante), and eliminated the Fool. Most notably, he restored the happy ending of the Lear legend. He did this by having Edgar and Cordelia fall in love, explaining:

'Twas my good Fortune to light on one Expedient to rectifie what was wanting in the Regularity and Probability of the Tale, which was to run through the whole, A *Love* betwixt *Edgar* and *Cordelia*, that never chang'd word with each other in the Original. This renders *Cordelia's* Indifference and her Father's Passion in the first Scene probable. It likewise gives Countenance to *Edgar's* Disguise, making that a generous Design that was before a poor Shift to save his Life.[4]

Other reasons prompted Tate to change the ending. Apparently the number of dead bodies at the ends of tragedies had become the occasion for 'unseasonable Jests'; as Dryden had said, "tis more difficult to Save than 'tis to Kill: The Dagger and Cup of Poyson are alwaies in Readiness; but to bring the Action to the last Extremity, and then by probable Means to recover All, will require the Art and Judgment of a Writer . . .'[5] Thus, Lear has his kingdom restored and bequeaths it to the lovers, Edgar and Cordelia, while he, Kent, and Gloucester (whom Lear has persuaded not to commit suicide) retire to 'some cool Cell'. There, meditating upon 'Fortunes past', and cheered by 'the prosperous Reign / Of this celestial Pair', they will live out their lives.

From the very first scene, Tate's transformation of Shakespeare's text, both in language and dramatic structure, is revealing. Instead of Gloucester and Kent discussing the division of the kingdom, the play opens with Edmond's soliloquy:

> Thou Nature art my Goddess, to thy Law
> My Services are bound, why am I then
> Depriv'd of a Son's Right, because I came not
> In the dull Road that custom has prescrib'd?
> Why Bastard, wherefore Base, when I can boast
> A Mind as gen'rous, and a Shape as true
> As honest Madam's Issue? why are we

[1] 'Additional prompt-books of Shakespeare from the Smock Alley Theatre', *MLR* 45 (1950), 65. Compare R. C. Bald, 'Shakespeare on the stage in Restoration Dublin', *PMLA* 56 (1941), 369–78.
[2] Derrick, 'Stage History', p. 35.
[3] *Ibid.*, pp. 53–4; but Peter Blayney suggests instead that stage practice may be responsible for some quarto readings.
[4] From the dedication to Thomas Boteler, Esq., in *Five Restoration Adaptations of Shakespeare*, ed. Christopher Spencer, 1965, p. 203.
[5] *Ibid.*, p. 204. Tate quotes from Dryden's Preface to *The Spanish Fryar*.

Held Base, who in the lusty stealth of Nature
Take fiercer Qualities than what compound
The scanted Births of the stale Marriage-bed?
Well then, legitimate *Edgar*, to thy right
Of Law I will oppose a Bastard's Cunning.
Our Father's Love is to the Bastard *Edmond*
As to Legitimate *Edgar*; with success
I've practis'd yet on both their easie Natures:
Here comes the old Man chaf't with th'Information
Which late I forged against my Brother *Edgar*,
A Tale so plausible, so boldly utter'd,
And heightned by such lucky Accidents,
That now the slightest circumstance confirms him,
And Base-born *Edmond* spight of Law inherits.

By regularising Shakespeare's language and 'clarifying' it to suit the more refined taste of his age, Tate also flattened it considerably. At the same time, he simplified the sub-plot and the characters. Edmond's intrigue has already occurred; now as Gloucester and Kent enter, the old earl rejects Kent's intercession on behalf of Edgar, whose alleged treachery he believes. Delighted, Edmond displays a more two-dimensional, rapacious character. Later, he even attempts to assault Cordelia (see illustration 8).

Regardless of what we may now think of Tate's redaction, actors and audiences preferred his version of the play, especially its happy ending, for the next century and a half.[1] It is an extreme instance of what Shakespeare's text, like any theatrical script, had been subject to from the beginning: actors, managers, and directors, as well as authors, have always felt free to alter the 'book' of a play to suit exigencies, dramatic or otherwise, that they anticipate or experience. Nor was Tate's version itself immune. As more and more editions of Shakespeare's works began appearing, starting with Nicholas Rowe's in 1709, dissatisfaction with Tate's adaptation grew. Joseph Addison was not alone in criticising the mangling of Shakespeare's tragedy in Tate's version.[2]

King Lear in the eighteenth century is thus a curious combination of Shakespeare and Tate. The Folio text, moreover, may not have been totally eclipsed. If the Smock Alley prompt-book was actually used for professional theatre performances, and if it dates from a period later than the Restoration, then something closer to *King Lear* as we know it was acted in the eighteenth century, too.[3] It was in its 'Tatefied' form,

---

[1] Compare Thomas Davies, *Dramatic Miscellanies*, 1783, II, 262–3: 'The passion of Edgar and Cordelia is happily imagined; it strongly connects the main plot of the play and renders it more interesting to the spectators; without this, and the consequent happy catastrophe, the alteration of Lear would have been of little worth; besides, after those turbulent scenes of resentment, violence, disobedience, ingratitude, and rage, between Lear and his two eldest daughters, with the king's consequent agony and distraction, the unexpected interview of Cordelia and Edgar in act III. gives a pause of relief to the harassed and distressed minds of the audience . . . I have seen this play represented twenty or thirty times, yet I can truly affirm that the spectators always dismissed the two lovers with the most rapturous applause.'

[2] See *The Spectator*, No. 40, 16 April 1711, and Arthur John Harris, 'Garrick, Colman, and *King Lear*', *SQ* 22 (1971), 59–62.

[3] Another prompt-copy in the Folger Shakespeare Library (Lear, 30) consists of the Tonson edition of 1734 incompletely marked. Whether it was actually used, and by whom, is unknown, but evidently Tate's adaptation of 1681 did not entirely monopolise the stage. Aaron Hill's quotations in *The Prompter* for

8 Susanna Maria Cibber as Cordelia, saved by Edgar from Edmond's ruffians in the storm, in Tate's adaptation (c. 1743)

however, that *King Lear* rose in popularity, though it did not rival the other great Shakespearean tragedies. In the Augustan period, 1700–28, *Hamlet, Macbeth*, and *Julius Caesar* were performed more frequently: 151, 132, and 105 times, respectively, to *Lear's* 87 performances.[1] *Lear* therefore does not appear in G. W. Stone's list of the top twenty-one plays – that is, those with a hundred or more performances (the bias of

Tuesday, 7 October 1735, moreover, are not from the Tate version. See *The Prompter: A Theatrical Paper (1734–1736)*, ed. William W. Appleton and Kalman A. Burnim, 1966, pp. 100–5.
[1] George Winchester Stone, Jr, 'The making of the repertory', in *The London Theatre World, 1660–1800*, ed. Robert D. Hume, 1980, p. 197.

the time clearly favoured comedy and melodrama). But by the Garrick era, 1747–76, the situation had changed. *Romeo and Juliet* and *Richard III* (in Cibber's version) were among the most popular plays (335 and 223 performances), trailing only Gay's *The Beggar's Opera* (395 performances). *Lear* (141 performances) had climbed in favour, while *Julius Caesar* with 27 had much declined. *Hamlet* continued to hold the stage well with 203 performances, as did *Macbeth* (139 performances). The differences derive partly from a change in taste, but perhaps more from the success of David Garrick, the age's premier actor, who took many of the leading roles and made them his own, especially Hamlet and King Lear.[1]

The several versions of Garrick's *Lear* show how fluid the play remained in the hands of a capable and dynamic actor-manager. The text continued to evolve as Garrick restored more and more of Shakespeare's original while tenaciously clinging to Tate's ending,[2] much against the advice of George Colman, who worked with him at Drury Lane before moving on to Covent Garden in 1768. With the love story curtailed and the Fool still altogether absent, increased emphasis fell on the already dominant role of the king. This suited the taste of Garrick's audiences, who enjoyed virtuoso acting. A high point came early in the play, when Lear curses Gonerill in 1.4. Following Tate's structure, which eliminated 1.5, but restoring most of Shakespeare's language, Garrick used this speech as the climax of Act 1, a moment of extreme emotionality. At 'Blasts and fogs upon thee' a contemporary observer 'could not avoid expecting a paralytic Stroke would wither every Limb of *Goneril*'.[3] Garrick continued playing on the emotions, or rather milking them, so that when he finally burst into tears at the end of the scene, the effect was stupendous. For the next hundred years, this moment became a crucial one for every actor who followed Garrick in the role.[4]

The theatre is never without its rivalries, and the eighteenth century was no exception. Garrick's Lear was challenged by Spranger Barry and William Powell, and his efforts to recover Shakespeare's text were rivalled, too – by George Colman, for example, in his edition of 1768. Beginning with the opening scene, Colman restored more of Shakespeare's original than anyone so far had done. But he was ahead of his time; his adaptation, performed at Covent Garden, was a failure. The public still preferred Tate's version, especially the Edgar–Cordelia love story, which Colman all but eliminated.[5] Eventually, yielding to Francis Gentleman's critique in 1770, Garrick further modified Tate's *Lear* but cast Barry in the leading role instead of himself.[6] The points at issue were mainly the disputed love scenes between Cordelia and Edgar, though given the

[1] *Ibid.*, pp. 202–3.
[2] For a brief analysis of this evolution from Tate to Garrick's last version, see George Winchester Stone, Jr, 'Garrick's production of *King Lear*: a study in the temper of the eighteenth-century mind', *SP* 45 (1948), 96–101. Restoration of Shakespeare's originals, at least in part, had already begun with other plays: see George C. D. Odell, *Shakespeare from Betterton to Irving*, 2 vols., 1920, I, 339–47.
[3] Joseph Pittard, *Observations on Mr. Garrick's Acting* (1758), in *Shakespeare: The Critical Heritage*, ed. Brian Vickers, 1976, IV, 318.
[4] Bratton, p. 23. For further details of Garrick's delivery and others', see *ibid.*, pp. 97–9 and 225–7, and Rosenberg, pp. 127–30.
[5] Odell, *Betterton to Irving*, I, 380–1.
[6] Harris, 'Garrick, Colman and *King Lear*', pp. 63–6.

temper of the times, neither Colman nor Garrick could reinstate the Fool or replace
Tate's ending with Shakespeare's.[1] Those restorations awaited the courage of the next
century.

After Garrick's retirement from the stage in 1776, John Philip Kemble essayed King
Lear in 1788, and his sister, Sarah Siddons, played Cordelia. Although at first he used
Garrick's text, Kemble later went back to Tate, reversing the direction that Garrick
and Colman had taken. For this he receives the severest condemnation from Genest.[2]
His production at Drury Lane in 1795 was elaborate (see below). Doubling had long
since become unnecessary, and increased numbers of supers filled the cast: the first
court scene consisted of four gentlemen, three knights, a physician, a captain of the
guard, a herald, four ladies (in addition to Tate's Arante), two pages, and an unspecified
number of guards, besides the principal characters.[3]

Kemble continued playing Lear from time to time and from version to version
until 1810, when performances were discontinued in London owing to George III's
growing mental disorder. When the sovereign died in 1820, theatre managers vied with
one another to restage the play. By this time, the criticisms of Charles Dibdin, Leigh
Hunt, Charles Lamb, William Oxberry, and others, including the eminent German
critic August Wilhelm von Schlegel, weighed heavily against Tate's adaptation and its
derivatives. But it would be years before anything like a true restoration of Shakespeare's
text could be heard on the English stage.[4]

Junius Brutus Booth at Covent Garden on 13 April 1820 was the first to portray
Lear after King George III's death; his performance paled before Edmond Kean's
at Drury Lane eleven days later and soon closed. What Kean lacked in physique
he more than compensated for in passion and articulation.[5] His was the first great
romantic representation of the role. Although it did not altogether please Leigh Hunt
and some others, it was obviously a great advance over Kemble's and much closer to
Garrick's, which in many ways anticipated Kean's conception.[6] He excelled in The
Curse (1.4.230–44) and in the storm scenes, but perhaps his most moving scene was
the reconciliation with Cordelia in Act 4, which utterly silenced the audience, struck
dumb with admiration. *Blackwood's Magazine* reported that 'The mild pathos of his
voice and the touching simplicity of his manner when he kneels down before her and
offers to drink the poison if she has it for him, can never be forgotten.'[7]

[1] See the 'Advertisement' to Colman's edition, sig. A2–4.
[2] John Genest, *Some Account of the English Stage, 1660–1830*, 1832, VIII, 131–4, 185. Derrick, 'Stage History',
p. 137, thinks the anti-French feeling aroused by the Napoleonic wars led Kemble to adopt Tate's version,
where Edgar replaces the King of France as Cordelia's suitor. The love story, moreover, lessened the
emphasis upon the king, whose madness could remind audiences of what ailed George III.
[3] Derrick, 'Stage History', pp. 153, 168–9, n. 14.
[4] See Carol Jones Carlisle, *Shakespeare from the Greenroom*, 1969, pp. 266–74, and *Leigh Hunt's Dramatic
Criticism, 1808–1831*, ed. L. H. Houtchens and C. W. Houtchens, 1949, pp. 15–20.
[5] H. N. Hillebrand, *Edmond Kean*, 1933, p. 191, quotes Crabbe Robinson: 'Kean's defects are lost in this
character, and become almost virtues. He does not need vigour or grace as Lear, but passion – and this never
fails him.' Compare the review in *The Times*, 25 April 1820; reprinted in Gāmini Salgādo, *Eyewitnesses of
Shakespeare: First Hand Accounts of Performances 1590–1890*, 1975, pp. 280–2.
[6] *Leigh Hunt's Dramatic Criticism*, pp. 297–8; Bratton, p. 30.
[7] Cited in F. W. Hawkins, *The Life of Edmond Kean*, 1869, II, 137.

Kean had wanted to retain Shakespeare's tragic conclusion, but Elliston (manager at Drury Lane) demurred for three years. When he did agree, legend has it that the audience tittered to see the diminutive actor struggling under the weight of Mrs W. West's Cordelia, and the production reverted to Tate's ending after only three performances. The 'Shakespeare' ending may not have been altogether abandoned in later productions, and in London in 1834 William Charles Macready revived it.[1]

Macready was the next important Lear. Immediately following his London success as Richard III, when Covent Garden was preparing to stage *Lear* in 1820, he was offered the lead but preferred to play Edmond opposite J. B. Booth instead. Not until August 1833, when on tour in the provinces, did he attempt Lear – and then not very successfully.[2] The following spring he acted the part for the first time in London, restoring much of Shakespeare's language and Kean's ending, but not the Fool. That event awaited January 1838 when, at the off-hand suggestion of his colleague, George Bartley, he cast a nineteen-year-old actress, Priscilla Horton, in the role.[3]

Criticism of Tate's version had at last triumphed, though a Tatefied *King Lear* continued to hold the boards in America (where Macready, disgusted, saw it with Forrest as Lear in 1843) and elsewhere.[4] Victorian England scarcely saw the *Lear* of Shakespeare's Jacobean audience, however. Textual matters aside,[5] the production as a production was vastly different. Victorians enjoyed spectacle, as Macready (and later Charles Kean) understood, and his productions at Covent Garden were nothing if not spectacular. Castles sat upon the stage, Druid circles adorned the landscape, and the storm scenes were ferocious. Macready, 'gigantic', was 'very enthusiastically' received.[6] Playing opposite a reluctant Helen Faucit as Cordelia, he made Lear one of his greatest roles.

Although he restored the Fool and Shakespeare's language, Macready retained Tate's dramatic structure and cut the text heavily. His was a virtuoso performance. Samuel Phelps, who staged *Lear* in 1845 at Sadler's Wells, made fewer cuts, kept Shakespeare's sequence of scenes, and attempted ensemble performance.[7] Charles Kean's production a dozen years later reverted to something like Macready's text (a third of Shakespeare's lines gone) but now spectacle threatened to overwhelm text, a phenomenon not unknown in our own time. Thus, though 'Shakespeare' was on the boards at last, bardolatry did not extend to sanctifying his text.

---

[1] Carlisle, *Shakespeare from the Greenroom*, p. 273; Hillebrand, *Kean*, p. 234; G. K. Hunter, Introduction to Cornmarket Press facsimile of Cumberland's 1830 edition, 1970; Odell, *Betterton to Irving*, II, 154–6.
[2] *The Diaries of William Charles Macready, 1833–1851*, ed. William Toynbee, 1912; reprinted 1969, I, 58.
[3] *Ibid.*, I, 483.
[4] Bratton, p. 31; Charles Shattuck, *Shakespeare on the American Stage: From the Hallams to Edwin Booth*, 1976, p. 77.
[5] On Macready's text, see Odell, *Betterton to Irving*, II, 195–7.
[6] *Diaries of Macready*, p. 442; Bratton, pp. 34–6. In his rave review in *The Examiner*, 4 February 1838 (reprinted in Salgādo, *Eyewitnesses of Shakespeare*, pp. 283–7), Charles Dickens especially praised the inclusion of the Fool.
[7] Bratton, pp. 36–7; Odell, *Betterton to Irving*, II, 272–3.

FINDING THE SET DESIGN

From the bare boards of the Globe to the huge Victorian sets, *King Lear* had come a long way. In Shakespeare's day, such spectacle as there was centred mainly upon costumes and a few effects. For *King Lear*, only a few props were needed: a throne (if one was used) and a map of some sort in 1.1, stocks for Kent in 2.2, and a chair (for which the throne in 1.1 could substitute) to carry Lear on stage in 4.6.[1] The hovel from which Edgar emerges in 3.4 was probably suggested by curtains at the rear of the stage. Costumes were elaborate but reflected contemporary, not historical, design (Lear comments upon his daughter's elegant attire at 2.4.262). Further spectacle was provided, as the quarto title page suggests, by 'the sullen and assumed humor of Tom of Bedlam' – Edgar in his disguise as a madman – and by the king during the storm. Armies, represented by two or three soldiers, flags, and a drum, appear in Acts 4 and 5, but the battle scene occurs off-stage and is deliberately underplayed. For Shakespeare's audience, prepared to listen as well as see, theatre meant language, words, poetry.

With the advent of movable scenery during the Restoration, things began to change. Although costuming remained elegant, it was still contemporary in style, not historical. Only later did intricate, historically oriented set designs dominate theatrical productions, but even then much was anachronistic. In 1795 John Philip Kemble's staging of *King Lear* at Drury Lane found him wearing a white wig and mustachios, a jewelled and feathered hat, false shoulders, and a lace collar and white stockings.[2] The production had fifteen different scene locations effected by painted flats raised and lowered from fly-galleries installed the year before.[3]

A taste for historical 'illustration' had grown since the days of Garrick. Charles Kean's production reflected the current passion for 'archaeological' representation. Baffled by how to set the play in the pre-history of Lear's reign, Kean decided on the 'Anglo-Saxon' era of A.D. 800 as 'a date sufficiently remote' and one that could secure 'uniformity of character in the accessories of this great drama'.[4] The choice thus depended upon what could be known as against what could only be guessed about the mythical age of King Lear.

Noting how the 'spectacular' could 'overlay the dramatic' at the cost of 'poetic and histrionic' effects, the *Illustrated London News* proclaimed that in Kean's production this danger was overcome, even as the engineer and the painter were accorded the widest scope for their talents.[5] It was spectacular nevertheless, and Charles Kean, though lacking his father's talent, apparently rose to the occasion. But despite his efforts, and despite several visits from the royal family, performances ended after eight weeks, a run not long enough to recoup the expense of producing the play.[6]

---

[1] The stage direction at 5.3.204, *Gonerill and Regans bodies brought out*, may suggest a litter or bier for each one, or perhaps dummies, if the actors were now needed as supers. Compare T. J. King, *Shakespearean Staging, 1599–1642*, 1971, p. 19.
[2] Bratton, p. 61.
[3] David Rostron, 'John Philip Kemble's "King Lear" of 1795', in *The Eighteenth-Century English Stage*, ed. Kenneth Richards and Peter Thomson, 1972, p. 153.
[4] Preface to Kean's edition of 1858.
[5] 24 April 1858; reprinted in Salgādo, *Eyewitnesses of Shakespeare*, p. 287.
[6] Bratton, p. 38.

Spectacle, antiquarianism, and textual cutting culminated in Henry Irving's production of *King Lear* in 1892. The elaborate staging necessarily resulted in cuts; but other cuts, such as eliminating Gloucester's blinding, were the result of Victorian taste. At Ford Madox Brown's suggestion, Irving set his production in the period just after the Romans left Britain, so as to imply both greatness and decay. Druidical priests and Viking warriors mingled on the stage among ruined Roman villas and temples. Like Macready, Irving arranged the text and the production to set himself off to best advantage, and like Macready he attempted a psychological interpretation. But the role was beyond his powers. The elaborate set designs notwithstanding, the production (which never toured) was not a success, nor was it ever revived. Its greatest emotional impact was Ellen Terry's achievement as Cordelia in the reconciliation scene that ends Act 4.[1]

After Irving's relative failure, *King Lear* fell into some disfavour, although Robert Bruce Mantell did well in the role in America from 1905 until his death in 1928.[2] Norman McKinnel was less successful at the Haymarket in 1909, but this production, by Herbert Trench, was important for its reaction against 'archaeological' realism. Experiments abroad and the efforts of William Poel and others to revive 'Elizabethan' staging had begun to make their mark. Meanwhile, Gordon Craig and his followers advocated a 'poetic' or 'symbolic' setting for Shakespeare that would provide the proper atmosphere and ambience for the plays. Although the two schools opposed each other, the one calling for a simple, bare stage, the other for suggestive set designs, both agreed on the need for smoother performances uninterrupted by long intervals that elaborate scene-shifting required. For the Haymarket, Charles Ricketts used looming monoliths, colour tones of grey, and variously illuminated backcloths that became a model for designers and producers for several decades.[3]

Experimentation has continued throughout the century, much enhanced by technological advances in lighting and scenery construction. In 1936, for Komisarjevsky's production at Stratford-upon-Avon, lighting was mainly used; flights of narrow, angled steps almost filled the stage, and Lear's fantastically-columned throne was the only furniture. Although reviewers and actors were not altogether happy with the set, critics thought that the bareness and Komisarjevsky's lighting strengthened the sense of elemental forces at work in the play.[4] George Devine's production in 1955, starring John Gielgud, became notorious for the sets by the Japanese-American designer, Isamu Noguchi. The entire play was performed against a background of geometrical or symbolic shapes that emphasised the drama's timeless, out-of-this-world quality. Costuming was grotesque: the strangely holed cloaks that Lear and others wore reminded some of Henry Moore sculptures.[5] If the explicit aim was to give language its preeminent

[1] Carlisle, *Shakespeare from the Greenroom*, p. 303; Bratton, pp. 38–9; Odell, *Betterton to Irving*, II, 387–8, 404, 446–7.
[2] Derrick, 'Stage History', pp. 261–4; compare Shattuck, *Shakespeare on the American Stage*, II: *From Booth and Barrell to Sothern and Marlowe*, 1987, pp. 235–43.
[3] Bratton, pp. 42–3; Derrick, 'Stage History', pp. 211–13. Compare Cary M. Mazer, *Shakespeare Refashioned: Elizabethan Plays on Edwardian Stages*, 1981, pp. 50–9, 107–10.
[4] Sally Beauman, *The Royal Shakespeare Company: A History of Ten Decades*, 1982, pp. 147–8; Bratton, p. 60.
[5] Bratton, p. 62.

place (as the programme note stated), it did not succeed, for audiences found the set and costume designs distracting. Only Claire Bloom as Cordelia (like Ellen Terry in Irving's production) conveyed anything of human warmth.[1]

King Lear has not escaped modern-dress productions. In 1976, with Donald Sinden in the lead, Trevor Nunn directed the play in the costumes and settings of 1914 – the last era, he thought, in which a monarch could conceivably give away his kingdom. Sinden as Lear wore a uniform and his family formal court attire; he entered 'stumping like an aged Hindenburg, chewing a cigar and creakily lowering himself into his seat'.[2] Six years later at Stratford, Adrian Noble staged the play in a supposedly timeless period, but visual allusions to the Falklands War then in progress, as in the type and colour of the soldiers' uniforms, gave the production a contemporary relevance. So did Samuel Beckett's influence, which was everywhere apparent, as in the oil drums or dustbins used in the mock trial scene (3.6), the pool of water in which the two old men bathe their feet in 4.5, the boots Lear leaves behind afterwards, and especially the representation of the Fool (see below). Throughout the performance, as Alan Sinfield observed, an 'assault on the transcendence' usually ascribed to the tragic hero was uppermost. An extremely physical production, the point was 'not insight into a further reality, there is no further reality – just the material world in which people and systems do things to you . . .'[3]

FINDING THE CHARACTERS AND THE OVERALL INTERPRETATION

Just as styles in staging have changed over the centuries, so has each age discovered new ways of representing the characters in *King Lear*, particularly the character of the king. Changes reflect changing tastes in art and drama, the abilities of specific actors, and directorial 'concepts'. Lacking eye-witness accounts, we can only guess at how Burbage portrayed Lear at the Globe or Blackfriars. In the next age, which favoured heroic drama, Betterton played the part (in Tate's version) as an essentially angry if regal old man. Breaking with tradition, Garrick broadened the emotional range of the part to a more complex characterisation much closer to the Shakespearean original, which he carefully studied. Indeed, even as he retained much of Tate's text, Shakespeare's seems to have influenced him more.[4] Madness, rage, complacency, pathos, indignation all contributed to his characterisation of the old king, but pathos was the dominant emotion (see illustration 9). In this age of 'sentiment', Garrick hoped to gain audience sympathy and commiseration, and he succeeded admirably.[5]

Kemble emphasised the age and physical decrepitude of the old king, not his titanism, but his Lear was still dignified and stately. In his *Life of Kemble*, James Boaden complains that however excellent the actor was in 1788, he subsequently 'quenched with infirmity

[1] Audrey Williamson, *Contemporary Theatre, 1953–1956*, n.d., pp. 122–3; J. C. Trewin, *Shakespeare on the English Stage, 1900–1964*, 1964, p. 221.
[2] *The Times*, 1 December 1976; cited by Bratton, p. 62.
[3] Alan Sinfield, '*King Lear* versus *Lear* at Stratford', *Critical Quarterly* 24, 4 (1982), 10.
[4] Compare Stone, 'Garrick's production', p. 92.
[5] Leigh Woods, *Garrick Claims the Stage*, 1984, pp. 35–6. For contemporary testimonials, see Arthur Colby Sprague, 'Garrick as King Lear', *Shakespearian Players and Performances*, 1953, pp. 21–40.

9   Garrick as King Lear in the storm, with Kent and Edgar but without the Fool. A painting by Benjamin
Wilson (1761)

the insane fire of the injured father'.[1] Kemble's unfortunate tendency was to simplify,
to eschew subtlety in favour of a single dominant passion, and his voice, uncertain and
unreliable at best, was inadequate to convey the depths of Lear's passion. On the other
hand, Kemble brought to the role a conscientiously studied performance, capable of
brilliant effects, which Macready admired. His greatest moments were The Curse in
Act 1 and his dialogue with Edgar as Tom o'Bedlam (played by his brother Charles) in
Act 3, but his performance overall never equalled Garrick's.[2]

Edmond Kean's romantic conception of King Lear had a profound influence both at
home and abroad. Like his predecessor, George Frederick Cooke, Kean toured America
on several occasions, beginning in 1820–1. During his second American tour, in 1825,
Edwin Forrest, then an aspiring actor, played opposite him in *Othello* and in other
Shakespearean tragedies. Forrest, who was soon to be recognised as America's greatest
actor, never forgot this formative experience. 'Until now Forrest had seen no actor who
represented in perfection the impassioned school of which Kean was the master', an

[1] Cited in Salgādo, *Eyewitnesses of Shakespeare*, p. 280. Compare Rostron, 'Kemble's "King Lear"',
  pp. 160–1.
[2] Rostron, 'Kemble's "King Lear"', pp. 163–6.

early biographer remarked. 'He had known Cooke in the decline of his powers, but his own judgment was immature. Here indeed was a revelation.'[1] At nineteen, Forrest had already played Lear, creditably though not outstandingly, and he determined to make it his 'great character'.[2] Partly owing to what he learned from Kean, he succeeded.

Although Edwin Booth's greatest role was Hamlet, his Lear was also note-worthy, both in America and in London, where he performed in 1881. Like Garrick, he began playing the role early in life, using Tate's version, as his father, Junius Brutus Booth, had done. But he dropped the part from his repertory in 1860 and did not revive it until many years later, this time in a Shakespearean version. His most famous scene was the Awakening:

I remember him, – indeed, who that saw him could ever forget? – sitting on a stool; his attenuated figure, his haggard face, his beseechful eyes, his bewildered glance at his clothing, his timid, hesitant, forlorn manner as he gazed on *Cordelia*, the doubting, questioning look which bespoke the slow recurrence of memory, the piteous, feeble movement of the hands, one upon the other, and the pathos of the heart-breaking voice . . .[3]

But if Booth was impressive in the final acts, his countryman, John Edward McCullough, was more impressive in the first half of the play. Unlike other Lears of his time, who played a robust monarch only gradually descending into dementia, McCullough saw Lear as a man verging on madness from the start, menaced by a disease which overtakes him rapidly. His representation was unique, and other aspects of his portrayal were, in Winter's words, 'inexpressibly touching'.[4] Moreover, McCullough was one of the first American actors to discard Tate's version and find in Shakespeare's the original structure and power that the play embodies.[5]

The strength of Forrest and the 'subtle intelligence' of Booth were combined, according to the American critic Towse, in Samuel Phelps's enactment of Lear in mid century. Whereas Macready played Lear as arrogant and domineering in Act 1, and afterwards tried to show how Lear learned through suffering, Phelps emphasised Lear's suffering from the beginning, probed the depths of his despair, and did not try to explain it. More aged father than king, his grief and madness were nonetheless regal. He won the approval of many critics besides Towse, whose praise is couched in a paradox generated by the still lingering attitude of Charles Lamb: 'His Lear . . . was one of the most satisfying interpretations of that unactable conception that I have seen.'[6]

In the twentieth century, especially since the Second World War, *King Lear* has been more often revived and more variously represented than at any previous time in its history. John Gielgud, for example, played the role in four productions, each one different, beginning with the Old Vic in 1931 when he was only twenty-six. Harcourt Williams directed, Ralph Richardson played Kent, and Robert Speaight, Edmond. Like Garrick, Booth, and Forrest, Gielgud gave promise of greater things to come. Commentators

[1] Lawrence Barrett, *Edwin Forrest*, 1881, p. 40.
[2] James Rees, *The Life of Edwin Forrest*, 1874, p. 82; compare Bratton, p. 31.
[3] William Winter, *Shakespeare on the Stage: Second Series*, 1915, p. 447.
[4] *Ibid.*, p. 461.
[5] Shattuck, *Shakespeare on the American Stage*, 1, 129.
[6] Shirley S. Allen, *Samuel Phelps and Sadler's Wells Theatre*, 1971, pp. 173–5, who quotes Towse.

remarked upon the intelligence of his interpretation and his fine speaking-voice.[1] In 1940 Gielgud again attempted the role at the Vic, this time under the guidance, if not direction, of Harley Granville-Barker, who came over from Paris for ten rehearsals. Only the limitations of his physique and perhaps too much reliance upon intellectual control prevented Gielgud from supreme mastery, although by his own account he felt that this was the one time he truly touched Lear.[2]

Gielgud played Lear twice more, in 1950 at Stratford-upon-Avon (see illustration 10), with excellent performances by Alan Badel as the Fool and Peggy Ashcroft as Cordelia, and in 1955 at the Palace Theatre, with a Stratford company that had toured Europe. The first of these was still influenced by Granville-Barker; the second was the notorious Noguchi one. Gielgud changed his conception so that his initial entrance, formerly strong and menacing, was now that of a weak and mentally deranged old man. As he has said, there is no one way to play the part, but this interpretation was not successful, despite excellent performances by others and the moving and emblematic scene at Dover between the shattered, aimlessly wandering king and the blind earl, played by George Devine. The production was a disaster, mainly because the sets and costumes overwhelmed everything else.[3]

The variety of approaches notwithstanding, what some have called a 'definitive' *King Lear* appeared during the war years. In 1943, Donald Wolfit brought his production to London from the provinces, where it had been touring (see Ronald Harwood's play, *The Dresser*, largely based on Wolfit's touring as Lear). Praising the revival the following year, James Agate enumerated Lear's qualities:

First, majesty. Second, the quality Blake would have recognized as moral grandeur. Third, mind. Fourth, he must be a man, and what is more, a king, in ruins. There must be enough voice to dominate the thunder, and yet it must be a spent voice. Lear must have all of Prospero's 'beating mind', but a mind enfeebled like his pulse . . .[4]

For Agate, Wolfit's Lear was the greatest tragic performance he had seen on the British stage since the death of Irving, and his vote was seconded by others. But, Speaight notes, by this time the theatre had moved on and 'was nervous of giants',[5] as some subsequent productions of *Lear* have shown.

Like Gielgud, Laurence Olivier played Lear more than once, and with unequal success. His first attempt, with the Old Vic in 1946, he also directed, to mixed reviews. Olivier was 'a comedian by instinct and a tragedian by art', Agate claimed, and his old, testy, and capricious king showed a quizzical sense of humour. Felix Barker, Olivier's biographer, thought this was mainly a device to help him get through the absurdity of

---

[1] James Agate, *Brief Chronicles*, 1943, p. 196. Agate much preferred the still younger William Devlin who, at twenty-two, opened at the Westminster Theatre in 1934 and was, Benson excepted, the best Lear Agate had ever seen up to then (pp. 197–201).
[2] Trewin, *Shakespeare on the English Stage*, p. 186; Agate, *Brief Chronicles*, pp. 201–2.
[3] John Gielgud, *An Actor and His Time*, 1979, pp. 95, 169, 212. Compare Alan S. Downer, 'A comparison of two stagings: Stratford-upon-Avon and London', *SQ* 6 (1955), 432–3.
[4] Cited in Ronald Harwood, *Sir Donald Wolfit, C.B.E.*, 1971, pp. 165–6. Harwood describes the genesis, performance, and reception of the production, pp. 157–67.
[5] Robert Speaight, *Shakespeare on the Stage*, 1973, p. 229.

10   John Gielgud as Lear and Alan Badel as the Fool in Anthony Quayle's production at the Shakespeare Memorial Theatre, Stratford-upon-Avon (1950)

Lear's division of the kingdom in 1.1, but the humour was pervasive.[1] Despite moments of great imagination and power, for example at Dover, his rendition was too lightweight: 'Instead of the pathos of great strength crumbling, he offered the misfortune of bright

---

[1]   *The Oliviers*, 1953, p. 294. Compare Charles Landstone, 'Four Lears', *S.Sur.* 1 (1948), 98.

wits blurred.'[1] When Olivier performed the role for the last time, in the television adaptation (1983), he was too frail and ill, although flashes of his old fire still emerged. Perhaps his most memorable scene (involving a bit of un-Shakespearean stage business) was of the mad old king in Act 4 catching and disembowelling a rabbit, and then eating its innards raw.

By far the most widely discussed and influential post-war production of *King Lear* was Peter Brook's for the Royal Shakespeare Company in 1962. Profoundly affected by Jan Kott, whose view was that of a middle-European survivor of the Second World War, Brook interpreted the play existentially. Speaight says Simone Jollivet had attempted as much in her adaptation, produced by Charles Dullin in Paris in 1945, but Brook did it better.[2] He cut the text carefully, following the Folio more closely than the quarto, so that the servants' dialogue at the end of 3.7 was gone along with the scene in Act 4 found only in the quarto. In addition, he cut many of Edmond's lines in the last scene, including 'Some good I mean to do', and kept his body on stage after his death. At the end Edgar, left alone with his brother's corpse, lugged it off-stage 'like a slaughtered pig'.[3] Paul Scofield as Lear was austerely effective, as were Alec McCowen as the Fool, Irene Worth as Gonerill, and Alan Webb as Gloucester (see illustration 11). Brook directed from the standpoint of 'moral neutrality', with the intention of provoking questions, not providing answers.[4] The flat white set and simple leather costumes enhanced the alienation that this deliberately Brechtian production contrived to impart. The results were 'revolutionary':

Instead of assuming that Lear is right, and therefore pitiable, we are forced to make judgements – to decide between his claims and those of his kin. And the balance, in this uniquely magnanimous production, is almost even. Though he disposes of his kingdom, Lear insists on retaining authority; he wants to exercise power without responsibility, without fulfilling his part of the feudal contract. He is wilfully arrogant, and deserves much of what he gets ... This production brings me closer to Lear than I have ever been; from now on, I not only know him but can place him in his harsh and unforgiving world.[5]

While King Lear dominates his play, other characters are important as well and lend themselves to various interpretations, which influence, or are influenced by, the overall conception. To focus only on the Fool as he has appeared in different productions: he is often played as a simple-minded child, but Frank Middlemass showed in the BBC-TV series that he can appear as an old man, long allied to his master. Marius Goring played him as 'an anxious, frightened jester fighting a losing battle', his attendance upon Lear 'urgent and sympathetic'.[6] In Olivier's stage production Alec Guinness was 'neither

---

[1] Kenneth Tynan, cited by Richard Findlater, *The Player Kings*, 1971, p. 221. Compare Speaight, *Shakespeare on the Stage*, p. 230.
[2] Speaight, *Shakespeare on the Stage*, pp. 232–3.
[3] *Ibid.*, p. 284.
[4] Kenneth Tynan, *A View of the English Stage: 1944–63*, 1975, p. 343.
[5] From Kenneth Tynan's review in the *Observer*, November 1962; reprinted in *Peter Brook: A Theatrical Casebook*, compiled by David Williams, 1988, pp. 23–7.
[6] T. C. Kemp, 'Acting Shakespeare: modern tendencies in playing and production', *S.Sur.* 7 (1954), 127.

11 Act 1, Scene 1: Peter Brook's Royal Shakespeare Company production (1962), with Paul Scofield as Lear

prancing jester nor piping grotesque', but 'wry, quiet, true, with a dog's devotion'.[1] Antony Sher was an astonishingly original Fool in Adrian Noble's 1982 production for the Royal Shakespeare Company (see illustration 12). From the opening tableau the Fool commanded attention: he and Cordelia were discovered on the throne together with a length of rope around their necks ('And my poor fool is hanged'). Sher wore a Charlot costume of baggy trousers and oversized shoes, a red button nose, white clown's make-up, and crumpled hat. With Lear (Michael Gambon) he performed vaudeville routines and played a Grock violin. During the mock trial in 3.6, while raving against his daughters, Lear plunged a dagger into his Fool who was standing, like a character in Beckett's *Endgame*, in an empty oil drum, into which he slowly subsided and died.[2]

Sher's outlandish, vaudevillian performance made political sense, as Nicholas Shrimpton observed: the Fool was 'an artist who uses his skills as an entertainer to win himself a platform'. More than that, with Lear he formed 'an old-established cross-talk act, long accustomed to claiming the spotlight for their banter'. The disadvantage, however, was that after the Fool's death in Act 3, following the extraordinary

[1] J. C. Trewin, 'Giving the countersign', in *Olivier: In Celebration*, ed. Gary O'Connor, 1987, p. 38.
[2] See Antony Sher, 'The Fool in *King Lear*', in *Players of Shakespeare 2*, ed. Russell Jackson and Robert Smallwood, 1988, pp. 151–65.

12   Antony Sher as the Fool (in the oil drum, left) and Michael Gambon as Lear in the Royal Shakespeare
Company production (1982)

representation of the storm, the play tended to lose both éclat and coherence.[1] A more
conventional Fool – the consummate Shakespearean Fool in *Lear*, though many critics
disagreed – was Linda Kerr Scott's at the RSC in 1990 (see illustration 13). Small in
stature, with pop-eyes, bare windmilling arms, and a scampering, knock-kneed walk,
she was endearingly funny and affectionate, speaking in a Glaswegian accent and drawing from the role all that binds the Fool to Lear. Closely following the Folio text, the
production showed the Fool abandoned at the end of 3.6, mouthing inaudible nonsense,
as Kent and Gloucester hurried the sleeping Lear away. One of two women to essay the
role (the other was Emma Thompson) in a season that saw three major productions of
the play, Scott revived a tradition dating back to 1838, when Macready cast Priscilla
Horton in the role.[2]

KING LEAR ABROAD

Like other Shakespeare plays, *King Lear* has a stage history outside England. In the late
seventeenth century it seems to have been performed in Smock Alley, Dublin, where
in the next century Thomas Sheridan occasionally acted the lead in Tate's version or,

---

[1] Nicholas Shrimpton, 'Shakespeare performances in Stratford-upon-Avon and London, 1981–2', *S.Sur.*
36 (1983), 152–3.
[2] For these three productions see J. L. Halio, 'Five days, three *King Lears*', *Shakespeare Bulletin* 9 (Winter
1991), 19–21.

13   Linda Kerr Scott as the Fool and John Wood as King Lear in Nicholas Hytner's production for the
Royal Shakespeare Company (1990)

as theatre manager, arranged for others to do so. In 1752, when Lewis Hallam and his wife led their company of actors to Williamsburg, Virginia, to perform plays by Shakespeare and others, *Lear* was included in the repertoire (again, in Tate's version). They performed also in New York, Philadelphia, and Charleston, South Carolina.[1] In France, Jean-François Ducis (1733–1816) followed Tate in rewriting Shakespeare (if anything, more drastically) for a production in Versailles and Paris. Brizard played the lead, clean-shaven, against an elaborate set.[2] In Germany, Schiller's version of *Lear* was presented at Weimar, and Ludwig Devrient (1784–1832) was one of the outstanding Lears of the century, emphasising the milder aspects of the character. At the Burgtheater in Austria he was rivalled by Adolf von Sonnethal. In 1889 Jocza Savits experimented in Munich with Elizabethan staging, which favourably impressed – and directly influenced – William Poel and, in France, Antoine, who in 1904 produced the play uncut in a translation by Pierre Loti.[3] German productions of *King Lear* have continued throughout the twentieth century as well, and the contemporary composer Aribert Reimann has transformed it into an opera, which had its British première at the Coliseum in London in January 1989. One reviewer called it 'an opera of shattering theatrical power'. In the storm scenes, for example, 'the chord-clusters build up and spread in huge, roaring, opaque columns of sound . . . obliterating the last traces of rationality of Lear's mind'.[4]

The most notable Italian performers in the nineteenth century were Ernesto Rossi and Tommaso Salvini. Both brought their interpretation to England, Rossi in 1876 and 1882, Salvini in 1884, and both played their roles in Italian. Rossi used an English-speaking supporting cast, although in 1882 he experimented in the last two acts by speaking in laboured but clear and accurate English. If Rossi emphasised Lear's madness from the outset, Salvini varied his character as the vigorous king in Act 1, the disquieted and sympathetic father in Act 2, the afflicted and enfeebled human being thereafter. His performance was much better received than Rossi's, especially in the closing scene.[5]

In Russia, Ivan Choucherine adapted Ducis's version of *Lear* in 1807, using Gothic settings. Greater productions awaited the next century, particularly Salomon Mikhoels's in 1935 and Grigori Kozintsev's in 1941, in which Lear's humanity was stressed as his regality decayed.[6] In New York in 1892 the Russian immigrant, Jacob Gordin, scored a rousing success on the Yiddish stage with *The Jewish King Lear*, consolidating Shakespeare's double plot and transforming setting, myth, and characters to his own didactic purposes.[7]

Using electronic music and elaborate costumes, make-up and set design, J. A. Seazer (a disciple of Shuji Terayama) staged *King Lear* in Japanese at the Tokyo Globe Theatre in 1991. The production preserved the basic structure of Shakespeare's play

[1] Shattuck, *Shakespeare on the American Stage*, 1, 3–10.
[2] Speaight, *Shakespeare on the Stage*, p. 88.
[3] *Ibid.*, pp. 105–9, 183.
[4] Malcolm Hayes, *Sunday Telegraph*, 29 January 1989, p. 17.
[5] Derrick, 'Stage History', pp. 194–8.
[6] Speaight, *Shakespeare on the Stage*, pp. 112, 222.
[7] Leonard Prager, 'Of parents and children: Jacob Gordin's *The Jewish King Lear*', *American Quarterly* 18 (1966), 506–16.

but included additional scenes, mostly in mime, at the start of the action and intermittently throughout – a rousing 'Festival of Fools' at the beginning, for example, and later 'Roses of Sterile Women', a dance by Gonerill and Oswald designed to reveal Gonerill's extreme sexuality. Dance, in fact, along with operatic singing and extravagant lighting, made this a kind of multi-media spectacular; the overall effect was stunning. Seazer achieved an effective translation of Shakespeare's play into other, quite different, cultural terms without sacrificing any of the tragedy's essential qualities.

KING LEAR ON SCREENS LARGE AND SMALL

Films of *King Lear* begin with the silent cinema in America and Italy (1909–10), but the most notable are Peter Brook's (1969), Grigori Kozintsev's (1971), and Akira Kurosawa's adaptation *Ran* (1985).[1] After touring with his stage version of *Lear*, Brook filmed the play in Jutland at the same time as Grigori Kozintsev began filming it in Russia. For his film, Brook transposed scenes, reassigned speeches, and made still deeper cuts in the text, nearly eliminating Cordelia's role. In addition, he used various cinematic effects to drive home the absurdity and despair he strove for on the stage. Tendentious as the interpretation is, it nevertheless conveyed great power, especially in the scene at Dover between Lear and Gloucester, which Robert Hapgood has called the most memorable scene in any Shakespearean film to date. Unlike the two tramps in *Waiting for Godot*, whom they resembled, the 'tender camaraderie of these two tough old losers', set against a landscape of unutterable bleakness, moved even the hardest heart.[2]

Kozintsev's film was wholly different. Not surprisingly, he emphasised the socialist aspects of the play – for example, by having numbers of poor peasants ('poor naked wretches') sheltering in a leaky shed that became Lear's refuge in the storm scenes. For Kozintsev, Shakespeare's Lear (played by Yuri Jarvet), 'despite his inordinate fate, cannot be separated from the sufferings of the many'. Through 'the depth of his emotions and the power of his intellect', however, Lear learns 'to understand not only his own mistakes but to comprehend the very essence of the unjust society which he himself created'.[3] For the musical score, Kozintsev engaged Dmitri Shostakovich, as he had done for *Hamlet*, but rejected the use of musical 'character themes', preferring instead more general ones, such as 'the Voice of Truth' or 'the Voice of Evil'.[4] In this film, which won universal acclaim, the Fool enters with Lear in 1.1 and does not disappear after 3.6; he remains at the end, playing his wooden pipe, until a litter-bearer carrying the dead king roughly boots him out of the way.

Departing much further from Shakespeare's texts than the other two films, Kurosawa's *Ran* ('Chaos') is set in feudal Japan (like his *Throne of Blood*, which was based upon *Macbeth*). Freely adapted from Shakespeare's original, *Ran* eliminates the Gloucester plot, and instead of three daughters, Hidetora (Lear) has three sons. Together with their wives, they combine the character traits of Lear's offspring and

---

[1] See Charles W. Eckert, *Focus on Shakespearean Films*, 1972, pp. 169–70.
[2] Robert Hapgood, 'Shakespeare on film and television', in *The Cambridge Companion to Shakespeare Studies*, ed. Stanley Wells, 1986, pp. 282–3.
[3] Cited by Peter Morris, *Shakespeare on Film*, Ottawa: Canadian Film Institute, 1972, p. 35.
[4] Grigori Kozintsev, *King Lear: The Space of Tragedy*, tr. Mary Mackintosh, 1977, p. 246.

Gloucester's, heightening the savagery of Shakespeare's *King Lear* and increasing its violence. The eldest and weakest son's wife, Lady Kaede, seeks revenge against Hidetora for destroying her parents, and then against Jiro, the jealous second son, for having her husband assassinated. In her viciousness, she has Jiro's wife, gentle Lady Sue, beheaded. Although Lady Sue has her own motives for revenge – Hidetora has also destroyed her family and has had her brother's eyes gouged out – she is a devoted Buddhist and refuses to hate. At the end, after an insane Hidetora and his hermaphrodite Fool Kyoami disappear into the smoking ruins of his fortress, Lady Sue's brother appears at the edge of a cliff, drops a scroll with the Buddha's portrait on it, and refuses to leap, waiting instead for his sister's return to life. The English-language caption here, in italics, is: 'The human condition'.[1]

King Lear has also been adapted for television, first in a much shortened version by Peter Brook for the American *Omnibus* programme in 1953, with Orson Welles as Lear. Two decades later, Joseph Papp's production at the Delacorte Theatre in New York City was televised, with James Earl Jones as Lear and Raul Julia as Edmond. This multi-ethnic version recalls the success of Ira Aldridge a century earlier, when the American-born black actor played Lear in Russia.[2] The next production, one made expressly for television, was in 1982, when Jonathan Miller directed Michael Hordern as Lear for the BBC-TV series, *The Shakespeare Plays*. As television differs from film, Miller's version differs from Brook's, Kozintsev's, or Kurosawa's, principally in avoiding large-scale or panoramic scenes. Given its recognised (and recognisable) limitations, the production succeeds, as in the extremely moving last scene.[3]

Finally, at the end of his career, Laurence Olivier performed Lear for Granada Television, directed by Michael Elliott (1983). Olivier tried to play Lear as a virile old man heroically overcoming difficulty and dying in the conviction that Cordelia still lived (the text was altered to enforce the interpretation).[4] Diana Rigg stunningly conveyed Regan's beauty and viciousness; David Threlfall as Edgar/Tom o'Bedlam swirled hideously around in mud during the storm; but the Fool's part, played by John Hurt, was considerably curtailed.

EDWARD BOND'S *LEAR*

The search for new meanings sometimes culminates in the composition of an entirely new text, not merely an adaptation such as Tate's *King Lear* or Kurosawa's *Ran*. An example is Edward Bond's *Lear* (1971), revived in 1982 by the Royal Shakespeare Company at The Other Place while Adrian Noble's production was performed at the main house. Using the basic Lear myth, Bond intensified the cruelty and violence in Shakespeare's play as well as the lasciviousness of the elder daughters (the only ones his Lear has). At the same time, Lear's descent into madness and his agonising

---

[1] Hapgood, 'Shakespeare on film', p. 286; Jack Jorgens, 'Kurosawa's *Ran*: a Samurai *Lear*', *SFNL* 10 (1986), 1, 4.

[2] See Herbert Marshall and Mildred Stock, *Ira Aldridge: The Negro Tragedian*, 1958, pp. 236–7, 244, 286–7. Aldridge used Tate's version.

[3] In '*King Lear* without tears', *SFNL* 7 (1983), 2, Steven Urkowitz commented, however, that a number of Shakespeare's directions were either altered or ignored, diminishing the tragedy.

[4] Marion Perret, 'The making of *King Lear*', *SFNL* 8 (1984), 7.

growth in self-knowledge remain the central focus. Instead of a Fool, Bond invents the Gravedigger's Son, who is killed early on but returns as a ghost to accompany Lear through his pilgrimage, gradually shrinking in stature as Lear's insights mount. The play ends as Lear, physically blinded, is shot while tearing apart the wall he had once foolishly built to protect his realm.

Bond justifies his use of violence on the grounds that 'an unjust society must be violent', and in his view contemporary society is grossly unjust. He rejects the criticism that his play is either pessimistic or resigned: Lear's experience discovering truth, imparted to the audience, should properly be seen as 'an opportunity'. Grasping this truth, 'you don't have to go on doing things that never work in the hope that they may one day – because now you know why they *can't*'.[1] Hence Lear begins dismantling the wall whose construction has oppressed his people for years. But since others, also driven by motives of power and security, have now taken over the kingdom, and they in turn insist on building the wall, the ex-king is shot.

Bond's play, like performances of it by the RSC and others, is both a commentary upon and an extension of Shakespeare's, a forthright transformation of *King Lear* into contemporary terms.[2] As the foregoing stage history has selectively demonstrated, this is what actors, producers, and directors have done, one way or another, from the very first: probed, examined, refashioned, reenacted it to discover all the play has to offer. For this reason – and others having to do with the variables of performance – no production can ever be definitive. Shakespeare's theatre continues to evolve, and the success of any production should be measured in direct proportion to what we learn from it.

Recent stage, film, and critical interpretations

At the start of his retrospective review of *Lear* scholarship and criticism (1980–2000), Kiernan Ryan remarks that since the 1960s *King Lear* has 'usurped the throne occupied till then by *Hamlet* as Shakespeare's masterpiece and the keystone of the canon'.[3] In support of this view he cites R. A. Foakes who, in *Hamlet versus Lear*, comments: 'I suspect that for the immediate future *King Lear* will continue to be regarded as the central achievement of Shakespeare, if only because it speaks to us more largely than the other tragedies to the anxieties and problems of the modern world.'[4] This view is shared not only by many critics but also by theatre producers and directors, who have of late often revived a play once thought to be unactable.[5] In the summer of 1990 not one but three acting productions of *King Lear* held the boards in Britain: the Royal Shakespeare Company's production in Stratford-upon-Avon, with John Wood as Lear; the Royal National Theatre's in London, with Brian Cox as Lear; and the Renaissance Theatre's in Birmingham and elsewhere, with a surprisingly effective Richard Briers

---

[1] Author's Preface to *Lear* in Edward Bond, *Plays: Two*, Methuen Paperback, 1978, p. 11.
[2] Compare Ruby Cohn, *Modern Shakespeare Offshoots*, 1976, pp. 254–66.
[3] '*King Lear*: a retrospect, 1980–2000', *S.Sur.* 55 (2002), 1.
[4] *Hamlet versus Lear*, 1993, p. 224.
[5] See p. 32, above.

14   David Calder as Kent, Ian Hughes as the Fool, Simon Russell Beale as Edgar, Robert Stephens as King
Lear, in the 1993 Royal Shakespeare Company production, directed by Adrian Noble

as Lear.[1] The number of outstanding productions of *King Lear* in the years since then
has also been very impressive.

One of the best productions was staged by the Royal Shakespeare Company in
Stratford-upon-Avon in 1993. It was directed by Adrian Noble, who had also directed
a quite different production of the play with Michael Gambon as Lear and Anthony
Sher as the Fool at the RSC in 1982.[2] In this production, Robert Stephens played the
title role in what was unquestionably the greatest performance of his career. A strong
supporting cast that included David Calder as Kent, David Bradley as Gloucester,
Owen Teale as Edmond, Simon Russell Beale as Edgar, and Ian Hughes as the Fool
won high critical acclaim along with Stephens. In a review Michael Davies claimed that
'this *Lear* is one of the most technically accomplished pieces ever staged at Stratford,
complete with a huge hanging globe, real rain in the powerful storm scene, and a map
of old England spread across the stage'.[3] That hanging globe proved a distraction –
or worse – to some in the audience, especially when, after Gloucester's blinding, it
opened and what were apparently the seeds of time poured out, or as though 'the thick
rotundity o'th'world' had cracked and all nature's 'germens' spilled onto the stage

[1] See above, p. 49 and footnote 2.
[2] See pp. 48–9, above.
[3] *Daily Mail*, 21 May 1993.

(3.2.7–8).[1] Nevertheless, as Charles Spencer observed, the 'wonder, humility and joy' of the reconciliation scene (4.6) was 'breathtakingly captured', making the final scene 'almost unbearable to watch'.[2] Irving Wardle believed that 'No production since Peter Brook's, thirty years ago . . . revealed the play's dimensions so fully.'[3]

If, as Michael Billington rightly remarked, *King Lear* is 'the Everest of acting',[4] others have attempted to scale its heights with some measure of success or, occasionally, failure: for some, like Stephens and others who have genuine performance capability, the play can inspire the best in them as actors; for others, it can be a perilous undertaking fraught with pitfalls. In 1997 once again three productions of the play graced the stage, this time in close geographical proximity to each other. Under Richard Eyre's direction, Ian Holm played Lear in London at the Royal National Theatre – a production that seemed deliberately to underplay the play's imposing grandeur. Staged in the Cottesloe Theatre, the smallest venue of the National, it attempted to convey 'a timeless world', where the governing idea was 'a moral and political anatomy that tears off masks, clothes and disguises to show humanity as it really is'.[5] This was fine, except that 'the production itself seem[ed] to shrink from accepting the moral chaos of the universe. Indeed, it [sought] almost to explain that universe by turning Edgar [played by Paul Rhys] into a choric figure: he [was] discovered on stage at the outset and summarized the action at the end of both halves.'[6] On the other hand, Holm's acting was excellent, given the directorial concept. As John Gross viewed it, this Lear was a man 'who cherishes his illusions as long as he possibly can. The shedding of those illusions [was] all the harder to bear'; 'the fear of impending mental breakdown' was thus powerfully signalled.[7] The production was later filmed and shown on television and is available on videotape.

A few months later, down the road at the Young Vic (located on the Cut, a street near Waterloo Station), Kathryn Hunter played Lear in a production that originated at Leicester's Haymarket Theatre and elicited 'remarkably varied' responses from reviewers. To render plausible a woman's enactment of the role, the play began as a dream or hallucination of an old woman in a geriatric hospital. Robert Smallwood's account sounds accurate:

The performance was indisputably a curiosity, but not, I think, a freak. It was highly effective in its presentation of Lear's journey towards increased awareness; it was intelligent and often incisive in its handling of language . . . Lear began clearly off his rocker and remained a strutting, peevish, rather nasty little person until he got out of [his] absurd ill-fitting suit and into a white hospital robe for the reconciliation with Cordelia.[8]

---

[1] See Nicholas De Jong, *Evening Standard*, 21 May 1993, and compare Charles Spencer, *Daily Telegraph*, 22 May 1993.
[2] *Daily Telegraph*, 22 May 1993.
[3] 'A giant among kings', *Independent on Sunday*, 23 May 1993. See p. 47 above, for Brook's *Lear*.
[4] *Guardian*, 22 May 1993.
[5] Michael Billington, *Guardian*, 29 March 1997.
[6] *Ibid*.
[7] *Sunday Telegraph*, 30 March 1997.
[8] 'Shakespearean performances in England', *S.Sur.* 51 (1998), 246.

The supporting cast was good, and the entire setting was contemporary, given its inception in a modern geriatric hospital.[1]

At the Old Vic shortly thereafter (also on the Cut), Peter Hall directed Alan Howard as Lear. (As Billington commented, it is getting just as crowded around the Shakespearean as the Himalayan peak.)[2] Howard had not played in Shakespeare for some years, but Smallwood found his performance 'undiminished in thoughtfulness, in verbal inquisitiveness and experimentation, and in vocal (particularly *vibrato*) athleticism'.[3]

This was a Lear apparently much in need of physical contact. He frequently touched Poor Tom's bare arms and shoulders, as if puzzled and worried by their nakedness. He kissed his elder daughters . . . on each cheek then, lengthily, on the mouth, after their love speeches . . . Cordelia held his hand throughout her failure to express her love and . . . again held his hand for much of her interview with her prospective husbands . . . All this physical affection made the wild and whirling rage of his rejection seem unbelievable, a performance merely.

The production overall was 'always clear, intelligent, and unpretentious. Yet somehow it never quite caught fire.'[4]

Two years later Nigel Hawthorne played Lear in a production directed by Yukio Ninagawa and jointly sponsored by the Royal Shakespeare Company and the Saitama Arts Foundation in Japan. Reviewers savaged Hawthorne's performance and the production generally. Paul Taylor blamed the director (whose former Shakespearean productions, in Japanese, were universally extolled); Benedict Nightingale questioned Hawthorne's fitness to play Lear since, in his view, Hawthorne is 'essentially benign as an actor'.[5] As if stung by these negative reviews, Hawthorne rose to the occasion on the night after the production's opening and was reportedly magnificent.[6] Although the cast was composed mainly of western actors, they were dressed in Noh costumes and performed in what was considered Noh theatre style.

Shortly afterwards, on the other side of the Atlantic, at the Shakespeare Theatre in Washington, D.C., Michael Kahn directed Ted van Griethuysen as Lear in a more traditional conception of the play – with one notable exception. Monique Holt, a deaf mute wearing short, spiky, blonde hair, played Cordelia, and the Fool spoke the lines (which she signed with her hands) in the opening scene and later. Holt, a diminutive Korean woman, captured beautifully the inability of Cordelia to convey her meaning to her father in 1.1, and in other ways also suggested Cordelia's fragile vulnerability

---

[1] In 'Liberal Shakespeare and illiberal critiques: Necessary Angel's *King Lear*', *Shakespeare in Canada*, ed. Diane Brydon and Irena R. Makaryk, 2002, pp. 212–30, Michael McKinnie writes about a cross-cast production of *King Lear* in Toronto in the spring of 1995 directed by Richard Rose, with Janet Wright as Lear and the roles of Kent, Edmond, and Albany also performed by women, while Gonerill was played by a man. The casting was purportedly based on merit and not, as some reviewers believed, on 'a type of employment equity' (p. 214). The central theme of the play, according to Rose, was 'an ascent from barbarism to humanism', although McKinnie says that the humanist teleology was often frustrated by the 'periodic dissonance between the cross-casting and the text' and by other considerations (*ibid.*).
[2] *Guardian*, 22 May 1993.
[3] Smallwood, 'Shakespeare performances', p. 248.
[4] *Ibid.*
[5] As reported in the *Sheffield Star* and the *Birmingham Post* on 29 October 1999.
[6] See Suzanne Chambers, *Sunday Express*, 30 October 1999.

15   Monique Holt as Cordelia and Floyd King as Lear's Fool in the Shakespeare Theatre's 1999 production of *King Lear*, directed by Michael Kahn

at the beginning. In the reconciliation scene, where again the Fool appeared to speak her lines, she was even more effective. On the whole, the production was a stunning success and played well into the year 2000.

In the summer of 2001, Shakespeare's Globe staged *King Lear* for the first time in its venue on Bankside, near where Shakespeare's own audiences had witnessed performances of the play. Directed by Barry Kyle and designed by Hayden Griffin, this production was a 'ruralist *Lear*, responsive to the play's pastoral elements'.[1] The gaily painted *frons scaena* was accordingly all boarded up, and a tall post, surmounted by a wooden wheel (the wheel of fortune, perhaps?), was placed in the yard. Several significant passages were spoken by actors who climbed on the post, as Edmond did when delivering his soliloquy at the beginning of 1.2, or when Edgar in 2.3 spoke his soliloquy deciding to disguise himself as Poor Tom. But the position of the wheel in the yard might also have suggested, at least to some, that the audience were 'the ultimate arbiters of fortune'.[2] The rich, almost filmic musical background seemed to give intimations of Lear's approaching madness and supplied all the sounds of the storm. Peter McEnery, who played the Fool, carried a small banjo-like instrument, which 'made one aware of how much music there is in this play, a fact that made his departure even more regrettable than usual'.[3] The Fool's hanging body, revealed behind the central doors at the end of 3.6, explained – for better or worse – the Fool's disappearance after this scene.[4] Michael Gould as Edmond was so effective in endearing himself to the audience as 'a swaggering, confident villain', that he tended to overbalance the play; by comparison, Julian Glover was a 'middleweight, colonel-like Lear'.[5]

In 2002 at what was once Stratford's 'Other Place', now turned into an academy for training young actors, Declan Donnellan directed the students in *King Lear*. As the *Sunday Times* reported,[6] Donnellan

reads the play as a tragedy of terrible absurdity. Lear [Monso Anozie] is boisterous, irascible, and self-adoring . . . The division of the kingdom sounds like a joke till it all sinks in . . . The storm scene, superbly staged by Nick Ormerod, is all the more harrowing for Lear's almost childlike fury and the way he declines into petulant, smiling madness; a big, innocent infant in an uncomprehending tantrum, pottering about under an angry black sky.

The verse-speaking was excellent, and the prose, too, evidently reflecting good RSC training. Michael Billington found a 'curious exhilaration in seeing sixteen young actors perform' and noted how Donnellan grasped the essential point: that this is a play 'of unfathomable contradictions'.[7]

In 2002 the Stratford Festival of Canada in Stratford, Ontario, also mounted *King Lear*, with Christopher Plummer in the lead, a production that later transferred to

---

[1] Michael Dobson, 'Shakespeare performances in England, 2001', *S.Sur.* 55 (2002), 303.

[2] Lois Potter, 'Shakespeare performed', *SQ* 53 (2002), 101.

[3] *Ibid.*, p. 97.

[4] Dobson, 'Shakespeare performances', p. 305, believes it also indicates that the Fool hanged himself. See p. 48 above, for the way the Fool died in Adrian Noble's 1982 production.

[5] Dobson, 'Shakespeare performances', p. 305.

[6] 13 October 2002.

[7] *Guardian*, October 2002.

New York's Lincoln Center in March 2004. The following comments focus on the New York production in which Plummer was generally considered to have given the performance of a lifetime.[1] In this fast-paced staging, Ben Brantley comments, 'nothingness is the backdrop against which the worldly domestic and political feuds of *Lear* take place. It threatens and eventually devours all but a few of the play's principal characters. And you get the sense that even the survivors are just marking time until darkness comes for them, too.' Hardly any scenery was used, and the costumes suggested not the pre-history of the original tale, but a Christian setting, Shakespeare's own period or the Restoration. The director, Jonathan Miller, declared that 'Christianity is essential to the play. Although it's only there by allusion, not by explicit mention. The whole idea of gaining through loss is a specifically Christian notion – that it's only by enduring the hideous ordeal of loss that any of these people gain.'[2] Mahon notes (p. 122) some unusual – and to him 'crucial' – cuts in the Folio text used as the basis for the script: Cordelia's opening asides (1.1.57, 71–3); Gloucester's speech on the 'superfluous and lust-dieted man' (4.1.62–6), which parallels Lear's speech at 3.4.28–36; and Edgar's account of his father's death (5.3.172–90). The production was obviously centred on King Lear himself who, in Plummer's 'lacerating, double-edged' portrayal, was 'a man of prodigious will and fading powers'.[3]

King Lear has continued to hold its attraction for actors and directors. In 2004, the RSC again mounted a production, a somewhat controversial one, directed by Bill Alexander with Corin Redgrave in the leading role. As Benedict Nightingale saw it, Redgrave's Lear was 'a smug, spoilt, playful, rather silly man' at the start, who laughed a lot, especially with John Normington's (elderly) Fool.[4] He was given to sudden mood swings and appeared as 'a man who, if not yet clinically senile, [was] certainly heading that way' (*ibid.*) The play was set in the early twentieth century; recent productions seem to have tried to bring the action and hence the significance of tragedy as close to us today as possible. Other critics also tended to discredit Redgrave's interpretation of the role. Charles Spencer, for example, bemoaned Lear's lack of rage along with no terrible fear of his encroaching madness. Instead, this Lear was 'a who has never grown up, a spoilt child', played without any 'sense of growing spiritual illumination'.[5] John Gross, on the other hand, found the production 'For the most part, an impressive affair . . . marked by energy and clarity.' Redgrave's Lear was very intelligently conceived, though he failed to scale the heights.[6] Indeed, Paul Taylor was torn between admiration for and misgivings about the performance, finding Redgrave's a 'subtle, highly intelligent but less than emotionally shattering performance'. Nevertheless, Lear's 'racked intoning of the word "never" over and over Cordelia's corpse [was] absolutely heartbreaking in its despairing wonder at the brutal irrevocability of life'. As for Normington's Fool,

---

[1] See, e.g., Ben Brantley, '*King Lear*: a fiery fall into the abyss', *New York Times*, 5 March 2004, and John Mahon, '*King Lear* at Lincoln Center', *Shakespeare Newsletter* 53 (Winter 2003/2004), 112, 122.

[2] Cited from *Lincoln Center Theater Review* by Mahon, '*King Lear* at Lincoln Center', p. 122.

[3] Brantley, 'Fiery fall'.

[4] *Guardian*, 2 July 2004.

[5] Charles Spencer, 'Redgrave's sniffy Lear', *Daily Telegraph*, 2 July 2004.

[6] John Gross, *Sunday Telegraph*, 4 July 2004.

Taylor felt that he achieved the rare distinction of actually making his jokes sound funny as well as wise.[1] The storm was staged very effectively. Far from drowning out Lear's words, it punctuated his lines appropriately as I have never before heard it done. Another interesting touch came in 3.6 when, just before he disappears from the play, the Fool handed his bauble over to Edgar.

At the Oregon Shakespeare Festival in Ashland, Oregon – home of the oldest Shakespeare festival in America – James Edmondson directed *King Lear* in the same summer of 2004. He had played Lear a few years earlier in Ashland, in 1997, but now Kenneth Albers assumed the leading role. Together they decided to examine the 'personal' tragedy of King Lear – 'Lear as a noble and gifted ruler who in his old age has become so self-righteous, imperious and obstinate that he creates the weapons of his own destruction.'[2] Albers performed Lear's descent into madness as 'a portrayal of the tricks that an aging mind plays, a Shakespearean examination of early Alzheimer's disease within the context of political and familial disaster' (*ibid.*). As the storm echoes his descent into madness, Lear becomes increasingly sane and humane. The ending of the play was 'uncompromising' – no redemption but 'splendor in the ashes . . . the kind of Shakespeare we need. It has its effect honestly, sans tricks or flash, and so is deeply satisfying.'[3]

The Oregon Shakespeare Festival's *King Lear* reminds us of the many regional productions of this mighty drama, in America, the British Isles, and around the world – too many to enumerate here – but a few may at least be mentioned.[4] In 1998, for example, Tom Courtney played King Lear at the Royal Exchange Theatre, Manchester, and Warren Mitchell enacted the role at the West Yorkshire Playhouse in November 1995. *King Lear* has also lent itself recently to several interesting adaptations, among them *The Tale of Lear*, performed by the Suzuki Company of Toga, Japan, with an all-male cast and staged at London's Barbican in November 1994. *The Yiddish Queen Lear* appeared at the Southwark Playhouse in May 1999 and later at the Pascal Theatre Company in Bridewell, London, in October 2001. A new opera of *King Lear* was staged at the Alexander Theatre in Helsinki, in September 2000. And at the Grand Theatre of the Hong Kong Cultural Centre in 1994 Daniel Yang directed the largest-scale production ever in Chinese. Yang made history by using two casts for his production – one speaking Mandarin, the other Cantonese – in his own translation, which was based mainly on the Folio text. Yang shortened the script by about 900 lines to keep the play within a reasonable acting time, emphasising, as he says in the programme notes, that the play is 'above all about learning'.

Given the intense interest in *King Lear* and in its productions on stage, a growing number of books and essays have appeared since the original publication of this edition.

---

[1] *Independent Review*, 5 July 2004.
[2] Roberta Kent, 'Compassion, grace infuse *King Lear*', *Ashland Daily Tidings*, 23 June 2004.
[3] Bill Varble, Medford *Mail Tribune*, 20 June 2004.
[4] The annual volumes of *Shakespeare Survey* list productions in Britain recorded by Niky Rathbone. Productions, mainly in the United States but also elsewhere, are reviewed in *Shakespeare Bulletin*, and *Shakespeare Jahrbuch* records those in Europe. The annual bibliography of *Shakespeare Quarterly* also lists many productions and reviews from all over the world for each Shakespeare play.

Marvin Rosenberg's groundbreaking volume of performance criticism, *The Masks of King Lear* (1972), has led the way to further studies about performances. These include two books by actors who have played the leading role in recent productions. In *The Lear Diaries* (1992) Brian Cox recounts his experience playing Lear. As he says in the Preface, the book 'is a diary of a year's work at the Royal National Theatre, in rehearsal, performance, and finally on tour'. Cox is careful to explain that 'a diary is a work of fiction, a version of the truth perceived through the bias, the prejudice, the bile of the diarist' (p. 1). Nevertheless, despite the different impressions and recollections of other members of the cast, whom Cox consulted, the book records many aperçus, such as Cox's recall of opening night. He says he then experienced for the first time 'a feeling that the play was playing me. . . . I really felt my emotional centre was open to the play, and the play and the part just took command and drove me. As a result it was a very rough and bumpy ride' (p. 84). Rough and bumpy though it was, the audience reaction was 'overwhelming'. Oliver Ford Davies's *Playing Lear* (2003) is based on his rather different experience performing the role at the Almeida Theatre in 2002. The subtitle reveals his approach: 'An insider's guide from text to performance'. His chapters proceed step by step from 'First reading' through a brief survey of previous 'Lears in performance' to several rehearsal diaries and a conversation with the director, Jonathan Kent, two months after the run ended. Davies notes that from the very first preview he was struck by how closely the audience listened: 'I have never felt so much concentration in the theatre', and he attributes this phenomenon to the power of myth. He remembers that at a number of moments in the play even the bored and wriggling members of the audience held quite still, especially during the Dover Beach scene after Lear says: 'I know thee well enough; thy name is Gloucester' (4.5.169).[1]

Meanwhile, scholarship and criticism have proceeded apace. While some students may regard close reading of the text as old-fashioned, a throwback to the (not-so-) New Criticism of the 1950s, many books and articles in fact provide readers with just that. James Lusardi and June Schlueter's *Reading Shakespeare in Performance: 'King Lear'* (1991) is close reading with a difference insofar as it combines performance criticism with close attention to the text. In 'exploring the range of interpretations that performance provides' (p. 15), their book refers both to past performances of the play and to imagined ones. For example, the authors contend that 'a production in which either or both of the sisters [Gonerill and Regan] grow into evil is every bit as possible and as plausible as one in which the two are implacably wicked from the start'. They back up this view with a close examination of the sisters' professions of love in 1.1 and with reference to a performance by Sheila Allen and Pippa Guard.[2]

The subtitle of R. A. Foakes's *Hamlet versus Lear: Cultural Politics and Shakespeare's Art*, really tells what the book is about. He confronts many of the trends in contemporary criticism, attacking their defects and deficiencies while at the same time noting their contributions to the ways we read – or view – Shakespeare's plays. But Foakes's main

---

[1] Oliver Ford Davies, *Playing Lear*, 2003, p. 169. With these diaries, compare two earlier ones: Grigori Kozintsev, *'King Lear': The Space of Tragedy: The Diary of a Film Director*, translated by Mary Mackintosh, 1977, and Maurice Good, *Every Inch a Lear: A Rehearsal Journal of 'King Lear' with Peter Ustinov and the Stratford Festival Company Directed by Robin Philips*, 1982.

[2] James Lusardi and June Schlueter, *Reading Shakespeare in Performance: 'King Lear'*, 1991, pp. 61–2.

interest is in Shakespeare's artistry, rejecting the post-structuralist dismissal of aesthetic issues as 'irrelevant'. His readings of *Hamlet* and *King Lear*, which come at the end of the book, therefore emphasise the evolving form of those plays – their artistic design – rather than the political or experiential knowledge they may impart. His analysis is far more concerned with such matters as dramatic unity. He says, for example: 'Our sense of unity in a play like *King Lear* is fostered by our imaginative recreation of the trajectory of an action that unfolds in time, and of the way the narrative shape seems to gather momentum as it leads to a conclusion that in retrospect seems inevitable' (p. 136). The volume is full of such insights, even as he rejects the notion promulgated by the two-text theory that Q and F are two different plays, notwithstanding the admittedly heavy revision he recognises in F.[1]

Several collections of essays that have appeared reprint previously published essays or chapters from books, while others offer altogether new essays, and still others compilations of both old and new works. Kiernan Ryan's collection includes previously published essays and extracts from books on a variety of subjects by Arnold Kettle, Howard Felperin, Leonard Tennenhouse, Annabel Patterson, Leah Marcus, and others. Noteworthy among them are Kathleen McLuskie's 'The patriarchal bard: feminist criticism and *King Lear*' and Terry Eagleton's 'Language and value in *King Lear*', which tend to show recent trends in cultural materialism and gender studies.[2] *Critical Essays on Shakespeare's 'King Lear'* (1996) edited by Jay L. Halio divides the essays into three groups: 'The two texts of *King Lear*', 'Critical and scholarly approaches to *King Lear*', and '*King Lear* in performance'. Although most essays are reprints of journal articles and chapters in books, the collection also includes new essays by Alexander Leggatt on 'Madness in *Hamlet*, *King Lear*, and Early Modern England' and Lois Potter on 'Macready, the two-text theory, and the RSC's 1993 *King Lear*'.

Shakespeare Survey 55 has as its title '*King Lear* and its afterlife' and begins with Kiernan Ryan's survey of criticism and scholarship, 1800–2000, noted above. Of the fifteen essays on *King Lear* in the volume, the first four after Ryan's do not, strictly speaking, follow the announced theme. They include Richard Knowles's scholarly essay, 'How Shakespeare knew *King Lear*', William O. Scott's 'Contracts of love and affection; Lear, old age, and kingship', Andrew Gurr's 'Headgear as a paralinguistic signifier in *King Lear*' and Drew Milne's 'What becomes of broken-hearted Lear: *King Lear* and the dissociation of sensibility'. The remaining essays range broadly from William Carroll's essay on how Shakespeare's Tom o'Bedlam evolved into a musical-hall character in the nineteenth century to Iska Alter's essay on Yiddish appropriations of *King Lear* and R. A. Foakes's fine comparison of *King Lear* and Beckett's *Endgame*. Thomas Cartelli believes that *King Lear* is closer to Brecht's *Mother Courage* than to *Endgame* as he compares Edward Bond's *Lear* to Shakespeare's play in 'Shakespeare in pain: Edward Bond's *Lear* and the ghosts of history'. In 'Some Lears' Richard Proudfoot also considers several Shakespearean offshoots, while in the last essay in this group, ' "Think about Shakespeare": *King Lear* on the Pacific Cliffs', Mark Houlahan reflects on Shakespearean offshoots in New Zealand, Australia, and elsewhere.

---

[1] See pp. 97–111.
[2] New Casebooks: *King Lear*, 1992.

Among recent books on Shakespeare's life and work, one of the most widely read and discussed is Harold Bloom's *Shakespeare: The Invention of the Human* (1998). While some scholars and critics may disagree with Bloom's interpretations or approaches – he is a self-confessed 'unreconstructed humanist' – others have found many of his insights penetrating and compelling. His chapter on *King Lear* is one of the best in the book. In confronting the greatness of *King Lear*, Bloom shows a broadness of vision that others who approach *Lear* from various ideological vantage points, such as cultural materialism, feminism, or psychoanalysis, clearly lack. Like Harold Goddard, the critic he most closely resembles and to whom he acknowledges a debt, he draws parallels and contrasts from Ecclesiastes and the Book of Job, William Blake, W. B. Yeats, Milton, Flaubert, W. H. Auden, Samuel Johnson, William Hazlitt, Nietzsche, Goethe, and others. Love is very much the theme of Bloom's discourse on *King Lear*. In this, he is not very original, though many of his observations on love, especially as they pertain to the principal characters, are. 'The crucial foregrounding of the play, if we are to understand it at all', he says, 'is that Lear is lovable, loving, and greatly loved, by anyone at all worthy of our own affection and approbation' (p. 479). Those unworthy are, of course, Goneril, Regan, Cornwall, Edmond, and Oswald. Whatever else we may think of Lear, we seldom regard him as a loving or lovable man. But, as Bloom claims, it is Lear's enormous capacity for love that lies at the heart of his tragedy. Like many who have anything like his capacity for loving, Lear expects, demands, reciprocation; and when it is not forthcoming, bafflement turns instantly into outrage and outrageousness.

In this context, Bloom notes 'Cordelia's recalcitrance in the face of incessant entreaties for a total love surpassing even her authentic regard for her violently emotional father'. Moreover, 'Cordelia's rugged personality is something of a reaction formation to her father's overwhelming affection' (p. 479). Contributing also to the play's immensity, Bloom says, is the figure of excess or overthrow that never abandons Shakespeare's text; 'except for Edmund, everyone either loves or hates too much' (p. 482). While excess is nothing new in Shakespearean drama, in *King Lear* the dramatist takes it to extremes heretofore unsuspected and unexamined.

Before Lear goes mad his consciousness is 'beyond ready understanding: his lack of self-knowledge, blended with his awesome authority, makes him unknowable by us'. Bloom continues: 'Bewildered and bewildering after that, Lear seems less a consciousness than a falling divinity, Solomonic in his sense of glory, Yahweh-like in his irascibility' (p. 482). Comparisons to Solomon and Yahweh do not seem to overstate the case, surely not if we comprehend the greatness of man that has emerged and indeed grown from the beginning of the play. Bloom is right: 'Lear, surging on through fury, madness, and clarifying though momentary epiphanies, is the largest figure of love desperately sought and blindly denied ever placed upon a stage or in print' (p. 506). That is the measure of his and the play's greatness, and it is, just as Bloom claims, measureless.[1]

---

[1] For a fuller critique on Bloom's essay, from which some lines in the foregoing paragraphs have been taken, see my essay, 'Bloom's Shakespeare', in *Harold Bloom's Shakespeare*, ed. Christy Desmet and Robert Sawyer, 2001, pp. 19–31.

Textual analysis, part I

In Register C, folio 161b, of the Company of Stationers of London, under the date 26 November 1607, the following entry appears:

Na. Butter Entred for their copie vnder thandes of Sr Geo.
Io. Busby Buck knight & Thwardens A booke called. M^r
        William Shakespeare his historye of Kinge Lear
        as yt was played before the kinges maiestie at
        Whitehall vppon St Stephans night at christmas
        Last by his mai^{ties} servantes playinge vsually
        at the globe on Banksyde   vj^d

The play was subsequently printed in quarto by Nicholas Okes for Nathaniel Butter during the period from mid December 1607 to early January 1608.[1] The title page of this first quarto (Q) reads:

M. William Shak-speare: / *HIS* / True Chronicle Historie of the life and / death of King LEAR and his three / Daughters. / *With the vnfortunate life of* Edgar, *sonne* / and heire to the Earle of Gloster, and his / sullen and assumed humor of / TOM of Bedlam: / *As it was played before the Kings Maiestie at Whitehall upon* / S. Stephans *night in Christmas Hollidayes.* / By his Maiesties seruants playing vsually at the Gloabe / on the Bancke-side. / [Printer's device, McKerrow 316] / *LONDON,* / Printed for *Nathaniel Butter,* and are to be sold at his shop in *Pauls* / Church-yard at the signe of the Pide Bull neere / S^t. *Austins* Gate. 1608.

This quarto, also known as the 'Pied Bull' quarto, contains forty-two unnumbered leaves (signatures A2 B–L4). It has occasioned controversy about its authority, the nature of the copy from which it derives, and its relation to the version in the Folio (F).

A second quarto (Q2), printed in 1619 by William Jaggard, bears the false date and imprint, 'Printed for *Nathaniel Butter.* / 1608.' It was one of a group of ten plays intended originally as a collection of works by Shakespeare (or attributed to him) to be published by Jaggard's friend, Thomas Pavier. Essentially a reprint of Q, the Pavier quarto is nevertheless important because of its possible influence on the printing of the Folio text and for a unique reading of a part line inserted before 4.5.189. The third quarto, a poor reprint of Q2, was published in 1655 by Jane Bell and has no textual authority whatsoever.

The third edition of the play (F) appeared in 1623. It occupies pages 283–309 (signatures qq2^r–ss3^r) of the tragedies, situated between *Hamlet* and *Othello.* The text differs significantly from Q, lacking some 285 lines and containing about another 115 not found in Q. Moreover, many different readings of individual words and phrases appear, punctuation and lineation vary decidedly, and speech designations are sometimes altered. F was long regarded as the authoritative text and Q a pirated one, but many scholars now believe that the quarto and Folio represent different versions of the play, F being a revision of the text found in Q and a form the play took on the boards after its initial performances. This version was reprinted in 1632 (F2), 1663 (F3), and 1685 (F4). Although these reprints correct some errors, they introduce others, and none

---

[1] Blayney, pp. 148–9.

has any textual authority. Not until 1709, when Nicholas Rowe edited a new collection of Shakespeare's works, was the text scrutinised again. Rowe used F4 as his copy-text, adding stage directions, scene locations, and other details, while also frequently correcting lineation and punctuation. It is with his edition that the history of modern printed editions of the play may be said to begin.[1]

THE Q TEXT

King Lear was the first play that Nicholas Okes, who had only recently become a master printer, attempted to print. Inexperience may explain, in part, the poor quality of Q, but difficult copy must also share the responsibility. Early theories held that this copy was a reported text of some kind, a version of the play taken down from memory ('memorial reconstruction') or by shorthand by someone in the theatre. W. W. Greg, for example, in a study of the variants among the twelve extant copies of Q, maintained that the text derived from a shorthand report,[2] a position he had arrived at earlier in an important journal essay.[3] While agreeing that Q represents a pirated text, Leo Kirschbaum argued instead that the copy derived from a memorial reconstruction, not shorthand[4] – a position also taken by G. I. Duthie, who concluded that no available system was capable of recording a performance with the fullness and accuracy of Q.[5] Citing many examples of what they considered anticipations, recollections, transpositions, substitutions, and other indications of memorial reconstruction, Kirschbaum and Duthie were convinced that Q with its manifold imperfections could not have come into being in any other way.

Meanwhile, Madeleine Doran had taken the opposite view in *The Text of 'King Lear'* (1931). She held that the quarto text derived directly from Shakespeare's rough draft, or foul papers,[6] which contained many revised and rewritten passages. This theory partly explained the poor printing in Okes's shop while at the same time it afforded Q more textual authority than it could possibly have as a reported text. Many scholars had already conceded that the Pied Bull quarto was too good for a 'bad' quarto (such as Q *Hamlet*), though it was not up to the standard of the authorised, or 'good', quartos of Shakespeare's plays (such as Q2 *Hamlet*). It was therefore a 'doubtful' quarto, an anomaly perhaps unique in the bibliography of the period.[7]

---

[1] Steven Urkowitz notes that some handwritten collations of Q and F exist on a copy of F3 that may have been prepared as a prompt-book for Dublin's Smock Alley Theatre in the 1670s, and Nahum Tate collated Q and F for his adaptation of the play. But Alexander Pope was the first *editor* to begin conflating the two texts, a tradition that has remained almost unbroken up to the present time. See Urkowitz, 'Editorial tradition', pp. 24–5.

[2] See Greg, *Variants*, pp. 138, 187.

[3] 'The function of bibliography in literary criticism illustrated in a study of the text of *King Lear*', *Neophilologus* 18 (1933), 241–62.

[4] *The True Text of 'King Lear'*, 1945, esp. pp. 6–7.

[5] *Elizabethan Shorthand and the First Quarto of 'King Lear'*, 1949. The case for memorial reconstruction is argued at length in Duthie's critical edition of the play, pp. 6, 21–116.

[6] In 'Narratives about printed Shakespeare texts: "foul papers" and "bad" quartos', *SQ* 41 (Spring 1990), 65–86, Paul Werstine questions the use of this term, especially as W. W. Greg 'idealised' it, referring to it as the author's final draft before a fair copy was made. 'Foul papers' could exist in a variety of states; see in particular *ibid.*, pp. 71–2.

[7] Greg, *Editorial Problem*, second edn, 1951, pp. 77–101. Compare Duthie, p. 76, who cites David Lyall Patrick's study, *The Textual History of 'Richard III'*, 1936.

In what amounts to a kind of compromise among these competing theories, Alice Walker proposed that Q *Lear* derived from a transcript of Shakespeare's foul papers stolen by the boy actors who played Gonerill and Regan. In dictating the play to each other, they occasionally depended more upon their memory than on the manuscript before them and thus memorially 'contaminated' some of the scenes, such as 1.1 and 5.3, where their roles were prominent. This theory received considerable support from no less an authority than Greg, though even he recognised a number of serious difficulties inherent in it and argued for further work on the problem.[1]

The challenge has been met by a number of recent studies. The first published was Michael Warren's essay,[2] which argued not only that Q and F represent alternative versions of the play, but that Q for all its problems is an authoritative text. The next published study was P. W. K. Stone's *The Textual History of 'King Lear'* (1980). Also advancing the alternative versions hypothesis, Stone argued (pp. 13–40) that Q nevertheless represented a reported text, though not a memorial reconstruction. He attributed the multitude of aural errors, mislineation, and faulty punctuation to a long-hand, not stenographic, report by someone in the theatre who attended the play more than once. This report was then used as copy by Okes's compositors, who committed further errors, especially where the manuscript was difficult to follow.

Steven Urkowitz's book, *Shakespeare's Revision of 'King Lear'*, also appeared in 1980. Although Madeleine Doran had long since withdrawn her view on the provenance of Q,[3] Urkowitz revived her 'foul papers' theory and brought further arguments to bear in support of it, as in his analyses of misassigned speeches, 'anomalous' spellings, punctuation, and mislined verse. He successfully demolished Alice Walker's theory of 'memorial contamination' of foul papers and concluded that Q was printed directly from Shakespeare's drafts and not from a transcript of them.[4] His study also strongly supported Warren's argument against the single 'ideal' text theory in favour of the two-text hypothesis.

Peter W. M. Blayney's exhaustive study of Nicholas Okes and Q *Lear* was published in 1982. It represents the first part of a complete investigation of the texts of Shakespeare's tragedy (part two has necessarily been delayed to take into account new work on F by other scholars). Eschewing any preconceptions about the provenance or authority of Q, and roundly criticising Greg for such preconceptions in his earlier studies, Blayney thoroughly examined the quarto text both in itself and in the context of other work produced by Okes and his immediate predecessors, particularly during the years 1605–9. His goal was to allow the evidence 'to speak for itself'[5] – that is, to discover in detail the true nature of the quarto text as a bibliographical phenomenon. Only on that basis, Blayney believed, could a reliable and accurate comparative textual analysis of Q and F proceed.

[1] Greg, *SFF*, pp. 381–3. Compare Charlton Hinman's 'Note to the second impression' of *King Lear, 1608 (Pied Bull Quarto)*, Shakespeare Quarto Facsimiles, 1964.
[2] Warren, 'Albany and Edgar', pp. 95–107.
[3] In a review of Greg's *Variants* in *RES* 17 (1941), 474.
[4] Urkowitz, pp. 7–11, 191–2.
[5] Blayney, p. 8.

Although Blayney in the first part of his study does not engage directly with the textual problems of Q, certain of his findings are relevant here. For example, without specifying the exact nature of the manuscript copy used for printing Q, he remarks that it was evidently very difficult copy.[1] Okes therefore abandoned casting-off (for setting by formes, the usual procedure) in favour of setting seriatim. This procedure resulted in shortages of type from time to time. Moreover, since Okes's shop had not previously printed a play-text from manuscript, different conventions of printing needed to be imposed during setting. Blayney confirmed E. A. J. Honigmann's contention that more than one compositor worked on Q *Lear*,[2] although the second compositor did not become involved until late, after the interruption caused by the Christmas holidays. Blayney identifies them as B and C and suggests that C, who worked more slowly and less competently than B, may have been an apprentice.[3]

Difficult copy and inexperience in setting a play-text from manuscript doubtless led to numerous errors, some of which were discovered after press-work began, as Greg surmised.[4] Hence, sheet B is invariant and C (i) is in three states. Press-correction began in earnest with sheet D (o) but declined after reaching maximum efficiency in sheet E (o). Possibly because just one press was used in perfecting (i.e. printing on the blank side of a sheet already printed on one side), variants appear in only one forme of sheets C–H.[5] Sheet K, which has variants in both inner and outer formes, is exceptional. Sheets B, I, and L are invariant. Either the variant states of these sheets have not survived, or proof-correction occurred on those formes to Okes's satisfaction before press-work began.

Since the proofreader was free to work with or without reference to copy, which may have been indecipherable or just not handy, he could make a calculated guess, as in the correction of Q uncorr. 'crulentious' to Q corr. 'tempestious'.[6] Moreover, his corrections were not always accurately made by the compositors – or indeed made at all.[7] Although Q *Lear* shows evidence of an unusual amount of proof-correction, it was after all just a play, of by no means the same importance as, say, a sermon, such as John Pelling's 'Of the Providence of God' (1607), which took precedence over *Lear* in the schedule of printing and publication.[8]

Blayney's study of Q *Lear* indicates, or at least strongly implies, that publication of the quarto by no means assured Butter that windfall returns lay in store. The play was already a year old, although the title page advertisement and dating tend to obscure that fact. Unlike many popular sermons (and some plays, including a few of Shakespeare's), *Lear* was not immediately reprinted; the second edition did not appear until the abortive collection projected by Thomas Pavier eleven years later. If it was not a highly

[1] *Ibid.*, p. 184.
[2] 'Spelling tests and the first quarto of *King Lear*', *The Library*, 5th ser., 20 (1965), 310–15.
[3] Blayney, p. 186.
[4] *Variants*, pp. 43–57, 191–2.
[5] *Ibid.*, pp. 44–57.
[6] *Ibid.*, p. 164. Compare F 'contentious', 3.4.6.
[7] Blayney, pp. 245–7.
[8] *Ibid.*, pp. 81 ff.

profitable commodity, then, the case for 'stolne, and surreptitious' copy[1] accordingly weakens.

THE F TEXT

The other authoritative text for *King Lear*, one which is generally recognised as at least better printed than Q, is the text that Heminge and Condell included in the Folio of 1623. Using cast-off copy, Compositors B and E in Jaggard's printing shop set by formes, as Charlton Hinman showed and as subsequent scholarship has confirmed, modifying only slightly the specific formes or part-formes set by either one. Textual scholars now believe that Compositor B, more experienced but more prone to take liberties in setting from copy, set pages qq2, 3^v, 5, rr1^v (column b), 2^v, 3^v–6^v, or (in the Folio numbered pagination) pages 283, 286, 289, 294b, 296, 298–304.[2] These pages correspond to 1.1.1–83, 1.2.19–135, 1.4.183–293, 2.4.138–93, 3.1.3–3.2.89, 3.4.74–4.5.271. Compositor E, whom Hinman identified as an apprentice,[3] set the rest of the play, or almost twice as much as B.

That Compositor E's pages were more carefully proofread than B's is hardly surprising, since E was only an apprentice. Hinman has recorded the corrections, which tend to show the kinds of mistakes an apprentice might make.[4] Jaggard was also more interested in the appearance of the pages than the accuracy of the text,[5] and (as in the printing of Q) miscorrections could occur. For example, at 1.1.164 uncorrected Folio (F uncorr.) reads 'To come betwixt our sentence, and our power', where corrected Folio (F corr.) has '. . . sentences, and . . .' As Hinman explains, F corr. is clearly wrong.[6] What probably happened is that Compositor E mistook the 'dele' sign in the margin for an 's' and, instead of removing the extraneous comma intended for deletion, added an 's' to 'sentence,' corrupting sense and metre in so doing.

THE COPY FOR F

P. A. Daniel first advanced the theory in 1885 that F was set from an annotated copy of Q, one that had been collated against a theatrical manuscript, probably the prompt-book. Sir Edmond Chambers endorsed the theory,[7] and Greg accepted it. Using the evidence

---

[1] This is the phrase used by Heminge and Condell in their preface to the Folio to stigmatise previously published editions of Shakespeare's plays. It is an obvious seller's ploy, as the full context reveals. See 'To the Great Variety of Readers', Folio sig. A3^r. But the question of how Okes obtained the manuscript remains open.

[2] Hinman, II, 271, 277, 293. T. H. Howard-Hill, 'New light on Compositor E of the Shakespeare First Folio', *The Library*, 6th ser., 2 (1980), 159, 173–8, modified two of Hinman's attributions for the text of *Lear*, assigning ss1 and ss3 to Compositor E.

[3] Hinman, I, 200–26. Hinman first set out his findings in 'The prentice hand in the tragedies of the Shakespeare First Folio: Compositor E,' *SB* 9 (1957), 3–20, but modified his attributions in the later work.

[4] Hinman, I, 304–12. Hinman's summary on p. 325 shows that of 23 pages in *Lear*, 13 were proof-corrected; of 51 variants, 45 were in material set by Compositor E. Recalculated according to Howard-Hill's reattributions, all but one of the variants occur in material set by E.

[5] Hinman, I, 235–9. Hinman identifies the proof-corrector as none other than Isaac Jaggard himself (who took over the running of the printing-house from his father at about this time) and notes that correction was usually not made against copy.

[6] Hinman, I, 304–6.

[7] Chambers, I, 465.

of errors reproduced in F from Q, Greg maintained that the annotated quarto contained at least one sheet (D) in the corrected state and two sheets (H and K) in the uncorrected state (possibly sheets E and G also). The state of sheets C and F he could not determine, and sheets B, I, and L are invariant in all extant copies.[1]

More recently, some scholars have argued that the exemplar used for providing the Folio copy was not annotated Q but an annotated copy of Q2. Although she maintained that F was printed from manuscript copy, Madeleine Doran suspected that because of the number of correspondences between Q2 and F that could not otherwise be explained, Q2 must have been consulted by the F compositor from time to time.[2] Stone rejected this hypothesis, although his research indicated that Q2 was used in some manner for F. After analysing the evidence, he concluded that Compositor E used an annotated copy of Q2 for his share in the pages of *Lear*, while B used manuscript copy.[3] In this conclusion, Stone concurred with Hinman, who argued that E was too inexperienced to set from manuscript, which was left for his partner, B.[4]

Although he first agreed with Stone's conclusions,[5] Gary Taylor later reconsidered the case and, reassessing the evidence, changed his view, arguing that both B and E used annotated Q2 copy while setting the Folio text.[6] To support this revised hypothesis, he analysed substantive variants in Q and F *Lear*, and considered various kinds of other evidence, such as comparisons of spellings and punctuation in the compositors' stints when they used known printed copy (e.g. Q3 *Richard III*) and when they used manuscript copy (e.g. *Hamlet*). He recognised, meanwhile, that the persistence of some Q errors in F, such as '*Historica*' (2.4.53), might derive from the manuscript Jaggard used to annotate Q2 if Shakespeare (or whoever was responsible for preparing that manuscript) was negligent and let them stand. The same argument would apply to common errors in punctuation and lineation.[7] Errors shared only by Q2 and F would be harder to dismiss, and Taylor cites in particular the bungled attempts in Q2 and F to reline correctly 4.6.1–3, where (in his analysis) the errors in F result from Compositor E's inability to follow the annotator's marks. In Q, the passage reads:

> (thy goodnes,
> *Cord.* O thou good *Kent* how shall I liue and worke to match
> My life will be too short and euery measure faile me.

Q2 tried to improve the setting at least visually, though not metrically, by removing the turnover:

---

[1] Greg, *Variants*, pp. 138–49. The summary of findings appears on p. 148.
[2] Doran, pp. 110 ff.
[3] Stone, pp. 129–40. In Appendix DI, pp. 257–67, as elsewhere, Stone assigns pages SS1 and SS3 to Compositor B instead of E, apparently unaware of Howard-Hill's reattributions, with which Stone's tallies fit more closely, obviating the need for any special pleading. Stone's conclusions are supported by MacD. P. Jackson, 'Printer's copy for Folio *Lear*', in *Division*, pp. 346–9.
[4] Hinman, I, 220–6; 'The prentice hand', pp. 3–20.
[5] 'The Folio copy for *Hamlet, King Lear*, and *Othello*', *SQ* 34 (Spring 1983), 44–61.
[6] 'Folio compositors and Folio copy: *King Lear* and its context', *PBSA* 79 (1985), 17–74.
[7] *Ibid.*, p. 23.

> *Cord.* O thou good *Kent,*
> How shall I liue and worke to match thy goodnesse,
> My life will be too short, and euery measure faile me.

According to Taylor, the annotator marked the line-division properly, inserting slash marks after 'worke' and 'short', but Compositor E misunderstood the correction and ended the verse lines both where Q2 ended them and where the slash marks indicated. What resulted in F was:

> *Cor.* O thou good *Kent,*
> How shall I liue and worke
> To match thy goodnesse?
> My life will be too short,
> And every measure faile me.

Compositor E, however, may have been otherwise influenced, as Taylor acknowledges in a footnote;[1] he might have been deliberately stretching his copy to fill up space, the result of inaccurate casting-off of copy.[2]

Similarly, much of the other evidence Taylor uses to demonstrate the dependence of F upon annotated Q2 is subject to alternative interpretation or explanation. For example, both Q2 and F alter the stage direction at 3.7.0. Q reads: *Enter Cornwall, and Regan, and Gonorill, and Bastard.* Q2 reads: *Enter Cornwall, Regan, Gonorill, and Bastard.* F reads: *Enter Cornwall, Regan, Gonerill, Bastard, and Seruants.* More has occurred in F than the simple alteration of *and Regan, and*; this could derive from annotated Q2 but might as easily derive from manuscript copy. Again, the link Taylor cites at 4.5.252, which he calls a progressive error from Q to Q2 to F, certainly looks like one, as he says.[3] But the 'progression' from a comma to a colon to a full stop in the line, 'there is nothing done, If he returne', need not be a *linked* progression. Q's majuscule 'If' may have independently influenced the Q2 compositor and the F collator to introduce heavier punctuation, as indeed occurs throughout Q2 and F.

Nevertheless, the weight of evidence Taylor produces tends heavily in the direction of annotated Q2 copy for both Folio compositors. Much of this weight, however, derives from shared Q2/F spellings of fairly common words[4] and from similar kinds of evidence, such as altered speech ascriptions[5] and punctuation.[6] Of course, neither the resemblances between Q2 and the presumed copy for F, nor any other extant bibliographical evidence can *prove* that Q2 was Compositor B's copy as well as E's; other alternatives are possible, as Taylor says.[7] For example, a transcript prepared from annotated Q2 that incorporated many substantive readings from some other manuscript may have been used as Folio copy, or the compositors may have had before them both a copy of Q2 and

---

[1] *Ibid.*, p. 26, n. 9.
[2] Compare Hinman, II, 507–8.
[3] Taylor, 'Folio compositors', p. 29.
[4] *Ibid.*, pp. 30–41, 57–65.
[5] *Ibid.*, pp. 41–5, 52–5.
[6] *Ibid.*, pp. 65–9.
[7] *Ibid.*, p. 56. Compare *Textual Companion*, p. 531.

an independent manuscript or transcription.[1] The manuscript copy, if there was one, had to be quite different from the kind of manuscript copy used for *Hamlet* and *Othello*, but some kind of manuscript copy for F *King Lear* cannot be entirely ruled out.[2] The main point is that Q2 was a major influence on the printing of F, however it was used.

In the course of his argument Taylor tries to counter Trevor Howard-Hill's findings.[3] From the evidence of spelling, punctuation, and speech ascriptions, Howard-Hill claimed that F used manuscript copy primarily but with some reference to Q2. Arguing that dependence on Q should reveal itself in F's spelling of unusual words, he examined the Folio texts of other plays, those known to be set from printed copy by both B and E, i.e. *Titus Andronicus* and *Romeo and Juliet*. He showed that the compositors, regardless of their experience or lack of it, tended to follow copy whenever they encountered a strange or unusual word. This tendency is not reflected in a comparison of such words in Q, Q2, and F; hence, the evidence discredits printed copy as the basis for F *Lear*.

In his search for more positive evidence to indicate manuscript copy, Howard-Hill resorted to Doran's list of errors in F most readily explained by postulating manuscript copy in Secretary hand.[4] He cites in particular the misreading 'strangenesse' (2.1.86) for the correct reading 'strange newes' that both quartos supply and goes on to argue for an intermediate transcript between the quartos and the Folio.[5] The theory he finally proposes is one of the alternatives noted above, that the manuscript underlying F derives from a copy of Q2 used to interpret the playhouse prompt-book that was transcribed for use in Jaggard's printing-house. The prompt-book, now many years old, was probably damaged, as Greg and others have claimed in order to explain anomalous readings and errors. Thus, for orthography and accidentals, the transcriber would be most influenced by Q2; for substantives and the unusual spellings, the prompt-book would have greater influence. The process of scanning first the quarto, then the manuscript (to locate additions and corrections) best accounts, in Howard-Hill's view, for the mixture of forms that characterises the Folio text.[6]

A fresh transcript would seem to be decidedly more desirable for printer's copy than a heavily annotated exemplar of a quarto, given the myriad changes that distinguish F from Q and Q2. Howard-Hill rejects the other possible alternative theory, supported by Taylor, that the manuscript copy for F was prepared by first collating Q2 against the

---

[1] Compare Doran, pp. 110–12.

[2] Taylor, 'Folio compositors', pp. 71–4.

[3] Howard-Hill, 'The problem of manuscript copy for Folio *King Lear*', *The Library*, 6th ser., 4 (1982), 1–24.

[4] Doran, pp. 91–5. Howard-Hill also notes Stone's use (p. 55) of the same material.

[5] Other misreadings Doran mentions that indicate manuscript copy for F include 'Reuenge' for Q 'reneag' (2.2.69), 'painting' for Q 'panting' (2.4.28), 'Fenitar' for Q 'femiter' (4.3.3). These represent the clearest examples, but compare the many other possibilities she cites. Granted, some of them could be simple misreadings of corrections on printed copy, e.g. F 'Somnet' for Q 'sommons', Q2 'summons' (4.5.57). But where the quarto is correct and the Folio is clearly wrong, as in the examples singled out above, misreading of manuscript copy and not of a correction is fairly certainly the case, although Duthie, pp. 13–14, argues otherwise: the collator saw 'Reneag' in his copy of Q, compared it with the playhouse manuscript, misread 'Reneag' there as 'Reueng', crossed out 'Reneag' in Q and substituted 'Reuenge', which the compositor then set up. But why would the collator deliberately substitute a word which made little sense, in the context, for one which made perfectly good sense, other errors (e.g. Q 'stir' for F 'fire') in the passage notwithstanding?

[6] Howard-Hill, 'The problem of manuscript copy', p. 23.

prompt-book and then copying the annotated exemplar to provide a clean transcript for the printer. Howard-Hill's objection to this alternative is not only that it assumes the collator failed to see early on that what he was producing was unacceptable as printer's copy; but also, more importantly, that the collator failed to correct the numerous errors that persist in F when he had the playhouse copy before him. Moreover, the failure of many distinctive Q spellings to survive in F as well as the similarity of the non-distinctive orthography of Q2 and F suggested to him that his proposed theory (actually, the procedure long ago suggested by Madeleine Doran) was closer to the mark.

In the still unpublished second volume of his study of the texts of *King Lear*, Peter Blayney also weighs the evidence for and against annotated Q2 as copy for F. Like Howard-Hill, he had come to the conclusion that manuscript, not printed, copy was what both Folio compositors used, although he argues that the manuscript was neither the original prompt-book nor a transcript of it; it was a transcription, rather, of an annotated exemplar of Q either annotated by the reviser or altered by the reviser as he copied it out. This transcription then became the new prompt-book. As for the number of minor agreements between Q2 and F, many of them can be explained without recourse to Q2 as copy for F. Nevertheless, several short stretches of text reveal a 'run' of Q2/F agreements that appear more significant than merely the sum of their parts. One such run occurs in the stretch of text 4.5.218–34. While the preponderance of Q2/F agreements in quasi-substantives, punctuation, and spellings clearly demonstrates F's indebtedness to Q2 as against Q, however, it does not *prove* Q2 was itself the copy for F. As Doran and Howard-Hill argue, it need only have been consulted during the setting of F. Blayney's extensive examination of punctuation demonstrates that F could not have been punctuated without *constant* reference to a copy of Q2 (his emphasis) by Compositor E, who set most of the work, and probably frequent reference to it (or another copy) by Compositor B. After considering other kinds of evidence, especially the spellings of abbreviated speech headings in both Q2 and F, Blayney concluded that the copy for F probably derived from a transcription of annotated Q.[1]

That manuscript copy was used together with an exemplar of Q2 in some fashion now seems, on the evidence, the most plausible theory upon which to proceed. Manuscript copy best explains a number of misreadings and errors in F, although the exact relation of the manuscript to the prompt-book is still unclear. Whether the manuscript was the prompt-book itself or a transcription of it made by consulting Q2 or possibly even an autograph or scribal fair copy (made for presentation or some other purpose),[2] we shall probably never know for certain, but both a manuscript and an exemplar of Q2 influenced the setting of the Folio.[3] The numerous deletions from Q in the manuscript, including a whole scene, strongly suggest theatrical adaptation; hence, the manuscript copy for F

[1] I am greatly indebted to Dr Blayney for generously providing me with the relevant chapter of his typescript for *The Texts of 'King Lear' and Their Origins*, vol. 2.

[2] Taylor, '*King Lear* and its context', p. 74. Compare Stone's chapter, 'The manuscript "copy" for F', esp. pp. 104–12.

[3] Compare *Textual Companion*, pp. 530–1. Greg disregarded Q2 as a mere reprint of Q and argued that F had to be set from an exemplar of Q with K4^v in the uncorrected state. His evidence focused on the omission of 'and appointed guard' inserted and partially turned over in Q corr. but lacking in both Q uncorr. and F (*Variants*, pp. 140–1). In 'Q1 and the copy for Folio *Lear*', *PBSA* 80 (1986), 427–35, Howard-Hill argues

very likely was, or derived from, a prompt-book, despite the fact that several prompt-book indicators are missing, such as the names of actors, duplicated stage directions, and warnings for the use of some stage properties.[1] In general, then, substantive readings and alterations derive from the manuscript; accidentals and orthography from Q2.

The implications of this distinction for an editor are important. As Howard-Hill has said, 'Depending upon whether the copy was manuscript or print, the editor may more exactly determine the sources of textual corruption and resolve cruxes.'[2] If the copy for F was (or derived from) an authoritative playhouse manuscript, then the editor can with some confidence correct mistakes that originate in certain misreadings (such as minim errors) and try to determine non-authorial interventions (such as theatrical cuts or actors' interpolations). Although accidentals and orthography will have little or no bearing on the preparation of a modern-spelling text, the editor must be on the lookout for mislined verse, ambiguous or erroneous speech headings, and the like. Especially if the copy was the playhouse prompt-book (or a transcription of it) modified by the book-keeper and then collated against an exemplar of Q2, the tendency will be to retain F readings against Q variants, except where the collator or compositor has bungled his job. The editor must then determine between the original Q reading and the intended reading that F has garbled in so far as it can be 'decoded'. In the example of Q 'strange newes' versus F 'strangenesse', noted above, the editor will adopt Q's reading, since not altered copy but a misreading of the manuscript underlies the F variant. On the other hand, where both Q and F have acceptable readings, F will be preferred as the presumably authoritative alteration or revision of the original text: 'presumably', because we cannot always know certainly that it was the author who effected the change, as in F 'sterne' for Q 'dearne' (3.7.62). Finally, in a few instances where both Q and F are doubtful, Q may provide a guide to the intended alteration or correction. For example, at 1.1.104, Q 'mistresse' has been clumsily altered to F 'miseries', whereas 'misteries' (F2 'mysteries') was probably the intended reading.

F AND Q TRANSMISSION

Strong support for a revision-hypothesis has grown among scholars and has led to the discrete editing of Q and F *Lear* as differing versions of the play, as in the complete Oxford Shakespeare. It is possible, however, that differences between Q and F are

that Greg's case does not hold up, since the F collator might have missed the insertion in the margin of his manuscript, just as Okes's compositor did. But if the manuscript was the theatre prompt-book, a fair copy of the corrected foul papers, why would the words again be inserted in the margin, unless of course the person who prepared the fair copy also missed the insertion and then, like the proof-corrector of Q, went back and added it in the margin in such a way that it could be overlooked once more by the F compositor. This is perhaps too coincidental to be plausible, especially since Q2, the exemplar which was collated, has the words which are missing in Q uncorr. and F. Howard-Hill therefore argues that the words were inserted in the prompt-book in such a manner as to be ambiguous. Since underlining was used to indicate deletion as well as interlineal insertion, Compositor E understandably became confused by the apparent conflict in authority and opted to follow the prompt-book, which apparently marked 'and appointed guard' for deletion.

[1] Taylor, '*King Lear* and its context', p. 74; *Textual Companion*, p. 530. But compare Stone, pp. 107–11, who comments on several of these omissions but finds that on the whole F reflects prompt-book derivation.

[2] Howard-Hill, 'The problem of manuscript copy', p. 3.

mixed and cumulative, and that autonomy can be claimed for neither in isolation. If Q derives from Shakespeare's own rough draft – his foul papers in some state or other – it can be argued that this version, as reflected in Q, was not a finished product but just a stage in the development of the play. Changes doubtless occurred when a fair copy of the manuscript was made either by Shakespeare or by a scribe, and when the fair copy became the prompt-book further alterations were introduced, a practice no doubt typical of theatrical production then as now.[1] These alterations included deletions of varying lengths, additions and amplifications, rewriting and recasting as well as substitutions. Moreover, changes need not have occurred all at once.[2] Theatrical practice demonstrates that playscripts tend to evolve over time, especially after initial performances, and now and then when a play is revived.[3] The author may have been a willing participant in any or all of the alterations, or he may not have been: the text as found in the Folio version may reflect one or more compromises between him and his fellow shareholders in the King's Men.

Finally, other stages in the transmission of the text, for which we have no record, may have intervened between the initial performances (not fully represented by Q) and the text as it exists in F. It is possible, for example, that after Butter issued the Pied Bull quarto, Shakespeare got hold of a copy and began tinkering with it, revising many individual words and phrases and altering some passages and scenes on a larger scale as well.[4] Stylistic evidence, particularly a study of the vocabulary used in substitutions and additions, indicates that revision was by Shakespeare and that it was quite late.[5] Adding these new revisions to the prompt-book, already marked up with alterations, must have seemed impractical, and a new prompt-book was prepared by collating the annotated quarto and the old prompt-book. This new prompt-book (or a transcript of it) became the copy for F, which was printed in consultation with Q2, copies of which were available in Jaggard's printing-house.

Demonstrating with certainty each step in the transmission of the text is difficult, and evidence is admittedly sensitive to editorial predisposition. The presentation of materials in this section of textual analysis is meant to provide a perspective for their interpretation. The proposed stemma somewhat simplifies transmission from foul papers to Folio. Some intervening stages have been postulated, but to include every possibility would unduly complicate matters without shedding sufficient light on the problems involved. Briefly, then, the following stemma is a graphic representation of the transmission of the *King Lear* text:

---

[1] In a review otherwise severely critical of many of the essays in *Division*, Richard Knowles supports the claims of Jackson (pp. 333–5) that revisions could have occurred during the rehearsal process. See Knowles, 'The case for two *Lears*', *SQ* 36 (Spring 1985), 117.

[2] Compare Taylor, 'Date and authorship', p 351: 'Indeed, even to speak of "*the* date" and "*the* authorship" of the redaction presumes something we have no right to presume: that all the changes between the Quarto and Folio versions were made at the same time and by the same man.'

[3] For a modern instance, see Thomas Clayton, 'The texts and publishing vicissitudes of Peter Nichols's *Passion Play*', *The Library*, 6th ser., 9 (1987), 365–83, which includes references to Tom Stoppard's *Jumpers* as well.

[4] See Kerrigan, pp. 195–245, and Taylor, 'Date and authorship', pp. 351–468.

[5] Compare Taylor, 'Date and authorship', pp. 376–95, 462–4.

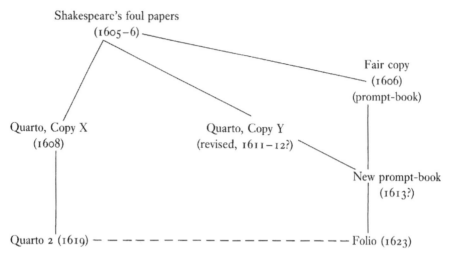

The solid lines on the stemma indicate direct transmission; the broken line indicates collateral influence. Dates for revision are estimates, therefore queried. The stemma shows essentially three separate but related lines of transmission. The first, from foul papers to Q2, is firmly established. The second, from foul papers through revised Q to F, is admittedly speculative. The third, from foul papers to fair copy and prompt-books 1 and 2 culminating in F, is also speculative but, like the second line, seems the best way to take account of available evidence. Collation of the old prompt-book with revised Q is necessary to explain all the revisions, including changes in vocabulary, speech ascriptions, deletions, and other alterations involving both authorial 'tinkerings' and production decisions.

THE NATURE OF INTERVENTIONS

The kinds of intervention by the author or others in the text of *King Lear* (and any other Shakespearean or Elizabethan play-text) are simple in outline but become intricate and extensive when set down in detail. Conclusive evidence is often impossible to marshal; one must proceed by using knowledge of printing practices and theatrical experience; stylistic analysis; and finally supposition, logic, and inference. Since available evidence is frequently ambiguous, alternative explanations are possible. The purpose here is to explain specifically the types of difference between Q and F and the nature of the Folio text as a revised acting version of the play.

OMISSIONS AND CUTS

Omission of one or more lines usually, but not necessarily, indicates a cut. Cuts may originate with a revising author, scribe, or book-keeper; or they may originate in the printing-house, where a compositor may have skipped a line accidentally or, finding copy badly cast-off, may have deliberately dropped a line. The omission after 1.1.98, for example, could be the result of eye-skip by the Folio compositor,[1] or it may be the result of revision, eliminating a redundancy from lines 94–5 (and an irregular half-line):[2]

[1] As Duthie, p. 166, and Stone, p. 233, believe.
[2] Compare Taylor, 'Censorship', p. 87.

> Why have my sisters husbands, if they say   94
> They love you all? . . .
> Sure, I shall never marry like my sisters   98
> [To love my father all].

Omission of several lines often signals a theatrical cut, marked in the prompt-book with a stroke through the text and a vertical line in the margin. The marks could have been misunderstood, and either too much or too little deleted (see below, p. 84). Adjoining lines sometimes invited or required rewriting, as at 1.4.185–91, erroneously printed as prose in the quarto and otherwise in need of correction (see below, p. 80). More often, blocks of lines (in one instance, the entire scene following 4.2) were cut. Where there is no disruption in the adjoining lines, we may suspect a theatrical cut, but *King Lear* is seldom abridged simply to shorten the play. Although the Folio text is some 200 lines shorter than Q, reducing performance time cannot have been the only or even the principal reason for many of the deletions, which demonstrably alter the ethos of several characters and are sometimes offset by additions or amplifications. True, most of the cuts occur in the latter half of the play, from 3.6 onwards, where anxiety about wearying the audience might have been a factor.[1] These include the omissions at the end of 3.6, the concluding lines of Acts 3 and 4, and at 5.3.195. But elsewhere, as in the cuts in Gonerill's speeches or Kent's, many of the alterations directly if subtly change characterisations and suggest authorial rather than theatrical intervention.[2]

AMPLIFICATIONS AND ADDITIONS

Amplifications that elaborate the style or content of an existing speech or passage may sometimes be distinguished from additions of entirely new material, which modify character or dramatic structure. As Thomas Clayton has shown, Lear's first long speech, amplified in F (1.1.31–49), contains additions closely correlated with substantive variants.[3]

Q: *Lear*. Meane time we will expreſſe our darker purpoſes,
The map there; know we haue diuided
In three, our kingdome; and tis our firſt intent,
To ſhake all cares and buſines of our ſtate,   35
Confirming them on yonger yeares,
The two great Princes *France* and *Burgundy*,
Great ryuals in our youngeſt daughters loue,
Long in our Court haue made their amorous ſoiourne,
And here are to be anſwerd, tell me my daughters,

---

[1] Taylor, 'War', p. 29, notes that although F contains significant additions to the Q text in 1.1, 1.4, 2.4, and 3.2, between the beginning of 3.6 and the end of 4.3 the Folio omits 157 lines while adding only seven; i.e. approximately half of the F omissions occur in these scenes. Compare Jackson, p. 331, and David Richman, 'The *King Lear* quarto in rehearsal and performance', *SQ* 37 (1986), 381–2.

[2] See, for example, Warren, 'Albany and Edgar', pp. 95–105, and McLeod, pp. 164–88. Taylor, 'War', pp. 28–30, shows how the cuts in Acts 3–4 'streamline the plot', strengthen the 'narrative momentum', and otherwise tighten the dramatic structure of the play.

[3] Clayton, pp. 121–41. See also the edited parallel passages, pp. 87–94 below.

Which of you fhall we fay doth loue vs moft,
That we our largeft bountie may extend,
Where merit doth moft challenge it,
Gonorill our eldeft borne,fpeake firft *?*

F: *Lear.* Meane time we fhal expreffe our darker purpofe.
Giue me the Map there. Know, that we haue diuided
In three our Kingdome : and 'tis our faft intent,
To fhake all Cares and Bufineffe from our Age,
Conferring them on yonger ftrengths, while we   35
Vnburthen'd crawle toward death. Our fon of *Cornwal*,
And you our no leffe louing Sonne of *Albany*,
We haue this houre a conftant will to publifh
Our daughters feuerall Dowers, that future ftrife
May be preuented now. The Princes, *France & Burgundy*,   40
Great Riuals in our yongeft daughters loue,
Long in our Court, haue made their amorous foiourne,
And heere are to be anfwer'd. Tell me my daughters
(Since now we will diueft vs both of Rule,
Intereft of Territory, Cares of State)   45
Which of you fhall we fay doth loue vs moft,
That we, our largeft bountie may extend
Where Nature doth with merit challenge. *Generill*,
Our eldeft borne, fpeake firft.

The complex effects of this amplification are essentially threefold: (1) anticipation of
Lear's firmness, as in the alteration of Q 'our first intent' to F 'our fast intent' (line
33),[1] and the added 'We haue this houre a constant will' (line 38); (2) provision of
more detailed and rational-sounding motives for abdication, as in the desire to confer
responsibility of the realm on 'yonger strengths' (line 35) and the wish to prevent 'future
strife' by immediately publishing the daughters' dowries (lines 38–40); (3) contributions
to the patterns of imagery involving clothing and nakedness, as in the announcement
that Lear will 'divest' himself of rule, territory, and responsibility for the state (lines
44–5). Careful comparison of the entire speech in F with its shorter – and different –
form in Q, combined with other changes later in the Folio version of the play that
Clayton notes, strongly suggest, though they cannot prove, authorial second thoughts
and subsequent revision.[2]

Similarly, alterations in Gonerill's character involve not only cuts but additions and
amplifications as well. While basically she remains an ungrateful daughter, headed
(as in Q) for collision with her equally strong-willed father, her nature in F is softer.
If she seems in Q 1.3–4 almost out of control raging against her father, in F she is cooler, a

---

[1] Of course, 'first' could be a misreading of 'fast', which F corrects; but compare 'I am firm' (240), which F
    adds.
[2] Compare Jackson, pp. 332–9, for another analysis, which comes to similar conclusions. He cites E. A. J.
    Honigmann, *The Stability of Shakespeare's Text*, 1965, who notes how Shakespeare's 'afterthoughts' some-
    times made his revised verses irregular.

woman much more capable of responding to provocation 'slowly and in proportion', as Randall McLeod says.[1] The omissions after 1.3.15 are complemented by revision of 1.4.267 (F 'Pray you content' for Q 'Come sir no more') and the addition of 1.4.276–87, which shows her mastering emotion and countering Albany's demurrer with rational argument. Again, in 2.4, F alters Gonerill's entrance from her aggressive behaviour in Q, still harping on mistreatment of her servant, to a more restrained initial silence, broken only by coming to her sister's defence (2.4.188).[2] Gonerill's speech on entering is given to Lear in F, with an appropriate change in wording (2.4.181):

Q: *Duke.* What meanes your Grace?   *Enter Gon.*
     Gon. Who ſtruck my ſeruant, *Regan* I haue good hope
     Thou didſt not know ant.
        Lear. Who comes here? O heauens!
     If you doe loue old men, if you ſweet ſway allow
     Obedience, if your ſelues are old, make it your cauſe,
     Send downe and take my part,
     Art not aſham'd to looke vpon this beard?
     O *Regan* wilt thou take her by the hand?
        Gon. Why not by the hand ſir, how haue I offended?

F: *Enter Gonerill.*
        Lear. Who ſtockt my ſeruant? *Regan*, I haue good hope
     Thou did'ſt not know on't.
     Who comes here? O Heauens!
     If you do loue old men; if your ſweet ſway
     Allow Obedience; if you your ſelues are old,
     Make it your cauſe: Send downe, and take my part.
     Art not aſham'd to looke vpon this Beard?
     O *Regan*, will you take her by the hand?
        Gon. Why not by'th'hand Sir? How haue I offended?

Michael Warren has shown how Albany's character is also affected by both deletions and additions in F.[3] In Act 1, Albany seems not quite so weak in F as he does in Q, mainly because in 1.4 F adds a few judiciously spoken lines in his dialogue with Gonerill and Lear. For example, Albany cautions Gonerill, 'Well, you may fear too far' (1.4.282), and he urges patience to the furious Lear (217). These additions, which somewhat strengthen his moral character, contrast with the later weakening that occurs in Acts 4 and 5. The outrage against his wife's treatment of Lear in 4.2 is substantially reduced; and in 5.3 Albany seems less sure of himself in his role as commander. Together with corresponding alterations in Edgar's role, they make ceding the kingdom to the younger man appropriate.[4]

---

[1] McLeod, pp. 175–81.
[2] *Ibid.*, p. 181.
[3] Warren, 'Albany and Edgar', pp. 99–101.
[4] Compare Urkowitz, pp. 80–128. His fuller analysis of the differences between Q and F Albany comes to conclusions similar to Warren's, but he tends to see every change in F as a deliberate alteration of character, whereas some changes, such as the cut following 5.3.195, may have been dictated as much – or more – by

REWRITING, SUBSTITUTION, AND RECASTING

Passages might be changed significantly either by local emendations or the substitution of new text, and recasting could involve moving speeches, changing the order of dialogue, and altering speech headings. Local emendations, sometimes of little or no significance, occur throughout the Folio text of *King Lear*, as in the alteration of the number of days Lear gives Kent in which to depart (1.1.167). Such minor (and minute) changes, or tinkerings, are typical of an author, as Kerrigan has shown,[1] not of a theatrical abridger, who would scarcely care how many days Lear gave Kent to leave the kingdom (four days in Q, five in F).

At 2.4.17, two brief speeches in Q are omitted in F; in their place F adds a new line (see below, pp. 267–8). At 3.1.14–21, eight lines in F replace twelve and a half lines in Q. Although some editors believe both sets of lines in these examples were intended for inclusion in F[2] (and appear thus in modern conflated texts), they are badly spliced and otherwise point to substitution, not amplification (see below, p. 269).

Recasting is clearly evident in a number of places in the Folio *King Lear*. At 1.4.183–92, F recasts Lear's speech (printed as prose in Q), making several corrections, cutting some lines at the end, and assigning to the Fool an important response (see below, p. 267):

Q: whoop *Iug* I loue thee.
   Lea'. Doth any here know mee? why this is not *Lear*, doth
   Lear walke thus? fpeake thus? where are his eyes, either his notion, weaknes, or his difcernings are lethergie, fleeping, or wakeing; ha! fure tis not fo, who is it that can tell me who I am? *Lears*
   fhadow? I would learne that, for by the markes of foueraintie,
   knowledge, and reafon, I fhould bee falfe perfwaded I had
   daughters.
   Foole. Which they, will make an obedient father.
   Lear. Your name faire gentlewoman?
   Gon. Come fir, this admiration is much of the fauour of other

F: Whoop Iugge I loue thee.
   Lear. Do's any heere know me?
   This is not *Lear*:
   Do's *Lear* walke thus? Speake thus? Where are his eies?
   Either his Notion weakens, his Difcernings
   Are Lethargied. Ha! Waking? 'Tis not fo?
   Who is it that can tell me who I am?
   Foole. *Lears* fhadow.
   Lear. Your name, faire Gentlewoman?
   Gon. This admiration Sir, is much o'tn' fauour

---

considerations of theatrical shortening. Of course, all such alterations modify character; it is a question of assessing the motives – and the source – that underlie the changes, and these are often impossible to determine with certainty.

[1] Kerrigan, pp. 205–17.
[2] For example, Duthie, pp. 394–5; compare Stone, pp. 70–5.

The reassignment of Gonerill's speech on entering at 2.4.181 has already been noted, but not the revision that goes with it (see above, p. 79). In 5.3 a good deal of rewriting and recasting has occurred, most notably at the very end. Lear's last words are new, one of his speeches is reassigned to Kent, a stage direction is added, and several other alterations of the text appear:[1]

Q: *Lear.* And my poore foole is hangd, no, no life, why fhould a
    dog, a horfe, a rat of life and thou no breath at all, O thou wilt
    come no more, neuer, neuer, neuer, pray you vndo this button,
    thanke you fir, O, o,o,o.   *Edg.* He faints my Lord, my Lord.
        Lear. Breake hart, I prethe breake. *Edgar.* Look vp my Lord.

F: *Lear.* And my poore Foole is hang'd: no, no, no life?
    Why fhould a Dog, a Horfe, a Rat haue life,
    And thou no breath at all ? Thou'lt come no more,
    Neuer, neuer, neuer, neuer, neuer.
    Pray you vndo this Button. Thanke you Sir,
    Do you fee this? Looke on her? Looke her lips,
    Looke there, looke there.   *He dies.*
        Edg. He faints, my Lord, my Lord.
        Kent. Breake heart, I prythee breake.

Finally, F assigns the last speech in the play to Edgar rather than Albany, their difference in rank notwithstanding. This is one of the alterations that concern the modified characters of both men (see p. 276 below).

THE TIMING OF INTERVENTIONS

Previous discussions of the evolution of the F text have tended to freeze the revisions at a single point in time, although (as noted) theatrical practice demonstrates that changes could be introduced at intervals over an extended period.[2] There seems little necessity, therefore, to fix precisely upon a single moment for all the differences between Q and F. Hypothetically, several stages in the evolution of the text may be posited, from pre-performance alterations to playhouse adaptations and finally to preparation for publication.

Pre-performance alterations

The process of alteration or revision could have begun with the transcription of foul papers to produce a fair copy. If Shakespeare himself transcribed his autograph draft, he might have begun tinkering with it then. Probably, however, a playhouse scribe was commissioned to prepare a fair copy for use as the prompt-book. In that event, alterations would have occurred from the scribe's failure to interpret the manuscript or from

---

[1] See Clayton, pp. 128–38.
[2] See above, p. 75, and compare Knowles, 'The case for two *Lears*', pp. 119–20, who believes changed playing
    conditions could account for variations, for example, in 4.6.

his deliberate intervention for the sake of lucidity or tidiness.[1] As Stone remarks,[2] the nature of Q misreadings suggests that the manuscript copy was sometimes illegible, not because of sloppiness or crowding or wilful distortion but because of hasty composition. A number of the corrections or alterations in F may be the result, then, of scribal intervention in the preparation of fair copy rather than authorial revision. Impossible though it may be to determine when and by whom these changes were introduced, Q 'straied', F 'strain'd' (1.1.163) and Q 'bitt', F 'kill' (4.1.37) – to cite just two examples from Stone's list of Q misreadings – may represent scribal corrections or 'tidyings' of Shakespeare's autograph.[3]

Playhouse adaptations
It is likely that during the rehearsal process the author, the book-keeper, or some other member of the company introduced other alterations. To the book-keeper fell the responsibility for recording routine clarifications of performance, such as the insertion of entrances and exits, speech assignments, sound effects, and the use of properties. The Q text notoriously lacks many such designations, especially entrances and exits, most of which F supplies, also adding or altering a number of other stage directions, as at 1.1.28 and 2.1.36.[4] In addition, the book-keeper would have the responsibility for indicating deletions from the prompt-book, although others in the company might have suggested the cuts. Elimination of the scene following 4.2, for example, could have been proposed during the first rehearsals. For all its lovely poetry, as in the Gentleman's lines on Cordelia (Appendix, p. 304 below, xx, 12–24), the scene adds little to the forward progress of the action; it is essentially a lyric interlude. Whether or not it was ever performed, or whether Shakespeare or another member of his company suggested the cut, we may never know. Likewise, the deletions in the last scene, such as the Captain's two-line speech after 5.3.35 or Edgar's longer passage after 195, might have been proposed by Shakespeare or someone else as inessential material that could be omitted.

It is also possible – indeed likely, on the basis of stylistic analysis – that major revisions including many additions and 'tinkerings' occurred sometime after the King's Men occupied the Blackfriars private theatre in 1609. If Shakespeare was asked to introduce act intervals for performance there, he might have taken that occasion to revise and correct the text, especially if he used a copy of Q.[5] At that or some other time, it might have been decided to eliminate many of the references to France as the invading power.

[1] Stone, pp. 105–6, attributes to a playhouse scribe precisely such indifferent variants as later appear in F, but he believes they were introduced at a later stage, i.e. in the preparation of the new prompt-book c. 1613.
[2] Stone, p. 177.
[3] Of course, Stone attributes the manuscript not to Shakespeare, but to a reporter.
[4] F simplifies or omits a number of Q's descriptive stage directions, as at 2.2.37, 3.3.0, 3.7.80. Many of the omissions may have occurred through compositor error, or the book-keeper or collator may have considered them redundant, as at 4.5.194, 233, 239. Altered stage directions may also indicate a change in staging or playing conditions, as at 4.3.0, 4.6.21. See below, pp. 83–4, and compare Taylor, 'War', p. 30, and Knowles, 'The case for two *Lears*', p. 119.
[5] George Walton Williams, review of *Division of the Kingdoms* in *Medieval and Renaissance Drama in English* 2 (1985), 347. Compare Taylor, 'Date and authorship', p. 428, and Stone, p. 107.

Was censorship involved? Gary Taylor has argued that if a censor intervened, he would have been more likely to cast a critical and disapproving eye upon other matters in the play, specifically those alluding to domestic problems that date from the accession of James I.[1] Since France under Henri IV and Britain under James I were now at peace and had been for years, an invasion set long ago in virtual pre-history would hardly be stepping on sensitive political corns. Or would it? Of course, as Taylor reminds us, at a time when England had much to fear from foreign invasion, the old play *King Leir* (*c.* 1590) was more explicit concerning the French landings in Britain than Shakespeare's *King Lear* is, even in the quarto. Moreover, England under James I was at peace not only with France, but with all the great powers of Europe. Nevertheless, diplomatic relations between Henri and James were never easy or relaxed. James was concerned about the war between Spain and the Dutch and the role France played in it, as well as about payment of the French debt to Britain. Since an incident involving protocol at one of Queen Anne's masques had strained or at least chilled diplomatic relations between the two countries,[2] discretion might advise the muting of hostilities in a play performed by the king's own company, especially if, like the masque, the performance would be at court. In the light of James's known pursuit of policies favouring peace, this deliberate muting becomes still more credible. Although we do not know and perhaps cannot know how it happened or when it happened, the fact is that almost all references to France and the French king as the invader in *King Lear* disappear in the Folio text; the omissions are undoubtedly made with a purpose.[3]

Changed playhouse conditions, such as a change of cast, an actor's indisposition, special performances for particular audiences, tours, and so forth may also have led to alterations in the text. The changes in both the cast and the sound effects in 4.6 may owe something to such changed conditions. The quarto's 'Doctor' becomes the 'Gentleman' of 3.1, and the call for music to awaken Lear is omitted. If the play was taken on tour, perhaps the musicians (except those for trumpet and drums) were left

---

[1] 'Censorship', p. 80. Taylor later acknowledges (pp. 102–5) that censorship occasioned the cut after 1.4.119, since the lines contain pointed allusions to King James's mismanagement of the realm. But see Philip J. Finkelpearl, ' "The comedians' liberty": the censorship of the Jacobean stage reconsidered', *ELR* 16 (1986), 123–38.

[2] Maurice Lee, *James I and Henri IV: An Essay in English Foreign Policy, 1603–1610*, 1970, p. 103. Lee's essay details the perennial difficulties in James's foreign policy regarding France under Henri IV.

[3] Doran, p. 73, notes that 'references to invasion by a foreign power remain untouched when the power is unnamed and when the circumstances of the invasion are shrouded in vagueness', but 'they are generally missing from the folio when France is directly named'. She believes that this is evidence of censorship, since the Master of the Revels was 'on guard to catch any matter in plays which might be offensive to the court or to foreign ambassadors'. But knowing this, the King's Men could themselves have made the alterations without having been told to do so. In 'War', p. 31, Taylor analyses these differences between quarto and Folio and makes several astute observations, but he does not speculate upon political or other motivations for the changes that are essentially extrinsic to the drama. Finkelpearl, ' "The comedians' liberty" ', does not treat *King Lear* but discusses the many loopholes in the system and quotes abundant testimony to show that scandalous and libellous plays were, in fact, performed; objectionable material apparently could be added *after* licensing. Furthermore, while the deletion of verbal allusions to France suggests self-censorship by the King's Men, on the other hand F introduces visual indications of nationality in altered stage directions, e.g. at 4.3.0, 5.1.0, 5.2.0, as Honigmann notes in 'Do-it-yourself-*Lear*', *New York Review of Books*, 25 October 1990, p. 59.

behind and the cast reduced.[1] Again, this is entirely speculative: unfortunately, we have sparse records of performance for *King Lear* in the early seventeenth century (see above, p. 32). It bears repeating that just as no single motive or person need have been responsible for all the alterations in the Folio, no single occasion is necessary to mark them. On the contrary, some evidence points to several stages of alteration. At 1.4.119, Q has fifteen lines of dialogue between Lear and his Fool. F lacks the passage, except for the first three lines, which were probably marked for omission as well, since an obvious hiatus is left; but Compositor E missed the notation or it was not indicated clearly enough on his manuscript.[2] The three lines in F, however, vary not only in accidentals but in two substantive readings:

Q: *Lear.* A bitter foole.
    Foole. Doo'ſt know the difference my boy, betweene a bitter foole, and a ſweete foole.
    Lear. No lad, teach mee.
    Foole. That Lord that counſail'd thee to giue away thy land,
Come place him heere by mee, doe thou for him ſtand,

The ſweet and bitter foole will preſently appeare,
The one in motley here, the other found out there.
    Lear. Do'ſt thou call mee foole boy ?

    Foole. All thy other Titles thou haſt giuen away, tha_thou waſt borne with.
    Kent. This is not altogether foole my Lord.
    Foole. No faith, Lords and great men will not let me, if I had a monopolie out, they would haue part an't, and Ladies too, they w:ll not let me haue all the foole to my ſelfe, they'l be ſnatching; giue me an egge Nuncle, and ile giue thee two crownes.

F: *Lear.* A bitter Foole.
    Foole, Do'ſt thou know the difference my Boy, be-tweene a bitter Foole, and a ſweet one.

    Lear. No Lad, teach me.
    Foole. Nunckle, giue me an egge, and Ile giue thee two Crownes.

What apparently happened was that a reviser originally altered the passage, which at a later time was marked for deletion in the playhouse manuscript (by a vertical line in the left-hand margin and a diagonal line through the passage).[3] Possibly the marks did not extend fully enough or clearly enough from the beginning of the passage; hence,

---

[1] Compare Greg, *SFF*, pp. 386–7. Taylor argues, however, that musicians regularly toured and in any case no evidence exists of *Lear* going on tour (*Textual Companion*, p. 538).

[2] Compare Stone, p. 234. Taylor, 'Censorship', pp. 106–7, seconded by Kerrigan, pp. 218–19, rejects Stone's conjecture and believes Shakespeare intended the lines to stand in F as they are.

[3] Alternatively, as Professor Howard-Hill advises me, a revising author might have begun adjusting the passage, then decided it was better to omit it altogether.

Compositor E mistakenly set the first three lines that were intended for omission along with the rest of the passage. In the process, besides changing the spelling of 'Doo'st' and capitalising 'boy' and 'foole', he kept the variant readings introduced earlier: the added 'thou' and the substitution 'one' for 'foole'.

Preparation for publication

Since Shakespeare had died several years before publication of the Folio collection was planned by his fellows, and since he apparently showed no interest in the publication of his plays during his lifetime, preparation of copy for the printing of either Q or F by the author may be ruled out. The book-keeper, the Folio compilers, or a printing-house editor, however, might have taken some care to see that the manuscript was properly prepared before printing began. Q gives little evidence that Okes or anyone else in his printing-house edited the manuscript before printing began. Q2, on the other hand, shows some attempts to correct lineation and other Q errors, and F (also printed by Jaggard) shows further attempts to correct, regularise, and otherwise update spelling and punctuation, not always accurately, as we have seen. The heavier Folio punctuation and capitalisation are doubtless the work of Compositors B and E and reflect Jaggard's house style, although the heavier use of parentheses might be a scribe's. Italics for stage directions are common for Q and F, but F uses italics for the letters in 1.2 and 4.5 as well. Either the author, an editor, or the book-keeper had introduced act and scene divisions in the copy for F, but whoever it was forgot to renumber the last scene in Act 4 correctly (see Commentary 4.6.0). Compositors might attempt local emendation – certainly B might, though not E – but neither was above stretching or compressing his copy to fit his measure, or breaking or combining verse lines as the available space required (see above, p. 69). Most likely we owe the better state of the Folio text more to the relative tidiness of the prompt-book manuscript, collated and corrected in the theatre, than to the attentions of a printing-house editor or the compositors.

THE TEXTUAL DATA AND EDITORIAL PROCEDURE

Variants are of two kinds, substantive and accidental. For the editor of a modern-spelling text, orthography and punctuation usually have little significance, although some ambiguous spellings in the copy-text may require decisions or emendations, as in the spelling of F 'mettle' (1.1.64), which could be 'mettle' or 'metal' (Q has 'mettall'), and the use of question marks, which were often used for exclamation marks. Where accidentals of this kind may have substantive implications, they are recorded in the collation.

More important than accidentals are the nearly 1,500 substantive variants between Q and F that require choices for a modernised text. Where both readings are acceptable, F is usually preferred, in accordance with the revision-hypothesis generally accepted for this edition, but both readings are recorded in the collation. Q readings usually preferred by editors are discussed in the Commentary, as in the case of Q 'rash'/F 'sticke' (3.7.57) and Q 'dearne'/F 'sterne' (3.7.62). Where F is clearly wrong and Q right, the Q reading is adopted, as at 3.6.27, Q 'Bobtaile tike'/F 'Bobtaile tight', though the spelling is modernised. Again, these variants are all recorded in the collation.

Quarto and Folio compared: some parallel passages

The many detailed changes that occur between Q and F are graphically illustrated in the series of parallel passages below, which are edited with collation (but no other annotation) and modernised, like the rest of this edition. Words, phrases, lines unique to one text or the other appear in bold type, with spaces left to indicate where cut or added passages appear. The reader may thereby get a general idea of the revision process, whereas the Textual Analysis (Part 2, pp. 265–91 below) and the Commentary provide more detailed information.

In the first pair of passages, the revision of stage directions as well as Lear's opening speeches are prominent. Not only are additions and deletions noticeable, but words and phrases are altered, for various reasons (see Textual Analysis, pp. 77–9 above). In the next pairs of passages, similar changes occur that, again, may be variously explained. As the collation reveals, the Folio sometimes corrects the quarto, and vice versa. Other emendations of both Q and F may also be required for clarity or sense, as in the emendations of Tom o'Bedlam's mad rant. In the final example, Shakespeare apparently took some pains to alter Lear's last speech, substituting for the long sigh in Q ('O, o, o, o') lines that emphasise the changes in his character by the end of the play. Two important speech ascriptions are also altered. The first makes ambiguous in F what was straightforward in Q (does Kent wish his heart, or Lear's, to break?); the second gives the concluding lines in F to Edgar rather than Albany and thus makes an important thematic and political statement. An appropriate final stage direction is added or restored.

Were a fully annotated and collated parallel-text edition feasible, the reader could study all of the changes between Q and F in detail. Since this is not possible, the passages presented here must serve to show the nature of at least some of the changes that support the revision theory on which this edition is based. For a complete demonstration of the changes, the reader may consult *The Complete 'King Lear'*, ed. Michael Warren, 1990, where the texts of quarto and Folio are presented in parallel form in facsimile reproduction, including the corrected and uncorrected states of each passage in which they occur. Unlike the present sampling, however, it provides no emendation or collation, and of course no annotation, although a useful introduction and bibliography are included.

[Quarto: Act 1, Scene 1]

Sound a Sennet. Enter one bearing a Coronet, then Lear, then the Dukes of Albany
and Cornwall, next Gonerill, Regan, Cordelia, with Followers

LEAR Attend **my** lords of France and Burgundy, Gloucester.
GLOUCESTER I shall, my **liege.**   [*Exit*]   30
LEAR Meantime we shall express our darker **purposes.**
      The map there. Know, we have divided
      In three our kingdom, and 'tis our **first** intent
      To shake all cares and business **of** our **state,**
      Confirming them on younger **years.**   35

      The **two great** princes, France and Burgundy,   40
      Great rivals in our youngest daughter's love
      Long in our court have made their amorous sojourn,
      And here are to be answered. Tell me, my daughters,

      Which of you shall we say doth love us most,
      That we our largest bounty may extend   45
      Where **merit** doth **most** challenge **it?** Gonerill,
      Our eldest born, speak first.

30 SD *Exit*] F; *not in* Q; *Exeunt Gloucester with Edmond. / Capell*   48–9 Gonerill, / Our . . . first] F; Gonerill, our . . . first
Q (*one line*)

[Quarto: Act 1, Scene 2]

GLOUCESTER He cannot be such a monster.   85
EDMOND **Nor is not, sure.**
GLOUCESTER **To his father, that so tenderly and entirely loves him.**
    Heaven and earth! Edmond, seek him out: wind me into him, I pray
    you. Frame **your** business after your own wisdom. I would unstate
    myself to be in a due resolution.
EDMOND **I shall** seek him, sir, presently, convey the business as I shall **see**
    means, and acquaint you withal.   90
GLOUCESTER These late eclipses in the sun and moon portend no good to
    us. Though the wisdom of nature can reason thus and thus, yet nature
    finds itself scourged by the sequent effects. Love cools, friendship falls
    off, brothers divide. In cities, mutinies; in countries, **discords;** palaces,
    treason; the bond cracked **between** son and father.   95

[Folio: Act 1, Scene 1]

> *Sennet. Enter* KING LEAR, CORNWALL, ALBANY, GONERILL, REGAN,
> CORDELIA, *and Attendants*

LEAR Attend the lords of France and Burgundy, Gloucester.
GLOUCESTER I shall, my lord.   *Exit*   30
LEAR Meantime we shall express our darker purpose.
  Give me the map there. Know, that we have divided
  In three our kingdom, and 'tis our fast intent
  To shake all cares and business from our age,
  Conferring them on younger strengths while we   35
  Unburdened crawl toward death. Our son of Cornwall,
  And you our no less loving son of Albany,
  We have this hour a constant will to publish
  Our daughters' several dowers, that future strife
  May be prevented now. The princes, France and Burgundy,   40
  Great rivals in our youngest daughter's love,
  Long in our court have made their amorous sojourn,
  And here are to be answered. Tell me, my daughters
  (Since now we will divest us both of rule,
  Interest of territory, cares of state),   45
  Which of you shall we say doth love us most,
  That we our largest bounty may extend
  Where nature doth with merit challenge? Gonerill,
  Our eldest born, speak first.

[Folio: Act 1, Scene 2]

GLOUCESTER He cannot be such a monster.   85

  Edmond, seek him out: wind me into him, I pray you. Frame the
  business after your own wisdom. I would unstate myself to be in a due
  resolution.
EDMOND I will seek him, sir, presently, convey the business as I shall find
  means, and acquaint you withal.   90
GLOUCESTER These late eclipses in the sun and moon portend no good to
  us. Though the wisdom of nature can reason it thus and thus,
  yet nature finds itself scourged by the sequent effects. Love cools,
  friendship falls off, brothers divide. In cities, mutinies; in countries,
  discord; in palaces, treason; and the bond cracked 'twixt son and   95

Find out this villain, Edmond, it shall lose thee nothing. Do it carefully.   100
And the noble and true-hearted Kent banished; his offence, honesty.
Strange, strange!   [*Exit*]

101 offence, honesty.] F; offence honest, Q   102 SD] F; *not in* Q

[Quarto: Act 2, Scene 2]

CORNWALL   Fetch forth the stocks!
          As I have life and honour, there shall he sit till noon.
REGAN Till noon? Till night, my lord, and all night too.
KENT Why, madam, if I were your father's dog,
          You **could** not use me so.
REGAN   Sir, being his knave, I will.   125
                              [*Stocks brought out*]
CORNWALL This is a fellow of the selfsame **nature**
          Our sister speaks of. Come, bring away the stocks.
GLOUCESTER Let me beseech your grace not to do so.   128
          His fault is much, and the good king, his master,
          Will check him for't. Your purposed low correction
          Is such as basest and contemned'st wretches
          For pilferings and most common trespasses   128d
          Are punished with. The king must take it ill
          That **he's** so slightly valued in his messenger
          Should have him thus restrained.
CORNWALL   I'll answer that.
REGAN My sister may receive it much more worse
          To have her gentleman abused, assaulted.
          For following her affairs. – Put in his legs.   133a
                     [*Kent is put in the stocks*]
          Come, my **good** lord, away.
                     [*Exeunt all but Gloucester and Kent*]

121–2 Fetch . . . noon] F *lineation; divided* honour, / There Q   122 sit] F, Q *corr.;* set Q *uncorr.*   124–5 Why . . . so] F
lineation; as prose Q   125 SD] F; *after 125 Dyce; not in* Q   127 speaks] F; speake Q   128c–d Is . . . trespasses] *Pope's
lineation; two lines divided* valued / In Q   128c basest] Q *corr.;* belest Q *uncorr.*   128c contemned'st] *Capell;* contaned Q
uncorr.; temnest Q *corr.,* Q2   128e–131 Are . . . that] *Oxford lineation; lines end* . . . with, / . . . valued / . . . restrained. / . . .
that. Q   133a SD] *After 127, Rowe; not in* Q, F   134 Come . . . away] F *assigns this line to Cornwall*   134 SD] *Dyce; Exit*
Q2, F; *not in* Q

father. This villain of mine comes under the prediction: there's son against father. The king falls from bias of nature, there's father against child. We have seen the best of our time. Machinations, hollowness, treachery, and all ruinous disorders follow us disquietly to our graves. Find out this villain, Edmond, it shall lose 100 thee nothing. Do it carefully. And the noble and true-hearted Kent banished; his offence, honesty. 'Tis strange. *Exit*

[Folio: Act 2, Scene 2]

CORNWALL   Fetch forth the stocks!
      As I have life and honour, there shall he sit till noon.
REGAN Till noon? Till night, my lord, and all night too.
KENT Why, madam, if I were your father's dog,
      You **should** not use me so.
REGAN   Sir, being his knave, I will.   125
                  Stocks brought out
CORNWALL This is a fellow of the selfsame **colour**
      Our sister speaks of. Come, bring away the stocks.
GLOUCESTER Let me beseech your grace not to do so.

      The king his master **needs** must take it ill
      That **he**, so slightly valued in his messenger,
      Should have him thus restrained.
CORNWALL   I'll answer that.
REGAN My sister may receive it much more worse
      To have her gentleman abused, assaulted.   133

                 [Kent is put in the stocks]
CORNWALL Come, my lord, away.
              [Exeunt all but Gloucester and Kent]

133 SD] *After 127 Rowe; not in* Q, F   134 SD] *Dyce; Exit.* F, Q2; *not in* Q

[Quarto: Act 4, Scene 1]

GLOUCESTER   Sirrah, naked fellow.
EDGAR Poor Tom's a-cold. [*Aside*] I cannot **dance** it **farther.**
GLOUCESTER Come hither, fellow.
EDGAR Bless thy sweet eyes, they bleed.
GLOUCESTER Know'st thou the way to Dover?   55
EDGAR Both stile and gate, horseway and footpath. Poor Tom hath been
    scared out of his good wits. Bless **the good man** from the foul fiend.
    Five fiends have been in poor Tom at once: of lust, as Obidicut;
    Hobbididence, prince of dumbness; Mahu, of stealing; Modo, of
    murder; Flibbertigibbet, of mopping and mowing, who since   58c
    possesses chambermaids and waiting-women. So, bless thee,
    master!
GLOUCESTER Here, take this purse, thou whom the heavens' plagues
    Have humbled to all strokes. That I am wretched   60
    Makes thee the happier. Heavens deal so still.
    Let the superfluous and lust-dieted man
    That **stands** your ordinance, that will not see
    Because he does not feel, feel your power quickly.
    So distribution should **under** excess,   65
    And each man have enough. Dost thou know Dover?
EDGAR Ay, master.
GLOUCESTER There is a cliff whose high and bending head
    Looks **firmly** in the confinèd deep.
    Bring me but to the very brim of it,   70
    And I'll repair the misery thou dost bear
    With something rich about me. From that place
    I shall no leading need.

52 a-cold] *Rowe;* a cold Q, F   56–58c Both . . . master] *As prose* F; *entire passage as verse, lines ending* . . . foot-path, / . . .
wits, / . . . fiend, / . . . once, / . . . dumbnes, / . . . of / . . . chambermaids / . . . maister. Q   58c Flibbertigibbet] *Pope;*
Stiberdigebit Q   58c mopping and mowing] *Theobald;* Mobing, & *Mohing* Q   72–3 With . . . need] F *lineation; lines end*
. . . me, / . . . need Q

[Folio: Act 4, Scene 1]

GLOUCESTER   Sirrah, naked fellow.
EDGAR Poor Tom's a-cold. [*Aside*] I cannot **daub** it **further**.
GLOUCESTER Come hither, fellow.
EDGAR [*Aside*] **And yet I must**. – Bless thy sweet eyes, they bleed.
GLOUCESTER Know'st thou the way to Dover?   55
EDGAR Both stile and gate, horseway and footpath. Poor Tom hath been
    scared out of his good wits. Bless thee, **goodman's son**, from the foul
    fiend.

GLOUCESTER Here, take this purse, thou whom the heavens' plagues
    Have humbled to all strokes. That I am wretched   60
    Makes thee the happier. Heavens deal so still.
    Let the superfluous and lust-dieted man
    That **slaves** your ordinance, that will not see
    Because he does not feel, feel your power quickly.
    So distribution should **undo** excess,   65
    And each man have enough. Dost thou know Dover?
EDGAR Ay, master.
GLOUCESTER There is a cliff whose high and bending head
    Looks **fearfully** in the confinèd deep.
    Bring me but to the very brim of it,   70
    And I'll repair the misery thou dost bear
    With something rich about me. From that place
    I shall no leading need.

54 And . . . bleed] *Capell's lineation and punctuation; two lines divided* must: / Blesse F   **57** scared] Q; scarr'd F   **57** thee,
goodman's son,] thee good mans sonne, F; the good man Q

[Quarto: Act 5, Scene 3]

LEAR And my poor fool is hanged. No, no, life?
      Why should a dog, a horse, a rat have life,   280
      And thou no breath at all? **O thou wilt** come no more,
      Never, never, never. Pray you, undo
      This button. Thank you, sir. **O, o, o, o.**

EDGAR   He faints. My lord, my lord!   285
LEAR Break, heart, I prithee break.
EDGAR   Look up, my lord.
KENT Vex not his ghost. O, let him pass. He hates him
      That would upon the rack of this tough world
      Stretch him out longer.   [*Lear dies*]
EDGAR   O, he is gone indeed.
KENT The wonder is he hath endured so long.   290
      He but usurped his life.
ALBANY Bear them from hence. Our present business
      Is **to** general woe. Friends of my soul, you twain
      Rule in this kingdom and the gored state sustain.
KENT I have a journey, sir, shortly to go: 295
      My master calls, and I must not say no.
ALBANY The weight of this sad time we must obey,
      Speak what we feel, not what we ought to say.
      The oldest have borne most; we that are young
      Shall never see so much, nor live so long.   300
                            [*Exeunt with a dead march*]

279–81 And . . . more] F *lineation; as prose* Q   280 have] F; of Q   282–3 Never . . . O] *Oxford lineation; as prose* Q   287–9
Vex . . . longer] F *lineation; lines end* . . . passe, / . . . wracke, / . . . longer. Q   289 SD] *Oxford; not in* Q (*compare* F)   300
SD] F; *not in* Q

[Folio: Act 5, Scene 3]

LEAR And my poor fool is hanged. No, no, **no** life?
　　　　Why should a dog, a horse, a rat have life,　　　　　　　　　280
　　　　And thou no breath at all? **Thou'lt** come no more,
　　　　Never, never, never, **never, never.**
　　　　Pray you, undo this button. Thank you, sir.
　　　　Do you see this? Look on her! Look, her lips.
　　　　Look there, look there.　　　　　　　　　　　*He dies*
EDGAR　　　　　　　　　　He faints. My lord, my lord!　　　　285
KENT Break, heart, I prithee break.
EDGAR　　　　　　　　　　Look up, my lord.
KENT Vex not his ghost. O, let him pass. He hates him
　　　　That would upon the rack of this tough world
　　　　Stretch him out longer.
EDGAR　　　　　　　　　　He is gone indeed.
KENT The wonder is he hath endured so long.　　　　　　　290
　　　　He but usurped his life.
ALBANY Bear them from hence. Our present business
　　　　Is general woe. Friends of my soul, you twain
　　　　Rule in this **realm** and the gored state sustain.
KENT I have a journey, sir, shortly to go:　　　　　　　　　295
　　　　My master calls **me**; I must not say no.
EDGAR The weight of this sad time we must obey,
　　　　Speak what we feel, not what we ought to say.
　　　　The oldest **hath** borne most; we that are young
　　　　Shall never see so much, nor live so long.　　　　　　300
　　　　　　　　　　　　Exeunt with a dead march

NOTE ON THE TEXT

The text for this edition is based on the First Folio (1623), not on the first quarto (1608). The quarto and Folio texts, while in the main running parallel to each other, are also significantly different in places: some words, phrases, and passages are unique in each, and some show minor alterations of various kinds. Some modern scholars argue that the differences – in which the Folio omits some of the quarto and adds new material – constitute evidence that the Folio is a revised version of the play, largely carried out by Shakespeare himself. In the present edition, spelling has been modernised, and abbreviations and punctuation regularised. The spelling of characters' names in speech headings and stage directions is made uniform and consistent with spellings used in F; hence, Edmond, Gonerill. Punctuation has been kept as light as possible, except where syntax requires clarification; significant departures from punctuation in the copy-text are recorded in the collation.

In the format for the collation, the authority for this edition follows immediately after the lemma (the quotation from the text, enclosed by a square bracket). Other readings follow in chronological order. Significant departures from F are noted in the collation by an asterisk, and all Q-only passages (not found in F) are presented in an Appendix, pp. 293–309 below. Discussions of substantial passages unique to either Q or F appear in the Textual Analysis, pp. 265–91 below.

Elisions in F are generally retained, when consistent with the metre. All *-ed* endings are assumed to be elided, where they would be today, except when the metre requires otherwise and *-èd* is used. Other elisions are often signalled in the Commentary. Although Shakespeare was at the height of his powers when writing *King Lear*, and irregular lines (short or long) may be found throughout the text, the iambic pentameter line has been taken as the normal verse structure, and relineation is made accordingly. This means that sometimes two half-lines, found to equal a single pentameter or (occasionally) hexameter line, will be so arranged in the text.[1]

The present edition generally omits locations for each scene or a detailed time scheme for the play. In keeping with its emphasis on the play as a performance script, especially for a modern audience, every effort is made to stress the fluid and rapid movement from scene to scene as well as within scenes. Although act and scene designations (which the Folio introduces) may appear as impediments to that end, they can be regarded as useful aids for tracking events in the play, nothing more.

---

[1] On joining half-lines, see George T. Wright, *Shakespeare's Metrical Art*, 1988, pp. 103–5, 143–5, and compare David Bevington (ed.), *Ant.*, 1990, pp. 266–70.

The 'Through Line Numbers', as established by Charlton Hinman in *The Norton Facsimile: The First Folio of Shakespeare*, copyright © by W. W. Norton & Company, Inc., are used in this volume with the kind permission of Norton & Co. They appear at the top of each page of the play text and include the first and last lines on those pages according to Hinman's Folio numbering.

The Tragedy of King Lear

LIST OF CHARACTERS

LEAR, *King of Britain*
GONERILL ⎫
REGAN ⎬ *Lear's daughters*
CORDELIA ⎭
The King of FRANCE
The Duke of BURGUNDY
The Duke of ALBANY, *husband to Gonerill*
The Duke of CORNWALL, *husband to Regan*
The Earl of GLOUCESTER
EDGAR, *his elder son*
EDMOND, *his bastard son*
The Earl of KENT
CURAN, *a courtier*
A GENTLEMAN
OSWALD, *Gonerill's steward*
An OLD MAN, *Gloucester's tenant*
A CAPTAIN
A HERALD
FOOL, *in Lear's service*
Knights, Gentlemen, Soldiers, Attendants, Messengers, Servants

THE TRAGEDY OF KING LEAR

1.1 *Enter* KENT, GLOUCESTER, *and* EDMOND

KENT I thought the king had more affected the Duke of Albany than Cornwall.

GLOUCESTER It did always seem so to us: but now in the division of the kingdom, it appears not which of the dukes he values most, for qualities are so weighed that curiosity in neither can make   5
choice of either's moiety.

KENT Is not this your son, my lord?

GLOUCESTER His breeding, sir, hath been at my charge. I have so often blushed to acknowledge him, that now I am brazed to't.

KENT I cannot conceive you.   10

GLOUCESTER Sir, this young fellow's mother could; whereupon she grew round wombed, and had indeed, sir, a son for her cradle ere she had a husband for her bed. Do you smell a fault?

Title] F; M. William Shak-speare / HIS / Historie, of King Lear. Q   Act 1, Scene 1   1.1] *Actus Primus. Scoena Prima.*
F; *not in* Q   0 SD] F; *Enter Kent, Gloster, and Bastard.* Q   4 kingdom] F; kingdomes Q   5 qualities] F; equalities Q   9
to't] too't F; to it Q

Act 1, Scene 1

0 SD GLOUCESTER F spells the name this way in some SDs and *Gloster* in others. In SHS, *Glouc.* is most frequently used, though Compositor E tends to prefer *Glo.* or *Glost.* In dialogue, 'Glouster' is Compositor B's preferred spelling, 'Gloster' Compositor E's. Q consistently uses 'Gloster', which reflects the proper pronunciation.

0 SD EDMOND This is the F spelling here and at 21; in 1.2 and afterwards F usually uses *Bastard* in SDs and *Bast.* in SHS, like Q, but either 'Edmond' or (especially in Acts 3–5) 'Edmund' in the dialogue, where Q uses 'Edmund' consistently. The name was probably suggested by Father Edmonds, the exorcist in Harsnett's *Declaration*, and by Edmond Peckham, in whose home the exorcisms took place.

1 affected inclined to, loved.

1 Albany When Brute, the first King of Britain, divided his realm, he gave his youngest son Alban-act the territory north of the Humber as far as Caithness. Thus it was called Albania and later Albany.

3–4 but . . . kingdom Lear has not revealed all

of the plan to his closest advisers. Compare 'darker purpose' (31). As these lines and 32–3 indicate, Lear has already divided up the realm; hence, the love contest that follows is a sham and not really meant to determine who gets what share. It appears from 81 that he intends to favour Cordelia, and the incentive in 47–8 is false.

4 values rates.

5 qualities i.e. their qualities. F changes Q's 'equalities'.

5 weighed balanced.

5–6 that . . . moiety that the most careful examination of either one's portion cannot determine any preference.

5 curiosity careful examination, scrutiny.

6 moiety share, portion.

8 breeding (1) upbringing, (2) parentage.

9 brazed brazened, hardened.

10 conceive understand. Gloucester plays on the biological sense.

11–13 Sir . . . bed Gloucester's coarse humour must be offensive to Edmond, if he overhears his father speaking thus, as Rosenberg assumes (p. 12).

KENT   I cannot wish the fault undone, the issue of it being so proper.

GLOUCESTER   But I have a son, sir, by order of law, some year elder   15
than this, who yet is no dearer in my account; though this knave
came something saucily to the world before he was sent for, yet
was his mother fair, there was good sport at his making, and the
whoreson must be acknowledged. Do you know this noble
gentleman, Edmond?   20

EDMOND   No, my lord.

GLOUCESTER   My lord of Kent; remember him hereafter as my
honourable friend.

EDMOND   My services to your lordship.

KENT   I must love you and sue to know you better.   25

EDMOND   Sir, I shall study deserving.

GLOUCESTER   He hath been out nine years, and away he shall
again. The king is coming.

Sennet. Enter KING LEAR, CORNWALL, ALBANY, GONERILL,
REGAN, CORDELIA, *and Attendants*

LEAR   Attend the lords of France and Burgundy, Gloucester.

GLOUCESTER   I shall, my lord.   *Exit*   30

---

16 account;] *Theobald;* account, Q, F   17 to] F; into Q   22 Kent; remember] Kent: / Remember F; Kent, remember
Q   28 SD] F; *Sound a Sennet, Enter one bearing a Coronet, then Lear, then the Dukes of Albany, and Cornwell, next Gonorill,
Regan, Cordelia, with followers.* Q   30 lord] F; Leige Q   30 SD] F; *not in* Q; *Exeunt Gloucester and Edmond.* / Capell

14 **fault** (1) transgression, (2) lost scent, as in
hunting, (3) female genitals (Rubenstein, King).
Compare *Venus and Adonis* 691–6, where 'fault' is
used in sense (2), and *AYLI* 4.1.174, where 'fault'
is used in senses (1) and (3).

14 **issue** (1) result, (2) offspring.

14 **proper** (1) good-looking, (2) right.

15 **order of law** i.e. legitimate.

15 **some year** about a year; compare 1.2.5.

16 **account** estimation.

16 **knave** fellow; often applied to servant or
menial. Hence, with an implication of low condition (see *OED* sv *sb* 2).

17 **something** somewhat.

19 **whoreson** bastard son (like 'knave' above,
said jocularly).

26 **study deserving** 'I shall make every effort
to be worthy of your favour' (Kittredge). But the
words carry an ominous implication.

27 **out** abroad. Renaissance nobles often sent
their children to be brought up in other noble-
men's homes, sometimes in their own country,
sometimes abroad.

27–8 **away . . . again** 'Perhaps these words seal
Gloucester's doom' (Muir).

28 SD **Sennet** A set of notes played on a trumpet
or cornet to signal a ceremonial entrance or exit.

28 SD GONERILL F spelling of this name is consistent. Compare the older form 'Gonorill' preferred by Q.

28 SD Q indicates that a 'coronet' is carried
in as part of the procession – the one intended
for Cordelia, Perrett and Muir believe. It is not
clear why F omits this part of the SD. See 133 n.
below.

29 **Attend** Wait upon, escort. Lear's entrance
will be conditioned as much by the size and stature
of the actor playing the role as by his interpretation
of it. See Rosenberg, pp. 22–32.

30 SD Most modern editions include Edmond in
this exit, but neither Q nor F gives any indication
when he leaves. In the light of subsequent events
and the development of his character, there may
be justification in keeping him on stage throughout these momentous proceedings until the general
exodus at 261. Compare Granville-Barker, p. 229.

LEAR   Meantime we shall express our darker purpose.
        Give me the map there. Know, that we have divided
        In three our kingdom, and 'tis our fast intent
        To shake all cares and business from our age,
        Conferring them on younger strengths while we   35
        Unburdened crawl toward death. Our son of Cornwall,
        And you, our no less loving son of Albany,
        We have this hour a constant will to publish
        Our daughters' several dowers, that future strife
        May be prevented now. The princes, France and
              Burgundy,   40
        Great rivals in our youngest daughter's love,
        Long in our court have made their amorous sojourn,
        And here are to be answered. Tell me, my daughters
        (Since now we will divest us both of rule,
        Interest of territory, cares of state),   45

---

31 shall] F; will Q   31 purpose] F; purposes Q   32 Give me] F; *not in* Q   32 that] F; *not in* Q   33 fast] F; first
Q   34 from our age] F; of our state Q   35 Conferring] F; confirming Q   35 strengths] F; yeares Q   35–40 while we . . .
now.] F; *not in* Q   40 The princes] F; The two great princes Q   44–5 (Since . . . state)] F; *not in* Q

31–49 Meantime . . . first See Textual Analysis,
pp. 77–9 above, for Folio revisions in this passage.
   31 we The royal plural.
   31 darker purpose secret intention. The sinis-
ter sense of 'darker' is submerged.
   32 Give me the map Perrett (p. 144), following Koppel, says that Gloucester or Kent carries the map in when they enter, discussing the
division. Mack (pp. 89–90) argues that despite its
many interrogatives, the play's dominant rhetorical
mood is imperative. Berlin (p. 92) disagrees: Lear's
progress is *from* imperative *to* interrogative, 'from a
sure sense of self to a confrontation with mystery'.
   33 In three i.e. into three parts, but not equal
thirds. See 3–4 n.
   33 fast (1) firmly fixed, (2) swift.
   34–5 To shake . . . strengths This is Lear's
motivation for dividing the kingdom in Q. F
expands it and adds a further motive at 44–5.
'Q's "state" compresses several relevant meanings,
including the political and the personal . . . F
unfolds the implications in "state", partly by developing the hint in Q's "Confirming"' (Jackson,
p. 333).
   36 crawl Lear speaks figuratively. Although
some actors have made him appear weak and senile
from the outset, Lear's old age appears vigorous
throughout this scene and later, certainly in F. Gary
Taylor, 'Censorship', p. 96, discusses F's 'deliberate
retrenchment of anything which might too directly

suggest senility, the comic *senex iratus*, or the dod-
dering old man . . .'
   36 son i.e. son-in-law. In the sources, none of
the daughters has a husband until after the love
contest.
   38 constant will unswerving intention. Charac-
teristically, as at 33, Lear speaks in absolute terms.
   38 publish publicly proclaim.
   39 several separate (*OED* sv *adj* 1).
   39–40 that . . . now The wisdom of Lear's
motive here is arguable. Shakespeare's audience
would have recognised the dangers, and James I
would have been particularly concerned (see p. 1
above). NS cites Matt. 12.25: 'Every kingdom
divided against itself is brought to desolation.' In
any event, Lear's good intention does not succeed. At 2.1.6–11, Curan speaks of impending wars
between the dukes, and at 3.1.11 Kent mentions
'division' between them.
   40 prevented forestalled.
   40 France and Burgundy Shakespeare assumes that in the time of which he writes France was
not a unified kingdom and that the Duke of Burgundy shared equal status with the King of France.
Their rivalry for Cordelia's hand is Shakespeare's
invention.
   44 both Used elsewhere by Shakespeare before
more than two nouns, as in *WT* 4.4.56.
   45 Interest Possession; compare *John* 4.3.147,
where 'interest' = ownership.

Which of you shall we say doth love us most,
That we our largest bounty may extend
Where nature doth with merit challenge? Gonerill,
Our eldest born, speak first.

GONERILL   Sir, I love you more than word can wield the matter,   50
Dearer than eyesight, space, and liberty;
Beyond what can be valued, rich or rare,
No less than life, with grace, health, beauty, honour;
As much as child e'er loved, or father found;
A love that makes breath poor, and speech unable;   55 ·
Beyond all manner of so much I love you.

CORDELIA   [*Aside*] What shall Cordelia speak? Love, and be silent.

LEAR   Of all these bounds even from this line, to this,
With shadowy forests and with champains riched
With plenteous rivers and wide-skirted meads,   60
We make thee lady. To thine and Albany's issues
Be this perpetual. What says our second daughter,
Our dearest Regan, wife of Cornwall?

REGAN   I am made of that self-mettle as my sister
And prize me at her worth. In my true heart   65

---

48 nature doth with merit challenge? Gonerill,] F; merit doth most challenge it, / *Gonorill* Q   50 Sir, I love] F; Sir I do love Q   50 word] F; words Q   51 and] F; or Q   54 as] F; a Q   54 found] F; friend Q   57 SD] *Pope*; not in Q, F   57 speak?] F; doe, Q   59 shadowy] F; shady Q   59–60 and with . . . rivers] F; *not in* Q   61 issues] F; issue Q   63 of] F; to Q   64 I] F; Sir I Q   64 that self-mettle as my sister] F; the selfe same mettall that my sister is Q

48–50 Where . . . matter Metrically irregular lines. F's revision of Q is incomplete or incompletely transcribed. In 48 'Gonerill' is elided (= 'Gon'rill'); in 50 'Sir' may be an actor's interpolation (Schmidt, *Zur Textkritik*, cited by Furness).
48 Where . . . challenge Where natural affection along with desert may claim it as due.
50 more . . . matter more than language can convey.
51 eyesight, space, and liberty King notes the dramatic irony behind Gonerill's first comparison, to 'eyesight', and her demand at 3.7.5 that Gloucester should be blinded, which perhaps explains the curious inclusion of this abstraction with the others.
51 space, and liberty 'freedom from confinement, and the enjoyment of that freedom' (Hunter).
53 grace favour, happiness.
55 breath poor (1) speech inadequate, (2) language impoverished, i.e. by love (King).
55 unable incapable, weak.

56 Beyond . . . much i.e. 'I love you beyond limits, and cannot say it is *so much*, for how much soever I should name, it would yet be more' (Johnson).
58 Of . . . to this Lear points to the map (32).
59–60 and . . . rivers Q's omission is probably the result of the compositor's eye-skip. See Textual Analysis, p. 277 below.
59 champains level, open country; compare Italian *campagna*.
59 riched enriched.
60 wide-skirted meads broad meadows.
64 self-mettle (1) self-same spirit (mettle), (2) self-same substance (metal). Shakespeare uses 'mettle' and 'metal' interchangeably, often playing on both senses regardless of spelling. Compare *2H4* 1.1.116: 'For from his metal was his party steeled'. The pun conveys dramatic irony: Regan's mettle/metal, like her sister's, is hard (King).
65 prize . . . worth estimate my value to be the same as hers. Kittredge believes the form is imperative: 'value me'.

I find she names my very deed of love.
Only she comes too short, that I profess
Myself an enemy to all other joys
Which the most precious square of sense possesses,
And find I am alone felicitate   70
In your dear highness' love.
CORDELIA [*Aside*]   Then poor Cordelia,
And yet not so, since I am sure my love's
More ponderous than my tongue.
LEAR   To thee and thine hereditary ever
Remain this ample third of our fair kingdom,   75
No less in space, validity, and pleasure
Than that conferred on Gonerill. Now our joy,
Although our last and least, to whose young love
The vines of France and milk of Burgundy
Strive to be interested. What can you say to draw   80

66–7 I . . . profess] F; *two lines divided short, / That* Q   67 comes too] F; came Q   *69 possesses] Q; professes F   71 SD]
Pope; not in Q, F   73 ponderous] F; richer Q   77 conferred] F; confirm'd Q   77 Now] F; but now Q   78 our last and
least, to whose young] F; the last, not least in our deere Q   78 least,] *Hanmer;* least; F   79–80 The vines . . . interested]
F; *not in* Q   *80 interested] *Jennens;* interest F   80 draw] F; win Q

66 very deed actual document (from which she
can read her love).
   67 that in that.
   69 the most precious square of sense Of
uncertain meaning, the phrase has been variously
interpreted. Riverside glosses 'square of sense' as
figurative for 'the human body' or 'human life'
and cites *FQ* II, ix, 22. In Pythagorean terms, the
square is an emblem of the material world, or the
world of sense, the physical universe; the circle,
an emblem of the conceptual world, even God
Himself. (See S. K. Heninger, *Touches of Sweet
Harmony*, 1974, p. 111, and compare Leonardo's
famous drawing of the human figure inscribed
within a square superimposed upon the same figure
with outstretched limbs inscribed within a circle –
a design that derives from Vitruvius. See G. L.
Hersey, *Pythagorean Palaces*, 1976, pp. 88 ff.)
   69 possesses Most modern editors follow Q
since the F compositor may have erred through the
proximity of 'professe' in 67.
   70 felicitate made happy.
   73 More ponderous Weightier. A short, hypermetrical line at the end of a speech is not unusual in
Shakespeare's mature drama. On short and shared
lines (like 71, also), see George T. Wright, *Shake-

speare's Metrical Art*, 1988, pp. 116–42. Wright
notes the variety of Shakespeare's metrics in *King
Lear* and analyses a passage (138–48 below) on
pp. 104–5.
   76 validity value. Compare 5–6.
   78 our last and least In revising (or correcting)
Q, F makes a more clear-cut distinction in Lear's
attitude to Cordelia and reintroduces the France–
Burgundy rivalry for her love. Cordelia was not
only the youngest daughter but smallest in stature,
hence 'least' in both senses.
   79 milk of Burgundy Furness and others cite
Eccles: 'The pastures of Burgundy, the effect
for the cause'. But Burgundy was a great wine-
producing country, then as now, and 'milk' contrasting with 'vines' may signify a rich wine; compare 'Bristol milk'. Compare 253, however, where
the King of France refers to 'waterish Burgundy',
and n.
   80 interested Most modern editors emend F's
'interest', a variant spelling of the past participle
form of 'interess' = 'to admit to a privilege' (*OED
Interess v* 1: '*to be interested*, to have a right or
share', quoting this passage).
   80 draw win. 'The gambling metaphor is significant' (NS).

A third more opulent than your sisters? Speak.
CORDELIA   Nothing, my lord.
LEAR   Nothing?
CORDELIA   Nothing.
LEAR   Nothing will come of nothing, speak again.   85
CORDELIA   Unhappy that I am, I cannot heave
    My heart into my mouth: I love your majesty
    According to my bond, no more nor less.
LEAR   How, how, Cordelia? Mend your speech a little,
    Lest you may mar your fortunes.
CORDELIA   Good my lord,   90
    You have begot me, bred me, loved me. I
    Return those duties back as are right fit,
    Obey you, love you, and most honour you.

---

81 opulent] Q; opilent F   81 Speak.] F; *not in* Q   83–4 LEAR Nothing? / CORDELIA Nothing.] F; *not in* Q   85 Nothing]
F; How, nothing Q   86–8 Unhappy . . . less] F; *as prose*, Q   88 no more] F; nor more Q   89 How, how, Cordelia? Mend]
F; Goe to, goe to, mend Q   90 you] F; it Q   91–2 You . . . fit] *Pope's lineation; lines divided* me. / I Q, F

81 **A third more opulent** This exposes the pretence of the contest, since only a third remains.
Contrary to modern usage of the word 'third', these
thirds are three very unequal parts of the whole. If
it is more opulent, the division of the realm and
the awards must have been decided beforehand.
The ways Lear may address, or 'tempt', Cordelia
in these lines are numerous and various (see Rosenberg, pp. 55–6). Nevertheless, Cordelia refuses to
humour her father and adheres rigidly to her 'bond'
of filial duty.
    81 **Speak** Cordelia's first response may be
silence (compare 57). F's addition, besides completing the line metrically, increases the dramatic tension occasioned by Cordelia's hesitation. Jill Levenson contrasts Cordelia's response to that of most
of her precursors in the Lear story and relates it to
folktale and scriptural sources ('What the silence
said: still points in *King Lear*', in Clifford Leech
and J. M. R. Margeson (eds.), *Shakespeare 1971*,
1972, pp. 215–29).
    82 **Nothing** J. S. Gill, *N&Q* 31 (1984), 210,
suggests Matt. 27.12–14 as a possible analogue or
source for Cordelia's response, and Matt. 27.11–26
as a whole for the love test.
    83 **Nothing?** Lear's question may reflect
incredulity or unsure hearing or both. The F additions (83–4) not only make Cordelia's response
emphatic, but provide the actor playing Lear with
space for further reaction.
    85 **Nothing . . . nothing** Proverbial: *Ex nihilo*

nihil fit (Tilley N285).
    86–7 **I cannot heave . . . mouth** Noble and
Shaheen both cite Ecclus. 21.26: 'The heart of
fooles is in their mouth: but the mouth of the
wise is in his heart'; but compare Sidney's *Arcadia*
(1590), Bk 11, ch. 2, where Zelmane begins speaking 'with such vehemencie of passion, as though
her harte would clime into her mouth, to take her
tongues office'. On Cordelia's linguistic behaviour
and later Kent's, Colie (p. 126) cites 1 John 3.18:
'let vs not loue in worde, nether in tongue onely,
but in dede and trueth'.
    87–8 **I love . . . less** Compare *King Leir*, 279–
80: 'But looke what love the child doth owe the
father, / The same to you I beare, my gracious
Lord' (Bullough, p. 344). On Cordelia's reply as it
evolved from Geoffrey to Shakespeare, see Perrett,
pp. 228–40; also see p. 10, n. 2, above.
    88 **bond** i.e. the bond between child and par-
ent, filial obligation. Salingar (pp. 96–7) discusses
the ambiguity in 'bond' = (1) fetter, (2) covenant,
legal agreement.
    91–3 **You . . . honour you** Cordelia explains
what she means by her 'bond'. Shaheen compares
the Catechism: 'To love, honour, and succour my
father and mother', and Eph. 6.1–2, Exod. 20.12,
and Deut. 5.16. Seeing Cordelia as a 'dramatized
emblem', Reibetanz notes Cordelia's reply as a close
paraphrase of the wedding response (pp. 30–1) – a
fact noticed also by some psychoanalytically oriented critics.

Why have my sisters husbands, if they say
They love you all? Happily, when I shall wed,   95
That lord whose hand must take my plight shall carry
Half my love with him, half my care and duty.
Sure, I shall never marry like my sisters.
LEAR But goes thy heart with this?
CORDELIA   Ay, my good lord.
LEAR So young, and so untender?   100
CORDELIA So young, my lord, and true.
LEAR Let it be so, thy truth then be thy dower.
For by the sacred radiance of the sun,
The mysteries of Hecate and the night,
By all the operation of the orbs   105
From whom we do exist and cease to be,
Here I disclaim all my paternal care,
Propinquity and property of blood,
And as a stranger to my heart and me
Hold thee from this forever. The barbarous Scythian,   110
Or he that makes his generation messes
To gorge his appetite, shall to my bosom

94–8 Why . . . sisters.] F; *lines end* . . . you all, / . . . hand / . . . him, / . . . neuer / . . . father all. Q 98 sisters.] F; sisters, to loue my father all. Q 100 untender?] F; vntender, Q 104 mysteries] F2; mistresse Q miseries F 104 night,] F; might, Q 111–13 Or . . . relieued] F; *lines end* . . . generation / . . . appetite / . . . relieued Q 112 to my bosom] F; *not in* Q

94–8 Why . . . sisters Cordelia's logic here is irrefutable, but Lear is in no mood for logic. He only registers what seems to him his daughter's cold response to a repeated invitation to tell the world how much she really loves him, as her sisters have just done. As 99 and 100 show, he cannot believe what he hears or understand what is happening.
95 Happily i.e. haply, perchance. F's spelling (a variant form) suggests a possible pun, though the pronunciation is disyllabic.
96 plight troth-plight, promise to wed.
98 Sure The sarcastic effect of 'Sure' is better appreciated in America, where the idiom has survived, than in Britain (King). Q's additional half-line makes Cordelia's point more emphatic but repeats the sense of 95. See Textual Analysis, p. 76–7 above.
99 thy heart King notes a possible pun on Cordelia's name (Latin *cor, cordis* = 'heart'). In the next twenty lines Lear twice refers to his heart as severed from her (109, 120).
101 true In the preceding line, Hunter detects a play on 'untender' = (1) hard, (2) inflexible,

stiff in opinion; 'true' would then = (1) unerring, (2) growing straight.
104 mysteries secret rites.
104 Hecate Pagan goddess of the lower world, patroness of witchcraft (usually performed at night) and of the moon, she appears in *Mac* 3.5 and 4.1.
105 operation of the orbs The movement, and therefore astrological influence, of the heavenly bodies.
108 Propinquity and property of blood i.e. close relationship, kinship, consanguinity.
110 from this from this time (Steevens). But Lear may be gesturing from his breast. In *Ham.* 2.2.156, Polonius similarly gestures, using demonstrative pronouns.
110 Scythian Inhabitant of Asia known from classical times for barbaric practices. Tamburlaine, in Marlowe's play, was a fierce Scythian shepherd whose cruelty was dramatised but did not include cannibalism.
111–12 Or he . . . appetite A reference to the barbaric custom among some cannibalistic peoples of feeding upon their infant children or their

Be as well neighboured, pitied, and relieved,
As thou my sometime daughter.
KENT   Good my liege –
LEAR Peace, Kent,   115
Come not between the dragon and his wrath.
I loved her most, and thought to set my rest
On her kind nursery. Hence and avoid my sight!
So be my grave my peace, as here I give
Her father's heart from her. Call France. Who stirs?   120
Call Burgundy. – Cornwall and Albany,
With my two daughters' dowers digest the third.
Let pride, which she calls plainness, marry her.
I do invest you jointly with my power,
Pre-eminence, and all the large effects   125
That troop with majesty. Ourself by monthly course,
With reservation of an hundred knights
By you to be sustained, shall our abode
Make with you by due turn; only we shall retain
The name and all th'addition to a king: the sway,   130

---

114 liege –] *Rowe;* Liege. Q, F   115–16 Peace . . . wrath.] F; *one line* Q (*turned over*)   121 Burgundy. –] *Theobald;* Burgundy, Q, F   122 dowers . . . the] F; dower . . . this Q   124 with] F; in Q   129 turn . . . shall] F; turnes . . . still Q   130 th'addition] F; the additions Q   130 king: the sway,] F; King, / The sway, Q

parents ('generation' = either 'offspring' or 'progenitors'; 'messes' = 'dishes of food'). According to Harrison's *Description of Britain*, ch. 4, the ancient Scots were of mixed Scythian and Spanish blood, and practised cannibalism (Perrett, p. 292).

114 sometime former.

114 liege sovereign.

116 dragon . . . wrath Although the dragon was on the crest of ancient British kings (Kittredge; NS), Shakespeare may refer simply to a type of fierceness (as in *Cor.* 4.7.23), and to wrath as a property of that fierceness, not its object.

117 set my rest Another metaphor from gambling (compare 80). In the card game primero, to set up one's rest meant 'to stand upon the cards in one's hand', thus to stake one's all. But as Kittredge and others note, 'rest' also carried the suggestion of repose, to which Lear looked forward in retirement. These ambiguities are present in *Rom.* 4.5.6–7, 5.3.110.

118 nursery i.e. care. The inversion of roles involving Lear's second childhood is the subject of much psychoanalytical commentary.

118 Hence Get away, leave; addressed to

Cordelia, who disobeys.

120 Who stirs? i.e. jump to it! 'The courtiers are shocked into immobility' (Muir).

122 digest consume, assimilate.

123 Let pride . . . marry her i.e. let her pride, which she terms candour, be her dowry and get her a husband.

125 all . . . effects all the outward shows, accompaniments. Compare *Ado* 2.3.107. But note the qualifiers below.

126–9 Ourself . . . turn Although Shakespeare borrowed the idea of a retinue from an earlier source than *King Leir* (probably the *Mirour for Magistrates*), he increased the number to a hundred knights and added the stipulation of alternating monthly visits (Perrett, pp. 187–90). How Gonerill and Regan react here to Lear's unexpected stipulation of monthly visits is open to interpretation.

127 reservation '*Law.* The action or fact of reserving or retaining for oneself some right or interest in property which is being conveyed to another' (*OED* sv 2); Compare 2.4.245.

130 addition titles, honours.

Revenue, execution of the rest,
Beloved sons, be yours; which to confirm,
This coronet part between you.

KENT   Royal Lear,
Whom I have ever honoured as my king,
Loved as my father, as my master followed,   135
As my great patron thought on in my prayers –

LEAR The bow is bent and drawn, make from the shaft.

KENT Let it fall rather, though the fork invade
The region of my heart. Be Kent unmannerly
When Lear is mad. What wouldst thou do, old man?   140
Think'st thou that duty shall have dread to speak
When power to flattery bows? To plainness honour's
    bound,
When majesty falls to folly. Reserve thy state,
And in thy best consideration check
This hideous rashness. Answer my life, my judgement: 145
Thy youngest daughter does not love thee least,

---

133 between] F; betwixt Q   136 prayers –] *Rowe;* prayers. Q; praiers. F   138–46 Let . . . least] F (*except 142, divided*
bowes. / To); *nine lines ending* . . . rather, / . . . heart, / . . . man, / . . . dutie / . . . bowes, / . . . folly, / . . .
consideration / . . . life / . . . least, Q   140 mad] Q2, F; man Q   140 wouldst] F4; wouldest F, F2–3; wilt Q   142 When
. . . bound] *Johnson's lineation; two lines divided* bowes / To F   143 Reserve thy state] F; Reuerse thy doome Q

131 **Revenue** Accented on second syllable.
133 **This coronet** Shakespeare uses 'coronet'
for the diadem of a nobleman in *1H6* 5.4.134,
JC 1.2.238, and elsewhere. In *H5* 2 Chorus 10
and in *Temp.* 1.2.111–16 he explicitly contrasts
'crowns and coronets'. In view of 131, moreover,
it is unlikely that Lear gives his sons-in-law his
own crown to divide between them (compare Greg,
SFF, p. 384 n.), although in stage performances he
sometimes does this, ironically emphasising the folly
of dividing his kingdom by so doing. Probably Lear
refers to the coronet he meant for Cordelia, which
an attendant carries during the entry procession,
as Q directs (28 SD n.) See Perrett, pp. 151–4, and
Rosenberg, p. 67, for stage business here, and compare G. W. Williams, 'Lear's coronet', *American
Notes & Queries* 9 (1971), 99–100, who argues that
'coronet' means Lear's crown.

137 **make from** i.e. let go. Lear's metaphor
refers to Kent's elaborate preamble; impatient, he
wants Kent to get to the point. But some commentators (e.g. Muir, Kittredge) interpret the passage
differently and gloss 'make from' as 'avoid', i.e. get
out of the way of (the arrow of) my anger.

138 **fork** An arrowhead with two forward points,
or 'forkhead'.

140 **When . . . old man?** Abandoning the figure
of parrhesia, or respectful protest (Joseph, p. 276),
Kent changes his idiom to direct, blunt address,
using the familiar second-person pronoun, appropriate only to subordinates and children, and an
appellation ('old man') that is stunning in its impu-
dence.

142 **plainness** blunt, frank speaking; as at 123
and 2.2.91.

143 **Reserve thy state** i.e. do not relinquish
your kingdom. Furness cites Johnson: 'I am
inclined to think that *Reverse thy doom* was Shakespeare's first reading, as more conducive to the
present occasion, and that he changed it afterwards to "Reserve thy state," which conduces
more to the progress of the action.' Other commentators (e.g. Duthie, p. 125; Granville-Barker,
p. 303) suggest that in F Kent is thinking more
of Lear's safety than of Cordelia, who in the Q
reading is uppermost. Jackson (p. 338) says the
F readings stress Lear's political folly in surren-
dering his kingdom; Q, more closely following the
source play, emphasises his error in condemning
Cordelia.

145 **Answer . . . judgement** Let my life be
answerable for my opinion.

Nor are those empty-hearted whose low sounds
Reverb no hollowness.
LEAR   Kent, on thy life no more.
KENT My life I never held but as a pawn
To wage against thine enemies, ne'er feared to lose it,   150
Thy safety being motive.
LEAR   Out of my sight!
KENT See better, Lear, and let me still remain
The true blank of thine eye.
LEAR Now by Apollo –
KENT   Now by Apollo, king,
Thou swear'st thy gods in vain.
LEAR   O vassal! Miscreant!   155
ALBANY, CORNWALL Dear sir, forbear.
KENT Kill thy physician, and thy fee bestow
Upon the foul disease. Revoke thy gift,
Or whilst I can vent clamour from my throat,
I'll tell thee thou dost evil.
LEAR   Hear me, recreant,   160
On thine allegiance hear me.

147–8 low sounds / Reverb] F; low, sound / Reuerbs Q   150 thine] F; thy Q   *150 ne'er feared] *Oxford (Furness conj.)*; nere feare F; nor feare Q   151 motive] F; the motiue Q   154 Apollo –] Q2; Appollo, Q; Apollo, F   154–5 Now . . . vain.] F; *one line* Q   155 O vassal! Miscreant] F; Vassall, recreant Q   156 ALBANY . . . forbear] F; *not in* Q   156 SH CORNWALL] *Cor.* F; CORDELIA *Halio, Oxford*   157–60 Kill . . . evil.] F; *lines end* . . . Physicion, / . . . disease, / . . . clamour / . . . euill. Q   157 Kill] F; Doe, kill Q   157 thy fee] F; the fee Q   158 gift] F; doome Q   160–1 Hear . . . me.] *Capell's lineation; one line* Q, F   160 recreant] F, *not in* Q   161 thine] F; thy Q

148 **Reverb no hollowness** Do not reverber-
ate hollowly; with a quibble on 'hollowness' =
'emptiness' and 'insincerity' (Riverside). Compare
H5 4.4.67–9: 'I did never know so full a voice issue
from so empty a heart; but the saying is true, "The
empty vessel makes the greatest sound." '
  149 **pawn** stake; as in a wager.
  150 **wage** wager, risk. The preposition 'against'
may suggest some form of waging war (Muir), and
'pawn' (149) may involve a metaphor from chess
(Capell).
  152–3 **See . . . eye** Kent, as the wise counsellor,
asks Lear to continue using him as his instrument
for seeing better. 'Blank' refers to the white centre
of a target, the concentric rings of which resemble
the pupil of an eye. Like Cordelia, Kent disobeys
Lear's command to get out.
  154 **Apollo** An appropriate pagan god, Apollo
was the archer god and the sun god, or the god
of clear seeing (Hunter). He was also the god of
diseases and their cure; compare 157–8.

155 **vassal** base wretch.
  155 **Miscreant** Villain (literally, infidel); as in
R2 1.1.39. Some editions (e.g. NS) follow Rowe
and add SD, *Laying his hand on his sword*, as occa-
sioning Albany and Cornwall's interjection (156).
But other stage business suggesting violence is
possible (Rosenberg, p. 72; compare Urkowitz,
pp. 32–3).
  156 SH CORNWALL F's *Cor.* can indicate either
Cordelia or Cornwall. Following Goldring's suggestion (pp. 143–51), Oxford makes Cordelia the
speaker here and later (see 182 SH n. below).
  157–8 **Kill . . . disease** Compare *Ham.* 3.4.145–
9, where Shakespeare uses the disease metaphor for
moral corruption, and 4.3.65–7, where he uses it
for mental disorder.
  158 **Revoke thy gift** Seeing what has happened,
Kent opposes the plan of dividing the kingdom,
regardless of what he may have thought earlier (see
3–4 n. above).
  160 **recreant** traitor.

That thou hast sought to make us break our vows,
Which we durst never yet; and with strained pride,
To come betwixt our sentence and our power,
Which nor our nature nor our place can bear,   165
Our potency made good, take thy reward.
Five days we do allot thee for provision
To shield thee from disasters of the world,
And on the sixth to turn thy hated back
Upon our kingdom; if on the tenth day following   170
Thy banished trunk be found in our dominions,
The moment is thy death. Away! By Jupiter,
This shall not be revoked.
KENT   Fare thee well, king, since thus thou wilt appear,
     Freedom lives hence, and banishment is here.   175
     [*To Cordelia*] The gods to their dear shelter take thee,
         maid,
     That justly think'st and hast most rightly said.
     [*To Gonerill and Regan*] And your large speeches may your
         deeds approve,
     That good effects may spring from words of love.
     Thus Kent, O princes, bids you all adieu,   180
     He'll shape his old course in a country new.   *Exit*

Flourish. Enter GLOUCESTER *with* FRANCE *and* BURGUNDY
[*and*] *Attendants*

CORDELIA   Here's France and Burgundy, my noble lord.

162 That] F; Since Q   162 vows] F; vow Q   163 strained] F; straied Q   164 betwixt] F; betweene Q   *164 sentence] Q,
F *uncorr.*, F2; sentences F *corr.*   167 Five] F; Foure Q   168 disasters] F; diseases Q   169 sixth] F4; fift Q; sixt F   170
tenth] F; seventh *Collier*   174 Fare] F; Why fare Q   *174 since] Q; sith F   175 Freedom] F; Friendship Q   176 SD]
Hanmer; not in Q, F   176 dear shelter] F; protection Q   177 justly think'st] F; rightly thinks Q   177 rightly said] F;
justly said Q   178 SD] *Hanmer; not in* Q, F   181 SD.1 *Exit*] F; *not in* Q   181 SD.2] F; *Enter France and Burgundie with
Gloster.* Q   182 SH CORDELIA] *Halio, Oxford; Cor.* F; *Glost.* Q

162 **That** Seeing that.
163 **strained** excessive.
166 **Our . . . good** i.e. our royal power being effected. Lear has not yet relinquished his kingship (note 'our dominions', 171), as the subsequent dialogue with Burgundy and France also shows.
171 **trunk** torso, body.
174–81 **Fare . . . new** 'After the storm comes the equanimity of Kent's rhymed couplets' (Craig, cited by NS).
174 **since thus** Crowding may have prompted Compositor E to substitute awkward 'sith' for Qq 'since' (*Textual Companion*, p. 532), thus avoiding a turned-over line.
175 **Freedom . . . here** An early indication of

topsy-turviness, or inverted order, in the play. (See NS, p. xxviii.)
178 **approve** make good, confirm.
179 **effects** deeds, actions.
181 **old course** customary conduct.
181 SD.2 *Flourish* A fanfare; compare '*Sennet*', 28 SD.
182 SH CORDELIA F alters Q's *Glost.* to *Cor.*, which most editors take to indicate Cornwall. Cordelia seems a more appropriate speaker, since Burgundy and France are her suitors. See 156 n., and compare Duthie, p. 168, who adopts Q's SH, and Urkowitz, pp. 39–40.
182 **Here's** A singular verb preceding a plural subject appears often in Shakespeare; compare 3.3.16.

LEAR   My lord of Burgundy,
    We first address toward you, who with this king
    Hath rivalled for our daughter. What in the least   185
    Will you require in present dower with her,
    Or cease your quest of love?
BURGUNDY   Most royal majesty,
    I crave no more than hath your highness offered,
    Nor will you tender less?
LEAR   Right noble Burgundy,
    When she was dear to us, we did hold her so,   190
    But now her price is fallen. Sir, there she stands.
    If aught within that little seeming substance,
    Or all of it, with our displeasure pieced
    And nothing more, may fitly like your grace,
    She's there, and she is yours.
BURGUNDY   I know no answer.   195
LEAR   Will you with those infirmities she owes,
    Unfriended, new adopted to our hate,
    Dowered with our curse, and strangered with our oath,
    Take her, or leave her?
BURGUNDY   Pardon me, royal sir,
    Election makes not up in such conditions.   200
LEAR   Then leave her, sir, for by the power that made me,
    I tell you all her wealth. [*To France*] For you, great king,
    I would not from your love make such a stray

183–93 My . . . pieced,] F; *ten lines ending* . . . towards you, / . . . daughter, / . . . present / . . . loue? / . . . what / . . . lesse? / . . . to vs [*turned over*] / . . . fallen, / . . . little / . . . peec'st, Q   184 toward . . . this] F; towards . . . a Q   187 Most] F; *not in* Q   188 hath] F; what Q   194 more] F; else Q   196 Will] F; Sir will Q   198 Dowered] F; Couered Q   199 her?] *Rowe;* her. Q, F   199–200 Pardon . . . conditions.] F; *divided* vp / On such Q   200 in] F; on Q   202 SD] *Pope; not in* Q, F

184 address toward direct our speech toward (Schmidt).
    185 rivalled competed.
    189 less? Modern editors change the question mark, found in both Q and F, to a full stop, which makes Burgundy's reply sound too peremptory. Caught off guard by Lear's question, the duke does not know what to make of it and responds with a query of his own.
    190 so i.e. dear, worth much (with a pun on 'dear' = 'beloved').
    192 that little seeming substance The ambiguity of 'seeming' (it can go with either 'little' or 'substance') suggests two interpretations: either

(1) that person who rejects the slightest hint of insincerity, or (2) that small piece of unreality (that looks like a person).
    193 pieced added, eked out.
    194 like please.
    196 infirmities i.e. disabilities (enumerated in 197–8).
    196 owes owns, has.
    198 strangered made a stranger, disowned.
    200 Election . . . conditions No choice (election) is possible under the terms thus set out.
    202 tell (1) report to, (2) count (Hunter).
    202 For As for.
    203 make such a stray be so aberrant.

To match you where I hate; therefore beseech you
T'avert your liking a more worthier way   205
Than on a wretch whom nature is ashamed
Almost t'acknowledge hers.

FRANCE   This is most strange,
That she whom even but now was your best object,
The argument of your praise, balm of your age,
The best, the dearest, should in this trice of time   210
Commit a thing so monstrous to dismantle
So many folds of favour. Sure, her offence
Must be of such unnatural degree
That monsters it, or your fore-vouched affection
Fall into taint; which to believe of her   215
Must be a faith that reason without miracle
Should never plant in me.

CORDELIA   I yet beseech your majesty –
If for I want that glib and oily art,
To speak and purpose not, since what I well intend,   220
I'll do't before I speak – that you make known
It is no vicious blot, murder, or foulness,
No unchaste action or dishonoured step
That hath deprived me of your grace and favour,

---

205 T'avert] F; To auert Q   207 t'acknowledge] F; to acknowledge Q   207–13 This . . . degree] F; *six lines ending* . . . now / . . . praise, / . . . deerest, / . . . thing, / . . . fauour, / . . . degree, Q   208 she whom] F; she, that Q   *208 best] Q; *not in* F   210 The best, the] F; most best, most Q   214 your fore-vouched affection] F; you for voucht affections Q   215 Fall] F; Falne Q   217 Should] F; Could Q   218–21 majesty – / If . . . speak – that] Maiestie, / If . . . speake, that Q; Maiesty. / If . . . speake, that F; majesty, / (If . . . speak) that *Theobald*   *220 well] Q; will F   221 make known] F; may know Q   223 unchaste] F; vncleane Q

204 **To** As to.
204 **beseech** I beseech.
205 **T'avert** To redirect.
205 **more worthier** Double comparatives and superlatives are common in Shakespeare. Compare e.g. 2.2.92, 3.2.62.
208 **whom** i.e. who. Compare *Temp.* 5.1.76–8.
208 **best object** most favoured object (to gaze upon). Compare *MND* 4.1.170, *Cym.* 5.4.55–6.
209 **argument** theme, subject.
211–12 **dismantle . . . favour** The image is of removing many layers of clothing that drape, or enfold, Cordelia in her father's favour. On the imagery of clothing and divestment, see Heilman, pp. 67–87.
214 **monsters it** i.e. makes it (the offence) monstrous.
214 **fore-vouched affection** previously proclaimed love.

215 **Fall into taint** i.e. must (from 213) now appear to be insincere, hence discredited.
215 **her** 'Emphatic. Of the two alternatives France chooses the second, for the first is to him incredible' (Kittredge).
215–17 **to believe . . . me** i.e. to believe Cordelia guilty of so monstrous an offence requires a faith that reason alone cannot instil in me; it would require a miracle to get me to believe it.
219 **If for** If (it is) because. Cordelia's broken or ungrammatical syntax (as well as her somewhat repetitious speech) may be the result of her emotional state, as some commentators believe.
219 **want** lack (also at 225).
220 **purpose** intend (to fulfil).
222 **vicious blot** moral stain.
223 **dishonoured** dishonourable.

But even for want of that for which I am richer –   225
A still-soliciting eye, and such a tongue
That I am glad I have not, though not to have it,
Hath lost me in your liking.

LEAR   Better thou
Hadst not been born than not t'have pleased me better.

FRANCE Is it but this? A tardiness in nature,   230
Which often leaves the history unspoke
That it intends to do? My lord of Burgundy,
What say you to the lady? Love's not love
When it is mingled with regards that stands
Aloof from th'entire point. Will you have her?   235
She is herself a dowry.

BURGUNDY   Royal king,
Give but that portion which yourself proposed,
And here I take Cordelia by the hand,
Duchess of Burgundy.

LEAR Nothing, I have sworn; I am firm.   240

BURGUNDY I am sorry then, you have so lost a father
That you must lose a husband.

CORDELIA   Peace be with Burgundy;
Since that respect and fortunes are his love,
I shall not be his wife.

FRANCE Fairest Cordelia, that art most rich being poor,   245
Most choice forsaken, and most loved despised,
Thee and thy virtues here I seize upon.

225 for want] Q, F; the want *Hanmer*   225 richer] F; rich Q   227 That] F; As Q   228–9 Better thou / Hadst . . . better.] *Pope's lineation;* Better thou hadst, / Not . . . better. F; Goe to, goe to, better thou hadst not bin borne, / Then . . . better. Q   229 t'have] F; to haue Q   230 but this?] F; no more but this, Q   231–6 Which . . . dowry.] F; *five lines ending* . . . to do [*turned under*] / . . . Lady? / . . . sta[n]ds [*turned under*] / . . . haue her? / . . . dowre. Q   231 Which] F; That Q   *232 do?] *Pope;* do, Q; do: F   233 Love's] F; Loue is Q   234 regards] F; respects Q   235 th'entire point. Will] *Steevens;* the intire point wil Q; th'intire point, will F   236 a dowry] F; and dowre Q   236–9 Royal . . . Burgundy.] F; *three lines ending* . . . portion / . . . Cordelia / . . . Burgundie, Q   236 king] F; Leir Q; Lear Q2   240 I am firm.] F; *not in* Q   242–4 Peace . . . wife.] F; *two lines divided* respects / Of Q   243 respect and fortunes] F; respects / Of fortune Q

225 **for which** i.e. for lack of which.
226 **still-soliciting** always importuning, begging.
228 **liking** 'Cordelia deliberately uses a colder word than love' (Muir, following Kittredge).
230 **tardiness in nature** i.e. slowness in disposition.
231 **history** 'Frequently used for what passes in the inner life of man' (Schmidt 1879, cited by Furness). Used in this sense in *MM* 1.1.28, *R3* 3.5.28.
233–5 **Love . . . point** Compare Sonnet 116, where Shakespeare develops the idea more fully.
234–5 **mingled . . . point** adulterated with

considerations (such as a dowry) completely irrelevant to the main issue (love).
243 **Since that** Since.
243 **respect and fortunes** consideration of wealth (hendiadys). Compare 1.2.45, etc., and Q 'respects / Of fortune'.
245–6 **most rich . . . despised** Noble and Shaheen compare the paradoxes in 2 Cor. 6.10: 'As poore, and yet making many rich: as hauing nothing, and yet possessing all things'. Shaheen adds 2 Cor. 8.9: 'Our Lord Iesus Christ, that he being riche, for your sakes became poore'.

Be it lawful I take up what's cast away.
Gods, gods! 'Tis strange, that from their cold'st neglect
My love should kindle to inflamed respect.   250
Thy dowerless daughter, king, thrown to my chance,
Is queen of us, of ours, and our fair France.
Not all the dukes of waterish Burgundy
Can buy this unprized precious maid of me.
Bid them farewell, Cordelia, though unkind;   255
Thou losest here a better where to find.
LEAR   Thou hast her, France, let her be thine; for we
Have no such daughter, nor shall ever see
That face of hers again. Therefore be gone,
Without our grace, our love, our benison.   260
Come, noble Burgundy.

Flourish. Exeunt [Lear, Burgundy, Cornwall, Albany, Gloucester,
     Edmond, and Attendants]

FRANCE   Bid farewell to your sisters.
CORDELIA   The jewels of our father, with washed eyes
Cordelia leaves you. I know you what you are,
And like a sister am most loath to call
Your faults as they are named. Love well our father: 265
To your professèd bosoms I commit him.
But yet, alas, stood I within his grace,
I would prefer him to a better place.

251 my] F; thy Q   **253** of] F; in Q   **254** Can] F; Shall Q   **257–8** Thou . . . see] F; *divided* thine, / For we Q   **260**
benison.] F; benizon? Q   *****261** SD] *This edn; Exit Lear and Burgundie.* Q; *Flourish. Exeunt.* F; *Exeunt Lear, Burgundy,*
Cornwal, Albany, Gloster, and Attendants. / Capell   **262–5** The . . . father:] F; *lines end* . . . father, / . . . you are, [*turned*
over] / . . . faults / . . . Father, Q   **265** Love] F; vse Q

249–60 Gods . . . benison The couplets not only
conclude the major action of this scene, they also
formalise the attitudes involved, as Hunter notes.
Reibetanz, p. 32, regards this speech of 'rhymed
paradoxy' as evidence that France is 'from another
world' than Lear's dark one.
 250 inflamed respect passionate regard.
 251 thrown . . . chance cast to my luck (another
gambling metaphor).
 253 waterish (1) well-watered (with streams
and rivers), (2) weak, insipid. Compare 79 n.: the
king may be casting a slur on the wine of Burgundy
as well!
 254 unprized precious unvalued, unappreci-
ated (by others) but dear (to me).
 255 though unkind i.e. though they have been
unkind or unnatural.
 256 here . . . where Used as nouns. Kittredge
compares *Oth.* 1.1.137.

260 benison blessing.
 261 SD *Exeunt* 'Lear seems to take his leave, but
in fact he flees . . . Flight – and pursuit – will weave
throughout the whole play now, its effect will be
. . . pervasive' (Rosenberg, p. 79). Drawing parallels with classical Greek tragedy, Fredson Bowers
considers the climactic aspects of this scene in 'The
structure of *King Lear*', *SQ* 31 (1980), 7–20.
 262 jewels A term of endearment (NS), spoken
sarcastically?
 262 washed eyes (1) tear-filled eyes, (2) eyes
cleared of illusion, cleansed, as in *R3* 4.4.389–90,
Ado 4.1.153–4.
 265 as . . . named by their actual names.
 266 your professèd bosoms i.e. the nurture
and love you have declared (as opposed to what
you may really feel and intend).
 268 prefer recommend.

So farewell to you both.

REGAN　Prescribe not us our duty.

GONERILL　　　　　　　　Let your study　　　　270
Be to content your lord, who hath received you
At fortune's alms. You have obedience scanted,
And well are worth the want that you have wanted.

CORDELIA　Time shall unfold what plighted cunning hides;
Who covers faults, at last with shame derides.　　　275
Well may you prosper.

FRANCE　　　　　　　Come, my fair Cordelia.

Exeunt France and Cordelia

GONERILL　Sister, it is not little I have to say of what most nearly
appertains to us both. I think our father will hence tonight.

REGAN　That's most certain, and with you; next month with us.

GONERILL　You see how full of changes his age is; the observation　280
we have made of it hath not been little. He always loved our
sister most, and with what poor judgement he hath now cast
her off appears too grossly.

REGAN　'Tis the infirmity of his age; yet he hath ever but slenderly
known himself.　　　285

---

269 both.] F; both? Q　**270** SH REGAN] F; *Gonorill.* Q　**270** duty.] F; duties? Q　**270** SH GONERILL] F; *Regan* Q　**270–3**
Let . . . wanted.] F; *lines end* . . . Lord, / . . . almes, / . . . scanted, / . . . wanted. Q　**273** want] F; worth Q　**274** plighted]
F; pleated Q　**275** covers] Q, F; cover'd *Hanmer, Capell*　**275** with shame] F; shame them Q　**276** my] F;
not in Q　**276** SD *Exeunt*] F3; *Exit* Q, F, F2　***277–8** Sister, . . . tonight.] *As prose, Capell; three verse lines ending* . . . say,
/ . . . both, / . . . night. Q, F　**277** little] F; a little Q　***281** not] Q; *not in* F　**283** grossly] F; grosse Q

---

270 study aim, endeavour.

272 At fortune's alms As a charity, a poor gift of fortune.

272 scanted stinted, slighted.

273 the want . . . wanted the absence of that which you have lacked (i.e. love). Bevington says 'want' may also refer to her dowry. The alliteration and word-play (anadiplosis) emphasise Gonerill's sarcasm.

274 Time . . . hides Martha Andresen notes Cordelia's version of the Renaissance commonplace *sententia Veritas filia temporis* ('Truth the daughter of Time') and its relation to divestiture imagery ('"Ripeness is all": sententiae and commonplaces in *King Lear*', in *Some Facets*, pp. 155–6).

274 plighted pleated, folded, hence concealed (Onions). Compare 211–12.

275 Who . . . derides The F reading is acceptable. As Duthie says, 'The F version of the speech sounds more awkward and stilted than that of Q: but the speech is a sententious one, and it may well have left Shakespeare's pen more rather than less stilted.' 'Who' takes 'Time' as its antecedent, not

'cunning', and 'faults' is the object of both 'covers' and 'derides' (Schmidt, cited by Duthie). NS and Oxford emend 'covers' to 'covert', following Mason (cited by Furness), so that 'cunning' is still responsible for covering faults. But Sisson, p. 231, defends the F reading: 'Time at first covers faults, but at last (unfolds them and) derides them with shame.'

276 Well . . . prosper Again, spoken sarcastically. Noble and Shaheen cite Prov. 28.13: 'He that hideth his sinnes, shall not prosper.' Shaheen notes that the Authorised Version (1611) uses 'coureth' instead of 'hideth'.

278 will hence will go hence (a common ellipsis).

279 with you Lear has not actually stipulated with whom he will first reside (126–9), but Regan rightly assumes that Gonerill, as the eldest daughter, will be first.

281 not Compositor E has apparently dropped the negative in this crowded line (and column), but Schmidt 1879 and Oxford follow F.

283 grossly obviously.

GONERILL The best and soundest of his time hath been but rash;
  then must we look from his age to receive not alone the
  imperfections of long-engraffed condition, but therewithal the
  unruly waywardness that infirm and choleric years bring with
  them.   290
REGAN Such unconstant starts are we like to have from him as this
  of Kent's banishment.
GONERILL There is further compliment of leave-taking between
  France and him. Pray you, let us sit together. If our father carry
  authority with such disposition as he bears, this last surrender   295
  of his will but offend us.
REGAN We shall further think of it.
GONERILL We must do something, and i'th'heat.

                                                        Exeunt

1.2 *Enter* EDMOND

EDMOND Thou, Nature, art my goddess; to thy law
  My services are bound. Wherefore should I

287 from his age to receive] F; to receiue from his age Q 288 imperfections] F; imperfection Q 288 long-engraffed]
Pope; long ingraffed F; long ingraft Q 289 the unruly] F; vnruly Q 294 Pray you, let us sit] F; pray lets hit Q; pray
you let vs sit F 295 disposition] F; dispositions Q 297 of it] F; on't Q Act 1, Scene 2 1.2] *Scena Secunda*. F; *not
in* Q 0 SD] *Enter Bastard*. F; *Enter Bastard Solus*. Q 1–26 Thou . . . news?] F; *as prose* Q 1 SH EDMOND] *Bast*. Q, F
(*generally throughout*)

286 The best . . . rash Even when in his prime
and in good health, i.e. not infirm of age (284),
Lear has been impetuous.
  287 look expect.
  287 alone only.
  288 imperfections . . . condition faults
implanted for a long time in his disposition. Q's
'ingrafted' is closer to modern spelling; 'engraffed'
is an older variant form.
  291 unconstant starts sudden fits (of passion).
  293 compliment ceremony.
  294 sit together take counsel with one another
(Schmidt). See *R3* 3.1.173, *Per.* 2.3.92. Q's 'hit' =
'agree' or 'strike' is more generally adopted by
editors, but F makes sense and does not require
emendation. McLeod (pp. 157–65) questions
Duthie's preference for 'hit' on several important
grounds.
  294 carry bear, manage.
  295–6 last surrender . . . us i.e. his recent
yielding of authority will become a problem for us.
Gonerill is concerned that despite his abdication
Lear will still try to wield power.
  298 do As opposed to Regan's 'think' (Muir).
  298 i'th'heat at once. Apparently, Gonerill and
Regan fail to decide on a plan for immediate action.
Scenes 3 and 4 show Gonerill taking the offensive
against Lear and his hundred knights only after a

period of time has elapsed and she has endured
disruptions to her household.

Act 1, Scene 2

  0 SD Gloucester's castle is the only location
definitely named, besides Dover, though Perrett
(p. 258) questions the description of Gloucester's
house as a 'castle' by Rowe and subsequent editors.
  1–22 Thou . . . bastards Edmond's soliloquy is
in the manner of the Vice of the old Morality plays
or Richard's opening soliloquy in *R3*, except that
he does not address the audience quite as directly
as they do while he reveals his vicious intentions.
Like Richard III, Edmond shares the Elizabethan
Machiavel's rationalism and ability to manipulate
others. See Danby, p. 63.
  1 Nature The natural son of Gloucester,
Edmond naturally takes Nature as his deity. See
Danby, pp. 15–53, who discusses the conflicting
concepts of Nature in Shakespeare's time. Heilman says nature for Edmond is 'a vital force, the
individual will, sexual vigor'. Compare Elton: 'In
his libertine naturalism, Edmund witnesses [to]
the Jacobean disintegration of natural law and ethical
absolutes' (p. 126).
  1 law i.e. as opposed to religion's laws and those
of society.

Stand in the plague of custom and permit
The curiosity of nations to deprive me?
For that I am some twelve or fourteen moonshines   5
Lag of a brother? Why 'bastard'? Wherefore 'base'?
When my dimensions are as well compact,
My mind as generous, and my shape as true
As honest madam's issue? Why brand they us
With 'base'? with 'baseness'? 'bastardy'? 'base, base'?   10
Who in the lusty stealth of nature take
More composition and fierce quality
Than doth within a dull, stale, tired bed
Go to th'creating a whole tribe of fops
Got 'tween a sleep and wake? Well then,   15
Legitimate Edgar, I must have your land.
Our father's love is to the bastard, Edmond,
As to th'legitimate. Fine word, 'legitimate'.

4 me?] F; me, Q   6 brother?] F; brother, Q   6 'base'?] F; base, Q   9 issue?] F; issue, Q   10 With 'base'? with 'baseness'?
'bastardy'? 'base, base'?] With Base? With basenes Barstardie? Base, Base? F; base, base bastardie? Q   13 dull, stale, tired]
F; stale dull lyed Q   14 th'creating] F; the creating of Q   15 a sleep] Q, F; asleep *Capell*   15 then,] F; the Q   16 land.]
land, Q, F   17 love] Q; loue, F   18 th'legitimate] F; the legitimate Q   18 Fine word, 'legitimate'] F; *not in* Q

3 **custom** convention, usage with the force of
law.
   4 **curiosity of nations** 'Edmund probably owes
his word, *curiosity* – which he appears to use here in
the sense of capricious refinement, with an overtone
of officious meddling – to Florio, and the attitude
behind it to Montaigne, who insistently contrasts
Nature and Custom' (Salingar, p. 122). Salingar
cites relevant passages from the *Essais*, and Muir
from the *Apology for Raymond Sebonde*.
   4 **me?** Most editors continue the query to 6,
but F appears right in making the break here.
Edmond is vexed at being 'deprived', or denied
an inheritance; he then considers the two counts
against him: he is a younger brother, and he is illegitimate.
   5 **For that** Because.
   5 **moonshines** months.
   6 **Lag of** Behind, later than.
   6 **Why . . . 'base'** His bastardy concerns
Edmond more than Edgar's seniority. Hence, in
the following lines he wrings from the terms 'bastard' and 'base' and their derivatives (the two terms
are not, however, etymologically related) as much
of their meaning as he can, both through the figure of repetition and through what seems to him
logical questioning. (Compare Falstaff on 'honour',
1H4 5.1.127–41.) Edmond challenges the assump-

tion that being base-born implies being base in
other respects. Salingar, pp. 123–4, believes this
passage is indebted in part to Montaigne's essay,
'Upon Some Verses of Virgil'.
   7 **dimensions** bodily proportions; as in *MV*
3.1.61.
   7 **compact** composed, formed.
   8 **generous** i.e. lofty, magnanimous, as befits a
gentleman; as in *Ham.* 4.7.135.
   8 **true** proper, correct, 'truly stamped' (Muir).
   9 **honest** chaste.
   11 **lusty . . . nature** 'stealthy enjoyment of natural sexual appetite' (Riverside).
   11–12 **take . . . quality** Either (1) receive
more physical and mental ingredients and energetic
traits, or (2) require a greater and more vigorous
physical and mental constitution. Both senses of
'take' may be active here.
   13 **a dull . . . bed** i.e. the result of a long marriage.
   14 **fops** fools.
   15 **Got** Begot.
   15 **a sleep** Capell's emendation, making one
word, is unnecessary.
   17–18 **Our father's . . . legitimate** The warrant for this statement is Gloucester's speech,
1.1.17–8 (Hunter).

Well, my legitimate, [*Takes out a letter*] if this letter speed
And my invention thrive, Edmond the base   20
Shall to th'legitimate. I grow; I prosper;
Now gods, stand up for bastards!

Enter GLOUCESTER

GLOUCESTER   Kent banished thus? and France in choler parted?
And the king gone tonight? Prescribed his power,
Confined to exhibition? All this done   25
Upon the gad? Edmond, how now? What news?
EDMOND   So please your lordship, none. [*Putting up the letter*]
GLOUCESTER   Why so earnestly seek you to put up that letter?
EDMOND   I know no news, my lord.
GLOUCESTER   What paper were you reading?   30
EDMOND   Nothing, my lord.
GLOUCESTER   No? What needed then that terrible dispatch of it
into your pocket? The quality of nothing hath not such need to
hide itself. Let's see. Come, if it be nothing, I shall not need
spectacles.   35

---

19 SD] *This edn; not in* Q, F   21 to th'] F; tooth' Q; top th' *Capell* (*conj. Edwards*)   23 thus? . . . parted?] F; thus, . . . parted, Q   24 tonight?] F; to night Q   24 Prescribed] F; subscribd Q   25 exhibition?] F; exhibition, Q   26 gad?] F; gadde; Q   27 SD] *Rowe; not in* Q, F   32 needed] F; needes Q   32 terrible] Q2, F; terribe Q

19 **speed** succeed.

20 **invention** device.

21 **Shall to th'legitimate** i.e. shall advance to, or take the place of, usurp, the legitimate. Nichols (cited by Furness) first proposed this interpretation of the Q, F reading in 1861–2 as against Edwards's emendation, 'top th' legitimate', which editors since Capell have generally adopted. Sisson, without citing Nichols, also defends the original reading, and articles by Thomas Clayton and Malcolm Pittock, both in *N&Q* 31 (June 1984), 207–10, present cogent arguments for 'disemending' the text. As Clayton says, 'Though differently arrived at, the forceful complementarity claimed for "top" . . . is there still' (p. 208). Moreover, other F alterations in this passage make it unlikely that the Q reading was overlooked (pp. 207–8); and as Pittock shows, *OED* gives numerous examples of an ellipsis after 'to' (p. 209).

22 **Now . . . bastards** Heilman (pp. 102 and 314 n. 16) notes the ambiguities here: since 'stand up' may refer to male sexual tumescence (as in *Rom.* 2.1.25, 3.3.88), Edmond's prayer becomes a phallic ritual; and he proceeds immediately to behave in the pejorative sense of 'bastard'.

23 **thus?** F's question marks throughout this speech, except for the last one, may be intended as exclamation points, as Muir interprets them, but a querying or wondering tone seems more appropriate for Gloucester here.

23 **in choler** Apparently something went wrong during the 'compliment of leave-taking' referred to at 1.1.293.

23 **parted** departed.

24 **tonight** last night; as in *Rom.* 1.4.50, *MV* 2.5.18.

24 **Prescribed** Limited, restricted.

25 **Confined to exhibition** Limited to an allowance. Compare *TGV* 1.3.68–9.

26 **Upon the gad** i.e. suddenly, as if pricked or goaded (a gad is a sharp spike or spear).

28 **put up** stow, conceal.

31 **Nothing** The word reverberates throughout the first half of the play. Compare 1.1.82–5, 1.4.113–15, 2.2.148, 2.3.21.

32 **terrible dispatch** extremely hasty disposition.

35 **spectacles** Spectacles are a symbol of what Gloucester does need. He does not see through Edmond's plot and shows himself entirely 'credulous' (Heilman, pp. 45, 154).

EDMOND I beseech you, sir, pardon me; it is a letter from my
brother that I have not all o'erread; and for so much as I have
perused, I find it not fit for your o'erlooking.

GLOUCESTER Give me the letter, sir.

EDMOND I shall offend either to detain or give it. The contents, as   40
in part I understand them, are too blame.

GLOUCESTER Let's see, let's see.

EDMOND I hope for my brother's justification he wrote this but as
an essay or taste of my virtue.
                        [*Gives him the letter*]

GLOUCESTER *Reads* 'This policy and reverence of age makes the   45
world bitter to the best of our times, keeps our fortunes from us
till our oldness cannot relish them. I begin to find an idle and
fond bondage in the oppression of aged tyranny, who sways not
as it hath power but as it is suffered. Come to me, that of this I
may speak more. If our father would sleep till I waked him, you   50
should enjoy half his revenue forever and live the beloved of
your brother. Edgar.' Hum! Conspiracy! 'Sleep till I waked
him, you should enjoy half his revenue.' My son Edgar, had he
a hand to write this? a heart and brain to breed it in? When
came you to this? Who brought it?   55

EDMOND It was not brought me, my lord; there's the cunning of it.
I found it thrown in at the casement of my closet.

GLOUCESTER You know the character to be your brother's?

EDMOND If the matter were good, my lord, I durst swear it were
his: but in respect of that, I would fain think it were not.   60

---

36 SH EDMOND] *Bast.* F; *not in* Q *uncorr.; Ba.* Q *corr.*   37 and] F; *not in* Q   38 o'erlooking] ore-looking F; liking Q   40–1
I . . . blame.] *As prose* Q; *three verse lines ending* . . . giue it: / . . . them, / . . . blame. F   44 SD] *This edn; not in* Q,
F   45 SD] F; *not in* Q, *which inserts* /A Letter / *after* 44   45–52 This . . . brother.] F *prints in italics,* Q *in roman*   45 and
reverence] F; *not in* Q   52 Sleep] F; slept Q   *52 waked] wakt Q; wake F   55 you to this] F; this to you Q

38 **o'erlooking** inspection, perusal.
  41 too blame too blameworthy. As recorded in
OED Blame *v* 5, the dative infinitive, *to blame*, was
much used as the predicate after *be*. In the sixteenth
and seventeenth centuries, the *to* was misunderstood as *too*, and *blame* was taken as an adjective
meaning 'blameworthy, culpable'. Compare *1H4*
3.1.175: 'In faith, my lord, you are too willful
blame', cited *OED*, Schmidt. Bevington emends
'to blame', but says the Q/F reading, followed here,
may be correct.
  44 essay or taste trial or sample, i.e. test.
'Essay' is etymologically the same as 'assay'.
  45 policy . . . age policy of revering the old:

hendiadys (Schmidt). 'Policy' suggests 'a clever
trick on the part of the aged' (Kittredge).
  46 best . . . times best years of our lives.
  47–8 idle and fond useless and foolish.
  48–9 who . . . suffered which rules not as
though it had real power, but because it is permitted to do so.
  57 casement A window opening on hinges.
  57 closet private room; as in *Ham.* 2.1.74,
3.2.331.
  58 character handwriting.
  59 matter substance (of the letter's contents).
  60 that i.e. the 'matter'.
  60 fain gladly, willingly.

GLOUCESTER It is his.

EDMOND It is his hand, my lord, but I hope his heart is not in the contents.

GLOUCESTER Has he never before sounded you in this business?

EDMOND Never, my lord. But I have heard him oft maintain it to 65
be fit that, sons at perfect age, and fathers declined, the father
should be as ward to the son, and the son manage his revenue.

GLOUCESTER O villain, villain – his very opinion in the letter!
Abhorred villain, unnatural, detested, brutish villain – worse
than brutish! Go, sirrah, seek him: I'll apprehend him. 70
Abominable villain, where is he?

EDMOND I do not well know, my lord. If it shall please you to
suspend your indignation against my brother till you can derive
from him better testimony of his intent, you should run a
certain course; where if you violently proceed against him, 75
mistaking his purpose, it would make a great gap in your own
honour and shake in pieces the heart of his obedience. I dare
pawn down my life for him that he hath writ this to feel my
affection to your honour and to no other pretence of danger.

GLOUCESTER Think you so? 80

EDMOND If your honour judge it meet, I will place you where you
shall hear us confer of this and by an auricular assurance have
your satisfaction, and that without any further delay than this
very evening.

---

61 his.] F; his? Q   64 Has] F; Hath Q   64 before] F; heretofore Q   65 heard him oft] F; often heard him Q   66 declined]
F; declining Q   66 the father] F; his father Q   67 his] F; the Q   70 sirrah] F; sir Q   70 I'll] F; I Q; I, Q2; Ay, *Cam.*   72
lord. If] F; Lord, if Q   74 his] F; this Q   78 that he hath writ] F; he hath wrote Q   79 other] F; further Q

62 **hand** handwriting.
64 **sounded** searched, examined: a nautical
metaphor (Kittredge).
66 **perfect** fully mature.
66–7 **father . . . revenue** Citing references to
Pettie, Florio, and Montaigne, Muir suggests that
this notion (that aged parents should be under the
guardianship of their children) was not unfamil-
iar in Shakespeare's time; indeed, it is now Lear's
position, as Verity (cited by NS) remarks. Compare Lady Wildgoose's action against her father,
Sir Brian Annesley (p. 4 above).
69 **Abhorred** Abhorrent. 'Participles in *-ed* are
common in this use' (Kittredge).
69 **detested** detestable.
70 **sirrah** Familiar term of address to children
or subordinates.

71 **Abominable** The Q/F spelling, 'Abhom-
inable', reflects the Elizabethan belief that the term
derived from Latin *ab* + *homine*, 'away from man',
hence 'unnatural', 'execrable'.
74–5 **you . . . course** your course of action would
be sure.
75 **where** whereas.
76 **gap** breach.
77 **shake . . . obedience** i.e. utterly destroy the
essence of his devotion.
78 **pawn** stake.
78 **feel** test.
79 **pretence of danger** dangerous purpose.
Compare *Mac.* 2.3.131.
81 **meet** fitting, proper.
82 **auricular assurance** i.e. certainty derived
from hearing directly.

GLOUCESTER   He cannot be such a monster. Edmond, seek him   85
out: wind me into him, I pray you. Frame the business after
your own wisdom. I would unstate myself to be in a due
resolution.

EDMOND   I will seek him, sir, presently, convey the business as I
shall find means, and acquaint you withal.   90

GLOUCESTER   These late eclipses in the sun and moon portend no
good to us. Though the wisdom of nature can reason it thus
and thus, yet nature finds itself scourged by the sequent effects.
Love cools, friendship falls off, brothers divide. In cities,
mutinies; in countries, discord; in palaces, treason; and the   95
bond cracked 'twixt son and father. This villain of mine comes
under the prediction: there's son against father. The king falls
from bias of nature, there's father against child. We have seen
the best of our time. Machinations, hollowness, treachery, and
all ruinous disorders follow us disquietly to our graves. Find   100
out this villain, Edmond, it shall lose thee nothing. Do it
carefully. And the noble and true-hearted Kent banished; his
offence, honesty. 'Tis strange.   *Exit*

85 monster.] F *omits three lines here*   86 the] F; your Q   89 will] F; shall Q   90 find] F; see Q   92 it] F; *not in* Q   95 discord; in palaces] F; discords, Pallaces Q   95 and the] F; the Q   96 'twixt] F; betweene Q   96–100 This . . . graves.] F; *not in* Q   97 prediction:] prediction F   97 father.] Father, F   103 honesty. 'Tis strange.] F; honest, strange, strange! Q   103 SD] F; *not in* Q

85 **monster** F omits two lines here found in Q. See Textual Analysis, p. 265 below.
86 **wind me** insinuate yourself (ethical dative construction; compare *Oth.* 1.1.49).
86 **Frame** Fashion.
87–8 **I . . . resolution** I would divest myself of estate and rank to be resolved sufficiently of doubt. Gloucester's anxiety resembles Othello's in *Oth.* 2.3 and 3.3, and like Othello he jumps too quickly to conclusions. Like Iago, Edmond preys upon this weakness and even proposes eavesdropping (81–3; compare *Oth.* 4.1.81 ff.), although he apparently changes his plan (2.1.20 ff.). Edmond makes his fortune by two letters and is undone by a third (Mack, p. 95; see 3.5.8, 5.1.39).
89 **presently** immediately.
89 **convey** carry out.
90 **withal** therewith.
91 **late eclipses** A possible allusion to the eclipse of the moon on 27 September and of the sun on 2 October 1605 (see p. 1 above). Eclipses were regarded by superstitious men like Gloucester as auguries of evil, giving warning of such things as the machinations of the Catholic conspirators who intended to blow up king and parliament. The Gunpowder Plot, however, was uncovered in November 1605 – before it could be carried out.

92–3 **Though . . . effects** Nature is used in two senses here: (1) human nature, specifically human reason as embodied in natural philosophy, or science; (2) the world of nature, including but not limited to the world of humankind. Thus: human reason can explain these events scientifically, but all nature is afflicted nevertheless by what subsequently happens ('Love cools', etc.).
95 **mutinies** riots, insurrections.
96–100 **This . . . graves** On the absence of these lines in Q, see Textual Analysis, p. 278 below.
97–8 **son . . . child** This recalls Matt. 10.21: 'The brother shall betray the brother to death, and the father the sonne, and the children shal rise against their parents, and shal cause them to die.' See also Mark 13.8, 12; Luke 12.52–3, 21.16; Micah 7.6, and compare part 3 of the homily 'Against Disobedience and Wilfull Rebellion' (Shaheen).
98 **bias of nature** 'natural course or tendency. A figure from bowling. The *bias* is the curve that the bowl makes in its course' (Kittredge).
99 **best . . . time** our best years; as at 46.
99 **hollowness** emptiness, insincerity; as in Kent's reference to Gonerill's and Regan's speeches, 1.1.148.
100 **disquietly** unquietly.
103 **honesty** 'love of truth, upright conduct' (Schmidt).

EDMOND This is the excellent foppery of the world, that when we
are sick in fortune, often the surfeits of our own behaviour, we   105
make guilty of our disasters the sun, the moon, and stars; as if
we were villains on necessity, fools by heavenly compulsion,
knaves, thieves, and treachers by spherical predominance,
drunkards, liars, and adulterers by an enforced obedience of
planetary influence; and all that we are evil in, by a divine   110
thrusting on. An admirable evasion of whoremaster man, to lay
his goatish disposition on the charge of a star! My father
compounded with my mother under the Dragon's tail, and my
nativity was under *Ursa major*, so that it follows, I am rough and
lecherous. I should have been that I am had the maidenliest   115
star in the firmament twinkled on my bastardising.

Enter EDGAR

Pat: he comes, like the catastrophe of the old comedy. My cue

---

105 surfeits] F; surfeit Q   **106** stars] F; the Starres Q   **107** on] F; by Q   **108** treachers] F; Trecherers Q   **108** spherical]
F; spirituall Q   **108** predominance,] Q; predominance. F   **111** whoremaster man] Q; Whore-master-man F   **112** on] F;
to Q   **112** a star!] a Starre, F; Starres: Q   **115** I should] F; Fut, I should Q   **115** maidenliest] F3; maidenlest Q, F, F2   **116**
in] F; of Q   **116** bastardising.] F; bastardy Q   **116** SD] Q2, F; *in margin* Q   **117** Pat: he] F; *Edgar, and out hee* Q   **117**
My cue] F; mine Q

---

104 excellent (1) supreme, (2) splendid (from
Edmond's point of view: Hunter).
104 foppery foolishness.
105 sick in fortune i.e. down on our luck.
105 surfeits excesses.
107 on by; as in *LLL* 1.1.148.
107 heavenly compulsion i.e. astrological
influence.
108 treachers traitors.
108 spherical predominance Under the astrological concept of 'planetary influence' (110), if at
the time of one's birth a heavenly body was especially powerful because of its ascendant position,
one's disposition and destiny were accordingly controlled, or 'enforced'.
109 of to.
110–11 divine thrusting on supernatural
imposition.
111 whoremaster lecherous.
111–12 lay . . . charge of impute his lustful tendencies to (Schmidt). To Elizabethans, goats were
emblematic of lechery.
113 compounded copulated.
113 Dragon's tail The constellation Draco, an
especially malevolent astrological sign.
114 nativity birth.
114 *Ursa major* The constellation Great Bear, or
Big Dipper, in which (astrologically) Mars is pre-
dominant but shares influence with Venus, making

it a malign constellation producing temperaments
that are not only daring and impetuous ('rough'),
but also lascivious ('lecherous'), as Hunter notes.
115 See collation. The omission of 'Fut' (a
variant of the expletive 'foot' = 'Christ's foot')
is probably the result of purging away profan-
ity in accordance with the 'Acte to Restraine
Abuses of Players' in 1606 (Duthie, p. 170). Taylor
concurs and argues for restoration ('Censorship',
pp. 78, 109–10).
117 Pat See collation. Because Q crowds *Enter
Edgar* into the margin immediately beside 'Edgar'
in Edmond's speech, some editors believe the F
collator may have become confused and dropped
Edmond's summons which, Duthie argues, p. 171,
makes 'Pat' pointless. The effect of Edmond's
speech, however, does not depend on such a direct
summons, and the F reading may stand.
117 catastrophe . . . comedy Early Tudor
plays often lacked dramatic motivation; the catastrophe, or concluding episode, often arrived quite
arbitrarily to suit the playwright's need to end a
play. Armado uses 'catastrophe' in *LLL* 4.1.77 to
refer to the concluding episode of an action.
117 cue Edmond deliberately adopts theatrical
language in keeping with the role he is about
to play. On stage-managing in *King Lear*, see
Reibetanz, pp. 57–67.

is villainous melancholy, with a sigh like Tom o'Bedlam. – O
these eclipses do portend these divisions. Fa, sol, la, me.

EDGAR   How now, brother Edmond, what serious contemplation   120
are you in?

EDMOND   I am thinking, brother, of a prediction I read this other
day, what should follow these eclipses.

EDGAR   Do you busy yourself with that?

EDMOND   I promise you, the effects he writes of succeed un-   125
happily. When saw you my father last?

EDGAR   The night gone by.

EDMOND   Spake you with him?

EDGAR   Ay, two hours together.

EDMOND   Parted you in good terms? Found you no displeasure in   130
him by word nor countenance?

EDGAR   None at all.

EDMOND   Bethink yourself wherein you may have offended him,
and at my entreaty forbear his presence until some little time
hath qualified the heat of his displeasure, which at this instant   135
so rageth in him that with the mischief of your person it would
scarcely allay.

EDGAR   Some villain hath done me wrong.

EDMOND   That's my fear. I pray you have a continent forbearance
till the speed of his rage goes slower; and as I say, retire with   140
me to my lodging, from whence I will fitly bring you to hear my
lord speak. Pray ye, go; there's my key. If you do stir abroad, go
armed.

118 sigh] Q2, F; sith Q   118 Tom o'] F; them of Q   119 Fa . . . me.] F; *not in* Q   124 with] F; about Q   125 writes]
F; writ Q   125–6 unhappily.] F (*which omits seven lines here*); vnhappily, Q   126 When] F; when Q   127 The] F; Why,
the Q   129 Ay,] I, F; *not in* Q   131 nor] F; or Q   134 until] F; till Q   136 person] F; parson Q   137 scarcely] F; scarce
Q   139–44 I . . . brother?] F; *not in* Q

118 villainous wretched.

118 Tom o'Bedlam A common name for a real
or pretended madman (Bedlam, or Bethlehem, was
a London lunatic asylum). See 2.3.14.

119 divisions (1) conflicts (as in 94–6), (2) a
musical run.

119 Fa . . . me Edmond vocalises to himself, pretending to be unaware of Edgar's approach
while he is busy about something else, possibly
a book on astrology he is reading, as the subsequent dialogue suggests (Taylor, 'Censorship',
p. 86). Some commentators, e.g. Hunter, think
Edmond is deliberately singing across the interval
of an augmented fourth, or 'the devil in music', a
most unpleasant sound suggesting the disharmony
of 'divisions' (or the sound of a bedlamite?).

125 effects results (of the eclipses).

125 succeed follow.

125–6 unhappily Taylor suggests that Edmond
snaps his book shut and (in F) abruptly changes
the subject. F omits seven lines here found in Q;
see Textual Analysis, pp. 265–6 below, and 96–100.

131 countenance bearing, demeanour.

134 forbear avoid.

135 qualified mitigated, reduced.

136–7 with . . . allay i.e. even with bodily harm
to you his rage would not subside much.

139–45 I pray . . . Brother See Textual Analysis, p. 278 below, on the lines missing from Q.

139 have . . . forbearance 'restrain yourself and
keep out of his presence' (Kittredge).

141 fitly at a suitable time.

142 abroad outside, out-of-doors.

EDGAR Armed, brother?

EDMOND Brother, I advise you to the best. I am no honest man, if 145
there be any good meaning toward you. I have told you what I
have seen and heard – but faintly, nothing like the image and
horror of it. Pray you, away.

EDGAR Shall I hear from you anon?

EDMOND I do serve you in this business. 150

Exit [Edgar]

A credulous father and a brother noble,
Whose nature is so far from doing harms
That he suspects none; on whose foolish honesty
My practices ride easy. I see the business.
Let me, if not by birth, have lands by wit. 155
All with me's meet that I can fashion fit. *Exit*

1.3 *Enter* GONERILL *and [her] Steward* [OSWALD]

GONERILL Did my father strike my gentleman for chiding of his
fool?

OSWALD Ay, madam.

GONERILL By day and night, he wrongs me; every hour
He flashes into one gross crime or other 5
That sets us all at odds. I'll not endure it.
His knights grow riotous, and himself upbraids us

---

145 best.] F; best, goe arm'd Q 146 toward] F; towards Q 150 SD] *As* Q; *after 149* Q2; *Exit* F (*after 149*) **Act 1, Scene**
3 1.3] *Scena Tertia.* F; *not in* Q 0 SD] *Collier (subst.); Enter Gonerill, and Steward* F; *Enter Gonorill and Gentleman* Q *3
SH] *Ste.* F; *Gent.* Q (*throughout*) 3 Ay,] *Rowe;* I F; Yes Q 4–5 By . . . other] F; *divided* me, / Euery Q 7 upbraids] F;
obrayds Q

147–8 **image and horror** true picture of the
actual horror (hendiadys).

154 **practices** plots, machinations. Edmond
then uses an equestrian metaphor.

154 **I see the business** Edmond's plot now
becomes clear.

156 **All . . . fit** Everything is all right with me
that I can frame to my own purposes.

Act 1, Scene 3

0 SD In the fictional narrative, enough time is
supposed to have passed for Gonerill to experience
the disruptions in her household she says Lear and
his knights have caused.

0 SD OSWALD F consistently uses *Steward* in SDS
and SHS; Q uses *Gentleman* and *Gent.* in this scene
but *Steward* and *Stew.* in the next. At 1.4.268 and
281 Gonerill calls for Oswald, whose name was the
Anglo-Saxon word for a steward. He is foppishly
dressed, probably in Albany's cast-off garments
(NS).

1–2 **Did . . . fool** This is not only the first mention of the Fool, but the first mention of disorderliness caused by Lear and his entourage, giving
Gonerill the excuse to act as she does.

4 **By . . . night** Either (1) an oath (compare 1.1.103–4), or (2) constantly (compare 'every
hour'). F punctuation favours (1); Q, omitting the
comma, favours (2).

5 **flashes** breaks out.

5 **crime** offence.

7 **His . . . riotous** The absence of actual
evidence for this behaviour in the play has led
some commentators, e.g. Kittredge, to discredit
Gonerill's assertion, but some stage and film versions, such as Peter Brook's, have graphically presented Lear's train as unruly. In any event, a hundred knights and squires given to hunting and
other sports would doubtless cause some problems, which Gonerill decides to exacerbate, forcing
a confrontation with her father.

On every trifle. When he returns from hunting,
I will not speak with him. Say I am sick.
If you come slack of former services,   10
You shall do well; the fault of it I'll answer.
[*Horns within*]

OSWALD   He's coming, madam, I hear him.

GONERILL   Put on what weary negligence you please,
You and your fellows: I'd have it come to question.
If he distaste it, let him to my sister,   15
Whose mind and mine I know in that are one.
Remember what I have said.

OSWALD   Well, madam.

GONERILL   And let his knights have colder looks among you:
What grows of it no matter. Advise your fellows so.   20
I'll write straight to my sister to hold my course.
Prepare for dinner.

Exeunt

1.4   *Enter* KENT [*disguised*]

KENT   If but as well I other accents borrow
That can my speech defuse, my good intent

8 trifle. When] F; trifell when Q   11 SD] *Capell (after 12); not in* Q, F   13–16 Put . . . one.] F; *as prose* Q   14 fellows:]
F; fellow seruants, Q   14 to] F; *in* Q   15 distaste] F; dislike Q   15 my] F; our Q   16 one.] one, Q, F; F *omits four lines
here*   17 Remember . . . said.] F; *as prose* Q   17 have said.] F; tell you. Q   18 Well] F; Very well Q   19–20 And . . . so.]
Hanmer's lineation; as prose Q, F   20 so.] so, Q, F; F *omits one and a half lines here*   21–2 I'll . . . dinner.] *This edn; as
prose* Q, F   21 course.] F; very course, Q   22 Prepare] F; goe prepare Q   22 SD] F; *Exit.* Q   Act 1, Scene 4   1.4] *Scena
Quarta.* F; *not in* Q   0 SD *disguised*] *Rowe; not in* Q, F   1–7 If . . . labours.] F; *as prose* Q   1 well] Q; will F

8 **hunting** The provision for Lear's hunting
appears in Layamon's *Brut*, which also includes a
hunting episode (Muir).
    9 **Say I am sick** A transparent 'social' lie.
    10 **come slack of** slacken, fall short of.
    11 **answer** be answerable for.
    12 **I hear him** Capell introduces SD, *Horns
within*, which many editors follow. (Compare 1.4.7
SD.)
    13 **weary negligence** tiresome or irksome
neglect (of service).
    14 **come to question** i.e. come to a head, made
an issue of.
    15 **distaste** dislike.
    15–16 **let . . . one** Apparently, though they may
not have decided upon any immediate course of
action, Gonerill and Regan have agreed not to put
up with much from Lear for very long. (Compare
1.1.298 n.)
    16 **one** F omits four lines here found in Q and

two more after 19; see Textual Analysis, p. 266
below.
    21 **straight** at once, straightaway.

Act 1, Scene 4
    0 SD KENT [*disguised*] Kent reappears, his
countenance altered (4) and wearing clothing more
suitable for the servant, 'Caius', than for an earl. He
also tries to disguise his voice by adopting a different accent (usually the actor adopts a rustic brogue,
according to Rosenberg, p. 96) and a blunt, plainspoken manner. The Elizabethan convention of
'impenetrable disguise' operates here and throughout the rest of the play, until Kent drops the disguise in 5.3. Lear never identifies Caius with Kent,
even at the end, when Kent wishes it (5.3.257–63).
    1 **as well** i.e. as well as I have disguised myself
otherwise.
    2 **defuse** confuse, disorder; a variant of 'diffuse'.
    2 **my good intent** i.e. to serve his master, Lear.

May carry through itself to that full issue
For which I razed my likeness. Now, banished Kent,
If thou canst serve where thou dost stand condemned,   5
So may it come thy master, whom thou lov'st,
Shall find thee full of labours.

Horns within. Enter LEAR, [*Knights,*] *and Attendants*

LEAR Let me not stay a jot for dinner. Go, get it ready.

[Exit an Attendant]

How now, what art thou?
KENT A man, sir.   10
LEAR What dost thou profess? What wouldst thou with us?
KENT I do profess to be no less than I seem, to serve him truly that
will put me in trust, to love him that is honest, to converse with
him that is wise and says little, to fear judgement, to fight when
I cannot choose, and to eat no fish.   15
LEAR What art thou?
KENT A very honest-hearted fellow, and as poor as the king.
LEAR If thou be'st as poor for a subject as he's for a king, thou art
poor enough. What wouldst thou?
KENT Service.   20
LEAR Who wouldst thou serve?
KENT You.

---

*4 razed] raz'd Q; raiz'd F   6 So . . . come] F; not in Q   6 lov'st] F; louest Q   7 labours] F; labour Q   7 SD] Rowe;
Hornes within. Enter Lear and Attendants. F; Enter Lear Q   8 SD] Malone; not in Q, F   18 be'st] F; be Q   18 he's] F; he
is Q   18 thou art] F; thar't Q*

3 full issue complete or satisfactory outcome.
4 razed erased, obliterated. Muir suggests a quibble on 'razor'.
4 likeness appearance.
4 banished Kent 'In case the audience have not recognized his voice, he announces his identity' (Hunter).
6 So . . . come Either (1) let it then happen that, or (2) it may happen thus.
7 SD Horns within Lear has been hunting (compare 1.3.8).
7 Knights That knights as well as attendants accompany Lear is clear from SHS at 44 ff. (Duthie).
8 stay wait.
10 man (1) a fully human being, (2) a servant. Compare *Ham.* 1.2.187: ''A was a man, take him for all in all.'
11 profess set up for, claim as a calling or trade. Kent plays on the sense 'proclaim, declare' in his reply.
13 converse associate, consort. Shaheen com-

pares Ecclus. 9.17: 'Let thy talke be with the wise', and Prov. 13.20, 17.27–8.
14 fear judgement Many commentators assume a reference to the Last Judgement. (Noble and Shaheen cite Psalms 1.5; Noble adds Jer. 8.7.) Kittredge says such an allusion may accord with the pagan religion of Lear's time, though not the following reference to abstaining from fish, which is anachronistic (Catholics ate fish but not meat on Fridays, the day of the Crucifixion). Kent may, however, simply be declaring his desire to serve well, fearing his master's censure.
15 cannot choose i.e. cannot help it.
15 eat no fish Three not incompatible glosses are possible. Kent means: (1) he is no papist (Warburton); (2) he is 'a jolly fellow, and no lover of such meagre diet as fish' (Capell; compare *2H4* 4.3.90–5); (3) he is no womaniser.
17 as . . . king Kent risks the joke, but Lear takes it good-humouredly.

LEAR   Dost thou know me, fellow?

KENT   No, sir; but you have that in your countenance, which I
would fain call master.   25

LEAR   What's that?

KENT   Authority.

LEAR   What services canst thou do?

KENT   I can keep honest counsel, ride, run, mar a curious tale
in telling it, and deliver a plain message bluntly. That which   30
ordinary men are fit for, I am qualified in, and the best of me is
diligence.

LEAR   How old art thou?

KENT   Not so young, sir, to love a woman for singing, nor so old to
dote on her for anything. I have years on my back forty-eight.   35

LEAR   Follow me; thou shalt serve me, if I like thee no worse
after dinner. I will not part from thee yet. Dinner, ho, dinner!
Where's my knave? my fool? Go you and call my fool hither.

[Exit an Attendant]

Enter OSWALD

You, you sirrah, where's my daughter?

OSWALD   So please you –   *Exit*   40

LEAR   What says the fellow there? Call the clotpoll back.

[Exit a Knight]

Where's my fool? Ho, I think the world's asleep.

[Enter KNIGHT*]*

How now? Where's that mongrel?

KNIGHT   He says, my lord, your daughter is not well.

28 thou] F; *not in* Q   31 me] me, Q, F   34 sir] F; *not in* Q   *37 dinner. I] Jennens; dinner, I Q, F   38 SD.1] Dyce (following
Capell); not in* Q, F   38 SD.2 *Enter* OSWALD] *Capell (subst.); Enter Steward.* Q, F *(after 39)*   39 You, you] You you F;
you, Q   40 SD] F; *not in* Q   41 clotpoll] Clot- / pole F; clat-pole Q   41, 42 SD] *Dyce; not in* Q, F   44 SH] F; *Kent.* Q;
daughter] Q; Daughters F

24 **countenance** demeanour, bearing.
25 **fain** gladly, willingly.
29 **keep honest counsel** keep honourable con-
fidences.
29–30 **mar . . . telling it** Proverbial: 'A good
tale ill told is marred in the telling' (NS, citing
Tilley T28). Kent underscores his plainspokenness
here.
29 **curious** elaborate, intricate.
34 **to** as to.
36–7 **thou . . . dinner.** Q/F punctuation is
ambiguous, but Lear's capricious attitude is clearer
with a full stop after 'dinner'.
37 **Dinner, ho** Lear repeatedly calls for dinner,
and modern editors insert directions for attendants

to exit, but no dinner is served (Rosenberg, p. 100).
Gonerill's instructions in 1.3 to slack off service are
taking effect.
38 **knave** boy. The word, often used familiarly,
could imply affection (Kittredge) and does not necessarily refer to the Fool's age. Compare 1.1.16 and
below, 80. At 3.4.26 Lear addresses the Fool as 'boy'
but may be using the word similarly.
40 **So please you** A deliberate snub.
41 **clotpoll** blockhead. A 'clot' or (in dialect)
'clat' = 'a clod of earth'; 'poll' = head.
44 SH KNIGHT Here and later F assigns speeches
to a Knight, where Q assigns 44 to Kent and 46,
49–53, 55–6, 62–3 to a servant. Duthie notes
the Lear/Kent alternation of speeches (9–36) and

LEAR   Why came not the slave back to me when I called him?   45

KNIGHT   Sir, he answered me in the roundest manner, he would not.

LEAR   He would not?

KNIGHT   My lord, I know not what the matter is, but to my judgement your highness is not entertained with that cer-   50
emonious affection as you were wont. There's a great abatement of kindness appears as well in the general dependants as in the duke himself also, and your daughter.

LEAR   Ha? Sayest thou so?

KNIGHT   I beseech you pardon me, my lord, if I be mistaken, for   55
my duty cannot be silent when I think your highness wronged.

LEAR   Thou but rememberest me of mine own conception. I have perceived a most faint neglect of late, which I have rather blamed as mine own jealous curiosity than as a very pretence   ʼ
and purpose of unkindness. I will look further into't. But   60
where's my fool? I have not seen him this two days.

KNIGHT   Since my young lady's going into France, sir, the fool hath much pined away.

LEAR   No more of that, I have noted it well. Go you and tell my daughter I would speak with her.   65

[Exit an Attendant]

Go you, call hither my fool.

[Exit an Attendant]

46, 49, 55, 62 SH] F; *seruant.* Q   48 He] F; A Q   52 of kindness] F; *not in* Q   54 Sayest] F; say'st Q   57 rememberest] remember'st Q; remembrest F   60 purpose] F; purport Q   61 my] F; this Q   *62 lady's]* Rowe; Ladies Q, F   64 well] F; *not in* Q   65 SD, 66 SD.1] *Dyce; not in* Q, F

says Q's SH for Kent here is a misassignment, but the others are the result of F's abridgement of the number of speaking characters. On altered SHS, see Textual Analysis, p. 80 above.

46 roundest bluntest, most plainspoken. Compare 'round' in Polonius's admonition to Gertrude, *Ham.* 3.4.5, and in King Henry's to Williams, *H5* 4.1.203.

50 entertained treated. Although Gonerill has just given instructions to slight Lear (1.3.13–14) and the action between Scenes 3 and 4 is continuous, Shakespeare conveys the illusion of a greater passage of time.

50–1 ceremonious affection 'combination the affection due to a father and the ceremony appropriate to a king' (Hunter).

52 general dependants i.e. household staff as a whole.

52–3 as in the duke This charge is inconsistent

with Albany's claim to be 'guiltless' (228) and with his general behaviour. Either the Knight is deliberately exacerbating the situation, or Shakespeare emphasises Lear's isolation (Hunter).

57 rememberest remindest.

57 conception thought.

58 faint neglect Either Lear minimises what the Knight has seen as 'a great abatement' (51–2) because he dreads the consequences of a confrontation, or the Knight, again, has exaggerated the situation.

59 jealous curiosity suspicious fastidiousness, i.e. paranoid concern over trifles.

59–60 pretence and purpose deliberate intention (synonyms).

62–3 Since . . . away The Knight calls attention to the affection between the Fool and Cordelia, whose roles may have been doubled. (See pp. 32–3 above.)

Enter OSWALD

Oh, you, sir, you, come you hither, sir, who am I, sir?

OSWALD   My lady's father.

LEAR   'My lady's father'? My lord's knave, you whoreson dog, you
slave, you cur!   70

OSWALD   I am none of these, my lord, I beseech your pardon.

LEAR   Do you bandy looks with me, you rascal?

[Strikes him]

OSWALD   I'll not be strucken, my lord.

KENT   [*Tripping him*]   Nor tripped neither, you base football player.

LEAR   I thank thee, fellow. Thou serv'st me, and I'll love thee.   75

KENT   Come, sir, arise, away, I'll teach you differences. Away,
away. If you will measure your lubber's length again, tarry; but
away, go to! Have you wisdom?

[Pushes Oswald out]

So.

LEAR   Now, my friendly knave, I thank thee; there's earnest of thy   80
service.

[Gives Kent money]

Enter FOOL

FOOL   Let me hire him, too; here's my coxcomb.

[Offers Kent his cap]

---

66 SD.2 *Enter* OSWALD] *Johnson* (*subst.*); *not in* Q; *Enter Steward.* F (*after 67*)   71 I . . . pardon.] *As one line* Q; *divided*
Lord, / I F   71 these] F; this Q   71 your pardon.] F; you pardon me. Q   72 SD] *Rowe* (*subst.*); *not in* Q, F   73 strucken]
F; struck Q   74 SD] *Rowe* (*subst.*); *not in* Q, F   75 I thank . . . love thee.] *As one line* Q; *divided* fellow. / Thou F   76
arise, away] F; *not in* Q   *78–9 go to! Have you wisdom? So.] *Theobald* (*subst.*); goe too, haue you wisdome, so F; you
haue wisdome. Q,   *78 SD] *Theobald* (*subst.*); *not in* Q, F   80 my] F; *not in* Q   81 SD.1] *Capell* (*subst.*); *not in* Q, F   82
SD] *Rowe* (*subst.*); *not in* Q, F

---

72 **bandy** bat back and forth (as in tennis), exchange. NS adds SDS, *glares* and *glares back*, at 68 and 70. Oswald's insolence moves Lear to strike him.

74 **base football player** Tennis was played by aristocrats, football by the lower classes. Thomas Elyot, *The Boke of the Governour* (1531), warns 'al noble men' against football, 'wherein is nothinge but beastly furie and extreme violence' (NS).

76–9 **Come . . . So** Kent roughly picks Oswald up and shoves him out.

76 **differences** distinctions (of rank, position).

77 **measure . . . length** Kent sent Oswald sprawling to the ground (74), where he lay at full

length. Shakespeare uses the term in *MND* 3.2.429 and similarly in *Rom.* 3.3.69–70.

77 **lubber** clumsy lout.

80 **earnest** earnest-money, i.e. part payment to bind a bargain.

82 **coxcomb** professional jester's cap. The cap evidently varied somewhat, though its salient feature was a crest made of red flannel in the shape of a cock's comb. It may also have had a bell, ass's ears, and/or feathers attached. (See p. 6 above.) The Fool offers the symbol of his office to Kent as someone who deserves it for following Lear, but Kent demurs (84).

LEAR How now, my pretty knave, how dost thou?

FOOL [*To Kent*] Sirrah, you were best take my coxcomb.

LEAR Why, my boy?   85

FOOL Why? For taking one's part that's out of favour. [*To Kent*]
Nay, and thou canst not smile as the wind sits, thou'lt catch
cold shortly. There, take my coxcomb; why, this fellow has
banished two on's daughters and did the third a blessing
against his will; if thou follow him, thou must needs wear my   90
coxcomb. How now, nuncle? Would I had two coxcombs and
two daughters.

LEAR Why, my boy?

FOOL If I gave them all my living, I'd keep my coxcombs myself.
There's mine; beg another of thy daughters.   95

LEAR Take heed, sirrah, the whip.

FOOL Truth's a dog must to kennel. He must be whipped out,
when the Lady Brach may stand by th'fire and stink.

LEAR A pestilent gall to me.

FOOL Sirrah, I'll teach thee a speech.   100

LEAR Do.

FOOL Mark it, nuncle:

---

84 SD] *Oxford; not in* Q, F   85 LEAR Why, my boy?] F; Kent. Why Foole? Q   86 Why?] F; Why Q   86 one's] F, Q2;
on's Q   86 SD] *Oxford; not in* Q, F   88–9 has banished] F; hath banisht Q   89 did] F; done Q   94 all my] F; any Q   97
Truth's] F; Truth is Q   97 dog must] F; dog that must Q   98 the Lady Brach] F; Ladie oth'e brach Q   98 by th'] F;
by the Q   99 gall] F; gull Q   102–12 Mark . . . score.] F *lineation; as prose* Q   102 nuncle] F; vncle Q

85 LEAR **Why, my boy?** Duthie, p. 171,
attributes the changed SH in F to compositor eye-
skip from 85 to 93 (and then back to 86). This
seems unlikely in view of F's other alterations in
the passages that follow.

87 **and** if; a common variant of 'an'.

87–8 **thou . . . shortly** i.e. if you cannot ingra-
tiate yourself with the powers that prevail, you will
soon be out in the cold and suffering.

89 **banished** Compare 1.1.175.

89 **on's** of his.

89–90 **blessing . . . will** Cordelia is now out of
Britain and Queen of France – hardly the cursed
existence Lear intended for her.

90 **must needs** A redundancy used for emphasis (as often).

91 **nuncle** A contraction of 'mine uncle' (the
usual address of a jester to his master).

94 **If . . . myself** NS cites Tilley A187: 'He that
gives all before he dies is a fool.' Two coxcombs is
the equivalent of a double fool.

95 **There's mine** The Fool now offers his coxcomb to Lear.

96 **the whip** Fools, like children, were whipped
when they went too far out of line. Compare *AYLI*
1.2.84–5.

97–8 **Truth . . . stink** The Fool identifies
himself with truth, imagined as an unwelcome,
lowly dog chased out of the house into a rude
shelter; whereas the bitch, flattery ('brach' =
bitch), enjoys a privileged place. The Fool hints
at Gonerill or Regan, 'braches of noble rank,
and sycophantic' (Sisson, p. 231), and implies
an identification between Truth and Cordelia
(Muir).

99 **pestilent gall** plaguey irritant. Lear probably refers to the Fool's gibes, though he may be
thinking of Oswald and his fellows or his own
foolish behaviour. In any event, the Fool tactfully
changes strategy here.

100 **Sirrah** Some editions follow Rowe and
add a SD, *To Kent*. But the Fool seems to address
Lear, who responds, not Kent. The Fool's licence
permits him to address Lear as 'Sirrah'.

> Have more than thou showest,
> Speak less than thou knowest,
> Lend less than thou owest,   105
> Ride more than thou goest,
> Learn more than thou trowest,
> Set less than thou throwest,
> Leave thy drink and thy whore,
> And keep in-a-door,   110
> And thou shalt have more,
> Than two tens to a score.

KENT   This is nothing, fool.

FOOL   Then 'tis like the breath of an unfeed lawyer; you gave me nothing for't. Can you make no use of nothing, nuncle?   115

LEAR   Why, no, boy; nothing can be made out of nothing.

FOOL   [*To Kent*] Prithee, tell him so much the rent of his land comes to; he will not believe a fool.

LEAR   A bitter fool.

FOOL   Nuncle, give me an egg, and I'll give thee two crowns.   120

LEAR   What two crowns shall they be?

FOOL   Why, after I have cut the egg i'th'middle and eat up the meat, the two crowns of the egg. When thou clovest thy crown i'th'middle and gav'st away both parts, thou bor'st thine ass on

---

113 SH] F; *Lear.* Q   114 'tis] F; *not in* Q   115 nuncle?] F; vncle? Q   116 Why . . . nothing.] Q; *two lines divided* Boy, / Nothing F   117 SD] *Rowe; not in* Q, F   119 fool.] *This edn;* F *erroneously includes three lines here meant for exclusion (see p. 79 above), then omits fifteen lines*   120 Nuncle, . . . egg,] F; giue . . . Nuncle, Q   122 i'th'] F; in the Q   123 crown] Q; Crownes F   124 i'th'] F; it'h Q   124 gav'st] F; gauest Q   124 bor'st] F; borest Q   124 thine] F; thy Q   124–5 on thy] F; at'h Q

103–12 Have . . . score This counsel of prudence is set in sing-song rhyme to emphasise its conventional wisdom, and accordingly earns Kent's response.

105 thou owest you own.

106 thou goest you walk; as at 3.2.92, where 'going' means walking.

107 Learn . . . throwest i.e. don't believe everything you hear.

108 Set . . . throwest i.e. don't gamble away your last penny.

110 in-a-door indoors. NS compares *MV* 2.5.53–5 on staying home and saving money.

111–12 thou . . . score i.e. you will grow richer (Riverside).

113 nothing i.e. no big news. As at 85, F changes Q's SH. Kent's interruption is dramatically apt.

114 unfeed lawyer Alludes to the proverb 'A

lawyer will not plead but for a fee' (Tilley L125); 'breath' = speech, hence pleading.

115 use usury, interest. Compare *Ado* 1.1.278–9.

116 nothing . . . nothing Compare 1.1.84–5.

117 his land Ironic: Lear is landless. He feels the Fool's gibe (119).

119 fool F includes three lines here that should probably have been cut along with the passage of twelve lines found only in Q that immediately follows: see Textual Analysis, p. 84 above.

121 two crowns Compare 'two coxcombs', 91. The two crowns are obviously the two halves of the eggshell, but Lear is deliberately acting as a stooge (Muir).

123–4 When . . . parts Compare 1.1.133 and n. The Fool alludes not to Lear's parting of the coronet but to the division of the kingdom.

thy back o'er the dirt. Thou hadst little wit in thy bald crown   125
when thou gav'st thy golden one away. If I speak like myself in
this, let him be whipped that first finds it so.
[*Sings*] Fools had ne'er less grace in a year,
　　　　For wise men are grown foppish,
　　　　And know not how their wits to wear,   130
　　　　Their manners are so apish.
LEAR   When were you wont to be so full of songs, sirrah?
FOOL   I have used it, nuncle, e'er since thou mad'st thy daughters
thy mothers; for when thou gav'st them the rod and put'st down
thine own breeches,   135
[*Sings*] Then they for sudden joy did weep,
　　　　And I for sorrow sung,
　　　　That such a king should play bo-peep,
　　　　And go the fools among.
Prithee, nuncle, keep a schoolmaster that can teach thy fool to   140
lie. I would fain learn to lie.
LEAR   And you lie, sirrah, we'll have you whipped.

---

126 gav'st] F; gauest Q   128 SD] *Rowe; not in* Q, F   128 grace] F; wit Q   130 And] F; They Q   130 to] F; doe Q   133
e'er] ere F; euer Q   134 mothers] F; mother Q   134 gav'st] F; gauest Q   136 SD] *Rowe; not in* Q, F   136 Then they]
Theobald; then they Q, F (*as part of preceding prose*) 136–9 for . . . among.] F *lineation; as prose* Q   139 fools] Q; Foole
F   141 learn to] F; learne Q *uncorr.;* learneto Q *corr.*   142 And] F, Q; If Q2   142 sirrah] F; *not in* Q

124–5 thou . . . dirt An allusion to the fable of
the old man who foolishly, out of a mistaken sense
of kindness, carried his ass on his back instead of
letting it carry him. The Fool's comments insistently point up inversions or perversions of the
natural order.
126–7 If . . . so i.e. let him who calls this foolish
be whipped, not me. Compare 96–7. The Fool's
baldness (to prevent lice) gives extra point to the
passage if he removes his coxcomb to 'speak like
myself in this' (Wiles, p. 190).
126 like myself i.e. like a fool.
128–31 Fools . . . apish i.e. fools have never been
more out of favour since wise men have become
foolish and do not behave properly, their style
becoming ridiculously imitative (of fools). Compare
Lyly, *Mother Bombie* 2.3: 'I thinke Gentlemen had
neuer lesse wit in a yeere' (Capell, cited by Furness). NS, citing Tilley F535, 'Fools had never less
wit in a year', says the Fool is parodying either
Lyly or the original proverb; hence the F reading
is correct.
128 grace favour.
129 foppish foolish.
131 apish foolishly imitative. The off-rhyme
with 'foppish' seems deliberate: see Kökeritz,
p. 225.

133 used it i.e. made it a practice. Muir cites
Ham. 3.2.45.
133–4 thou . . . mothers i.e. you made your
children your parents (another inversion, or per-
version, of the natural order).
134–5 thou . . . breeches i.e. the right to
chastise has been transferred from parent to
child.
136–9 Then . . . among The Fool adapts
the first stanza of the familiar old *Ballad of John
Carelesse*: 'Some men for sodayne ioye do wepe,/
And some in sorow syng: / When that they lie in
daunger depe, / To put away mournyng' (Hyder
E. Rollins, '"King Lear" and the ballad of "John
Careless"', *MLR* 15 (1920), 87–90).
138 bo-peep 'A nursery play with a young
child, who is kept in excitement by the nurse
or playmate alternately concealing herself (or her
face), and peeping out for a moment at an unexpected place, to withdraw again with equal sud-
denness' (*OED*). Apparently, the game was also
played with naturals, or fools. Compare Skel-
ton, *Image Hypocrisy*: 'Thus youe make vs sottes
/ And play with vs boopeepe' (cited Tilley
B540).
142 And If.

FOOL I marvel what kin thou and thy daughters are: they'll have
me whipped for speaking true, thou'lt have me whipped for
lying, and sometimes I am whipped for holding my peace. I had   145
rather be any kind o'thing than a fool, and yet I would not be
thee, nuncle; thou hast pared thy wit o'both sides and left
nothing i'th'middle. Here comes one o'the parings.

Enter GONERILL

LEAR How now, daughter! What makes that frontlet on? You are
too much of late i'th'frown.   150

FOOL Thou wast a pretty fellow when thou hadst no need to care
for her frowning; now thou art an O without a figure. I am
better than thou art now; I am a fool, thou art nothing. [*To
Gonerill*] Yes, forsooth, I will hold my tongue, so your face bids
me, though you say nothing.   155

[*Sings*] Mum, mum:
    He that keeps nor crust, nor crumb,
    Weary of all, shall want some.
That's a shelled peascod.

GONERILL Not only, sir, this, your all-licensed fool,   160
    But other of your insolent retinue
    Do hourly carp and quarrel, breaking forth
    In rank and not-to-be-endurèd riots. Sir,

---

144 thou'lt] F; thou wilt Q   145 sometimes] F; sometime Q   146 o'] F; of Q   147 o'] F; a Q   148 i'th'] F; in the Q   148
o'] F; of Q   149–50 How . . . frown.] F; *as verse, two lines divided* on, / Me Q   149 on? You] F; on, / Me thinks you
Q   150 of late] F; alate Q   150 i'th'] F; it'h Q   152 frowning] F; frowne Q   152 now thou] F, Q *corr.;* thou, thou Q
uncorr., Q2   153–4 SD] *Pope; not in* Q, F   156 SD] *Rowe; not in* Q, F   156–7 Mum . . . crumb,] *Capell's lineation; one
line* Q, F   157 nor crust] F; neither crust Q   *157 nor crumb] nor crum Q; not crum F   158–9 Weary . . . peascod.]
Rowe's lineation; one verse line Q, F   160–73 Not . . . proceeding.] F *lineation; as prose* Q   *163 In . . . Sir,] *Capel (without
hyphens);* in ranke & (not to be indured riots,) Sir Q; In ranke, and (not to be endur'd) riots Sir. F

143–5 I marvel . . . peace An example of the
'crocodile's argument', one that harms the opponent whichever way he chooses (Joseph, p. 202).
146–8 yet . . . middle i.e. if a fool is only a
half-wit, Lear is less: he has given his wits away
along with everything else.
149 What . . . on Gonerill enters wearing a
frontlet = 'a cloth or bandage containing some
medicament' (*OED* sv *sb* ıc; compare 44 above and
1.3.9, where Gonerill instructed Oswald to tell Lear
she is sick). A frontlet also = a 'frowning cloth', i.e.
a forehead band worn by ladies at night to prevent
or smooth out wrinkles (*OED sb* ıa). Lear quibbles on the two senses of 'frontlet', asking Gonerill

why she is wearing the cloth and commenting on
her demeanour.
152 O without a figure i.e. a cipher; a zero
with no number before it to give it value (NS).
154 forsooth An expletive: in truth, truly.
156 Mum, mum Hush, hush; softly.
157–8 He . . . some i.e. he who foolishly gives
everything away, because he is tired of it all, shall
at the end of the day want some of it back.
159 shelled peascod empty pea-pod, i.e.
nothing.
160 all-licensed free to say or do anything.
162 carp find fault, cavil.
163 rank gross, excessive.

I had thought by making this well known unto you
To have found a safe redress, but now grow fearful,   165
By what yourself too late have spoke and done,
That you protect this course, and put it on
By your allowance; which if you should, the fault
Would not 'scape censure, nor the redresses sleep;
Which in the tender of a wholesome weal   170
Might in their working do you that offence
Which else were shame, that then necessity
Will call discreet proceeding.

FOOL   For you know, nuncle,
The hedge-sparrow fed the cuckoo so long,   175
That it's had it head bit off by it young.
So out went the candle, and we were left darkling.

LEAR   Are you our daughter?

GONERILL   I would you would make use of your good wisdom,
Whereof I know you are fraught, and put away   180
These dispositions, which of late transport you
From what you rightly are.

---

167 it] F; *not in* Q   169 redresses] F; redresse Q   170 Which] F; that Q   173 Will] F; must Q   173 proceeding] F; proceedings Q   174 know] F; trow Q   175–6 The . . . young.] *Pope's lineation; as prose* Q, F   176 it's] F; it Q   176 by it] F; beit Q   179–82 I . . . are.] F *lineation; as prose* Q   179 I] F; Come sir, I Q   180 Whereof . . . fraught,] Q; (Whereof . . . fraught), F   181 which] F; that Q   181 transport] F; transforme Q

164 I . . . you The line is hypermetrical unless the first two words are elided (= I'd) as well as 'known unto' (= known to). Similarly, in the next line, 'To have' = T'have. In correcting Q's prose, the F editor or reviser failed to make all the necessary adjustments to verse.

165 safe sure.

166 too late very recently.

167 put it on encourage it.

168 allowance i.e. failure to censure.

168–73 which . . . procceding i.e. if you do approve of all this, then you are to blame and redress will be forthcoming, although the steps I take, designed to maintain a healthy state ('wholesome weal'), may offend you as they are carried out. In other circumstances these steps might indeed be shameful, but in this instance they will be considered an act of necessary discretion. Gonerill's rhetoric conveys 'an impression of cold venom' (Hunter). Her speech is formal, convoluted, and abstract; but Lear gets the point, which leaves him – and Kent – speechless; hence, the Fool fills the silence (Rosenberg, p. 117).

170 Which i.e. the redresses.

170 tender care.

175–6 The hedge-sparrow . . . young The cuckoo proverbially laid its eggs in other birds' nests, and its chicks were notorious for their murderous gluttony. (See *1H4* 5.1.59–64.) The Fool alludes figuratively to Gonerill's illegitimacy (compare 209) or usurpation and certainly to her ingratitude in taking over half the realm. The baby-talk ('it . . . it') heightens the grotesqueness.

177 So . . . darkling Possibly this is a nonsense tag to take off the edge of the Fool's bitter couplet, but even so it conveys a sense of disaster. 'Lear's folly has produced a figurative darkness in the kingdom, and darkness can be very frightening' (NS, p. xxx). The image of the snuffed candle may come from the Lear story in *FQ* II, x, 30 (Knight, cited by Furness).

177 darkling in the dark.

180 fraught furnished (literally, freighted).

181 dispositions moods, humours; as in *AYLI* 4.1.114.

181 transport passionately carry away; as in *WT* 3.2.158.

FOOL   May not an ass know when the cart draws the horse? Whoop,
  Jug, I love thee!
LEAR   Does any here know me? This is not Lear: 185
  Does Lear walk thus? speak thus? Where are his eyes?
  Either his notion weakens, his discernings
  Are lethargied – Ha! Waking? 'Tis not so!
  Who is it that can tell me who I am?
FOOL   Lear's shadow.   190
LEAR   Your name, fair gentlewoman?
GONERILL   This admiration, sir, is much o'th'savour
  Of other your new pranks. I do beseech you
  To understand my purposes aright:
  As you are old and reverend, should be wise.   195
  Here do you keep a hundred knights and squires,
  Men so disordered, so deboshed and bold,
  That this our court, infected with their manners,
  Shows like a riotous inn; epicurism and lust
  Makes it more like a tavern or a brothel   200
  Than a graced palace. The shame itself doth speak
  For instant remedy. Be then desired
  By her, that else will take the thing she begs,
  A little to disquantity your train,

---

*183–4 Whoop . . . thee!] Q (*subst.*); *as separate verse line* F (*see Commentary*)   185 Does . . . Lear:] *Rowe's lineation; as prose* Q; *two lines divided* me? / This F   185 Does] F; Doth Q   185 This] F; why this Q   186–9 Does . . . am?] F *lineation; as prose* Q   186 Does] F; doth Q   187 notion weakens,] F; notion, weaknes, *or* Q   188 lethargied –] *Rowe;* Lethargied. F; lethergie, Q   188 Ha! Waking?] F; sleeping *or* wakeing; ha! sure Q   *188 so!] so? F; so, Q   190 FOOL Lear's shadow.] F; *no* SH *in* Q, *which continues as Lear's prose speech with four lines not in* F   190 shadow.] F; shadow? Q   192–210 This . . . daughter.] F *lineation; as prose* Q   192 This admiration, sir,] F; Come sir, this admiration Q   192 o'th'] F; of the Q   194 To] F; *not in* Q   195 old] Q; Old, F   197 deboshed] F; deboyst Q   200 Makes it] F; make Q   200 *or* a] F; *or* Q   201 graced] F; great Q   202 then] F; thou Q

183 **May . . . horse** As Lear remains stunned by
what he is hearing, the Fool again interposes, referring sarcastically to the proverbial inversion of the
cart and the horse.
 183–4 **Whoop . . . thee** Gonerill makes a threat-
ening gesture that elicits this mock protestation of
love, possibly the tag from an old song.
 184 **Jug** Nickname for Joan, often = whore, as
in *Cambyses* 251–2: 'Rufe. I wil give thee sixpence
to lye one night with thee. *Meretrix.* Gogs hart,
slave, doost thinke I am a sixpenny jug?' (NS).
 187 **notion** understanding.
 187–8 **discernings . . . lethargied** intellectual faculties or ability to discriminate is dulled,
paralysed. Moved almost to incoherence, Lear does
not complete the either/or construction. Compare
2.4.263.
 188–90; **Ha . . . shadow** On F's revisions, see
Textual Analysis, p. 267 below.

188 **Ha! Waking?** Lear pinches or shakes himself to be sure he is not asleep and dreaming.
 192 **admiration** (pretended) astonishment,
wonderment. Compare *Ham.* 1.2.192.
 192 **savour** characteristic (literally, taste).
 193 **Of other your** Of your other (anastrophe).
 193 **pranks** childish misbehaviour. Gonerill's
terminology reflects her attitude to her father.
 195 **should** you should.
 196–200 **Here . . . brothel** Compare 1.3.7 n.
 197 **disordered** disorderly.
 197 **deboshed** Variant of 'debauched'.
 197 **bold** impudent.
 199 **epicurism** gluttony.
 201 **graced** endowed with graces, favoured,
adorned with honour (Onions).
 202 **desired** requested.
 204 **disquantity** reduce the size or number of.

And the remainders that shall still depend   205
To be such men as may besort your age,
Which know themselves and you.
LEAR   Darkness and devils!
Saddle my horses; call my train together. –
Degenerate bastard, I'll not trouble thee;
Yet have I left a daughter.   210
GONERILL You strike my people, and your disordered rabble
Make servants of their betters.

Enter ALBANY

LEAR   Woe that too late repents!
Is it your will? Speak, sir. Prepare my horses.
Ingratitude! Thou marble-hearted fiend,
More hideous when thou show'st thee in a child   215
Than the sea-monster.
ALBANY Pray, sir, be patient.

---

205 remainders] F; remainder Q 207 Which] F; That Q 207 devils!] Q; Diuels. F 211–12 You . . . betters] *Rowe's lineation; as prose* Q, F 212–16 Woe . . . sea-monster.] F *lineation; as prose* Q 212 Woe] F; We Q 212 repents!] F; repent's, O sir, are you come? Q *213 will? Speak, sir.] *Johnson;* will, speake Sir? F; will that wee Q 213 my] F; any Q 215 show'st] shew'st F; shewest Q 217 ALBANY Pray . . . patient.] F; *not in* Q, *which continues Lear's speech without* SH

---

205 remainders . . . depend i.e. the rest of your followers.
206 besort suit, befit.
207 Which . . . you Who know their places and yours.
207 Darkness and devils Lear explodes with anger at this point. Peter Brook staged the scene thus: 'Incensed by [Gonerill's] words, Lear overturns the dinner-table and storms out. This is the cue for general pandemonium as the knights, following their master's example, tip chairs, throw plates and generally demolish the chamber' (C. Marowitz, 'Lear Log', *Tulane Drama Review* 8 (1963), 113). This representation is extreme (Rosenberg, p. 121). Lear's knights may appear disorderly in varying degrees; compare 218–21 below and Booth, p. 50.
208 Saddle . . . together Lear's servants seem frozen here; thus, he must order them again at 227 (see n.) and 244. Nevertheless, Oxford adds SD *Exit one or more.*
212 Woe i.e. woe to him who.
213 Speak, sir Albany is astonished at what is happening.
213 Prepare my horses Again, no SD appears, though Oxford repeats *Exit one or more.* Either the servants ignore Lear's commands, or his attendants

and knights are paralysed by events. At 227 Lear urges his people out, but their departure seems further delayed until 244.
216 sea-monster No monster of the deep has been satisfactorily identified, but the ocean, traditionally a home of horrors, was also cold and pitiless. The sea-monster that destroyed Hippolytus probably best fits the context (Hunter). In the 1581 translation of Seneca's *Phaedra*, it has a 'marble neck' and is sent as a punishment for filial ingratitude.
217 ALBANY . . . patient See Textual Analysis, p. 279 below.
217 be patient Coverdale's definition of patience is 'the precious pearl', the Christian virtue that guards against forsaking charity and falling into wrath (Danby, p. 29). 'Lear's passion rises. Albany – always the "moral fool" – calls out the advice from the devotionalists appropriate for the occasion . . . Patience is the only remedy in cases such as Lear's. Lear, however, flings into the angry venom of his outburst against Goneril. Patience is something he has yet to learn' (Danby, p. 177). Compare Hoeniger, who notes that patience is the only virtue that can cure intemperate passion (p. 325). At 2.4.264 Lear prays for patience, and by 4.5.170 he preaches it to Gloucester.

LEAR   [*To Gonerill*]   Detested kite, thou liest!
My train are men of choice and rarest parts,
That all particulars of duty know,
And in the most exact regard support   220
The worships of their name. O most small fault,
How ugly didst thou in Cordelia show!
Which, like an engine, wrenched my frame of nature
From the fixed place, drew from my heart all love,
And added to the gall. O Lear, Lear, Lear!   225
Beat at this gate that let thy folly in
And thy dear judgement out. Go, go, my people.

ALBANY   My lord, I am guiltless as I am ignorant
Of what hath moved you.

LEAR   It may be so, my lord.
Hear, Nature, hear, dear goddess, hear: 230
Suspend thy purpose, if thou didst intend
To make this creature fruitful.
Into her womb convey sterility,
Dry up in her the organs of increase,
And from her derogate body never spring   235
A babe to honour her. If she must teem,
Create her child of spleen, that it may live

---

217 SD] *Rowe; not in* Q, F   217 liest!] F; list Q; lessen Q2   218 train are] F; traine, and Q   222 show!] F; shew? F; shewe, Q   223 Which] F; that Q   225 Lear, Lear, Lear!] F; *Lear, Lear!* Q   228 SH] F; Duke. Q (*throughout scene*)   229 Of . . . you.] F; *not in* Q   226–41 It . . . away!] F *lineation; as prose* Q   230 Hear] F; harke Q   230 goddess, hear] F; Goddesse, Q

217 **kite** A carrion bird particularly despised by Shakespeare. Muir cites Armstrong, *Shakespeare's Imagination*, 1946, pp. 12, 17.

218 **choice and rarest parts** select and special qualities.

220–1 **in . . . name** i.e. on every single point justify and uphold their honourable reputation.

221 **worships** dignity, honour. 'Abstract nouns are often pluralized when they refer to more than one person' (Kittredge).

223 **engine** mechanical contrivance; here, one used for levering, not the rack.

223–4 **wrenched . . . place** i.e. pried loose the structure of my being from its foundations. The metaphor is of an overturned edifice or building. Lear implies that Cordelia was the centre of his being.

225 **gall** bitterness; literally, bile, secreted by the liver.

226 **Beat . . . gate** Pope and others add SD *Striking his head*.

227 **Go . . . people** Some editors add SD *Exeunt*

Kent and Knights, but their departure appears further delayed until 244.

230 **Nature** The goddess Lear appeals to is very different from Edmond's (1.2.1). It is closer to a personification of the orthodox Elizabethan conception of nature as described, for example, by Richard Hooker in *Of the Laws of Ecclesiastical Polity*, 1.iii: '. . . God being the author of Nature, her voice is but his instrument' (cited by Danby, p. 26). Lear's curse is very much like those of the Old Testament. Hunter cites Deut. 28.15, 18. In the eighteenth century (in Tate's adaptation), this was regarded as a high point of the drama.

230 **dear** precious.

235 **derogate** debased (Onions); but compare Cotgrave: *derogé* 'disabled; also . . . abolished in part'. If Gonerill's 'organs' were dried up, her body would be 'derogate' in the latter sense.

236 **teem** be fruitful, have offspring.

237 **of spleen** i.e. entirely of malice, as in *Cor.* 4.5.91.

And be a thwart disnatured torment to her.
Let it stamp wrinkles in her brow of youth,
With cadent tears fret channels in her cheeks,   240
Turn all her mother's pains and benefits
To laughter and contempt, that she may feel
How sharper than a serpent's tooth it is
To have a thankless child. Away, away!
              Exeunt [*Lear, Kent, Knights, and Attendants*]
ALBANY   Now, gods that we adore, whereof comes this?   245
GONERILL   Never afflict yourself to know more of it,
But let his disposition have that scope
As dotage gives it.

                    Enter LEAR

LEAR   What, fifty of my followers at a clap?
              Within a fortnight?
ALBANY   What's the matter, sir?   250
LEAR   I'll tell thee. [*To Gonerill*] Life and death! I am ashamed
That thou hast power to shake my manhood thus,
That these hot tears, which break from me perforce,
Should make thee worth them. Blasts and fogs upon thee!
Th'untented woundings of a father's curse   255

---

238 thwart disnatured] F; thourt disuetur'd Q   240 cadent] F; accent Q   242 feel] F; feele, that she may feele Q   244 Away, away!] F; goe, goe, my people? Q   244 SD] *This edn; not in* Q; *Exit* F; *Exit Lear and Attendants* Rowe (*after 265*)   245 Now . . . this?] Q; *two lines divided* adore, / Whereof F   246–8 Never . . . it.] F *lineation; as prose* Q   246 more of it,] F; the cause, Q   248 As] F; that Q   248 SD] F; *not in* Q   249–50 What . . . fortnight?] F *lineation; as prose* Q   250 What's] F; What is Q   251 I'll . . . ashamed] *Rowe's lineation; two lines divided* thee: / Life F   251 SD] *Theobald; not in* Q, F   252–65 That . . . forever.] F *lineation (except 254); as prose* Q   253 which] F; that Q   254 Should . . . thee!] *Rowe's lineation; two lines divided* them. / Blasts F   254 thee worth them. Blasts] F; the worst blasts Q   254–5 thee! / Th'untented] F; the vntender Q *uncorr.;* the vntented Q *corr.*

---

238 **thwart** perverse, cross-grained.
238 **disnatured** unnatural, lacking natural feelings.
240 **cadent** falling.
240 **fret** make or form by wearing away.
241 **pains** care.
243 **How . . . is** The wording recalls Ps. 140.3: 'Thei haue sharpened their tongues like a serpent' (Malone).
247 **disposition** mood, humour.
248 **As** That.
249–50 **What . . . fortnight** Gonerill has said nothing to Lear about halving his train; presumably someone informs him of her order in the brief time he is off-stage, and the news drives him back for further confrontation. But Hunter rightly dis-

counts explanations that depend upon realism and praises instead 'the bold foreshortening that makes the loss of fifty followers seem the consequence of an absence during which only four lines are spoken'.
249 **at a clap** at one stroke.
250 **Within a fortnight?** Either this is part of the ultimatum, or it suggests the length of time Lear has been with Gonerill so far.
253–4 **That these . . . them** That you appear to be worth the tears that uncontrollably fall from me.
254 **Blasts** Gusts of pestilential foul air.
255 **untented** untentable, i.e. too deep for probing with a tent (probe or absorbent wedge used for cleaning wounds: *OED sb³* 1 and 2).

Pierce every sense about thee. Old fond eyes,
Beweep this cause again, I'll pluck ye out
And cast you with the waters that you loose
To temper clay. Ha! Let it be so.
I have another daughter,   260
Who I am sure is kind and comfortable.
When she shall hear this of thee, with her nails
She'll flay thy wolvish visage. Thou shalt find
That I'll resume the shape which thou dost think
I have cast off forever.   *Exit*

GONERILL   Do you mark that?   265
ALBANY   I cannot be so partial, Gonerill,
To the great love I bear you –
GONERILL   Pray you, content.
What, Oswald, ho!
You, sir, more knave than fool, after your master.
FOOL Nuncle Lear, nuncle Lear, tarry, take the fool with thee.   270
A fox, when one has caught her,
And such a daughter,
Should sure to the slaughter,

---

256 Pierce] F; peruse Q *uncorr.*; pierce Q *corr.*   256 thee. Old] F; the old Q   257 ye] F; you Q   258 cast you] F; you cast
Q   258 loose] F; make Q   259 clay.] F; clay, yea, i'st come to this? Q   259 Ha! . . . so.] F; *not in* Q   260 I have another]
F; yet haue I left a Q   261 Who] F; whom Q   265 forever.] F; for euer, thou shalt I warrant thee. Q   265 SD] F; *not in*
Q   265 that?] F; that my Lord? Q   266–7 I . . . you –] F *lineation; as prose* Q   267 you –] *Theobald* (*subst.*); you, Q; you.
F   267 Pray you, content.] F; Come sir no more, Q   268 What, Oswald, ho!] F; *not in* Q   269 You, sir,] F; you, Q   270
Nuncle . . . thee] *As prose* Q; *two verse lines divided: Lear, / Tarry*, F, *Oxford*   270 tarry,] F; tary and Q   270 with thee]
F; with Q   271–5 A fox . . . after.] F *lineation; as prose* Q

256 **fond** foolish (as often).
257 **Beweep this cause again** If you cry over
this once more.
258 **loose** let loose, release. But 'lose' is also possible, as the spellings were interchangeable. Muir
suggests a quibble.
259 **temper** soften by moistening. Compare
2H6 3.1.311: 'And temper clay with blood of
Englishmen'.
259–60 **Ha! . . . daughter** An example of F
substitution for Q. Compare Duthie, pp. 36, 172,
and Stone, p. 234, who believe the Q half-line was
accidentally omitted and should be restored. Some
metrical disruption is manifest, but short lines are
not uncommon in F, similar substitutions occur
elsewhere (see Textual Analysis, pp. 78–9 above),
and other evidence of revision appears; hence,
conflation (which does not perfect the metre) is
unwarranted.
261 **comfortable** able to comfort, comforting.

267 **Pray you, content** Gonerill cuts Albany
off in mid sentence in both Q and F, but the manner in F is somewhat gentler, as Duthie, p. 35, and
McLeod, pp. 176–7, agree. On F's alterations of
Gonerill's role, see Textual Analysis, p. 73 above.
270 **take . . . thee** 'An absolutely perfect pun.
The literal sense is obvious; but the phrase was a
regular farewell gibe: "Take the epithet 'fool' with
you as you go!" ' (Kittredge).
271–5 **A fox . . . after** The rhymes here may
have been phonetically exact, possibly involving
a patchwork of colloquial pronunciations. Neither
the *l* in 'halter' nor the *f* in 'after' was pronounced.
Compare Ben Jonson's rhymes, *water: daughter:
slaughter: after* in 'On the Birth of the Lady Mary',
which Elizabethans would not have regarded as
vulgar or rustic, but 'undoubtedly a source of
amusement and appreciative comment' (Kökeritz,
p. 183; compare Cercignani, p. 211).
273 **sure to** certainly go to.

If my cap would buy a halter;
So the fool follows after.   *Exit*   275
GONERILL   This man hath had good counsel. A hundred knights?
'Tis politic and safe to let him keep
At point a hundred knights? Yes, that on every dream,
Each buzz, each fancy, each complaint, dislike,
He may enguard his dotage with their powers   280
And hold our lives in mercy. Oswald, I say!
ALBANY   Well, you may fear too far.
GONERILL   Safer than trust too far.
Let me still take away the harms I fear,
Not fear still to be taken. I know his heart.
What he hath uttered I have writ my sister: 285
If she sustain him and his hundred knights
When I have showed th'unfitness –

                        Enter OSWALD

                                    How now, Oswald?
What, have you writ that letter to my sister?
OSWALD   Ay, madam.
GONERILL   Take you some company and away to horse.   290
Inform her full of my particular fear,
And thereto add such reasons of your own
As may compact it more. Get you gone,
And hasten your return.

                                    [*Exit Oswald*]

---

275 SD] F; *not in* Q   276–87 This . . . th'unfitness –] F; *not in* Q   276 This . . . knights?] *Rowe's lineation; two lines divided* Counsell, / A F   *278 knights?] *Hanmer;* Knights: F   287 th'unfitness –] *Rowe;* th'vnfitnesse. F   287 SD] F; *not in* Q   287 How now, Oswald?] F; What Oswald, ho. Oswald. Here Madam. Q   288 that] F; this Q   289 Ay,] I F; Yes Q   290–300 Take . . . well.] F *lineation; as prose* Q   291 fear] F; feares Q   294 And hasten] F; and after Q *uncorr.,* Q2; & hasten Q *corr.*   294 SD] *Rowe; not in* Q, F

---

274 halter hangman's noose.
276–87 This . . . unfitness On F's addition. see Textual Analysis, p. 279 below.
276 This man i.e. Lear. Gonerill speaks sarcastically.
278 At point In (armed) readiness.
279 buzz whisper, rumour.
280 enguard put a guard around, protect.
281 in mercy in fee, at (his) mercy.
282 fear . . . trust too far Compare 'Fear is one part of prudence' (Tilley F135, cited by NS).
283 still always (as often).
284 Not . . . taken Rather than constantly live in fear of being overtaken by those dangers. Gonerill

uses the rhetorical device of antimetabole (Joseph, p. 81). Compare *Tro.* 3.3.178–9.
288 What . . . writ At 1.3.21, Gonerill says she will write to her sister at once, but the letter cannot contain what Lear has just said, and presumably she means she has commissioned Oswald to write for her.
291 full fully.
291 particular own.
293 compact strengthen, confirm.
294 return Although Gonerill orders Oswald to return, she meets him instead at Gloucester's castle (2.4).

No, no, my lord,
This milky gentleness and course of yours,   295
Though I condemn not, yet under pardon
You are much more ataxed for want of wisdom,
Than praised for harmful mildness.
ALBANY How far your eyes may pierce I cannot tell;
Striving to better, oft we mar what's well.   300
GONERILL Nay then –
ALBANY Well, well, th'event.

Exeunt

1.5 *Enter* LEAR, KENT, *and* FOOL

LEAR Go you before to Gloucester with these letters. Acquaint my
daughter no further with anything you know than comes from

---

294 No, no] F; Now Q   295 milky] F; mildie Q *uncorr.;* milkie Q *corr.*   296 condemn] F; dislike Q   *297 You are] F2; y'are Q; Your are F   *297 ataxed for] ataxt for *Duthie, conj. Greg;* alapt Q *uncorr.,* Q2; attaskt for Q *corr.;* at task for F   298 praised] F; praise Q   300 better, oft] F; better ought, Q   302 th'event] the'uent F; the euent Q   Act 1, Scene 5   1.5] *Scena Quinta.* F; *not in* Q   *0 SD] Q2; *Enter Lear.* Q; *Enter Lear, Kent, Gentleman, and Foole.* F

---

295 milky . . . course mild and gentle course of action (hendiadys). Compare *Tim.* 3.1.54.

296 Though . . . not 'But she does' (NS).

296 under pardon pardon me.

297 ataxed taxed, censured: a famous crux. Greg, *Variants,* pp. 153–5, has convinced most recent editors that Q uncorr. 'alapt' is probably a misprint for 'ataxt' (*t* and *x* were often confused with *l* and *p*). The press readers wrongly corrected the word in Q corr. and F, although Q corr. 'attaskt' can be construed as a variant of 'ataxt', and F 'at task' may be a sophistication or regularisation of Q corr. (Hunter). Noting the common origin of 'task' and 'tax' and their interchangeable spellings, T. Howard-Hill conjectures that F 'at task' derived from 'ataxt' through an intermediate manuscript 'in which the spelling may have already been varied' ('The problem of manuscript copy for Folio *King Lear*', *The Library,* 6th ser., 4 (1982), 21–2). Compare 3.2.15, where F reads 'taxe' for Q 'taske'.

298 harmful mildness i.e. leniency, which results in further harm being done.

299 How . . . tell i.e. I cannot tell how perceptive you are or how well you can predict future events.

300 Striving . . . well Compare 'Let well enough alone' (Tilley w260), Bodenham, *Belvedere* (1600): 'Some men so strive in cunning to excell, / That oft they marre the worke before was well' (Dent, p. 246) and Sonnet 103.9–10.

302 Well . . . event i.e. let's await the outcome. Albany has no stomach here for continuing the quarrel.

Act 1, Scene 5

0 SD Although F includes *Gentleman* in the SD, most editors delete it, as Lear directs Kent, not his Gentleman or Knight, to carry his letters. The Gentleman has no speaking role and is not needed until 38, where Theobald inserts his entrance. Oxford, following Jennens, retains the Gentleman here and has Lear give him letters for Gloucester and Kent a letter for Regan, after which each exits. While this arrangement attempts to resolve the problem of Regan and Cornwall's residence (see below), Gloucester in the next scene gives no indication of receiving word from Lear, as Regan does (2.1.122).

1 before i.e. before me, ahead.

1 Gloucester Perhaps Lear refers not to the Earl of Gloucester but to the town of that name, near where Cornwall and Regan may have a residence (Perrett, pp. 167–72). Bradley, p. 449, notes that Cornwall is Gloucester's 'arch and patron', 2.1.58. But NS sees a slip here for 'Cornwall' and emends accordingly. Shakespeare may simply have anticipated the later action.

1 these letters this letter; compare Latin *litterae,* a similar plural form with a singular meaning; see also 3 and 5 below, and 4.5.237, 244.

1–3 Acquaint . . . letter Compare 1.4.288–93. Lear does not distrust Kent; unlike Gonerill, he is trying to keep a lid on the situation. Hunter implausibly says Lear distrusts Regan and does not want to give her any ammunition against him.

her demand out of the letter. If your diligence be not speedy, I
shall be there afore you.

KENT   I will not sleep, my lord, till I have delivered your letter.   5

Exit

FOOL   If a man's brains were in's heels, were't not in danger of
kibes?

LEAR   Ay, boy.

FOOL   Then, I prithee, be merry; thy wit shall not go slipshod.

LEAR   Ha, ha, ha.   10

FOOL   Shalt see thy other daughter will use thee kindly, for though
she's as like this as a crab's like an apple, yet I can tell what I
can tell.

LEAR   What canst tell, boy?

FOOL   She will taste as like this as a crab does to a crab. Thou   15
canst tell why one's nose stands i'th'middle on's face?

LEAR   No.

FOOL   Why, to keep one's eyes of either side 's nose, that what a
man cannot smell out, he may spy into.

LEAR   I did her wrong.   20

FOOL   Canst tell how an oyster makes his shell?

LEAR   No.

FOOL   Nor I neither; but I can tell why a snail has a house.

LEAR   Why?

FOOL   Why, to put 's head in, not to give it away to his daughters,   25
and leave his horns without a case.

4 afore] F; before Q   6 were in's] F; where in his Q   6 were't] *Rowe;* wert Q, F   9 not] F; nere Q   12 crab's] F; crab is
Q   12 can tell what] F; con, what Q   14 What canst] F; Why what canst thou Q   14 boy?] F; my boy? Q   15 She will]
F; Sheel Q   15 does] F; doth Q   16 canst] F; canst not Q   16 stands] F; stande Q   16 i'th'] F; in the Q   16 on's] F; of
his Q   18 one's] F; his Q   18 of] F; on Q   19 he] F; a Q   25 put 's] F; put his Q   25 daughters] F; daughter Q

3 **demand** question.
3 **out of** from, suggested by.
6 **were't** i.e. his brains, taken as singular.
7 **kibes** chilblains. The Fool refers first to Kent's
promise of speedy service, then (11–13) to Lear's
foolish journey that shows he has no wit, even in
his heels.
9 **thy . . . slipshod** your brains will not have to
wear slippers (because of chilblains); you are witless
to begin with (in going to Regan and thinking to
find succour there). The joke has sometimes been
used as a cue for actors playing the Fool to do
handstands or somersaults (Rosenberg, p. 137).
11 **Shalt** Thou shalt.
11 **kindly** (1) affectionately, (2) according to her
kind (the same as Gonerill's).
11–15 **though . . . to a crab** The Fool makes an
ironic joke, continuing the play on 'kindly': only a
fool could think there is any real difference between
Regan and Gonerill. Though Regan and Gonerill

look slightly different, they are essentially the same.
12 **like this** i.e. like this daughter.
12 **crab** crab-apple; a small, sour wild apple.
Wright (cited by Furness) quotes Lyly, *Euphues*:
'The sower Crabbe hath the shew of an Apple as
well as the sweet Pippin.'
15–19 **Thou . . . into** An example of the Fool's
rapidly shifting focus though the answer to his
question adheres to the main issue of perception.
16 **on's** of his.
20 **I . . . wrong** Lear broods on his treatment of
Cordelia. Compare 'O most small fault' (1.4.221).
D. G. James, *The Dream of Learning*, 1951, pp. 94–
6, believes Lear refers to Gonerill.
23–5 **why a snail . . . in** Compare Tilley, s580:
'Like a snail he keeps his house on his head' (NS).
25 **put 's** put his.
26 **horns** An allusion to the cuckold's horns;
being cuckolded was the inevitable fate of married
men, according to the standard (and much

LEAR   I will forget my nature. So kind a father! Be my horses ready?

FOOL   Thy asses are gone about 'em. The reason why the seven
stars are no mo than seven is a pretty reason.

LEAR   Because they are not eight.   30

FOOL   Yes, indeed, thou wouldst make a good fool.

LEAR   To take't again perforce. Monster ingratitude!

FOOL   If thou wert my fool, nuncle, I'd have thee beaten for being
old before thy time.

LEAR   How's that?   35

FOOL   Thou shouldst not have been old till thou hadst been wise.

LEAR   O let me not be mad, not mad, sweet heaven!
Keep me in temper, I would not be mad.

[*Enter* GENTLEMAN]

How now, are the horses ready?

GENTLEMAN   Ready, my lord.   40

LEAR   Come, boy.

FOOL   She that's a maid now, and laughs at my departure,
Shall not be a maid long, unless things be cut shorter.

Exeunt

---

28 'em] F; them Q   29 mo] F; more Q   31 indeed] F; *not in* Q   36 till] F; before Q   37–9 O . . . ready?] *Pope's lineation;*
as prose Q, F   37 not mad] F; *not in* Q   38 Keep] F; I would not be mad, keepe Q   38 SD] *Theobald; not in* Q, F   39 How
now,] F; *not in* Q   40 SH] F; *Seruant.* Q   41 boy.] F; boy. *Exit.* Q   42 that's] F; that is Q   43 unless] F; except Q   43 SD]
F; *Exit.* Q

repeated) Elizabethan joke. The legitimacy of
Lear's elder daughters is again brought into question, and Lear's destitution predicted.

27 forget lose.

27 nature Either (1) generally: character,
disposition; or (2) specifically: paternal instincts;
or (3) both.

28 asses An obvious quibble.

28–9 The reason . . . reason An example of
the fallacy of begging the question, i.e. when the
conclusion, or question to be proved, stands as one
of the premises (Joseph, p. 198).

29 mo more.

31 thou . . . fool 'There is bite in Fool's answer
. . . Fool's jokes are not working, line by line Lear
slips further away from communication . . . as Fool
incites Lear to sanity, he baits him, too, and the
pitch rises' (Rosenberg, p. 139).

32 To take't again i.e. to resume his
sovereignty. Lear's mutterings, when he does not
directly respond to the Fool, are not fully coherent. As at 20 'her' could refer to either Cordelia or

Gonerill, here Lear may be thinking of Gonerill's
rescinding the privileges she agreed to grant him
(Steevens).

32 perforce by force.

37–8 O . . . mad The fear is occasioned by
'wise' = in one's right mind, in the Fool's preceding gibe (NS). Lear's passion is rising, and
the 'unnatural' events are approaching a climax.
Hoeniger describes Lear's madness in Renaissance
terms as 'acute hypochondriac melancholy developing into mania' (p. 330) and traces it from here
through 4.5.

42–3 She . . . shorter The Fool addresses the
audience and warns *naifs* against a simplistic (i.e.
merely humorous) interpretation of his role and (by
extension) of all experience. He puns on 'departure' (pronounced like 'departer' and rhyming
with 'shorter': Kökeritz, pp. 169, 226; Cercignani,
pp. 114, 263), and on the bawdy sense of 'things',
perhaps putting his bauble (= a phallus) between
his legs as he mimes the lines (Wiles, pp. 190–1).

2.1 *Enter* EDMOND *and* CURAN, *severally*

EDMOND Save thee, Curan.

CURAN And you, sir. I have been with your father and given him notice that the Duke of Cornwall and Regan his duchess will be here with him this night.

EDMOND How comes that?   5

CURAN Nay, I know not. You have heard of the news abroad? I mean the whispered ones, for they are yet but ear-kissing arguments.

EDMOND Not I; pray you, what are they?

CURAN Have you heard of no likely wars toward 'twixt the Dukes   10
of Cornwall and Albany?

EDMOND Not a word.

CURAN You may do then in time. Fare you well, sir.   *Exit*

EDMOND The duke be here tonight! The better, best.
This weaves itself perforce into my business.   15
My father hath set guard to take my brother,
And I have one thing of a queasy question
Which I must act. Briefness and Fortune, work!
Brother, a word, descend; brother, I say!

Act 2, Scene 1   2.1] *Actus Secundus. Scena Prima.* F; *not in* Q   0 SD] F; *Enter Bast. and Curan meeting.* Q   2–4 And . . . night.] *As prose* Q; *four verse lines ending* . . . bin / . . . notice / . . . Duchesse / . . . night. F   *2 you] Q; *your* F   3 Regan] F; *not in* Q   4 this] F; *to* Q   *6 abroad?] *Duthie*; abroad, Q, F   7 they] F; there Q   7 ear-kissing] F; *eare-bussing* Q   9 Not I;] F; *Not,* I Q   10–11 Have . . . Albany?] Q; *not in* Q2, *which also omits* 12; *two verse lines divided* toward, / 'Twixt F   10 toward] F; towards Q   10 Dukes] F; two Dukes Q   13 You . . . sir.] Q; *two lines divided* time. / Fare F   13 do] F; *not in* Q   13 SD] F; *not in* Q   14–27 The . . . yourself.] F *lineation; as prose* Q   *14 better,] *Rowe*; better Q, F   18 I must act. Briefness and Fortune, work] F; must aske breefnes and fortune helpe Q

Act 2, Scene 1

0 SD *severally* Edmond and Curan enter separately from different entrances.

1 **Save thee** i.e. God save thee (a common greeting).

1 **Curan** Though unusual, as Hunter says, for so minor a character to have a proper name, it is not unprecedented (compare Conrad in *Much Ado*). Curan is apparently one of Gloucester's men and thus known by name to Edmond.

6 **news abroad** talk going around.

7 **ear-kissing** Q's 'bussing' may be a misreading for 'kissing' since *k* could be misread as *b* – as e.g. at 4.1.37: Q 'bitt', F 'kill'. Minim misreadings, *i* for *u*, and vice versa, are common. On the other hand, 'kissing' may be a Folio sophistication (Duthie, p. 192, adopting Q). The two words mean the same, but 'bussing' has the advantage of a possible pun on 'buzzing' (Collier, cited by Furness). Nevertheless, the F reading is perfectly acceptable.

8 **arguments** subjects, topics.

10–11 **wars . . . Albany** A leitmotiv from here on, showing disorder in domestic politics and confuting one of Lear's reasons for giving up the throne (1.1.39–40).

10 **toward** impending.

14 **The better, best** i.e. this is better, in fact the best news yet.

17 **queasy question** i.e. delicate nature.

18 **Briefness and Fortune** Whereas Fortune was a standard allegorical figure, Edmond here personifies another 'natural' force, speed. During this speech following Curan's exit, Edmond moves towards his imagined lodging, where he has hidden Edgar (1.2.140–2).

19 **descend** This is the only occasion in the play where some kind of 'above' seems to be used. Possibly Edgar drops down from the Lord's Room above the rear centre stage, where he is hidden by spectators seated there. Edmond is again stage-managing the action, manipulating people and events.

Enter EDGAR

My father watches: O sir, fly this place.   20
Intelligence is given where you are hid;
You have now the good advantage of the night.
Have you not spoken 'gainst the Duke of Cornwall?
He's coming hither, now i'th'night, i'th'haste,
And Regan with him. Have you nothing said   25
Upon his party 'gainst the Duke of Albany?
Advise yourself.
EDGAR   I am sure on't, not a word.
EDMOND I hear my father coming. Pardon me,
In cunning, I must draw my sword upon you.
Draw, seem to defend yourself. Now, quit you well.   30
[*Shouting*] Yield! Come before my father! – Light ho,
here! –
Fly, brother! – Torches, torches! – so, farewell.

                                        Exit Edgar

Some blood drawn on me would beget opinion
Of my more fierce endeavour.
                [*Wounds his arm*]
                        I have seen drunkards
Do more than this in sport. Father, father!   35
Stop, stop! No help?

*19 SD] *Theobald; in margin before 15* Q; after 18* F   **20** sir,] F; *not in* Q   **23** Cornwall?] F; *Cornwall* ought, Q   **24** i'th'night] F; *in the night* Q   **24** i'th'haste] F; *it'h hast* Q   **26** 'gainst] F; *against* Q   **27** yourself.] F; *your –* Q   **28–36** I . . . help?] F *lineation (except 30); as prose* Q   **29** cunning] F; *crauing* Q   **30** Draw . . . well.] *Capell's lineation; two lines divided* your selfe, / Now F   **30** Draw] F; *not in* Q   **31** SD] *This edn; not in* Q, F   **31** ho] F; *here* Q   **32** brother! – Torches,] Brother, Torches, F; *brother flie, torches,* Q   **32** SD] F; *not in* Q   **34** SD] Rowe; *not in* Q, F   **36** No] Q, F; Ho Oxford

21 Intelligence Information.

23 spoken 'gainst Edmond is not wildly speculating, but planting seeds of doubt in Edgar's mind concerning his safety, as he does at 25–6.

24 i'th'haste i.e. in haste.

27 on't of it.

29–30 In cunning . . . yourself Playing on his brother's naïvety, as in 1.2, Edmond implies that his 'cunning', or craft, is used on Edgar's behalf, though in fact the opposite is true. Rosenberg, pp. 142–3, questions whether Edmond here intends to kill Edgar (the 'queasy question', 17) and claim self-defence. But citing the duel in 5.3, Rosenberg notes that Edgar, a better swordsman, frustrates Edmond's design, unless Edmond himself has a change of heart at the last moment. 33–4 sug-

gest, however, that the duel is a sham from first to last, even though Edmond might be better off with Edgar dead.

30 quit you acquit yourself; with a possible play on the sense 'leave'.

33–4 beget . . . endeavour i.e. cause people to think that my efforts were fiercer than they actually were in the struggle.

34–5 drunkards . . . sport Young gallants sometimes stabbed their own arms so that they could drink the healths of their mistresses in blood (Collier, cited by Furness). Several references to the practice appear in dramatic literature; e.g. Steevens cites a relevant passage from Marston's *The Dutch Courtesan* 4.1, and Kittredge cites Middleton's *A Trick to Catch the Old One* 5.2.198.

Enter GLOUCESTER, *and Servants with torches*

GLOUCESTER   Now, Edmond, where's the villain?
EDMOND Here stood he in the dark, his sharp sword out,
    Mumbling of wicked charms, conjuring the moon
    To stand auspicious mistress.
GLOUCESTER   But where is he?
EDMOND Look, sir, I bleed.
GLOUCESTER   Where is the villain, Edmond?   40
EDMOND Fled this way, sir, when by no means he could –
GLOUCESTER Pursue him, ho! Go after.
                                                 [*Exeunt Servants*]
                                    'By no means' what?
EDMOND Persuade me to the murder of your lordship,
    But that I told him the revenging gods
    'Gainst parricides did all the thunder bend,   45
    Spoke with how manifold and strong a bond
    The child was bound to'th'father; sir, in fine,
    Seeing how loathly opposite I stood
    To his unnatural purpose, in fell motion
    With his preparèd sword he charges home   50
    My unprovided body, latched mine arm;

---

36 SD] F; *Enter Glost.* Q   36 where's] F; *where is* Q   37–9 *Here . . . mistress.*] F *lineation; as prose* Q   38 Mumbling] F; *warbling* Q   39 stand] F; *stand's* Q, *Oxford; stand his* Q2   *41 could –] Q; *could.* F   42 ho] F; *not in* Q   42 SD] *Dyce* (*subst.*); *not in* Q, F   43–84 *Persuade . . . capable.*] F *lineation; as prose* Q   44 revenging] F; *reuengiue* Q   45 the thunder] F; *their thunders* Q   46 manifold] F; *many fould* Q   47 to'th'] F; *to the* Q   47 fine] F; *a fine* Q   49 in] F; *with* Q   51 latched] F; *lancht* Q

---

36 SD *with torches* Note the ironies of (a) Edmond's call for torches (32), when he does not really want to reveal what is happening, and (b) Gloucester's entrance with them, and their failure to illuminate what he most needs to see (Heilman, p. 46).

38–9 *Mumbling . . . mistress* Edmond is playing upon Gloucester's superstitious nature, but the lines also show Shakespeare beginning to imagine Edgar as Tom o'Bedlam. Compare 1.2.118.

38–9 *moon . . . mistress* Edmond alludes to Hecate. See 1.1.104 n.

39 *stand* be; 'his' is understood, though Q prints 'stand's' and Q2 'stand his'.

41 *this way* Edmond points in the wrong direction, of course, giving Edgar time to flee, just as in the preceding lines he has been deliberately stalling despite his father's repeated demands to know where Edgar is.

44 **revenging** avenging.
45 **bend** aim. The metaphor is from archery; compare 1.1.137.
47 **in fine** finally.
48 **loathly opposite** loathingly opposed.
49 **fell motion** fierce, deadly thrust.
50 **preparèd** unsheathed.
50 **charges home** makes a home thrust at (Muir).
51 **unprovided** i.e. unprotected, unarmed.
51 **latched** caught. In defending the F reading against Q's 'lancht' (= lanced), Duthie, p. 137, regrets that his best evidence is a 1535 quotation from a Scottish author cited by *OED* Latch *sb* 2. But compare *OED sb* 4, 'to receive . . . a blow'; Bishop Hall in 1649: 'A man that latches the weapon in his own body to save his Prince'; and *Mac.* 4.3.195, also cited by *OED* under *sb* 4.

And when he saw my best alarumed spirits
Bold in the quarrel's right, roused to th'encounter,
Or whether ghasted by the noise I made,
Full suddenly he fled.
GLOUCESTER   Let him fly far,   55
Not in this land shall he remain uncaught;
And found, dispatch. The noble duke my master,
My worthy arch and patron, comes tonight.
By his authority I will proclaim it,
That he which finds him shall deserve our thanks,   60
Bringing the murderous coward to the stake;
He that conceals him, death.
EDMOND When I dissuaded him from his intent
And found him pight to do it, with cursed speech
I threatened to discover him. He replied,   65
'Thou unpossessing bastard, dost thou think,
If I would stand against thee, would the reposal
Of any trust, virtue, or worth in thee
Make thy words faithed? No; what I should deny
(As this I would, ay, though thou didst produce   70
My very character) I'd turn it all
To thy suggestion, plot, and damnèd practice;
And thou must make a dullard of the world,

52 And] F; but Q   53 quarrel's right,] F; quarrels, rights Q   53 th'] F; the Q   54 ghasted] *Knight;* gasted Q, F   55 Full] F; but Q   *56–7 uncaught, / And found, dispatch. The]* Steevens *(subst.);* vncaught / And found; dispatch, the F; vncaught and found, dispatch, the Q   61 coward] F; caytife Q   67 would the reposal] F; could the reposure Q   *69 I should] Q; should I F   70 *ay,] I, Q; *not in* F   72 practice] F; pretence Q

52 **best alarumed spirits** i.e. best energies called to arms (Kittredge).
54 **ghasted** frightened, scared. Compare *Oth.* 5.1.106. Muir suggests a possible pun on 'ghosted', since Edgar 'vanished like a ghost at cock-crow'. The two words are nevertheless etymologically distinct.
55 **Full** An intensive (= 'very', 'extremely').
55–7 **Let . . . dispatch** Either (1) however far he flies, we'll catch him and kill him, or (2) let him fly far from this land, for if he dares to remain I'll see that he is caught and exiled (Davenport, p. 20).
57 **And found, dispatch** i.e. and once he is found, he will be summarily executed.
58 **arch and patron** chief patron (hendiadys).
61 **to the stake** i.e. to the place of execution.
64 **pight** firmly set, determined; an archaic form of the past participle of 'pitch', as in 'to pitch a tent'. Compare *Tro.* 5.10.24 for its literal use.

64 **cursed** angry.
65 **discover him** i.e. reveal his purpose.
66 **unpossessing** Illegitimate children could not inherit property.
67 **I would** I should.
67 **reposal** placing.
68 **virtue, or worth** 'These words are not the objects of *of*; they are in the same construction as *reposal*: "Would our father's putting any confidence in you, or would any virtue or worthiness on your part", etc.' (Kittredge).
69 **faithed** believed.
71 **character** handwriting.
72 **practice** evil machination. Compare 106 below.
73–6 **thou . . . seek it** i.e. you must think the world is pretty stupid for people not to think that what you stood to gain from my death was a powerful incentive for you to seek it (by this stratagem).

If they not thought the profits of my death
Were very pregnant and potential spirits   75
To make thee seek it.'
                              Tucket within
GLOUCESTER   O strange and fastened villain!
Would he deny his letter, said he?
Hark, the duke's trumpets. I know not why he comes.
All ports I'll bar, the villain shall not 'scape;
The duke must grant me that. Besides, his picture   80
I will send far and near, that all the kingdom
May have due note of him; and of my land,
Loyal and natural boy, I'll work the means
To make thee capable.

            Enter CORNWALL, REGAN, *and Attendants*

CORNWALL   How now, my noble friend, since I came hither,   85
Which I can call but now, I have heard strange news.
REGAN If it be true, all vengeance comes too short

---

75 spirits] F; spurres Q   76 SD] F; *after 77, Malone; not in* Q   76 O strange] F; Strong Q   77 said he?] F; I neuer got
him, Q   *78 why] Q; wher F   82 due] F; *not in* Q   84 SD] F; *Enter the Duke of Cornwall.* Q   85–94 How . . . father?] F
lineation; as prose Q   *86 strange news.] Q; strangenesse F

75 **pregnant and potential spirits** i.e. spirits fertile and powerful in incitement. Many editors, ignoring a possibly mixed metaphor ('pregnant spurs'), adopt Q's reading as better suiting
the sense. Duthie, p. 173, thinks the F collator or
compositor may have misread 'spurres' and thus
miscorrected Q. But Sisson, p. 232, argues that the
sense and language of the whole speech points to
'spirits', with 'pregnant and potential' fitting evil
spirits and referring back to 'damnèd practice' (72).
Shakespeare often juxtaposes 'potent' and 'spirits'
(Muir, adopting F, as does Riverside).
    76 SD **Tucket within** Most editors place SD after
77, but space considerations did not force Compositor B to insert it earlier, and Gloucester's preoccupation with Edmond's news naturally suggests
a delayed response. A tucket (from Italian *toccata*)
is a succession of notes on a trumpet distinguished
from a flourish. Gloucester recognises the particular melody or sequence as Cornwall's (78).
    76 **strange** (1) monstrous (of human species),
(2) unnatural, alienated (of human kinship).
    76 **fastened** confirmed, hardened.
    77 **said he?** F's substitution for Q's 'I neuer

got him' leaves an irregular line, but conflation,
as Duthie recommends (p. 173) and many editors read, does not help metrically. Duthie believes
'said he?' was meant as an addition, not a substitution, and was misinterpreted by the scribe or collator preparing copy for F. Gloucester's agitation
lends itself to hypermetrical speech, interrupted
by the trumpet announcing Cornwall and Regan's
arrival.
    79 **ports** seaports; but possibly gates of walled
towns, too.
    80–1 **his picture . . . near** Before xerography
or even photography, this method of apprehend-
ing malefactors was used. Furness cites *Nobody and
Somebody* (1606): 'Let him be straight imprinted to
the life: / His picture shall be set on euery stall, /
And proclamation made, that he that takes him, /
Shall haue a hundred pounds of *Somebody.*'
    83 **natural** The ambiguity – (1) naturally loyal
and loving, (2) illegitimate – is further compounded
since 'natural' could also refer to a legitimate
child. Thus Gloucester may already indicate that
Edmond is his heir (Muir).
    84 **capable** i.e. legally able to inherit patrimony.

Which can pursue th'offender. How dost, my lord?

GLOUCESTER   O madam, my old heart is cracked, it's cracked.

REGAN   What, did my father's godson seek your life?   90
He whom my father named, your Edgar?

GLOUCESTER   O lady, lady, shame would have it hid.

REGAN   Was he not companion with the riotous knights
That tended upon my father?

GLOUCESTER   I know not, madam; 'tis too bad, too bad.   95

EDMOND   Yes, madam, he was of that consort.

REGAN   No marvel, then, though he were ill affected.
'Tis they have put him on the old man's death,
To have th'expense and waste of his revenues.
I have this present evening from my sister   100
Been well informed of them, and with such cautions,
That if they come to sojourn at my house,
I'll not be there.

CORNWALL   Nor I, assure thee, Regan.
Edmond, I hear that you have shown your father
A child-like office.

EDMOND   It was my duty, sir.   105

GLOUCESTER   He did bewray his practice, and received
This hurt you see, striving to apprehend him.

CORNWALL   Is he pursued?

GLOUCESTER   Ay, my good lord.

CORNWALL   If he be taken, he shall never more   110
Be feared of doing harm. Make your own purpose

---

88 th'] F; the Q   89 O] F; *not in* Q   89 it's] F; is Q   92 O] F; I Q   94 tended] F; tends Q   96 of that consort] F; *not in* Q   99 th'expense and waste] F; these – and wast Q *uncorr.*; the wast and spoyle Q *corr.*   99 his] F, Q *corr.*; this his Q *uncorr.*   102–3 That . . . there.] F *lineation; one line* Q   103–5 Nor . . . office.] F *lineation; as prose* Q   104 hear] F; heard Q   104 shown] shewne F; shewen Q   105 It was] F; 'Twas Q   106 bewray] F; betray Q   110–16 If . . . on.] F *lineation; as prose* Q

88 **dost** i.e. dost thou. Since Regan never again addresses Gloucester in the second-person familiar, Furness believes the F2 emendation, 'does', should be adopted, though his text follows Q/F.

90 **my father's godson** Regan begins to make a series of associations connecting Edgar and Lear with mischief and disorder. Compare 93–4.

94 **tended upon** Although many editors follow Theobald and emend 'tended' to 'tend', thus preserving the metre, Abbott 472 (cited by Furness, Duthie) indicates that *-ed* was often not pronounced after a *d* or *t*; hence, the emendation, which also changes the tense, is unnecessary.

96 **consort** band, company; accented on second syllable.

97 **though** if.

97 **ill affected** badly disposed, disloyal.

98 **put him on** put him on or up to.

99 **th'expense** the spending.

99 **revenues** Accented on second syllable.

101 **them** i.e. Lear's knights.

103 **assure thee** be assured.

105 **child-like office** filial service.

106 **bewray** expose, reveal.

111–12 **Make . . . please** i.e. carry out your plan to capture Edgar, using whatever means in my name you please.

How in my strength you please. For you, Edmond,
Whose virtue and obedience doth this instant
So much commend itself, you shall be ours;
Natures of such deep trust we shall much need;   115
You we first seize on.

EDMOND   I shall serve you, sir,
Truly, however else.

GLOUCESTER   For him I thank your grace.

CORNWALL   You know not why we came to visit you?

REGAN   Thus out of season, threading dark-eyed night?
Occasions, noble Gloucester, of some prize,   120
Wherein we must have use of your advice.
Our father he hath writ, so hath our sister,
Of differences, which I best thought it fit
To answer from our home. The several messengers
From hence attend dispatch. Our good old friend,   125
Lay comforts to your bosom and bestow
Your needful counsel to our businesses,
Which craves the instant use.

GLOUCESTER   I serve you, madam;
Your graces are right welcome.

                                          Exeunt. Flourish

116–17 I . . . else.] *Pope's lineation; one line* Q, F   116 sir] F; *not in* Q   119 threading] F; threatning Q   120 prize] F; prise Q *uncorr.;* poyse Q *corr.*   123 differences] F, Q *corr.;* defences Q *uncorr.*   123 best] F, Q *uncorr.;* lest Q *corr.*   *123 thought] Q; though F   124 home] F, Q *corr.;* hand Q *uncorr.*   126–8 Lay . . . use.] F *lineation; two lines divided* councell / To Q   127 businesses] F; busines Q   128–9 I . . . welcome] F; *one line* Q   129 SD] F; (*Exeunt* Q (*after* vse, *127*)

114 ours The royal plural.
115 we . . . need Cornwall alludes to impending broils with either Lear or Albany (Hunter).
116 seize on 'take legal possession of (a vassal)' (NS); but Cornwall may not be using the term technically.
118 you? Many editions (e.g. Muir, Oxford) follow Rowe and change the question mark to a dash, making Regan cut Cornwall off in mid speech. But by interposing herself and relegating Cornwall to second fiddle, Regan does not necessarily interrupt her husband (NS).
119 out of season i.e. untimely travel by night.
119 threading dark-eyed night A precise metaphor conveying the difficulties of travel along unlit roads and byways, with a quibble on the eye of a needle (NS).
120 prize importance. See collation. Oxford reads 'poise': Taylor argues, against Greg, that here

and again at 123 Q's press-corrections are authoritative and were simply overlooked by the F collator ('Date and authorship', pp. 362–3). Duthie, pp. 139–40, rejects Q corr. 'poyse', since he believes F's 'prize' came from a playhouse manuscript.
123 which Not the differences, or quarrels, but the letters (Delius, cited by Muir).
124 To . . . home Regan leaves her home so that she will have an easier way to put Lear off and to consult with Gonerill. But, dramaturgically, her arrival and Cornwall's at Gloucester's castle bring all the principal characters of the main plot together (except Cordelia and Albany) for the climactic episodes that end this act and the next (Bradley, p. 449).
124 from i.e. away from.
125 attend dispatch are waiting to be sent back (with replies).
128 craves . . . use demands immediate action.

2.2 *Enter* KENT *[disguised] and* OSWALD, *severally*

OSWALD   Good dawning to thee, friend. Art of this house?
KENT   Ay.
OSWALD   Where may we set our horses?
KENT   I'th'mire.
OSWALD   Prithee, if thou lov'st me, tell me.   5
KENT   I love thee not.
OSWALD   Why, then I care not for thee.
KENT   If I had thee in Lipsbury pinfold, I would make thee care for
   me.
OSWALD   Why dost thou use me thus? I know thee not.   10
KENT   Fellow, I know thee.
OSWALD   What dost thou know me for?
KENT   A knave, a rascal, an eater of broken meats, a base, proud,
   shallow, beggarly, three-suited, hundred-pound, filthy worsted-
   stocking knave; a lily-livered, action-taking, whoreson glass-   15
   gazing, superserviceable, finical rogue; one-trunk-inheriting

---

Act 2, Scene 2   2.2] *Scena Secunda.* F; *not in* Q   0 SD] *severally*] F; *not in* Q   1 dawning] F; deuen Q *uncorr.;* euen Q *corr.*   1 this] F; the Q   5 lov'st] F; loue Q   *14 three-suited, hundred-pound,] three snyted hundred pound Q *uncorr.;* three shewted hundred pound Q *corr.;* three-suited-hundred pound F; three-suited, hundred pound F2   14–15 worsted-stocking] woosted-stocking F; wosted stocken Q *uncorr.;* worsted-stocken Q *corr.*   15 action-taking] F; action taking knaue, a Q   16 superserviceable, finical] F; superfinicall Q   *16 one-trunk-inheriting] F3; one truncke inheriting Q; one Trunke-inheriting F, F2

Act 2, Scene 2

1 **dawning** Q uncorr. 'deuen' (colloquial) was unnecessarily changed to Q corr. 'euen' (NS). F's neologism, 'Good dawning', is 'possibly an invention . . . to suit Oswald's euphuistic style' (Stone, p. 194). In any event, as 26–7 indicate, it is night-time before dawn.

1 **of this house** i.e. a servant here. Why Kent answers affirmatively is not clear, unless it is to give occasion for further attacks on Oswald (Hunter).

5 **if . . . me** A conventional, if affected, way of saying please (Hunter).

7–8 **care . . . care** A quibble: (1) like, (2) heed (NS).

8 **Lipsbury pinfold** Probably a pun on 'between my teeth' (Nares, cited by Furness). No town of Lipsbury is known; 'pinfold' = pound, or pen, for confining stray cattle or sheep.

10 **use** treat.

13 **broken meats** Leftover food or scraps, such as a menial would eat.

14 **three-suited** Servingmen were allotted three suits of clothes. Compare 3.4.120–2 and Jonson, *Epicoene, or The Silent Woman* 3.1.38–42 (Mrs Otter scolds her husband, whom she treats as a dependant): 'Who giues you your maintenance,

I pray you? Who allowes you your horsemeat, and man's-meat? your three sutes of apparell a yeere? your foure paire of stockings, one silke, three worsted?' (Wright, following Steevens; cited by Furness).

14 **hundred-pound** A large amount for a servingman, but probably a hit at James I's profuse creation of knights (Muir). Compare Middleton's *The Phoenix* 4.3.55: 'How's this? am I used like a hundred-pound gentleman?' (Steevens, cited by Furness).

14–15 **worsted-stocking** Silk stockings were very dear; servingmen wore woollen ones.

15 **lily-livered** cowardly.

15 **action-taking** i.e. preferring litigation to fighting.

15–16 **glass-gazing** given to self-admiration, vain.

16 **superserviceable** ready and willing to serve beyond one's duties, even dishonourably (Kent soon calls him a bawd and a pander). Compare 4.5.240–2.

16 **finical** fussily fastidious.

16 **one-trunk-inheriting** possessing only enough things to fill a single trunk.

slave; one that wouldst be a bawd in way of good service, and
art nothing but the composition of a knave, beggar, coward,
pander, and the son and heir of a mongrel bitch, one whom
I will beat into clamorous whining if thou deniest the least   20
syllable of thy addition.

OSWALD Why, what a monstrous fellow art thou, thus to rail on
one that is neither known of thee nor knows thee!

KENT What a brazen-faced varlet art thou to deny thou knowest
me! Is it two days since I tripped up thy heels and beat thee   25
before the king? Draw, you rogue! For though it be night, yet
the moon shines. I'll make a sop o'th'moonshine of you,
[*Drawing his sword*] you whoreson cullionly barber-monger,
draw!

OSWALD Away, I have nothing to do with thee.   30

KENT Draw, you rascal. You come with letters against the king,
and take Vanity the puppet's part against the royalty of her
father. Draw, you rogue, or I'll so carbonado your shanks –
draw, you rascal, come your ways!

OSWALD Help, ho, murder, help!   35

KENT Strike, you slave! Stand, rogue! Stand, you neat slave, strike!

OSWALD Help, ho, murder, murder!

---

19 one] F; *not in* F Q   *20 clamorous] Q *corr.*; clamarous Q *uncorr.*; clamours F   20 deniest] F; denie Q   21 thy] F; the
Q   22 Why] F; *not in* Q   23 that is] F; that's Q   23 thee!] thee. Q; thee? F   24 brazen-faced] F; brazen fac't Q   25 me!]
mee, Q; me? F   25 days . . . thee] F; dayes agoe since I beat thee, and tript vp thy heeles Q   26 yet] F; *not in* Q   27 o'th']
F; of the Q   27 of you] F; a'you, draw Q   28 SD] *After 29, Rowe; not in* Q, F   31 come with] F; bring Q   *33 shanks –]
Rowe; shankes, Q; shanks, F   36 strike!] strike? Q *corr.*; strike. Q *uncorr.*, F   37 murder, murder!] murther, murther. F;
murther, helpe. Q

---

17 be a bawd . . . service i.e. do anything, no
matter how dishonourable, and consider it good
service.

18 composition compound.

19 heir 'A fine touch! – not merely the *son*,
but the *heir*, inheriting all the mongrel's qualities'
(Kittredge).

21 addition A mark of distinction, something
added to a man's name or coat-of-arms to denote
his rank, title (Onions); here used ironically.

24 varlet rogue, rascal.

27 sop o'th'moonshine Kent threatens to beat
Oswald so badly that he will be worthless except to
soak up moonlight. He may also allude to sopping
up 'eggs in moonshine', a dish of fried eggs and
onions (Nares, cited by Furness).

28 cullionly despicable.

28 barber-monger frequenter of barbershops;
hence, a vain fop.

32 Vanity the puppet's part Vanity as a proud,
self-admiring woman was emblematic, virtually

interchangeable with the figure of Pride (one of the
Seven Deadly Sins). The figure appears often in
Renaissance iconography, though not in any extant
Morality plays, as commentators (following Johnson) have been misled into believing (Meagher,
pp. 252–3). Kent refers to Gonerill thus because
as part of her costume she wears a hand-mirror
(compare 3.2.33–4); but Meagher fails to connect
Gonerill's vanity with her servant Oswald's, which
Kent detests. 'Puppet' is also a 'contemptuous term
for a person (usually a woman)' (*OED* sv *sb* 1,
cited by NS). Compare 'poppet' = darling, pet,
or dolled-up woman.

33 carbonado cut crosswise for broiling.

34 come your ways come on, come along; as
in *Tro.* 3.2.44. Kent tries to get Oswald to fight,
but he comically keeps backing away, refusing the
encounter. (Some editors follow Rowe and insert a
SD after 36: *Beats him.*)

36 neat elegant, foppish.

Enter EDMOND, CORNWALL, REGAN, GLOUCESTER, *Servants*

EDMOND   How now, what's the matter? Part!

KENT   With you, goodman boy, if you please; come, I'll flesh ye;
come on, young master.   40

GLOUCESTER   Weapons? Arms? What's the matter here?

CORNWALL   Keep peace, upon your lives; he dies that strikes
again. What is the matter?

REGAN   The messengers from our sister and the king?

CORNWALL   What is your difference – speak!   45

OSWALD   I am scarce in breath, my lord.

KENT   No marvel, you have so bestirred your valour, you cowardly
rascal. Nature disclaims in thee: a tailor made thee.

CORNWALL   Thou art a strange fellow – a tailor make a man?

KENT   A tailor, sir, a stone-cutter, or a painter could not have made   50
him so ill, though they had been but two years o'th'trade.

CORNWALL   Speak yet, how grew your quarrel?

OSWALD   This ancient ruffian, sir, whose life I have spared at suit
of his grey beard –

KENT   Thou whoreson zed, thou unnecessary letter! My lord, if you   55
will give me leave, I will tread this unbolted villain into mortar
and daub the wall of a jakes with him. Spare my grey beard,
you wagtail?

37 SD] F; *Enter Edmond with his rapier drawne, Gloster the Duke and Dutchesse.* Q   38 Part!] Part. F; *not in* Q   39 if] F;
and Q   39 ye] F; you Q   43 What is] F; what's Q   44 king?] F; King. Q   45 What is] F; Whats Q   50 A] F; I, a Q   51
they] F; hee Q   51 years] F; houres Q   51 o'th'] o'th' F3; oth' F, F2; at the Q   52 SH] F; *Glost.* Q   53 ruffian] F; ruffen
Q   *54 grey beard –] *Rowe* (subst.); gray-beard. Q, F   55–6 you will] F; you'l Q   57 wall] F; walles Q

37 SD Since Edmond's name precedes those of
the others, who outrank him, he may actually enter
first and try to separate Kent and Oswald (who may
have drawn his sword by now). Oxford alters the
SD accordingly. See collation: in Q, Edmond enters
with his rapier drawne.

39 With you Kent here turns to Edmond, chal-
lenging him.

39 goodman boy A contemptuous term of
address for a presumptuous young man.

39 flesh initiate (i.e. into tasting blood, fighting);
as in *1H4* 5.4.130.

45 difference quarrel.

48 disclaims in thee disavows, renounces having any part in you.

48 a tailor made thee Referring to Oswald's
fancy clothes but hollow character, Kent alludes
to the proverb, 'The tailor makes the man' (Tilley
T17), as Guiderius does in *Cym.* 4.2.81–3, describing Cloten.

51 years Q's 'houres' is a vulgarisation; 'Shake-

speare knows that art is long' (Greg, *Editorial Problem*, p. 91).

55 unnecessary letter The letter *z* is 'unnecessary' because its function is largely taken over by
s; dictionaries of the time ignored the letter, which
is not used in Latin (Muir). As a parasite, Oswald
is 'unnecessary'.

56 unbolted (1) unsifted (of flour or cement),
hence (2) unmitigated, or (3) undiscovered,
unexamined; (4) released of fetters or bolts (as a
villain should not be); (5) effeminate, impotent (i.e.
lacking a 'bolt').

57 jakes privy.

58 wagtail '(used as a term of contempt) obsequious person' (Onions); compare *OED* sv *sb* 3b,
'contemptuous term for a profligate or inconstant
woman'. Oswald is too scared to stand still and,
hopping about, resembles the actions of a bird,
the wagtail (Kittredge). Kent may also strike out
against him again, prompting Cornwall's response.

CORNWALL Peace, sirrah.
    You beastly knave, know you no reverence?   60
KENT Yes, sir, but anger hath a privilege.
CORNWALL Why art thou angry?
KENT That such a slave as this should wear a sword,
    Who wears no honesty. Such smiling rogues as these,
    Like rats, oft bite the holy cords a-twain,   65
    Which are too intrince t'unloose; smooth every passion
    That in the natures of their lords rebel,
    Being oil to fire, snow to the colder moods,
    Renege, affirm, and turn their halcyon beaks
    With every gall and vary of their masters,   70
    Knowing naught, like dogs, but following.
    A plague upon your epileptic visage!
    Smile you my speeches, as I were a fool?

59–60 Peace . . . reverence?] F *lineation; one line* Q 60 know you] F; you haue Q 61 hath] F; has Q 64 Who] F; That Q 65 the holy] F; those Q 65 a-twain] F; in twaine Q *66 too intrince] *Capell;* to intrench, Q; t'intrince, F 66 t'unloose] F; to inloose Q 68 Being] F; Bring Q 68 fire] F; stir Q 68 the] F; their Q *69 Renege] Reneag Q; Reuenge F 70 gall] F; gale Q 71–3 Knowing . . . fool?] F *lineation; two lines divided* epilepticke [*turned over*] / Visage Q 71 dogs] F; dayes Q 73 Smile] smoyle Q; Smoile F

---

61 anger . . . privilege Tilley L458, citing *John* 4.3.32: 'Impatience hath his privilege' (NS).

63 sword A symbol of manhood.

64 smiling rogues Compare *Ham.* 1.5.105–7, where Hamlet refers to Claudius as 'a smiling damned villain'.

65 rats, oft bite Compare Tilley M135: 'A mouse in time may bite in two a cable' (NS).

65 holy cords i.e. sanctified bonds (of matrimony). 'Kent hints that Oswald is "duteous to the vices" of his mistress' (NS).

65 a-twain in two.

66 too intrince too intertwined, tightly bound (compare 'intrinsicate', *Ant.* 5.2.304, and Stone, pp. 52–3). F's contraction may have been influenced, wrongly, by the contraction later of the preposition. *t'* for the adverb is not normal (*Textual Companion*, p. 534), though it is common for the preposition. Both words could be spelled the same, as they are in Q. (Compare Doran, p. 93, and Duthie, pp. 385–7.) Moreover, 'are' should be elided so that 'too' receives the accent.

66 smooth flatter, humour (Onions).

67 rebel i.e. against reason, which should control the passions.

68 Being Although in NS Duthie withdrew his earlier defence of F, his argument still makes excellent sense. Citing *2H6* 5.2.51–5, he says that 'flatterers *are* oil to the flame of their masters' wrath . . . just as when their masters are in, say,

a melancholy mood, which is a cold mood, the flatterers are snow to that mood, keep it cold' (pp. 142–3).

69 Renege Deny. Compare 4.5.94–7. Q is clearly right here; F results from Compositor E's misreading copy (Doran, p. 91; compare Duthie, pp. 13–14).

69 halcyon beaks The bird is the kingfisher, which when hung up by the neck or tail could serve as a weathervane. Compare Marlowe's *The Jew of Malta* 1.1.38–9: 'But now how stands the wind? / Into what corner peeres my Halcion's bill?' (Steevens, cited by Furness). Flatterers thus shift with their masters' passions.

70 gall and vary Most editors accept Q's 'gale' and treat the words as hendiadys. Duthie cites *OED*'s reference to 'gall-wind' and retains 'gall', since his is an old-spelling edition (NS adopts 'gale'). Oxford reads 'gall' (= 'a state of mental soreness or irritation', *OED sb²* 2), despite F2's emendation supporting Q (*Textual Companion*, p. 534). The hendiadys may then signify 'varying irritation', a less easy metaphor but not less Shakespearean.

72 epileptic visage 'Oswald pale, and trembling with fright, was yet smiling and trying to put on a look of lofty unconcern' (Muir).

73 Smile you i.e. smile you at.

73 as as if.

Goose, if I had you upon Sarum Plain,
I'd drive ye cackling home to Camelot.   75
CORNWALL   What, art thou mad, old fellow?
GLOUCESTER   How fell you out? Say that.
KENT   No contraries hold more antipathy
      Than I and such a knave.
CORNWALL   Why dost thou call him knave?
      What is his fault?
KENT   His countenance likes me not.   80
CORNWALL   No more perchance does mine, nor his, nor hers.
KENT   Sir, 'tis my occupation to be plain.
      I have seen better faces in my time
      Than stands on any shoulder that I see
      Before me at this instant.
CORNWALL   This is some fellow   85
      Who, having been praised for bluntness, doth affect
      A saucy roughness, and constrains the garb
      Quite from his nature. He cannot flatter, he;
      An honest mind and plain, he must speak truth.
      And they will take it, so; if not, he's plain.   90
      These kind of knaves I know, which in this plainness
      Harbour more craft and more corrupter ends
      Than twenty silly-ducking observants
      That stretch their duties nicely.

74 if] F; and Q   75 drive ye] F; send you Q   79–80 Why . . . fault?] F *lineation; one line* Q   80 What is] F; what's Q   80 fault?] F; offence. Q   81 nor . . . nor] F; or . . . or Q   84 Than] Then F; That Q   85–94 This . . . nicely.] F *lineation; nine verse lines ending* . . . praysd / . . . ruffines, / . . . nature, / . . . plaine, / . . . so, / . . . know / . . . craft, / . . . ducking / . . . nisely. Q   85 some] F; a Q   87 roughness] F; ruffiness Q   89 An . . . plain,] F; he must be plaine, Q   *90 take it,] *Rowe*; take it F; tak't Q   93 silly-ducking] F; silly ducking Q

74–5 **Goose . . . Camelot** Though the passage is variously interpreted, the main sense is clear. Oswald's laughter suggests the cackling of a goose and hence associations with Sarum (= Salisbury) Plain, not far from Winchester, where Camelot may have been located. But it is not certain that geese were, in fact, found on Sarum Plain, or why Shakespeare should make that association. Capell suspected an allusion to 'Winchester goose', i.e. a syphilitic person, but Muir thinks the association must have been largely unconscious and doubts that it would have been picked up by an audience. Compare E. A. Armstrong, *Shakespeare's Imagination*, 1963, pp. 57–8.
  80 **likes** pleases.
  86 **affect** put on, assume.
  87–8 **constrains . . . nature** i.e. he distorts the

style of plain speech from its inherent function, sincerity, and makes it a cloak for craftiness and corrupt ends (92) (Clarke, cited by Furness). In Shakespeare 'garb' = 'style, fashion (of speech or behaviour); never = "fashion in dress" ' (NS).
  88 **his** its.
  90 **And . . . plain** i.e. if people will take it, fine; if not, his excuse is that he's plainspoken.
  92 **craft** craftiness.
  92 **more corrupter** Double comparatives, like double superlatives, are common in Shakespearean and Elizabethan usage.
  93 **silly-ducking observants** obsequious servants who foolishly keep bowing.
  94 **stretch . . . nicely** strain the exercise of their duties to a fine point.

KENT Sir, in good faith, in sincere verity,   95
    Under th'allowance of your great aspect,
    Whose influence like the wreath of radiant fire
    On flick'ring Phoebus' front –
CORNWALL   What mean'st by this?
KENT To go out of my dialect, which you discommend so much. I
    know, sir, I am no flatterer. He that beguiled you in a plain   100
    accent was a plain knave, which for my part I will not be,
    though I should win your displeasure to entreat me to't.
CORNWALL What was th'offence you gave him?
OSWALD I never gave him any.
    It pleased the king his master very late   105
    To strike at me upon his misconstruction,
    When he, compact, and flattering his displeasure,
    Tripped me behind; being down, insulted, railed,
    And put upon him such a deal of man
    That worthied him, got praises of the king   110
    For him attempting who was self-subdued,
    And in the fleshment of this dread exploit
    Drew on me here again.

---

95 faith] F; sooth Q   95 in] F; or in Q   96 great] F; graund Q   *98 flick'ring] *Duthie* (*subst.*); flitkering Q; flicking F; flickering *Pope*   *98 front –] *Rowe*; front. Q, F   98 mean'st] F; mean'st thou Q   99 dialect] F; dialogue Q   103 What was th'] F; What's the Q   104–6 I . . . misconstruction,] F *lineation; two verse lines divided* maister / Very Q   107 compact,] F; coniunct Q   109 man] F; man, that, Q   112 fleshment] F; flechuent Q   *112 dread] Q; dead F

95–8 Sir . . . front Kent parodies the style and manner of one of the 'silly-ducking observants', adopting the idiom of an Oswald (or an Osric).

95 sincere verity A deliberate redundancy for 'good faith'.

96 aspect (1) countenance, (2) astral position and influence (in astrology); accent is on the second syllable. Kent's inflated speech compares Cornwall to a powerful planet or star.

97 influence Another astrological term (compare 1.2.110).

98 Phoebus' front The sun's forehead. Phoebus was the sun god.

99 dialect idiom, manner of speaking.

100–1 He . . . knave Kent alludes to the person Cornwall described above, 85–94, and disassociates himself accordingly.

102–2 though . . . to't Unsatisfactorily explained. Kent probably means that nothing, not even the incentive of Cornwall's further displeasure, could induce him to be the kind of 'plain knave' Cornwall has described.

105 very late most recently.

106 misconstruction misunderstanding, misconstruing.

107 compact in league with, in cahoots with (the king).

108 being . . . railed i.e. I being down, he insulted and railed at me.

109 put . . . man i.e. struck such an attitude of manliness.

110 That worthied him Either (1) that it made him appear very worthy, (2) that it raised him to honour or distinction (Onions), or (3) that it made a hero of him (NS). It is not clear, as Muir notes, whether the verb derives from the adjective (Abbott), or from the noun 'worthy' = hero (Schmidt), or from Middle English *wurthien* = dignify (Perrett).

111 For . . . subdued 'For attacking a man who offered no resistance' (NS).

112 fleshment 'Excitement resulting from a first success' (Onions). Compare 39 above.

112 dread exploit Oswald speaks ironically.

KENT   None of these rogues and cowards
But Ajax is their fool.
CORNWALL   Fetch forth the stocks!
You stubborn, ancient knave, you reverend braggart,   115
We'll teach you.
KENT   Sir, I am too old to learn:
Call not your stocks for me. I serve the king,
On whose employment I was sent to you.
You shall do small respects, show too bold malice
Against the grace and person of my master,   120
Stocking his messenger.
CORNWALL   Fetch forth the stocks!
As I have life and honour, there shall he sit till noon.
REGAN   Till noon? Till night, my lord, and all night too.
KENT   Why, madam, if I were your father's dog,
You should not use me so.
REGAN   Sir, being his knave, I will.   125
                    Stocks brought out
CORNWALL   This is a fellow of the selfsame colour
Our sister speaks of. Come, bring away the stocks.
GLOUCESTER   Let me beseech your grace not to do so.
The king his master needs must take it ill

113–14 None . . . fool.] F *lineation; one line* Q   114 Ajax] F; A'Iax Q   114 Fetch] F; Bring Q   114 stocks!] F; stockes
ho? Q   115 ancient] F; ausrent Q *uncorr.;* miscreant Q *corr.*   116–18 Sir . . . you.] F *lineation; two lines divided* me, / I
Q   116 Sir,] F; *not in* Q   118 employment] F; imployments Q   119 shall] F; should Q   119 respects] F; respect Q   121
Stocking] F; Stobing Q *uncorr.;* Stopping Q *corr.*   121–2 Fetch . . . noon.] F *lineation; divided* honour, / There Q   122
sit] F, Q *corr.;* set Q *uncorr.*   124–5 Why . . . so.] F *lineation; as prose* Q   125 should] F; could Q   125 SD] F; *after 127,*
Dyce and most later editors (except Oxford); *not in* Q   126 colour] F; nature Q   127 speaks] F; speake Q   128 so.] so, Q, F
(F *omits four lines here*)   129–31 The . . . restrained.] F *lineation; two lines divided* valued / In Q   129 his master needs]
F; *not in* Q

114 **Ajax** Kent's muttered response arouses
Cornwall's fierce outburst because he believes Kent
identifies him with the foolish Greek warrior who
is easily duped by others (as in *Tro.*) (NS). Kent's
pun, intentional or otherwise ('Ajax' – 'a jakes'),
does not help matters.

114 **stocks** An ancient form of punishment for
servants. In the fifth Earl of Huntington's household, disorderliness or unseemly behaviour towards
one's betters was punished first by a spell in the
stocks, as recorded in Rawdon Hastings MSS. iv
(G. M. Young, *Times Literary Supplement*, 30 Sept.
1949, p. 633; cited by Muir).

115 **reverend** old. Cornwall is being sarcastic.

117 **I . . . king** Kent reminds Cornwall that he
is not his servant, but the king's (and thus should
be treated with more consideration).

120 **grace and person** The position he holds
as king and himself personally.

125 **should** would.

125 **being** i.e. since you are.

126 **colour** stripe, complexion.

127 **sister** i.e. Gonerill. Elizabethans took the
marriage ceremony literally, husband and wife
becoming 'one flesh'; hence, a sister-in-law was a
sister.

127 **Come . . . stocks** Some editors take this as
the cue to bring out the stocks and move the previous SD (125) here. But the change is unnecessary;
Cornwall sees the stocks at this point and directs
them to be brought up.

129–31 **The king . . . restrained** For F's revision and cuts here and at 133, see Textual Analysis,
p. 267 below.

That he, so slightly valued in his messenger,   130
Should have him thus restrained.
CORNWALL   I'll answer that.
REGAN   My sister may receive it much more worse
   To have her gentleman abused, assaulted.
                              [*Kent is put in the stocks*]
CORNWALL   Come, my lord, away.
                     [*Exeunt all but Gloucester and Kent*]
GLOUCESTER   I am sorry for thee, friend; 'tis the duke's pleasure,   135
   Whose disposition all the world well knows
   Will not be rubbed nor stopped. I'll entreat for thee.
KENT   Pray do not, sir. I have watched and travelled hard.
   Some time I shall sleep out, the rest I'll whistle.
   A good man's fortune may grow out at heels.   140
   Give you good morrow.
GLOUCESTER   The duke's to blame in this; 'twill be ill taken.   *Exit*
KENT   Good king, that must approve the common saw,
   Thou out of heaven's benediction com'st
   To the warm sun.   145
   Approach, thou beacon to this under globe,
   That by thy comfortable beams I may

---

130 he] F; hee's Q   133 gentleman] F; Gentlemen Q   133 assaulted.] F; assalted Q; F *omits one line here*   133 SD] *After*
134, Rowe; not in Q, F   134 SH] F; *not in* Q, *where line is part of Regan's speech*   134 my] F; my good Q   134 SD] *Dyce;*
Exit. F; *not in* Q   *135 duke's*] Dukes Q; Duke F   138 Pray] F; Pray you Q   139 out] F; ont Q   142 The . . . taken.] Q
lineation; two lines divided this, / 'Twill F   *142 to*] Q; too F   142 taken] F; tooke Q   142 SD] F; *not in* Q   143 saw] F,
Q *corr.;* say Q *uncorr.*   144 com'st] F; comest Q

133 SD *Kent . . . stocks* '[T]he Morality-play
icon of virtue martyred in the stocks becomes an
icon of social transposition, of the confusion of
moral values' (Salingar, p. 99; compare Mack, pp.
55–6).
   134 *Come . . . away* Cornwall addresses
Gloucester who, unhappy about the situation,
remains behind for a few moments.
   137 *rubbed* A term from bowls, meaning
impeded or deflected. Kittredge compares *R2*
3.4.3–5.
   138 *watched* stayed awake, been up.
   140 *A good . . . heels* With mordant humour
Kent reflects that the usual metaphor, or saying,
has become reality, for him, being in the stocks
(Furness). Compare Tilley H389. Colie compares
Job 13–27.
   141 *Give* i.e. may God give.
   142 *to blame* to be blamed; but see collation

and compare 1.2.41, where 'too blame' = too
blameworthy.
   143 *approve* confirm, prove the truth of.
   143 *saw* saying, proverb.
   144–5 *Thou . . . sun* Proverbial for going from
good to bad (compare Tilley G272, who quotes
Florio: '"Da baiante a ferrante": From bad to
worse, out of gods blessing into the warme sun,
out of the parlor into the kitchin'). Perhaps used
ironically: bad as Gonerill is, Lear is heading for
worse. Muir cites *King Leir* 1154: 'he came from
bad to worse'. Daybreak reminds Kent of the
proverb.
   146 *thou beacon* The sun. Its beams may be
'comfortable' (147), i.e. comforting, in so far as they
will provide light for Kent to read Cordelia's letter,
whereas 'the warm sun' (145) in context suggests
less beneficent exposure to the elements.

Peruse this letter. Nothing almost sees miracles
But misery. I know 'tis from Cordelia,
Who hath most fortunately been informed   150
Of my obscurèd course, and shall find time
For this enormous state, seeking to give
Losses their remedies. All weary and o'er-watched,
Take vantage, heavy eyes, not to behold
This shameful lodging. Fortune, goodnight,   155
Smile once more, turn thy wheel. [*He sleeps*]

2.3 *Enter* EDGAR

EDGAR I heard myself proclaimed,
And by the happy hollow of a tree
Escaped the hunt. No port is free, no place
That guard and most unusual vigilance
Does not attend my taking. Whiles I may 'scape   5
I will preserve myself, and am bethought

---

148 miracles] F; my rackles Q *uncorr.*; my wracke Q *corr.*   **150** most] F, Q *corr.*; not Q *uncorr.*   *151 course, and] Q; course. And F   *152 For] *Rowe;* From Q, F   **152** enormous] F; enormious Q   **153** their] F, Q *corr.*; and Q *uncorr.*   **153** o'er-watched] F; ouerwatch Q   **154** Take] F, Q *corr.*; Late Q *uncorr.*   **156** Smile once more,] F; smile, once more Q   *156 SD] *sleepes* Q; *not in* F   **Act 2, Scene 3   2.3]** *Steevens; not in* Q, F *(see Commentary)*   **1** heard] F; heare Q   **4** unusual] Q; vnusall Q2, F   **5** Does] F; Dost Q   **5** Whiles] F; while Q

148–9 Nothing . . . misery The most miserable are almost the only ones to witness miracles ('for, when we are in despair, any relief seems miraculous' (Kittredge)).

151–3 and . . . remedies A famous crux. Many editors follow Jennens and assume that Kent is reading excerpts from Cordelia's letter, or that the passage is corrupt and some words are missing. Perhaps Kent cannot fully make out the contents of the letter since it is not yet light enough (Muir). But such considerations may be irrelevant: 'Who' (150) can be understood as the subject of this clause, too. Rowe's emendation, 'For' for 'From', is simple and easy and makes sense of the lines (*Textual Companion*, p. 515).

152 enormous state monstrous situation, one full of enormities.

153 o'er-watched exhausted, used too much for 'watching'; compare 138 above.

154 Take vantage Take advantage (of your fatigue and fall asleep).

155 shameful lodging i.e. the stocks.

156 turn thy wheel Compare 5.3.164, where

Edmond also refers to Fortune's wheel.

156 SD He sleeps The SD, from Q, indicates that Kent remains asleep in the stocks as Edgar enters and gives his soliloquy. Modern editors follow Q, keeping Kent on stage (as he would have been at the Globe) during Edgar's speech. 'The juxtaposition is symbolic, not illusionistic, making a point about two banished men who must disguise themselves and endure humiliation while villains prosper' (D. Bevington, *Action Is Eloquence*, 1984, p. 121).

Act 2, Scene 3
0 SD Although the action is continuous, and probably the Globe stage would not be cleared, Edgar's soliloquy warrants a scene to itself; therefore, I preserve the traditional scene numbering.
1 proclaimed publicly declared (an outlaw).
2 happy opportune.
3 port Compare 2.1.79, where Gloucester orders all ports closed to Edgar.
5 attend my taking stand ready to capture me.
6 am bethought have an idea.

To take the basest and most poorest shape
That ever penury in contempt of man
Brought near to beast. My face I'll grime with filth,
Blanket my loins, elf all my hairs in knots,   10
And with presented nakedness outface
The winds and persecutions of the sky.
The country gives me proof and precedent
Of Bedlam beggars, who with roaring voices
Strike in their numbed and mortifièd arms,   15
Pins, wooden pricks, nails, sprigs of rosemary;
And with this horrible object, from low farms,
Poor pelting villages, sheep-cotes, and mills,
Sometimes with lunatic bans, sometime with prayers,
Enforce their charity. 'Poor Turlygod! Poor Tom!'   20
That's something yet: Edgar I nothing am.   *Exit*

---

10 elf] F; else Q   10 hairs in] F; haire with Q   12 winds] F; wind Q   12 persecutions] F; persecution Q   15 numbed
. . . arms] F; numb'd and mortified bare armes Q *corr;* numb'd mortified bare armes Q *uncorr.*   16 Pins] F, Q *corr.;* Pies
Q *uncorr.*   16 wooden pricks] wodden prickes Q; Wodden-prickes F   17 from] F, Q *corr.,* Q2; frame Q *uncorr.*   17 farms]
F; seruice Q   *18 sheep-cotes] sheep-coates Q; Sheeps-Coates F   19 Sometimes] F; Sometime Q   20 Turlygod] F, Q
corr., Q2; *Tuelygod* Q *uncorr.*

8 in contempt of man holding humanity in
contempt.

10 elf twist, tangle into 'elflocks' (*Rom.* 1.4.90).

11 presented exposed, exhibited.

11 outface brave, confront. As Edgar utters
these lines, he strips off his clothes and decorates
himself accordingly. The action is moreover significant if Edgar throws off conspicuously rich attire
(as a nobleman's son) to become 'nothing'. 'On this
pivot, Edgar's inward journey turns: he gives up,
not only clothes and person, but also a way of life,
from best to worst, and the peripety is evidently
steep' (Rosenberg, p. 151).

13 proof example.

14 Bedlam beggars 'Abram men', or
vagabonds, who feigned madness or who actually
were discharged from Bedlam (i.e. Bethlehem
Hospital, the lunatic asylum in London) and
licensed to beg. Furness cites Awdeley's *Frater-
nitye of Vacabondes* (1565): 'An Abraham man is
he that walketh bare armed, and bare legged, and
fayneth hym selfe mad, and caryeth a packe of
wool, or a stycke with baken on it, or such lyke
toy, and nameth himself poore Tom.' Furness also
quotes a longer passage adapted from Harman's
Caueat or Warening for Commen Cvrsetors (1567)

in Dekker's *Belman of London* (1608), which
gives a more detailed description corroborating
Shakespeare's.

15 numbed i.e. with cold.

15 mortifièd deadened to pain. See collation.
Duthie accepts the Q reading, which 'adds an effective touch to the picture' (it also helps the metre),
and explains F's omission as compositor oversight
(p. 175). But accenting *-ed* in 'mortified' makes the
metre regular.

16 pricks skewers.

17 object spectacle.

17 low lowly, humble.

18 pelting paltry, mean.

19 bans curses.

20 Turlygod Unexplained. Oxford prefers Q
uncorr. 'Tuelygod' and suggests some possible
derivations for the word (*Textual Companion*,
pp. 515–16). See collation.

21 That's . . . am i.e. Poor Tom is at least something, however base and despicable; I renounce my
identity as Edgar, who is doomed in any case.
The rhyme, 'Tom' – 'am', is probably dialectal
(Kökeritz, p. 224; compare Cercignani, pp. 113–
14); Edgar doubtless means to disguise his voice as
well as his person.

2.4 *Enter* LEAR, FOOL, *and* GENTLEMAN

LEAR 'Tis strange that they should so depart from home
   And not send back my messenger.
GENTLEMAN   As I learned,
   The night before there was no purpose in them
   Of this remove.
KENT [*Waking*]   Hail to thee, noble master.
LEAR Ha!   5
   Mak'st thou this shame thy pastime?
KENT   No, my lord.
FOOL Ha, ha, he wears cruel garters. Horses are tied by the heads,
   dogs and bears by th'neck, monkeys by th'loins, and men by
   th'legs: when a man's overlusty at legs, then he wears wooden
   nether-stocks.   10
LEAR What's he that hath so much thy place mistook
   To set thee here?
KENT   It is both he and she,
   Your son and daughter.
LEAR No.
KENT Yes.   15
LEAR No, I say.
KENT I say, yea.

Act 2, Scene 4 2.4] *Steevens; not in* Q, F   0 SD] F; *Enter King.* Q   1 home] F; hence Q   *2 messenger] Q; Messengers
F   2 SH] F; *Knight.* Q   2–4 As . . . remove.] F; *two lines divided* was / No Q   3 in them] F; *not in* Q   4 this] F; his Q   4
SD] *Staunton; not in* Q, F   5–6 Ha! . . . pastime] *Steevens's lineation; one line* Q, F   5 Ha!] F; How, Q   6 thy] Q; ahy
F   6 KENT No, my lord.] F; *not in* Q   7–10 Ha, ha . . . nether-stocks.] *As prose* F; *five verse lines ending* . . . garters, /
. . . beares / . . . men / . . . at legs, / . . . neatherstockes Q   7 he] F; looke he Q   7 heads] F; heeles Q   8 by th'neck]
F; Byt'h necke Q   8 by th'loins] F; bit'h loynes Q   8–9 by th'legs:] F; Byt'h legges, Q   *9 man's] mans Q; man F   9
wooden] Q; wodden F   11–12 What's . . . here?] *Rowe's lineation; three lines ending* . . . he, / . . . mistooke / . . . heere?
F; *as prose* Q   12–13 It . . . daughter.] F; *one line* Q   17 yea.] F *omits two half-lines here*

Act 2, Scene 4
0 SD The action may be regarded as continuous from 2.2 (see 2.2.156 SD n.). Lear and the others at first do not see Kent in the stocks; he awakens at 4.

0 SD GENTLEMAN Q designates this speaker as *Knight*, a member of Lear's reduced entourage (see 56 below). The speech headings are simply alternative appellations for the same small-part actors (Duthie, p. 83).

1 they i.e. Regan and Cornwall.
2 messenger i.e. Kent.
4 remove change of residence.
6 pastime amusement; i.e. is this your idea of a joke?
7 cruel garters The Fool refers of course to

the stocks, with a pun on 'crewel', thin worsted material. Compare *Two Angry Women of Abington* (1599): 'heele haue / His Cruel garters crosse about the knee' (Muir).

9 overlusty at legs too eager to use his legs (for running away from service or indenture); with a quibble on the deadly sin of lust.
10 nether-stocks stockings. Upper-stocks were breeches (Kittredge).
11 place (1) rank (as king's messenger), (2) proper place for you to be (Hunter).
12 To As to.
13 son son-in-law; compare 2.2.127 n.
14–19 LEAR . . . swear ay See Textual Analysis, p. 80 above.

LEAR   By Jupiter, I swear no.
KENT   By Juno, I swear ay.
LEAR   They durst not do't:
They could not, would not do't. 'Tis worse than murder,   20
To do upon respect such violent outrage.
Resolve me with all modest haste which way
Thou mightst deserve or they impose this usage,
Coming from us.
KENT   My lord, when at their home
I did commend your highness' letters to them,   25
Ere I was risen from the place that showed
My duty kneeling, came there a reeking post,
Stewed in his haste, half breathless, panting forth
From Gonerill, his mistress, salutations;
Delivered letters spite of intermission,   30
Which presently they read. On those contents
They summoned up their meiny, straight took horse,
Commanded me to follow and attend
The leisure of their answer, gave me cold looks;
And meeting here the other messenger,   35
Whose welcome I perceived had poisoned mine –
Being the very fellow which of late
Displayed so saucily against your highness –
Having more man than wit about me, drew.
He raised the house with loud and coward cries.   40
Your son and daughter found this trespass worth
The shame which here it suffers.

19 KENT By . . . ay.] F; *not in* Q   20 could not, would] F; would not, could Q   23 mightst] F; may'st Q   23 impose]
F; purpose Q   26 showed] shewed Q, F   *28 panting] Q; painting F   31 those] F; whose Q   32 meiny] F; men Q   33–4
Commanded . . . looks;] F; *divided* leasure / Of Q   37 which] F; that Q   42 The] F; This Q

21 **upon respect** Either (1) against proper
regard and deference (due to a king's messenger),
or (2) deliberately, upon consideration (compare
MV 1.1.74; *John* 3.4.90).
22 **Resolve me** i.e. free me from uncertainty or
ignorance, satisfy, inform (Schmidt).
22 **modest** moderate.
24 **us** The royal plural.
25 **commend** deliver.
27 **reeking** steaming, sweating.
28 **panting** Duthie, p. 176, rightly suspects
a minim misreading of manuscript copy. Oxford
retains F 'painting', defended in *Textual Companion*, p. 534.

30 **spite of intermission** in spite of interrupt-
ing me. Note that Cornwall and Regan not only
permit the interruption, they extend it by reading
the letters Oswald delivers.
31 **presently** immediately.
32 **meiny** body of retainers (Onions).
38 **Displayed** Acted, exhibited himself.
39 **more man than wit** more manliness or
courage than sense.
39 **drew** i.e. his sword.
40 **raised** woke up.

FOOL   Winter's not gone yet, if the wild geese fly that way.
   Fathers that wear rags
    Do make their children blind,   45
   But fathers that bear bags
    Shall see their children kind.
   Fortune, that arrant whore,
   Ne'er turns the key to th'poor.
  But for all this, thou shalt have as many dolours for thy 50
  daughters as thou canst tell in a year.

LEAR   O how this mother swells up toward my heart!
  Hysterica passio! Down, thou climbing sorrow,
  Thy element's below. Where is this daughter?

KENT   With the earl, sir, here within.

LEAR   Follow me not, stay here. 55

               Exit

GENTLEMAN   Made you no more offence but what you speak of?

KENT   None.
  How chance the king comes with so small a number?

FOOL   And thou hadst been set i'th'stocks for that question,
  thou'dst well deserved it.   60

KENT   Why, fool?

43–51 FOOL Winter's . . . year.] F; *not in* Q 43 wild] F2; wil'd F 44–9 Fathers . . . poor.] *Pope's lineation; three lines ending* . . . blind, / . . . kind. / . . . poore. F *53 *Hysterica*] F4; *Historica* Q, F, F2; *Hystorica* F3 55 here] F; *not in* Q 55 stay here.] F; stay there? Q 55 SD] F; *not in* Q 56 SH] F; *Knight.* Q 56 Made . . . of?] *One line* Q; *two lines divided* offence, / But F 56 but] F; then Q 57 None] F; No Q (*as part of 53*) 58 the] Q; the the F 58 number] F; traine Q 59 And] F, Q; If Q2 59 i'th'] F; in the Q 60 thou'dst] F; thou ha'dst Q

43–51 FOOL . . . year See Textual Analysis, pp. 279–80 above, for F addition.

43 Winter's . . . way i.e. we're in for more trouble (bad weather), judging from these portents.

43 wild geese A possible allusion to Sir John and Lady Grace Wildgoose? See p. 4 above.

44–9 Fathers . . . poor Oxford inserts SD *Sings* before these lines (as later at 71). Possibly the verses were sung, but neither Q nor F indicates this, they do not sound like traditional ballad material (Hunter, p. 340), and actors often speak the lines, though in sing-song fashion.

45 blind i.e. to their father's needs.

46 bags money bags.

49 turns the key opens the door (as a prostitute would, admitting someone to her favours).

50 dolours (1) griefs, (2) dollars (from German *thaler*, a silver coin first struck in 1515 and worth about three marks, or about 15 pence).

50 for on account of, owing to (Muir).

51 tell (1) count, (2) relate.

52 mother hysteria. Compare 114 below. Richard Mainy, mentioned by Harsnett, suffered from the mother, also known as *Passio Hysterica*, which Harsnett describes as a disease that 'riseth . . . of a wind in the bottome of the belly, and proceeding with a great swelling, causeth a very painfull colicke in the stomack, and an extraordinary giddiness in the head' (NS, citing Muir, 'Samuel Harsnett and *King Lear*', RES 2 (1951), 14).

53 *Hysterica passio* Hysteria, or the 'mother' (see 52 n.). In his chapter on 'The development of Lear's madness', Hoeniger traces the medical history of the illness, its symptoms, and Shakespeare's borrowing from Harsnett.

54 element sphere; place; 'a visceral symbol of the breakdown in hierarchy, when the lower elements climb up to threaten or destroy the superior ones' (Hunter).

58 How chance How comes it.

FOOL   We'll set thee to school to an ant, to teach thee there's no
labouring i'th'winter. All that follow their noses are led by their
eyes but blind men, and there's not a nose among twenty but
can smell him that's stinking. Let go thy hold when a great   65
wheel runs down a hill, lest it break thy neck with following.
But the great one that goes upward, let him draw thee after.
When a wise man gives thee better counsel, give me mine
again; I would have none but knaves follow it, since a fool gives
it.   70

<blockquote>

That sir which serves and seeks for gain
    And follows but for form,
Will pack when it begins to rain
    And leave thee in the storm.
But I will tarry, the fool will stay,   75
    And let the wise man fly;
The knave turns fool that runs away,
    The fool no knave, perdy.
</blockquote>

KENT   Where learned you this, fool?

FOOL   Not i'th'stocks, fool.   80

Enter LEAR *and* GLOUCESTER

LEAR   Deny to speak with me? They are sick, they are weary,

63 i'th'] F; in the Q   64 twenty] F; a 100. Q   *65 hold] Q; hold, F   66 following.] F; following it, Q   67 upward] F;
vp the hill Q   68 wise man] Q; wiseman F   68 gives] F *corr.*, Q; giue F *uncorr.*   68 counsel,] Q, F *uncorr.;* counsell F
corr.   *69 have] Q; hause F   71 which] F; *that* Q   71 and seeks] F; *not in* Q   73 begins] F; begin Q   76 wise man] Q;
wiseman F   80 i'th'] F; in the Q   80 fool] F; *not in* Q   *80 SD] *As in* Q; *after 78* F   81 Deny . . . weary,] *One line* Q; *two
lines divided* me? / They F   81 They are . . . they are] F; th'are . . . th'are Q

62–3 We'll . . . winter The Fool alludes to the
proverbial ant, mentioned by Aesop, gathering its
food in harvest time (i.e. during times of plenty),
not in winter. Compare Prov. 6.6, 30.25 (cited by
Noble, NS, Shaheen). As he falls from prosperity,
Lear offers less attraction to hangers-on, as Kent
ought to realise. Even a blind man, the Fool continues, can detect someone's decaying fortunes ('him
that's stinking' (65)).

64 twenty i.e. twenty blind men.

65–6 great wheel Compare *Ham.* 3.3.17–22,
where Rosencrantz uses the image similarly.

71–2 That . . . form Compare *Oth.* 1.1.49–
55: Iago describes himself to Roderigo as one of
those self-serving individuals, 'throwing but shows
of service on their lords'.

71 sir man.

73 pack pack up and leave.

75–8 But . . . perdy The Fool plays on different
senses of 'fool', 'wise man', and 'knave', using them

both ironically and straightforwardly. In one sense
it is mere foolishness for anyone to hang on to the
'great wheel' while it rolls down-hill; 'The better
part of valour is discretion', as Falstaff says (*1H4*
5.4.120). This is one kind of wisdom. Against it the
Fool posits absolute fidelity – adversity and self-
interest notwithstanding. The paradox that concludes the lines resolves itself thus: the knave is
foolish, finally, for running away and exposing his
true colours, and he is foolish in any higher moral
sense; the loyal fool – whatever else he may be – is
at least no knave, i.e. guilty of disloyalty and gross
self-interest.

78 perdy by God (from French *par Dieu*).

81 Deny Refuse.

81–2 They . . . they . . . They The pronouns
perhaps are stressed, as Lear may be sardonic; he,
after all, has 'travelled twice as far, wearily, unfed,
sickening in mind and body' (Rosenberg, p. 157).

They have travelled all the night? Mere fetches,
The images of revolt and flying off.
Fetch me a better answer.
GLOUCESTER   My dear lord,
You know the fiery quality of the duke,   85
How unremovable and fixed he is
In his own course.
LEAR Vengeance, plague, death, confusion!
'Fiery'? What 'quality'? Why Gloucester, Gloucester,
I'd speak with the Duke of Cornwall and his wife.   90
GLOUCESTER Well, my good lord, I have informed them so.
LEAR 'Informed them'? Dost thou understand me, man?
GLOUCESTER Ay, my good lord.
LEAR The king would speak with Cornwall, the dear father
Would with his daughter speak! Commands – tends –
service!   95
Are they 'informed' of this? My breath and blood!
'Fiery'? The 'fiery duke'? Tell the hot duke that –
No, but not yet; maybe he is not well:
Infirmity doth still neglect all office

82 have travelled all the] F; traueled hard to Q   82 fetches,] F *corr.*; fetches F *uncorr.*; Iustice, Q   83 The] F; I the
Q   84–90 My . . . wife.] F; *as prose* Q   88 plague, death] F; death, plague Q   89 'Fiery'? What 'quality'?] F; What fierie
quality, Q   91–2 Well . . . man?] F; *not in* Q   94 The . . . father] *As in* Q; *two lines divided: Cornwall,* / *The* F   94
father] F, Q *corr.*; fate Q *uncorr.*   95 his] F, Q *corr.*; the Q *uncorr.*   95 Commands – tends – service!] *This edn;* commands,
tends, service. F; come and tends seruise, Q *uncorr.*; commands her seruice, Q *corr.*   96 Are . . . blood!] F; *not in* Q   97
'Fiery'? The 'fiery duke'?] F; The fierie Duke, Q *uncorr.*; Fierie duke Q *corr.*   97 that –] F; that *Lear,* Q   98 No] F, Q
corr.; Mo Q *uncorr.*   99–102 Infirmity . . . forbear,] F; *three lines ending* . . . health / . . . oprest / . . . forbeare, Q

82 fetches (1) contrivances, dodges, tricks, (2)
(an allusion to) the nautical manoeuvre of 'tack-
ing', by which a vessel sails indirectly to wind-
ward by alternating between two oblique courses,
or 'tacks'. Milton uses a similar image to describe
Satan's approach to Eve in the Garden of Eden
(*Paradise Lost,* IX.510 ff.).
83 images . . . off Lear sees in their refusal
to see him the sign or symbol of serious disobedience, tantamount to 'revolt' and desertion, the
breakdown of order.
85 quality character, disposition.
91–2 GLOUCESTER . . . man See Textual
Analysis, p. 280 below, for F's addition here and at
96.
95 Commands – tends – service See collation. Q corr. is generally regarded as a proof-
corrector's guess carried over into Q2, since 'tends'
could not be a misreading of 'her'. Q uncorr.,
'come and tends seruise', is possibly a misreading of
what was in the original manuscript, which F may
recover: 'tends', an aphetic form of 'attends' =

waits for. (See Greg, *Variants,* pp. 161–2; Duthie,
pp. 143–4; but Duthie in NS adopts the Q corr.
reading, withdrawing his earlier note.) Hunter suggests that 'commands true seruise', or something
like it, may have been in the copy for Q, but he
follows F.
97 'Fiery'? The 'fiery duke'? See collation.
Again, the Q corrector erred and F (which restores
or adds 96) may reflect the original wording (Greg,
Variants, p. 162). Blayney, however, conjectures that
in Q corr. the line, with punctuation emended,
should have read: 'Fierie? the Duke? Tell the hot
Duke that *Lear* – '; he then explains how the compositor might have failed to make corrections the
proofreader had marked. He conjectures, further,
that the second 'fiery?' was retained in F through
faulty proof-correction or compositor error
(pp. 245–6).
97 hot i.e. hot-tempered. Lear plays on 'fiery'.
99–100 Infirmity . . . bound i.e. illness invari-
ably makes us neglect duties which, when well, we
are obliged to perform.

Whereto our health is bound. We are not ourselves   100
When nature, being oppressed, commands the mind
To suffer with the body. I'll forbear,
And am fallen out with my more headier will,
To take the indisposed and sickly fit
For the sound man. – Death on my state! Wherefore   105
Should he sit here? This act persuades me
That this remotion of the duke and her
Is practice only. Give me my servant forth.
Go tell the duke and's wife I'd speak with them,
Now, presently: bid them come forth and hear me,   110
Or at their chamber door I'll beat the drum
Till it cry sleep to death.

GLOUCESTER   I would have all well betwixt you.   *Exit*

LEAR   Oh me, my heart! My rising heart! But down.

FOOL   Cry to it, nuncle, as the cockney did to the eels when she put   115
'em i'th'paste alive; she knapped 'em o'th'coxcombs with a stick
and cried, 'Down, wantons, down!' 'Twas her brother that in
pure kindness to his horse buttered his hay.

Enter CORNWALL, REGAN, GLOUCESTER, [*and*] *Servants*

LEAR   Good morrow to you both.

---

101 commands] F; Cômand Q   104–7 To . . . her] F; *three lines ending* . . . man, / . . . here? / . . . & her [*turned under*] Q   109 Go] F; *not in* Q   109 I'd] I'll'd F; Ile Q   113 SD] F; *not in* Q   114 Oh . . . down.] F; O my heart, my heart. Q   115 cockney] F; Coknay Q *uncorr.*; Cokney Q *corr.*   116 'em i'th'] F; vm it'h Q   116 paste] F; past Q *uncorr.*; pâst Q *corr.*   116 knapped 'em o'th'] F; rapt vm ath Q   118 SD] F; *Enter Duke and Regan.* Q

100–102 We . . . body Compare 3.4.11–14, where Lear also notes psychosomatic effects.

102–5 I'll . . . man i.e. I'll desist, for I am upset that my violent impulse ('will') mistook the unhealthy condition for the well man. But this rationalisation and the calm it induces are short-lived, as Lear catches sight again of Kent in the stocks and is reminded of the insult it represents.

105 state royal power.

107 remotion keeping aloof or remote; as in *Tim.* 4.3.342. But Lear may refer to Cornwall and Regan's removal from their home to Gloucester's (Malone, cited by Furness).

108 practice craft, trickery; as at 2.1.72.

109 and's and his.

110 presently immediately, at once.

112 Till . . . death i.e. till sleep is destroyed by the noise. Muir compares *Mac.* 2.2.39.

114 Oh . . . down A further symptom, or aggravation, of the 'mother', *hysterica passio*; compare

52–3 above and n.

115–18 Cry . . . hay NS identifies two examples here of foolish tender-heartedness relevant to Lear's earlier dealings with his daughters: (1) the cockney cook who could not bear to kill eels before baking them in a pie, and when they tried to wriggle out, she could only rap them on the head and cry, 'Down'; (2) her brother, who thought he was favouring his horse by buttering its hay but actually was doing the opposite (horses dislike grease). Now that Lear's heart distresses him by 'rising', he is as ludicrous as the cockney crying 'Down!' For possible borrowing from or allusion to Lyly's *Euphues*, see Muir.

116 coxcombs heads.

117 wantons playful, frisky creatures.

118 SD Cornwall and Regan may be in night gowns, or they may be fully clothed, giving the lie to their 'social excuse' (Rosenberg pp. 161–2). But whatever Regan wears, she is 'gorgeous' (261).

CORNWALL Hail to your grace.

Kent here set at liberty

REGAN I am glad to see your highness.   120

LEAR Regan, I think you are. I know what reason
I have to think so. If thou shouldst not be glad,
I would divorce me from thy mother's tomb,
Sepulch'ring an adultress. [*To Kent*] O are you free?
Some other time for that. Belovèd Regan,   125
Thy sister's naught. Oh Regan, she hath tied
Sharp-toothed unkindness, like a vulture here –
I can scarce speak to thee – thou'lt not believe
With how depraved a quality – oh Regan!

REGAN I pray you, sir, take patience. I have hope   130
You less know how to value her desert
Than she to scant her duty.

LEAR Say? How is that?

REGAN I cannot think my sister in the least
Would fail her obligation. If, sir, perchance
She have restrained the riots of your followers,   135
'Tis on such ground and to such wholesome end
As clears her from all blame.

LEAR My curses on her.

REGAN O sir, you are old,
Nature in you stands on the very verge
Of his confine. You should be ruled and led   140

---

119 SD] F; *not in* Q   *121 you] Q; your F   123 divorce] F, Q *corr.;* deuose Q *uncorr.*   *123 mother's] mothers Q; Mother
F   123 tomb,] F; fruit, Q *uncorr.;* tombe Q *corr.*   124 SD] *Rowe; not in* Q, F   124 O] F; yea Q   126 sister's] F; sister is
Q   127 here] F; heare Q   128 thou'lt] F; thout Q   129 With] F; Of Q   129 depraved] F; deptoued Q *uncorr.;* depriued
Q *corr.*   130 you] F; *not in* Q   132 scant] F; slacke Q   132–7 Say? . . . blame.] F; *not in* Q   139–43 Nature . . . return;]
F *lineation; four lines ending* . . . confine, ['fine' *turned over*] / . . . discretion, / . . . your selfe, / . . . returne, Q   139 in]
F; on Q   140 his] F, *Oxford;* her Q, *Duthie*

124 **Sepulch'ring** Entombing.
126 **naught** wicked.
126–9 **Oh . . . Regan** The dashes (where F uses
commas or, at 129, a period) emphasise the gasping
cadences that Lear's overwrought condition produces.
126–7 **tied . . . here** The image of a vulture
gnawing at Lear's innards derives from the torture
of Prometheus, familiar to Shakespeare's contemporaries. Harsnett mentions it, as Muir notes, along
with Ixion's wheel (compare 4.6.44).
129 **quality** nature, disposition.

130 **take patience** Standard Renaissance counsel. Compare 1.4.217 and n.
130–2 **I . . . duty** i.e. I hope you are less able
to estimate her merit than she is capable of slight-
ing her duty. The double negative, 'less know' and
'scant', makes the syntax difficult, but the sense is
clear.
132–7 LEAR **. . . blame** On F's addition, see
Textual Analysis, p. 280 below.
135 **She have** i.e. she may have.
135 **riots** carousals.
140 **his confine** its limit, boundary area.

By some discretion that discerns your state
Better than you yourself. Therefore I pray you
That to our sister you do make return;
Say you have wronged her.

LEAR   Ask her forgiveness?
Do you but mark how this becomes the house?   145
[*Kneels*] 'Dear daughter, I confess that I am old;
Age is unnecessary: on my knees I beg
That you'll vouchsafe me raiment, bed, and food.'

REGAN   Good sir, no more: these are unsightly tricks.
Return you to my sister.

LEAR [*Rising*]   Never, Regan.   150
She hath abated me of half my train,
Looked black upon me, struck me with her tongue
Most serpent-like upon the very heart.
All the stored vengeances of heaven fall
On her ingrateful top! Strike her young bones,   155
You taking airs, with lameness.

CORNWALL   Fie, sir, fie.

LEAR   You nimble lightnings, dart your blinding flames
Into her scornful eyes! Infect her beauty,
You fen-sucked fogs, drawn by the powerful sun

---

142 pray you] F; pray Q   144 her.] F; her Sir? Q   145 but] F; *not in* Q   146 SD] *Hanmer* (*subst.*); *after 147, Johnson; not in* Q, F   150 SD] *Collier; not in* Q, F   150 Never] F; No Q   154–6 All . . . lameness.] F; *two lines divided* top, [*turned over*] / Strike Q   156 Fie, sir, fie.] F; Fie fie sir. Q   157 SH] F; *not in* Q, *but line indented*   159 fen-sucked] F; Fen suckt Q

141 **discretion** i.e. a discreet person, the abstract for the concrete (Furness, who compares 3.4.26, 'houseless poverty').
141 **state** mental and physical condition; with a possible ironic play upon 'power, royalty' (Hunter).
144 **Ask her forgiveness?** Lear is stunned by Regan's response.
145 **house** Either (1) family, or (2) royal line.
146–8 **Dear . . . food** Deliberate bathos. Lear is hurt and angry but still has enough wit left for sarcasm.
147 **Age is unnecessary** Lear aptly summarises Gonerill's and Regan's Darwinian outlook, in which survival of the fittest rules and the elderly are superfluous (compare Heilman, p. 143).
148 **vouchsafe** grant in condescension (Schmidt).
149 **tricks** i.e. rhetorical devices.
151 **abated** deprived.

155 **top** head.
155 **young bones** unborn child. Compare *King Leir* 844–7: Leir tries to excuse Gonorill's 'tutchy' behaviour by saying 'she breeds young bones'. Cursing Gonerill's unborn child is appropriate in the context of 'ingrateful top': Lear is obsessed with filial ingratitude. Compare 1.4.230–44, where Lear similarly curses Gonerill and a child she might bear, which he hopes will be deformed and torment her as she torments him. In both contexts, the serpent image occurs. But 'young bones' may refer to Gonerill herself; compare Gascoigne's *Supposes* 4.2.4: 'A rope stretche your yong bones', referring to a young man (Perrett, pp. 275–6).
156 **taking airs** blasting, pernicious vapours.
158–9 **Infect . . . sun** Noxious vapours produced by the sun's rays upon swampy fens were, like 'taking airs' (156), thought to be infectious.

To fall and blister.   160
REGAN   O the blessed gods! So will you wish on me
        When the rash mood is on.
LEAR   No, Regan, thou shalt never have my curse.
        Thy tender-hefted nature shall not give
        Thee o'er to harshness. Her eyes are fierce, but thine   165
        Do comfort and not burn. 'Tis not in thee
        To grudge my pleasures, to cut off my train,
        To bandy hasty words, to scant my sizes,
        And in conclusion, to oppose the bolt
        Against my coming in. Thou better know'st   170
        The offices of nature, bond of childhood,
        Effects of courtesy, dues of gratitude.
        Thy half o'th'kingdom hast thou not forgot
        Wherein I thee endowed.
REGAN   Good sir, to th'purpose.
LEAR   Who put my man i'th'stocks?
                        Tucket within
CORNWALL   What trumpet's that?   175
REGAN   I know't, my sister's. This approves her letter
        That she would soon be here.

---

160 blister] F; blast her pride Q; blister her *Muir*   **161–2** O . . . on.] Q *lineation; divided* Gods! / So F   **162** mood is on.] F; mood – Q   **164–7** Thy . . . train,] F *lineation; three lines ending* . . . or'e / . . . burne [*turned over*] / . . . traine, [*turned under*] Q   **164** Thy tender-hefted] F; The tĕder hested Q   **170** know'st] F; knowest Q   **173** o'th'] F; of the Q   *175 SD Tucket within*] Collier; *after 174* F; *not in* Q   **176** letter] F; letters Q

160 fall and blister i.e. the action of the fogs and their effect. Furness compares *Temp.* 1.2.323–4: 'A south-west blow on ye, / And blister you all o'er!' The intransitive verbs have led editors to various emendations, unnecessarily, since F makes sense as it stands.

164 tender–hefted 'A heft or haft is a handle, and a nature tender-hefted is one which is set in a tender handle or delicate bodily frame' (Wright, cited by Furness); hence 'womanly, gentle' (Muir). Note Regan's differences from Gonerill: '. . . her particular style of dress, her more feminine mode of offering tenderness to Lear, her kind manner toward Gloster, and, probably, Edmund, have so far in the text masked her capacity for hurt and hate . . . In the theatre she has been most effective – partly because it contrasts her with Goneril – when she has seemed sweet; in fact bittersweet, emasculating Lear with an insistent, tender concern' (Rosenberg, pp. 162–3).

168 bandy Compare 1.4.72 and n.

168 scant my sizes reduce my allowances. Compare 'sizar' = 'a poor scholar who used to obtain allowances from the college butteryhatch' (Muir).

169 oppose set over against, i.e. to lock. Compare *Tim.* 3.4.79: 'What, are my doors oppos'd against my passage?' Of course, this is exaggerated; Gonerill did not lock Lear out, although later Regan (297), seconded by Cornwall (301), will order Gloucester's doors shut up against Lear and his followers.

171 offices of nature duties that nature expects us to fulfil; specifically those relating to filial 'bonds'.

172 Effects Manifestations.

174 to th'purpose i.e. get to the point.

175 Who . . . stocks Lear repeats the question (181) and does not receive an answer until his third demand (191).

175 SD Tucket within See 2.1.76 SD n.

176 approves confirms.

Enter OSWALD

Is your lady come?

LEAR   This is a slave whose easy-borrowed pride
　　　Dwells in the sickly grace of her he follows.
　　　Out, varlet, from my sight!

CORNWALL　　　　　　　　What means your grace?　　　　180

Enter GONERILL

LEAR   Who stocked my servant? Regan, I have good hope
　　　Thou didst not know on't. Who comes here? O heavens!
　　　If you do love old men, if your sweet sway
　　　Allow obedience, if you yourselves are old,
　　　Make it your cause; send down and take my part.　　　185
　　　[*To Gonerill*] Art not ashamed to look upon this beard?
　　　O Regan, will you take her by the hand?

GONERILL   Why not by th'hand, sir? How have I offended?
　　　All's not offence that indiscretion finds,
　　　And dotage terms so.

LEAR　　　　　　　　O sides, you are too tough!　　　　190

177 SD] *Dyce; after* that? (*175*) Q; *after* Stockes? (*175*) F   179 sickly] F3; fickly F, F2; fickle Q   179 her he] F; her a Q *uncorr.;* her, a Q *corr.*   180 varlet] F, Q *corr.;* varlot Q *uncorr.*   180 SD] F, Q; *after* on't (*182*) *Johnson, Duthie, and most later editors*   181 SH] F; *Gon.* Q   181 stocked] F; struck Q   182 Thou . . . heavens!] *Pope's lineation; two lines divided ant. / Lear.* Who Q; *two lines divided* on't. / Who F   182 on't] F; ant Q   183–5 If . . . part.]. F *lineation; lines end* . . . allow / . . . cause, / . . . part, Q   183 your] F; you Q   184 you] F; *not in* Q   186 SD] *Johnson; not in* Q, F   187 will you] F; wilt thou Q   188 by th'] F; by the Q

178 **easy-borrowed** Either (1) cool, derived; (2) easily-assumed. Most editors follow Theobald and insert a hyphen, as Muir does, though he questions it and thinks 'easy' may mean 'coolly-impudent'.

179 **sickly** See collation. The copy for F corrected Q, most likely, but the compositor got the wrong ligature, probably through foul-case error. NS and Oxford reject 'fickle' on semantic grounds as well: the dig at Gonerill could result in sympathy for Oswald, which is certainly not desirable in this or any other context. By contrast, 'sickly grace' = diseased grace, a possible oxymoron, which could also mean 'causing sickness or ill health' (*Textual Companion*, p. 534).

180 **varlet** rogue, rascal.

180 SD *Enter* GONERILL. Many editors follow Johnson and move Gonerill's entrance to 182 after 'here', but in the growing tumult, Lear may not at first see her. On the differences between Q and F, see Textual Analysis, p. 79 above.

182 **on't** of it.

184 **Allow** Sanction, approve of.

185 **it** i.e. what is due to parents and the elderly.

186 **Art** Art thou.

186 **beard** Symbol of aged reverence.

187 **O . . . hand** '. . . with four quick shocks – his sudden recall of the outrage upon his servant, the sound of a trumpet, the sight of Oswald, the sight of Goneril – [Lear] is brought to a stand and to face the realities arrayed against him. This must be made very plain to us. On the one side stand Goneril and Regan and Cornwall in all authority. The perplexed Gloucester stands a little apart. On the other side is Lear, the Fool at his feet, and his one servant, disarmed, freed but a minute since, behind him. Things are at their issue' (Granville-Barker, pp. 289–90). Striking as this conception of the staging is, alternative kinds of blocking are also possible here and at 193.

189 **indiscretion** want of discernment or judgement. Schmidt compares *Ham.* 5.2.8: 'Our indiscretion sometime serves us well / When our deep plots do pall.'

190 **sides** 'the sides of the chest, strained by the swellings and passions of the heart' (Hunter).

Will you yet hold? How came my man i'th'stocks?
CORNWALL   I set him there, sir; but his own disorders
　　　　Deserved much less advancement.
LEAR　　　　　　　　　　　　　You? Did you?
REGAN   I pray you, father, being weak, seem so.
　　　　If till the expiration of your month　　　　　　　195
　　　　You will return and sojourn with my sister,
　　　　Dismissing half your train, come then to me.
　　　　I am now from home and out of that provision
　　　　Which shall be needful for your entertainment.
LEAR   Return to her? and fifty men dismissed?　　　200
　　　　No, rather I abjure all roofs and choose
　　　　To wage against the enmity o'th'air,
　　　　To be a comrade with the wolf and owl,
　　　　Necessity's sharp pinch. Return with her?
　　　　Why, the hot-blooded France, that dowerless took　205
　　　　Our youngest born – I could as well be brought
　　　　To knee his throne and, squire-like, pension beg
　　　　To keep base life afoot. Return with her?
　　　　Persuade me rather to be slave and sumpter
　　　　To this detested groom.
GONERILL　　　　　　　　　At your choice, sir.　　　210

---

191 Will . . . stocks?] *As in* Q; *two lines divided* hold? / How F　191 i'th'] F; it'h Q　192 sir] F, Q; *not in* Q2　202 o'th']
F; of the Q　205–6 Why . . . brought] F; *divided* dowerles / Tooke Q　*205 hot-blooded] F *uncorr.*, Pope; hot-bloodied
F *corr.*; hot bloud in Q　207 beg] F; bag Q

192 disorders misconduct.

193 much less advancement Cornwall is
sarcastic: he believes Kent deserved much more
severe punishment.

193 You? Did you? Uttered more in contempt
than outrage or shock. 'Gielgud, hands clenched
behind his back, strode up to face Cornwall, spat
You!, passed, rounded on him contemptuously to
finish the line' (Rosenberg, p. 170). But Regan
immediately interrupts that colloquy, reasserting
herself (compare 2.1.119) and thereby turning
Lear's attention back to her and her sister.

199 entertainment reception and care.

201–4 I abjure . . . pinch A self-fulfilling
prophecy: by the end of the scene Lear does precisely this.

202–3 To wage . . . owl Theobald transposed these lines, and Oxford follows suit, making
'Necessity's sharp pinch' (204) the object of 'wage'.

But 'Necessity's sharp pinch', if anything, should
be the subject, not object, of 'wage', which here
is used intransitively to signify 'wage war, struggle'. As it stands, however, the phrase, 'Necessity's
sharp pinch', is in apposition to 'To be a comrade
with the wolf and owl', i.e. cohabiting with wild
animals is the result of grim necessity. The lines
thus do not require transposition.

202 enmity o'th'air e.g. storms and in general
the harsh condition of 'houseless poverty' (3.4.26).

204 Necessity's sharp pinch Compare Florio's
Montaigne: 'Necessitie must first pinch you by the
throat' (Muir).

205 hot-blooded passionate.

207 knee kneel before.

207 squire-like like a vassal or servant.

209 sumpter drudge (literally, packhorse).

210 groom i.e. Oswald.

LEAR I prithee, daughter, do not make me mad.
　　　I will not trouble thee, my child. Farewell.
　　　We'll no more meet, no more see one another.
　　　But yet thou art my flesh, my blood, my daughter,
　　　Or rather a disease that's in my flesh,　　　　　　　　　215
　　　Which I must needs call mine. Thou art a boil,
　　　A plague-sore, or embossèd carbuncle
　　　In my corrupted blood. But I'll not chide thee;
　　　Let shame come when it will, I do not call it.
　　　I do not bid the thunder-bearer shoot,　　　　　　　　220
　　　Nor tell tales of thee to high-judging Jove.
　　　Mend when thou canst, be better at thy leisure;
　　　I can be patient, I can stay with Regan,
　　　I and my hundred knights.

REGAN　　　　　　　　　　　　　Not altogether so.
　　　I looked not for you yet, nor am provided　　　　　　225
　　　For your fit welcome. Give ear, sir, to my sister,
　　　For those that mingle reason with your passion
　　　Must be content to think you old, and so –
　　　But she knows what she does.

LEAR　　　　　　　　　　　　Is this well spoken?

REGAN I dare avouch it, sir. What, fifty followers?　　　230
　　　Is it not well? What should you need of more?
　　　Yea, or so many, sith that both charge and danger
　　　Speak 'gainst so great a number? How in one house
　　　Should many people under two commands
　　　Hold amity? 'Tis hard, almost impossible.　　　　　235

211 I] F; Now I Q   215 that's in] F; that lies within Q   216 boil] bile Q; Byle F   217–18 A . . . thee;] F; *divided* my / Corrupted Q   217 or] F; an Q   224–7 Not . . . passion] F *lineation; lines end* . . . yet, / . . . welcome, / . . . those / . . . passion, Q   224 so] F; so sir Q   225 looked] F; looke Q   226 sir] F, Q; *not in* Q2   228 you] F; you are Q   228 so –] *Rowe;* so, Q, Q, F   229 spoken] F; spoken now Q   *230 What,] *Rowe;* what Q, F   233 Speak] F; Speakes Q   233 one] F; a Q

211–24 I . . . knights Lear quickly moves through several contrasting emotions and attitudes, from quiet withdrawal and acceptance, to passionate recognition of relationship immediately followed by vigorous rejection, to hard-won self-control and an attempt, again, to accept the situation and try to make the best of it.

217 embossèd swollen; from French *embosser* 'to swell, or arise in bunches, hulches, knobs' (Cotgrave, cited by Furness).

217 carbuncle In medical terminology an 'inflammatory, circumscribed, malignant tumour . . . It differs from a boil in having no central core' (*OED* sv *sb* 3, citing this passage).

218 corrupted i.e. by disease.

220 thunder-bearer Jupiter.

220 shoot i.e. throw thunderbolts.

224 hundred knights Although his train is diminished (compare 58 above), Lear still thinks of it as intact.

227 mingle . . . passion view your impulsive behaviour with calm rationality. Indeed, cool rationality characterises Regan's and Gonerill's speeches throughout the rest of the scene, culminating in Lear's appeal, 'O reason not the need', 257 ff.

230 avouch it declare it to be true.

232 sith that since.

232 charge expense.

GONERILL Why might not you, my lord, receive attendance
       From those that she calls servants, or from mine?
REGAN Why not, my lord? If then they chanced to slack ye,
       We could control them. If you will come to me
       (For now I spy a danger) I entreat you   240
       To bring but five and twenty; to no more
       Will I give place or notice.
LEAR I gave you all.
REGAN   And in good time you gave it.
LEAR Made you my guardians, my depositaries,
       But kept a reservation to be followed   245
       With such a number. What, must I come to you
       With five and twenty? Regan, said you so?
REGAN And speak't again, my lord. No more with me.
LEAR Those wicked creatures yet do look well-favoured
       When others are more wicked. Not being the worst   250
       Stands in some rank of praise. [*To Gonerill*] I'll go with
       thee;
       Thy fifty yet doth double five and twenty,
       And thou art twice her love.
GONERILL   Hear me, my lord:
       What need you five and twenty? ten? or five?
       To follow in a house where twice so many   255
       Have a command to tend you?
REGAN   What need one?
LEAR O reason not the need! Our basest beggars
       Are in the poorest thing superfluous.
       Allow not nature more than nature needs,

---

238 Why . . . ye,] *As in* Q; *two lines divided* Lord? / If F   238 ye] F; you Q   *239 control] Q; comptroll F   240 (For . . . danger)] F; For . . . danger, Q   249 look] F; seem Q   251 SD] *Hanmer; not in* Q, F   256 need] F; needes Q   257 need!] need: F; deed, Q   259 needs,] Q; needs: F

238 **slack ye** i.e. lessen their attendance on you.
242 **notice** cognisance, recognition.
243 **I . . . all** Compare *King Leir* 2144: 'Ah, cru-ell *Ragan*, did I giue thee all?' (Muir). Actors at this point often move between the extremes of love and hate, tenderness and rage, gently reproachful pathos and stern obstinacy, astonishment and dis-traction (Rosenberg, p. 173).
244 **guardians . . . depositaries** Synonyms for trustees (of his estate). Muir compares Florio's *Montaigne*, 'depositary and guardian'.
245 **reservation** reserved right; compare 1.1.127.
249 **well-favoured** attractive, handsome.
255 **follow** attend you, be your followers.

257 **O . . . need** Ignoring his own earlier attempts to quantify love, Lear appeals to his daughters not to compute his 'need' by rational-ist criteria, since it cannot truly be thus calculated. It is beyond practical measures.
257–8 **Our . . . superfluous** The little that the lowest and most destitute persons have is (by that way of calculating 'need') not absolutely necessary to keep them alive.
259–60 **Allow . . . beast's** Calculated by the lowest common denominators of 'need', human requirements do not differ from animal needs, and in that process human worth becomes downgraded to the level of a beast's.

Man's life is cheap as beast's. Thou art a lady;   260
If only to go warm were gorgeous,
Why nature needs not what thou gorgeous wear'st,
Which scarcely keeps thee warm. But for true need –
You heavens, give me that patience, patience I need.
You see me here, you gods, a poor old man,   265
As full of grief as age, wretched in both;
If it be you that stirs these daughters' hearts
Against their father, fool me not so much
To bear it tamely. Touch me with noble anger,
And let not women's weapons, water drops,   270
Stain my man's cheeks. No, you unnatural hags,
I will have such revenges on you both
That all the world shall – I will do such things –
What they are, yet I know not, but they shall be
The terrors of the earth! You think I'll weep;   275
No, I'll not weep,
                     Storm and tempest
I have full cause of weeping, but this heart
Shall break into a hundred thousand flaws
Or ere I'll weep. O fool, I shall go mad.
             Exeunt [*Lear, Gloucester, Kent, Gentleman, and Fool*]
CORNWALL   Let us withdraw; 'twill be a storm.   280
REGAN   This house is little. The old man and's people
         Cannot be well bestowed.
GONERILL   'Tis his own blame; hath put himself from rest

---

260 life is] F; life as Q; life's as Q2   262 wear'st] F; wearest Q   263 need –] *Warburton (subst.);* need, Q; need: F   265 you gods,] (you Gods) Q, F   265 man] F; fellow Q   268 so] F; to Q   269 tamely] F; lamely Q   270 And] F; O Q   273 shall –] F, Q2; shall, Q   *274 are, yet] Q2; are yet, F   275 earth!] earth? F; earth, Q   276–8 No . . . flaws] *Jennens's lineation; two lines divided* weeping, / But Q, F   276 SD] *After* weeping (*277*) F; *not in* Q   278 into . . . thousand] F; in a 100. thousand Q; in a thousand Q2   278 flaws] F; flowes Q   *279 SD] *This edn; Exeunt Lear, Leister, Kent, and Foole* Q; *Exeunt* F   281 and 's] F2; an'ds F; and his Q   *283 blame;] *Boswell;* blame Q, F

260–3 Thou . . . warm Lear addresses Regan: If warmth was the only measure of elegance, then you would not need the elegant apparel you have on, which hardly keeps you warm. Lear contrasts two different kinds of 'need' here, one for basic animal requirements, the other for human dignity and pride.

263 But for true need This phrase is 'very important, for it underscores the existence of values entirely different from demonstrable material needs – higher needs (his own need, at the moment, is for symbols of respect and love) which must be imaginatively grasped and cannot be mechanically computed' (Heilman, p. 169). Eloquent as Lear's

appeal is, he cannot sustain it, but breaks down into self-pity, angry, impotent threats, and near incoherence as he fears approaching insanity.

264 patience See 1.4.217 n.

268 fool . . . much i.e. do not make me such a fool as.

271 you . . . hags Lear now turns back to Gonerill and Regan.

278 flaws fragments.

279 Or ere Before.

282 bestowed accommodated, housed.

283 blame fault.

283 hath he hath.

283 put . . . rest deprived himself of repose.

And must needs taste his folly.

REGAN For his particular, I'll receive him gladly,   285
But not one follower.

GONERILL   So am I purposed.
Where is my lord of Gloucester?

CORNWALL Followed the old man forth.

Enter GLOUCESTER

He is returned.

GLOUCESTER The king is in high rage.

CORNWALL   Whither is he going?

GLOUCESTER He calls to horse, but will I know not whither.   290

CORNWALL 'Tis best to give him way; he leads himself.

GONERILL My lord, entreat him by no means to stay.

GLOUCESTER Alack, the night comes on, and the high winds
Do sorely ruffle; for many miles about
There's scarce a bush.

REGAN   O sir, to wilful men,   295
The injuries that they themselves procure
Must be their schoolmasters. Shut up your doors.
He is attended with a desperate train,
And what they may incense him to, being apt
To have his ear abused, wisdom bids fear.   300

CORNWALL Shut up your doors, my lord; 'tis a wild night,
My Regan counsels well: come out o'th'storm.

Exeunt

286 SH] F; *Duke.* Q   286–7 So . . . Gloucester?] F *lineation; one line* Q   286 purposed] F; puspos'd Q   288 SH] F; *Reg.*
Q   288 SD] *After 287* Q, F; *at end of line, Capell*   289–90 CORNWALL Whither . . . horse,] F; *not in* Q   290 but] F;
& Q   291 SH] F; *Re.* Q   291 best] F; good Q   293 high] F; bleak Q   294–5 Do . . . bush.] F *lineation; one line* Q   294
ruffle] F; russel Q   295 scarce] F; not Q   301 wild] Q; wil'd F   302 Regan] F; *Reg* Q   302 o'th'] F; at'h Q

284 **taste** experience (the consequences of).
285 **For his particular** As far as he himself is
concerned.
289–91 **The king . . . himself** See Textual
Analysis, p. 281 below.
290 **will** will go.
291 **give him way** not to obstruct him, give him
his head.
291 **leads himself** i.e. follows no lead or guidance but his own, is headstrong.
294 **ruffle** rage, bluster. Q's 'ruff el' is probably the result of a simple misreading of 'ff' as 'ff'
(Duthie, p. 394); 'ruffle' is in Harsnett (Muir).
295–7 **to wilful . . . schoolmasters** The harm
that headstrong men bring on themselves must

teach them a lesson (about how to behave).
298 **He . . . train** Regan assumes that Lear's
'riotous' knights are still with him, or perhaps she
is just making excuses for her conduct (Muir).
299–300 **being . . . abused** i.e. Lear being susceptible to misleading stories or lying tales.
300 **wisdom bids fear** i.e. prudence urges us
to take precautions.
301 **Shut . . . doors** Cornwall's repetition
of Regan's request, or command (297), indicates Gloucester's hesitation or reluctance to comply, though in the end, perhaps prompted by
Cornwall's men, he signals his servants to obey.
Compare Rosenberg, p. 182.

3.1 *Storm still. Enter* KENT [*disguised*] *and a* GENTLEMAN, *severally*

KENT Who's there, besides foul weather?
GENTLEMAN One minded like the weather, most unquietly.
KENT I know you. Where's the king?
GENTLEMAN Contending with the fretful elements;
    Bids the wind blow the earth into the sea,   5
    Or swell the curlèd waters 'bove the main,
    That things might change or cease.
KENT   But who is with him?
GENTLEMAN None but the fool, who labours to out-jest
    His heart-struck injuries.
KENT   Sir, I do know you,
    And dare upon the warrant of my note   10
    Commend a dear thing to you. There is division,
    Although as yet the face of it is covered
    With mutual cunning, 'twixt Albany and Cornwall,
    Who have – as who have not, that their great stars
    Throned and set high? – servants, who seem no less,   15

Act 3, Scene 1   3.1] *Actus Tertius. Scena Prima.* F; *not in* Q   0 SD] F; *Enter Kent and a Gentleman at seuerall doores.*
Q   1 Who's there, besides] F; *Whats here beside* Q   4 elements] F; *element* Q   7 cease.] F *omits eight and a half lines*
here   10 note] F; *Arte* Q   12 is] F; *be* Q   14–21 Who . . . furnishings –] F *substitutes these lines for thirteen lines in* Q (*see*
p. 269 below)   14 have – as] have (as *Theobald;* haue, as F   15 high? –] high?) *Theobald;* high? *Rowe;* high; F

Act 3, Scene 1

0 SD *Storm still* At the Globe, thunder was
created by rolling an iron ball, or cannon-ball ('a
roul'd bullet'), on a sheet of metal, or by drums
beating, or by both; lightning was suggested by a
squib, or firework, set off. (See Andrew Gurr, *The
Shakespearean Stage, 1574–1642,* 2nd edn, 1980,
p. 170, and compare Rosenberg, pp. 183–6; Bratton,
pp. 26–30.)

0 SD GENTLEMAN Whether or not this is the
same Gentleman who entered with Lear and the
Fool in 2.4 is unclear but not of great importance.
He has little to say in 2.4, and both Q and F omit an
exit for him when Lear, Kent, and the Fool leave
(279 SD). Like Kent, he may have become separated
from the others in the stormy night. Although Kent
recognises him as trustworthy, i.e. loyal to the king,
and he was probably played by the same actor,
Oxford regards him as a new character and designates him 'First Gentleman'. Compare Perrett,
pp. 198–9.

4 Contending (1) physically struggling against,
(2) competing in violence and anger (Hunter).

6 main mainland (Onions).

7 things i.e. everything, the world. Compare
3.2.6–9.

7 cease F lacks eight lines here found in Q: see
Textual Analysis, pp. 268–9 below.

8–9 out-jest . . . injuries dispel by jests or jokes
the injuries (by his daughters) that have struck him
to the heart. 'It is the Fool's tragedy that his efforts
to cheer up his master serve only to emphasize
Lear's folly and its dreadful results' (Kittredge).

10 note notice, observation.

11 Commend Entrust.

11 dear important.

11 division conflict, a parting of the ways.

14–21 Who . . . furnishings On the substitution of these lines in F for Q's, see Textual Analysis,
p. 269 below.

14–15 as who . . . high i.e. like all those who
have been so fortunate as to rise to positions of
greatness and power. Presumably, 'throned and set
high' is a past participial phrase = 'since they have
been throned and set high'.

15 who . . . less i.e. who seem to be just servants
(but are really spies).

>   Which are to France the spies and speculations
>   Intelligent of our state. What hath been seen,
>   Either in snuffs and packings of the dukes,
>   Or the hard rein which both of them hath borne
>   Against the old kind king; or something deeper,   20
>   Whereof, perchance, these are but furnishings –
> GENTLEMAN   I will talk further with you.
> KENT   No, do not.
>   For confirmation that I am much more
>   Than my out-wall, open this purse and take
>   What it contains. If you shall see Cordelia –   25
>   As fear not but you shall – show her this ring,
>   And she will tell you who that fellow is
>   That yet you do not know. Fie on this storm!
>   I will go seek the king.
> GENTLEMAN   Give me your hand. Have you no more to say?   30
> KENT   Few words, but to effect more than all yet:
>   That when we have found the king – in which your pain
>   That way, I'll this – he that first lights on him
>   Holla the other.

Exeunt

---

*21 furnishings –] *Rowe;* furnishings. F   22 further] F; farther Q   23 am] F; *not in* Q   *24 out-wall,] Q *corr.;* outwall Q *uncorr.;* out-wall; F   27 that] F; your Q   30 Give . . . say?] *As in* Q; *two lines divided* hand, / Haue F   32 in . . . pain] F; *not in* Q   33 That way, I'll this – he] That way, Ile this: He F; Ile this way, you that, he Q   33 on him] F; *as part of 34* Q   34 Holla] F; hollow Q

16 speculations observers, spies (abstract for concrete).

17 Intelligent of Bearing or giving information about.

18 snuffs huffs, resentments.

18 packings plots, conspiracies. Compare the verb 'pack' = to plot, scheme, intrigue, and *Shr.* 5.1.121: 'Here's packing . . . to deceive us all!' (Muir). The word also appears in *King Leir* 1932.

19 hard rein An equestrian metaphor, signifying severe curbing, with a possible pun on 'reign'.

20 something deeper This is not disclosed because Kent's speech is cut off by the Gentleman, who apparently does not wish to hear any more, forcing Kent to offer reassurances. In Q, Kent interrupts himself at 21 to shift from internal division to foreign invasion. Compare Urkowitz, p. 70.

21 furnishings extrinsic considerations, or pretexts.

22 I . . . you A 'courteous postponement or dismissal of a request' (Delius, cited by Furness). The Gentleman is being prudent.

24 out-wall exterior appearance.

25 If . . . shall In F, Kent does not send the Gentleman to Cordelia, but knowing her approach, he knows that Lear's followers will meet her.

27 fellow A term of address often used for servants, though Schmidt and Muir gloss 'companion', and Furness cites *TN* 3.4.60–78. where the word is understood in both senses.

30 Give . . . say The Gentleman is won over, but Kent has said enough and, in any case, is now intent on finding Lear.

31 to effect in importance.

32–3 in which . . . this i.e. to find the king your effort (pain) lies that way, mine this way. Kent motions accordingly.

3.2 *Storm still. Enter* LEAR *and* FOOL

LEAR   Blow, winds, and crack your cheeks! Rage, blow,
       You cataracts and hurricanoes, spout
       Till you have drenched our steeples, drowned the cocks!
       You sulph'rous and thought-executing fires,
       Vaunt-couriers of oak-cleaving thunderbolts,   5
       Singe my white head; and thou all-shaking thunder,
       Strike flat the thick rotundity o'th'world,
       Crack nature's moulds, all germens spill at once
       That makes ingrateful man.
FOOL   O nuncle, court holy water in a dry house is better than this   10
rain-water out o'door. Good nuncle, in, ask thy daughters
blessing. Here's a night pities neither wise men nor fools.

Act 3, Scene 2   3.2] *Scena Secunda.* F; *not in* Q   0 SD *Storm still.*] F; *not in* Q   2–9 You . . . man.] F; *lines end* . . .
drencht, / . . . sulpherous and / . . . vaunt-currers to / . . . head, / . . . flat / . . . natures / . . . make / . . . man.
Q   2 cataracts] F; caterickes Q   2 hurricanoes] Hyrricano's F; Hircanios Q   3 our] F; The Q   *3 drowned] Q; drown
F   4 sulph'rous] F; sulpherous Q   5 Vaunt-couriers of] F; vaunt-currers to Q   7 Strike] F; smite Q   7 o'th'] F; of the
Q   8 moulds] F; Mold Q   9 makes] F; make Q   10–12 O . . . fools.] F *lineation; four verse lines ending* . . . house / . . .
doore, / . . . blessing, / . . . foole. Q   10 holy water] Q *corr.;* holly water Q *uncorr.;* holy-water F   11 o'] F; a Q   11 in,]
F; in, and Q   *12 wise men] Wisemen F; wise man Q   12 fools] F; foole Q

Act 3, Scene 2

0 SD *Storm still* 'The quality of Lear's resistance . . . is determined by his design in the
total action. The Lear who is weak, very cold,
already partly unbalanced must begin to find
unexpected strengths in his ordeal . . . The
titanic Lears begin to deteriorate under the ero-
sion within and without . . . [A] Lear too
old and weak cannot plausibly ride the storm,
a Lear too stalwart cannot be subdued to the
image – even self-image – of a poor, infirm,
weak old man, unless a massive factor of self-
pity is thrown into the equation' (Rosenberg,
pp. 188–9).
   1 crack your cheeks The winds are personified, with cheeks ballooned, as in old maps.
   2 cataracts flood-gates of heaven.
   2 hurricanoes waterspouts.
   3 drenched . . . cocks Lear demands a second deluge. Rosenberg, pp. 191–2, notes the sexual
undercurrent that runs through this speech.
   3 cocks weathercocks.
   4 thought-executing fires i.e. lightning whose
swiftness exceeds thought (compare *Temp.* 1.2.201–
3), or whose fearsomeness extinguishes it. The
lightning flash precedes the actual bolt, or missile,
hurled by the thunder.
   5 Vaunt-couriers Forerunners. Harsnett uses
the term (Muir).
   5 oak-cleaving thunderbolts A favourite

Shakespearean image: Muir cites *Temp.* 5.1.44–6,
Cor. 5.3.152–3, *MM* 2.2.115–16.
   7–9 Strike . . . man Delius (cited by Furness)
compares the spherical earth with the 'roundness of
gestation'; the lines continue the image of nature's
orgasm (3 n. above).
   8 Crack . . . moulds Break the forms nature
uses in the process of creation.
   8 germens seeds; as in *Mac.* 4.1.59. 'Lear
wishes to prevent the birth of any more people,
so that the ungrateful race of man will die out'
(Muir).
   8 spill spill out; hence, destroy.
   10 court holy water i.e. the flattery of the
court. Compare Cotgrave: '*Eau beniste de Cour.*
Court holy water; complements, faire words,
flattering speeches' (Malone, cited by Furness).
Arthur Kinney, 'Conjectures on the composition
of *King Lear*', *S.Sur.* 33 (1980), 20, cites Iustus
Lipsius, *Sixe Bookes of Politickes or Civil Doctrine*,
trans. William Jones (1594), 3.8, '*How a Prince
ought to behaue him selfe in hearing counsel*': 'Let
him freelie permit his Counsellers, to speake their
minde boldlie, not louing *this court holy vvater.
Flattery doth more often subuert & ouerthrow the
wealth of a kingdome, then an open enemie . . . That
Emperour is miserable from vvhom the troth is hidden.*'
   11–12 ask . . . blessing i.e. ask a blessing from
your daughters. The verb here takes two objects;
compare 5.3.10 (Kittredge).

LEAR Rumble thy bellyful; spit, fire; spout, rain!
Nor rain, wind, thunder, fire are my daughters.
I tax not you, you elements, with unkindness.   15
I never gave you kingdom, called you children.
You owe me no subscription. Then let fall
Your horrible pleasure. Here I stand your slave,
A poor, infirm, weak, and despised old man;
But yet I call you servile ministers,   20
That will with two pernicious daughters join
Your high-engendered battles 'gainst a head
So old and white as this. O, ho! 'tis foul.

FOOL He that has a house to put 's head in has a good head-piece.
[*Sings*] The codpiece that will house   25
Before the head has any,
The head and he shall louse;
So beggars marry many.
The man that makes his toe

---

15 tax] F; taske Q   **17–23** You . . . foul.] F; *lines end* . . . plesure [*turned under*] / . . . weak & / . . . seruile / . . . ioin'd / . . . white / . . . foule. Q   **17** Then] F; why then Q   **21** will] F; ioin'd Q   **22** battles] F; battel Q   **23** ho!] F; *not in* Q   **24** put 's] F; put his Q   **25** SD] *Capell; not in* Q, F   **25–32** The . . . wake.] *Johnson's lineation; four verse lines ending* . . . any; / . . . many. / . . . make, / . . . wake. F; *as prose* Q

14 fire Disyllabic.
15 tax charge, accuse.
17 subscription submission, allegiance.
18–23 Here . . . as this Lear shifts in these lines from self-pity to defiance to a mixture of both pity and defiance.
20 ministers agents.
22 high-engendered i.e. coming from on high (the heavens).
22 battles battalions, armies.
24 head-piece (1) helmet, head-covering, (2) brain.
25 SD *Sings* Although Hunter, p. 340, finds these lines unsuitable for music and thus does not include Capell's SD, he agrees that 72–5 below are sung and cites the SD from *TN*. The storm is apparently not a consideration to Shakespeare in either case. Compare 72–5 n.
25–32 The codpiece . . . wake In the first quatrain the Fool comments on the danger of the sexual appetite overcoming prudence; i.e. reckless fornication leads to forced marriages, beggary, and disease. The second quatrain comments on another foolish inversion of values that eventually leads to misery. Compare the proverb, 'Let not at thy heart what should be at thy heel' (Tilley H317). The Fool alludes to Lear's favouring of Gonerill and Regan over Cordelia, but he also continues the theme of

sexual licence contrasted with real love (see 29 n. below).
25 codpiece (1) fool, (2) euphemism for the penis (as in *MM* 3.2.115). The codpiece (suggested here by 'head-piece') was part of men's clothing worn at the crotch, partly to hide, partly to emphasise the penis and scrotum. Court fools often wore exaggerated versions of the codpiece (compare 38 below). Wiles, p. 190, suggests that the Fool does not wear one but puts his bauble between his legs to mime the lines.
25 house i.e. fornicate.
26 any any house, i.e. adequate provision.
27 louse i.e. become lousy.
28 many The Fool refers to the paradox of 'the Beggarman and his long line of doxies. He "marries" so many because he is poor (the result of an initial imprudence), and not vice versa. The four lines give a kind of condensed Rake's Progress . . .' (Danby, p. 111). But 'many' may also refer to lice; or the word order may be inverted for the sake of rhyme: 'many beggars marry after this fashion' (NS).
29 toe Danby, p. 111, considers the toe a symbol of the phallus, paralleling 'codpiece'. The line thus contrasts sexual promiscuity with love ('heart' (30)).

What he his heart should make, 30
Shall of a corn cry woe,
And turn his sleep to wake.
For there was never yet fair woman but she made mouths in
a glass.

Enter KENT [*disguised*]

LEAR No, I will be the pattern of all patience. 35
I will say nothing.
KENT Who's there?
FOOL Marry, here's grace and a codpiece; that's a wise man and a
fool.
KENT Alas, sir, are you here? Things that love night 40
Love not such nights as these. The wrathful skies
Gallow the very wanderers of the dark
And make them keep their caves. Since I was man
Such sheets of fire, such bursts of horrid thunder,
Such groans of roaring wind and rain I never 45
Remember to have heard. Man's nature cannot carry
Th'affliction nor the fear.
LEAR   Let the great gods,
That keep this dreadful pudder o'er our heads,

---

31 of] F; haue Q 33 but] F, Q *corr.*; hut Q *uncorr.* 34 SD] F; *after 35* Q *38 wise man] wiseman Q; Wiseman F 40–6
Alas . . . carry] F *lineation; eight lines ending* . . . here? / . . . these, / . . . of the / . . . caues, / . . . fire, / . . . grones
of / . . . remember / . . . cary. Q 40 are] F; sit Q 42 wanderers] F; wanderer Q 43 make] F; makes Q 45 never] F;
ne're Q 47 Th'] F; The Q 47 fear] F; force Q 47–58 Let . . . sinning.] F *lineation; eleven lines ending* . . . dreadful /
. . . now, / . . . within thee / . . . Iustice, / . . . periur'd, and / . . . incestious, / . . . couert / . . . life, / . . . centers, /
. . . grace, / . . . sinning. Q 48 pudder] F; Powther Q; Thundering Q2

33–4 For . . . glass A diversionary tactic by the
Fool following his rather pointed satire (Furness);
an oblique allusion to the vanity and hypocrisy of
Gonerill and Regan (Muir; compare 2.2.32 n.). To
'make mouths in a glass' is to practise smiling or
grimacing in a mirror; it can also signal contempt,
as in *Ham.* 4.4.50.

38 Marry A common exclamation, derived from
'by the Virgin Mary'.

38 grace and a codpiece An apparent reference to Lear (the king's grace) and the Fool (compare 25 n.), ambiguous because of Lear's foolish
behaviour and the Fool's references to him as a
fool, as in the previous song. 'This is the dialectic
of man, stretched to its limits: man is love and lust,
wisdom and folly' (Rosenberg, p. 195).

40 are you here Q's 'sit you here' may reflect
the interpretative attitude Lear assumes above as
the 'pattern of all patience' (35–6) (compare *TN*
2.4.114–15). F's change lets the emphasis fall on

'here' but does not necessarily require Lear to keep
standing (Urkowitz, 'Editorial tradition', pp. 36–7).

42 Gallow Terrify.

42 wanderers . . . dark wild nocturnal animals.

46–7 Man's . . . fear Kent's words underscore
Lear's titanism. The upheaval in physical nature
reflects the upheavals in international relations
(conflict with France), the state (division between
the dukes), the family, and the individual. According to Kent, the storm is beyond normal human
endurance, not only for what it does (causes affliction, i.e. physical buffeting), but for what it means
(the 'fear') – the aspect of the storm that Lear con-
centrates upon in the lines that follow.

46 carry bear, endure.

48 pudder Variant of 'pother' = turmoil,
tumult. 'Pother' historically rhymed with 'other',
'smother', 'brother' and was sometimes spelled
'puther', 'pudder' (*OED*).

Find out their enemies now. Tremble, thou wretch,
That hast within thee undivulgèd crimes   50
Unwhipped of justice. Hide thee, thou bloody hand,
Thou perjured and thou simular of virtue
That art incestuous. Caitiff, to pieces shake,
That under covert and convenient seeming
Has practised on man's life. Close pent-up guilts,   55
Rive your concealing continents and cry
These dreadful summoners grace. I am a man
More sinned against than sinning.

KENT   Alack, bare-headed?
Gracious my lord, hard by here is a hovel.
Some friendship will it lend you 'gainst the tempest.   60
Repose you there, while I to this hard house –
More harder than the stones whereof 'tis raised,
Which even but now, demanding after you,
Denied me to come in – return and force
Their scanted courtesy.

LEAR   My wits begin to turn.   65
Come on, my boy. How dost, my boy? Art cold?
I am cold myself. – Where is this straw, my fellow?
The art of our necessities is strange,

---

52 simular] F; simular man Q   53 incestuous] F; incestious Q   53 to] F; in Q   55 Has] F; hast Q   56 concealing
continents] F; concealed centers Q   58 than] then F; their Q   58–65 Alack . . . courtesy.] F *lineation; as prose* Q   61
while] F; whilst Q   62 harder than] F; hard then is Q   62 stones] F; stone Q   63 you] F; me Q   65 wits begin] F; wit
begins Q   68–70 The . . . heart] F; *lines end . . . can, / . . . poore, / . . . heart* Q

49 Find . . . now The fear caused by the storm
will lead guilty creatures (criminals and malefactors) to reveal themselves as enemies of the gods.
Compare 46–7 above.
    51 of by.
    51 bloody hand i.e. murderer (metonymy).
    52 simular counterfeiter, pretender. Compare
Tyndale's Prologue to Rom. in his New Testament
(1526): 'Christ . . . calleth them [the Pharisees]
ypocrites, that is to safe Simulars' (*OED*).
    53 Caitiff Wretch.
    54 seeming hypocrisy.
    55 practised on plotted against.
    55 Close pent-up guilts Crimes kept secret.
    56 Rive . . . continents Slit open the containers
that hide you.
    56–7 cry . . . grace beg for mercy from these
terrible agents of vengeance. A summoner was a
minor official who summoned offenders to ecclesiastical courts.

57 grace mercy (Schmidt).
    57 I Emphatic (Kittredge). Lear contrasts him-
self with those murderers, hypocrites, and other
'pent-up guilts'.
    59 Gracious my lord My gracious lord; com-
pare 1.1.90.
    61 hard pitiless, unyielding.
    61 house household.
    63 demanding after asking for.
    65 My . . . turn 'From this point he becomes
aware of the sufferings of others' (NS).
    66–7 Come . . . myself Salvini in the role
of Lear took off his cloak here and wrapped it
around the shivering Fool, who may be near col-
lapse (Rosenberg, p. 197).
    68–9 The art . . . precious Poverty (necessity)
is an unusual alchemist; it can transform worthless
things into precious ones.

And can make vile things precious. Come, your hovel. –
Poor fool and knave, I have one part in my heart   70
That's sorry yet for thee.
FOOL [*Sings*] He that has and a little tiny wit,
   With heigh-ho, the wind and the rain,
  Must make content with his fortunes fit,
   Though the rain it raineth every day.   75
LEAR   True, boy. – Come, bring us to this hovel.
        [*Exeunt Lear and Kent*]
FOOL   This is a brave night to cool a courtesan. I'll speak a pro-
phecy ere I go:
  When priests are more in word than matter;
  When brewers mar their malt with water;   80
  When nobles are their tailors' tutors,
  No heretics burned, but wenches' suitors,
  Then shall the realm of Albion
  Come to great confusion.
  When every case in law is right;   85
  No squire in debt nor no poor knight;
  When slanders do not live in tongues,

---

69 And] F; *that* Q   69 your] F; *you* Q   70 in] F; *of* Q   71 That's sorry] F; *That sorrowes* Q   72 SD] *Capell; not in* Q,
F   72–5 He . . . day.] F; *as prose* Q   72 and] F; *not in* Q   75 Though] F; *for* Q   76 boy] F; *my good boy* Q   76 SD]
Capell; Exit. F; *not in* Q   77–93 FOOL This . . . time.] F; *not in* Q   83–4 Then . . . confusion.] *Pope's lineation; placed
here by NS; as one line following* 90 F (*see* Commentary)

72–5 He . . . day Adapted from Feste's song, *TN*
5.1.387–92. 'The Fool may be referring to Lear, or
to himself' (Muir).
 74 Must . . . fit Either (1) must make his happiness fit his fortunes (Kittredge), or (2) must be
content with the fortunes suitable to such a person.
 77 This . . . courtesan A pun on 'night' and
'knight' may explain why the comment on the
weather takes this form (Hunter). It would also
partly explain the medieval parody that follows.
 77 brave fine.
 79–92 When . . . feet These lines and those
immediately preceding and following them were
long suspected of being a non-Shakespearean theatrical interpolation. See Textual Analysis, p. 281
below. Warburton was the first to detect two
prophecies (79–84: a satire of England under James
I; 85–92: utopia), and to propose the relineation
that is followed here and in NS. Wittreich, echo-
ing Malone, argues that the lines were deliberately
scrambled (p. 62).
 79 When . . . matter i.e. when clergymen talk
more for the sake of talking than to say something.

The pseudo-Chaucerian verse imitated here is cited
in Puttenham's *Arte of English Poesie* (1589) in the
section on merismus or 'the distributor', i.e. amplification (Taylor, 'Date and authorship', p. 383).
 81 nobles . . . tutors aristocrats teach their
tailors. Compare *Shr.* 4.3.86–95: Petruchio has
instructed and now criticises a tailor (Kittredge).
 82 heretics (1) religious dissenters, (2) lovers.
Compare Donne,'The Indifferent': 'Poore Here-
tiques in love there bee, / Which thinke to stablish
dangerous constancie.'
 82 burned A quibble on 'infected with venereal
diseases' (NS).
 83–4 Then . . . confusion See collation. If they
were a marginal insertion in copy, the lines may
have confused the compositor, who set them as one
line in the wrong place (NS).
 83 Albion An old name for Britain.
 85 right (1) just, or (2) genuine (NS). Legal procedures, then as now, were notoriously complex.
 86 nor no Double negatives do not cancel each
other out.
 87 live i.e. make a permanent residence in.

Nor cutpurses come not to throngs;
When usurers tell their gold i'th'field,
And bawds and whores do churches build,   90
Then comes the time, who lives to see't,
That going shall be used with feet.
This prophecy Merlin shall make, for I live before his time.

Exit

3.3   *Enter* GLOUCESTER *and* EDMOND

GLOUCESTER Alack, alack, Edmond, I like not this unnatural
dealing. When I desired their leave that I might pity him, they
took from me the use of mine own house, charged me on pain
of perpetual displeasure neither to speak of him, entreat for
him, or any way sustain him.   5
EDMOND Most savage and unnatural!
GLOUCESTER Go to, say you nothing. There is division between
the dukes, and a worse matter than that. I have received a letter
this night – 'tis dangerous to be spoken – I have locked the
letter in my closet. These injuries the king now bears will be   10

Act 3, Scene 3   3.3] *Scaena Tertia.* F; *not in* Q   0 SD] F; *Enter Gloster and the Bastard with lights.* Q   1–5 Alack . . .
him.] F; *six verse lines ending* . . . this, / . . . leaue / . . . from me/ . . . paine / . . . of him, / . . . sustaine him. Q   3
took] F; tooke me Q   4 perpetual] F; their Q   5 or] F; nor Q   7–17 Go . . . careful.] F; *thirteen verse lines ending* . . .
the Dukes, [*turned over*] / . . . receiued / . . . spoken, / . . . iniuries / . . . home / . . . landed, / . . . him, and / . . .
talke / . . . of him / . . . gon / . . . threatned me, / . . . there is / . . . careful. Q   7 There is] F; ther's a Q   7 between]
F; betwixt Q

88 Nor . . . throngs A crowd was an irresistible target for pickpockets, or cutpurses, as they were then called, because money was kept in a purse strung from a girdle.

89 usurers moneylenders, notorious for secrecy.

89 tell count.

90 bawds . . . build i.e. when these low characters are religiously and philanthropically motivated.

92 going . . . feet i.e. normality shall reign and perversions end.

92 going walking.

93 This . . . time A third prophecy. The Lear legend antedates Arthurian legend by centuries.

Act 3, Scene 3

0 SD Enter . . . EDMOND Q's addition, *with lights*, requires the actors to enter the Globe stage carrying torches – a conventional sign to indicate night scenes and perhaps here to suggest a scene indoors.

1–2 unnatural dealing i.e. Gonerill's and

Regan's treatment of their father.

2–5 When . . . him By pitying the king, Gloucester begins to make his move in the conflict between father and daughters; as a result, his guests confiscate his house and threaten still worse if he continues to express compassion for Lear or tries to help him.

2 pity take pity on, relieve.

6 Most . . . unnatural In the context of the entire scene, these words are ironic, but they must be said without deliberate irony.

7 Go to An exclamation: 'Quiet! Enough!'

8 worse matter Possibly the French invasion, although the suggestion of some vague, ominous threat is like Kent's 'something deeper' (3.1.20). Compare also 'strange things toward' (16 below).

8 a letter See 3.5.8–9. Like Kent, Gloucester is in communication with Cordelia and the French forces.

10 closet private room.

revenged home. There is part of a power already footed. We
must incline to the king. I will look him and privily relieve him.
Go you and maintain talk with the duke, that my charity be not
of him perceived. If he ask for me, I am ill and gone to bed. If I
die for it – as no less is threatened me – the king my old master   15
must be relieved. There is strange things toward, Edmond;
pray you be careful.   *Exit*
EDMOND   This courtesy, forbid thee, shall the duke
        Instantly know, and of that letter too.
        This seems a fair deserving, and must draw me   20
        That which my father loses: no less than all.
        The younger rises when the old doth fall.   *Exit*

3.4 *Enter* LEAR, KENT [*disguised*], *and* FOOL

KENT   Here is the place, my lord. Good my lord, enter.
       The tyranny of the open night's too rough
       For nature to endure.   *Storm still*
LEAR   Let me alone.
KENT   Good my lord, enter here.
LEAR   Wilt break my heart?
KENT   I had rather break mine own. Good my lord, enter.   5

---

11 There is] F; Ther's Q   11 footed] F; landed Q   12 look] F; seeke Q   14 bed. If] bed; if *Rowe*²; bed, if F; bed, though Q   15 for it] F; for't Q   16 There is strange things toward, Edmond;] there is / Some stra̅ge thing toward, *Edmund* Q; There . . . toward *Edmund*, F   18–22 This . . . fall.] F *lineation; four verse lines ending* . . . know [*turned under*] / . . . deseruing / . . . lesse / . . . fall. Q   21 all.] all, Q, F   22 The] F; then Q   22 doth] F; doe Q   **Act 3, Scene 4** 3.4] *Scena Quarta.* F; *not in* Q   1–3 Here . . . endure.] F *lineation; as prose* Q   2 The] F, Q *corr.*; the the Q *uncorr.*   3 SD] F; *not in* Q   4 here] F; *not in* Q   5 I . . . enter.] *As in* Q; *two lines divided* owne, / Good F

11 **home** to the full, thoroughly.
11 **footed** landed.
12 **look** i.e. look for.
14 **of** by.
14 **If . . . bed** A 'social lie': compare 2.4.81–2.
14–16 **If . . . relieved** Gloucester takes his stand, aware of the risks, but now fully committed, morally and otherwise. In assuming the major initiative in the preservation of Lear, he risks more than the disguised Kent, and henceforth it is he who is the suffering servant, 'punished unjustly for his fidelity to human values' (Warren, 'Diminution', p. 63).
16 **toward** coming, about to happen.
17 SD *Exit* 'With a touch, an embrace, [Gloucester] goes to face the lightning' (Rosenberg, p. 200). Edmond watches him leave, with a knowing smile and even, perhaps, contempt.
18 **courtesy** i.e. to Lear.
18 **forbid** forbidden to.

20 **This . . . deserving** My action bids fair to merit a good reward.
20–1 **draw . . . all** Edmond calculates correctly: see 3.5.14.
22 **The . . . fall** Compare Tilley R136: 'The rising of one man is the falling of another' (NS).

Act 3, Scene 4
0 SD In Trevor Nunn's Royal Shakespeare Company production (1968), Eric Porter as Lear, though gaunt and haggard, carried the Fool on stage in his arms, anticipating the end, when he would enter carrying Cordelia (Rosenberg, p. 201).
1 **the place** Compare 3.2.59.
2 **open night** night in the open.
3 **For . . . endure** Kent's repeated theme (compare 3.2.46–7). But Lear persists in opposing his nature against the storm's.
4 **Wilt** Wilt thou.

LEAR Thou think'st 'tis much that this contentious storm
        Invades us to the skin: so 'tis to thee.
        But where the greater malady is fixed,
        The lesser is scarce felt. Thou'dst shun a bear,
        But if thy flight lay toward the roaring sea,   10
        Thou'dst meet the bear i'th'mouth. When the mind's free,
        The body's delicate. This tempest in my mind
        Doth from my senses take all feeling else,
        Save what beats there: filial ingratitude.
        Is it not as this mouth should tear this hand   15
        For lifting food to't? But I will punish home.
        No, I will weep no more. In such a night
        To shut me out? Pour on, I will endure.
        In such a night as this! O Regan, Gonerill,
        Your old kind father, whose frank heart gave all –   20
        O that way madness lies; let me shun that;
        No more of that.
KENT   Good my lord, enter here.
LEAR Prithee, go in thyself, seek thine own ease.
        This tempest will not give me leave to ponder
        On things would hurt me more; but I'll go in.   25

---

6 contentious] F; crulentious Q *uncorr.*; tempestious Q *corr.* *7 skin: so] skin.so F *uncorr.*; skinso F *corr.*; skin, so Q   9 Thou'dst] F; thou wouldst Q2 *10 thy] Q; they F   10 roaring] F; roring Q *corr.*; raging Q *uncorr.*, Q2   11 i'th'] F; it'h Q *12 body's] bodies Q, F *12 This] Q *corr.*; the Q *uncorr.*, Q2, F   14 beats] F, Q *corr.*; beares Q *uncorr.*, Q2   14 there: . . . ingratitude] there . . . ingratitude, F *uncorr.*; there, . . . ingratitude F *corr.*; their . . . ingratitude Q   16 to't] F, Q; to it Q2   16 home] F; sure Q   17–18 In . . . endure.] F; *not in* Q   19–21 O . . . that;] F *lineation; three verse lines ending . . .* father / . . . lies, [*turned over*] / . . . that. Q   20 gave] F; gaue you Q   21 lies] Q, F *corr.*; lie F *uncorr.*   22 here] F; *not in* Q   23 thine own] F; thy one Q

---

8 **greater malady** i.e. his mental torment, as 11–14 explain.
8 **fixed** set, established.
11 **i'th'mouth** i.e. face to face.
11–14 **When . . . ingratitude** Compare Montaigne, *Apology for Raymond Sebond*, iv.70: 'our senses are . . . many times dulled by the passions of the mind' (Muir).
11 **free** i.e. of pain, undisturbed, untroubled.
12 **delicate** sensitive.
14 **beats** (1) throbs, as of thought, (2) rages, as of a storm (Muir).
15–16 **Is . . . to't** Is it not as if my mouth should attack my hand for bringing food to it? The image suggests the absurd rebellion of one part of the body against another (compare *Cor.* 1.1.96 ff.). Lear conceives of

the family – himself and his daughters – as an organic whole.
16 **home** thoroughly, to the full.
18 **Pour . . . endure** Lear asserts his titanism, his defiance against nature and all it can do to him. On F's addition, see Textual Analysis, p. 282 below.
20 **frank** (1) liberal, bounteous (of giving), (2) open, without guile.
21 **that way** i.e. dwelling upon his foolish generosity and his daughters' ingratitude.
23 **Prithee . . . ease** Lear has begun to consider others first, a marked change in his attitude and behaviour.
25 **things . . . more** Lear refers to filial ingratitude and his own foolishness. Compare 21 above.
25 **would** that would.

In, boy, go first. You houseless poverty –
Nay, get thee in; I'll pray, and then I'll sleep.

Exit [*Fool*]

Poor naked wretches, wheresoe'er you are
That bide the pelting of this pitiless storm,
How shall your houseless heads and unfed sides,   30
Your looped and windowed raggedness defend you
From seasons such as these? O I have ta'en
Too little care of this. Take physic, pomp,
Expose thyself to feel what wretches feel,
That thou mayst shake the superflux to them   35
And show the heavens more just.

Enter FOOL

EDGAR [*Within*] Fathom and half; fathom and half; poor Tom!
FOOL Come not in here, nuncle! Here's a spirit! Help me, help
me!

26–7 In . . . sleep.] F; *not in* Q 26 poverty –] *Rowe;* pouertie, F 27 SD] *Johnson (subst.); Exit.* F *(after 26); not in* Q 29
storm] F; night Q *31 looped] loopt Q; lop'd, F 36 SD] *This edn; Enter Edgar, and Foole.* F; *The Fool runs out from the
hovel. / Theobald (after 39; after 37, Capell); not in* Q 37 EDGAR Fathom . . . Tom!] F; *not in* Q 37 SD] *Theobald; not
in* F

26–7 **In, boy . . . sleep** See Textual Analysis.
pp. 282–3 below. The lines, added or restored in
F, underscore Lear's changing attitude and lead
directly and naturally into his prayer, which is
interrupted poignantly by insistent concern for his
Fool.

26 **houseless poverty** Compare 'Poor naked
wretches' (28 ff.). Here, concrete and abstract
are combined in a typically Shakespearean phrase.
Compare 31 below.

27 **I'll pray** 'In the night's bleak exposure he
kneels down, like a child at bedtime, to pray'
(Granville-Barker, p. 292). But most editions,
except Oxford, omit a SD.

28–36 Macready deliberately pointed this speech
at Queen Victoria during a performance she
attended (Bratton, p. 143).

29 **bide** endure.

30 **sides** Not the sides of the chest, as at 2.4.190,
but the part of the body principally fed by nour-
ishment, as in *Tim.* 4.3.12 (Schmidt).

31 **looped . . . raggedness** More yoking
of concrete and abstract: the ragged clothes of
the poor are full of loopholes and openings
(windows).

32–3 **O . . . this** By assuming responsibility
for the wretched state of his subjects, Lear takes
a major step forward in understanding himself.

33 **physic** medical treatment, possibly a purge.

33 **pomp** Abstract for concrete, i.e. rich and

powerful persons accustomed to splendour and
luxury.

34–6 **Expose . . . just** This is the 'physic' Lear
prescribes: the great ones of the earth should subject themselves to the experiences of the poor (as
Lear himself now does); the action will lead them
to surrender unnecessary possessions ('superflux'),
and by giving them to the poor demonstrate how
heaven can be more just than we realise. Compare Gloucester's speech, 4.1.62–6, where the same
point is made.

37 SD **Enter** FOOL Q has no SD, while F has
both Edgar and the Fool enter here, though Kent
later calls Edgar (as Poor Tom) to come forth at
42–3. A line (37) is also missing from Q, which
seems (like the Bedlam's entrance) a response to
Lear's prayer (see Textual Analysis, p. 283 below).
Theobald's emendations suggest a plausible staging of the scene: the Fool comes running out of
the hovel badly frightened by what he sees there –
the hideous figure of the Bedlam beggar, who utters
a despairing cry from within. His hovel is an imagined place, entered perhaps from a trap (as in the
1990 Renaissance Theatre Company production) or
from behind curtains upstage centre.

37 **Fathom . . . half** 'Edgar speaks as if he were
a sailor sounding the depth of the water in the hold
of a leaking ship. He is almost "swamped" by the
storm' (Kittredge).

38 **spirit** supernatural being, demon.

KENT   Give me thy hand. Who's there?   40

FOOL   A spirit, a spirit! He says his name's Poor Tom.

KENT   What art thou that dost grumble there i'th'straw? Come forth.

[*Enter* EDGAR, *disguised as a madman*]

EDGAR   Away, the foul fiend follows me. Through the sharp hawthorn blow the winds. Humh! Go to thy bed and warm   45
thee.

LEAR   Didst thou give all to thy daughters? And art thou come to this?

EDGAR   Who gives anything to Poor Tom, whom the foul fiend hath led through fire and through flame, through ford and   50
whirlpool, o'er bog and quagmire; that hath laid knives under his pillow and halters in his pew; set ratsbane by his porridge; made him proud of heart to ride on a bay trotting-horse over four-inched bridges, to course his own shadow for a traitor. Bless thy five wits, Tom's a-cold! O do, de, do, de, do de. Bless   55

41 a spirit] F; *not in* Q   41 name's] F, Q; name is Q2   42 i'th'] F; in the Q   43 SD] *Theobald; not in* Q, F   44 Through] F; thorough Q   45 blow the winds.] F; blowes the cold wind, Q   45 Humh!] F; *not in* Q   45 bed] F; cold bed Q   47 Didst thou give] F; Hast thou giuen Q   47 thy] F; thy two Q   *50 through fire] Q; though Fire F   50 through flame] F; *not in* Q   *50–1 ford and whirlpool] foord, and whirli-poole Q; Sword, and Whirle-poole F   51 hath] F; has Q   52 porridge] F; pottage Q   *55 Bless] Q; Blisse F   55 O . . . de.] F; *not in* Q   *55 Bless] Q; blisse F

44 **Away** i.e. keep away. As someone followed or attended by demons, Edgar warns the others off.

44–5 **Through . . . winds** See collation. Hunter follows Q and inserts 'cold' before 'winds', citing the same phrase at 89 below. Oxford omits 'cold' here but with Q inserts it before 'bed' in the next sentence, following *Shr.* Induction 1.9–10 (see *Textual Companion*, p. 535). F's omission of 'cold' in both places may seem odd (Duthie, p. 148), but the lines are satisfactory without the adjective; if anything, they are stronger for the omissions.

45 **Humh** Edgar, half-naked, shivers with cold (Kittredge).

45–6 **Go . . . thee** See 44–5 n. above. Duthie, p. 149, thinks an actor may have interpolated 'cold' before 'bed' to make an antithesis. He follows F both here and earlier, though NS retains Q's 'cold' before 'winds'.

47–8 **Didst . . . this** Lear's monomania becomes evident, and his descent into madness is aided by the image of the Bedlam beggar. 'Immediately after the *Poor naked wretches* speech [Lear] finds a figure with whom he can wholly identify himself and whose role (of madman) he can take over' (Hunter).

49–58 **foul fiend . . . there** As Theobald first noted, many details of this speech are indebted to Harsnett's *Declaration*. See also Muir, 'Samuel Harsnett and *King Lear*', *RES*, n.s., 2 (1951),

17. Suicide, a result of the sin of despair, was a favourite temptation of the devil. Compare Marlowe, *Dr Faustus* 2.2.20–2: 'then swordes and kniues, / Poyson, gunnes, halters, and invenomd steele / Are layde before me to dispatch my selfe' (Steevens, cited by Muir).

50 **ford** 'Sword' in F is an apparent manuscript misreading (Duthie, p. 178). All the other dangers are natural phenomena: 'Sword' is exceptional; Q's 'foord' is doubtless right.

51 **that** i.e. he that.

52 **pew** A 'gallery in a house or outside a chamber window – not a pew in church' (Kittredge; from Old French *puye*, 'parapet, balustrade, balcony' (*OED*); compare Cotgrave, *Appuye*: 'An open, and outstanding terrace, or gallery, set on th'outside with railes to lean vpon').

52 **porridge** thick soup.

53–4 **ride . . . bridges** i.e. perform a difficult feat, like walking a tight-rope.

54 **course** chase. Compare the image of a cat chasing its own tail (NS) and Tilley s281, 'To be afraid of one's own shadow'.

55 **five wits** These are common wit, imagination, fantasy, estimation, and memory. They were sometimes confused with the five senses, though not in Sonnet 141.9–10.

55 **O do . . . de** Sounds of chattering teeth.

thee from whirlwinds, star-blasting, and taking. Do Poor Tom
some charity, whom the foul fiend vexes. There could I have
him now, and there, and there again, and there.

                         Storm still

LEAR   What, has his daughters brought him to this pass?
       Couldst thou save nothing? Wouldst thou give 'em all?   60
FOOL   Nay, he reserved a blanket, else we had been all shamed.
LEAR   Now all the plagues that in the pendulous air
       Hang fated o'er men's faults, light on thy daughters!
KENT   He hath no daughters, sir.
LEAR   Death, traitor! Nothing could have subdued nature   65
       To such a lowness but his unkind daughters.
       Is it the fashion that discarded fathers
       Should have thus little mercy on their flesh?
       Judicious punishment: 'twas this flesh begot
       Those pelican daughters.   70
EDGAR Pillicock sat on Pillicock Hill; alow, alow, loo, loo.
FOOL   This cold night will turn us all to fools and madmen.

---

56 star-blasting] F; starre-blusting Q   58 and there again, and there.] F; and and there againe Q   58 SD] F; *not in* Q   *59
What, has] What, Q; Ha's F   60 Wouldst] F; didst Q   60 'em] F; them Q   63 light] F; fall Q   69 begot] F; *begins next
line* Q   71 Pillicock Hill] F; pelicocks hill Q   71 alow, alow, loo, loo.] F; a lo lo lo. Q

56 **star-blasting** In astrology, the adverse influence of malignant stars, which could afflict one with
disease.
56 **taking** The state of becoming infected,
blasted.
57–8 **There . . . there** 'Edgar makes grabs at
different parts of his body as if to catch vermin –
or devils' (Kittredge).
59 **What, has** See collation. On metrical and
other grounds, Duthie, pp. 15–16, recommends
combining Q and F. Q may have inadvertently omitted 'has'; in correcting Q, the F collator or compositor may have misread the correction as a substitution instead of an addition.
59 **pass** predicament, extremity (Schmidt).
61 **reserved** NS suggests an allusion to Lear's
'reservation' of a hundred knights.
62–3 **all . . . faults** The idea that infectious
plagues were airborne was commonplace, as was
the notion of 'star-blasting' (56), the infliction of
disease as a punishment for malefactors.
63 **fated** destined (i.e. to fall).
63 **light** alight, fall.
65 **subdued** reduced; accent on the first syllable.
65 **nature** i.e. human nature.

67–8 **Is . . . flesh** Lear refers to Edgar's mortified
body (see 2.3.15–16). In his monomania, he insists
Edgar must be the victim of ungrateful and cruel
daughters, despite Kent's statement (64). Edwin
Booth as Lear drew a thorn or spike from Edgar's
arm and stuck it in his own (Sprague, cited by NS).
69 **Judicious** Fitting, well-judged.
69–70 **'twas . . . daughters** The bawdry that
Lear utters in his madness (e.g. 4.5.108–25) may
be traced to this perception.
70 **pelican daughters** The pelican was proverbial for feeding its young with its own flesh and
blood, and the young were proverbial for cruelty
to their parents.
71 **Pillicock . . . Hill** Edgar's fragment, suggested by 'pelican', may be part of a nursery rhyme:
'Pillycock, Pillycock sat on a hill; / If he's not
gone, he sits there still' (Collier, cited by Furness).
Compare 'Pillicock' = (1) term of endearment, darling, (2) the penis; 'Pillicock Hill' = female genitals
(Partridge).
71 **alow . . . loo** Variously explained. Furness
suggests the sound of a cockcrow; Kittredge, a wild
'halloo' as if to a hawk; Perrett, a Bedlam's horn;
etc., etc.

EDGAR Take heed o'th'foul fiend, obey thy parents, keep thy
words' justice, swear not, commit not with man's sworn spouse,
set not thy sweet heart on proud array. Tom's a-cold.   75
LEAR What hast thou been?
EDGAR A servingman, proud in heart and mind, that curled my
hair, wore gloves in my cap, served the lust of my mistress'
heart, and did the act of darkness with her. Swore as many
oaths as I spake words, and broke them in the sweet face of   80
heaven. One that slept in the contriving of lust and waked to
do it. Wine loved I dearly, dice dearly, and in woman out-
paramoured the Turk. False of heart, light of ear, bloody of
hand; hog in sloth, fox in stealth, wolf in greediness, dog in
madness, lion in prey. Let not the creaking of shoes nor the   85

---

*74 words' justice] *Schmidt 1879;* words Iustice F; words iustly Q; word justly *Pope;* word's justice *Knight*   75 sweet
heart] Q; Sweet-heart F   *77 servingman,] Q; Seruingman? F   82 I dearly] F; I deeply Q

73 foul fiend Possibly suggested by similar-sounding 'fool' in the preceding line (NS, citing Kökeritz, p. 75, who also notes word-play in *3H6* 5.6.18–20).

73–5 obey . . . array A version of five of the Ten Commandments; specifically, to honour one's parents, not to commit false witness, take the Lord's name in vain, commit adultery, or engage in covetousness. Compare also 1 Tim. 2.9: '. . . that they aray them selues in comely apparell, with shamefastnes and modestie, not with . . . golde, or pearles, or costly apparell' (Noble, Shaheen).

73–4 keep . . . justice Duthie, p. 150, originally defended the F reading, but in NS favours Q. Muir retains F, but makes 'words' singular possessive. The sense seems to be 'keep the integrity of your utterances', i.e. do not lie or bear false witness. The parody of the Commandments strengthens the F reading. Muir and Shaheen compare the Catechism, 'bee true and iust in all my dealing'.

75 proud array fancy clothes.

77–88 A servingman . . . fiend Compare Donne's Elegy IV (*c.* 1595) (Davenport, p. 21).

77 servingman Either (1) servant, or (2) lover; possibly both. The description of a dandified servant as courtier fits Oswald as well.

77 proud in heart Shaheen compares Prov. 16.5: 'All that are proude in heart, are an abomination to the Lord', and 21.4: 'A hautie loke, and a proude heart, which is the light of the wicked, is sinne.' 'Proud' could also signify 'lustful' (Booth, p. 164, n. 19).

77–8 curled my hair Malone (cited by Furness) quotes a long passage from Harsnett, p. 54, in which Master Mainy 'curled his hair' and otherwise demonstrated the sin of pride. The passage continues, as the present one does, with a catalogue of deadly sins represented by devils in the shape of animals, including the dog and the wolf, which Shakespeare may have remembered.

78 wore . . . cap i.e. wore the favours of his mistress like a courtly lover or gallant.

81 slept . . . lust i.e. dreamt of plotting lascivious deeds.

82 dearly . . . dearly See collation. F's repetition appears intentional and emphatic.

82–3 out-paramoured the Turk i.e. had more lovers than the Turkish sultan had in his harem.

83 light of ear 'credulous of evil, ready to receive malicious reports' (Johnson, cited by Furness); i.e. a gossip-monger. Kittredge quotes from *The Schole-House of Women*: 'So light of eare they be and sowre, / That of the better they neuer record, / The worse reherce they word by word.'

84–5 hog . . . prey Edgar gives an abbreviated list parodying the Seven Deadly Sins, which were often represented by animals. Compare 77–8 n. above, and Florio, *Second Fruites*, p. 165: 'lyon for surquedry, goate for letcherie, dragon for crueltie' (cited by Muir).

85 prey preying.

85–6 Let . . . silks The sounds a woman makes as she walks. Creaking shoes were fashionable (Kittredge).

rustling of silks betray thy poor heart to woman. Keep thy foot
out of brothels, thy hand out of plackets, thy pen from lender's
books, and defy the foul fiend. Still through the hawthorn
blows the cold wind, says suum, mun, nonny. Dauphin, my boy,
boy, *cessez!* let him trot by.   90

Storm still

LEAR Thou wert better in a grave than to answer with thy uncovered body this extremity of the skies. Is man no more than
this? Consider him well. Thou ow'st the worm no silk, the beast
no hide, the sheep no wool, the cat no perfume. Ha! Here's
three on's are sophisticated; thou art the thing itself. Unaccom-   95
modated man is no more but such a poor, bare, forked animal
as thou art. Off, off, you lendings! Come, unbutton here.

---

86 rustling] F; ruslngs Q 86 woman] F; women Q 87 brothels] F; brothell Q 87 plackets] F; placket Q 88 books] F; booke Q 89 says suum, mun, nonny] F; hay no on ny Q 89–90 Dauphin, my boy, boy, *cessez!*] *This edn;* Dolphin my boy, my boy, caese Q; Dolphin my Boy, Boy *Sesey:* F; Dauphin, my boy! Boy, *cessez;* Oxford 90 SD] F; *not in* Q 91 Thou] F; Why thou Q 91 a] F; thy Q 92 than] then F; but Q 93 ow'st] F; owest Q 94 Ha!] Ha? F; *not in* Q 97 lendings! Come, unbutton here.] F; leadings, come on be true. Q *uncorr.,* Q2; lendings, come on Q *corr.*

87 **plackets** (1) slits or openings in petticoats, (2) a euphemism for the female pudendum (Partridge).

87–8 **pen . . . books** A sure way to fall into trouble was to borrow from moneylenders.

89 **suum, mun, nonny** The first two words suggest the sound of the wind (Knight, cited by Furness). The third word is used often in ballad refrains. (Steevens apparently invented a ballad about a battle in France in which the French king did not want to risk his son the Dauphin: see Furness.) Some editions, e.g. NS, conflate emended Q and F, 'suum, mun, hay nonny nonny', since Edgar utters the kind of nonsense that could end in a ballad tag. For 'nonny-nonny' NS quotes *OED:* 'meaningless refrain, formerly often used to cover indelicate allusions'. Compare *Ham.* 4.5.166, *Ado* 2.3.69.

89–90 **Dauphin . . . by** Unexplained. See collation. Johnson was the first to suggest French *cessez* for F '*Sesey*', but the reference to the Dauphin of France is unclear. Johnson thought it referred to a servant or attendant, others that it is from a ballad or song, but evidence is absent. John Crow suggested to Muir that 'Dolphin' (Dauphin) could mean the devil; he quoted a Noah mystery play: 'I pray to Dolphin, prince of dead, / Scald you all in his lead.' The identification with the devil derives from English hatred of the French, and Edgar often refers to devils or fiends who accompany or torment him.

91 **answer** respond, encounter.

92–3 **Is . . . well** Compare Hebrews 2.6: 'What is man, that thou shouldest bee mindfull of him? or the sonne of man that thou wouldest consider him?' (Noble, Shaheen). Nearly the same words appear in Ps. 8.4. G. C. Taylor cites parallels from Montaigne's *Apology for Raymond Sebonde*, iii.250, 268; vi.189–90 (in Florio's translation, quoted in Muir, NS).

94 **cat** i.e. the civet cat, from whose glands ingredients for perfume are obtained.

95 **sophisticated** adulterated, artificially altered.

95–6 **Unaccommodated** Unfurnished with the trappings of civilisation, i.e. unadorned with clothes.

96 **forked** two-legged. Compare *2H4* 3.2.311, where Falstaff describes Justice Shallow as 'a forked radish'.

97 **lendings** clothes, i.e. the borrowings mentioned in 93–4. Lear begins tearing off his clothes, the 'ironic conclusion' to the divestiture begun in 1.1 of everything but the name of king and the reservation of a hundred knights (Heilman, p. 76). Now he strips down to 'nothing'.

97 **Come . . . here** Perhaps a delirious command to a groom, but more likely Lear speaking to himself. Compare 5.3.283. *Hysterica passio* is evidently afflicting Lear. As he tears off his clothing, Kent and the Fool try to restrain him. See collation and compare Clayton, pp. 127–8; Stone, pp. 225–6. Furness suggests 'unbutton here' may be a SD.

FOOL   Prithee, nuncle, be contented; 'tis a naughty night to swim
in. Now a little fire in a wild field were like an old lecher's heart
– a small spark, all the rest on's body cold. Look, here comes a   100
walking fire.

Enter GLOUCESTER *with a torch*

EDGAR   This is the foul Flibbertigibbet; he begins at curfew and
walks till the first cock. He gives the web and the pin, squints
the eye, and makes the harelip; mildews the white wheat, and
hurts the poor creature of earth.   105
[*Chants*] Swithold footed thrice the wold,
He met the nightmare and her ninefold;

98 contented; 'tis] F; content, this is Q   100 on's] F; in Q   101 SD] F (*after 97*); *Enter Gloster.* Q   102 foul] F; foule
fiend Q   102 Flibbertigibbet] F; *Sriberdegibit* Q *uncorr.*; *fliberdegibek* Q *corr.*; *Sirberdegibit* Q2   *103 till the] Q; at F   103
gives] F, Q *corr.*; gins Q *uncorr.*, Q2   103 web and the pin, squints] F; web, the pin- / queues Q *uncorr.*; web, & the pin,
squemes Q *corr.*; web, the pinqueuer Q2   104 harelip] Hare-lippe F; harte lip Q *uncorr.*, Q2; hare lip Q *corr.*   106 SD]
This edn; not in Q, F; [*Sings*] / *Oxford*   106–10 Swithold . . . thee!] *Capell's lineation; four lines ending* . . . old, / . . .
nine-fold; / . . . -plight, / . . . thee. F; *as prose* Q   106 Swithold] F; swithald Q   *106 wold] *Theobald*; old Q, F   107
He . . . nightmare] F, Q *corr.*; a nellthu night more Q *uncorr.*; anellthu night More Q2

98 **naughty** wicked.
98 **swim** Perhaps suggested by Lear's move-
ments and the wet weather.
99 **little fire . . . heart** As the Fool sees
Gloucester advancing through the field, the comparison is dramatically apt. Accordingly, some
editions, e.g. NS, move the SD for Gloucester's
entrance to 99 after 'swim in'.
99 **wild** uncultivated, not bearing crops (NS).
101 **walking fire** i.e. someone carrying a torch.
Here the Fool begins his lapse into silence.
Upstaged initially by Edgar as Poor Tom in both
Q and F, the Fool later – in Q – tries to regain
his position, but not in F, as the texts diverge significantly (Kerrigan, p. 226; see Textual Analysis,
p. 270 below).
102 **Flibbertigibbet** A dancing devil in
Harsnett.
102 **curfew** 9 p.m.
103 **first cock** midnight.
103 **web . . . pin** cataract of the eye. Compare
OED Web *sb* 7.
103 **squints** i.e. causes to squint. See collation. Q
corr. 'squemes' may be a miscorrection of Q uncorr.
'-queues' for 'squenies' or 'squenes' (Duthie,
p. 193); compare 4.5.132. Greg, *Variants*, pp. 165–
7, believes F 'squints' is a sophistication, but other
evidence suggests authorial revision (*Textual Companion*, p. 536). Muir, who prints 'squinies', cites
Armin's use of 'squiny' as well as 'squened' in
his *Nest of Ninnies* (1608) and 'squeaning' in *The*

Italian Taylor (1609), also cited by Greg.
104 **white wheat** grain almost ripe for harvest-
ing. Compare John 4.35: 'loke on the regions: for
they are white already vnto haruest' (NS).
105 **creature** Collective for 'creatures'.
106 **Swithold** Most editors see 'Swithold' as
a contraction of 'St Withold', mentioned in *The
Troublesome Raigne of Iohn King of England* (1591):
'Sweete S. *Withold* of thy lenitie, defend vs from
extremitie' (1184). The saint, of whom only this is
known, was apparently a protector from harms in
general. Oxford emends to 'Swithune', following
Tate. Swithune, or Swithun (also spelled Swithin),
was a popular English saint famous for healing and
associated with rain (*Textual Companion*, p. 518,
arguing for common *a/u* and *l/* minim misreadings
in Q of 'Swithune' – and presumably *e/d* misreading as well). Q's 'swithald' and F's '*Swithold*' rein-
force each other, however, and the precedent in *The
Troublesome Raigne* is persuasive, since (as *Textual
Companion* recognises) Tate may have been only
simplifying.
106 **footed thrice** The saint walks over the
downs three times (a magical number).
106 **wold** upland plain, or downs; Q/F 'old' suggests the dialectal pronunciation.
107 **nightmare . . . ninefold** The nightmare
was 'a female spirit or monster supposed to beset
people and animals by night, settling upon them
when they are asleep and producing a feeling of
suffocation by its weight' (*OED* Nightmare *sb* 1).

Bid her alight
And her troth plight,
And aroint thee, witch, aroint thee!   110
KENT How fares your grace?
LEAR What's he?
KENT Who's there? What is't you seek?
GLOUCESTER What are you there? Your names?
EDGAR Poor Tom, that eats the swimming frog, the toad, the   115
tadpole, the wall-newt, and the water; that in the fury of his
heart, when the foul fiend rages, eats cowdung for salads,
swallows the old rat and the ditch-dog, drinks the green mantle
of the standing pool; who is whipped from tithing to tithing,
and stocked, punished, and imprisoned; who hath had three   120
suits to his back, six shirts to his body,
Horse to ride, and weapon to wear;
But mice and rats and such small deer
Have been Tom's food for seven long year.
Beware my follower. Peace, Smulkin; peace, thou fiend!   125
GLOUCESTER What, hath your grace no better company?

108 alight] a-light F; O light Q, Q2   109 troth plight] Q; troth-plight F   110 aroint] F; arint Q (*both times*)   110 witch]
F, Q *corr.*; with Q *uncorr.*, Q2   116 tadpole] tode pold Q *uncorr.*; tod pole Q *corr.*; Tod-pole F   116 wall-newt] F, Q *corr.*;
wall-wort Q *uncorr.*, Q2   120 stocked, punished,] F; stock-punisht Q   *120 had] Q; *not in* F   122 Horse . . . wear;] F;
part of preceding prose Q   124 Have] F; Hath Q   125 Smulkin] F; snulbug Q

Note the derivation from Anglo-Saxon 'mare' =
incubus, which has nothing to do with 'mare' =
she-horse (Kittredge). But Q corr. 'nine fold' (F
nine-fold) may = 'nine fole' (i.e. 'foal') (Tyrwhitt,
cited by Furness). Excrescent -*d* is common in
Shakespeare, as in 'vilde' for 'vile' (129). Oxford
prints 'foal'. Capell thought the 'nine-fold' referred
to the attendant train of imps or familiars. Nine, as
a multiple of three, is another magic number. NS
and others cite a similar charm to cure the nightmare from Scot's *Discoverie of Witchcraft* (1584) and
elsewhere.
    108 **Bid her alight** i.e. get down off the
sleeper's chest.
    109 **troth plight** i.e. promise to do no more
harm.
    110 **aroint thee** Command to the demon (or
witch who invoked her) to be gone, as in *Mac.*
1.3.6.
    111–13 **How . . . seek?** Kent addresses Lear
first, then Gloucester. Sisson, p. 237, believes the
first query is properly Gloucester's; but since Lear,
now subdued, has just undergone a vigorous struggle, the question by Kent is appropriate.
    116 **wall-newt** wall-lizard.

    116 **water** i.e. water-newt.
    116–17 **in the fury . . . rages** i.e. when the mad
fit is upon him.
    118 **ditch-dog** dead dogs thrown into ditches
(Delius, cited by Furness).
    118–19 **green mantle . . . pool** scum from a
stagnant pond. Compare *MV* 1.1.89.
    119–20 **whipped . . . imprisoned** Vagabonds
under a statute of 1572 could be punished in these
ways until driven back to wherever they belonged
or whoever would take them in.
    119 **tithing** A rural district originally containing
ten households.
    120 **stocked** i.e. placed in the stocks.
    120–1 **three . . . body** Compare 2.2.14 n. on a
servingman's allowance.
    123–4 **mice . . . year** Compare the popular
romance, *Bevis of Hampton*: 'Ratons and myce and
soche smale dere / That was hys mete that seven
yere' (Capell, cited by Kittredge).
    123 **deer** game in general.
    125 **Smulkin** A minor devil (in mouse's form
in Harsnett, p. 140).
    126 **What . . . company** This speech and
Gloucester's next two are directed to Lear.

EDGAR　The Prince of Darkness is a gentleman. Modo he's called,
　and Mahu.
GLOUCESTER　Our flesh and blood, my lord, is grown so vile,
　That it doth hate what gets it.　　　　　　　　　　　　　　130
EDGAR　Poor Tom's a-cold.
GLOUCESTER　Go in with me. My duty cannot suffer
　T'obey in all your daughters' hard commands.
　Though their injunction be to bar my doors
　And let this tyrannous night take hold upon you,　　　　135
　Yet have I ventured to come seek you out
　And bring you where both fire and food is ready.
LEAR　First let me talk with this philosopher.
　What is the cause of thunder?
KENT　Good my lord, take his offer; go into th'house.　　　140
LEAR　I'll talk a word with this same learnèd Theban.
　What is your study?
EDGAR　How to prevent the fiend, and to kill vermin.
LEAR　Let me ask you one word in private.

---

128 Mahu.] F; ma hu – Q　129–30 Our . . . it.] *Pope's lineation; as prose* Q, F　129 blood . . . vile] F; bloud is growne
so vild my Lord, Q　132–7 Go . . . ready.] F *lineation; as prose* Q　133 T'] F; to Q　137 fire and food] F; food and fire
Q　140 Good . . . house.] Q; *two lines divided* offer, / Go F　140 Good my] F; My good Q　140 th'] F; the Q　141–2
I'll . . . study?] F *lineation; as prose* Q　141 same] F; most Q

127 **Prince . . . gentleman** Said apparently in
reply to Gloucester's question.

127–8 **Modo . . . Mahu** Modu, another name
for the devil in Harsnett, was 'a graund Com-
maunder, Mustermaister over the Captaines of the
seaven deadly sinnes', and Maho was 'generall
Dictator of hell' (Harsnett, p. 46; compare *ibid.*,
p. 166). Edmond Blunden, *Shakespeare's Signifi-
cances* (cited by Muir), says that Modo may have
reminded Shakespeare of a passage in Horace, *Epistles*, 2.1.210–13, which describes the tragic poet and
concludes with references to Thebes and Athens
(compare 'learned Theban' (141), and 'good Athenian' (164 below)). Harsnett, moreover, quotes and
translates from Horace's next epistle on 'Dreames
and Magicall affrights'; both epistles are connected
by mention of terror and magic (Muir). The passage describing the tragic poet is one 'above all others' in Horace that Shakespeare could be expected
to have known (NS).

129 **flesh and blood** i.e. children. Gloucester's
comment may occasion Edgar's cry.

130 **gets** begets.

132 **suffer** bear, endure.

133 **in all** in every respect.

137 **bring . . . ready** Gloucester wants to escort
Lear to a more suitable place than Edgar's hovel,
possibly a servants' chamber in his castle or a sturdy
outbuilding on his estate.

138 **philosopher** student of natural philosophy,
scientist. G. S. Gordon, *Shakespearian Comedy*,
1944, pp. 126–8, says that formerly kings kept
philosophers just as they kept a fool and other court
officers (Muir, NS). Lear takes Edgar as a member
of his court and questions him in the manner of
medieval instructional procedures (dialogue or catechism). The cause of thunder was a typical question. Compare 1.5.15 ff., where the Fool parodies
the procedure.

139 **What . . . thunder** A stock question,
prompted undoubtedly by the storm.

141 **learnèd Theban** Greek scholar. Compare
127–8 n.

142 **study** (1) field of research, (2) object of main
attention.

143 **prevent** (1) anticipate, and thus (2) avoid,
escape.

143 **fiend . . . vermin** Compare 57–8 n. above.

144 **in private** Lear and Edgar here converse
apart.

KENT Importune him once more to go, my lord.   145
    His wits begin t'unsettle.
GLOUCESTER   Canst thou blame him?
    Storm still
    His daughters seek his death. Ah, that good Kent,
    He said it would be thus, poor banished man!
    Thou sayst the king grows mad; I'll tell thee, friend,
    I am almost mad myself. I had a son,   150
    Now outlawed from my blood; he sought my life
    But lately, very late. I loved him, friend;
    No father his son dearer. True to tell thee,
    The grief hath crazed my wits. What a night's this!
    I do beseech your grace –
LEAR   O, cry you mercy, sir. –   155
    Noble philosopher, your company.
EDGAR Tom's a-cold.
GLOUCESTER In, fellow, there, in t'hovel; keep thee warm.
LEAR Come, let's in all.
KENT   This way, my lord.
LEAR   With him;
    I will keep still with my philosopher.   160
KENT Good my lord, soothe him; let him take the fellow.
GLOUCESTER Take him you on.
KENT Sirrah, come on. Go along with us.
LEAR Come, good Athenian.
GLOUCESTER No words, no words. Hush.   165

145–6 Importune . . . t'unsettle] F *lineation; as prose* Q **145** once more] F; *not in* Q **146** t'] F; *to* Q **146** SD] F; *not in* Q **147** Ah,] F; O Q **149** sayst] sayest Q, F **151** he] F; a Q **152** friend;] (Friend) F; friend Q **153** True] F, Q; truth Q2 **154–5** The . . . grace –] F *lineation; divided* wits, / What Q **155** grace –] *Capell (subst.);* Grace. Q; grace. F **155–6** O . . . company.] F *lineation; one line* Q **155–6** mercy, sir. – / Noble] F; mercie noble Q ***158** in t'] in't Q; into th' F **159–60** With . . . philosopher.] F *lineation; one line* Q **159–60** him; / I will keep still] F; him I wil keep stil, Q **161** Good . . . fellow.] *As in* Q; *two lines divided* him: / Let F

147 His . . . death Perhaps Gloucester interprets 2.4.295–302 to mean this. At 3.6.45, however, after returning from his castle to get help for the king, he says he has heard of 'a plot of death upon him'.
    151 outlawed . . . blood i.e. disowned and disinherited.
    152–3 I loved . . . dearer Gloucester's behaviour in 1.2 and 2.1 hardly bears out this statement, but his self-delusion is characteristic.
    155–65 I . . . Hush Gloucester addresses Lear and tries to lead him away from the Bedlamite. But Lear demurs and wishes to stay with Edgar, where-

upon Gloucester again tries to separate them by urging Edgar back into his hovel. Lear insists on keeping with Edgar even as Kent intercedes and also tries to lead him away. Lear, in fact, never enters the hovel (Perrett, p. 260), but at the end of the scene is led elsewhere, taking Edgar and the others with him (160–4).
    155 cry you mercy I beg your pardon.
    161 soothe humour; used by Harsnett (p. 185) in this sense (Muir).
    164 Athenian i.e. philosopher; compare 127–8 n.

EDGAR   Child Roland to the dark tower came.
His word was still 'Fie, fo, and fum;
I smell the blood of a British man.'

Exeunt

3.5 *Enter* CORNWALL *and* EDMOND

CORNWALL   I will have my revenge ere I depart his house.

EDMOND   How, my lord, I may be censured, that nature thus gives
way to loyalty, something fears me to think of.

CORNWALL   I now perceive it was not altogether your brother's evil
disposition made him seek his death, but a provoking merit set   5
a-work by a reprovable badness in himself.

EDMOND   How malicious is my fortune, that I must repent to be
just! This is the letter which he spoke of, which approves him
an intelligent party to the advantages of France. O heavens, that
this treason were not, or not I the detector!   10

CORNWALL   Go with me to the duchess.

EDMOND   If the matter of this paper be certain, you have mighty
business in hand.

---

166 tower came] F; towne come Q   168 SD] F; *not in* Q   Act 3, Scene 5   3.5] *Scena Quinta*. F; *not in* Q   0 SD EDMOND]
F; *Bastard*. Q   1 his] F; the Q   8 just!] iust? Q, F   8 letter which] F; letter Q   9 heavens,] heauens Q; Heavens! F   10
this] F; his Q   10 were not,] F; were Q

166–8 Child . . . man 'Tom has the last
word. Silent Fool is usually seen separated inexorably from his master, following forlornly behind'
(Rosenberg, p. 228; compare Kerrigan, pp. 226–30).
Edgar combines fragments presumably from two
lost ballads: the first line alludes to the exploits
of the epic hero, Roland, famous in the twelfth-
century *Chanson de Roland*. The second and third
lines derive from some version of *Jack the Giant
Killer*. 'British Roland is entering the Giant's Castle, where his blood (kinship) is in danger of being
smelt (detected)' (NS).

166 Child Title of candidate for knighthood
(Kittredge).

166 dark tower Possibly refers to Gloucester's
castle, which is proving quite 'dark'.

167 word password.

167–8 Fie . . . man The Giant's speech is 'given,
by an intentional incongruity, to the heroic Child
Rowland' (Muir); the tower may have suggested the
story of the beanstalk (Hunter). It is all very ominous, the apparent nonsense notwithstanding; the
foreboding is borne out in 3.7. In dramatic function, Edgar's speech parallels the Fool's prophecy
at the end of 3.2.

168 British Instead of 'English', as in the traditional tag; possibly a concession to legendary history, or to the efforts of James I to unify the realm.

Act 3, Scene 5
2 censured judged.
2–3 nature . . . loyalty Edmond subordinates
the 'natural' loyalty of a child to his father in favour
of loyalty to the duke (from whom he 'naturally'
expects advancement).
3 something fears somewhat frightens.
4–6 I now . . . himself The syntax is unclear,
but the sense seems to be: I see now that it was
not only your brother's innate wickedness, but
Gloucester's deserving, which could incite his son's
reprehensible wickedness to kill him.
5 merit desert (in bad sense) (Schmidt).
7–8 How . . . just The irony here doubles back
on itself.
8 approves him proves him to be.
9 an intelligent party a spy, giving information, intelligence.
12 this paper Gloucester's letter (8).

CORNWALL True or false, it hath made thee Earl of Gloucester.
Seek out where thy father is, that he may be ready for our   15
apprehension.
EDMOND [*Aside*] If I find him comforting the king, it will stuff his
suspicion more fully. – I will persever in my course of loyalty,
though the conflict be sore between that and my blood.
CORNWALL I will lay trust upon thee, and thou shalt find a dearer   20
father in my love.

Exeunt

3.6 *Enter* KENT [*disguised*] *and* GLOUCESTER

GLOUCESTER Here is better than the open air; take it thankfully. I
will piece out the comfort with what addition I can. I will not be
long from you.
KENT All the power of his wits have given way to his impatience;
the gods reward your kindness!   5

Exit [*Gloucester*]

Enter LEAR, EDGAR [*disguised as a madman*], *and* FOOL

EDGAR Fraterretto calls me, and tells me Nero is an angler in the
lake of darkness. Pray, innocent, and beware the foul fiend.
FOOL Prithee, nuncle, tell me whether a madman be a gentleman
or a yeoman.

17 SD] *Theobald; not in* Q, F   *20 dearer] Q; *deere* F   21 SD] F; *Exit.* Q   Act 3, Scene 6   3.6] *Scena Sexta.* F; *not in*
Q   0 SD] F; *Enter Gloster and Lear, Kent, Foole, and Tom.* Q   4 to his] F; *to* Q   5 reward] F; *deserue* Q   5 SD.1] *Capell;*
Exit F *(after 3); not in* Q   5 SD.2 *Enter . . .* FOOL] F; *not in* Q (*but see 0* SD)   6 Fraterretto] F; *Freteretto* Q   7 Pray, innocent,
and] *Johnson;* pray Innocent, and F; pray innocent Q

16 **apprehension** arrest.
17 **comforting** i.e. in legal sense of 'supporting,
helping' (Muir).
18 **persever** The form used by Shakespeare,
with the accent on the second syllable (*OED*).
19 **blood** i.e. filial feeling.

Act 3, Scene 6
2 **piece out** augment, supplement.
4 **have** 'wits' influences the plural form.
4 **impatience** 'lack of self-control; passion'
(NS).
5 **gods . . . kindness** But what Gloucester
gets in 3.7 is cruelly different (Rosenberg, p. 231).
Compare 5.3.230.
6 **Fraterretto** Another of the dancing devils in
Harsnett (p. 49).
6–7 **Nero . . . darkness** After introducing
Fraterretto and other 'devils of the round, or
Morice', Harsnett associates them with 'the Fidler'
(p. 49), clearly the Emperor Nero, who fiddled
while Rome burned and is imagined condemned

to hell for many crimes against his family and
the Empire. Nero's angling, however, comes from
Chaucer's *Monk's Tale* (F. E. Budd, 'Shakespeare,
Chaucer, and Harsnett', *RES* 11 (1935), 421–9).
Angling in the 'lake of darkness', moreover, may
allude not only to the Stygian lake, which Harsnett
mentions in the same context, but also to the murder of Agrippina, whose womb Nero 'slitte, to
biholde / Wher he conceyved was' (*Monk's Tale,*
485–6). Compare Hamlet's allusion to this crime.
Ham. 3.2.390–6. The vision of hell is continued in
Lear's speech (13–14), where he imagines tortures
for Gonerill and Regan.
7 **Pray . . . fiend** Perhaps addressed to the Fool,
who briefly revives and tries vainly to recapture
Lear's attention.
8 **madman** A possible pun, 'mad' – 'made'
(Schmidt, cited by Muir). Kökeritz, pp. 126–7, 164,
notes similar puns elsewhere, e.g. *TN* 3.4.52–7 and
TNK 3.5.72–7 (compare Cercignani, pp. 236–7). A
'made man' is one whose success in life is assured
(*OED* Made *ppl a* 7).

LEAR A king, a king!   10

FOOL No, he's a yeoman that has a gentleman to his son; for he's a
    mad yeoman that sees his son a gentleman before him.

LEAR To have a thousand with red burning spits
    Come hizzing in upon 'em!

EDGAR Bless thy five wits.   15

KENT O pity! Sir, where is the patience now
    That you so oft have boasted to retain?

EDGAR [*Aside*] My tears begin to take his part so much
    They mar my counterfeiting.

LEAR The little dogs and all,   20
    Tray, Blanch, and Sweetheart – see, they bark at me.

EDGAR Tom will throw his head at them. – Avaunt, you curs!
    Be thy mouth or black or white,
    Tooth that poisons if it bite,
    Mastiff, greyhound, mongrel grim,   25
    Hound or spaniel, brach or him,
    Bobtail tyke or trundle-tail,

11–12 FOOL No . . . him.] F; *not in* Q   13–14 To . . . 'em!] F *lineation; as prose* Q (*continuing 10*)   18 SD] Rowe; *not in* Q, F   19 They] F; Theile Q   22 Tom . . . curs] *As in* Q; *divided* you / Curres F   23–8 Be . . . wail;] F *lineation (except 22–3); three lines ending* . . . bite, / . . . him, / . . . waile, Q   *25–6 mongrel grim, / Hound] Rowe (*subst.*); Mongrill, Grim, / Hound F; mungril, grim-hoũd Q   *26 him,] Q; Hym: F; lym; *Hanmer (see Commentary)*   *27 Bobtail tyke] Bobtaile tike Q; Or Bobtaile tight F   *27 trundle-tail] Q2; trũdletaile Q; Troudle taile F

11–12 FOOL . . . **before him** See Textual Analysis, pp. 283–4 below. Davenport, p. 21, compares Joseph Hall's satire on the doting Lolio, a yeoman, in *Virgidemiae* (1598), Bk IV, sat. ii: 'Old driueling *Lolio* drudges all he can, / To make his eldest sonne a Gentleman . . .' Lolio's son, like Lear's two elder daughters, is ungrateful.

13 **a thousand** i.e. devils, or demons. Compare Lear's hundred knights.

14 **hizzing** F's spelling seems a deliberate attempt at onomatopoeia, i.e. the whizzing sound of the red-hot weapons (Kittredge).

14 **upon 'em** On F's omission of the mock trial that follows in Q, see Textual Analysis, p. 270 below.

15 **Bless . . . wits** See 3.4.55 n.

20–1 **The little . . . me** Lear imagines that even his lapdogs, possibly bitches as their names suggest, have turned against him.

22 **throw his head** Unexplained, but the expression (repeated at 29) may mean to shake one's head wildly or to face menacingly. 'Head' could mean hair, or the antlers of a deer (Edgar mentions his 'horn' (32)). See also 29 n.

23 **or . . . or** either . . . or.

26 **brach** bitch. Compare 1.4.98.

26 **him** i.e. male dog. Hanmer's emenda-

tion, 'lym' (= lymmer, a species of bloodhound), generally accepted, is unnecessary. Furthermore, Blayney's lengthy analysis (in the unpublished second volume of *The Texts of 'King Lear'*) shows that the philological evidence brought to bear in support of Hanmer's emendation breaks down. 'Lyam' means 'leash'; hence, 'lyam-hound' or 'lime-hound' = 'leash-hound'. According to Hanmer, 'lyam' or 'lym' also means 'leash-hound', which is about as plausible, Blayney says, as the analogous claim that 'fox' means 'fox-hound' or that 'cart' means 'carthorse'. *OED* errs in citing, out of context, 'lyam' as meaning any kind of dog; in context, the quotation from 1486 may mean something quite different, but the entry itself may be wrong.

27 **Bobtail tyke** A small dog with its tail cut short, or 'bobbed'. Q 'tike' is obviously right; F 'tight' makes no sense and may be a misreading and miscorrection of 'tike' > 'tite' > 'tight' (Duthie, p. 179).

27 **trundle-tail** A dog with a long, curly tail. F's 'Troudle' is apparently the result of a turned letter, since 'trondle' is a variant spelling of 'trundle' (Q2). Compare Duthie, p. 180.

Tom will make him weep and wail;
For with throwing thus my head,
Dogs leap the hatch, and all are fled.   30
Do, de, de, de. *Cessez!* Come, march to wakes and fairs and
market towns. Poor Tom, thy horn is dry.

LEAR   Then let them anatomise Regan; see what breeds about her
heart. Is there any cause in nature that makes these hard-
hearts? [*To Edgar*] You, sir, I entertain for one of my hundred,   35
only I do not like the fashion of your garments. You will say
they are Persian; but let them be changed.

KENT   Now, good my lord, lie here and rest a while.

LEAR   Make no noise, make no noise. Draw the curtains: so, so.

---

28 him] F; them Q   29–30 For . . . fled.] F *lineation; as prose* Q   *29 head,] Q; head; F   *30 leap] Q; leapt F   31–2 Do . . . dry] *As prose* Q; *two lines divided* Fayres / And F   31 Do, de, de, de] F; loudla doodla Q   *31 *Cessez!*] *This edn;* sese: F; Sessey / Johnson; not in Q   33–7 Then . . . changed.] F; *five verse lines ending* . . . her [*turned over*] / . . . hardnes, / . . . hundred, / . . . say, / . . . chang'd. Q   *34 makes] Q; make F   34–5 these hard-hearts] F; this hardnes, Q; these hard hearts *Rowe*   35 SD] *Capell; not in* Q, F   35 entertain] F; entertaine you Q   36 garments. You will] F; garments youle Q   37 Persian] F; Persian attire Q   38 and rest] F; *not in* Q   39–40 Make . . . morning.] *As prose* F; *two verse lines divided* so, / Weele Q   39 so, so.] so, so, F; so, so, so, Q

29 throwing . . . head Edgar either throws his horn ('head'), or, putting the horn on his head, pretends to attack or scare away the dog (Muir). In Edmond Kean's staging and Macready's, he threw a straw head-dress at imaginary dogs (Bratton, p. 229).

30 hatch Lower half of a divided door.

31 Do . . . de Compare 3.4.55. Edgar's teeth chatter again.

31 wakes 'local annual festival of an English parish observed . . . as an occasion for making holiday, entertainment of friends, and often for village sports, dancing, and other amusements' (*OED* Wake *sb*[1] 4b). Beggars and rogues did well at such gatherings; compare *WT* 4.3.102: Autolycus 'haunts wakes, fairs, and bear-baitings'.

32 thy horn is dry Formula for begging drink, carried in the ox horn beggars wore about their necks. Perhaps it also means, as Steevens thought, that Edgar has exhausted his repertoire of Tom o'Bedlam; in fact, this is his last speech in the scene.

33–4 Then . . . heart An acceptable non sequitur, given the context of mad speeches, though Duthie, p. 8, argues that as it continues the mock trial in Q, the words retained in F are rendered pointless after the trial is cut.

33 anatomise dissect. In the theatre, Lear usually acts out the dissection, plunging a dagger into the imaginary body, holding up the heart, etc. (Rosenberg, p. 236). In the Royal Shakespeare Company production in 1982, directed by Adrian Noble (who retained the mock trial), Lear here

thrust his dagger into a cushion the Fool held over his stomach, mortally wounding him. The action thus accounted for the Fool's disappearance from the play after 3.6.

33–4 what . . . heart i.e. what grows around her heart (to harden it).

34–5 hard-hearts See collation and *Textual Companion*, p. 536: 'the compound was current as a verb and adjective (*OED*), and on the analogy of *hard-head*(s) could easily have been understood as a substantive'. Hard hearts were well known theological phenomena, caused by a fall from grace (Hunter); but Lear seeks an anatomical explanation.

35 entertain engage.

35 my hundred i.e. hundred knights.

37 Persian i.e. gorgeous; but compare 'Theban', 'Athenian' (3.4.141, 164), and next note. Blunden believed the allusion is to Horace, *Odes*, 1.38: 'Persicos odi, puer, apparatus' ('I dislike Persian pomp') (NS). A Persian embassy visited England early in James I's reign (Muir).

37 changed Compare Dan. 6.8: 'Seale the writing, that it not be changed, according to the lawe of the Medes and Persians, which altereth not' (Shaheen). The immutability of Medean and Persian laws had become proverbial in Shakespeare's day.

39 Draw . . . so, so Lear, exhausted, imagines he is in a luxurious, canopied bed speaking to his servant. Perhaps Edgar or Kent and the Fool mime the action; hence, 'so, so' (Rosenberg, p. 237).

We'll go to supper i'th'morning. [*He sleeps*]   40
FOOL And I'll go to bed at noon.

Enter GLOUCESTER

GLOUCESTER Come hither, friend. Where is the king my master?
KENT Here, sir, but trouble him not; his wits are gone.
GLOUCESTER Good friend, I prithee take him in thy arms.
I have o'erheard a plot of death upon him.   45
There is a litter ready. Lay him in't
And drive toward Dover, friend, where thou shalt meet
Both welcome and protection. Take up thy master;
If thou shouldst dally half an hour, his life
With thine and all that offer to defend him   50
Stand in assurèd loss. Take up, take up,
And follow me, that will to some provision
Give thee quick conduct. Come, come away.

Exeunt

---

40 i'th'morning.] F; it'h morning, so, so, so, Q   40 SD] *Oxford; not in* Q, F   41 FOOL And . . . noon.] F; *not in* Q   *41 SD] As in Capell; after 37* F; *after 40* Q   42 Come . . . master?] *As in* Q; *two lines divided* Friend: / Where F   46–53 There . . . away.] F *lineation; six lines ending* . . . frend / . . . master [*turned under*] / . . . with thine / . . . losse, / . . . prouision / . . . conduct. Q   46 in't] F, Q; in it Q2   47 toward] F; towards Q   51 Take up, take up,] F; Take vp to keepe Q *uncorr.*, Q2; Take vp the King Q *corr.*   52 me,] F, Q *corr.*; me Q *uncorr.*   53 conduct.] F *omits four lines here*   53 come away.] F *omits thirteen and a half lines here*   53 SD] F; Q *continues scene*

40 We'll . . . morning This 'inversion-utterance' (NS) is a characteristic of the Fool (see 41 n.), who has been tutoring Lear to face harsh realities, not curtain them off. Whatever other significance they have, the words may refer, literally, to the lack of food (which Gloucester was supposed to provide), and imply 'We'll eat later.'

41 I'll . . . noon The Fool's last line, not in Q, is an 'inversion-statement' (NS, p. xxxii), an appropriate response to Lear's speech. Its underlying significance has been much discussed. It may be proverbial for 'I'll play the fool' (Tilley B197), with a quibble on 'bed' = grave (the Fool, exhausted by events and feeling himself supplanted by Poor Tom, feels his heart breaking). Or Lear's apparent withdrawal from the actual world to the world of hallucination, indicated by the preceding line, culminates here in the Fool's acquiescence in defeat, his 'acceptance of unreality – a purposive pretence that things are other than they are' (Hilda Hulme, *Explorations in Shakespeare's Language*, 1962,

p. 71). Other meanings are possible, including the Fool's intention to abandon his master, since he can no longer help him (Kerrigan, pp. 228–9). In any case, the F addition – if it is one and not a Q oversight – provides the Fool with an appropriate exit line from the play. See Textual Analysis, p. 284 below.

41 SD *Enter* GLOUCESTER See collation. Most editors follow Q and delay Gloucester's entrance. It is unlikely that, given his sense of urgency, Gloucester would stand quietly by for several lines; moreover, he apparently does not see or hear Lear, after whom he enquires (Taylor, 'Censorship', p. 117, n. 48).

45 upon against.

46 litter Evidently, a wheeled vehicle pulled by horses; note 'drive' (47).

52–3 provision . . . conduct i.e. Gloucester will quickly lead Kent to where he will find supplies and other necessaries for the trip.

3.7 *Enter* CORNWALL, REGAN, GONERILL, EDMOND, *and Servants*

CORNWALL [*To Gonerill*] Post speedily to my lord your husband;
show him this letter. The army of France is landed. – Seek out
the traitor Gloucester.

                                          [*Exeunt some Servants*]

REGAN Hang him instantly.

GONERILL Pluck out his eyes.   5

CORNWALL Leave him to my displeasure. Edmond, keep you our
sister company. The revenges we are bound to take upon your
traitorous father are not fit for your beholding. Advise the
duke, where you are going, to a most festinate preparation:
we are bound to the like. Our posts shall be swift and intel-   10
ligent betwixt us. Farewell, dear sister; farewell, my lord of
Gloucester.

                   [*Gonerill and Edmond start to leave*]

                          Enter OSWALD

How now, where's the king?

Act 3, Scene 7   3.7] *Scena Septima.* F; *not in* Q   o sD] F; *Enter Cornwall, and Regan, and Gonorill, and Bastard.* Q   1
sD] *Furness; not in* Q, F   1–3 Post . . . Gloucester.] *As prose* F; *two lines divided letter [turned over]* / The Q   3 traitor] F;
vilaine Q   3 sD *Capell (subst.); not in* Q, F   6–12 Leave . . . Gloucester.] *As prose* F; *six lines of verse ending . . . company.*
[*turned under*] /. . . father, /. . . going [*turned under*] /. . . like, /. . . betwixt vs, / . . . *Gloster,* Q   7–11 revenges] F;
reuenge Q   *8 Advise] Q; Advice F   9 festinate] F2; festuant Q, Q2; festiuate F   10 posts] F; post Q   10 intelligent] F;
intelligence Q   12 sD.1] *This edn; not in* Q, F   12 sD.2] F; *Enter Steward.* Q (*after 13*)

Act 3, Scene 7

o SD Edmond may be dressed in different attire
now, grandly, like the earl he intended to be, though
he will aim still higher. Gonerill and Regan may
also have changed dress to appear more queenly,
accentuating at the same time a growing compet-
itiveness between them as much for the new earl
as for sole sovereignty in the kingdom (Rosenberg,
p. 240).

1 Post speedily Ride quickly.

2 this letter i.e. the letter Gloucester mentioned
to Edmond, who retrieved it and used it to inform
against him: see 3.3.10; 3.5.8.

5 Pluck out his eyes Editors generally pass
over this line in silence, despite the strange punishment Gonerill demands, which Cornwall later exe-
cutes. Psychoanalytically oriented critics, however,
see blinding, particularly the tearing out of eyes, as
a symbol of castration (N. Holland, *Psychoanalysis
and Shakespeare*, 1966, pp. 217–18). In the Middle
Ages blinding as well as castration was a penalty
for rape (Bridget Lyons, 'The subplot as simplifi-
cation in *King Lear*', *Some Facets*, p. 28). Compare
5.3.162–3. That Gonerill is an emasculating female
is evident from her treatment of Albany in 1.4 and

later in 4.2. Blinding as punishment – not for treason, but for adultery – is ironically appropriate for
Gloucester. Compare the homily 'Agaynst Whore-
dome, and Adultery' in *Certain Sermons or Homilies*
(1547): 'Emong the Locrensians the adulterers had
bothe theyr eyes thrust oute' (ed. Ronald B. Bond,
1987, p. 183). See also J. L. Halio, 'Gloucester's
blinding', *SQ* 43 (1992), 221–3.

7 sister i.e. sister-in-law; see 2.2.127 n.

7 bound (1) prepared, ready, (2) obliged,
destined (?).

9 festinate preparation hasty preparation (for
war). See collation. A minim misreading results in
Q 'festuant' (for 'festinant'? See Stone, p. 182, and
compare Duthie, p. 401, and *Textual Companion*,
p. 519). Either Compositor B similarly misread
copy, or more likely F 'festiuate' is the result of
a turned letter.

10 bound to 'on our way to' (Kittredge).

10 posts messengers.

10–11 intelligent bearing information.

12 Gloucester Edmond: compare 3.5.14. But
Oswald still refers to Edmond's father by that title
(14 below).

OSWALD   My lord of Gloucester hath conveyed him hence.
Some five or six and thirty of his knights,   15
Hot questrists after him, met him at gate,
Who, with some other of the lord's dependants,
Are gone with him toward Dover, where they boast
To have well-armèd friends.
CORNWALL   Get horses for your mistress.   20

[Exit Oswald]

GONERILL   Farewell, sweet lord, and sister.
CORNWALL   Edmond, farewell.

[Exeunt Gonerill and Edmond]
[To Servants]   Go seek the traitor Gloucester.
Pinion him like a thief; bring him before us.

[Exeunt other Servants]
Though well we may not pass upon his life
Without the form of justice, yet our power   25
Shall do a curtsy to our wrath, which men
May blame but not control.

Enter GLOUCESTER and Servants

Who's there – the traitor?
REGAN   Ingrateful fox! 'tis he.
CORNWALL   Bind fast his corky arms.
GLOUCESTER   What means your graces? Good my friends, con-
sider   30

---

14 hence.] hence, Q; hence F   15–19 Some . . . friends.] F *lineation; as prose* Q   16 questrists] F; questrits Q   *17 lord's]
Pope; Lords Q; Lords, F   18 toward] F; towards Q   20 SD] *Staunton; not in* Q; F   22 SD.1] *Staunton (subst.); Exit Gon.*
and Bast. Q *(after 21); Exit* F *(after 21)*   22 SD.2 *To Servants*] *Oxford; not in* Q, F   23 SD] *Capell; not in* Q, F   24 well] F;
not in Q   26–7 Shall . . . control.] F *lineation; divided* blame / But Q   26 curtsy] curt'sie F; curtesie Q   *27 control] Q;
comptroll F   27 SD] F; *Enter Gloster brought in by two or three,* Q *(after* traytor?)   30–1 What . . . friends.] Q *lineation;
three lines ending . . .* Graces? / . . . Ghests: / . . . Friends. F

---

15 **Some . . . knights** Apparently, Lear's retinue
has not yet entirely dissolved, though the play is
generally vague about their number, whereabouts,
and final disposition. According to Oswald, some
three dozen join with Gloucester's men (17) to
form a suitable entourage for Lear's trip to Dover,
whence they seem to disappear or merge with the
forces supporting the king.

16 **questrists** Probably a Shakespearean coin-
age = 'questers'; but compare Latin *equestris*
= 'equestrian'. Taylor suggests 'questants', as in
AWW 2.1.16 ('Addenda' to *Division*, p. 488),
though Oxford follows F.

23 **thief** Robbery was then a more heinous crime
and punishment more severe than today.

24–5 **Though . . . justice** Cornwall is fully con-

scious of the travesty of justice he is about to commit in the ensuing 'trial'.

24 **pass upon** i.e. pass judgement upon.

25–6 **our power . . . wrath** i.e. our authority will
bend to our great anger. As his next clause shows,
Cornwall is also conscious that his illegal procedure will excite disapproval; but, hubristically, he
believes he can handle the consequences.

26 **curtsy** i.e. 'do a courtesy to, yield', not the
modern word meaning a feminine salutation made
by bending the knees and lowering the body.

29 **Bind** During the next few lines, the servants
tie Gloucester to a chair, with apparent reluctance,
since Cornwall repeats the command (32).

29 **corky** 'sapless, dry, and withered' (Muir,
citing Harsnett (p. 23), 'an old corkie woman').

You are my guests. Do me no foul play, friends.
CORNWALL Bind him, I say.
REGAN   Hard, hard! O filthy traitor!
GLOUCESTER Unmerciful lady as you are, I'm none.
CORNWALL To this chair bind him. Villain, thou shalt find –
                [*Regan plucks Gloucester's beard*]
GLOUCESTER By the kind gods, 'tis most ignobly done,   35
       To pluck me by the beard.
REGAN So white, and such a traitor?
GLOUCESTER   Naughty lady,
       These hairs which thou dost ravish from my chin
       Will quicken and accuse thee. I am your host.
       With robbers' hands my hospitable favours   40
       You should not ruffle thus. What will you do?
CORNWALL Come, sir, what letters had you late from France?
REGAN Be simple-answered, for we know the truth.
CORNWALL And what confederacy have you with the traitors
       Late footed in the kingdom?
REGAN   To whose hands   45
       You have sent the lunatic king. Speak.
GLOUCESTER I have a letter guessingly set down,
       Which came from one that's of a neutral heart,
       And not from one opposed.
CORNWALL   Cunning.
REGAN   And false.
CORNWALL Where hast thou sent the king?
GLOUCESTER   To Dover.   50

---

33 lady] Q; Lady, F   33 I'm none.] F; I am true. Q   34 To . . . find –] *As in* Q; *two lines divided* him, / Villaine, F   *34 find –] Q; finde. F   34 SD] *Johnson (subst.); not in* Q, F   35–6 By . . . beard.] F *lineation; as prose* Q   37–8 Naughty . . . chin] F; *one line (turned under)* Q   42 Come . . . France?] *As in* Q; *two lines divided* Sir. / What F   43 simple-answered] *Hanmer (subst.);* simple answerer Q; simple answer'd F   44–5 And . . . kingdom?] *Rowe's lineation; as prose* Q, F   45–6 To . . . Speak.] F *lineation; one line* Q   46 You have sent] F, Q; haue you sent Q2   46 king. Speak.] F; King speak? Q

32 **filthy** foul, contemptible.
36 **To . . . beard** This was a gesture of extreme insult and provocation: compare 75–6 below and *Ham.* 2.2.573.
37 **Naughty** Wicked. The word conveyed a stronger sense of evil in Shakespeare's time. Compare 2.4.126.
39 **quicken** come alive.
40 **hospitable favours** welcoming features, i.e. those of a host; compare *1H4* 3.2.136: 'And stain my favours in a bloody mask'.

41 **ruffle** treat roughly, disorder violently.
43 **simple-answered** direct, straightforward in reply.
45 **Late footed** Lately landed.
45–6 **To . . . Speak** Q2 inverts 'You have' to 'haue you', making Regan's speech a separate question – a plausible emendation, but not a necessary one, however consistent with Regan's independent character (Duthie, p. 402; compare Sisson, p. 237).
47 **guessingly set down** 'written without certain knowledge' (Muir).

REGAN   Wherefore to Dover? Wast thou not charged at peril –
CORNWALL   Wherefore to Dover? Let him answer that.
GLOUCESTER   I am tied to th'stake, and I must stand the course.
REGAN   Wherefore to Dover?
GLOUCESTER   Because I would not see thy cruel nails   55
Pluck out his poor old eyes, nor thy fierce sister
In his anointed flesh stick boarish fangs.
The sea, with such a storm as his bare head
In hell-black night endured, would have buoyed up
And quenched the stellèd fires.   60
Yet, poor old heart, he holp the heavens to rain.
If wolves had at thy gate howled that stern time,
Thou shouldst have said, 'Good porter, turn the key:
All cruels else subscribe.' But I shall see

51 Wherefore . . . peril –] *As in* Q; *two lines divided* Douer? / Was't F   *51 peril –] Q; perill. F   52 answer] F; first answere Q   53 I . . . course.] *As in* Q; *two lines divided* Stake, / And F   53 to th'] to'th' F; tot'h Q   54 Dover?] F; Douer sir? Q   57 anointed] F, Q *corr.;* aurynted Q *uncorr.,* Q2   57 stick] F; rash Q   58 as his bare] F; of his lou'd Q *uncorr.,* Q2; on his lowd Q *corr.*   59 hell-black night] *Pope;* Hell-blacke-night F; hell blacke night Q   59 buoyed] F; layd Q *uncorr.,* Q2; bod Q *corr.*   60–1 And . . . rain.] F *lineation; divided* heart, / Hee Q   60 stellèd] F, Q *corr.;* steeled Q *uncorr.,* Q2   61 holp] F; holpt Q   61 rain] F; rage Q   62 howled] F; heard Q   62 stern] F; dearne Q   64 subscribe] F; subscrib'd Q

51 **at peril** at risk (of death).
53 **I . . . course** Gloucester uses the image of a bear or bull tied to a post and baited by dogs, a common, cruel entertainment, referred to also in *TN* 3.1.118–20, *Mac.* 5.7.1–2.
53 **course** attack (one of a succession) by dogs.
57 **anointed** At a coronation, the sovereign was anointed with oil in the manner of biblical kings. Compare 1 Sam. 26.9 (Shaheen).
57 **stick** See collation. Although 'rash' (= slash violently) is a more vivid and accurate term for the action of a boar's tusks (Hunter), the F reading is perfectly acceptable. F's 'sticke' for Q's 'rash', like 'sterne' for 'deame' (62 below), is a sophistication, though not by the F scribe or compositor (Greg, *Editorial Problem*, pp. 99–100). Duthie agrees: 'sticke' is 'an editorial replacement of a difficult word by an easier one', but he does not identify the editor (pp. 17, 194). Muir believes the substitution might be an actor's, though Shakespeare could have made it 'to avoid the thrice repeated "sh"'; he adopts Q anyway.
58–60 **The sea . . . fires** In such a storm as the bareheaded king endured in total darkness, the sea itself would have swelled (in rage), reaching and extinguishing the very stars. Compare *Temp.* 1.2.4–5: 'the sea, mounting to th'welkin's cheek, / Dashes the fire out' (NS).
59 **buoyed** resin (like a buoy on a swell).
60 **stellèd** (1) fixed (from *OED* Stell *v* 2 = to fix,

place in position), or (2) starry (from Latin *stella* = star; compare *OED*); but either way, shining stars are meant.
61 **holp . . . rain** i.e. by his tears.
61 **holp** Obsolete form of 'helped'.
62 **stern** On the preference for Q 'dearne' by many editors, compare Q 'rashe', F 'sticke' (57 above and n.). The present instance may be a simpler (or more complicated) one, since either Q or F may involve only a typographical error. The compartment for the ligature of 'long-s' + 't' was very near that for the 'd' in an English type case. Far from substituting one word for another, the compositor may just have substituted one piece of type for another, though we cannot judge whether it was the Q or the F compositor who was at fault – if indeed a typo was actually involved (McLeod, p. 160). Sisson believes that, as with 'stick' for 'rash', revision occurred in rehearsal or for purposes of euphony; in a sense, he says, 'there is nothing to choose' (p. 238; 'dearne' = dire, dread: compare *Per.* 3 Chorus 15).
63–4 **Good . . . subscribe** A famous crux, partly because of the ambiguity in 'cruels' (= cruel creatures or cruel deeds); Q 'subscrib'd' versus F 'subscribe'; and the uncertainty about where the direct address ends. But the main sense seems clear. Gloucester says that on such a night Regan would have pitied wild animals howling outside her gates more than she did her father. Assuming F is correct

The wingèd vengeance overtake such children.   65
CORNWALL See't shalt thou never. Fellows, hold the chair.
  Upon these eyes of thine I'll set my foot.
GLOUCESTER He that will think to live till he be old,
  Give me some help! – O cruel! O you gods!
            [*Cornwall puts out one of Gloucester's eyes*]
REGAN One side will mock another: th'other, too.   70
CORNWALL If you see vengeance –
SERVANT   Hold your hand, my lord.
  I have served you ever since I was a child,
  But better service have I never done you
  Than now to bid you hold.
REGAN   How now, you dog!
SERVANT If you did wear a beard upon your chin   75
  I'd shake it on this quarrel. What do you mean?
CORNWALL My villain!
SERVANT Nay then, come on, and take the chance of anger.
            [*They draw and fight*]
REGAN [*To another Servant*] Give me thy sword. A peasant stand up
  thus!
                    Kills him

---

67 these] F; those Q   69 you] F; ye Q   69 SD] *Rowe (subst.); not in* Q, F   70 th'other] F; tother Q   *71 vengeance –] Q; vengeance.* F   72 you] F; *not in* Q   73–4 But . . . hold.] F *lineation; one line (turned over)* Q   75–6 If . . . mean?] F *lineation; as prose* Q   77 villain!] *Villaine?* F; *villaine.* Q; villein! *Oxford*   78 Nay] F; Why Q   *78 SD] draw and fight* Q *(after 77); not in* F   79 SD.1] *Oxford; not in* Q, F   79 thus!] thus? F; thus. Q   79 SD.2] F; *Shee takes a sword and runs at him behind.* Q

and direct address ends with 'subscribe', then: 'Good porter, turn the key (and open the gates to the wolves); all cruel creatures but you yield (to feelings of sorrow and compassion at a time like this).' For 'cruels' = cruel creatures, compare 'resolutes', *Ham.* 1.1.98; 'vulgars', *WT* 2.1.94; for 'subscribe' = yield, submit, compare *Tro.* 4.5.105 (Duthie, pp. 152–4, who ends direct address, like Kittredge, Muir, and Bevington, with 'key'; compare also Furness, Sisson). Stone, p. 197, proposes the emendation 'ile' (= I'll) for 'else', ending the direct address with 'key'. He glosses: 'All cruels [= cruel people or creatures] I'll (= I am, if necessary, willing to] subscribe [= countenance], but [*sc.* come what may] I shall see / The wingèd vengeance overtake such children.'

65 wingèd vengeance 'The vengeance of the gods, sweeping down upon them like a bird of prey' (Kittredge). Compare 2.4.154–5.

69 SD *Cornwall . . . eyes* For the various ways this action has been staged, see Rosenberg, p. 242–3, and Bratton, p. 157.

75–6 If . . . quarrel Compare 36 and n. above.

76 What do you mean? NS follows Kittredge, who assigns these words to Regan (after a conjecture by Craig) – unnecessarily, since her sense of outrage (and Cornwall's) is registered strongly enough elsewhere. Some stage business, unrecorded in Q or F, may prompt the servant's query to Cornwall. Thus, after 'quarrel' Hunter inserts SD *Cornwall draws his sword*, but most editors follow Q and have both men draw at 78.

77 villain (1) serf, (2) evil person.

78 take . . . anger take the risk (of good or bad success: Schmidt) that anger brings.

78 SD *They . . . fight* During the swordplay, the servant fatally wounds Cornwall before Regan is able to kill him (by running him through from behind, as Q directs). Compare 94–7.

SERVANT Oh, I am slain. My lord, you have one eye left   80
　　　To see some mischief on him. Oh!   [*He dies*]
CORNWALL Lest it see more, prevent it. Out, vile jelly!
　　　[*He puts out Gloucester's other eye*]
　　　Where is thy lustre now?
GLOUCESTER All dark and comfortless. Where's my son Ed-
　　　mond?
　　　Edmond, enkindle all the sparks of nature   85
　　　To quit this horrid act.
REGAN   Out, treacherous villain!
　　　Thou call'st on him that hates thee. It was he
　　　That made the overture of thy treasons to us,
　　　Who is too good to pity thee.
GLOUCESTER O, my follies! Then Edgar was abused.   90
　　　Kind gods, forgive me that, and prosper him.
REGAN Go thrust him out at gates, and let him smell
　　　His way to Dover.
　　　　　　　　Exit [a Servant] with Gloucester
　　　How is't, my lord? How look you?
CORNWALL I have received a hurt. Follow me, lady.
　　　[*To Servants*] Turn out that eyeless villain. Throw this
　　　slave   95
　　　Upon the dunghill. Regan, I bleed apace.
　　　Untimely comes this hurt. Give me your arm.
　　　　　　　　　　　　　　　　Exeunt

80–1 Oh . . . Oh!] F *lineation; as prose* Q   80 you have] F; yet haue you Q   *81 SD] Q2; *not in* Q, F   82 SD] *Rowe (subst.);*
not in Q, F   84 All . . . Edmond?] *As in* Q; *two lines divided* comfortlesse? / Where's F   *84 comfortless.] comfortles,
Q; comfortlesse? F   85–6 Edmond . . . act.] F *lineation; one line* Q   85 enkindle] F; vnbridle Q   86–9 Out . . . thee.] F
lineation; as prose Q   86 treacherous] F; *not in* Q   92–3 Go . . . you?] *Capell's lineation; three lines ending* . . . smell / . . .
Douer. / . . . you? F; *as prose* Q   93 SD] *Duthie; Exit with Glouster.* F; *not in* Q   95–7 Turn . . . arm.] F *lineation; lines
end* . . . vpon / . . . vntimely / . . . arme. Q   95 SD] *Oxford; not in* Q, F   96 dunghill] F; dungell Q   97 SD] F; *Exit.* Q;
F *omits nine lines here*

81 **mischief** injury, harm.
82 **prevent** i.e. I shall prevent.
85 **nature** i.e. filial loyalty and devotion.
86 **quit** repay, requite; as in *Ham.* 5.2.68.
88 **overture** disclosure. The article before the
noun is elided and the second syllable stressed:
'th'ovèrture'.
90 **abused** wronged.
91 **that** i.e. his misjudgement and mistreatment
of Edgar.
92 **smell** Emphatic (Kittredge).
93 SD **Exit . . . Gloucester** Although Cornwall
repeats Regan's command two lines later, F is probably right in placing the SD here; Cornwall's repetition is for emphasis.

93 **How . . . you** Regan's concern for Cornwall varies with interpretation. In some productions, intent on Edmond, she ignores Cornwall's
request for her arm (97) and walks coolly off. But
the language here suggests more than a modicum
of compassion for her husband.
93 **How look you** i.e. how are you feeling?
96 **dunghill** manure pile. The rebellious servant
receives ignominious treatment, denied the rites of
burial and cast unburied upon offal.
97 **Untimely** i.e. because of the invasion and
other problems.
97 SD **Exeunt** In modern stage productions, the
interval usually occurs here. On F's omission of
nine lines, see p. 271.

4.1 *Enter* EDGAR *[disguised as a madman]*

EDGAR   Yet better thus, and known to be condemned,
Than still condemned and flattered. To be worst,
The low'st and most dejected thing of fortune,
Stands still in esperance, lives not in fear.
The lamentable change is from the best;   5
The worst returns to laughter. Welcome, then,
Thou unsubstantial air that I embrace:
The wretch that thou hast blown unto the worst
Owes nothing to thy blasts.

Enter GLOUCESTER *and an* OLD MAN

But who comes here?
My father, parti-eyed? World, world, O world!   10
But that thy strange mutations make us hate thee,
Life would not yield to age.

Act 4, Scene 1   4.1] *Actus Quartus. Scena Prima.* F; *not in* Q   *2 flattered. To be worst,] *Pope;* flatter'd, to be worst: F;
flattered to be worst, Q   3 low'st] *Oxford;* lowest Q F   4 esperance] F; experience Q   6–9 Welcome . . . blasts.] F; *not
in* Q   9 SD] F; *Enter Glost. led by an old man.* Q (*after* age, *12*)   9–10 But . . . world!] *Pope's lineation;* F *begins new line
with* But *and divides* led? / World; *one line* Q   9 But who comes] F; Who's Q   *10 parti-eyed] *Oxford (Davenport conj.);*
parti, eyd Q *corr.;* poorlie, leed Q *uncorr.;* poorely led? Q2, F

Act 4, Scene 1
   0 SD *Enter* EDGAR Edgar has become detached
from Lear and his entourage, left behind deliberately, perhaps, since he is ignored at the end of 3.6.
In the fictional narrative, it is the next morning
(compare 32 below).
   1–4 Yet . . . fear Edgar says it is better to know
one's condemnation openly than to suffer it under
the false guise of flattery. When one is at the worst,
i.e. the very bottom of Fortune's wheel, one lives
always in hope, not fear (of falling further). See collation. Pope's punctuation helps clarify the sense
and is not inconsistent with F (compare Sisson, pp.
238–9). 'To be worst' is most likely in apposition
to 'The low'st'. Perrett, however, defends F punctuation (see Muir).
   1 thus i.e. a Bedlam beggar.
   3 dejected cast down.
   4 esperance hope.
   6 The worst . . . laughter Compare Dent,
p. 228, T216: 'When things are at the worst they
will mend.'
   6 laughter happiness, good times.
   6–9 Welcome . . . blasts See Textual Analysis,
p. 284 below.
   9 Owes . . . blasts i.e. has nothing left to be

swept away and therefore can embrace you freely.
   10 parti-eyed 'with his eyes "motley" or parti-
coloured, i.e. bleeding' (Riverside). A major crux:
see collation. Q corr. may reflect copy. Either (1)
the reviser or collator, working from an exemplar
of Q with sheet H in the uncorrected state, corrected
only the spelling he saw there; or (2) Q2, deriving
from Q uncorr., directly influenced F, especially if
the playhouse manuscript was illegible (see Greg,
Variants, p. 169; Textual Analysis, p. 73 above). F
makes sufficient, if feeble, sense; but many recent
editions, e.g. Hunter, Riverside, adopt emended Q
corr., whose comma might have been meant for
a hyphen, as sometimes happens in texts of foul-
papers provenance, or a hyphen might have been
misunderstood as a comma by the Q compositor
or corrector (Davenport, p. 21; compare *Textual
Companion*, pp. 519, 536.) Compare *LLL* 5.2.766:
'parti-coated presence of loose love'; *MV* 1.3.88:
'parti-coloured lambs'. From the description of the
Paphlagonian king and his son in Sidney's *Arcadia*,
Muir conjectures 'poorly 'rayd' but follows F.
   10–12 world . . . age i.e. life would not willingly yield to old age (and death) except that the
world's changes and vicissitudes make us welcome
release from them.

OLD MAN   O my good lord,
    I have been your tenant and your father's tenant
    These fourscore –
GLOUCESTER   Away, get thee away; good friend, be gone.   15
    Thy comforts can do me no good at all;
    Thee they may hurt.
OLD MAN   You cannot see your way.
GLOUCESTER   I have no way, and therefore want no eyes:
    I stumbled when I saw. Full oft 'tis seen,
    Our means secure us, and our mere defects   20
    Prove our commodities. Oh, dear son Edgar,
    The food of thy abusèd father's wrath:
    Might I but live to see thee in my touch,
    I'd say I had eyes again.
OLD MAN   How now? Who's there?
EDGAR   [*Aside*] O gods! Who is't can say 'I am at the worst'?   25
    I am worse than e'er I was.
OLD MAN   'Tis poor mad Tom.
EDGAR   [*Aside*] And worse I may be yet. The worst is not
    So long as we can say 'This is the worst.'
OLD MAN   Fellow, where goest?
GLOUCESTER   Is it a beggarman?
OLD MAN   Madman and beggar too.   30
GLOUCESTER   He has some reason, else he could not beg.
    I'th'last night's storm I such a fellow saw,

12–14 O . . . fourscore –] *Johnson's lineation; two lines divided* Tenant, / And F; *as prose* Q   *14 These fourscore –] this forescore – Q; these fourscore years. F   17 You] F; Alack sir, you Q   21 Oh] F; ah Q   25, 27, 37, 52, 54 SD] *Johnson; not in* Q, F   28 So] F; As Q   30 Madman] F; Mad man Q   31 He] F; A Q   32 I'th'] F; In the Q

14 **fourscore** – See collation. Compositor B, who set these lines in F, appears guilty of sophistication, completing a sentence meant to be interrupted, as Q indicates.
  17 **Thee . . . hurt** Gloucester is concerned for the Old Man's safety if he should be found aiding the proclaimed traitor. Compare 4.4.39–40.
  18–19 **I have . . . saw** 'Gloucester here summarizes his whole career' (Heilman, p. 44). When he had eyes, he could not see what he most needed to see and understand, and thus he erred; blind and knowing what he knows, his actions are now without purpose. Colie (pp. 131–2) compares Isa. 59.10, Matt. 13.13, and Job 5.14.
  20–1 **Our means . . . commodities** i.e. our

assets, or advantages, give us a false sense of security (overconfidence), whereas our very lacks, or deficiencies, turn out to be advantages. Compare *Mac.* 3.5.32–3: 'And you all know, security / Is mortals' chiefest enemy.' Dent, p. 244, compares w152: 'He that is secure is not safe', and *R2* 2.1.265–6.
  22 **abusèd** deceived.
  23 **to see . . . touch** i.e. to recognise by touching you. Compare 4.5.143. Kittredge paraphrases more freely: 'To hold thee in my embrace'.
  25–6 **Who is't . . . was** Compare 1–9 above. Edgar's shock is an object lesson to him against false optimism, as his next speech explicitly states.
  31 **reason** rational capacity, sanity.

Which made me think a man a worm. My son
Came then into my mind, and yet my mind
Was then scarce friends with him. I have heard more
    since.   35
As flies to wanton boys are we to th'gods;
They kill us for their sport.

EDGAR [*Aside*]   How should this be?
Bad is the trade that must play fool to sorrow,
Ang'ring itself and others. – Bless thee, master.

GLOUCESTER Is that the naked fellow?

OLD MAN   Ay, my lord.   40

GLOUCESTER Get thee away. If for my sake
Thou wilt o'ertake us hence a mile or twain
I'th'way toward Dover, do it for ancient love,
And bring some covering for this naked soul,
Which I'll entreat to lead me.   45

OLD MAN Alack, sir, he is mad.

GLOUCESTER 'Tis the time's plague when madmen lead the
    blind.
Do as I bid thee; or rather do thy pleasure.

---

35 Was . . . since.] *As in* Q; *two lines divided* him. / I F   36 flies to] F; flies are toth' Q   37 kill] F; bitt Q   37–9 How
. . . master.] F *lineation; as prose* Q   38 fool] F; the foole Q   39 others. – Bless] *Theobald;* others, blesse Q; others. Blesse
F   41 Get thee away] F; Then prethee get thee gon Q   42 hence] F; here Q   43 I'th'] F; Ith' Q   43 toward] F, Q; to
Q2   45 Which] F; Who Q   47 'Tis . . . blind.] *As in* Q; *two lines divided* plague, / When F

33 a man a worm Compare Job 25.6: 'How
much more man, a worme, euen the sonne of man,
which is but a worme?' (cited by Kittredge and
others. Shaheen compares Ps. 22.6: 'But I am a
worme, & not a man').
36–7 As flies . . . sport Often mistakenly
believed to sum up the basic philosophy or 'message' of the play, these lines represent, rather,
Gloucester's despairing viewpoint at this stage in
his development. Edgar will try to bring him out of
it, as he explains later (4.5.33–4). Here, Gloucester, deeply cynical, believes human beings are of no
greater significance or importance to the gods than
insects are to sportive children, who enjoy killing
them for fun. Shakespeare may have recalled Plangus's lament in Sidney's *Arcadia*, Bk II, ch. 12,
where human beings are called 'Balles to the starres, and thralles to Fortunes raigne'. Montaigne
uses a similar expression: 'The gods perdie doe
reckon and racket us men as their tennis-balles'
(Florio's translation, cited by Muir). Compare the
flykilling episode in *Tit.* 3.2.52 ff.
37 How . . . be Edgar is astonished by his
father's physical or mental condition, or both.

38–9 Bad . . . others Considering his father's
real misery, Edgar deplores the role he must
resume, one that upsets both himself and others.
NS regards this speech as Shakespeare's apology
to the audience, as well as Edgar's to himself, and
compares the Fool and Lear.
41 Get thee away See collation. Although Q
offers a metrically regular line, F repeats the earlier
command (15) and is no more abrupt here than
there or at 49 (but compare Duthie, p. 180, who
adopts Q). Werstine, p. 283, notes Compositor B's
omission of line beginnings elsewhere and thinks
he may have done so here, though conflation produces a metrically difficult line. Oxford considers
the tetrameter acceptable and follows F (*Textual
Companion*, p. 536).
47 'Tis . . . blind It is the curse of our time
when rulers (madmen) lead ignorant (blind) subjects. Gloucester makes a kind of parable out of his
situation (Kittredge).
48 Do . . . pleasure Gloucester alters his command, realising it is no longer appropriate for him
to order anyone to do anything.

Above the rest, be gone.

OLD MAN   I'll bring him the best 'parel that I have,   50

Come on't what will.   *Exit*

GLOUCESTER   Sirrah, naked fellow.

EDGAR   Poor Tom's a-cold. [*Aside*] I cannot daub it further.

GLOUCESTER   Come hither, fellow.

EDGAR   [*Aside*] And yet I must. – Bless thy sweet eyes, they bleed.

GLOUCESTER   Know'st thou the way to Dover?   55

EDGAR   Both stile and gate, horseway and footpath. Poor Tom hath
been scared out of his good wits. Bless thee, goodman's son,
from the foul fiend.

GLOUCESTER   Here, take this purse, thou whom the heavens'
plagues

Have humbled to all strokes. That I am wretched   60

Makes thee the happier. Heavens deal so still.

Let the superfluous and lust-dieted man

That slaves your ordinance, that will not see

Because he does not feel, feel your power quickly.

---

50 'parel] *Rowe;* Parrell Q, F   50 have,] Q2; haue Q, F   51 SD] F; *not in* Q   *52 a-cold] *Rowe;* a cold Q, F   52 daub] F; dance Q   52 further] F; farther Q   54 And . . . bleed.] *Capell's lineation; two lines divided* must: / Blesse F   54 And yet I must.] F; *not in* Q   54 must. – Bless] *Capell (subst.);* must: / Blesse F   56–8 Both . . . fiend.] *As prose* F; *three verse lines ending . . .* footpath, / . . . wits, / . . . fiend, Q   *57 scared] scard Q; scarr'd F   57 thee, goodman's son,] thee good mans sonne, F; the good man Q   58 fiend.] F *omits five lines here*   58 heavens'] heauens Q; heau'ns F   60–1 Have . . . still] F *lineation; divided* thee [*turned under*] / The Q   63 slaves] F; stands Q   64 does] F, Q; doth Q2

---

49 **Above the rest** Above all.

50 **'parel** apparel. Compare Marlowe, *Jew of Malta* 4.4: 'Here's goodly 'parrell, is here not?' (Muir; see Abbott 460, for dropped prefixes elsewhere.)

51 **Come . . . will** i.e. regardless of what happens as a result.

52 **daub it further** dissemble any longer. Compare Old French *dauber*, Latin *dealbare*, 'to whiten over, whitewash, plaster'; *R3* 3.5.29: 'So smooth he daub'd his vice with show of virtue'; and 2.2.57 above.

54 **And . . . must** See Textual Analysis, pp. 284–5 below.

55 **Dover** Gloucester is thinking of Dover as a suitable place for suicide (68–73), not as the place where he has sent Lear to meet the other 'traitors'. Perhaps Dover was suggested by the interrogation in 3.7: 'in his half-crazed state he has an irrational urge to end his life there' (Muir, p. xlix). But not only the exigencies of the plot require the meeting of all principal characters at Dover; the source in Sidney's *Arcadia* also included the desire of the Paphlagonian king to jump off a high rock (Moberly, cited by Furness; compare Bullough, p. 403).

56 **Both . . . footpath** 'Each kind of path has its appropriate obstacle – the stile for the footpath, the gate for the horse-way (bridle path)' (Hunter).

60 **humbled . . . strokes** i.e. made you susceptible to every misfortune.

61 **Heavens** i.e. may the heavens.

62–6 **Let . . . enough** Compare 3.4.33–6, where Lear expresses similar sentiments.

62 **superfluous** i.e. having too much, more than enough (hypallage, or transferred epithet: see Joseph, p. 56).

62 **lust-dieted** i.e. fed by pleasures.

63 **slaves your ordinance** 'makes your law subservient to his own desires' (Riverside). All men are commanded to help one another; the rich are especially enjoined to help the poor, not to ignore or exploit them. Compare the parable of Dives the rich man and Lazarus the beggar in Luke 16.19–31 and the marginal gloss at verse 19 in the Geneva Bible: 'By this storie is declared what punishment thei shal haue, which liue deliciously & neglect the poore.' Compare also Mark 10.21.

64 **feel, feel** (1) sympathise, (2) experience.

64 **quickly** A triple pun: (1) very soon, (2) while he is still alive, and (3) sharply, piercingly (NS).

So distribution should undo excess,   65
And each man have enough. Dost thou know Dover?
EDGAR Ay, master.
GLOUCESTER There is a cliff whose high and bending head
Looks fearfully in the confinèd deep.
Bring me but to the very brim of it,   70
And I'll repair the misery thou dost bear
With something rich about me. From that place
I shall no leading need.
EDGAR   Give me thy arm.
Poor Tom shall lead thee.

Exeunt

4.2 *Enter* GONERILL [*with*] EDMOND, *and* OSWALD, [*severally*]

GONERILL Welcome, my lord. I marvel our mild husband
Not met us on the way. – Now, where's your master?
OSWALD Madam, within; but never man so changed.
I told him of the army that was landed;
He smiled at it. I told him you were coming;   5
His answer was, 'The worse'. Of Gloucester's treachery,
And of the loyal service of his son
When I informed him, then he called me sot,
And told me I had turned the wrong side out.
What most he should dislike seems pleasant to him;   10
What like, offensive.
GONERILL [*To Edmond*] Then shall you go no further.

---

65 undo] F; vnder Q   69 fearfully] F; firmely Q   72–3 With . . . need.] F *lineation; divided* me, / From Q   73–4 Give . . . thee.] F *lineation; one line* Q   74 SD] F; *not in* Q   Act 4, Scene 2   4.2] *Scena Secunda.* F; *not in* Q   0 SD] *This edn; Enter Gonerill, Bastard, and Steward.* F; *Enter Gonorill and Bastard* Q (*which places Steward's entrance after* 2)   3–11 Madam . . . offensive.] F *lineation; as prose* Q   10 most he should dislike] F; hee should most desire Q   12 SD] *Hanmer; not in* Q; F

65 So . . . excess Thus (heaven's intervention having punished the rich for insensitivity to the poor), excesses will be eliminated by a redistribution of wealth.
65 distribution (1) administration (of justice), (2) sharing out (NS, citing *Cor.* 3.3.99).
68–9 a cliff . . . deep The cliff itself becomes the image of someone who, bending over its edge and looking down at the straits far below, is stricken with fear at the sight.
69 in into.
69 confinèd deep 'pent in straits' (Capell, cited by Furness). Dover is the closest point in Britain

to France on the other side of the Channel.

Act 4, Scene 2
1 Welcome, my lord Gonerill welcomes Edmond to her castle, although they arrive together.
4 the army i.e. the French forces. Compare 3.7.2.
8 sot fool.
9 turned . . . out A clothing metaphor: Oswald has inverted the treachery and treason.
11 What like i.e. what he should like.

It is the cowish terror of his spirit
That dares not undertake. He'll not feel wrongs
Which tie him to an answer. Our wishes on the way   15
May prove effects. Back, Edmond, to my brother.
Hasten his musters and conduct his powers.
I must change names at home and give the distaff
Into my husband's hands. This trusty servant
Shall pass between us. Ere long you are like to hear   20
(If you dare venture in your own behalf)
A mistress's command. Wear this; spare speech.
Decline your head. This kiss, if it durst speak,
Would stretch thy spirits up into the air.
Conceive, and fare thee well.   25

EDMOND   Yours in the ranks of death.

GONERILL   My most dear Gloucester.

                                        Exit [*Edmond*]

---

13 terror] F; curre Q *uncorr.*, Q2; terrer Q *corr.*   16 Edmond] F; *Edgar* Q   18 names] F; armes Q   21 (If . . . behalf)] F; If . . . behalfe Q   22 command] F, Q *corr.*; coward Q *uncorr.*, Q2   22 this; spare] F; this spare Q *uncorr.*, Q2; this, spare Q *corr.*   25 fare thee] F; far you Q; farye Q2   26–8 My . . . due] F *lineation; one line* Q, *which omits 27*   26 dear] F; deere Q *uncorr.*; deer Q *corr.*   26 SD] *As in Rowe; Exit.* F (*after* death.*); not in* Q

---

13 **cowish** cowardly.

14 **undertake** take responsibility (for some enterprise).

14–15 **He'll . . . answer** He will not notice injuries which would require him to respond manfully.

15–16 **Our . . . effects** Our desires as we travelled here together may be fulfilled. Gonerill hopes that Edmond will supplant Albany as her husband; ever the opportunist, Edmond has apparently encouraged that hope. Neither one knows yet of Cornwall's death: see 39 ff. below, especially 52–5.

16 **effects** realised facts, fulfilments.

16 **brother** brother-in-law.

17 **musters** levies of troops.

17 **conduct** escort, guide, accompany (compare *OED* sv *v* 1); *not* 'to lead as a commander' (Schmidt).

18 **change** exchange.

18 **names** titles (i.e. wife and husband). Compare *1H4* 3.4.64, *Temp.* 2.1.150 (Onions). Many modern editors adopt Q's 'armes' = weapons, or possibly = insignia (Craig, cited by Duthie). F's 'names' may be a misreading, as Jackson believes (p. 323). F. E. Budd, 'Shakespeare, Chaucer, and Harsnett', *RES* (1935), 427, notes a close parallel from Chaucer's *Monk's Tale*, where the Host recalls his wife's reproach: 'I wol have thy knyf, / And thou shalt have my distaf and go spinne' (B.3096–7). Though he adopts Q, Duthie consid-

ers F defensible: 'Goneril says that she must adopt the name of man and her husband the name of woman, and then goes on to refer to an exchange of symbols of husband and wife – she will give Albany the distaff and (this is implied) take from him the sword' (p. 181).

18 **distaff** 'cleft stick on which wool or flax was formerly wound; (used as the type for woman's work) wifely duties' (Onions). Compare *Cym.* 5.3.34.

20 **like** likely.

22 **mistress's command** (1) liege's, or (2) lover's order, presumably to get rid of Albany.

22 **Wear this** Gonerill here gives Edmond a favour to wear, such as a chain or scarf; but she may simply refer to a kiss.

23 **Decline your head** i.e. so that she can put the favour around his neck or kiss him.

24 **Would . . . air** This speech and the lines that follow contain several sexual innuendos (Heilman, p. 318, n. 15; Muir and Hunter agree). For 'stretch' and 'spirits' see Rubenstein.

25 **Conceive** Compare 1.1.10–11.

26–9 **Yours . . . body** See collation. In Q not only is 27 missing, but so is Edmond's exit. Gonerill's entire speech is thus directed in Q to her lover, not to herself as in F.

26 **Yours . . . death** Muir and others find a sexual pun on 'death' = orgasm, and compare 4.5.189. In other respects, the speech is prophetic (Rosenberg, p. 251).

Oh, the difference of man and man.
To thee a woman's services are due;
My fool usurps my body.
OSWALD Madam, here comes my lord.   [*Exit*]   30

Enter ALBANY

GONERILL   I have been worth the whistle.
ALBANY   O Gonerill,
You are not worth the dust which the rude wind
Blows in your face.
GONERILL   Milk-livered man,
That bear'st a cheek for blows, a head for wrongs;
Who hast not in thy brows an eye discerning   35
Thine honour from thy suffering –
ALBANY   See thyself, devil:

---

28 a] F, Q *corr.; not in* Q *uncorr.,* Q2   29 My . . . body.] F; My foote vsurps my body. Q *uncorr.;* A foole vsurps my bed. Q *corr.;* My foote vsurps my head. Q2   *30 SD.1 Exit] Exit Stew.* Q; *not in* F   30 SD.2 *Enter* ALBANY] F; *not in* Q   31 whistle.] F, Q *uncorr.;* whistling. Q *corr.*   31–2 O . . . wind] F *lineation; one line (turned under)* Q   33 face.] F *omits twenty lines here*   34 bear'st] F; bearest Q   35–6 Who . . . suffering –] F *lineation; divided* honour, / From Q, *which continues with six lines not in* F   *35 eye discerning] *Rowe;* eye-discerning F; eye deseruing Q   *36 suffering –] *Oxford;* suffering, Q; suffering. F   36–8 See . . . woman.] F *lineation; as prose* Q

28 a woman's services 'the service that a woman naturally gives to a *real* man' (Hunter).

29 My . . . body Though Albany is Gonerill's husband, she thinks him a 'fool' who does not deserve possession of her body (which Edmond, a real man, does). Thomas Clayton makes a good case for Q uncorr. 'My foote vsurps my body' as the original manuscript reading, miscorrected in Q corr. and further in Q2 ('Old light on the text of *King Lear*', *MP* 78 (1981), 347–67). F can be defended, but compare Greg, who concludes that 'My foole vsurps my bed' was what the copy for Q actually contained (*Variants*, pp. 170 ff.).

30 SD.1 F omits Q's *Exit Stew.* The omission is more likely an error by Compositor B, who needed to insert *Enter Albany* at this point and may have mistaken the added SD for a substitution (NS). Albany's entrance is missing in Q, but *Enter the Duke of Albany* appears in Q2 after Gonerill's speech (31). See Textual Analysis, p. 82 above.

31 worth the whistle i.e. worth finding, seeking out. See collation. The usual proverbial form may have led to miscorrection in Q corr. (Greg, *Variants*, p. 172; Duthie, p. 406; and Muir). Compare Heywood's *Proverbs*: 'It is a poore dogge that is not woorth the whystlyng' (Steevens, cited by Furness), and Tilley w311. In NS, Duthie adopts Q corr. and proposes the quibble: (1) entice, allure (*OED v* 7a *fig.*), (2) wait for (*OED v* 9).

32–3 You . . . face Albany compounds Gonerill's sarcasm and plays on 'worth the whistle'. For the marked change in his attitude, compare 1.4.266 ff.

32 rude (1) harsh, rough (Schmidt), (2) uncivil (compare *TGV* 5.4.60: 'Ruffian! Let go that rude uncivil touch').

33 face For F omissions here, see Textual Analysis, p. 271 below.

33 Milk-livered White-livered, i.e. cowardly. Cowardice was believed to be caused by lack of blood in the liver (Kittredge). Compare 2.2.15.

34 That . . . blows Compare Matthew 5.39 and Luke 6.29 on turning the other cheek (Shaheen).

35–6 eye . . . suffering i.e. you cannot see the difference between what can be honourably borne and what should be resented (Muir). Compare Hamlet's dilemma, *Ham.* 3.1.55–9.

36 See . . . devil In Q, Gonerill's speech continues for six more lines and comes to a proper conclusion (see Textual Analysis, p. 271 below). In F, Albany abruptly and vehemently breaks into the middle of her speech, holding up to her, perhaps, the mirror she carries by her side (see 2.2.32 n.). Shakespeare may be alluding to Renaissance iconography, in which the devil is sometimes portrayed standing behind the figure of Lady Vanity, his face rather than hers reflected in the mirror she gazes into (Meagher, p. 254).

Proper deformity shows not in the fiend
So horrid as in woman.
GONERILL   O vain fool!

Enter a MESSENGER

MESSENGER O my good lord, the Duke of Cornwall's dead,
Slain by his servant going to put out   40
The other eye of Gloucester.
ALBANY   Gloucester's eyes?
MESSENGER A servant that he bred, thrilled with remorse,
Opposed against the act, bending his sword
To his great master; who, thereat enraged,
Flew on him and amongst them felled him dead,   45
But not without that harmful stroke which since
Hath plucked him after.
ALBANY   This shows you are above,
You justicers, that these our nether crimes
So speedily can venge. But O, poor Gloucester!
Lost he his other eye?
MESSENGER   Both, both, my lord.   50
This letter, madam, craves a speedy answer:
'Tis from your sister.
GONERILL [*Aside*]   One way I like this well;

---

*37 shows] shewes Q *corr.*; seemes Q *uncorr.*, F   38 fool!] F *omits seven lines here*   38 SD] F; *Enter a Gentleman* Q   39 SH]
F; *Gent.* Q (*as throughout scene*)   39–41 O . . . Gloucester] F *lineation; as prose* Q   *41 eyes?] Q; eyes. F   42 thrilled] F;
thrald Q   *44 thereat enraged] Q; threat-enrag'd F   47–50 This . . . eye?] F *lineation; three lines ending* . . . Iustisers, /
. . . venge. / . . . eye. Q   *48 You justicers] Q *corr.*; your Iustices Q *uncorr.*, Q2; You Iustices F   50–1 Both . . . answer:]
F *lineation; one line* (*turned over*) Q   52 SD] *Johnson; not in* Q, F

37–8 **Proper . . . woman** The deformity of devils is appropriate to demons and therefore not so
horrid in them as in women (whose faces should
reflect more suitable feelings and attitudes). Muir
compares *King Leir* 2582: 'Thou fiend in likenesse
of a humane creature'.
   38 **O vain fool** 'vain' = silly; but the epithet
may reflect back upon Gonerill ironically if she is
a representation of Lady Vanity (see 2.2.32 n., and
Meagher, pp. 250–3).
   42 **bred** brought up (*OED* Breed *v* 10b).
   42 **thrilled** pierced, suddenly moved.
   42 **remorse** compassion, pity.
   43 **bending** directing.
   44 **To** Against.
   44 **thereat enraged** See collation. Q is prefer-
able here. As Oxford observes, 'F1 could as easily
result from Compositor B omitting a single type as

from a misreading of, or in, the manuscript' (*Textual Companion*, p. 537).
   45 **felled** he felled. Compare Abbott 399 on
ellipsis. The Messenger implies a struggle among
several of those present but does not mention
Regan's attack.
   47 **plucked him after** i.e. pulled him after his
servant (into death).
   48 **justicers** (divine) judges. See collation. Q
corr. is 'unquestionably correct' and is supported
by 'justicer' elsewhere in Q (Greg, *Variants*, p. 175;
see Appendix, p. 299 below, xii, 36).
   48 **nether** earthly.
   49 **venge** avenge.
   52 **One . . . well** In so far as Cornwall's death
removes an obstacle to Gonerill's taking
over the whole kingdom, she is pleased at the
news.

But being widow, and my Gloucester with her,
May all the building in my fancy pluck
Upon my hateful life. Another way   55
The news is not so tart. – I'll read, and answer.   *Exit*
ALBANY Where was his son when they did take his eyes?
MESSENGER Come with my lady hither.
ALBANY   He is not here.
MESSENGER No, my good lord; I met him back again.
ALBANY Knows he the wickedness?   60
MESSENGER Ay, my good lord; 'twas he informed against him
And quit the house on purpose that their punishment
Might have the freer course.
ALBANY   Gloucester, I live
To thank thee for the love thou showed'st the king,
And to revenge thine eyes. – Come hither, friend.   65
Tell me what more thou know'st.

                                           Exeunt

4.3 *Enter with drum and colours,* CORDELIA, GENTLEMAN, *and Soldiers*

CORDELIA Alack, 'tis he: why, he was met even now,
As mad as the vexed sea, singing aloud,

---

54 in] F; on Q   55–6 Upon . . . answer.] F *lineation; divided* tooke, / Ile Q   *56 tart. –] Capell (subst.);* tart. F; tooke,
Q   *56 SD] Q; not in* F   57 Where . . . eyes?] *As in* Q; *two lines divided* Sonne, / When F   63–4 Gloucester . . . king,] F
lineation; one line (turned over) Q   64 showed'st] shewedst Q; shew'dst F   65 thine] F; thy Q   65 eyes. –] *Capell;* eyes,
Q; eyes. F   66 know'st] F; knowest Q   66 SD] F; *Exit.* Q; F *omits a full scene here. See p. 77 above*   Act 4, Scene 3   4.3]
Scena Tertia. F; *not in* Q   0 SD] F; *Enter Cordelia, Doctor and others.* Q   *1 why,] why Q, F   2 vexed] F; vent Q

53 **my Gloucester** Gonerill's possessiveness is
patent.
54–5 **May . . . life** The dream that Gonerill's
imagination has constructed (of marrying Edmond)
may be demolished (if Regan takes her place); then
life (with Albany) will remain hateful to her.
55–6 **Another way . . . tart** An apparent redundancy, as she reverts to her attitude in 52.
59 **back** i.e. on his way back.
66 SD **Exeunt** F omits an entire scene following
4.2, probably to shorten the play in performance.
See Doran, p. 70, Duthie, p. 8, and Textual Analysis, p. 271 below.

Act 4, Scene 3
0 SD **Enter . . . CORDELIA** Cordelia's reappearance in the play in F differs significantly from her
reappearance in Q (Warren, 'Diminution', p. 67).
Here, she is at the head of an army, and although

she voices the humane concerns the Gentleman
attributes to her in Q's Scene 3, she is much more
the active exponent of her father's rights. In Q,
'Monsieur La Far' was named the leader of the
French army after the King of France suddenly
had to return home; in F, Cordelia leads the French,
and there is no mention of either her husband or
his proxy (Goldring, p. 149; compare Urkowitz,
p. 94).
0 SD **GENTLEMAN** See collation and compare
4.6.0 SD. Taylor ('War', p. 30) suggests that the
scene in Q is intimate rather than military, more
suitable for a doctor's presence than a military setting, where Shakespeare has surgeons rather than
doctors appear – a nice distinction.
1 **he** i.e. Lear, of whom they have been just
speaking.
2 **vexed** turbulent; compare *Ham.* 4.1.7: 'Mad
as the sea and wind when both contend'.

Crowned with rank fumitor and furrow-weeds,
With burdocks, hemlock, nettles, cuckoo-flowers,
Darnel, and all the idle weeds that grow   5
In our sustaining corn. A century send forth.
Search every acre in the high-grown field,
And bring him to our eye.
                                        [*Exit an Officer*]
                            What can man's wisdom
In the restoring his bereavèd sense?
He that helps him take all my outward worth.   10
GENTLEMAN   There is means, madam.
Our foster-nurse of nature is repose,
The which he lacks. That to provoke in him
Are many simples operative, whose power
Will close the eye of anguish.
CORDELIA   All blest secrets,   15
All you unpublished virtues of the earth,

---

*3 fumitor] *Oxford;* femiter Q; Fenitar F; fumiterr *Theobald;* fumitory *Hanmer* *4 burdocks] *Hanmer;* hor-docks Q; Hardokes F, F2; Hardocks F3–4; bur-docks *Capell* 6 century send] Centery send F; centurie is sent Q 8 SD] *Malone (following Capell); not in* Q, F 8 wisdom] F, Q; wisedom do Q2 9–10 In . . . worth.] *Pope's lineation; divided* him / Take Q, F 9 sense?] Q2; sence, Q; Sense; F 10 helps] F; can helpe Q 11 SH] F; *Doct.* Q 15–16 All . . . earth] F *lineation; one line* Q

---

3 fumitor fumitory, a weed (compare Old French *fumeterre,* medieval Latin *fumus terrae,* 'smoke of the earth', so-called because it springs from the earth in great quantity like smoke: see *OED*). *H5* 5.2.45 similarly lists 'rank femetary' along with darnel and hemlock. F's 'Fenitar' may derive from a minim misreading; Q 'femiter' may reflect Shakespeare's spelling (NS).

3 furrow-weeds i.e. weeds growing in ploughed land.

4 burdocks 'coarse weedy plant . . . bearing prickly flower-heads called burs, and large leaves like those of the dock' (*OED*). See collation. Q's 'hor-docks' is probably the result of misreading copy, an error compounded in F 'Hardokes' by the collator and/or compositor (see Stone, pp. 56, 101, 209; *Textual Companion,* p. 521).

4 cuckoo-flowers Variously identified as ragged robin, ladies' smocks, and bedlam cowslip. Ladies' smocks, or *Cardimine pratensis,* was used as long ago as the ancient Greeks and Romans and as recently as the last century for treating mental diseases (Muir).

5 Darnel Any troublesome weed (Furness); tares.

5 idle i.e. useless.

6 sustaining life-supporting, in contrast to 'idle weeds'.

6 century A hundred soldiers. The number

may faintly suggest the restoration of Lear's train (Perrett, p. 201).

7 high-grown field 'It is now, for symbolic purposes, high summer at Dover. The height of Lear's escape into "natural" chaos is supported by a natural riot of vegetation' (Hunter).

8 What . . . wisdom i.e. what can human knowledge accomplish.

10 worth wealth.

12 Our . . . nature i.e. what naturally nourishes and helps us. Shakespeare opposes a natural remedy – repose – to quack cures, such as scourging, charms, bleeding, scalp-shaving, etc., used by contemporary physicians (A. E. Kellogg, *Shakespeare's Delineation of Insanity, Imbecility, and Suicide,* 1866, cited by Furness).

13 provoke induce.

14 simples operative effective medicinal herbs. Compare 'simples' in *Rom.* 5.1.40.

15–16 All blest . . . earth Cordelia invokes the assistance of natural, or white, magic, dependent here on herbs and plants for its effectiveness. Compare Giambattista della Porta, *Magiae naturalis* (Naples, 1589); English trans., London, 1658: Bk 8, ch. 1, 'Of Medicines which cause sleep', pp. 217–18.

16 unpublished . . . earth i.e. secret, powerful herbs.

Spring with my tears; be aidant and remediate
In the good man's distress. – Seek, seek for him,
Lest his ungoverned rage dissolve the life
That wants the means to lead it.

Enter MESSENGER

MESSENGER   News, madam.   20
The British powers are marching hitherward.
CORDELIA   'Tis known before. Our preparation stands
In expectation of them. – O dear father,
It is thy business that I go about:
Therefore great France   25
My mourning and importuned tears hath pitied.
No blown ambition doth our arms incite,
But love, dear love, and our aged father's right.
Soon may I hear and see him.

                                                              Exeunt

4.4 *Enter* REGAN *and* OSWALD

REGAN   But are my brother's powers set forth?
OSWALD   Ay, madam.
REGAN   Himself in person there?
OSWALD   Madam, with much ado.
Your sister is the better soldier.   5

---

*18 good man's distress. –] *Capell* (*subst.*); good mans distresse, Q*; Goodmans desires: F   **20–1** News . . . hitherward.]
F *lineation; one line* (*turned under*) Q   **23** them. –] *Capell*; them, Q*; them. F   **24–5** It . . . France] *Johnson's lineation;
one line* Q, F   **26** importuned] F; important Q   **27** incite] F; in sight Q   **28** right.] right, Q*; Rite: F   **29** SD] F; *Exit.* Q
Act 4, Scene 4   4.4] *Scena Quarta.* F; *not in* Q   **3** there] F; *not in* Q   **4–5** Madam . . . soldier.] F *lineation; one line* Q   **5**
sister is] F, Q; sister's Q2

17 Spring . . . tears Cordelia figuratively and
literally waters the plants with her tears to encourage growth.
17 aidant and remediate helpful and reme-
dial. Shakespeare may have coined 'remediate' to
avoid the jingle with 'aidant' that 'remediant' would
cause (Muir; compare Wright, cited by Furness).
18 good man's distress See collation. F's error
cannot derive from Q; Compositor B misread
manuscript copy (see Textual Analysis, p. 74 above,
and compare Stone, pp. 101, 222).
19–20 Lest . . . it Cordelia is afraid that in his
madness Lear will kill himself.
19 rage madness, frenzy.
20 wants the means lacks sanity, reason.
22 preparation forces ready to fight; as in *Oth.*
1.3.14.
23–4 O . . . about Compare Luke 2.49: 'knewe
ye not that I must go about my fathers business?'

25 France i.e. the King of France.
26 importuned importunate, solicitous. Q's
'important' means the same, though it may be
a misreading of 'importund' (Duthie, p. 410) or
'importune' (also meaning importunate: Muir).
27–8 No . . . right Cordelia here proclaims her
reasons for coming to England – not the seizure of
political power for herself, but filial devotion and
the wish to restore her father's rights.
27 blown puffed up, inflated. Compare 1 Cor.
13.4–5: 'Loue suffreth long: it is bountiful . . . it
is not puffed vp: / It disdaineth not: it seketh not
her owne things . . .' (Muir).

Act 4, Scene 4
4 with much ado It has apparently required
considerable effort from Gonerill to get Albany,
uncertain where his duty lay, to take command of
his army and march on.

REGAN Lord Edmond spake not with your lord at home?
OSWALD No, madam.
REGAN What might import my sister's letter to him?
OSWALD I know not, lady.
REGAN Faith, he is posted hence on serious matter.   10
It was great ignorance, Gloucester's eyes being out,
To let him live. Where he arrives he moves
All hearts against us. Edmond, I think, is gone,
In pity of his misery, to dispatch
His 'nighted life, moreover to descry   15
The strength o'th'enemy.
OSWALD I must needs after him, madam, with my letter.
REGAN Our troops set forth tomorrow. Stay with us.
The ways are dangerous.
OSWALD   I may not, madam.
My lady charged my duty in this business.   20
REGAN Why should she write to Edmond? Might not you
Transport her purposes by word? Belike –
Some things – I know not what. I'll love thee much:
Let me unseal the letter.
OSWALD   Madam, I had rather –
REGAN I know your lady does not love her husband.   25
I am sure of that; and at her late being here

---

6 lord] F; Lady Q 6 home?] F; home. Q 8 letter] F; letters Q 13 Edmond] F; and now Q 14–16 In . . . enemy.] F
lineation; two lines divided life, / Moreouer Q 16 o'th'enemy.] F; at'h army. Q; of the Army. Q2 17 madam] F; not in
Q 17 letter] F; letters Q 18 troops set] F; troope sets Q 19–20 I . . . business.] F lineation; as prose Q 21–2 Why . . .
Belike –] As in Q; divided: Edmond? / Might F *22 Belike –] Oxford; belike Q; Belike, F *23 Some things –] Something –
Pope; Some things, F; Some thing, Q; Something Q2 23 much!] Oxford; much, Q; much F 24 I had] F; I'de Q

6–8 Lord . . . him Regan is curious about
Edmond's sudden departure and the reason Gonerill so swiftly sent a letter after him.
  6 lord See collation. Copy for Q probably had
'L.', which the compositor mistook for an abbrevi-
ation of 'Lady' (Duthie, p. 411; Stone, p. 38).
  8 import signify.
  10 Faith In faith (a common oath).
  11–12 It . . . live Compare 3.7.4. Regan initially
counselled death, which was practical, but Gonerill's sadism better suited Cornwall's temperament
and then excited Regan (King).
  11 ignorance folly.
  15 'nighted benighted; literally, because he is
blind, but Regan may also contemptuously imply
the figurative sense.
  17 after See collation. 'Madam' was possibly
meant to replace rather than follow 'him', but

the correction was misunderstood and the line
remained unmetrical (*Textual Companion*, p. 537).
  18–19 Stay . . . dangerous Regan's motive in
cajoling Oswald is related to her suspicion concerning the relationship between her sister and
Edmond. Compare 23–4 and n.
  20 charged . . . business i.e. lay particular
stress upon me to carry out her orders.
  22–3 Belike . . . what Regan is momentarily
unsure how to proceed, as her suspicions mount
regarding Gonerill and Edmond.
  22 Belike Probably.
  23–4 I'll . . . letter In the theatre these lines are
often accompanied by significant gestures, as Regan
attempts to seduce Oswald, caressing – even kissing – him while reaching for the letter he carries
on his person (Rosenberg, p. 261).

She gave strange oeilliads and most speaking looks
To noble Edmond. I know you are of her bosom.
OSWALD   I, madam?
REGAN   I speak in understanding. Y'are, I know't.   30
Therefore I do advise you take this note:
My lord is dead; Edmond and I have talked;
And more convenient is he for my hand
Than for your lady's. You may gather more.
If you do find him, pray you give him this;   35
And when your mistress hears thus much from you,
I pray desire her call her wisdom to her.
So, fare you well.
If you do chance to hear of that blind traitor,
Preferment falls on him that cuts him off.   40
OSWALD   Would I could meet him, madam, I should show
What party I do follow.
REGAN   Fare thee well.

Exeunt

4.5 *Enter* GLOUCESTER *and* EDGAR [*dressed like a peasant*]

GLOUCESTER   When shall I come to th'top of that same hill?
EDGAR   You do climb up it now. Look how we labour.

---

27 oeilliads] Eliads F; Iliads F2–4; aliads Q; oeiliads *Rowe*   29 madam?] F; Madam. Q   30 Y'are] F; for Q   *34 lady's]
Rowe; Ladies Q, F   37–8 I . . . well.] F *lineation; one line* Q   38 fare you well] F; farewell Q   *41 him] Q; *not in* F   41
should show] should shew F; would shew Q   42 party] F; Lady Q   42 SD] F; *Exit.* Q   Act 4, Scene 5   4.5] *Scena
Quinta.* F; *not in* Q   0 SD] *Theobald; Enter Gloucester, and Edgar.* F; *Enter Gloster and Edmund.* Q   1 I] F; we Q   2 up it
now.] F; it vpnow, Q; it vp now, Q2   2 labour.] F; labour? Q

27 **oeilliads** amorous glances (*OED*, Onions);
compare *Wiv.* 1.3.61, and Cotgrave: *Oeilliade*, 'An
amorous looke, affectionate winke, wanton aspect,
lustfull iert [= jerk], or passionate cast, of the eye;
a Sheepes eye'. *OED* and Muir cite Greene, *Dispu-
tation between a He and a She Cony-Catcher* (1592):
'amorous glaunces, smirking oeyliads'. Q's 'aliad'
involves *a/e* misreading.
27 **speaking looks** Muir compares the phrase
in Florio's *Montaigne*, iii.211.
28 **of her bosom** (1) in her confidence, (2) sexually intimate. Compare 5.1.11 n. and *R3* 1.2.13,
Richard III to Lady Anne: 'So I might live one
hour in your sweet bosom' (NS; Partridge, p. 77).
30 **understanding** knowledge (Schmidt).
31 **take this note** i.e. note this carefully.
32 **talked** i.e. come to an understanding
(Kittredge).
33 **convenient** suitable, fitting.
34 **You . . . more** You may infer more from
what I have said.

35 **give him this** Precisely what Regan gives
Oswald for Edmond is not clear. It may be a ring
or other token rather than a note, since Edgar
reads only one letter after rifling Oswald's pockets (4.5.250–8). Compare Furness, Muir, Hunter.
36 **thus much** i.e. what I have told you.
37 **I pray . . . to her** Compare *Wiv.* 3.3.118. The
image is the summoning of a subordinate. The repetition of 'her' propels the irony of this line into
sarcasm, which Regan hardly expects Oswald to
repeat (King).

Act 4, Scene 5
0 SD *dressed like a peasant* The Old Man in 4.1
has apparently kept his word and given Edgar new
apparel. See 4.1.50 and 222 below.
1 **that same hill** Compare 4.1.68–70.
2 **You . . . labour** Edgar's deception throughout
this scene may seem cruel, his explanation and

GLOUCESTER   Methinks the ground is even.

EDGAR   Horrible steep.
      Hark, do you hear the sea?

GLOUCESTER   No, truly.

EDGAR   Why, then your other senses grow imperfect   5
      By your eyes' anguish.

GLOUCESTER   So may it be indeed.
      Methinks thy voice is altered, and thou speak'st
      In better phrase and matter than thou didst.

EDGAR   Y'are much deceived. In nothing am I changed
      But in my garments.

GLOUCESTER   Methinks y'are better spoken.   10

EDGAR   Come on, sir, here's the place. Stand still. How fearful
      And dizzy 'tis to cast one's eyes so low.
      The crows and choughs that wing the midway air
      Show scarce so gross as beetles. Half-way down
      Hangs one that gathers samphire, dreadful trade!   15
      Methinks he seems no bigger than his head.
      The fishermen that walk upon the beach
      Appear like mice, and yon tall anchoring barque
      Diminished to her cock; her cock, a buoy
      Almost too small for sight. The murmuring surge,   20
      That on th'unnumbered idle pebble chafes,
      Cannot be heard so high. I'll look no more,

3–4 Horrible . . . sea?] F *lineation; one line* Q   7 speak'st] F; speakest Q   8 In] F; With Q   11 Come . . . fearful] *As in* Q; *two lines divided* Sir, / Heere's F   14 Show] Shew Q, F   *17 walk] Q; walk'd F   *18 yon] Q; yond F   21 th'] F; the Q   21 pebble] F; peeble Q   21 chafes] F; chaffes Q   22 so] F; its so Q

defence at 33–4 notwithstanding. Especially cruel is the attempt to rob Gloucester of confidence in the senses he still retains.
  6 anguish extreme pain; this may include both physical and mental pain. Compare Florio's *Montaigne*, iv.70: 'Our senses are not onely altered, but many times dulled, by the passions of the mind' (Muir).
  7–8 Methinks . . . didst Gloucester's observation is accurate. Edgar has dropped mad Tom's idiom and manner, and his tone of voice is accordingly different. He now speaks in blank verse.
  11–24 How . . . headlong Muir again compares Florio's *Montaigne*, iv.67–8, on the effect of dizzying heights. The details of the description, which Addison admired and to which Dr Johnson objected, are precisely what make the passage moving and persuasive, particularly to eyeless Gloucester. See Furness.

  13 choughs jackdaws, or possibly the Cornish chough or red-legged crow (Onions, cited by NS; pronounced 'chuffs'). Compare 'russet-pated choughs', *MND* 3.2.21.
  14 gross large.
  15 samphire St Peter's herb, or *herbe de Saint Pierre*, an aromatic plant growing along sea-cliffs, used in pickling and gathered by men suspended by ropes.
  18 yon See collation. Again at 114 and 145, F has 'yond' for Q's 'yon', a recurrent Folio mannerism that apparently reflects its modernising tendency rather than a concern for accuracy (Hunter).
  19 cock A small ship's-boat, cockboat.
  21 unnumbered innumerable.
  21 idle useless, barren.
  21 pebble Collective plural.

Lest my brain turn and the deficient sight
Topple down headlong.

GLOUCESTER   Set me where you stand.

EDGAR Give me your hand. You are now within a foot   25
Of th'extreme verge. For all beneath the moon
Would I not leap upright.

GLOUCESTER   Let go my hand.
Here, friend, 's another purse: in it, a jewel
Well worth a poor man's taking. Fairies and gods
Prosper it with thee. Go thou further off.   30
Bid me farewell, and let me hear thee going.

EDGAR Now fare ye well, good sir.

GLOUCESTER   With all my heart.

EDGAR [*Aside*] Why I do trifle thus with his despair
Is done to cure it.

GLOUCESTER [*Kneels*]   O you mighty gods!
This world I do renounce, and in your sights   35
Shake patiently my great affliction off.
If I could bear it longer and not fall
To quarrel with your great opposeless wills,
My snuff and loathèd part of nature should
Burn itself out. If Edgar live, O bless him.   40
Now, fellow, fare thee well.

EDGAR   Gone, sir; farewell.
[*Gloucester throws himself forward and falls*]

25–7 Give . . . upright.] *As in* Q*; lines end* . . . hand: / . . . Verge: / . . . vpright. F   **30** further] F*; farther* Q   **32** ye]
F*; you* Q   **33** SD] *Capell; not in* Q, F   **33–4** Why . . . it.] F *lineation; one line (turned over)* Q   **34** Is] F, Q*; tis* Q2   *34
SD] *He kneeles.* Q *(after* Gods,)*; not in* F   **39** snuff] F*; snurff* Q   **40** him] F*; not in* Q   **41–8** Gone . . . sir?] F *lineation; as
prose* Q   **41** SD] *Capell; He fals.* Q *(after* thee well)*; not in* F

23 turn spin, become giddy.
23 deficient failing, defective.
24 Topple i.e. topple me.
27 leap upright Having been pulled along, wearily climbing the 'hill' (1–2), Gloucester is in a crouching position. Edgar warns that to straighten or jump up suddenly could result in loss of balance and prove fatal.
28 another purse Compare 4.1.59, 72.
29–30 Fairies . . . **thee** Gloucester alludes to the superstition that fairies who guard hidden treasure can make it multiply miraculously in the possession of the discoverer (Kittredge). Compare *WT* 3.3.123.
36 patiently Gloucester, of course, is anything

but 'patient'. Compare 38 n., and p. 21 above.
38 opposeless Unaware of his futility as well as inconsistency, Gloucester opposes ('quarrels with') the gods by attempting suicide while at the same time asserting that their wills cannot be resisted (opposed).
39 snuff candle-end or smouldering wick.
39 loathèd . . . **nature** the fag end of life, characterised by senility and therefore disgusting.
40 Burn itself out i.e. end naturally.
41 SD Gloucester . . . *falls* Gloucester doubtless waits till he hears Edgar say he is gone before he throws himself forward. Q places the SD *He fals* after Gloucester's speech, where there is ample space, rather than in the midst of Edgar's speech. Why F

[*Aside*] And yet I know not how conceit may rob
The treasury of life, when life itself
Yields to the theft. Had he been where he thought,
By this had thought been past. – Alive or dead?   45
Ho, you sir, friend! Hear you, sir? Speak!
[*Aside*] Thus might he pass indeed. Yet he revives. –
What are you, sir?

GLOUCESTER   Away, and let me die.

EDGAR   Hadst thou been aught but gossamer, feathers, air,
So many fathom down precipitating,   50
Thou'dst shivered like an egg. But thou dost breathe,
Hast heavy substance, bleed'st not, speak'st, art sound.
Ten masts at each make not the altitude
Which thou hast perpendicularly fell.
Thy life's a miracle. Speak yet again.   55

GLOUCESTER   But have I fall'n or no?

EDGAR   From the dread summit of this chalky bourn.
Look up a-height: the shrill-gorged lark so far
Cannot be seen or heard; do but look up.

---

42 SD] *Capell; not in* Q, F   42 may] F; my Q   45 had thought] F, Q; thought had Q2   45 past. –] *Theobald*; past, Q; past. F   *46 Ho . . . Speak!] *This edn;* Hoa, you Sir: Friend, heare you Sir, speake: F; ho you sir, heare you sir, speak Q   47 SD] *Capell; not in* Q, F   49 Hadst . . . air,] *As in* Q; *two lines divided* ought / But F   49 gossamer] gosmore Q; Gozemore F; goss'mer *Pope*   50 So . . . precipitating,] Q; (So . . . precipitating) F   51 Thou'dst] F; Thou hadst Q   52 speak'st] F; speakest Q   56 fall'n] falne F; fallen Q   56 no?] F; no I Q   57 summit] Somnet F; sommons Q; summons Q2   *58 a-height] *Warburton;* a hight Q; a height F   59 up.] F; vp? Q

lacks the SD is unclear, unless Compositor B simply overlooked it. On staging-techniques, see Bratton, pp. 175–7; Derek Peat, '*King Lear* and the tension of uncertainty', *S.Sur.* 33 (1980), 46–9; and p. 22 above.

42–4 And yet . . . theft Edgar takes a calculated risk: the illusion ('conceit') of a death leap may have the same effect as the reality, especially when death is willed. But see W. Schleiner's discussion of 'cure by imagination' in *Melancholy, Genius, and Utopia in the Renaissance*, Wiesbaden, 1991, pp. 274–86.

43 treasury treasure; as in *2H6* 1.3.131.

45–6 Alive . . . Speak Edgar changes his tone of voice to suggest still another character as he moves into the next phase of ministering to Gloucester, who has apparently fainted but may appear to be dead.

47 pass die.

49 gossamer Disyllabic; compare Q, F spellings in collation.

50 fathom Plural.

53 at each i.e. end to end, one on top of the other. Stone conjectures that 'alenth' (= 'alength') stood in the copy, and Oxford adopts 'a-length'. But none of the early quartos and Folios emend, so the expression was probably understood as it stands.

55 Thy . . . miracle The theme of Edgar's ministrations to his father; compare 72–7.

57 summit F 'Somnet', a variant but erroneous spelling of 'summit' (*OED*), probably derives from Shakespeare's hand: see Duthie, p. 412.

57 bourn boundary; i.e. cliff bordering on the sea.

58 a-height on high; compare *R3* 4.4.86: 'One heaued a high, to be hurld downe belowe' (*William Shakespeare: The Complete Works (Original-Spelling Edition)*, ed. Stanley Wells and Gary Taylor, 1986).

58 shrill-gorged shrilly voiced.

GLOUCESTER Alack, I have no eyes.   60
    Is wretchedness deprived that benefit
    To end itself by death? 'Twas yet some comfort
    When misery could beguile the tyrant's rage
    And frustrate his proud will.
EDGAR   Give me your arm.
    Up; so. How is't? Feel you your legs? You stand.   65
GLOUCESTER Too well, too well.
EDGAR   This is above all strangeness.
    Upon the crown o'th'cliff what thing was that
    Which parted from you?
GLOUCESTER   A poor unfortunate beggar.
EDGAR As I stood here below, methought his eyes
    Were two full moons. He had a thousand noses,   70
    Horns whelked and waved like the enragèd sea.
    It was some fiend. Therefore, thou happy father,
    Think that the clearest gods, who make them honours
    Of men's impossibilities, have preserved thee.
GLOUCESTER I do remember now. Henceforth I'll bear   75
    Affliction till it do cry out itself
    'Enough, enough', and die. That thing you speak of,
    I took it for a man. Often 'twould say
    'The fiend, the fiend!' He led me to that place.
EDGAR Bear free and patient thoughts.

---

*63 tyrant's] tyrants Q; Tyranrs F   65 is't?] F; *not in* Q   *66 strangeness.] strangenes Q; strangenesse: Q2; strangenesse, F   *67 o'th'cliff what] of the cliffe what Q; o'th'Cliffe. What F   68 beggar] F; bagger Q   69 methought] F; me thoughts Q   70 He] F; a Q   71 whelked] *Hanmer (subst.);* welk't Q; welkt Q2; weal'd F   71 enragèd] F; enridged Q   73 make them] F; made their Q   78 'twould] F; would it Q; would he Q2   79 fiend!] fiend, Q; Fiend, F   80 Bear] F; Bare Q

63 beguile deceive, cheat.

63 tyrant's rage Gloucester alludes to the traditional defence of suicide among the Romans, particularly the Stoics under emperors like Nero or Domitian (Hunter).

69–72 Compare *Ham.* 1.4.69–78: Horatio warns Hamlet that a demon might drive him to insanity and to suicide by jumping off a cliff (Kittredge).

71 whelked convoluted, twisted.

71 enragèd Although most editors prefer Q's 'enridged' and regard F's 'enraged' as a 'vulgarisation (Hunter; compare Duthie, p. 182), F is acceptable. Moreover, Shakespeare describes the 'enraged' sea many times elsewhere and could as easily be responsible for F's adjective as Q's (*Textual Companion*, p. 537).

72 father i.e. old man.

73 clearest brightest, purest, most glorious (Schmidt; cited by Furness, Muir).

73–4 who . . . impossibilities i.e. who acquire honour and reverence by performing miracles. Compare Luke 18.27: 'The things which are vnpossible with me[n], are possible with God' (Furness; Shaheen cites Matt. 19.26 as well). Compare also 'Man's extremity is God's opportunity' (Kittredge; Tilley M471).

75 I . . . now It is not clear what Gloucester refers to – the patience he earlier rejected (35–40), or Tom o'Bedlam.

75–7 Henceforth . . . die i.e. from now on I shall bear affliction patiently until it wearies itself out and stops.

80 free not guilty or troubled.

Enter LEAR, [*mad*]

But who comes here? 80
The safer sense will ne'er accommodate
His master thus.

LEAR No, they cannot touch me for crying. I am the king himself.

EDGAR O thou side-piercing sight!

LEAR Nature's above art in that respect. There's your press- 85
money. That fellow handles his bow like a crow-keeper. Draw
me a clothier's yard. Look, look, a mouse! Peace, peace, this
piece of toasted cheese will do't. There's my gauntlet. I'll prove

---

*80 SD] Q (*subst., following 82*); Enter Lear. F   81–2 The . . . thus.] F *lineation; one line* Q   81 ne'er] F; neare Q   83 crying] F; coyning Q   85 Nature's] F; Nature is Q   87 piece of] F; *not in* Q   88 do't] F; do it Q*

80 SD *Enter* LEAR, *mad* Many editions expand Q's SD with a description of Lear fantastically dressed, crowned with weeds and flowers, etc. For various theatrical representations, see Rosenberg, pp. 267–8; Bratton, pp. 177–9. A change of garments here and in the next scene is appropriate to Lear's changed condition. Obviously, to have the Fool accompany him in this state would be both superfluous and distracting: another reason to terminate his role in Act 3. Compare 3.6.41 n.

81–2 **The safer . . . thus** i.e. no one in his right mind would be dressed like this.

81 **safer** sounder, saner (Onions). Compare *MM* 1.1.72; *Oth.* 4.1.269: 'Are his wits safe? Is he not light of brain?'

81 **accommodate** Compare 3.4.95–6, where Lear refers to 'unaccommodated man' in a different sense.

82 **His** Its.

83 **touch . . . crying** See collation. If the reading 'crying' is preferred, then 'touch' = (1) lay hands on, or (2) rebuke, censure, accuse. M. Warren sees an allusion to the special sense of laying the hand upon (a diseased person) for the cure of the 'king's evil', or scrofula (*OED* Touch *v* 2b) ('*King Lear*, IV.iv.83: the case for "crying" ', *SQ* 35 (1984), 320). If the chosen reading is 'coining', this would constrict the meaning of 'touch'. Since 'coining' means minting coins (a royal prerogative), Lear would then be understood as saying, 'since I am the king, I cannot be arrested ("touched") for forgery'. See Rosenberg, pp. 267–8, who also defends F's 'crying'.

84 **side-piercing** i.e. heart-rending (Schmidt), with a possible allusion to Christ on the cross. Compare John 19.34; in the Geneva Bible the

column heading reads 'Christs side perced'.

85 **Nature's . . . respect** A king is born, not made, and cannot lose his natural rights (Schmidt 1879, cited by Furness). But Lear may also allude to the natural propensity for emotional outlet. The relation between art and nature was frequently discussed, as in *WT* 4.4.87–103. The disjointed sentences in this speech and elsewhere suggest Lear's disordered mental state, although a submerged thread of sense often connects his utterance.

85–6 **press-money** Payment for enlistment or impressment into the king's army. Lear distributes his coins, real or imagined, to Gloucester and Edgar, or to soldiers he imagines standing by.

86 **That fellow** i.e. one of Lear's imaginary soldiers.

86 **crow-keeper** scarecrow, or a farm-boy assigned to keep crows off a field; here, an inept archer. *OED* cites *Dick of Devon* (1626), 2.4: 'Sure these can be no Crowkeepers nor birdscarers.' Compare *Rom.* 1.4.6.

87 **clothier's yard** i.e. full length of the arrow (36 inches).

87 **mouse** Perhaps imagined, through association with 'crow-keeper', though actual fieldmice were abundant then as now.

87 **Peace, peace** Addressed to the soldiers Lear imagines are startled into action.

88 **do't** i.e. catch the mouse.

88 **gauntlet** i.e. challenge (literally, a thrown glove).

88–9 **I'll . . . giant** I'll make good my cause against anyone, even a giant (let alone a mouse). Lear imagines himself as a mighty champion.

it on a giant. Bring up the brown bills. O well flowni'th' bird:
clout, i'th'clout! Hewgh! Give the word.   90
EDGAR Sweet marjoram.
LEAR Pass.
GLOUCESTER I know that voice.
LEAR Ha! Gonerill with a white beard? They flattered me like a
dog and told me I had the white hairs in my beard ere the black   95
ones were there. To say 'ay' and 'no' to everything that I said
'ay' and 'no' to was no good divinity. When the rain came to
wet me once and the wind to make me chatter, when the
thunder would not peace at my bidding, there I found 'em,
there I smelt 'em out. Go to, they are not men o'their words.   100
They told me I was everything; 'tis a lie, I am not ague-proof.
GLOUCESTER The trick of that voice I do well remember.
Is't not the king?

90 i'th'clout . . . Hewgh!] F; in the ayre, hagh, Q 94 Ha! . . . beard?] F; Ha *Gonorill*, ha *Regan*, Q 95 the white] F;
white Q *96–7 To say . . . was] *Oxford*; to say I and no, to euery thing I saide, I and no toe, was Q; to say I and no to
all I saide: I and no too was Q2; To say I, and no, to euery thing that I said: I, and no too, was F 99 'em] F; them Q
(*both times*) 100 o'] F; of Q 101 ague-proof] F; argue-proofe Q 102–5 The . . . cause?] F *lineation; as prose* Q

89 **brown bills** Halberds painted brown to prevent rust. Having assembled his archers, Lear
orders up his billmen.
89 **O . . . bird** Falconer's cry of approval
when his falcon was successful (Steevens, cited by
Furness); but Lear may refer to the feathered arrow
he imagines shot off.
90 **clout** Centre of target or mark, as in *LLL*
4.1.134.
90 **Hewgh** Whistling sound to indicate (1)
sound of the arrow through the air, or (2) cry of
astonishment (NS).
90 **word** password.
91 **Sweet marjoram** Edgar humours Lear with
this fanciful password, which may allude to the
wildflowers bedecking Lear and/or to 'a blessed
remedy for diseases of the brain' (Blunden, cited
by Muir).
94 **Gonerill . . . beard** Lear takes Gloucester for Gonerill in disguise (Kittredge), or he asks
how she could be so inhuman to her aged father
(Halliwell, cited by Furness). Either way, Lear is
prompted by the sight of white-bearded Gloucester, as F's alteration of Q indicates (see collation
and R. Warren, p. 50). Hunter adds a SD *He kneels*
after 93, so that Gloucester's obsequious or flattering attitude reminds Lear of Gonerill. But the hag
image is more complex, suggesting transsexuality

(Rosenberg, p. 270), a demon witch, the inversion
of child and parent, etc. Also: Gloucester was to
Edgar what Gonerill was to Lear, as Edgar says in
Q (see Appendix, p. 300 below, xiv, 9), and both are
lechers (King).
94–6 **They . . . there** Another abrupt mental
shift, prompted perhaps by recollection of Gonerill's flattery in 1.1. The image of the fawning dog
is typically Shakespearean (Spurgeon, p. 195). Lear
complains of the world's flattery that praises pre-
maturely a king's ripe wisdom. A white beard
symbolises the wisdom of age, which 'they' said
he had before he was old enough to grow any
beard.
97 **no good divinity** bad theology. Several biblical verses are possible sources or analogues. Compare Matt. 5.37: 'But let your communication be,
Yea, yea: Nay, nay. For whatsoeuer is more the[n]
these, commeth of euil.' Compare also Matt. 5.36:
'Nether shalt thou sweare by thine head, because
thou canst not make one heere white or blacke'
(Hunter), and James 5.12, 2 Cor. 1.18–19.
97–100 **When . . . out** Lear recalls the storm.
Compare *AYLI* 2.1.6–12 (NS).
101 **ague-proof** immune to severe chill. J. C.
Maxwell cites Florio's *Montaigne*, i.42: 'Doth the
ague . . . spare him [the king] more than us?' (NS).
102 **trick** peculiar characteristic.

LEAR   Ay, every inch a king.
When I do stare, see how the subject quakes.
I pardon that man's life. What was thy cause?   105
Adultery?
Thou shalt not die. Die for adultery? No,
The wren goes to't, and the small gilded fly
Does lecher in my sight.
Let copulation thrive: for Gloucester's bastard son   110
Was kinder to his father than my daughters
Got 'tween the lawful sheets.
To't, luxury, pell-mell, for I lack soldiers.
Behold yon simp'ring dame,
Whose face between her forks presages snow,   115
That minces virtue, and does shake the head
To hear of pleasure's name.
The fitchew nor the soilèd horse goes to't
With a more riotous appetite.

---

103 every] F; euer Q   106–8 Adultery . . . fly] *Capell's lineation; two lines divided* for Adultery? / No, F; *as prose* Q   107 die. Die] dye: dye F; die Q   108 to't] F; toot Q   109–12 Does . . . sheets.] *Johnson's lineation; three lines ending* . . . thriue: / . . . Father, / . . . sheets. F; *as prose* Q   109 Does] F; doe Q   113 lack] F, Q; want Q2   114–22 Behold . . . inherit;] *Capell's lineation; as prose* Q, F   *114 yon] Q; yond F   115 presages] F; presageth Q   116 does] F; do Q   117 To] F; *not in* Q   118 The] F; to Q   118 to't] F; toot Q

---

103 Ay . . . king Spoken with various emphasis and intonation, from regal reassertion to dreamy recollection of bygone glory (Rosenberg, pp. 271–2; Bratton, pp. 178–81).

104–23 When . . . fiend's Prompted by Gloucester's appearance, Lear begins a disquisition on adultery that combines sense and nonsense and varies the idiom of the absent Fool. Hunter notes the progression from 'natural' or illicit sexuality (adultery, copulation) to more violent representations of animal lust (pell-mell luxury, riotous appetite, centaurs). Lear's vision also includes the breakdown of normal safeguards (the king, lawful sheets, gods), culminating in unrestrained animal behaviour and damnation (124–5). The lineation reflects either Shakespeare's unrevised, roughed-out version of the speech, or (more probably) irregular verse, ending as prose and meant to accord with Lear's state of mind (Duthie, pp. 413–14).

104 the subject Collective, as in *MM* 3.2.136. Here = 'my people' (NS).

105 cause offence, charge. Compare *Oth.* 5.2.1 (NS).

107 Thou . . . adultery Compare Lev. 20.10 and John 8.4–5, where death is the penalty for adultery (Noble, Shaheen).

109 lecher fornicate.

113 luxury lechery, lust.

113 pell-mell i.e. promiscuously, randomly, like men plunging headlong into battle; hence, the association with soldiers (NS).

113 I lack soldiers Promiscuity will help fill the ranks of the king's army (Hunter).

114–23 Both Q and F print these lines as prose, but Johnson relined them as verse following the example of 103–13. (See 104–23 n. above.)

115 Whose . . . forks Usually taken to refer to the pudendum ('forks' = legs; compare 3.4.96). But H. C. Hart suggests that 'forks' may refer to instruments for holding up women's hair; compare Stubbes, *Anatomy of Abuses*, on women's hair 'vnderpropped with forks, wyers, and I can not tel what' (Muir).

115 presages snow forecasts chastity, frigidity.

116 minces virtue coyly affects virtue, chastity.

116–17 shake . . . name Compare Florio's *Montaigne*, iv.131: 'Wee haue taught Ladies to blush, onely by hearing that named, which they nothing feare to doe' (Muir).

118 fitchew (1) polecat, (2) prostitute.

118 soilèd 'Fed with fresh-cut green fodder' (Onions); hence, frisky.

Down from the waist they're centaurs,   120
Though women all above.
But to the girdle do the gods inherit;
Beneath is all the fiend's.
There's hell, there's darkness, there is the sulphurous pit,
burning, scalding, stench, consumption. Fie, fie, fie; pah, pah!   125
Give me an ounce of civet, good apothecary, sweeten my
imagination: there's money for thee.
GLOUCESTER   O, let me kiss that hand!
LEAR   Let me wipe it first; it smells of mortality.
GLOUCESTER   O ruined piece of nature! This great world   130
Shall so wear out to naught. Dost thou know me?
LEAR   I remember thine eyes well enough. Dost thou squiny at me?
No, do thy worst, blind Cupid, I'll not love.

*120 they're] th'are Q; they are F   123–4 Beneath . . . pit] *Globe's lineation; as prose* Q, F   124 there is] F; ther's Q   124 sulphurous] F; sulphury Q   125 consumption] F; consumation Q   *126 civet,] Q; Ciuet; F   126 sweeten] F; to sweeten Q   129 Let . . . mortality.] *As in* Q; *two lines divided* first, / It F   129 Let me] F; Here Q   130–1 O . . . me?] *Rowe's lineation; lines end* . . . world. / . . . naught. / . . . me? F; *as prose* Q   131 Shall] F; should Q   131 Dost thou] F; do you Q   132–4 I . . . it] *Muir's lineation; as prose* Q, F   132 thine] F; thy Q   132 at] F; on Q

120 **centaurs** Half human, half horse, the centaur was notorious for riot and lechery. In an infamous battle, mentioned in *MND* 5.1.44, centaurs attempted to carry off Hippodamia, bride of Theseus's friend Pirithous (Ovid, *Metamorphoses*, 12.210 ff.; summarised in North's Plutarch, *The Life of Theseus*).

122–3 **But . . . fiend's** Much Renaissance thought was preoccupied with humanity's double nature. Compare C. Carlile, *A Discourse of Peters life* (1580): 'Serverus said that a woman was the worke of the devil, and the upper part of a man of God, but from the navell downe of sathan: and therefore they that marrie doe fulfill the works of the devill' (Dent, p. 31). Exorcists hunted the devil through various parts of the woman's body; the girdle of a martyred saint, moreover, was allegedly used 'to confine the chief fiend to the lower part of the woman's body, her "hell"' (M. C. Bradbrook, *Shakespeare: The Poet in his World*, 1978, p. 196). Compare Virgil's description of Scylla: a fair virgin to the waist, a sea-monster below (*Aeneid*, 3.426–8).

122 **girdle** waist.

122 **inherit** possess, govern.

124–5 **hell . . . consumption** 'The obvious sexual references point to a climax of hysterical disgust at female sexuality' (Hunter).

124 **hell** (1) place of damnation, (2) slang for female genitals (Riverside).

125 **consumption** destruction.

125 **Fie . . . pah** 'The monosyllables are, of course, not voiced as such: they are inarticulate sounds of physical disgust that may be accompa-

nied by grimace, spitting, vomiting' (Rosenberg, p. 274).

126–7 **Give . . . thee** Lear now addresses Gloucester as an apothecary from whom he buys perfume to 'sweeten' his imagination, which engendered his foul vision of hell. Compare Marston, *The Fawne* (1606), 2.1: 'Sweeten your imaginations, with thoughts of – ah why women are the most giddie, uncertaine motions under heaven . . . onely meere chancefull appetite swayes them' (Muir).

126 **ounce** (1) one sixteenth of a pound (weight), (2) lynx (King).

126 **civet** Perfume made from the anal glands of civet cats. The association is suggested by Gloucester's bandages: civet cats have reddish eyes (King). NS suspects irony and compares *AYLI* 3.2.64–8.

130 **piece** masterpiece (probably, in view of Lear's former majesty); compare *Ant.* 5.2.98–9: 't'imagine / An Antony were nature's piece 'gainst fancy' (Schmidt 1879, cited by Furness).

130–1 **This . . . naught** The universe will, like Lear, disintegrate into ruin.

132 **I . . . enough** Lear is bitterly tendentious. His 'remembering' focuses on the absent organs and forces attention on them.

132 **squiny** squint. Compare 3.4.103 n.

133 **blind Cupid** 'Love is blind' is proverbial (Tilley L506; *MV* 2.6.36–7). But 'blind Cupid' also adorned the sign of a brothel, as Benedick indicates in *Ado* 1.1.253–4. Gloucester, as Edmond's father, his eye-sockets bandaged, reminds Lear of brothel love. In Sidney's *Arcadia*, Bk II, ch. 14, Cupid is 'an old false knaue', half man, half beast (Muir).

Read thou this challenge; mark but the penning of it.

GLOUCESTER   Were all thy letters suns, I could not see.   135

EDGAR   [*Aside*] I would not take this from report; it is,
And my heart breaks at it.

LEAR   Read.

GLOUCESTER   What – with the case of eyes?

LEAR   O ho, are you there with me? No eyes in your head, nor no   140
money in your purse? Your eyes are in a heavy case, your purse
in a light; yet you see how this world goes.

GLOUCESTER   I see it feelingly.

LEAR   What, art mad? A man may see how this world goes with no
eyes; look with thine ears. See how yon justice rails upon yon   145
simple thief. Hark in thine ear: change places, and handy-
dandy, which is the justice, which is the thief? Thou hast seen
a farmer's dog bark at a beggar?

GLOUCESTER   Ay, sir.

LEAR   And the creature run from the cur? There thou mightst   150
behold the great image of authority. A dog's obeyed in office.

134 this] F; that Q   134 but] F; *not in* Q   134 of it] F; oft Q   135 thy] F; the Q   135 see.] F; see one. Q   136 SD] *Hanmer;*
not in Q, F   136–7 I . . . it.] *Theobald's lineation; divided* report, / It F; *as prose* Q   *139 What –] *Oxford;* What! Q;
What, Q2; What F   144 this] F; the Q   145 thine] F; thy Q   *145 yon] Q; yond F   *145 yon] Q; yond F   *146 thine]
F; thy Q   146 change places, and] F; *not in* Q   147 justice] F; theefe Q   147 thief?] F; Iustice, Q   *150 cur? There]
Theobald; Cur: there F; cur, ther: Q   151 dog's obeyed] F; dogge, so bade Q; dogge, so bad Q2

134 this challenge Compare 88 above.
Whether Lear actually holds a piece of paper
(the proclamation for Gloucester's death,
as Staunton believed), or imagines one, is
uncertain, but irrelevant where unseeing
Gloucester is concerned. Compare 1.2.27 ff.
(Cavell).

134 penning style (Schmidt).

136 take this believe this spectacle.

139 case of eyes eye-sockets.

140 are . . . me (1) is that your meaning? (2)
are we both blind, i.e. are we both victims of
imperceptiveness? (Rosenberg, p. 275).

141 heavy case sad predicament; with quibbles
on 'heavy' and 'case'.

142 see (1) understand, (2) view.

143 feelingly (1) deeply, keenly, (2) with my
sense of touch.

144 What, art mad Taking Gloucester's 'feelingly' in sense (2), Lear is outraged that he should
complain of blindness, i.e. impaired perception,
since all senses are equally valid – and invalid.

145–6 See . . . thief An example of looking with
ears.

146 simple Either (1) humble, ordinary, or (2)
weak-witted.

146–7 handy-dandy A child's guessing game in
which an object is concealed in one hand; here =
'take your choice', the difference between justice
and thief is insignificant or indistinguishable, more
a matter of luck or chance than anything else. Dent,
p. 227, quotes Barclay's *Mirrour of good Maners*
(c. 1523), 34 (8–14): 'What difference betwene a
great thief and a small . . . The small thief is judged,
oft time the great is Judge'; compare *MM* 2.1.19–
23, 2.2.175–6. Florio's *Montaigne*, vi.85, has several
references to guilty judges, including an adulterer
passing sentence on another (Muir).

151 A . . . office i.e. response to authority is
governed by role or status, not intrinsic worth or
right; 'dog's' is emphatic. Compare Florio's *Montaigne*, iii.210: 'there are Nations, who receive and
admit a Dogge to be their King' (Muir).

Thou rascal beadle, hold thy bloody hand.
Why dost thou lash that whore? Strip thy own back.
Thou hotly lusts to use her in that kind
For which thou whip'st her. The usurer hangs the coz-
ener.   155
Through tattered clothes great vices do appear:
Robes and furred gowns hide all. Plate sin with gold,
And the strong lance of justice hurtless breaks;
Arm it in rags, a pygmy's straw does pierce it.
None does offend, none, I say none. I'll able 'em.   160
Take that of me, my friend, who have the power
To seal th'accuser's lips. Get thee glass eyes,

152–5 Thou . . . cozener.] *Pope's lineation; as prose* Q, F   153 thy] F; thine Q   154 Thou] F; thy bloud Q   155 cozener]
F; cosioner Q   156–63 Through . . . seem] *Rowe's lineation; as prose* Q, F   156 Through] Q; Thorough F   156 tattered
clothes] F; tottered raggs, Q   156 great] F; smal Q   157 furred gowns hide] F; furd-gownes hides Q   157–62 Plate . . .
lips.] F; *not in* Q   *157 Plate sin] *Theobald;* Place sinnes F

152–5 Thou . . . her Compare John 8.7
on the woman taken in adultery, and Rom. 2.1
on hypocrisy: 'Therefore thou art inexcusable, o
ma[n], whosoeuer thou art that iudgest: for in that
thou iudgest another, thou co[n]demnest thy self:
for thou that iudgest, doest the same things' (NS,
p. xxxvi).
152 beadle A minor parish officer who whipped
whores and other offenders.
154 kind manner.
155 The usurer . . . cozener Compare 'The
great thieves hang the little ones' (Tilley T119),
and 146–7 n. above. 'In this period usurers or
capitalists were acquiring respectability and
being appointed to offices such as that of magis-
trate, against the protests of preachers and poets'
(Hunter). Usury had become legal in 1571.
155 usurer moneylender.
155 cozener cheater.
156 Through F 'thorough' is probably the result
of a page-break, which required splitting the word
(*Textual Companion*, p. 537).
156 great See collation. Although Duthie,
p. 183, prefers Q's 'smal', Maxwell argues that F
restores the Shakespearean phrasing for Q's cliché;
he compares similar Q/F alterations elsewhere, e.g.
'houres'/'yeares', 2.2.51 (NS). Compare Furness:
'When looked at through tattered clothes, all vices
are great'; Hunter: 'it is not the smallness of their
vices that distinguishes the poor, but the exposure
to which they are subject'.
157 Robes . . . all i.e. judges and magistrates
get away with crimes which the poor cannot. Robes
and gowns are used both literally and metaphori-
cally. Compare the furred gowns of usurers, *MM*
3.2.7–8, and 155 n. above.

157–62 Plate . . . lips See Textual Analysis,
p. 285 below.
157 Plate sin Cover sin in armour plate. F
'Place' derives from easy *t/c* misreading; a singular noun, moreover, is required as the antecedent
of 'it' (159). Copy for F probably read 'sinne' (NS;
Duthie, p. 415). The imagery here and in the two
lines following is from jousting: compare *R2* 1.3.1
ff., especially 26–30, where 'plated in habiliments
of war' occurs.
159 pygmy's straw i.e. a weak weapon. In
the pseudo-Homeric epic *The Battle of the Frogs
and Mice* the frogs carried rushes for spears
(Hunter).
160 None . . . able 'em Again, Shakespeare
alludes to the woman taken in adultery, John 8.7,
the passage in scripture that also influenced Montaigne (Muir; compare 152–5 n. above). If everyone
sins, then no one does. As king, Lear can vouch
for ('able') everyone and exempt them from punishment. Lear 'needs to forgive so as to forgive
himself, too; needs to obviate the compulsion to
punish' (Rosenberg, p. 277).
161 Take . . . me Lear offers Gloucester an
imaginary pardon (Kittredge), information (Muir),
guarantee of immunity (Harbage, Bevington), or
imaginary money (NS): the context permits any of
these interpretations.
161 power i.e. either as king or as briber.
162–4 Get . . . not Lear returns to harping
upon blindness and false perception. The 'scurvy
politician' (= vile machiavel or schemer, as in *1H4*
1.3.241) pretends to perceptions he does not and
cannot have. Lear's fierce attack sets Gloucester
weeping.
162 glass eyes spectacles (Onions).

And, like a scurvy politician, seem
To see the things thou dost not. Now, now, now, now.
Pull off my boots. Harder, harder! So.   165
EDGAR [*Aside*] O matter and impertinency mixed,
   Reason in madness.
LEAR If thou wilt weep my fortunes, take my eyes.
   I know thee well enough; thy name is Gloucester.
   Thou must be patient. We came crying hither.   170
   Thou know'st the first time that we smell the air
   We wawl and cry. I will preach to thee: mark.
GLOUCESTER Alack, alack the day.
LEAR When we are born, we cry that we are come
   To this great stage of fools. This' a good block.   175
   It were a delicate stratagem to shoe

164–5 To . . . So.] *Capell's lineation; as prose* Q, F   164 dost] F; doest Q   164 Now . . . now.] F; no now Q   166 SD] *Capell; not in* Q, F   166–7 O . . . madness.] F; *one line* Q   166 impertinency mixed,] F; impertinencie mixt Q; impertinency, mixt Q2   168–72 If . . . mark.] F *lineation; as prose* Q   168 fortunes.] F; fortune Q   171 know'st] F; knowest Q   172 wawl] F; wayl Q   172 mark] F; mark me Q   174–9 When . . . kill!] F *lineation; as prose* Q   *175 This'] *Singer; this* Q; This F   176 shoe] shoot Q

164 Now . . . now Lear's tone changes as Gloucester weeps, and he tries to comfort the blind old man. See collation. Blayney conjectures that Q's 'No now' marks a lacuna, 'teares' being omitted (cited by *Textual Companion*, p. 522). But the emendation, however attractive, is unnecessary, as Q2 punctuation, 'No, now', shows that Q can make sense as well as F. Alternatively, the *w* may have been indistinct in Q's copy, as elsewhere (Duthie, p. 399).

165 Pull . . . So Lear commands Gloucester to pull off his boots, a reminiscence perhaps of his return from hunting in 1.4, though he may in fact be barefoot. 'So' may express (imagined) relief at being rid of the uncomfortable gear.

166 matter and impertinency i.e. sense and nonsense.

167 Reason in madness Compare *Ham.* 2.2.205–6; 4.5.174, 178.

168–75 If . . . fools Lear's tenderness towards Gloucester reaches its apogee as he recognises his old retainer and preaches patience to him, the virtue he had vainly tried to practise himself during his initial distress.

170–2 We . . . cry Compare Wisdom 7.6; also 7.3: 'When I was borne, I receyued the common ayre . . . crying and weeping at the first as all other doe' (Noble, Shaheen). Muir cites Plangus's lament in Sidney's *Arcadia*, Bk II, ch. 12, and Florio's *Montaigne*, i.107: 'So wept we, and so much did it cost us to enter into this life.' The thought is proverbial:

'We weeping come into the world, and weeping hence we go' (Tilley w889); compare 5.2.9–11.

172 wawl wail.

175 this . . . fools Shakespeare frequently compares the world to a stage, as in *AYLI* 2.7.136–66. Compare also Tilley, w882, 896.

175 This' This is.

175 block The association with 'felt' (177) suggests a hat. It may be Lear's, which he removes at 172 to begin his sermon – either the crown of weeds and wildflowers he has made (4.3.3–5), an actual hat bedecked with flora, or an imaginary one; or it may be Edgar's or Gloucester's. On the other hand, 'A troop of horse' (177) suggests a mounting-block; in some productions, Lear has mounted a stump to begin preaching (Furness); 'stage' (175) = scaffold, or a boulder or tree-stump that Lear mistakes and quibbles on (Muir). The associations are not mutually exclusive, and Lear's mind rapidly shifts from one association to another.

176–7 a delicate . . . felt Lord Herbert of Cherbury's *Life of Henry VIII* describes a joust in which horses were shod this way to prevent sliding (Malone, cited by Furness); here the stratagem is for a sneak attack.

176 delicate finely skilful, ingenious (Onions). Compare *Oth.* 4.1.187: 'So delicate with her needle'.

176 shoe See collation. Q 'shoot' probably derives from t/e misreading; Q copy may have had 'shooe' (Duthie, p. 415).

A troop of horse with felt. I'll put't in proof,
And when I have stol'n upon these son-in-laws,
Then kill, kill, kill, kill, kill, kill!

Enter a GENTLEMAN *[with Attendants]*

GENTLEMAN O here he is: lay hand upon him. Sir,   180
  Your most dear daughter –
LEAR No rescue? What, a prisoner? I am even
  The natural fool of fortune. Use me well.
  You shall have ransom. Let me have surgeons,
  I am cut to th'brains.
GENTLEMAN   You shall have anything.   185
LEAR No seconds? All myself?
  Why, this would make a man a man of salt,

---

177 felt.] F; fell, Q   177 I'll . . . proof,] F; *not in* Q   178 stol'n] F; stole Q   178 son-in-laws] Son in Lawes F, Q; sonnes in law Q2   *179 SD] *Rowe; Enter three Gentlemen.* Q; *Enter a Gentleman.* F   180–1 O . . . daughter –] F *lineation; one line* Q   180 hand] F; hands Q   *180 him. Sir,] *Johnson;* him, Sir.* F; him sirs, Q; him sirs. Q2   181 Your most dear daughter –] F; your most deere Q; *not in* Q2   182–5 No . . . brains.] F *lineation; as prose* Q   182 even] F; eene Q   184 ransom] F, Q; a ransom Q2   184 surgeons] F; a churgion Q   185 to th'] F; to the Q   186–91 No . . . that?] F; *two prose speeches in* Q, *which gives second* SH *before* I will die . . . , *where* Q2 *inserts:* Gent. Good Sir. *(not in* Q, F)   187 a man a man] F; a man Q

177 **felt** Q 'fell' probably derives from *l/t* misreading (Duthie, p. 415).
177 **I'll . . . proof** I'll put it to the test, try the experiment.
178 **son-in-laws** A possible colloquial plural (Doran, p. 97).
179 SD GENTLEMAN *with Attendants* See collation. Obviously, more than one person enters since a Gentleman stays behind to talk with Edgar (195 ff.). The stage business that follows is complicated. Lear has no way of knowing that the Gentleman means him no harm. He attempts to escape, especially as the Gentleman orders the others to 'lay hand upon him' (180). They hold him so gently that he easily breaks free, or they release their hold momentarily to kneel when he says 'I am a king' (190). Lear does not hear what the Gentleman says until 192, and then may not credit him; hence his flight, forcing pursuit.
180 **him. Sir** See collation. Since it is unlikely that the Gentleman would address Lear without a vocative, Johnson's emendation of the punctuation (anticipated by Rowe) appears correct.
183 **natural** (1) born (as in *3H6* 1.1.82), (2) idiot.
183 **fool of fortune** Compare *Rom.* 3.1.136: 'O, I am fortune's fool!' Note Lear's irony: just a moment ago he was leading a charge against the 'son-in-laws'; now he is a prisoner (Hunter).

183–4 **Use . . . ransom** A royal prisoner was worth much in ransom and was accordingly well treated (NS).
184 **surgeons** Trisyllabic. Abbott 479 scans the line: 'Yóu shall have ránsom. Lét me have súrgeóns.'
185 **cut to th'brains** Literally and figuratively: Lear imagines a head wound and feels a psychic one.
186–91 **No . . . that** See collation and Textual Analysis, p. 272 below. F omits an inessential half-line ('I and laying Autums dust'), but prints 188–91 as three lines. Modern editions that conflate Q and F also retain metrical anomalies. By conflating Q2 and F, and by various linebreaks, Furness, Riverside, and Halio come closer to providing regular scansion. Rearranging F, Oxford (followed here) provides nearly regular lineation, except for (1) an apparently excrescent 'What?' (189), found in both Q and F, and (2) a half-line (191). Compare Taylor, 'Date and authorship', pp. 363–4; Duthie, pp. 415–16.)
186 **seconds** supporters. Lear's sense of isolation is acute.
187 **a man a man** By adding 'a man', F corrects both sense and metre.
187 **salt** i.e. tears. Lear remains preoccupied with weeping.

To use his eyes for garden water-pots.
I will die bravely, like a smug bridegroom. What?
I will be jovial. Come, come, I am a king.   190
Masters, know you that?
GENTLEMAN You are a royal one, and we obey you.
LEAR Then there's life in't. Come, and you get it, you shall get it by
    running. Sa, sa, sa, sa!

                        Exit [running, Attendants following]

GENTLEMAN A sight most pitiful in the meanest wretch,   195
    Past speaking of in a king. Thou hast a daughter
    Who redeems nature from the general curse
    Which twain have brought her to.
EDGAR   Hail, gentle sir.
GENTLEMAN Sir, speed you: what's your will?
EDGAR Do you hear aught, sir, of a battle toward?   200
GENTLEMAN Most sure and vulgar: everyone hears that,
    Which can distinguish sound.
EDGAR   But, by your favour,
    How near's the other army?

188–91 To . . . that?] *Furness's lineation; three lines ending* . . . brauely, / . . . Iouiall: / . . . that? F; *as prose* Q 188
water-pots.] F; waterpots, I and laying Autums dust. Q; water-pottes, I and laying Autumnes dust. *Gent. Good Sir.*
Q2 189 smug] F; *not in* Q 191 Masters] F; my maisters Q 191 that?] F; that. Q 193–4 Then . . . running.] *As in*
Q; *two verse lines divided* get it, / You F 193 Come,] F; nay Q 193 by] F; with Q 194 Sa . . . sa!] F; *not in* Q 194
SD] *Capell (subst.); Exit King running.* Q; *Exit.* F 195–8 A sight . . . to.] F *lineation; as prose* Q 196 a daughter] F; one
daughter Q 198 have] F; hath Q 200 sir,] (Sir) F; *not in* Q 200 toward?] Q2; toward. Q, F 201–2 Most . . . sound.]
As in Q; *divided* heares / That Q2; vulgar: / Euery F 201 everyone] F, Q; euery ones Q2 201 hears that] F, Q; heares
Q2 202 Which] F; That Q 202 sound] F; sence Q 202–3 But . . . army?] F *lineation; one line* Q

189 **die** (1) end my life, (2) reach sexual climax.
Compare *Ant.* 4.14.99–101: 'but I will be / A bridegroom in my death, and run into't / As to a lover's
bed' (NS).

189 **bravely** (1) courageously, (2) handsomely,
in fine attire (as Lear regards his fantastic garb).

189 **smug** neat, trim, spruce.

190 **jovial** (1) majestic, Jove-like (*OED* sv *adj* 1),
(2) merry, convivial (*OED* sv *adj* 6). Compare *Mac.*
3.2.28.

193 **there's life in't** 'The case is not yet desperate' (Johnson, cited by Furness); i.e. Lear still
commands some shreds of respect as king.

193 **an** if.

193 **it** i.e. the ransom (NS).

194 **Sa . . . sa** An old hunting cry (French *ça*,
ça!) to urge dogs forward in the chase (Kittredge).

195–8 **A sight . . . to** The Gentleman's speech
is choric, spoken to the audience rather than to
anyone on stage; although the second sentence
uses direct address, it is a comment upon Lear's

situation, not spoken to him.

196 **speaking of** Oxford deletes 'of', which it
regards as inessential as well as hypermetrical, an
'easy compositorial interpolation' (*Textual Companion*, p. 523). But the Gentleman's speech, prose in
Q, is otherwise irregular and requires elisions – e.g.
'pit'ful', 'gen'ral' – to scan.

197 **nature** i.e. human nature.

197 **general** universal; with connotations of
original sin.

198 **twain** i.e. Gonerill and Regan. Danby,
p. 125, sees an indirect allusion to Adam and
Eve.

198 **her** i.e. human nature.

199 **speed you** (God) prosper you, give you
success.

200 **toward** impending.

201 **vulgar** i.e. a matter of common knowledge
(Kittredge).

203 **other army** i.e. the army of Gonerill and
Regan.

GENTLEMAN Near and on speedy foot: the main descry
    Stands on the hourly thought.
EDGAR   I thank you, sir. That's all.   205
GENTLEMAN Though that the queen on special cause is here,
    Her army is moved on.
EDGAR   I thank you, sir.

                              Exit [Gentleman]

GLOUCESTER You ever gentle gods, take my breath from me.
    Let not my worser spirit tempt me again
    To die before you please.
EDGAR   Well pray you, father.   210
GLOUCESTER Now, good sir, what are you?
EDGAR A most poor man, made tame to fortune's blows,
    Who by the art of known and feeling sorrows
    Am pregnant to good pity. Give me your hand;
    I'll lead you to some biding.
GLOUCESTER   Hearty thanks;   215
    The bounty and the benison of heaven
    To boot, and boot.

                   Enter OSWALD

OSWALD   A proclaimed prize! most happy!
    That eyeless head of thine was first framed flesh
    To raise my fortunes. Thou old, unhappy traitor,

---

204 speedy foot:] F; speed fort Q   204 descry] F; descryes, Q   205 Stands] F; Standst Q   205 thought] F; thoughts Q   *207 SD] *Johnson; Exit.* Q; *Exit.* F (*after* moved on.)   212 tame to] F; lame by Q   215–17 Hearty . . . boot.] F *lineation; as prose* Q   216 bounty] F, Q *corr.;* bornet Q *uncorr.*   216 the benison] F, Q *corr.* (the benizon)*; beniz Q *uncorr.*   216–17 heaven / To boot, and boot.] F; heauen to saue thee. Q *uncorr.;* heauen, to boot, to boot. Q *corr.,* Q2   217–21 A proclaimed . . . thee.] F *lineation; as prose* Q   217 happy!] happy, Q; happie F; happy: F2–4   218 first] F; *not in* Q *uncorr.*   219 old] F; most Q

---

204 on speedy foot marching rapidly.
204–5 the main . . . thought Most editors accept Johnson: 'The main body is expected to be descried every hour.' But Stone, pp. 47, 210, objects that this paraphrase depends upon unwarrantable glosses and says a line or two may be missing between 204 and 205.
205 Stands on Rests on, depends on (Kittredge); compare 5.1.58.
206 Though that Though.
208 take . . . me i.e. take my life before I am tempted to suicide again.
209 worser spirit evil side of my nature; with an allusion perhaps to 'evil angel'.
210 father old man; as at 72 above.
212 tame yielding, submissive; the image is of a whip used for taming animals (King).
213 art instruction, lesson.

213 known . . . sorrows Either (1) misfortunes experienced and sympathised with, or (2) sorrows I have known by feeling them (hendiadys) (King).
214 pregnant to 'ready, by intervention of sorrow, to give birth to pity' (King); receptive to (Onions). Compare *TN* 3.1.88–9: 'My matter hath no voice, lady, except to your own most pregnant and vouchsafed ear.'
215 biding abode, dwelling.
216 benison blessing.
217 To boot, and boot Gloucester plays on noun and verb: 'in addition' (*OED* Boot *sb*[1] 1) and '(may it) profit (you)' (*OED* Boot *v*[1] 3). Oswald may interrupt before Gloucester reaches his verb (King). Compare NS; Greg, *Variants*, p. 176; *Textual Companion*, p. 537.
217 happy opportune; compare 2.3.2.

Briefly thyself remember: the sword is out   220
That must destroy thee.
GLOUCESTER   Now let thy friendly hand
Put strength enough to't.
OSWALD   Wherefore, bold peasant,
Dar'st thou support a published traitor? Hence,
Lest that th'infection of his fortune take
Like hold on thee. Let go his arm.   225
EDGAR Chill not let go, zir, without vurther 'casion.
OSWALD Let go slave, or thou di'st.
EDGAR Good gentleman, go your gait, and let poor volk pass. And
chud ha' been zwaggered out of my life, 'twould not ha' been
zo long as 'tis by a vortnight. Nay, come not near th'old man.   230
Keep out, che vor'ye, or I s' try whether your costard or my
ballow be the harder; chill be plain with you.

221–2 Now . . . to't.] F *lineation; one line* Q   222–5 Wherefore . . . arm.] F *lineation; as prose* Q   223 Dar'st] F; durst
Q   224 that th'] F; the Q   226 Chill . . . 'casion.] *As in* Q; *two lines divided* Zir, / Without F   226 zir] F; sir Q   226
vurther 'casion] F; cagion Q   227 di'st] F; diest Q   228 and] F; *not in* Q   229 ha'] F; haue Q (*both times*)   229 zwaggered]
F; swagger'd Q   229 'twould] F; it would Q   230 zo] F; so Q   230 as 'tis] F; *not in* Q   230 vortnight] F; fortnight Q
uncorr.   230 th'] F; the Q   *231 out,] Q *uncorr.*; out Q *corr.*, F   231 che vor'ye] F; cheuore ye Q   231 I s'] ice F; ile
Q   231 whether] Q; whither F   231 costard] F; coster Q *uncorr.*; costerd Q *corr.*   232 ballow] F; battero Q *uncorr.*; bat Q
corr., Q2   232 chill] F; ile Q

220 Briefly thyself remember i.e. quickly
confess your sins and pray for forgiveness. Even
Oswald is loath to kill someone without giving the
victim an opportunity to prepare his soul for death.
Compare analogous situations in *Ham.* 3.3.73–86;
Oth. 5.2.26–32.
  221 friendly i.e. because Gloucester wants to
die.
  222–3 Wherefore . . . traitor Johnson and later
editors insert a SD here, e.g. *Edgar interposes*, as
the dialogue suggests. Oswald's epithet indicates
Edgar's changed habit and perhaps gives him a cue
for speaking in dialect. Oswald is more aggressive here than he was to Kent in 2.2, probably
because he feels superior to a mere peasant with no
schooling in weaponry, and because he anticipates
a reward for killing Gloucester (4.4.40) (King).
  223 published proclaimed.
  226–34 Chill . . . foins Edgar's dialect is borrowed mainly from Somersetshire, but Elizabethan
dramatists were no dialectologists: their purpose
was simply to write dialect that sounded rustic
enough to be funny or otherwise suit the dramatic occasion. Q2 and F introduce many more
dialectal spellings than Q, elaborating the indications of dialect typical of Jaggard's printing-house
(*Textual Companion*, p. 537); but from a philological standpoint the passage is merely a patchwork
of current colloquialisms and conventional stage
dialect (Kökeritz, pp. 37–9; compare Kittredge).

This dialect is identical with the Devonshire dialect
in *The London Prodigal* (1605), performed by the
King's Men (Muir).
  226 Chill I will.
  226 'casion occasion, cause. Oxford adopts Q's
'cagion', suspecting compositorial substitution of
the common for the unusual form (*Textual Companion*, p. 537). But possibly F was altered to make
the speech more comprehensible.
  228 go your gait get along, go your way.
  228 volk See collation. F is probably an uninten-
tional normalisation of Q 'voke' (*Textual Companion*, p. 537), but the pronunciation is not affected
(compare Kökeritz, p. 310).
  228–30 And chud . . . vortnight i.e. if I could
have been killed by boasting (swaggering), I would
not have lasted a fortnight.
  231 che vor'ye I warrant you (Kökeritz, 'Elizabethan *Che vor ye* "I warrant you"', *MLN* 57
(1942), 98 ff.).
  231 costard Slang for 'head' (literally, a large
apple).
  231 ballow cudgel (Onions). See collation.
Oxford prints 'baton', assuming a misreading in
F similar to that which led to Q uncorr. 'battero'
(*Textual Companion*, p. 538; compare Greg, *Variants*, pp. 176–7). But Wright, *English Dialect Dictionary* (cited by Muir, Kökeritz) records later use
in Nottingham and elsewhere.

OSWALD Out, dunghill!

[They fight]

EDGAR Chill pick your teeth, zir: come, no matter vor your foins.

OSWALD Slave, thou hast slain me. Villain, take my purse.   235
    If ever thou wilt thrive, bury my body,
    And give the letters which thou find'st about me
    To Edmond, Earl of Gloucester: seek him out
    Upon the English party. O untimely death, death.

[He dies]

EDGAR I know thee well – a serviceable villain,   240
    As duteous to the vices of thy mistress
    As badness would desire.

GLOUCESTER   What, is he dead?

EDGAR Sit you down, father; rest you.
    Let's see these pockets. The letters that he speaks of
    May be my friends. He's dead. I am only sorry   245
    He had no other deathsman. Let us see.
    Leave, gentle wax; and manners, blame us not:
    To know our enemies' minds, we rip their hearts;
    Their papers is more lawful.

Reads the letter

---

*233 SD] Q; not in F   234 zir] F; sir Q   234 vor] F; for Q   238–9 out / Upon the] F; out vpon / The Q uncorr.; out, vpon / The Q corr.   239 English] F; British Q uncorr.; Brittish Q corr.   239 death,] F; death! Q   *239 SD] Q; not in F   241–2 As duteous . . desire.] F lineation: one line (turned under) Q   243–7 Sit . . . . not:] F lineation: four verse lines ending . . . pockets / . . . friends, / . . . deathsmā / . . . not Q   243–4 you. / Let's] F; you lets Q uncorr.; you, lets Q corr.   244 these] F; his Q   244 The] F; These Q   244–5 of / May] F; of may Q uncorr.; of, may Q corr.   245 sorry] F; sorrow Q   *247 wax; and manners,] Capell (subst.); waxe, and manners Q; waxe, and manners: F   *247 not:] Pope; not Q, F   248 minds, we] F; minds wee'd Q uncorr.; minds,wee'd Q corr.   249 SD] F; not in Q uncorr.; A letter. Q corr.*

---

233 Out Out upon you! (Kittredge).

234 pick your teeth i.e. with his ballow (231), a 'Rabelaisian toothpick' (King), or possibly during the fight Edgar manages to get Oswald's dagger, with which he promises to pick the steward's teeth (Hunter); a proverbial threat (Tilley T424.1; Dent, p. 235).

234 foins sword-thrusts. Oswald is apparently fencing like a courtier. Compare Mercutio's description of Tybalt's fencing, *Rom.* 2.4.20–6 (NS).

237 letters letter; as at 244. See 1.5.1 n.

239 English See collation. Greg, *Variants*, p. 177, and Duthie, pp. 158–9, both believe this is the original Shakespearean reading. Greg speculates that Q 'British' resulted from an actor correcting the anachronism, but this hypothesis assumes memorial reconstruction. Compare 3.4.168: Shakespeare of course could be inconsistent, and the fact that he wrote 'British' there (as an apparent compliment to James) does not mean he could not have written 'English' here, even when

revising (Duthie; compare Stone, p. 116, n.7).

239 death, death Some editors, e.g. Bevington, break the line after the first 'death', making the second a separate line. But this division solves nothing metrically; both lines remain irregular. The odd exclamation may be an actor's interpolation; if so, the line should end 'untimely –' (NS).

240–2 I know . . . desire A further hint that Oswald has been more than a mere steward; compare 2.2.16–19, 3.4.77–82, and nn.

240 serviceable '(obsequiously) diligent in service' (NS); Kent calls him a 'superserviceable, finical rogue' (2.2.16).

245 my friends i.e may be useful.

246 deathsman executioner.

247 Leave . . . not Edgar opens the sealed letter. Compare Tilley B637, 'The breaking open of letters is the basest kind of burglary', and Malvolio's 'By your leave, wax', *TN* 2.5.91 (NS).

247 Leave i.e. by your leave, allow me.

249 Their papers i.e. to rip open their letters.

'Let our reciprocal vows be remembered. You have many   250
opportunities to cut him off. If your will want not, time and
place will be fruitfully offered. There is nothing done, if he
return the conqueror; then am I the prisoner, and his bed my
gaol, from the loathed warmth whereof, deliver me, and supply
the place for your labour.   255
                    Your (wife, so I would say)
                        affectionate servant,
                                            Gonerill.'
O indistinguished space of woman's will,
A plot upon her virtuous husband's life –   260
And the exchange my brother! Here in the sands
Thee I'll rake up, the post unsanctified
Of murderous lechers; and in the mature time
With this ungracious paper strike the sight
Of the death-practised duke. For him 'tis well   265
That of thy death and business I can tell.
                        [*Exit, dragging out the body*]
GLOUCESTER   The king is mad. How stiff is my vile sense,

250–7 Let . . . servant,] *As in* Q; *italics in* F   250 our] F; your Q   *252 done, if] done, If Q; done: If Q2; done. If
F   *253 conqueror; then] *Furness;* conquerour, then Q; Conqueror, then F; conqueror. Then *Pope*   254 gaol] F; iayle
Q *corr.;* gayle Q *uncorr.*   255–6 labour. / Your] F; labour, your Q   256 (wife, so . . . say)] F; wife (so . . . say) your
Q   257 servant,] Seruant. F; seruant and for you her owne for *Venter,* Q   259 O] Oh F; *Edg.* O Q   259 indistinguished]
Indistinguisht Q; indinguish'd F   259 will] F; wit Q   266 thy] F, Q; his Q2   266 SD] *Capell (subst.); not in* Q, F   267
The . . . sense,] *As in* Q; *two lines divided* mad: / How F

250 **reciprocal vows** Compare 4.2.20–6. Muir, p. 250, lists 'reciprocal' among the words in Florio's *Montaigne* not used by Shakespeare before 1603.

251 **him** i.e. Albany.

251 **will** (1) intention, purpose, (2) carnal desire, lust.

251 **want** lack.

252 **fruitfully** abundantly.

252–3 **There . . . conqueror** i.e. nothing important will have been accomplished if we win and Albany returns (and the sexual activity you and I anticipate is forestalled). See collation: Duthie, p. 184, comments that F's full stop after 'done' may have been influenced by Q's 'If', the capital an aberration which probably misled the collator.

255 **for your labour** (1) as a recompense for your work, (2) as a place for your (amorous) activity (Hunter).

257 **servant** lover. See collation, and Textual Analysis, pp. 272–3 below.

259 **O . . . will** 'O woman's lust, how limitless is thy range!' (Kittredge).

259 **indistinguished** indefinable, undiscernible (because vast).

262 **rake up** cover up, bury.

263 **mature time** when the time is right, at the proper occasion. The first syllable of 'mature' is accented.

264 **ungracious** i.e. because evil.

264 **strike** blast.

265 **death-practised** i.e. whose death has been plotted.

266 SD **Exit . . . body** Capell's SD is necessary: unless Edgar drags off the body here, two 'gross improbabilities' arise: (1) Edgar drags off the body as he simultaneously leads his blind father by the hand – a 'very clumsy exit, at best'; (2) Edgar's speech (273–5) uncharacteristically ignores Gloucester's lapse into gloominess (Urkowitz, pp. 158–9).

267 **stiff** unbending, obstinate.

267 **sense** 'mental power, faculty of thinking and feeling' (Schmidt); compare Sonnet 112.8: 'my steel'd sense'.

That I stand up and have ingenious feeling
Of my huge sorrows! Better I were distract,
So should my thoughts be severed from my griefs,   270
Drum afar off
And woes by wrong imaginations lose
The knowledge of themselves.

[*Enter* EDGAR]

EDGAR   Give me your hand.
Far off methinks I hear the beaten drum.
Come, father, I'll bestow you with a friend.

Exeunt

4.6 *Enter* CORDELIA, KENT [*disguised*], *and* GENTLEMAN

CORDELIA   O thou good Kent, how shall I live and work
To match thy goodness? My life will be too short,
And every measure fail me.
KENT   To be acknowledged, madam, is o'erpaid.

---

269 sorrows!] Sorrowes? F; sorowes, Q   270 severed] F; fenced Q   270 SD] F; *A drumme a farre off.* Q (*after* themselues 272)   272 SD] Capell (*subst.*); *not in* Q, F   272–3 Give . . . drum.] F *lineation; one line (turned under) in* Q   274 SD] F; *Exit.* Q   Act 4, Scene 6   4.6] *Scæna Septima.* F (*see* Commentary); *not in* Q   0 SD] F; *Enter Cordelia, Kent, and Doctor.* Q   1–3 O . . . me.] *Rowe's lineation; two lines divided* thy goodnes, [*turned over*] / My Q; *five lines ending* . . . Kent, / . . . worke / . . . goodnesse? / . . . short, / . . . me. F

268 **ingenious** intelligent, sensitive (Onions); in antithesis to 'mad'. But the word already had the meaning 'inventive, skilful' and thus 'suggests a clever inner destructive force contriving to remind Gloucester of, and intensify, his misery' (Rosenberg, p. 282).
269 **distract** mad.
270–2 **So . . . themselves** Thinking it would bring him relief, Gloucester longs for madness, a world of illusions ('wrong imaginations') divorced from the reality of his sorrows and their causes.
274 **bestow** lodge; compare *Mac.* 3.1.29.
274 **a friend** The mysterious friend never appears; perhaps Edgar and Gloucester never reach him, or are overtaken by events (King). Compare 5.2.1–2.

Act 4, Scene 6
4.6 F, which omits a scene after 4.2, incorrectly numbers this '*Scæna Septima*'. Possibly, after the long preceding scene, the collator forgot to alter the scene number as he had done for the three previous scenes. On the other hand, the F compositors suspended work on *Lear* at precisely the

page on which this scene begins (signature ss), and did not resume composition until the last pages of *Rom.* (which had been interrupted by problems involving *Tro.*) and all of *Tim.* were set. Conceivably, when he returned to *King Lear*, Compositor E forgot to continue altering scene numbers which Compositor B had begun. Compare Hinman, II, 281, 293–5; Doran, p. 70; Duthie, p. 418, Taylor, 'Date and authorship', pp. 417–18; Greg, *SFF*, p. 388.
0 SD *Enter* . . . GENTLEMAN See collation, and Appendix, p. 304 below, XX, 0 SD n. Rosenberg suggests, p. 283, that some hint of French costumes or décor in Cordelia's camp prompts Lear's question (75).
2 **My . . . short** Dramatic irony (King).
3 **measure** 'that by which extent or quantity is ascertained' (Schmidt); compare *Ant.* 1.1.1–2: 'this dotage of our general's / O'erflows the measure'. Every attempt at recompense will fail, Cordelia says, because Kent's goodness is immeasurable.
4 **To . . . o'erpaid** Recognition for his loyal service is all the recompense Kent wishes. But compare 9 below and n.

All my reports go with the modest truth,   5
Nor more, nor clipped, but so.
CORDELIA   Be better suited:
These weeds are memories of those worser hours.
I prithee, put them off.
KENT   Pardon, dear madam.
Yet to be known shortens my made intent.
My boon I make it that you know me not   10
Till time and I think meet.
CORDELIA   Then be't so, my good lord. – How does the king?
GENTLEMAN   Madam, sleeps still.
CORDELIA   O you kind gods,
Cure this great breach in his abusèd nature;   15
Th'untuned and jarring senses O wind up
Of this child-changèd father!
GENTLEMAN   So please your majesty,
That we may wake the king? He hath slept long.
CORDELIA   Be governed by your knowledge, and proceed   20
I'th'sway of your own will. Is he arrayed?

Enter LEAR [*asleep*] *in a chair carried by servants*

6–8 Be . . . off.] F *lineation; two lines divided* those / Worser Q   8 Pardon] F; Pardon me Q   12 Then . . . king?] *As in* Q;
two lines divided Lord: / How F   13 SH] F; *Doct.* Q (*throughout scene*)   14–15 O . . . nature;] F *lineation; one line* (*turned
over*) Q   14 gods,] Gods Q; Gods! F   16 Th'] F; The Q   16 jarring] F; hurrying Q   18–19 So . . . long.] F; *divided* king, /
He Q   19 That] F, Q; *not in* Q2   *19 king?] *Hanmer*; King, F, Q; King Q2   *19 long.] Q; long? F   21 SD] F (*subst.*); *not
in* Q

5–6 All . . . so Either (1) everything I have
said about what has happened is accurate and
unadorned, or (2) may everything said about me
be told simply and accurately.
  5 go with accord with.
  6 Nor . . . clipped Neither exaggerated nor
understated.
  6 suited dressed. Kent still wears servant's
clothes.
  7 weeds clothes.
  7 memories reminders.
  9 Yet . . . intent To be revealed now would be
premature and so contrary to my plan. Kent wants
Lear to make the connection with Caius, which
he fails to do (5.3.256–64). Whatever Kent's purpose in maintaining his disguise, Shakespeare's is
clear: he does not want 'to spoil Lear's reconciliation with Cordelia, by adding to it a recognition of
Kent' (Granville-Barker, p. 308).
  9 made formed.
  10 My boon . . . it The favour I request is.
  11 meet suitable, appropriate. Like Edgar,
Kent respects 'ripeness' (5.2.11), and may also

misjudge: compare 5.3.183.
  15 breach i.e. wound.
  16 Th'untuned . . . senses Shakespeare often
uses the metaphor of discord in music to portray
mental disorder, as in *Ham.* 3.1.157–8. Hendiadys:
'jarring' because 'untuned' (King).
  16 wind up i.e. tune by tightening the strings.
  17 child-changèd i.e. changed by his children
(Malone, cited by Furness); compare 'carecrazed
mother', *R3* 3.7.184.
  18 majesty Cordelia is Queen of France.
  21 I'th' . . . will As your desire directs you, i.e.
as you see fit.
  21 arrayed i.e. clothed in his royal robes (NS,
citing Granville-Barker, p. 298). But often he is
dressed 'in a purity of white' (Rosenberg, p. 284).
Compare 23 n. below.
  21 SD chair The chair may suggest or even be
a throne, as in Trevor Nunn's 1968 RSC production, which made this entrance parallel Lear's in
1.1 (Taylor, 'Date and authorship', p. 412; compare Bratton, p. 189).

GENTLEMAN Ay, madam: in the heaviness of sleep
    We put fresh garments on him.
    Be by, good madam, when we do awake him;
    I doubt not of his temperance.   25
CORDELIA O my dear father, restoration hang
    Thy medicine on my lips, and let this kiss
    Repair those violent harms that my two sisters
    Have in thy reverence made.
KENT   Kind and dear princess!
CORDELIA Had you not been their father, these white flakes   30
    Did challenge pity of them. Was this a face
    To be opposed against the warring winds?
    Mine enemy's dog,
    Though he had bit me, should have stood that night
    Against my fire. And wast thou fain, poor father,   35
    To hovel thee with swine and rogues forlorn
    In short and musty straw? Alack, alack,
    'Tis wonder that thy life and wits at once
    Had not concluded all. He wakes. Speak to him.

22 of] F; of his Q   24 Be by, good madam] F; *Gent.* Good madam be by, Q; *Kent.* Good Madam be by Q2   *25 not] Q; *not in* F   25 temperance] F *omits one and a half lines here*   26–8 O . . . sisters] F *lineation; two lines divided* lips, / And Q   31 Did challenge Q   32 opposed] F; exposd Q   *32 warring] Q, *Oxford; iarring F   32 winds?] F *omits three and a half lines here*   33–5 Mine . . . father,] *This edn (following* Q); *lines end* . . . bit me. / . . . fire, / . . . Father) F   33 enemy's] F; iniurious Q

23 **fresh garments** As elsewhere in Shakespeare, change of clothing signals a change in character or disposition, especially after significant absence. Compare *Cor.* 4.4.0 SD; Heilman, p. 82.
25 **not** See collation. Rhythm, metre, and sense argue that Q is correct. Compositor E apparently omitted 'not' accidentally, as at 1.1.287. Compare Duthie, p. 185; *Textual Companion*, p. 538.
25 **temperance** self-control. F omits a line and a half here: see Textual Analysis, pp. 273–4 below.
26 **restoration** Perhaps personified as a goddess.
29 **reverence** condition of being respected or venerated (Onions).
30 **flakes** thin or delicate hair. Compare Lyly, *Midas* (1592), 3.2: 'your mustachoes . . . hanging downe to your mouth like goates flakes' (Kittredge).
31 **challenge** demand.
32 **warring** See collation. F 'iarring' could be Compositor E's misreading of 'warring' combined with a recollection of 'iarring' (16). Compare Sisson, p. 243; Duthie, 185; *Textual Companion*, p. 538.
32 **winds** F omits three and a half lines here: see Textual Analysis, p. 274 below.
33–5 **Mine . . . fire** Compare 3.7.62–4.

33 **Mine enemy's dog** The irregular line results from cutting three and a half inessential though eloquent lines.
36 **To hovel . . . forlorn** See 3.6.0 SD n. Shaheen compares the parable of the Prodigal Son in Luke 15, an analogue or source developed by Susan Snyder, 'King Lear and the Prodigal Son', *SQ* 17 (1966), 361–9 (see above, pp. 11–12).
36 **rogues forlorn** outcast vagabonds. This reference justified Grigori Kozintsev's setting for 3.6 in his film, which shows the room Lear enters inhabited by poor, ragged vagrants.
37 **short** Because broken up by constant use as bedding (Kittredge). It would give less comfort and warmth than long, dry straw.
39 **all** i.e. all together, entirely.
39 **He wakes** These words signal the moment of greatest emotional tension in the play. How will Lear react to Cordelia? All eyes are fixed on him in silent expectation as slowly, very slowly he awakens and gains comprehension. (Compare Rosenberg, pp. 284–6, and E. A. J. Honigmann, *Myriad-Minded Shakespeare*, 1989, p. 86, where a parallel is drawn with Gloucester's reawakening after his attempted suicide in 4.5.)

GENTLEMAN Madam, do you; 'tis fittest.   40

CORDELIA How does my royal lord? How fares your majesty?

LEAR You do me wrong to take me out o'th'grave.

Thou art a soul in bliss, but I am bound
Upon a wheel of fire, that mine own tears
Do scald like molten lead.

CORDELIA   Sir, do you know me?   45

LEAR You are a spirit, I know. Where did you die?

CORDELIA Still, still far wide.

GENTLEMAN He's scarce awake. Let him alone a while.

LEAR Where have I been? Where am I? Fair daylight?

I am mightily abused. I should ev'n die with pity   50
To see another thus. I know not what to say.
I will not swear these are my hands. Let's see:
I feel this pin prick. Would I were assured
Of my condition.

CORDELIA   O look upon me, sir,

41 How . . . majesty?] *As in* Q; *two lines divided* Lord? / How F   42 o'th'] F; ath Q   *45 scald] Q; scal'd F   45 Sir, do you know] F; Sir know Q   46 You are] F; Yar Q; Y'are Q2   *46 spirit,] *Theobald*; spirit Q, F   46 Where] F, Q; when Q2   48 He's . . . while.] *As in* Q; *two lines divided* awake, / Let F   49 Where . . . daylight?] *As in* Q; *two lines divided* bin? / Where F   50 ev'n] F; ene Q   53–4 I . . . condition.] F *lineation; one line* Q   54–6 O . . . kneel.] F *lineation; as prose* Q

42 do . . . grave (1) commit a sacrilege by opening my grave, (2) hurt me by restoring me to life, (3) injure me by subjecting me to shame, (4) afflict me by bringing me out of the grave into consciousness of the afterlife (King).

44 wheel of fire This image is complex and syncretic, alluding to pagan, Christian, and other symbols not only of torture and suffering, but also of energy (Elton, pp. 236–8). Lear thinks he is damned and Cordelia is an angel in heaven: in this context, Ixion's wheel, which was sometimes placed in the heavens (Elton cites Christopher Middleton's *Historie of Heaven* (1596)), is especially relevant. There are other references to the sun (e.g. 1.1.103), and wheel images appear elsewhere (e.g. 2.2.156, 2.4.65–6, 5.3.164). For further discussion of the image's archetypal aspects, especially Jung's studies of the mandala, or magic circle, see James Kirsch, *Shakespeare's Royal Self*, 1966, pp. 283–6. Kirsch says the wheel of fire image could be understood as Lear's '*horoscope*, that is, his fundamental constitution; his Self is set on fire by his wild affects' (p. 285).

44 that so that.

44–5 mine . . . lead i.e. his tears, provoked by shame and guilt as well as suffering, are heated by the fire so that they scald.

46 Where See collation. NS and other editions

(e.g. Kittredge, Riverside) adopt Q2 'when'. Conceivably, copy for Q had 'when', which was misread as 'wher'. But Q/F 'where' makes no less sense, in context, than 'when'; hence the reviser or collator could easily have accepted it. Compare Duthie, p. 419, whose argument for Q/F Dover Wilson rejects in NS.

47 wide i.e. of the mark; hence, astray, mistaken. Compare *Tro.* 3.1.88: 'no such matter, you are wide'.

50 abused Lear could mean that he is (1) deluded, deceived, (2) taken advantage of, (3) illused, wronged, (4) misrepresented – or some combination of these senses (see *OED* Abuse *v* 4b, 2, 5, 3). Lear is in 'a strange mist of uncertainty' (Johnson, cited by Furness). Compare 'abusèd nature' (15), where the sense 'mistreated' is uppermost, and later (76), where 'wrong' or 'deceive' is meant. In 'do not mock me' (56) Lear fears he is being illused or misrepresented (as loving father or king).

53 pin prick Lear takes a brooch or some other ornament from his costume to test himself.

54–6 O look . . . kneel After 'sir' or during the next line, Cordelia kneels to receive her father's blessing, whereupon Lear rises from his chair and starts to kneel before her. The business is borrowed and modified from *King Leir* (2298–2304), where the kneeling is excessive and involves other

And hold your hand in benediction o'er me.   55
You must not kneel.

LEAR   Pray do not mock me:
I am a very foolish, fond old man,
Fourscore and upward,
Not an hour more nor less; and to deal plainly,
I fear I am not in my perfect mind.   60
Methinks I should know you and know this man;
Yet I am doubtful: for I am mainly ignorant
What place this is, and all the skill I have
Remembers not these garments, nor I know not
Where I did lodge last night. Do not laugh at me,   65
For, as I am a man, I think this lady
To be my child Cordelia.

CORDELIA   And so I am: I am.

LEAR   Be your tears wet? Yes, faith. I pray, weep not.
If you have poison for me, I will drink it.   70
I know you do not love me; for your sisters
Have, as I do remember, done me wrong.
You have some cause; they have not.

CORDELIA   No cause, no cause.

LEAR   Am I in France?

KENT   In your own kingdom, sir.   75

---

55 your hand] F *corr.;* yours hand F *uncorr.;* your hands Q   **56** You] F; no sir you Q   **56** me] F; *not in* Q   **58** Fourscore and upward,] F; Q *combines in one line with* and to deale plainly   **59** Not an hour more nor less] F; *not in* Q   **60** in . . . mind.] F, Q; perfect in my minde. Q2   **65** Do not] F, Q; Do no Q2   **68** am: I am.] F; am. Q   **69** Be . . . not.] *As in* Q; *two lines divided* wet. / Yes F

characters as well. 'Shakespeare compresses the moment, as he does the scene, to save sentiment from sentimentality' (Rosenberg, p. 288).

56 mock Because of the next lines, the sense 'ridicule' is usually understood; but Shakespeare also uses 'mock' in the sense 'defy; set at nought' (*OED* sv *v* 1c, citing *MV* 2.1.30 and *Ant.* 3.13.184), which the preceding line prompts; hence, the meanings combine.

57 fond silly (because in his dotage).

58–9 Fourscore . . . less Lear is still 'far wide', as he himself recognises (60); therefore, even his attempt to state his age is confused. He may well be an octogenarian, and is usually so portrayed. The F addition, 'Not . . . less', renders the lines irregular, but there is no reason to suspect they are inauthentic. See Textual Analysis, p. 286 below, and compare the debate in Furness.

58 upward more; compare *Wiv.* 3.1.56. 'Not . . . less' (59) contradicts this (King).

61 this man i.e. Kent, as Caius.

62 mainly entirely (Onions).

65 Do . . . me Lear misinterprets the smiles of Cordelia, Kent, and the Gentleman; they are smiles of compassion and understanding, not derision.

68 I am: I am Perhaps the second 'I am' was inserted to pad out the half-line to join with the preceding half-line (Stone, p. 63). Moreover, throughout this column of printing in F, Compositor E seems to be stretching copy. But the insertion, for all that, may be authentic and is certainly expressive. F's colon indicates a longer pause than the comma usually substituted in modern editions; therefore, it is retained.

75 France Lear recalls that the King of France married Cordelia.

LEAR Do not abuse me.
GENTLEMAN Be comforted, good madam. The great rage
    You see is killed in him. Desire him to go in.
    Trouble him no more till further settling.
CORDELIA Will't please your highness walk?   80
LEAR You must bear with me. Pray you now, forget
    And forgive. I am old and foolish.

                                       Exeunt

5.1 *Enter with drum and colours,* EDMOND, REGAN, *Officers and Soldiers*

EDMOND [*To an Officer*] Know of the duke if his last purpose hold,
    Or whether since he is advised by aught
    To change the course. He's full of alteration
    And self-reproving. Bring his constant pleasure.

                                       [*Exit Officer*]

REGAN Our sister's man is certainly miscarried.   5
EDMOND 'Tis to be doubted, madam.
REGAN   Now, sweet lord,
    You know the goodness I intend upon you.
    Tell me but truly, but then speak the truth,

---

76 me.] F; me? Q   **77–9** Be . . . settling.] F *lineation; as prose* Q   **78** killed] F; cured Q   **78** him.] F *omits one and a half lines here*   **80** Will't] *Rowe;* Wilt Q, F   **81–2** You . . . foolish.] *Oxford's lineation; three lines ending* . . . me: / . . . forgiue, / . . . foolish. F; *as prose* Q   **81** Pray you] F; pray Q   **82** SD] F *ends scene here, omitting a dozen lines found in* Q; *Exeunt. Manet Kent and Gent.* Q   Act 5, Scene 1   **5.1**] *Actus Quintus. Scena Prima.* F; *not in* Q   **0** SD] *After* F; *Enter Edmond, Regan, and their powers.* Q   **0** SD Officers] *This edn;* Gentlemen F   **1** SD] *This edn (Capell subst.); not in* Q, F; (To a Gentleman) *Duthie*   **3** He's] F, Q *uncorr.;* hee's Q *corr.;* he is Q2   **3** alteration] F, Q *corr.;* abdication Q *uncorr.*   **4** SD] *This edn (Capell subst.); not in* Q, F; *Exit Gentleman.* / *Duthie*

76 abuse (1) dupe, deceive, (2) mistreat, wrong. The past is coming back to him, with pain.
77 Be comforted Cordelia is overcome momentarily with emotion.
77 rage madness, frenzy.
78 in him F omits a line and a half here; see Textual Analysis, p. 274 below.
79 further settling i.e. until his wits have settled more.
80 walk withdraw.
82 foolish F omits the dialogue between Kent and the Gentleman that concludes the scene in Q. See Textual Analysis, p. 274 below.

Act 5, Scene 1
  0 SD *drum and colours* This is a standard military entrance, with flags flying and drum beating.
  0 SD *Officers* See collation. Officers were called 'Gentlemen' in Shakespeare's day, as F designates them.

1 his last purpose i.e. most recent intention (to fight with us against Cordelia and her army).
2 advised by aught persuaded by anything.
3 alteration vacillation. See collation. Not everyone accepts Greg's judgement (*Variants*, p. 177) that F is 'certainly correct'. Stone, p. 291, and Taylor, 'Date and authorship', p. 459, prefer Q *uncorr.* 'abdication' as the more pointed reading, which Oxford prints and which Rosenberg says 'has more energy, and is curiously prophetic' (p. 292).
4 constant pleasure i.e. fixed resolution.
5 sister's man i.e. Oswald.
6 doubted feared.
7 intend upon i.e. mean to confer upon.
8 Tell . . . truth Regan is suspicious that Edmond will equivocate or extenuate his position. In Q she remains uncertain and unconvinced by Edmond's protestations (see below).

Do you not love my sister?

EDMOND   In honoured love.

REGAN But have you never found my brother's way   10
    To the forfended place?

EDMOND   No, by mine honour, madam.

REGAN I never shall endure her. Dear my lord,
    Be not familiar with her.

EDMOND   Fear me not.
    She and the duke her husband –

Enter with drum and colours, ALBANY, GONERILL, *Soldiers*

ALBANY Our very loving sister, well bemet.   15
    Sir, this I heard: the king is come to his daughter,
    With others whom the rigour of our state
    Forced to cry out.

REGAN   Why is this reasoned?

GONERILL Combine together 'gainst the enemy;
    For these domestic and particular broils   20
    Are not the question here.

ALBANY Let's then determine with th'ancient of war

---

9 In] F; I, Q; I Q2   *11 forfended] Q; fore-fended F   11 place?] F *omits two and half lines here*   12–13 I . . . her.] F *lineation; one line (turned over) in* Q   13–14 Fear . . . husband –] *Capell's lineation; one line in* Q, F   *13 me] Q; *not in* F   *14 husband –] *Rowe;* husband. Q, F; F *omits a line and a half here*   14 SD] F; *Enter Albany and Gonorill with troupes* Q   16 Sir,] F; For Q   16 heard] F; heare Q   18 out.] F *omits five lines here*   20 and particular broils] F; dore particulars Q; doore particulars Q2   21 the] F; to Q   22–3 Let's . . . proceeding.] F *lineation; as prose in* Q; *divided* determine / With Q2   22 Let's] F; Let vs Q   22 th'ancient] F; the auntient Q; th'ensign *Oxford*

9 **honoured** i.e. honourable.

10 **brother** i.e. Albany.

11 **forfended place** forbidden place, i.e. Goner-ill's bed or 'bosom', as Q emphasises. Regan sus-pects her sister and Edmond of adultery, with rea-son (compare 4.2.15–29, 4.4.25–8, and nn.).

11 **place** F omits three lines here. For this cut and those a few lines later, see Textual Analysis, p. 275 below.

12 **I . . . her** i.e. I can't stand her. The antago-nism between Gonerill and Regan, which was care-fully concealed in 1.1 and 2.4, is now broken wide open by their rivalry for Edmond.

13 **me** Apparently accidentally omitted by Com-positor E.

14 **She . . . husband –** Many editors take the line as an announcement or exclamation, but Rowe and others see the speech dramatically inter-rupted by the entrance of the persons discussed.

F omits two lines here.

16 **the king** Albany, alone among those present, still refers to Lear as 'king'.

17 **rigour . . . state** harshness of our govern-ment.

18 **cry out** i.e. protest in pain. F omits five lines here.

18 **Why . . . reasoned** i.e. why are you going into all that? In its new context Regan's question takes on new meaning. See Textual Analysis, p. 275 below.

19–21 **Combine . . . here** Gonerill efficiently and swiftly focuses on the immediate problem and gets things moving. Compare 4.2.16–17.

19 **Combine together** i.e. unite Albany's army and Regan's.

20 **domestic** internal.

20 **particular broils** private quarrels.

22 **th'ancient of war** senior officers.

On our proceeding.
REGAN   Sister, you'll go with us?
GONERILL   No.
REGAN   'Tis most convenient. Pray, go with us.   25
GONERILL   [*Aside*] O ho, I know the riddle. – I will go.

Enter EDGAR [*dressed like a peasant*]

EDGAR   If e'er your grace had speech with man so poor,
   Hear me one word.
ALBANY   [*To the others*]   I'll overtake you.
                                                   Exeunt both the armies
                              Speak.
EDGAR   Before you fight the battle, ope this letter.
   If you have victory, let the trumpet sound   30
   For him that brought it. Wretched though I seem,
   I can produce a champion that will prove
   What is avouchèd there. If you miscarry,
   Your business of the world hath so an end,
   And machination ceases. Fortune love you.   35
ALBANY   Stay till I have read the letter.
EDGAR   I was forbid it.
   When time shall serve, let but the herald cry,
   And I'll appear again.   *Exit*

23 proceeding] F; proceedings Q   25 Pray] F; pray you Q   26 SD.1] Capell; not in Q, F   26 riddle. –] Capell (subst.); riddle, Q; Riddle. F   27 man] F, Q; one Q2   28 SD.1] Oxford; not in Q, F   28 SD.2 Exeunt . . . armies] F (after 26); Exeunt. Q (after word.); Exit. Q2 (after 26); Exeunt all but Albany and Edgar. / Cam.   35 And . . . ceases.] F; not in Q   *35 love] Q; loues F   36–8 I . . . again.] F lineation; as prose Q

23 proceeding i.e. battle plan. Albany apparently addresses Edmond, but unlike Q, F does not include a response; indeed, Edmond remains silent throughout this part of the dialogue. See Textual Analysis, p. 275 below.
23 Sister . . . us Regan tries to steer Gonerill away from the others, especially Edmond, with whom she does not trust her for a moment. Or perhaps she does not want Gonerill to participate in the council of war, close to Edmond (Muir).
23, 25 us The royal plural (compare 5.3.55–7), or herself and her troops.
25 convenient (1) expedient, (2) seemly (NS).
26 I . . . riddle i.e. I get your drift, insinuation. Here, Gonerill may recognise Regan's priority with Edmond and plan to kill her (Rosenberg, p. 293).
26 SD.2 *Enter* EDGAR Edgar is still dressed as a

peasant, though his speech is correct. He intercepts Albany as he is leaving with the others.
29 this letter i.e. the letter Oswald carried (4.5.250–8).
32 champion In chivalry, someone who undertakes a cause in single combat.
33 avouchèd asserted, declared.
33 miscarry lose the battle and die.
35 And . . . ceases See collation. The Q compositor, who set Albany's response on the same line with 'Fortune loue you', may have dropped a clause to save space.
35 machination intrigue. Compare 50–4 below.
35 love See collation. An easy compositorial error: 'The sense shows that Q is right' (Duthie, p. 186).

ALBANY   Why, fare thee well. I will o'erlook thy paper.

Enter EDMOND

EDMOND   The enemy's in view; draw up your powers.   40
Here is the guess of their true strength and forces
By diligent discovery; but your haste
Is now urged on you.
ALBANY   We will greet the time.   *Exit*
EDMOND   To both these sisters have I sworn my love,
Each jealous of the other as the stung   45
Are of the adder. Which of them shall I take?
Both? one? or neither? Neither can be enjoyed
If both remain alive. To take the widow
Exasperates, makes mad her sister Gonerill,
And hardly shall I carry out my side,   50
Her husband being alive. Now then, we'll use
His countenance for the battle, which being done,
Let her who would be rid of him devise
His speedy taking off. As for the mercy
Which he intends to Lear and to Cordelia,   55
The battle done, and they within our power,

39 o'erlook] ore-looke Q, F; looke ore Q2   **39** thy] F; the Q   **41** Here] F; Hard Q   **41** guess] F; quesse Q   **41** true] F; great Q   **42–3** By . . . you.] F *lineation; one line* Q   **44** sisters] F; sister Q   **45–7** Each . . . enjoyed] F *lineation; two lines divided* Adder, / Which [inioy'd *turned under*] Q   **45** stung] F; sting Q   **53** who] F; that Q   **54** the] F; his Q   **55** intends] F; entends Q; extends Q2

39 o'erlook look over, read. The text does not indicate whether Albany reads the letter or any part of it before Edmond enters. If he does, a new tension develops between him and Edmond, motivating his terse response at 43 (Rosenberg, p. 293; compare Urkowitz, p. 103, who argues that Edmond should rush in with his letter, or paper, before Albany has a chance to read the letter Edgar gives him).

39 SD *Enter* EDMOND Fully accoutred for battle, Edmond enters amidst growing sounds of war. Presumably, he has met with 'th'ancient of war' (22) while Albany conversed with Edgar.

41–2 Here . . . discovery Edmond offers Albany a written estimate of the enemy's army and its disposition. Again, the text fails to show whether Albany accepts it or not.

42 discovery spying, reconnaissance.

43 We . . . time Unlike Edmond, who is eager for battle, but like Kent and Edgar, with whom

he shows increasing affinities, Albany understands 'ripeness'.

43 greet embrace, welcome.

45 jealous suspicious.

47–8 Both . . . alive Edmond's hubris does not long permit him to think he can enjoy *both* sisters; if he is to enjoy either, then one must die.

50 carry . . . side make my game, achieve my goal (i.e. to become king: Edmond's ambitions have grown). But compare 'fulfil my side of the bargain with Goneril – satisfy her lust in return for advancement' (Muir).

52 countenance authority, support.

54 taking off murder.

54–5 mercy . . . Cordelia Till now, Albany has nowhere explicitly mentioned his intention regarding Lear and Cordelia, let alone revealed it to Edmond. Shakespeare introduces the information here partly to develop Albany's character, and to prepare for Edmond's treachery after the battle.

Shall never see his pardon; for my state
Stands on me to defend, not to debate.   *Exit*

5.2 *Alarum within. Enter with drum and colours,* LEAR, CORDELIA,
and Soldiers, over the stage, and exeunt

Enter EDGAR [*dressed like a peasant*] *and* GLOUCESTER

EDGAR   Here, father, take the shadow of this tree
For your good host; pray that the right may thrive.
If ever I return to you again
I'll bring you comfort.
GLOUCESTER   Grace go with you, sir.

Exit [*Edgar*]

Alarum and retreat within. Enter EDGAR

EDGAR   Away, old man! Give me thy hand; away!   5
King Lear hath lost, he and his daughter ta'en.
Give me thy hand. Come on.
GLOUCESTER   No further, sir; a man may rot even here.
EDGAR   What, in ill thoughts again? Men must endure

Act 5, Scene 2   5.2] *Scena Secunda.* F; *not in* Q   0 SD] F; *Alarum. Enter the powers of France ouer the stage, Cordelia with*
her father in her hand. / *Enter Edgar and Gloster.* Q   1 tree] F; bush Q   3–4 If . . . comfort.] F *lineation; one line* Q   4
SD.1 *Exit Edgar*] Pope; *Exit.* Q (*after* comfort), F   4 SD.2 *within*] F; *not in* Q   4 SD.2 *Enter* EDGAR] F; *not in* Q   8 further]
F; farther Q   9 What . . . endure] *As in* Q; *two lines divided* againe? / Men F

57 **Shall** i.e. they shall.
57 **state** situation, position.
58 **Stands on** Rests, depends on.

Act 5, Scene 2
0 SD.1–2 *Alarum . . . stage* Having shown
the British side, Shakespeare now has Cordelia's
army march with her father over the stage amidst
sounds of battle. This, again, is a standard military
entrance, but significantly altered from Q (see collation). Lear's strength and defiance are suggested,
not his weakness and infirmity; regally attired, he
may also carry a sword. After the army departs,
Edgar leads Gloucester on, while the battle occurs
off-stage.
1 **father** Compare 4.5.72 n., 243, 274. Although
Edgar has not yet revealed himself to Gloucester,
he favours this term of address.
2 **good host** i.e. one who gives shelter.
4 SD.2 *Alarum and retreat* Trumpet calls.
Gloucester is left alone on stage during the course
of the battle which, though brief, is long enough
to let the image of the solitary, blind, tormented
old man, early victim of the struggle, impress
itself upon the audience. Some modern produc-

tions present the clash of arms on stage or mime
the battle balletically (Rosenberg, p. 296; Bratton,
p. 197). But a stage empty except for this solitary figure is clearly Shakespeare's intention, i.e.
he preferred to minimise the battle and concen-
trate on larger issues. Compare Granville-Barker,
pp. 298–9.
8 **a man may rot** Gloucester lapses into despair
('ill thoughts') again.
9–11 **Men . . . all** Compare *Ham.* 5.2.219–22.
Edgar's counsel was proverbial in the Renaissance
and combined both pagan (especially Stoic) and
Judaeo-Christian attitudes (compare Eccles. 3.1–8:
'All things haue their time') (Elton, pp. 100–5).
Shakespeare uses the concepts of 'endurance' and
'ripeness' here very precisely. In essence, Edgar
tells Gloucester (as Hamlet tells Horatio) that Providence or the gods control our lives; hence, we must
endure the time of our death even as, perforce, we
endure the time of our birth. Providence, or the
gods, not man, determines when the time is 'ripe',
an idea which has little to do with modern theories
of maturation or development. Cordelia is hardly
'ripe' for death in any other sense (compare Berlin,
p. 91).

Their going hence even as their coming hither: 10
Ripeness is all. Come on.
GLOUCESTER   And that's true too.

Exeunt

5.3 *Enter in conquest with drum and colours* EDMOND; LEAR *and*
CORDELIA, *as prisoners;* Soldiers; CAPTAIN

EDMOND Some officers take them away: good guard,
            Until their greater pleasures first be known
            That are to censure them.
CORDELIA   We are not the first
Who with best meaning have incurred the worst.
For thee, oppressèd king, I am cast down,   5
Myself could else outfrown false fortune's frown.
Shall we not see these daughters and these sisters?
LEAR No, no, no, no! Come, let's away to prison.
         We two alone will sing like birds i'th'cage.
         When thou dost ask me blessing, I'll kneel down   10
         And ask of thee forgiveness: so we'll live,
         And pray, and sing, and tell old tales, and laugh
         At gilded butterflies, and hear poor rogues
         Talk of court news, and we'll talk with them too –
         Who loses and who wins; who's in, who's out –   15

11 all.] *Johnson;* all Q, F   11 GLOUCESTER And . . . too.] F; *not in* Q   11 SD] F; *not in* Q; *Exit.* Q2   Act 5, Scene 3
5.3] *Scena Tertia.* F; *not in* Q   0 SD] F; *Enter Edmond, with Lear and Cordelia prisoners.* Q   2 first] F; best Q   3–5 We . . .
down,] F *lineation; two lines divided* incurd [*turned over*] / The worst Q   5 I am] F; am I Q   8 No, no, no] F; No, no
Q   9 i'th'] F; it'h Q   12 and sing] F; *not in* Q2   *13 hear poor rogues] Q; heere (poore Rogues) F   15 who's in, who's]
F; whose in, whose Q

11 And . . . too Appearing only in F, these
words (which fill out the pentameter line) have been
attacked as a vacuous 'stopgap' (Stone, pp. 69–70),
and defended as emblematic of the play's complementarity (Peat, p. 44; compare Urkowitz, p. 44).

Act 5, Scene 3
  0 SD *Enter* . . . CAPTAIN See collation. Unlike Q,
F builds up the image of victorious Edmond, who
reaches the summit of his success and, from the
beginning of the scene, commands a much larger
share of audience attention – until the entrance of
Albany (38) (Taylor, 'War', pp. 32–3).
  1 **good guard** i.e. let them have careful guard.
  2 **their greater pleasures** the wishes of those
of higher rank.
  3 **censure** judge.
  4 **best meaning** i.e. rescuing Lear and restoring
him to his throne.

  5 **cast down** i.e. by Fortune; humbled. The figurative sense, dejected, is improbable at this date
(Brockbank, p. 5 n.).
  9 **cage** (1) birdcage, (2) prison (Muir).
  10–11 **When . . . forgiveness** A reminiscence,
perhaps, of the kneeling in *King Leir* (2298–2304).
Compare 4.6.54–6 and n.
  12 **old tales** folktales; as in *AYLI* 1.2.120, *WT*
5.2.61.
  13 **gilded butterflies** (1) gaily coloured butterflies, (2) lavishly adorned courtiers. Compare
Marston, *Antonio and Mellida* 4.1.49: 'Troopes of
pide butterflies, that flutter still / In greatnesse
summer, that confinne a prince' (Craig, cited by
Muir).
  13 **poor rogues** wretched creatures (Kittredge).
  F punctuation mistakenly assumes that 'Talk' in the
next line is a noun.

And take upon 's the mystery of things,
As if we were God's spies; and we'll wear out
In a walled prison packs and sects of great ones
That ebb and flow by th'moon.

EDMOND   Take them away.

LEAR Upon such sacrifices, my Cordelia,   20
The gods themselves throw incense. Have I caught thee?
He that parts us shall bring a brand from heaven
And fire us hence like foxes. Wipe thine eyes.
The goodyears shall devour them, flesh and fell,
Ere they shall make us weep. We'll see 'em starved first.   25
Come.

Ex[eunt Lear and Cordelia, guarded]

---

21 The . . . thee?] *As in* Q; *two lines divided* Incense. / Haue F   *24 goodyears] good yeares F; good Q   24 them] F; em
Q   24 flesh] F; fleach Q   25–6 Ere . . . Come.] *Pope's lineation; two lines divided* weepe? / Weele F; *one line* (come *turned
under*) Q   25 'em] F3; vm Q; em Q2; e'm F, F2   26 Come.] F, Q; *not in* Q2   26 SD] *Theobald; Exit.* F, Q2; *not in* Q

---

16 take . . . things assume the responsibility of understanding and explaining the hidden workings of the world.

17 God's spies Either (1) spies commissioned and enabled by God to pry into even the most deeply hidden secrets (Heath, cited by Furness), or (2) 'detached observers surveying the deeds of mankind from an eternal vantage point' (Bevington). Though both capitalise, neither F nor Q uses an apostrophe in 'Gods'. Perrett, pp. 250–1, argues for the plural possessive in this pagan setting, but this is 'surely pedantry' (NS).

17 wear out outlast, outlive (*OED* Wear *v* 9).

18 packs and sects cliques and parties (Muir).

19 That ebb . . . moon As the changeable moon governs the ever-shifting tides, so power and position at court shift, too. In prison, Lear believes, he and Cordelia will be insulated from such vicissitudes.

20 such sacrifices Either (1) their renunciation of the world (Bradley, pp. 289–90), or (2) Cordelia's sacrifice for Lear (Kittredge). Muir notes the suggestion of human sacrifice, which looks forward to the murder of Cordelia, and echoes the Old Testament stories underlying Lear's speech, e.g. Jephthah's daughter, who was sacrificed; Samson and the foxes; etc. Brockbank (p. 13) compares Heb. 13.16: 'To do good, & to distribute forget not: for with suche sacrifices God is pleased', which the Geneva Bible glosses: 'Thanksgiuing & doing good are our onlie sacrifices which please God.'

21 The gods . . . incense Lear imagines gods as priests performing a ritual.

21 Have . . . thee Lear still cannot believe his

luck and holds Cordelia ever more tightly. Compare the second song from Sidney's *Astrophel and Stella* (1591): 'Have I caught thee, my heavenly jewel?', which Falstaff quotes, *Wiv.* 3.3.43 (Brockbank, pp. 15–16).

22–3 He . . . foxes i.e. it will take divine assistance to separate us again. Shaheen cites Judges 15.4–5, but the story of Samson and the foxes is only obliquely relevant here, as it concerns Samson's revenge on the Philistines for causing a breach between him and his wife. Compare Harsnett, p. 97: 'to fire him out of his hold, as men smoke out a Foxe out of his burrow' (Kittredge).

24 goodyears malefic powers (*OED*); specifically, the plague or pox: see F. Rubenstein, 'They were not such good years', *SQ* 40 (1989), 70–4. An allusion to Pharaoh's dream (Gen. 41.1–36) seems remote; compare Taylor, 'Addenda' to *Division*, p. 489, who argues for the singular, which Oxford adopts.

24 fell skin; 'flesh and fell' = altogether (Onions).

25 Ere . . . weep Compare 2.4.268–71.

26 SD *Exeunt* Taylor argues ('War', p. 33) that only Edmond and the Captain remain; everyone else goes off with Lear and Cordelia. Moreover, Albany later says (96–8) that Edmond's army has been discharged. But it is not necessary to clear the stage entirely for Edmond and the Captain to talk apart, and the drummer is needed later for the concluding dead march. Oxford has the drummer re-enter with Albany, Gonerill, and Regan (38 SD.2), accompanied by a 'trumpeter', although F calls only for a *Flourish*.

EDMOND Come hither, captain. Hark.
   Take thou this note. Go follow them to prison.
   One step I have advanced thee; if thou dost
   As this instructs thee, thou dost make thy way   30
   To noble fortunes. Know thou this: that men
   Are as the time is; to be tender-minded
   Does not become a sword. Thy great employment
   Will not bear question: either say thou'lt do't,
   Or thrive by other means.
CAPTAIN   I'll do't, my lord.   35
EDMOND About it, and write 'happy' when th'hast done.
   Mark, I say, instantly, and carry it so
   As I have set it down.

              Exit Captain

Flourish. Enter ALBANY, GONERILL, REGAN, *[Officers,] Soldiers*

ALBANY Sir, you have showed today your valiant strain,
   And fortune led you well. You have the captives 40
   Who were the opposites of this day's strife.
   I do require them of you, so to use them
   As we shall find their merits and our safety
   May equally determine.
EDMOND   Sir, I thought it fit
   To send the old and miserable king   45
   To some retention and appointed guard,

---

29 One] F, Q *corr.;* And Q *uncorr.*   34 thou'lt] F; thout Q   36 th'hast] F; thou hast Q   38 down.] F *omits two lines here*   38
SD.1 *Exit Captain*] F; *not in* Q   38 SD.2 *Flourish . . . Soldiers*] F (*subst.*); Enter Duke, the two Ladies, and others. Q   38
SD.2 *Officers*] *This edn; not in* Q, F   39 showed] shew'd F; shewed Q; shewne Q2   40 well. You] well: you Q2, F; well you
Q *uncorr.;* well, you Q *corr.*   41 Who] F; That Q   42 I] F; We Q   42 require them] F; require then Q   *45–6 To . . .
guard,] *As in* Q2; *one line* Q *corr.* (pointed guard *turned under*); *one line* F, Q *uncorr.* (*which omit* and appointed guard)   45
send] F; saue Q *uncorr.*

28 **this note** Lear and Cordelia's death warrant, signed by Gonerill and Edmond: compare 226–9.

31 **noble fortunes** i.e. further advancement to nobility.

31–2 **men . . . is** A counsel of expediency, consistent with Edmond's philosophy.

33 **a sword** i.e. soldiers in wartime.

34 **question** discussion.

35 **my lord** F omits two lines here: see Textual Analysis, pp. 275–6 below.

36 **write 'happy'** count yourself fortunate.

37 **Mark** Attend.

37–8 **carry . . . down** manage it as I have indi-

cated, i.e. as if Cordelia had slain herself (compare 227–9).

39 **strain** Either (1) quality, or (2) lineage (compare *JC* 5.1.59).

41 **opposites** opponents (compare 143 below).

43 **merits** deserts.

46 **To . . . guard** Sec collation, and Textual Analysis, p. 73 above, n. 3. This line appears out of sequence and should possibly precede 45. Compare Halio, p. 164; Taylor, 'Date and authorship', pp. 361–2.

46 **retention** detention, imprisonment.

Whose age had charms in it, whose title more,
To pluck the common bosom on his side
And turn our impressed lances in our eyes
Which do command them. With him I sent the queen: 50
My reason all the same, and they are ready
Tomorrow, or at further space, t'appear
Where you shall hold your session.
ALBANY   Sir, by your patience,
I hold you but a subject of this war,
Not as a brother.
REGAN   That's as we list to grace him.   55
Methinks our pleasure might have been demanded
Ere you had spoke so far. He led our powers,
Bore the commission of my place and person,
The which immediacy may well stand up
And call itself your brother.
GONERILL   Not so hot.   60
In his own grace he doth exalt himself
More than in your addition.
REGAN   In my rights,
By me invested, he compeers the best.
ALBANY That were the most if he should husband you.
REGAN Jesters do oft prove prophets.

---

47 had] F; has Q   47 more,] F, Q *corr.;* more Q *uncorr.*   48 common bosom] F, Q *corr.;* coren bossom Q *uncorr.;* common blossomes Q2   48 on] F; of Q   51–2 My . . . t'appear] F *lineation; lines end . . . to morrow, / . . . shall hold* Q (*see 5.3.53 n.*)   52 t'] to Q   53 session.] F *omits five lines here*   54–5 I . . . brother.] F *lineation; one line* Q   56 might] F; should Q   59 immediacy] F; imediate Q   60–2 Not . . . addition.] F *lineation; as prose* Q   62 addition] F; aduancement Q   62–3 In . . . best.] F *lineation; one line* Q   62 rights] F; right Q   64 SH] F; Gon. Q

47 **Whose** Its antecedent is 'king' (45).
47 **title** (1) kingship, (2) legal right to possession of the land (Hunter).
48 **common bosom** hearts of the people.
48 **on** onto.
49–50 **turn . . . them** turn our forces against us, their leaders; literally, turn the weapons of our conscripted pikemen into our own eyes (with a reminiscence of Gloucester's blinding?).
53 **session** sitting of a court of justice. F omits four and half lines here: see Textual Analysis, p. 276 below.
53 **by your patience** i.e. pardon me.
54 **subject of** i.e. subordinate in.
55 **brother** equal.
55 **we list** I choose, please. Regan uses the royal plural; compare 5.1.23–5.
58 **Bore . . . person** Carried the authority of

my position and represented me personally.
59 **immediacy** direct connection; compare *Ham.* 1.2.109.
61 **grace** merit and honour (Kittredge); compare 55.
62 **your addition** i.e. the title or position you have bestowed.
63 **compeers** equals.
64 **That . . . you** i.e. he would be most fully invested with your rights (and Albany's equal) if he were your husband. See collation: Q gives this line to Gonerill, but the compositor very likely erred in assuming that the Regan/Gonerill alternation continued (Duthie, pp. 85, 161). Albany interrupts again later (76); the interruption here makes good dramatic sense.
65 **Jesters . . . prophets** Compare 'There is many a true word spoken in jest' (Tilley W772).

GONERILL   Holla, holla!   65
That eye that told you so, looked but asquint.
REGAN Lady, I am not well, else I should answer
From a full-flowing stomach. [*To Edmond*] General,
Take thou my soldiers, prisoners, patrimony.
Dispose of them, of me; the walls is thine.   70
Witness the world that I create thee here
My lord and master.
GONERILL   Mean you to enjoy him?
ALBANY The let-alone lies not in your good will.
EDMOND Nor in thine, lord.
ALBANY   Half-blooded fellow, yes.
REGAN [*To Edmond*] Let the drum strike, and prove my title thine.   75
ALBANY Stay yet, hear reason. Edmond, I arrest thee
On capital treason, and in thy attaint
This gilded serpent. For your claim, fair sister,
I bar it in the interest of my wife.
'Tis she is subcontracted to this lord,   80
And I, her husband, contradict your banns.

65–6 Holla . . . asquint.] F *lineation; one line* Q   65 Holla, holla!] *Theobald;* Hola, hola, Q, F   *66 asquint] a squint Q, F; a-squint *Rowe*   68 full-flowing] *Theobald;* full flowing Q, F   68 SD] *Oxford; not in* Q, F; – General, *Capell*   70 Dispose . . . thine.] F; *not in* Q   72 him?] F; him then? Q   *73 let-alone] *Capell;* let alone Q, F   75 SH] F; *Bast.* Q   75 SD] *Malone; not in* Q, F   75 thine] F; good Q   *77 thy attaint] thine attaint Q; thy arrest F   *78 sister,] sister Q; Sisters, F   79 bar] *Rowe;* bare Q, F   80 this] F, Q; her Q2   81 your] F; the Q   81 banns] Banes F, Q; bans *Malone*

---

66 That . . . asquint Gonerill alludes to the proverb, 'Love, being jealous, makes a good eye look asquint' (Tilley L498; Dent, p. 159, cites Florio, *Second Fruites*, 6.83: 'To much loue makes a sound eye oftentimes to see a misse').

68 full-flowing stomach i.e. a full ride of anger, resentment.

70 walls i.e. of the heart or person (typically conceived as a fortress besieged by a lover). On F's additional line, see Textual Analysis, p. 286 below.

73 let-alone (1) permission, (2) hindrance (NS).

74 Half-blooded Not only is Edmond a bastard, but his parenting was mixed, i.e. only one parent had noble blood.

75 Let . . . thine See collation. F alters not only the speech ascription, but the final word in the line. Instead of Edmond boldly defying Albany, Regan orders the drum to beat, so that the world will witness her action (69–72), and invites Edmond to establish his right to her title, putting the matter

to trial by combat if necessary. Compare Urkowitz, p. 109; Stone, p. 229.

76 thee To underscore his contempt, Albany henceforward uses the second-person familiar pronoun in addressing Edmond.

77 attaint (1) impeachment, (2) dishonour. Most modern editors agree that F 'arrest' is a mistaken repetition from the preceding line and Q is correct here. But compare Furness and Duthie, pp. 186–8.

78 gilded serpent i.e. Gonerill, 'gilded' because beautifully accoutred (and brilliantly: King).

79 I . . . wife With heavy irony, Albany as Gonerill's husband moves to protect his wife's 'interest', or rights.

80 subcontracted has a subsidiary or secondary contract (subsidiary, that is, to her marriage contract with Albany).

81 contradict your banns i.e. oppose the declaration of your intention to marry.

If you will marry, make your love to me,
My lady is bespoke.
GONERILL   An interlude!
ALBANY   Thou art armed, Gloucester; let the trumpet sound.
If none appear to prove upon thy person   85
Thy heinous, manifest, and many treasons,
There is my pledge!
                [*Throws down a glove*]
                    I'll make it on thy heart,
Ere I taste bread, thou art in nothing less
Than I have here proclaimed thee.
REGAN   Sick, O sick!
GONERILL   [*Aside*] If not, I'll ne'er trust medicine.   90
EDMOND   There's my exchange!
                [*Throws down a glove*]
                    What in the world he is
That names me traitor, villain-like he lies.
Call by the trumpet: he that dares, approach;
On him, on you – who not? – I will maintain
My truth and honour firmly.
ALBANY   A herald, ho!   95

Enter a HERALD

Trust to thy single virtue, for thy soldiers,

---

*82 love] Q; loues F   83 GONERILL An interlude!] F; not in Q   84 Thou . . . sound.] Rowe's lineation; two lines divided Gloster, / Let F; Q combines My . . . bespoke. (83) with Thou . . . Gloster, / in one line and omits SH and Let . . . sound   84 trumpet] F2; Trmpet F   85 person] F; head Q   87 make] F; proue Q   90 SD] Rowe; not in Q, F   90 medicine] F; poyson Q   91 SD] Malone (subst.); not in Q, F   87 make] F; proue Q   90 SD] Rowe; not in Q, F   91 he is] Q; hes F   93 the] F; thy Q   *93 dares, approach;] Oxford; dares approach; F; dares approach, Q   *94 you – who not? –] Furness; you, who not, Q, F; you, (who not?) Theobald   95 ho!] ho. F; ho. Bast. A Herald ho, a Herald. Q   95 SD] As in Theobald; after firmely. F; not in Q*

82 If . . . me Albany sarcastically advises Regan to direct her matrimonial intentions to him, as Edmond has spoken for Gonerill.
82 love See collation. Q appears correct. Faulty plurals (characteristic of Compositor E) occur elsewhere in F, e.g. 'Sisters' (78).
83 An interlude What a farce! (Kittredge). Interludes were brief plays usually comic, performed in the intervals of festivities, they are so called in *MND* 1.2.6, *TN* 5.1.372. On F's addition here, see Textual Analysis, p. 287 below.
84 let . . . sound See Textual Analysis, p. 287 below, and compare Taylor, 'War', p. 33.
87 pledge gage.
87 make it i.e. make it good.

88 in nothing in no single detail.
90 medicine poison. See collation. In F Gonerill's humour is grimmer.
91 What . . . is i.e. whoever and of whatsoever rank he is (compare Abbott 254).
95–107 A herald . . . Again See collation. In Q, Edmond insistently repeats the call for a herald, and it is he, not the Herald, who orders the second and third trumpet calls (106–7). Q has a Captain (not in F) order the first trumpet call. F's alterations show Albany still very much in charge. (See Textual Analysis, pp. 80–1 above, on recasting; Sisson, pp. 243–4, who supports F; Duthie, pp. 188–9.)
96 virtue strength, valour (compare Latin *virtus*).

All levied in my name, have in my name
Took their discharge.

REGAN   My sickness grows upon me.

ALBANY She is not well. Convey her to my tent.

                    [*Exit Regan, led by an Officer*]

Come hither, herald. Let the trumpet sound,   100
And read out this.

                    A trumpet sounds

HERALD *Reads* 'If any man of quality or degree within the lists of
the army will maintain upon Edmond, supposed Earl of
Gloucester, that he is a manifold traitor, let him appear by the
third sound of the trumpet. He is bold in his defence.'   105

                    First trumpet

Again.

                    Second trumpet

Again.

                    Third trumpet

        Trumpet answers within. Enter EDGAR, *armed*

ALBANY Ask him his purposes, why he appears
Upon this call o'th'trumpet.

HERALD   What are you?
Your name, your quality, and why you answer   110
This present summons?

EDGAR   Know, my name is lost,
By treason's tooth bare-gnawn and canker-bit.

97–8 All . . . discharge.] F *lineation; one line* (discharge *turned under*) Q 98 My] F; This Q 99 SD] *This edn (after
Theobald); not in* Q, F 100 hither] F; hether Q 100 trumpet] Q; Trumper F 101 this.] F; this. *Cap.* Sound trumpet?
Q 101 SD] F; *not in* Q 102 SD] F; *not in* Q 102–5 'If . . . defence.'] *As in* Q (*quotation marks added); in italics* F 102
within the lists] F; in the hoast Q 104 he is] F; he's Q 104 by] F; at Q 105 SD] F; *not in* Q, *which inserts / Bast.* Sound?
on new line 106 Again.] *Her.* Againe. F; Againe? Q 106 SD] F; *not in* Q 107 Again.] *Her.* Againe. F; *not in* Q 107
SD.1] F; *not in* Q 107 SD.2 Trumpet . . . armed] F; *Enter Edgar at the third sound, a trumpet before him.* Q 109 o'th']
F; oth' Q 109–11 What . . . summons?] F *lineation; two lines divided* qualitie? / And Q 110 name, your] F; name and
Q 111–14 Know . . . cope.] F *lineation; three lines ending* . . . tooth. / . . . mou't / . . . cope with all. Q 111 Know,] F;
O know Q 111 lost,] lost Q, F; lost; *Theobald* *112 tooth] *Theobald*; tooth. Q; tooth: Q2, F

102 degree rank.

102 lists Either (1) palisades, boundaries (*OED*
List *sb*³ 10), or (2) rolls, catalogue (*OED* List *sb*⁶;
compare *Ham.* 1.2.32).

107 SD.2 Enter . . . armed Edgar is in combat
armour, his beaver down barring recognition. In Q,
Edgar enters with *a trumpet before him*, apparently
the trumpet that answered the third call, though it
has no other function except possibly to respond
to Edmond's command (140). Neither Q nor F,

however – nor most modern editions – provide an
entrance for the trumpeter who sounds the calls at
105–7, and who must enter with either Albany (38
SD) or the Herald (95 SD). Compare 26 SD n. above.
Whereas in Q no trumpet answers and Edgar enters
at the third sound, F's staging seems calculated to
increase suspense (Peat, p. 50).

112 canker-bit i.e. destroyed (literally, eaten by
worms; as in Sonnets 70.7, 99.13).

Yet am I noble as the adversary
I come to cope.

ALBANY   Which is that adversary?

EDGAR What's he that speaks for Edmond, Earl of Gloucester?   115

EDMOND Himself. What sayst thou to him?

EDGAR   Draw thy sword,
That if my speech offend a noble heart
Thy arm may do thee justice. Here is mine.
Behold, it is the privilege of mine honour,
My oath, and my profession. I protest,   120
Maugre thy strength, place, youth, and eminence,
Despite thy victor-sword and fire-new fortune,
Thy valour and thy heart, thou art a traitor:
False to thy gods, thy brother, and thy father,
Conspirant 'gainst this high illustrious prince,   125
And from th'extremest upward of thy head
To the descent and dust below thy foot,
A most toad-spotted traitor. Say thou no,
This sword, this arm, and my best spirits are bent
To prove upon thy heart, whereto I speak,   130
Thou liest.

EDMOND   In wisdom I should ask thy name,
But since thy outside looks so fair and warlike,

---

113 Yet am I noble as] F; yet are I mou't / Where is Q; Where is Q2   114 cope] F; cope with all Q   114 Which] F, Q; What Q2   116 sayst] F; saiest Q   117–18 That . . . mine.] F *lineation; divided* arme / May Q   *119 Behold . . . honour,] *As in Pope;* Behold it is the priuiledge of my tongue, Q; Behold it is my priuiledge, / The priuiledge of mine Honours, F   *119 honour] *Oxford;* Honours F; tongue Q   120 and my] F, Q; and Q2   121 Maugre] F; Maugure Q   121 place, youth,] F; youth, place Q   *122 Despite] Q; Despise F   122 victor-sword] F; victor, sword Q   122 fire-new] *Rowe;* fire new Q, F   122 fortune] F; fortun'd Q   124 thy gods] F, Q; the gods Q2   125 Conspirant] F; Conspicuate Q   126 th'extremest] F; the'xtreamest Q   127 below thy foot] F; beneath thy feete Q   129–31 This . . . liest] F *lineation; two lines divided* spirits, / As bent Q   129 are] F; As Q; Is Q2

114 **cope** cope with, encounter.
115 **What's** Who is (Abbott 254; compare *H5* 4.3.18).
118 **Here is mine** Edgar draws his sword.
119 **Behold . . . honour** See collation. Either the compositor (Duthie, p. 422) or the collator (*Textual Companion*, p. 538) is responsible for unnecessary duplication in F.
119 **it** 'i.e. the drawing of a sword against an adversary, and the challenge of him to single combat' (NS).
119 **honour** personal integrity. While executing the change from Q 'my tongue', Compositor E (typically) pluralised the noun, thereby further altering the sense (*Textual Companion*, p. 538).

120 **oath . . . profession** i.e. as a knight.
121 **Maugre** In spite of.
122 **fire-new** i.e. brand new, freshly minted.
126–7 **from . . . foot** i.e. from top to toe.
127 **descent** lowest part, i.e. the sole.
128 **toad-spotted** i.e. stained or marked with infamy as a toad is with (supposedly) venomous spots.
131 **In wisdom . . . name** In chivalry, one was not bound to fight a social inferior. Edmond rejects prudence ('wisdom'), revealing his 'sentimental side' in accepting the old code of honour Edgar represents (Heilman, pp. 244–7). Compare 141–4 and 155–6 n. below.

And that thy tongue some say of breeding breathes,
What safe and nicely I might well delay
By rule of knighthood, I disdain and spurn.   135
Back do I toss these treasons to thy head,
With the hell-hated lie o'erwhelm thy heart,
Which, for they yet glance by and scarcely bruise,
This sword of mine shall give them instant way
Where they shall rest for ever. Trumpets, speak!   140
            Alarums. [They] fight. [Edmond falls]
ALBANY   Save him, save him.
GONERILL   This is practice, Gloucester;
By th'law of war thou wast not bound to answer
An unknown opposite. Thou art not vanquished,
But cozened and beguiled.
ALBANY   Shut your mouth, dame,

---

133 tongue] F; being Q   *133 some say] Q; (some say) F   134 What . . . delay] F; *not in* Q   135 rule] F; right Q   136 Back . . . head] F, Q; *not in* Q2   136 Back] F; Heere Q   136 these] F; those Q   137 hell-hated lie] F; hell hatedly Q   137 o'erwhelm] ore-whelme F; oreturnd Q   *138 scarcely] Q; scarely F   140 SD] *Capell; Alarums. Fights.* F (*after* saue him.); *not in* Q   141 SH ALBANY] Q, F; ALL *Oxford* (*conj. van Dam, Blayney*)   141–4 This . . . beguiled.] F *lineation; three lines ending* . . . armes / . . . opposite, / . . . beguild. Q   141 practice] F; meere practise Q   142 th'] F; the Q   142 war] F; armes Q   142 wast] F; art Q   142 answer] F, Q; offer Q2   144 cozened] F; cousned Q   144–7 Shut . . . it.] F *lineation; as prose* Q   144 Shut] F; Stop Q

---

133 **tongue** See collation. Q 'being' is probably a misreading of 'tong' (Duthie, p. 423).

133 **say** Aphetic form of 'assay' = proof, sample (Onions); hence, 'smack', 'air'. The F collator or compositor mistook the noun for a verb and, treating the expression as parenthetical, inserted brackets. Compare Duthie, pp. 195–6.

134 **What . . . delay** See Textual Analysis, p. 287 below, on line missing in Q.

134 **safe and nicely** legally and punctiliously.

135 **rule** See collation. Q 'right' may derive from misreading 'rit' for 'rule' in copy (compare Duthie, p. 423); or F may have altered Q (as often in this passage) to avoid the internal rhyme, 'right' – 'knighthood'.

137 **hell-hated lie** lie as hateful as hell. Q 'hell hatedly' derives from the compositor mistaking 'ly' (= 'lie') for an adverbial suffix (Duthie, p. 423).

138 **Which** i.e. those treasons (136). 'Which' is also the object of the verb in the next line, where 'them' is grammatically redundant (Kittredge).

138 **for** because.

138 **bruise** i.e. you.

139 **instant way** immediate passage.

140 **Where . . . for ever** i.e. in you.

140 **SD** A realistic duel must involve a fight, not just swordplay (Rosenberg, p. 305; compare

Bratton, p. 205).

141 **Save him** Albany apparently calls out to save Edmond from a *coup de grâce*, because he wants Edmond's confession (Johnson). Or he may be calling out to soldiers to save Edgar, momentarily in danger, as Gonerill with murder in her eyes accuses him of 'practice'. Blayney, following van Dam (see collation), regards Q/F *Alb.* as a misreading of *All*, which could also make sense dramatically.

143 **opposite** opponent; as at 41 above.

144 **cozened** cheated, duped.

144–51 **Shut . . . her** See collation. To Duthie, p. 43, the Q/F variants here were evidence of memorial reconstruction, but to more recent scholars they reveal differences in dramatic intention: e.g. in Q, Albany acts more straightforwardly throughout the passage; in F, his actions are more disjointed, hesitant, consistent with his 'pattern of delay' later in this scene (Urkowitz, pp. 111–15). Gonerill's final exit similarly shows 'a very clear differentiation': in Q, she leaves the stage defeated and shamefaced; in F, she is challenged but strong and defiant (McLeod, pp. 187–8). Speech headings and address have also aroused comment, as indicated below. On recasting speeches, see Textual Analysis, pp. 80–1 above.

Or with this paper shall I stop it. – Hold, sir.   145
Thou worse than any name, read thine own evil. –
No tearing, lady. I perceive you know it.
GONERILL   Say if I do; the laws are mine, not thine.
Who can arraign me for't?   *Exit*
ALBANY   Most monstrous! O,
Know'st thou this paper?
EDMOND   Ask me not what I know.   150
ALBANY   Go after her, she's desperate, govern her.
                                            [*Exit an Officer*]
EDMOND   What you have charged me with, that have I done,
And more, much more; the time will bring it out.
'Tis past, and so am I. But what art thou
That hast this fortune on me? If thou'rt noble,   155
I do forgive thee.

---

145 stop] F; stople Q   145 – Hold, sir.] hold Sir, F; *not in* Q   146 name] F; thing Q   147 No] F; nay no Q   147 know it] F; know't Q   148–9 Say . . . for't] F *lineation; one line* (me for't. *turned under*) Q   149 can] F; shal Q   149 SD] F; *Exit. Gonorill.* Q (*after 150*)   149–50 Most . . . paper?] *Capell's lineation; one line,* Q, F   149 O,] F; *not in* Q   150 SH] F; *Gon.* Q (*see Commentary*)   151 SD] Capell; *not in* Q, F   152 What . . . done,] *As in* Q; *two lines divided* with, / That F   155 thou'rt] F; thou bee'st Q

145 this paper i.e. the letter Edgar has given him (5.1.29).

145 Hold, sir These words, not in Q, show who is addressed. 'Hold' = take, receive (often with the implication of wait or desist: see Schmidt, and compare *TN* 3.3.38, *Mac.* 2.1.4).

146 Thou . . . evil Albany addresses Edmond, not Gonerill, since he does not use the familiar pronoun for her, as he now consistently does for Edmond. Only once (4.2.36), after she uses the familiar pronoun to him, does Albany address her thus (Urkowitz, p. 111).

146 thine own evil Edmond is thoroughly implicated in Gonerill's letter, which explicitly mentions their 'reciprocal vows' (4.5.250), although Gonerill takes the initiative in urging the further evil of Albany's murder.

147 No tearing Gonerill tries to tear the letter out of Albany's hands as he gives it to Edmond. Compare a similar incident in *King Leir* (2586).

148–9 the laws . . . for't Gonerill refers to her position as queen and to Albany as merely consort. The sovereign had no peer and therefore could not be tried: see *R2* 1.2.37–41, 3.2.54–7.

149 SD See collation. Q delays Gonerill's exit until after 'Ask me not what I know' (150), which it assigns to her, not Edmond. In F she exits defi-

antly asserting her superiority over Albany and law (McLeod, p. 187).

150 Know'st . . . paper In F, Albany's address to Edmond is clear, whereas in Q, with Gonerill still on stage, it is ambiguous and even contradictory: Albany has already indicated that Gonerill recognises the letter (147). Compare Furness.

150 SH EDMOND Q assigns this speech to Gonerill, who then exits vanquished, implying her guilt (McLeod, p. 188). In assigning the line to Edmond, F resolves any ambiguity and contradiction (see previous note). Edmond's response is not necessarily defiant, but may be 'a resigned admission' of guilt, delivered sombrely, i.e. 'You need not ask' (Urkowitz, p. 114). Perhaps the Q compositor mistakenly continued the Albany/Gonerill alternation; moreover, Gonerill's name after her exit in Q would be redundant if the speech were hers (Halio, p. 164; compare Duthie, pp. 189–90, and Muir, who follow Q).

151 Go . . . govern her Somewhat belatedly, Albany recognises Gonerill's despair and shows justified concern; this is consistent with his emerging pattern of delayed response.

155–6 If . . . thee Edmond implicitly repudiates his stance in 1.2 and reverts to traditional concepts of nobility and breeding (Hunter).

EDGAR   Let's exchange charity.
I am no less in blood than thou art, Edmond.
If more, the more th'hast wronged me.
My name is Edgar, and thy father's son.
The gods are just, and of our pleasant vices   160
Make instruments to plague us.
The dark and vicious place where thee he got
Cost him his eyes.

EDMOND   Th'hast spoken right; 'tis true.
The wheel is come full circle; I am here.

ALBANY Methought thy very gait did prophesy   165
A royal nobleness. I must embrace thee.
Let sorrow split my heart if ever I
Did hate thee or thy father.

EDGAR Worthy prince, I know't.

ALBANY Where have you hid yourself?   170
How have you known the miseries of your father?

EDGAR By nursing them, my lord. List a brief tale,
And when 'tis told, O that my heart would burst!

---

157 art,] F4; art Q, F **158** th'hast] F; thou hast Q **160** vices] F; vertues Q **161–3** Make . . . eyes.] F *lineation; two lines divided* vitious / Place Q **161** plague] F; scourge Q **162** thee he] F, Q; he thee Q2 **163–4** Th'hast . . . here.] F *lineation; as prose* Q **163** Th'hast] F; Thou hast Q **163** right; 'tis true] F; truth Q **164** circle] F; circled Q **167–8** Let . . . father.] F *lineation; one line* Q **167–8** ever I / Did] F; I did euer Q **169** know't] F, Q; know it Q2 **172–80** By . . . rings,] F *lineation; nine lines ending* . . . Lord, / . . . told / . . . proclamation / . . . neere, / . . . death, / . . . once. / . . . rags / . . . disdain'd / . . . rings, Q

---

156 Let's exchange charity Edgar's fierceness apparently abates, although his character 'has too much validity to be merely humble and gentle', and his speech reflects a 'bitter morality' that offers Edmond no solace (Rosenberg, p. 307).

158 If more i.e. since Edmond is 'half-blooded' (74).

159 My . . . son Edgar removes his helmet.

160–1 The gods . . . us Compare Wisdom 11.[13]: 'wherewith a man sinneth, by the same also shal he be punished', and Jer. 2.19: 'Thine owne wickednes shal correct thee, and thy turnings backe shal reproue thee' (Noble).

160 pleasant pleasure-giving.

162–3 The dark . . . eyes Edgar applies his statement of compensatory justice to the specific instance: the sinful fornication that bred Edmond led to events culminating in Gloucester's blinding.

162 dark (1) dim, unlit, (2) morally benighted.

162 vicious place Compare 'forfended place' (5.1.11) (King).

162 got begot.

164 The wheel . . . here More is suggested than

Fortune's wheel, which has returned Edmond to the bottom whence he began. Events have circled back so that he, who was the initiator and beneficiary of much evil, is now its victim. Compare Bradley, p. 15: 'That men may start a course of events but can neither calculate nor control it, is a *tragic* fact.'

165–6 Methought . . . nobleness Albany addresses Edgar, whose demeanour and very manner of walking, he says, suggest something kingly. Albany's specific terms, 'royal nobleness', are themselves prophetic: compare 293–4 below.

166 royal (1) dignified, (2) regal, kingly.

167 sorrow . . . heart Compare *R3* 1.3.299. where Queen Margaret uses the same expression.

169 Worthy Noble.

172 List Listen to.

173 O that . . . burst Emotionally overtaxed by now, Edgar uncharacteristically, like his father, yearns for death. But his work is not yet finished. (At 4.1.10–12, he said the opposite; see Rosenberg, p. 307, on Edgar's inconsistencies.)

The bloody proclamation to escape
That followed me so near (O, our lives' sweetness,   175
That we the pain of death would hourly die
Rather than die at once!) taught me to shift
Into a madman's rags, t'assume a semblance
That very dogs disdained; and in this habit
Met I my father with his bleeding rings,   180
Their precious stones new-lost; became his guide,
Led him, begged for him, saved him from despair,
Never – O fault! – revealed myself unto him
Until some half hour past, when I was armed.
Not sure, though hoping of this good success,   185
I asked his blessing, and from first to last
Told him our pilgrimage; but his flawed heart –
Alack, too weak the conflict to support –
'Twixt two extremes of passion, joy and grief,
Burst smilingly.

EDMOND   This speech of yours hath moved me,   190
And shall perchance do good. But speak you on,
You look as you had something more to say.

ALBANY   If there be more, more woeful, hold it in,
For I am almost ready to dissolve,
Hearing of this.   195

---

176 we] F; with Q   178 madman's] mad-mans Q, F   178 t'assume] F; To assume Q   181 Their] F; The Q   *182 despair,] Q; dispaire. F   183 fault] F; Father Q   187 our] F; my Q   194–5 For . . . this.] F *lineation; one line* Q   195 this.] F *omits eighteen lines here*

174 bloody proclamation Compare 2.1.55–7, 2.3.1–5.

175–7 O, our . . . once i.e. life is so precious to us that we prefer to prolong it, suffering agonies repeatedly, rather than to die quickly and be done. Compare *Cym.* 5.1.25–7.

177 shift change.

180 rings i.e. eye-sockets. The next line continues the metaphor.

183 O fault Edgar now realises he was wrong to delay reconciliation with his father. 'In effect, Edgar's way and time of telling killed his father' (Rosenberg, p. 308).

185 success outcome; i.e. victory in the duel.

187–90 his flawed . . . smilingly In Sidney's *Arcadia*, Bk II, ch. 10, the blind Paphlagonian king dies similarly of a broken heart, 'with many teares (both of ioy and sorrow)'.

187 flawed cracked, i.e. damaged by suffering.

190 Burst smilingly Gloucester's dying smile suggests not only joyful reunion with Edgar, but gladness that death has come to him at last. Gloucester's death prepares in some ways for Lear's, brought closer in F by substantial cutting after 195 (Clayton, p. 137; compare 196–201 n. below).

190–2 This . . . say Edmond 'becomes humanised' in the course of *King Lear*, discovering limitations and passions that being human involves, as this speech and others in the scene reveal (Reibetanz, p. 59).

191 shall . . . good Compare 217–25 below.

193 hold it in As if taking a cue from Albany, F cuts seventeen lines following this speech: see Textual Analysis, pp. 276–7 below.

194 dissolve i.e. in tears.

Enter a GENTLEMAN [*with a bloody knife*]

GENTLEMAN Help, help, O help!

EDGAR   What kind of help?

ALBANY   Speak, man.

EDGAR What means this bloody knife?

GENTLEMAN   'Tis hot, it smokes.
It came even from the heart of – O, she's dead.

ALBANY Who dead? Speak, man.

GENTLEMAN Your lady, sir, your lady; and her sister   200
By her is poisoned: she confesses it.

EDMOND I was contracted to them both; all three
Now marry in an instant.

EDGAR   Here comes Kent.

Enter KENT [*as himself*]

ALBANY Produce the bodies, be they alive or dead.
Gonerill's and Regan's bodies brought out
This judgement of the heavens, that makes us tremble,   205

---

195 SD] *Enter one with a bloudie knife,* Q; *Enter a Gentleman.* F   196 O help!] F; *not in* Q   196 SH EDGAR] F; *Alb.* Q   196 ALBANY Speak, man.] F; *not in* Q   197 SH EDGAR] F; *not in* Q, *which continues speech as part of previous line*   197 this] F; *that* Q   197–8 'Tis . . . dead.] *Steevens's lineation (Capell subst.); one line* Q, *which omits* O she's dead; *as prose* F   197 'Tis] F; *Its* Q   199 dead? Speak, man.] F; man, speake? Q   201 confesses] F; *hath confest* Q; *has confest* Q2   203 EDGAR Here comes Kent.] F; *after* pity 206 Q   203 Kent.] F; *Kent* sir. Q   203 SD] *Oxford (subst.); Enter Kent* Q, Q2, F (*after* 207 Q; *after* pity 206 Q2)   204 the] F; *their* Q   204 SD] F; *The bodies of Gonerill and Regan are brought in.* Q (*after 212; see Commentary*)   205 judgement] F; *Iustice* Q   205 tremble,] Q; tremble. F

196–201 Help . . . it See collation. Revision of this sequence in F gives Edgar two speeches. By sharing the interrogation with Albany, he begins taking over responsibility for events (compare Textual Analysis, p. 79 above; Urkowitz, pp. 116–17; and 222–5 below). Doran, pp. 53–4, 72, believed Shakespeare was responsible for the revision, as for the deletion of the lines following 195. The episode was modified by all eighteenth- and nineteenth-century actor-editors, who often cut it completely (Bratton, p. 209).

197 smokes steams. 'Fresh blood commonly "smokes" in Sh[akespeare]' (NS). The line is one of the most difficult for a modern audience to take seriously, unless very carefully controlled and modulated (Rosenberg, p. 309).

198 It . . . dead The line generates deliberate tension and suspense. Regan's death is expected, but by poison. Gonerill and Cordelia are other possible victims, but which one, and why?

200 Your lady Edmond's prophecy (4.2.26) is fulfilled.

203 marry unite; with a pun on sex and death (Rosenberg, p. 309, who compares 4.5.189).

203 EDGAR . . . Kent See collation. In Q, Edgar's line and Kent's entrance occur in the middle of Albany's speech. In F, Kent 'comes slowly down the stage while Albany is speaking' (Muir) – a more effective entrance. Moreover, in F's lineation the metre improves.

203 SD *Enter* KENT Kent now drops his disguise as Caius. He was last seen in 4.6 and may be imagined as having become separated from Lear and Cordelia during the battle.

204 SD *Gonerill's . . . out* See collation. Muir believes Q is right, allowing time for Albany's order to be obeyed. But Q's SD occurs at an awkward moment; in F, only a brief pause is needed, and 'This judgement of the heavens' (205) becomes immediately visual. The business is unfortunately often cut, destroying the tragic reprise of 1.1 when Lear enters (Bratton, p. 209; compare Granville-Barker, p. 277).

205–6 This judgement . . . pity i.e. this divine retribution is terrible (in swiftness and finality), but it does not evoke sorrow or compassion (since the victims deserved their fate).

       Touches us not with pity. – O, is this he?
       [*To Kent*] The time will not allow the compliment
       Which very manners urges.
KENT   I am come
       To bid my king and master aye good night.
       Is he not here?
ALBANY   Great thing of us forgot!   210
       Speak, Edmond; where's the king, and where's Cordelia?
       Seest thou this object, Kent?
KENT   Alack, why thus?
EDMOND   Yet Edmond was beloved.
       The one the other poisoned for my sake,
       And after slew herself.   215
ALBANY   Even so. – Cover their faces.
EDMOND   I pant for life. Some good I mean to do,
       Despite of mine own nature. Quickly send –
       Be brief in it – to th'castle; for my writ
       Is on the life of Lear and on Cordelia.   220
       Nay, send in time.
ALBANY   Run, run, O run!
EDGAR   To who, my lord? – Who has the office? Send
       Thy token of reprieve.

---

206 us] F, Q; *not in* Q2   206–8 O . . . urges.] F *lineation; two lines divided* allow / The *and with* SH *Alb.* / *before* O (*see*
5.3.203 n.) Q   206 is this] F; 'tis Q   207 SD] *Hanmer; not in* Q, F   208 Which] F; that Q   208–9 I . . . night.] F *lineation;*
one line Q   210–12 Great . . . Kent?] F, Q *lineation; as prose* Q2   210 thing] F, Q; things Q2   213–15 Yet . . . herself.] F,
Q *lineation; as prose* Q2   217–21 I . . . time.] F, Q *lineation; as prose* Q2   218 mine] F; my Q   219 Be brief in it – to th']
F; Be briefe, int toth' Q; bee briefe, into the Q2   222–3 To . . . reprieve.] *As in* Q; *divided* Office? / Send F, Q2   222
has] F; hath Q

206 O . . . he Albany finally sees Kent.
207–8 The time . . . urges Events do not permit the ceremony of greeting which mere courtesy
demands.
208–9 I am . . . night Kent is not interested in
ceremony; he is concerned only to see Lear.
210 Great . . . forgot Events before and after
the battle have distracted Albany from concern for
Lear and Cordelia. Kent's reminder, however, does
not lead to immediate action. Albany questions
Edmond, but then directs Kent's gaze to the bodies of Gonerill and Regan which, in Q, are brought
out here. In F, something else apparently motivates
Albany's interrupted response, 'some sudden erup-
tion of concern within himself' (Urkowitz, p. 119),
or 'involvement with his own repressed feeling' of
love for Gonerill (Rosenberg, p. 309). But Shakespeare may simply have made a characteristic minor
slip, one scarcely noticed in the theatre. Whatever

the case, Albany reveals an inability from here on to
take effective and timely action, which justifies his
relinquishment of the throne at the end. (Compare
144–51 n. and 151 n. above.)
212 this object i.e. the bodies of Gonerill and
Regan; 'object' = sight, spectacle.
213–16 Yet Edmond . . . faces Edmond's boast
here as at 202–3 deeply wounds Albany, who utters
a terse 'Even so'. Then, before ordering their faces
covered, 'Reminded of his great love, great hurt,
he takes one last look' (Rosenberg, p. 310).
215 after afterwards, later.
219 Be brief i.e. don't waste time.
220 on against.
221–3 Run . . . reprieve Albany's exhortation
to Edgar shows turmoil and confusion; it remains
for the younger man again to take charge and get
from Edmond the important details.

EDMOND Well thought on. Take my sword. The captain,
    Give it the captain.
EDGAR   Haste thee for thy life.   225
                                     [*Exit an Officer*]
EDMOND He hath commission from thy wife and me
    To hang Cordelia in the prison and
    To lay the blame upon her own despair,
    That she fordid herself.
ALBANY The gods defend her. Bear him hence a while.   230
                             [*Edmond is borne off*]

Enter LEAR *with* CORDELIA *in his arms* [*and the* OFFICER *following*]

LEAR Howl, howl, howl, howl! O, you are men of stones.
    Had I your tongues and eyes, I'd use them so,

224–5 Well . . . captain.] F, Q *lineation; one line* Q2 *224 sword. The captain,] *Oxford;* sword the Captaine Q; sword, Q2, F 225 SH] *Duke.* Q; *Alb.* Q2 225 SD] *This edn; Exit the Gentleman / Oxford; not in* Q, F 226–8 He . . . despair] *As verse* F, Q; *as prose* Q2 227–8 To . . . despair] F; *divided* lay / The Q 229 That . . . herself.] F, Q; *not in* Q2 230 SD.1 *Edmond . . . off*] *Theobald; not in* Q, F 230 SD.2 *and the* OFFICER *following*] *This edn; not in* Q, F *231 Howl . . . howl!] *As in* Q; F *omits one* howle *231 you] Q; your F 232 I'd] F; I would Q

224 The captain See collation. Like Q2, F omits these words, which Duthie, p. 424, believes the Q compositor erred in setting up too soon and then repeated in their proper place. More likely, Compositor E was influenced by Q2, whose compositor tried to correct the syntax, save space (making 224–5 one line), and avoid what seemed to him an awkward and unnecessary repetition. Edmond's gasping repetition, however, is dramatically effective and helps make the next line metrically complete, though half an iamb in 224 is sacrificed.

225 SH EDGAR Q assigns this speech to Albany, rightly according to Sisson, p. 244, and to Duthie, p. 191, who argues (1) that Edmond gives Edgar his sword, and (2) that Albany earlier bade him run to the castle. But F revises or corrects Q, allowing Edgar (who sends an officer with Edmond's sword) more authority. Compare 221–3 n.; Hunter; and 249 below, where the officer, not Edgar, confirms Lear's boast.

228 To lay . . . despair In the sources, e.g. Geoffrey of Monmouth, Cordeilla does commit suicide years later. See p. 2 above.

229 fordid killed.

230 Bear . . . while Edmond no longer matters (compare 269 below). He is borne off through one door as Lear enters through another.

230 SD.2 Enter . . . arms This image, often regarded as an inverted or secular pietà, is properly not a 'prefiguration' but 'a representative event of human history' (Brockbank, p. 14). Both Q and F

leave open the question of Cordelia's physical state, although many editors prejudice readers by following Rowe and inserting *dead* after CORDELIA. The ambiguity of Cordelia's state is crucial, as throughout the scene 'the audience continue to alternate between hope and despair' (Peat, pp. 49, 51; compare E. A. J. Honigmann, *Myriad-Minded Shakespeare*, 1989, pp. 90–2).

230 SD.2 and . . . following After repeated delays in the reprieve, the officer has arrived too late. He re-enters, trailing behind Lear (compare *Textual Companion*, p. 539).

231 Howl . . . howl See collation. Compositor E may have dropped the fourth 'howl' because the line was too long for his stick. The fourth 'howl' syllabically fills out the metre. In actual stage practice, however, 'howl' is not usually articulated as a word but rather as 'a voiced pain, often an animal ululation' (Rosenberg, p. 312; compare Bratton, p. 209).

231 stones i.e. insensitive as statues. The onlookers are all stunned into frozen silence and grief; in fact, the 'howls' are sometimes taken as demands that they cry out (Rosenberg, p. 312). Hunter believes the overall imagery is of a funerary chapel or pantheon of statues. (Perhaps Compositor E created another false plural, but elsewhere Shakespeare uses similar plurals, e.g. *R3* 3.7.224: 'I am not made of stones.')

232 eyes i.e. used for weeping along with wailing; or perhaps for lightning looks.

That heaven's vault should crack. She's gone for ever.
I know when one is dead and when one lives.
She's dead as earth.
                    [*He lays her down*]
                    Lend me a looking-glass;   235
If that her breath will mist or stain the stone,
Why then she lives.
KENT   Is this the promised end?
EDGAR Or image of that horror?
ALBANY   Fall and cease.
LEAR This feather stirs, she lives: if it be so,
      It is a chance which does redeem all sorrows   240
      That ever I have felt.
KENT   O my good master!
LEAR Prithee, away.
EDGAR   'Tis noble Kent, your friend.
LEAR A plague upon you murderers, traitors all.
      I might have saved her; now she's gone for ever.

---

235 SD] *Oxford; not in* Q, F   236–7 If . . . lives] F, Q *lineation; one line* Q2   237 Why then she] F, Q; she then Q2   239–41
This . . . felt.] F, Q *lineation; as prose* Q2   239 stirs, she lives:] F; stirs she liues, Q; stirs; She lives! *Capell*   241 O] F; A
Q   243–8 A . . . thee.] F, Q *lineation; as prose* Q2   243 you murderers] F; your murderous Q; you murdrous Q2

233 heaven's . . . crack Compare 3.2.1–9.

235–7 She's dead . . . lives Lear's oscillation between belief that Cordelia is dead and hope that she is not has led to controversy concerning whether he is finally deluded or not. 'The tension here, and it is the underlying tension in Lear until his death, lies between an absolute knowledge that Cordelia is dead, and an absolute inability to accept it' (Stampfer, p. 2). Compare also 284–5 n. below.

235 Lend me a looking-glass The stage business from here through the next fifteen lines is complicated and subject to various interpretation. Someone may actually give Lear a glass (perhaps one that Gonerill wears), or he hallucinates having one about him. If he has a glass, why does he refer to a feather four lines later, and where does it come from? Again, he may fantasise or pluck a feather from his garment or a plume from someone's helmet, as he earnestly tries to discover or restore some sign of life, however faint. Much depends on how the actor interprets Lear's state of mind and the fluctuating madness that still afflicts him, understandably, given the shock of Cordelia's hanging. Compare Meagher, pp. 248–9, 254–7; Rosenberg, p. 314; Stampfer, pp. 2–3.

236 stone 'mirror of polished stone or crystal' (Onions). Compare Webster, *The White Devil*

(1612), 5.2.38–40: 'Fetch a looking glasse, see if his breath will not stain it; or pull out some feathers from my pillow, and lay them to his lippes' (Steevens). Webster doubtless recalled Shakespeare's scene and was more explicit about the feather.

237 promised end (1) Judgement Day, the end of the world, (2) what Lear promised himself when he divided his kingdom (Hunter), (3) the outcome promised by what has occurred (compare p. 12 above).

238 Or image . . . horror Edgar understands Kent's question in sense (1); 'image' = likeness, representation.

238 Fall and cease Vocatives: either (1) let judgement come and all things end, or (2) may Lear fall and cease to be (rather than continue living a wretched existence) (Steevens).

239 This . . . lives Although most early editors adopt F's punctuation, as here, Capell takes the first clause as simply declarative and the second as a joyous exclamation. Many editions (e.g. NS) follow. But the line, which parallels 236–7, carries an implied 'if' at the beginning. Lear's uncertainty continues in the next lines, as he toils over Cordelia's body.

Cordelia, Cordelia, stay a little. Ha?   245
What is't thou sayst? – Her voice was ever soft,
Gentle, and low, an excellent thing in woman. –
I killed the slave that was a-hanging thee.
OFFICER 'Tis true, my lords, he did.
LEAR   Did I not, fellow?
I have seen the day with my good biting falchion   250
I would have made them skip. I am old now,
And these same crosses spoil me. [*To Kent*] Who are you?
Mine eyes are not o'th'best, I'll tell you straight.
KENT If fortune brag of two she loved and hated,
One of them we behold.   255
LEAR This' a dull sight. Are you not Kent?
KENT   The same,
Your servant Kent. Where is your servant Caius?
LEAR He's a good fellow, I can tell you that.
He'll strike, and quickly too. He's dead and rotten.
KENT No, my good lord, I am the very man –   260
LEAR I'll see that straight.
KENT That from your first of difference and decay
Have followed your sad steps.

---

246 sayst] F, Q2; sayest Q   247 woman] F; women Q   *249 SH OFFICER] Capell; Gent. F; Cap. Q · 249 my lords,] Q; (my Lords) F   249-53 Did . . . straight.] F lineation; as prose Q2   249-51 Did . . . now,] Lines end . . . day, / . . . would / . . . now, Q   250 have] F, Q; ha Q2   250 with my good] F, Q; that with my Q2   *251 them] Q; him F   252 SD] Oxford; not in Q, F   253 o'th'] F; othe Q   254 brag] F; bragd Q   254 and] F; or Q   256 This' . . . sight] F; not in Q   *256 This'] Schmidt 1879 (conj. S. Walker); This is F   256 you not] F; not you Q   256-7 The . . . Caius?] Capell's lineation; divided: Kent, / Where F; one line Q   258 you] F; not in Q   *260 man –] Pope; man. Q, F   262 first] F; life Q

245 **Cordelia . . . little** The eloquence and poignancy of this simple utterance are unsurpassed.

249 SH **OFFICER** See collation and compare 5.1.0 SD and 5.3.225 SD, 230 SD.2.

250-1 **I have . . . skip** Compare *Wiv.* 2.1.227–9, *Oth.* 5.2.261–4.

250 **falchion** A hooked, or curved, sword.

251 **them** See collation: Q makes better sense. Lear is speaking of his enemies generally, not Cordelia's executioner (Duthie, p. 191). An easy compositorial error.

252 **crosses** vexations, thwartings.

252 **spoil me** 'i.e. as a swordsman' (Muir).

253 **straight** straightaway.

254-5 **If . . . behold** Kent and Lear are looking at each other; hence, 'the two objects of fortune's love and her hate are, – himself, and his master . . .: of these two, says the speaker, you (the per-

son spoke to) "behold" one, and I another' (Capell, cited by Furness, NS).

256 **This'** This is.

256 **dull sight** Either (1) melancholy spectacle (referring to Cordelia's body), or (2) poor eyesight (Booth, pp. 31–2; compare 253 above).

256 **Are . . . Kent** Eyesight failing, Lear peers at Kent and is briefly diverted from Cordelia. Failing eyesight was a symptom of approaching death (Bucknill, cited by Hoeniger (p. 96)).

257 **Where . . . Caius** Kent earnestly wants Lear to make the connection. Compare 4.6.9 n.

261 **I'll . . . straight** I'll attend to that in a moment's time. Lear is still preoccupied with Cordelia. His 'welcome' (263) is similarly peremptory.

262 **your . . . decay** the beginning of your change and decline (of fortunes).

LEAR   You're welcome hither.
KENT Nor no man else. All's cheerless, dark, and deadly.
        Your eldest daughters have fordone themselves   265
        And desperately are dead.
LEAR   Ay, so I think.
ALBANY He knows not what he says, and vain is it
        That we present us to him.

                        Enter a MESSENGER

EDGAR   Very bootless.
MESSENGER Edmond is dead, my lord.
ALBANY   That's but a trifle here.
        You lords and noble friends, know our intent.   270
        What comfort to this great decay may come
        Shall be applied. For us, we will resign
        During the life of this old majesty
        To him our absolute power; [*To Edgar and Kent*] you, to
            your rights,
        With boot, and such addition as your honours   275
        Have more than merited. All friends shall taste
        The wages of their virtue, and all foes
        The cup of their deservings. O see, see!

263 You're] *Pope;* You'r Q; Your are F 264 Nor . . . deadly.] *As in* Q; *two lines divided* else: / All's F 265 fordone]
fore-done F; foredoome Q; foredoom'd Q2 266 Ay . . . think.] F; So thinke I to. Q 267 says] F; sees Q 267 is it] F; it
is Q 268 SD] F; *Enter Captaine.* Q (*after* bootlesse) 269–78 That's . . . see!] F *lineation* (*except 276–7*); *as prose* Q 271
great] F; *not in* Q 274 SD] *Malone; not in* Q, F 275 honours] F; honor Q 276–7 Have . . . foes] *Pope's lineation; divided*
shall / Taste F

263 **You're** See collation. F's sophistication has
gone awry; Q's 'you'r' is metrically superior. Compare Duthie, p. 379, and 231 above.
    264 **Nor . . . else** i.e. no one else deserves your
welcome if I don't. On double negatives, see Abbott
406. Some editors follow Rowe and continue from
Kent's preceding lines: 'I am the very man . . .
and no one else.' Booth believes the reference is
'unfixed and multiple . . . a vague and syntactically
unattached comment on the general scene' (p. 32).
    265 **fordone** killed. Q 'foredoome' may be a mis-
reading of 'foredoone' (Duthie, p. 425), or possibly
'foredoomd'.
    266 **desperately** in despair.
    266 **Ay . . . think** Although the bodies of Goner-
ill and Regan are on stage (204 SD), Lear, intent on
Cordelia, has paid no attention to them. He may
glance at them here before falling silent, tranced
perhaps, certainly bemused (compare 278 n.).
    268 **bootless** useless.
    270 **know our intent** Again, the wheel comes

full circle. Compare 1.1.32 ff. (NS).
    270 **our** Albany uses the royal plural appropri-
ately throughout this speech.
    271 **great decay** i.e. Lear, whose physical and
mental decline is increasingly apparent. Compare
'noble ruin', i.e. Antony, *Ant.* 3.10.18 (NS).
    275 **boot** something additional.
    275 **addition** title; quibbling on 'boot'.
    275 **honours** i.e. honourable deeds, conduct.
    276–8 **All . . . deservings** Albany's peroration
appears suitable for the end of a tragedy (compare
Mac. 5.9.26–41). But Shakespeare has more. Compare J. K. Walton, 'Lear's last speech', *S.Sur.* 13
(1960), 17, and John Shaw, '*King Lear*: the final
lines', *Essays in Criticism*, 16 (1966), 262–3.
    278 **O see, see** Some piece of stage business
refocuses everyone's attention on Lear. Perhaps,
having momentarily fallen into a tranced or tran-
quil state (266 n.), he awakens abruptly and, rock-
ing Cordelia in his arms, has begun speaking to
her.

LEAR And my poor fool is hanged. No, no, no life?
   Why should a dog, a horse, a rat have life,   280
   And thou no breath at all? Thou'lt come no more,
   Never, never, never, never, never.
   Pray you, undo this button. Thank you, sir.
   Do you see this? Look on her! Look, her lips.
   Look there, look there.   *He dies*

EDGAR   He faints. My lord, my lord! 285

KENT Break, heart, I prithee break.

EDGAR   Look up, my lord.

KENT Vex not his ghost. O, let him pass. He hates him
   That would upon the rack of this tough world
   Stretch him out longer.

EDGAR   He is gone indeed.

KENT The wonder is he hath endured so long.   290
   He but usurped his life.

ALBANY Bear them from hence. Our present business
   Is general woe. Friends of my soul, you twain
   Rule in this realm and the gored state sustain.

279–83 And . . . sir.] F *lineation; as prose* Q 279 No, no, no] F; no, no Q 280 have] F; of Q 281 Thou'lt] F; O thou wilt Q 282 Never . . . never.] F; neuer, neuer, neuer, Q 283 Pray you] F, Q; pray Q2 283 sir.] F; sir, O, o, o. Q; sir, O, o, o, o. Q2 284–5 Do . . . there.] F; *not in* Q 284 this? Look] F *corr.;* this, looke F *uncorr.* *284 her!] her? F 285 SD] F; *not in* Q 286 SH KENT] F; *Lear.* Q 287–9 Vex . . . longer.] F *lineation; lines end* . . . passe, / . . . wracke, / . . . longer. Q 287 hates him] F, Q; hates him much Q2 289 He] F; O he Q 293 Is] F; Is to Q 294 realm] F; kingdome Q 294 gored] F, Q; good Q2

279 And . . . hanged Lear appears to be in mid sentence. Since 'fool' was a common term of endearment, most commentators believe Lear refers to Cordelia (see Furness). But his term inevitably recalls the Fool, last seen in 3.6, whom he also loved. Moreover, the actor who played Cordelia probably doubled as the Fool. (See p. 35 above, and compare Bradley, p. 314; Rosenberg, p. 318, Booth, pp. 32–3).

283 Pray . . . button Compare 3.4.97 n. Although Lear may ask help to undo Cordelia's button, most commentators believe he is suffering a final attack of the 'mother' and wants the button at his own throat loosened. Kent obliges. (Q follows with death groans.)

284–5 Do . . . there In 1.1, Lear, egocentric, demanded that everyone's attention be focused upon himself, as he asked his daughters publicly to declare their love. Here, finally, he directs attention not to himself, but to the Other, to Cordelia, now more precious to him than his own life.

285–6 He . . . lord Edgar rushes to assist Lear,

trying to revive him, until he gives up at 289.

286 SH KENT See collation, and Textual Analysis, p. 81 above. 'What Shakespeare has done in revising is to transfer Lear's ultimate Quarto line . . . to Kent, thus utterly altering action, character, context, and significance' (Clayton, p. 135). Bradley, p. 309, suggests that Kent refers to his own heart.

287 ghost i.e. departing spirit. Medieval and Renaissance iconography typically depicts the spirit of a person departing at the point of death.

288 rack A torture machine upon which the victim was bound and stretched, forcing his limbs to become dislocated. Hunter believes 'tough' suggests 'rack' = the body, which encloses the spirit while a person lives. Lear's corporeal strength was great: compare 248–51.

289 longer (1) for a longer time, (2) with his body stretched further on the rack (Muir).

291 usurped stole (*OED* Usurp *v* 3).

294 gored bleeding, wounded.

KENT I have a journey, sir, shortly to go: 295
    My master calls me; I must not say no.
EDGAR The weight of this sad time we must obey,
    Speak what we feel, not what we ought to say.
    The oldest hath borne most; we that are young
    Shall never see so much, nor live so long.   300

Exeunt with a dead march

296 calls me;] F; cals, and Q   297 SH] F; *Duke.* Q   299 hath] F; haue Q   300 SD] F; *not in* Q

297 SH EDGAR See collation. Albany, the survivor with highest rank, would ordinarily utter the concluding lines. But Edgar owes him a reply, and the speech otherwise suits the younger man, especially as F alters his role: see Textual Analysis, p. 81 above.

297 **weight** heavy burden (sadness was 'heavy').

297 **obey** submit to, comply with.

298 **we** Perhaps the royal plural, as Edgar puts on the crown (Rosenberg, p. 323). Alternatively, the pronoun may include Albany, whose 'design of uncertainty' implies youth.

300 SD *dead march* 'A piece of solemn music played at a funeral procession, *esp.* at a military funeral; a funeral march' (*OED* Dead *adj* D.2).

TEXTUAL ANALYSIS, PART 2

Q has approximately 300 lines not in F, and F has about 100 lines not in Q. First, the longer Q passages omitted from F are here examined in detail (a) to determine what range of reasons there might have been for cutting them; (b) to trace connections between passages which might suggest comprehensive revision; and (c) to weigh the advantages and disadvantages of restoring them to the present modernised, Folio-based text. So that readers may consult the materials fully, all Q-only passages are presented (in edited form) in an Appendix, pp. 293–309 below. In the analyses that follow, most passages are shown in slightly reduced photo-facsimile; but for longer passages, especially those that do not involve complex bibliographical problems, the reader must refer to the Appendix. Analyses of F-only passages follow the section of Q-only passages.

Q-only passages

A number of these passages have been discussed in Part 1 of the Textual Analysis (pp. 65–85 above), but others require analysis, sometimes in conjunction with those previously considered. The lines in question are enclosed by square brackets in the facsimile reproductions.

(i) After 1.2.85:

> *Glost.* He cannot be fuch a monfter.
> [*Baft.* Nor is not fure.
> *Glost.* To his father,that fo tenderly and intirely loues him,
> heauen and earth !]*Edmund* feeke him out, wind mee into him, I
> pray you frame your bufines after your own wifedome, I would
> vnftate my felfe to be in a due refolution.

The omission from F appears deliberate, not accidental on the part of Compositor B, who set the passage. Theatrical cuts this early in the text are rare, and the column that B was setting on signature qq3ᵛ shows signs of crowding later on. On the other hand, the lines are not indispensable; moreover, another cut of several lines (complemented by a Folio addition, lines 96–100) occurs at 125. In view of these other alterations suggesting revision, the lines here may have been deleted by a reviser.

(ii) After 1.2.125:

> *Edg.* Doe you bufie your felfe about that?
> *Baft.* I promife you the effects he writ of,fucceed vnhappily,
> [as of vnnaturalneffe betweene the child and the parent, death,
> dearth, diffolutions of ancient amities, diuifions in ftate, mena-

ces and maledictions against King and nobles, needles diffidences,banishment of frieds,dissipation of Cohorts,nuptial breaches,and I know not what.

Edg. How long haue you beene a sectary Astronomicall?

Baf. Come, come,]when saw you my father laft ?

Edg. Why, the night gon by.

Since these lines essentially repeat Gloucester's speech 96 ff., added in F, they are
unnecessary here. Folio lineation, moreover, suggests that a cut has been made:

Edg. Do you busie your selfe with that ?

Baf. I promise you, the effects he writes of,succeede
vnhappily.

When saw you my Father laft?

Edg. The night gone by.

(iii) After 1.3.16:

Gon. Put on what wearie negligence you pleafe,you and your
fellow seruants, i'de haue it come in question, if he diflike it,let
him to our sifter, whose mind and mine I know in that are one,
[not to be ouerruld; idle old man that ftill would manage thofe
authorities that hee hath giuen away, now by my life old fooles
are babes again,& mufl be vs'd with checkes as flatteries,when
they are seene abufd]remember what I tell you.

Gent. Very well! Madam.

Gon. And let his Knights haue colder looks among you,what
growes of it no matter, aduife your fellowes fo, [I would breed
from hence occafions,and I fhall. that I may fpeake,]ile write
ftraight to my fifter to hould my very courfe, goe prepare for
dinner. *Exit.*

Two cuts in this passage are complemented by additions in the following scene. These
alterations and others affect Goneril's character in ways described above (pp. 78–9);
furthermore, local alterations, e.g. F 'Remember what I have said' (17) for Q 'remember
what I tell you' also point to a revising hand.

(iv) After 1.4.119 (see Textual Analysis, Part 1, pp. 84–5 above).

E. K. Chambers (1, 467) suggests that censorship as well as theatrical abridgement
may be responsible for the F omission. The overt satirical reference to monopolies
was dangerous under James I, especially in the bawdy context the Fool describes, and
censorship or the threat of it may have intervened. But after developing the argument
for censorship at length, Taylor ('Censorship', pp. 101–9) concedes that the passage as
abbreviated in F 'makes good dramatic sense' and does not argue for restoration of Q's
lines, as he does for 'Fut' at 1.2.115 ('Censorship', p. 110). If censorship was imposed,
Shakespeare could have recast the passage, but evidently he or his fellows found it was

better left out. Compare Kerrigan, pp. 218–19, who notes revisions elsewhere, such as the reassigned speech headings at 91 and 189, and changes in the Fool's psychology. For Compositor E's failure to delete the first three lines of the passage, see above, pp. 84–5.

(v) After 1.4.190 (see Textual Analysis, Part 1, p. 80 above).

As Urkowitz notes ('Editorial tradition', p. 34), Capell was the first to suggest that Shakespeare was responsible for revising this passage, a position supported by, for example, Kerrigan, p. 220. He argues that F's assignment of 190 to the Fool complements the cut and highlights 'Lear's shadow'. Although Q is good, F is better: 'it opens a gap between "Lear's shadow" and "Your name . . ." which is both painful and unignorable. The poetic space can scarcely be played across. Within it, the Fool's words resonate.'

(vi) After 2.2.128:

```
    Glost. Let me beseech your Grace not to doe so,
[ His fault is much, and the good King his maister
  VVill check him for't, your purpost low correction
  Is such,as baseft and temneft wretches for pilfring,
  And most common trespasses are punisht with,]
  The King must take it ill, that hee's so slightly valued
  In his messenger,should haue him thus restrained.
    Duke. Ile answer that.
    Reg. My sister may receiue it much more worse,
  To haue her Gentlemen abus'd, assalted
[ For following her affaires,put in his legges,]
  Come my good Lord away ?
```

Duthie, p. 174, believes that the first cut of four and a half lines is deliberate, and the patch (with appropriate relineation) is expert (compare Stone, p. 235). Revision appears to be at work here. The lines are not essential to the action, although they spell out the situation in fuller detail and show Gloucester pleading more earnestly. F also lacks a line after 133, which Duthie, p. 175, calls a compositor error. Since F otherwise alters Q, giving the next half-line to Cornwall (instead of continuing it as part of Regan's speech) and dropping 'good' from the term of address, the changes again seem to indicate revision.

(vii) After 2.4.17:

```
Q: Kent. It is both he and shee, your sonne & daugter.
   Lear. No.      Kent. Yes.
   Lear. No I say,      Kent. I say yea.
[ Lear. No no,they would not. Kent. Yes they haue.]
   Lear. By Iupiter I sweare no,they durst not do't,
  They would not, could not do't,tis worse then murder,
```

F: *Kent.* It is both he and she,
    Your Son, and Daughter.
      Lear. No.
      Kent. Yes.
      Lear. No I say.
      Kent. I say yea.
      Lear. By *Iupiter* I sweare no,

  [*Kent.* By *Iuno*, I sweare I,]
      Lear. They durst not do't:
  They could not, would not do't : 'tis worse then murther,

F omits two brief speeches and adds one – Kent's oath, introduced to parallel Lear's. Evidently the cut was made to allow for the addition, although some editors (e.g. Duthie, Muir) have found the speeches so impressive that they conflate. But, as Michael Warren says, conflation has no authority – unless, of course, we assume the collator accidentally skipped Q's crowded line. But within the puerile, see-saw argument between Lear and Kent, effective for three interchanges in either Q or F, a fourth seems tedious and unnecessary. Finally, if F's additional line was accidentally omitted by the Q compositor as well, a remarkable coincidence of errors results – possible, but unlikely.

(viii) After 3.1.7:

  Gent. Contending with the fretfull element,
Bids the wind blow the earth into the sea,
Or swell the curled waters boue the maine   (haire,
That things might change or ceafe, feares his white
Which the impetuous blasts with eyles rage
Catch in their furie, and make nothing of,
Striues in his little world of man to outscorne,
The too and fro conflicting wind and raine,
This night wherin the cub-drawne Beare would couch,
The Lyon, and the belly pinched Wolfe
Keepe their furre dry, vnbonneted he runnes,
And bids what will take all.]

The eight and a half lines missing from F represent theatrical abridgement, reducing the prominence Q gives the Gentleman. Moreover, the action he describes occurs in the immediately following scene. Duthie, p. 8, compares it to the cut at 5.3.195.

(ix) After 3.1.13:

Q: *Kent*, Sir I doe know you,
     And dare vpon the warrant of my Arte,
     Commend a deare thing to you, there is diuifion,.
     Although as yet the face of it be couer'd,
     With mutuall cunning, twixt *Albany* and *Cornwall*
     But true it is, from *France* there comes a power
     Into this fcattered kingdome, who alreadie wife in our
     Haue fecret feet in fome of our beft Ports, (negligéce,
     And are at point to fhew their open banner,
     Now to you, if on my credit you dare build fo farre,
     To make your fpeed to Douer, you fhall find
     Some that will thanke you, making iuft report
     Of how vnnaturall and bemadding forrow
     The King hath caufe to plaine,
     I am a Gentleman of blood and breeding,
     And from fome knowledge and affurance,
     Offer this office to you.
         Gent. I will talke farther with you.
         Kent, No doe not,

F: *Kent.* Sir, I do know you,
       And dare vpon the warrant of my note
       Commend a deere thing to you. There is diuifion
       (Although as yet the face of it is couer'd
       With mutuall cunning) 'twixt Albany, and Cornwall :
       Who haue, as who haue not, that their great Starres
       Thron'd and fet high; Seruants, who feeme no leffe,
       Which are to France the Spies and Speculations
       Intelligent of our State. What hath bin feene,
       Either in fnuffes, and packings of the Dukes,
       Or the hard Reine which both of them hath borne
       Againft the old kinde King ; or fomething deeper,
       Whereof (perchance) thefe are but furnifhings.
           Gent. I will talke further with you.
           Kent. No, do not:

Here is an instance (compare vii above) not of simple abridgement but of substitution (see p. 80). Both sets of lines are Shakespearean, although the Folio lines are in
a style more typical of Shakespeare's later work. Combining the passages, however,
not only gives Kent an inordinately long speech but, as Urkowitz notes, introduces
difficulties not found in either Q or F. For example, in Q, France does not know of the
king's mistreatment by his daughters and needs to be told, so Kent sends the Gentleman to Dover with the news; in F, France already knows, and Kent does not need to
(and therefore does not) send the Gentleman to Dover; in the composite text, France
has the news, and Kent sends the Gentleman to Dover with it anyway. Finally, although
they include mention of French spies, the Folio lines eliminate a reference to French
invasion and thus form part of a pattern of cuts that downplay this aspect of the plot
(see above, p. 83; on fragmented syntax, see Commentary notes to 3.1.14–15 and 20).

(x) After 3.6.14 (see Appendix, pp. 297–9 below, xii).

The omission of the 'mock trial' episode in F has aroused considerable controversy. Some scholars have argued for authorial revision, though the effect or rather the value of the cut in dramatic terms is debatable. For example, Roger Warren maintains that the omission of Lear's mad trial of Gonerill and Regan not only tightens the dramatic structure, but avoids duplication of Lear's mock justice in Act 4. Moreover, cutting the mad trial in 3.6 hurries the action forward to the 'thing itself', that is, the insane enactment of justice that immediately follows in 3.7, the trial and sentencing of Gloucester. But these putative gains may not be worth the loss of what, in the theatre, is a most impressive piece of drama. The parallel with events in 3.7 is sharp: the madness in 3.6 contrasts with the diabolical cruelty in 3.7. Furthermore, the quarto version of 3.6 completes Lear's descent into madness; the king does not appear again until much later in Act 4. Without appreciably shortening performance time (35 lines), removing the mock trial foreshortens a process that Lear has been struggling to contain since the end of Act 1. If Shakespeare was responsible for this cut, he may have had reason, as Warren argues, for his alterations. But authors – even Shakespeare – are not always the best judges of their own work, and theatre directors (who are notorious for making alterations of their own, regardless of whose play it is) seldom cut the mock trial in 3.6.

(xi) After 3.6.53 (see Appendix, pp. 299–300 below, xiii–xiv).

Better arguments can be made for cuts at the end of 3.6 – Kent's meditation on the sleeping king and Edgar's soliloquy – than for the omission of the mock trial. The argument for swiftly juxtaposing events in 3.6 with those in 3.7 is more pertinent here; moreover, the sense of urgency in Gloucester's begging the group to flee is enhanced. The effect of the Fool's last line, 'And I'll go to bed at noon', added in F, is not diluted by Kent's urging him to help carry Lear off. On the contrary, by ignoring the Fool, Kent and the others allow him to remain isolated and alone, overwhelmed by everything that has happened and now utterly spent.

Edgar's sententious closing soliloquy is also, in a more obvious sense, dispensable. As Granville-Barker says, the lines lower the dramatic tension and thus may adversely affect the following scene of Gloucester's blinding. The soliloquy is better postponed to the beginning of Act 4, especially if an act-interval comes at that point. Michael Warren has shown, moreover, that the omission of these lines paradoxically enhances Edgar's role, giving his opening soliloquy in 4.1, expanded in F, greater prominence. This prominence gains further by the deletion of the servants' dialogue at the end of 3.7. Indeed, Warren shows how other alterations in F affecting Edgar's role significantly change it in ways that traditionally conflated editions obscure ('Albany and Edgar', pp. 103–4; compare xxiv, p. 276 below, on the cut at 5.3.195). Furthermore, there appears to be in F a consistent pattern in reducing the passages of moral commentary found in Q. Altogether, these alterations suggest revision as well as theatrical abridgement.

(xii) After 3.7.97 (see Appendix, p. 300 below, xv).

F's omission of the servants' dialogue (nine lines) reduces the number of minor speaking parts, hurries the action to the next scene, and, like the omission of Edgar's soliloquy in 3.6, eliminates reflective commentary (see Doran, pp. 71, 77; Stone, p. 236). Moreover, as Urkowitz notes, p. 51, the servant's plan (to get Tom o'Bedlam to help Gloucester) conflicts with what actually happens in 4.1: the Old Man enters leading the earl, and the meeting with Poor Tom is accidental and in many ways ironic. If an interval was inserted at this point between Acts 3 and 4, the effect achieved in Q of juxtaposing Edgar's entrance and the compassion of the servants would be nullified, as Williams says; hence, the loss of their dialogue is of less consequence. But Granville-Barker, p. 331, regards the piece of dialogue as 'significant' and worth retaining.

(xiii) After 4.1.58:

> *Edg.* Both ſtile and gate, horſe-way, and foot-path,
> Poore *Tom* hath beene ſcard out of his good wits,
> Bleſſe the good man from the foule fiend,
> [Fiue fiends haue beene in poore *Tom* at once,
> Of luſt, as *Obidicut*, *Hobbididence* Prince of dumbnes,
> *Mahu* of ſtealing, *Modo* of murder, *Stiberdigebit* of
> Mobing, & *Mobing* who ſince poſſeſſes chamberinaids
> And waiting women, ſo, bleſſe thee maiſter.]

Edgar's identity as Poor Tom is by now well established and does not require further ravings of the kind extensively presented in Act 3; or, as Stone says, 'the reviser probably felt there was more in this speech than was dramatically justified' (p. 236).

(xiv) After 4.2.33 (see Appendix, pp. 301–3 below, xvii–xix).

Theatrical abridgement may have prompted the extensive cuts from Albany's and Gonerill's quarrel in this scene, but combined with the cuts, additions, and alterations elsewhere (see above, pp. 77–9), they seriously affect the ethos of these characters and suggest authorial revision. Several local emendations in the Folio text, especially at the entrance of Albany, tend to confirm this view.

(xv) After Act 4, Scene 2 (see Appendix, pp. 304–6 below, xx).

Theatrical abridgement again probably occasioned an extensive cut (56 lines) of expository but inessential material – an entire scene (see above, p. 82, and compare Doran, p. 70; Duthie, p. 8). The cut, however, along with other cuts in Acts 4 and 5, reduces the role of Kent and helps bring Edgar and Cordelia into greater prominence (Warren, 'Diminution', pp. 66–8). It also reduces the amount of moral commentary found in Q. Removing the scene resolves several dramatic problems, such as questions regarding Lear's actual whereabouts and his attitude towards Cordelia (Urkowitz, pp. 53–4). Compare Granville-Barker, p. 332: 'I could better believe that Shakespeare cut [the scene] than wrote it.'

(xvi) After 4.5.188:

Q: *Lear.* No feconds, all my felfe, why this would make a man
of falt to vfe his eyes for garden waterpots,⌊I and laying Autumns
duft.
    Lear.⌋I will die brauely like a bridegroome, what ? I will be
Iouiall, come, come, I am a King my maifters, know you that.
   Gent. You are a royall one, and we obey you.
   Lear. Then theres life int, nay and you get it you fhall get it
with running.   *Exit King running.*

Q2:   *Lear.* No feconds, all my felfe : why this would make a man
of falt to vfe his eyes for garden water-pottes, I and laying Autumnes duft.   *Gent.* Good Sir.
   Lear. I will dye brauely like a Bridegroome. What, I will bee
iouiall : Come, come, I am a King my mafters, know you that ?
   Gent. You are a royall one, and we obey you.
   Lear. Then theres life int, nay if you get it you fhall get it
with running.   *Exit King running.*

F: *Lear.* No Seconds ? All my felfe?
Why, this would make a man, a man of Salt
To vfe his eyes for Garden water-pots. I wil die brauely,
Like a fmugge Bridegroome. What ? I will be Iouiall :
Come, come, I am a King, Mafters, know you that ?
   Gent. You are a Royall one, and we obey you.
   Lear. Then there's life in't. Come, and you get it,
You fhall get it by running : Sa, fa, fa, fa.   *Exit.*

At first, Greg rejected Daniel's conjecture that the anomalous Q2 insertion may derive from a variant, corrected state of sheet 1 (no longer extant) in the exemplar of Q that served as copy for Q2 (*Variants*, pp. 188–90). Later he reluctantly reconsidered the possibility (Postscript, in *ibid.*, p. 192). Whether or not the Gentleman's speech originally stood in the copy for Q remains uncertain, since a press-corrector, seeing the error in two consecutive speeches by Lear, could have added it independently of copy; or the Q2 compositor could have added it (for the same reason). But either of these hypotheses seems less likely than that it was in the original manuscript. F was not here influenced by Q2. Working on an exemplar of Q with uncorrected sheet 1, the F reviser or collator solved the problem of Lear's consecutive speeches by fusing them, but left the lines metrically irregular. (See Commentary 4.5.186–91 and compare Taylor, 'Date and authorship', pp. 363–4, and Duthie, pp. 415–16.) Stone, p. 236, believes the reviser omitted the line after 188 because he found it obscure.

(xvii) After 4.5.257:

Q: your labour, your wite(fo I would fay)your affectionate feruant
⌈and for you her owne for *Venter*⌉*Gonoril.*
   Edg. O Indiftinguifht fpace of womans wit,

Q2:   *And supply the place for your labour.*
             Your wife (fo I would fay) & your affectionate feruant,
                                                    Goneril.

Edg. O vndiftinguifht fpace of womans wit,

F: *ply the place for your Labour.*
                     Your (Wife, fo I would fay) affectio-
                           nate Seruant. Gonerill.
          Oh indinguifh'd fpace of Womans will,

Both Q2 and F omit Q's words 'and for you her owne for *Venter*', perhaps because they
were incomprehensible (Stone, pp. 132, 146). Duthie, p. 416, regards Q's words as an
actor's mangled interpolation; citing 4.2.20, Muir thinks the words may conceal sense;
Halio, p. 162, suspects that a word such as 'life' may have dropped out after 'owne' in
Q. Unlike xvi above, the passage appears on variant sheet K but is found in all extant
copies of Q. The different emendations in Q2 and F suggest that both the Q2 editor or
compositor and the F reviser or collator independently deleted the nonsense line.

(xviii) After 4.6.25:

Gent. Good madam be by, when we do awake him
I doubt not of his temperance.
[*Cord.* Very well.
[*Doct.* Pleafe you draw neere, louder the muficke there,]
  Cor. O my deer father reftoratiõ hang thy medicin on my lips,
And let this kis repaire thofe violent harmes that my two fifters
Haue in thy reuerence made.
    Kent. Kind and deere Princeffe,
Cord. Had you not bene their father thefe white flakes,
Had challengd pitie of them, was this a face

To be expofd againſt the warring winds,
[To ſtand againſt the deepe dread bolted thunder,
In the moſt terrible and nimble ſtroke
Of quick croſſe lightning to watch poore *Perdu*,
With this thin helme,]mine iniurious dogge,
Though he had bit me, ſhould haue ſtood that night
Againſt my fire, and waſt thou faine poore father,

The first cut may have been prompted by changed playhouse conditions (see above, p. 83). However, music in Shakespeare often accompanies scenes of restored harmony, as in *MND* 5.1.395–400, *MV* 5.1.55 ff., *WT* 5.3.98. Perhaps on reflection Shakespeare now preferred silence at Lear's awakening (Taylor, 'Date and authorship', p. 413). The second cut of three and a half inessential though eloquent lines results in an irregular line caused, as Stone thinks, by a reviser's oversight and the copyist's subsequent attempt to avoid an obviously short line (p. 118, n. 10; see the play-text, p. 237 above).

(xix) After 4.6.78:

Doſt. Be comforted good Madame, the great rage you ſee is cured in him,[and yet it is danger to make him euen ore the time hee has loſt,]defire him to goe in, trouble him no more till further ſetling.' *Cord.* Wilt pleafe your highnes walke?

Duthie, pp. 419–20, suspects that the F compositor (B) is responsible for dropping these lines through eye-skip or faulty comprehension (compare Stone, p. 236). But considerable cutting follows afterwards (see below) and the alteration F 'killed' for Q 'cured' suggests revision, although the verse lines in F (see the play-text, p. 240 above) remain irregular.

(xx) After 4.6.82 (see Appendix, p. 307 below, xxiv).

F omits a dozen lines of dialogue here between Kent and the Gentleman, a cut 'precisely analogous' to those at the end of 3.6 and 3.7 (Stone, p. 237). The dialogue is about Cornwall's death, Kent's supposed whereabouts (he is still in disguise), and the impending battle between Cordelia's army and her sisters'. Urkowitz, pp. 54–5, notes how the elimination of these lines juxtaposes more sharply contrasting stage pictures: the 'gentle pageant of physical and familial restoration' that ends 4.6 and 'the harsh conjunction of authority and violence' that begins 5.1. But again, if an interval was inserted between the acts, this effect would be lost, or at least diminished. The deletion, however, obviates a potential inconsistency: Cordelia addresses Kent at the beginning of the scene in the presence of the Gentleman, who in the missing lines apparently does not know whom she is addressing.

(xxi) After 5.1.11:

Reg. But haue you neuer found my brothers way,
To the forfended place?   [*Baſt.* That thought abuſes you.
Reg. I am doubtfull that you haue beene coniunct and bo-
ſom'd with hir, as far as we call hirs.]
    Baſt. No by mine honour Madam.   (with her.
    Reg. I neuer ſhall indure hir, deere my Lord bee not familiar
    Baſt. Feare me not, ſhee and the Duke her husband.
        Enter Albany and Gonorill with troupes.
[*Gono.* I had rather looſe the battaile, then that ſiſter ſhould
looſen him and mee.]
    Alb. Our very louing ſiſter well be-met
For this I heare the King is come to his daughter
With others, whome the rigour of our ſtate
Forſt to crie out, [where I could not be honeſt
I neuer yet was valiant, for this buſines
It touches vs, as *France* inuades our land
Not bolds the King, with others whome I feare,
Moſt iuſt and heauy cauſes make oppoſe.
    Baſt. Sir you ſpeake nobly.]   *Reg.* Why is this reaſon'd *!*
    Gono. Combine togither gainſt the enemy,
For theſe domeſtique dore particulars
Are not to queſtion here.
    Alb. Let vs then determine with the auntient of warre on our
proceedings.   [*Baſt.* I ſhall attend you preſently at your tent.]
    Reg. Siſter you I goe with vs ?   *Gon.* No.
    Reg. Tis moſt conuenient, pray you goe with vs.
           K 3   *Gon*

Stone, p. 237, regards these cuts as 'deliberate pruning', as in 2.2 and 4.2, although
he recognises that the last one may be the result of copyist or compositor error. The
most significant cut is the longest one, where Albany says he will fight because the
French invade, not because he opposes Lear. Without these lines, Albany in F appears
less sure of his stance – a weakening of his character that correlates with cuts earlier in
Act 4 (see above). When Regan interrupts him impatiently, her line means something
different in F from what it means in Q, where she questions why Albany is moralising
over a decision already made; in F, she asks why he is raising a new issue (Urkowitz,
p. 99). The earlier cuts remove some slackness and gratuitous comment from the
dialogue.

(xxii) After 5.3.35:

Baſt. About it, and write happy when thou haſt don,
Marke I ſay inſtantly, and carie it ſo
As I haue ſet it downe.
    Cap. [I cannot draw a cart, nor eate dride oats,
If it bee mans worke ile do't.

The Captain's lines are a distracting and unnecessary bit of grim humour. Compare Stone, p. 237.

(xxiii) After 5.3.53:

> *Baſt.* Sir I thought it ſit,
> To ſend the old and miſerable King to ſome retention, and ap-
> Whoſe age has charmes in it,whoſe title more, (pointed guard,
> To pluck the common boſſome of his ſide,
> And turne our impreſt launces in our eyes
> Which doe commaund them,with him I ſent the queen
> My reaſon,all the ſame and they are readie to morrow,
> Or at further ſpace, to appeare where you ſhall hold
> Your ſeſſion at this time, wee ſweat and bleed,
> The friend hath loſt his friend and the beſt quarrels
> In the heat are curſt, by thoſe that foele their ſharp nes,
> The queſtion of *Cordelia* and her father
> Requires a fitter place.]
> *Alb.* Sir by your patience,
> I hold you but a ſubiect of this warre,not as a brother.

Edmond's speech in F (properly lined: see the play-text, pp. 247–8 above) is sufficient to justify his action; in Q, the speech continues beyond the point of impertinence. Albany's response is appropriate with or without the deleted lines, which are largely reflective and sententious. Compare Urkowitz, p. 107; Stone, p. 238.

(xxiv) After 5.3.195 (see Appendix, p. 309 below, xxxi).

F's omission of Edgar's seventeen lines describing his meeting with Kent does more than reduce the inexplicable delay between Edmond's announced intention to do some good and the actual attempt to save Lear and Cordelia. It also modifies the role of Edgar as 'the immature, indulgent man displaying his heroic tale of woe' in the face of Albany's desire not to hear anything 'more woeful'. Edgar thus emerges as a man worthier of the responsibility that becomes his at the close, certainly as F fashions it (Warren, 'Albany and Edgar', p. 104). The omission of these lines, moreover, more sharply juxtaposes the pathos of Gloucester's death with the deaths of Gonerill and Regan. Theatrical abridgement may have been a major motive in the cut, but artistic considerations were clearly involved as well.

F-only passages

F-only passages are essentially of two kinds: (1) passages restored to the text that were accidentally omitted from Q; (2) passages that could not have been accidentally omitted from Q and must have been added by a reviser. The first kind would have appeared in the original prompt-book along with a number of alternative manuscript readings (Doran, pp. 38–52); the other kind might have appeared there, if revision was early, or in the second playhouse manuscript (the result of collation with revised Q), if revision came later. Accidental omissions in Q usually involve passages of a line or two; more extensive F-only passages are most likely additions to the original text. In the passages reproduced below, F-only lines are marked by brackets.

(xxv) After 1.1.36 (see above, pp. 77–9).

(xxvi) After 1.1.59:

> *Lear.*Of all thefe bounds euen from this Line,to this,
> With fhadowie Forreſts,and with Champains rich'd
> With plenteous Riuers,and wide-skirted Meades
> We make thee Lady. To thine and *Albanies* iſſues
> Be this perpetuall. What ſayes our ſecond Daughter?

These words may have stood in the original manuscript but the Q compositor accidentally skipped from 'and' in 59 to 'and' in 60 (Doran, p. 57). Revisions at the beginning of the play, however, tend to be more frequent and fussy than they are elsewhere, and this could be a genuine addition (Stone, p. 239).

(xxvii) After 1.1.82:

> Q: Then that confirm'd on *Generill*,but now our ioy,
> Although the laſt,not leaſt in our deere loue,
> What can you ſay to win a third, more opulent
> Then your ſiſters.
>   *Cord.* Nothing my Lord.   (againe.
>   *Lear.* How, nothing can come of nothing, ſpeake
>   *Cord.* Vnhappie that I am, I cannot heaue my heart into my
> mouth,I loue your Maieſtie according to my bond,nor more nor
> leſſe.
>   *Lear.* Goe to,goe to,mend your ſpeech a little,
> Leaſt it may mar your fortunes,

> F: Then that confeir'd on *Generill.* Now our Ioy,
> Although our laſt and leaſt ; to whoſe yong loue,
> The Vines of France, and Milke of Burgundie,
> Striue to be intereſt. What can you ſy, to draw
> A third, more opilent then your Siſters? ſpeake.
>   *Cor.* Nothing my Lord.
>   *Lear.* Nothing ?
>   *Cor.* Nothing.
>   *Lear.* Nothing will come of nothing,ſpeake againe.
>   *Cor.* Vnhappie that I am,I cannot heaue
> My heart into my mouth:I loue your Maieſty
> According to my bond,no more nor leſſe.
>   *Lear.* How,how *Cordelia?*Mend your ſpeech a little,
> Leaſt you may marre your Foitunes.

Besides additions, other alterations in F clearly indicate revision here. The additions not only make Cordelia's response emphatic, they provide the actor playing Lear with space for further reaction.

(xxviii) 1.2.96–100:

> *Glou.* Thefe late Eclipfes in the Sun and Moone por-
> tend no good to vs : though the wifedome of Nature can
> reafon it thus, and thus, yet Nature finds it felfe fcourg'd
> by the fequent effects. Loue cooles, friendfhip falls off,
> Brothers diuide. In Cities, mutinies ; in Countries, dif-
> cord ; in Pallaces, Treafon ; and the Bond crack'd, 'twixt
> Sonne and Father. ⌈This villaine of mine comes vnder the
> prediction; there's Son againft Father, the King fals from
> by as of Nature, there's Father againft Childe. We haue
> feene the heft of our time. Machinations, hollowneffe,
> treacherie, and all ruinous diforders follow vs difquietly
> to our Graues.⌉ Find out this Villain, *Edmond*, it fhall lofe
> thee nothing, do it carefully : and the Noble & true-har-
> ted Kent banifh'd ; his offence, honefty.'Tis ftrange. *Exit*

An unlikely though not impossible accidental omission from Q (Doran, p. 58), these lines complement the cut later on at 1.2.125. See above, pp. 265–6; Stone, p. 239; and Taylor, 'Censorship', pp. 81–8.

(xxix) 1.2.139–44:

> Q: *Edg.* Some villaine hath done me wrong.
> *Baft.* Thats my feare brother, I aduife you to the beft, goe
> arm'd, I am no honeft man if there bee any good meaning to-
> wards you, I haue told you what I haue feene & heard, but faint-
> ly, nothing like the image and horror of it, pray you away {

> F: *Edg.* Some.Villaine hath done me wrong.
> *Edm.* That's my feare, ⌈I pray you haue a continent
> forbearance till the fpeed of his rage goes flower : and as
> I fay, retire with me to my lodging, from whence I will
> fitly bring you to heare my Lord fpeake : pray ye goe,
> there's my key : if you do ftirre abroad goe arm'd.
> ⌊*Edg.* Arm'd, Brother ?
> *Edm.*⌋ Brother, I aduife you to the beft, I am no honeft
> man, if ther oe any good meaning toward you: I haue told
> you what I haue feene, and heard : But faintly. Nothing
> like the image, and horror of it, pray fou away.

Stone, p. 240, and Doran, p. 63, agree that the omission from Q of the bracketed lines could hardly have been accidental. The different position of 'goe arm'd' in Q and F indicates a deliberate interpolation of matter not originally in Q.

(xxx) 1.4.217:

> *Enter Albany.*
> *Lear.* Woe, that too late repents:
> Is it your will, speake Sir? Prepare my Horses.
> Ingratitude! thou Marble-hearted Fiend,
> More hideous when thou shew'st thee in a Child,
> Then the Sea-monster.
> [*Alb.* Pray Sir be patient.
>   *Lear.*] Detested Kite, thou lyest.
> My Traine are men of choice, and rarest parts,
> That all particulars of dutie know,
> And in the most exact regard, support
> The worships of their name. O most small fault,

Besides several local corrections and changing Q's prose to verse, F interpolates Albany's speech, which 'punctuates' Lear's tirade (Urkowitz, p. 44) and gives the duke something to say soon after his entrance (Stone, p. 240). See also p. 79 above.

(xxxi) 1.4.229:

> And added to the gall. O *Lear, Lear, Lear*!
> Beate at this gate that let thy Folly in,
> And thy deere Iudgement out. Go,go,my people.
> *Alb.* My Lord, I am guiltlesse, as I am ignorant
> [Of what hath moued you.]
> *Lear.* It may be so,my Lord.

Albany's additional half-line completes his meaning and was probably omitted accidentally by the Q compositor, who printed almost the entire scene as prose and omitted the third '*Lear*' in 225 as well.

(xxxii) 1.4.276–87 (see the play-text, p. 139 above).

Duthie, p. 378, believes that Gonerill's speech was cut in Q to shorten the play in performance and restored in F (compare Stone, pp. 76–80). But others, e.g. McLeod, find the F-only lines consistent with changes elsewhere in Gonerill's speeches (see above, p. 266). Other alterations also strongly suggest revision here; for example, Gonerill's interruption of her husband and her summons to Oswald (281–2) are changed from Q and result in metrical irregularity (see collation, and Doran, pp. 65–6).

(xxxiii) 2.4.19 (see above, pp. 267–8).

(xxxiv) 2.4.43–51:

> Your Sonne and Daughter found this trespasse worth
> The shame which heere it suffers.   (way,
> [*Foole.* Winters not gon yet,if the wil'd Geese fly that
> Fathers that weare rags, do make their Children blind,

Bur Fathers that beare bags,fhall fee their children kind.
Fortune that arrant whore,nere turns the key toth' poore.
But for all this thou ifhalt haue as many Dolors for thy
Daughters,as thou canft tell in a yeare.]
   Lear. Oh how this Mother fwels vp toward my heart!
*Hiftorica paffio,*downe thou climing forrow,

Stone, p. 241, says the Fool's lines are an obvious theatrical interpolation not in the style of the reviser and added as an afterthought. He suggests that F's faulty lineation is the result of the lines' being written sideways in the margin of the prompt-book, as an addition of such length would be. Doran, p. 66, and others find the lines consistent with Shakespeare's style for the Fool; but if the reference to 'wild geese' is an allusion to the Wildgoose family (see p. 4 above), then the addition was probably early. The Folio lineation, obviously crowded, may result from faulty casting-off of copy for signature rr1^r, set by Compositor E. Taylor, 'Date and authorship', p. 396, and Kerrigan, p. 220, argue for both authenticity and dramatic aptness; Granville-Barker remarks that the Fool's song alters the dramatic effect as Lear 'stands speechless, his agony upon him' (p. 329).

(xxxv) After 2.4.90:

Q: why *Glofter,Glofter,* id'e fpeake with the Duke of *Cornewal,*and
  his wife.
   Gloft. I my good Lord.
   Lear. The King would fpeak with *Cornewal,*the deare father
  Would with his daughter fp eake,commands her feruice,
  Fierie Duke, tell the hot Duke that *Lear,*
  No but not yet may be he is not well,

F: Fiery? What quality ? Why *Glofter.Glofter,*
  I'ld fpeake with the Duke of *Cornewall,*and his wife.
  [*Glo.* Well my good Lord,I haue inform'd them fo.
  Lear. Inform d them ? Do'ft thou vnderftand me man.]
  Glo. I my good Lord.
  Lear. The King would fpeake with *Cornwall,*
  The deere Father
  Would with his Daughter fpeake,commands,tends,fer-
  [Are they inform'd of this ? My breath and blood:] (uice,
  Fiery? The fiery Duke,tell the hot Duke that ——
  No,but not yet,may be he is not well,

Besides the additional lines, the passage shows other signs of revision. According to Stone, p. 241, the reviser must have thought Gloucester's behaviour in Q needed verbal extenuation. The additional lines 91–2 are complemented by the further addition at 96. On the other variants here, sec Commentary.

(xxxvi) 2.4.132–7 (see the play-text, p. 166 above).

Since Regan speaks in convoluted syntax, amplification of her meaning was probably felt to be necessary for Lear's benefit (and for that of the audience), as Stone suggests,

p. 242, although he does not believe the addition is Shakespeare's. But in discerning a professional rivalry between the original author and a reviser. Stone may miss the rhetorical and dramatic point of the passage, which is developed more fully by the addition.

(xxxvii) 2.4.289–90:

Q: *Duke.* So am I puspos'd,where is my Lord of *Gloster?*   *Enter Glo*
     Reg. Followed the old man forth,he is return'd.
     Glo. The King is in high rage, & wil I know not whe-
     Re. Tis good to giue him way,he leads himfelfe.(ther.
     Gon. My Lord,intreat him by no meanes to ftay.
     Glo. Alack the night comes on,and the bleak winds

F: *Enter Glofter.*
     Corn. Followed the old man forth,he is return'd.
     Glo. The King is in high rage.
     [*Corn.* Whether is he going ?
       Glo. He cals to Horfe,but will I know not whether.
       Corn. 'Tis beft to giue him way,he leads himfelfe.
       Gon. My Lord,entreate him by no meanes to ftay.
       Glo. Alacke the night comes on,and the high windes

Again, besides the added lines, other signs of revision appear here, such as reassigned speech headings and local emendations. A reviser may have noticed the hypermetrical line in Q and made two regular lines using interpolated matter, as Stone thinks, p. 242; on the other hand, the hypermetrical line could have been the result of an accidental omission that F either recovers or substitutes for.

(xxxviii) 3.1.14–21 (see p. 269 above).

(xxxix) 3.2.77–93 (see the play-text, pp. 181–2 above).

Like the Fool's additional lines in 2.4 (xxiv above), 'Merlin's Prophecy' is sometimes considered spurious. For long it was regarded as an interpolation by the actor who played the Fool, a bit of irrelevant nonsense, food for the groundlings, as Cowden Clarke suggested (cited by Furness, p. 179). More recently, however, the lines have been defended as not only Shakespearean, but relevant to both the dramatic context and the Fool's changed character in F (Kerrigan, pp. 221–6). They parody some pseudo-Chaucerian verses found in Thynne's edition of Chaucer (1532) cited by Puttenham, in slightly different form, in *The Arte of English Poesie* (1589), which Shakespeare was apparently reading at about the time he wrote *The Winter's Tale* (Taylor, 'Date and authorship', pp. 382–6). The addition reflects this later source and, while not indispensable, adds to the ironic use of prophecy found elsewhere in the play.

(xl) 3.4.17–18:

Q: Is it not as this mouth fhould teare this hand
    For lifting food to't, but I will punifh fure,
    No I will weepe no more, in fuch a night as this !
    O *Regan, Gonorill*, your old kind father   (lies,
    Whofe franke heart gaue you all, O that way madnes
    Let me fhun that, no more of that.

F: Is it not as this mouth fh ould teare this hand
       For lifting food too't ? But I will punifh home;
       No, I will weepe no more; in fuch a night,

       To fhut me out ? Poure on, I will endure:]
       In fuch a night as this ? O Regan, Gonerill,
       Your old kind Father, whofe franke heart gaue all,
       O that way madneffe lies, let me fhun that :
       No more of that.

Probably the lines not found in Q are the result of compositor eye-skip, caused by the repetition of 'in such a night' and making Q's lines irregular. Stone, however, suspects revision, since Lear cannot know at this point that he has, in fact, been 'shut out' of Gloucester's castle (p. 243), and other indications of revision appear here and elsewhere in the scene (see xli–xlii below).

(xli) 3.4.26–7:

    Kent. Good my Lord enter here.
    Lear. Prythee go in thy felfe, feeke thine owne eafe,
    This tempeft will not giue me leaue to ponder
    On things would hurt me more, but Ile goe in,
    [In Boy, go firft. You houfeleffe pouertie,   *Exit.*
    Nay get thee in; Ile pray, and then Ile fleepe.]
    Poore naked wretches, where fo ere you are
    That bide the pelting of this pittileffe ftorme,
    How fhall your Houfe-leffe heads, and vnfed fides.

While the lines not in Q may again be the result of accidental omission, eye-skip is less likely here. Both Stone, p. 244, and Urkowitz, p. 44, see a reviser's hand at work. The '*Exit*' added in F may be the book-keeper's notation.

(xlii) 3.4.37:

> Your lop'd,and window'd raggednesse defend you
> From seasons such as these ? O I haue tane
> Too little care of this : Take Physicke, Pompe,
> Expose thy selfe to feele what wretches feele,
> That thou maist shake the superflux to them,
> And shew the Heauens more iust.
>
>   *Enter Edgar,and Foole.*
>
> *Edg.* Fathom,and halfe,Fathom and halfe;poore *Tom.*
>   *Foole.* Come not in heere Nuncle,here's a spirit,helpe
> me,helpe me.
>   *Kent.* Giue me thy hand,who's there ?

Edgar's interpolated scream dramatically motivates the Fool's terrified re-entrance. F also adds a stage direction, although Edgar's actual emergence follows the Fool's a few lines later (see Commentary).

(xliii) 3.6.11–12:

> *Foole.* Prythee Nunkle tell me,whether a madman be
> a Gentleman,or a Yeoman.
>   *Lear.* A King,a King.
>   [*Foole.* No, he's a Yeoman, that ha's a Gentleman to
> his Sonne : for hee's a mad Yeoman that sees his Sonne a
> Gentleman before him.
>   *Lear.*] To haue a thousand with red burning spits
> Come hizzing in vpon 'em.

Doran, p. 67, supposes that the F-only lines are original and that the Q compositor had difficulty with the passage and deliberately omitted it. Stone, p. 67, and Kerrigan, pp. 227–30, consider the passage evidence of revision, Lear's response to the Fool's question having apparently been regarded as insufficient by the reviser. Kerrigan is sure the lines are Shakespeare's and allude to the dramatist's father, John, a yeoman, for whom his son obtained a grant from the College of Arms in 1596. In 1602, however, after John Shakespeare's death, the grant was challenged by York Herald Ralph Brooke, and possibly William had to justify his own claim (through his father) to the title 'gentleman' when he was writing or revising his play. But no evidence has been found to this effect and, as Kerrigan says, what happened to Brooke's complaint is not known. If the reviser intended a personal allusion, then (like xxxiv above) the addition – if it was one – was probably early.

(xliv) 3.6.41:

Q: *Lear*. Make no noife,make no noife,draw the curtains,fo,fo,fo,
    Weele go to fupper it'h morning,fo,fo,fo,   *Enter Glofter*.
    Glof. Come hither friend, where is the King my maifter.

F: *Enter Glofter*.
    Kent. Now good my Lord,lye heere,and reft awhile.
    Lear. Make no noife, make no noife, draw the Cur-
    taines : fo,fo,wee'l go to Supper i'th'morning.
    [*Foole*. And Ile go to bed at noone.]
    Glou. Come hither Friend :
    Where is the King my Mafter?

Taylor speculates that the Fool's last, cryptic line was an early addition, perhaps inserted in the original prompt-book. By the time rehearsals began, Shakespeare knew that the Fool's role ended here and may have decided to give him a suitable concluding line ('Date and authorship', p. 405). Other alterations, further evidence of revision, surround the line, which is susceptible to several interpretations (see Commentary). Stone, pp. 244–5, and Kerrigan, pp. 228–9, accept the line as an interpolation, though Stone questions its authenticity.

(xlv) 4.1.6–9:

                        Enter Edgar.
    Edg. Yet better thus,and knowne to be contemn'd,
    Then ftill contemn'd and flatter'd,to be worft :
    The loweft, and moft deiected thing of Fortune,
    Stands ftill in efperance, liues not in feare :
    The lamentable change is from the beft,
    The worft returnes to laughter. [Welcome then,
    Thou vnfubftantiall ayre that I embrace :
    The Wretch that thou haft blowne vnto the worft,
    Owes nothing to thy blafts.]
                    Enter Gloufter,and an Oldman.

The lines at first appear more like a deliberate cut in Q than an addition to F (Stone, p. 245). But they complement the omission of Edgar's lines at the end of 3.7 (see above, p. 271), improve the metre, and make Edgar more vulnerable to the shock of seeing his newly blinded father.

(xlvi) 4.1.54:

    Glou. Sirrah, naked fellow.
    Edg. Poore Tom's a cold.. I cannot daub it further.
    Glou. Come hither fellow.
    [*Edg*. And yet I muft :]
    Bleffe thy fweete eyes, they bleede.
    Glou. Know'ft thou the way to Douer?

Edgar's half-line completes the sense of 'I cannot daub it further' and regularises the line metrically. Its omission in Q may be accidental, or its appearance in F may be a consequence of the correction 'daub' for Q 'dance'. Note also the cut after 58 (see above, p. 271).

(xlvii) 4.2.27:

Q: *Baſt.* Yours in the ranks of death.   (are dew
   Gon. My moſt deer *Gloſter,*to thee a womans ſeruices
  A foole vſurps my bed.
   Stew. Madam, here comes my Lord.   *Exit Stew.*
   Gon. I haue beene worth the whiſtling. (rude wind
   Alb. O *Gonoril,*you are not worth the duſt which the

F: *Baſt.* Yours in the rankes of death.   *Exit.*
   Gon. My moſt deere Gloſter.

  [Oh, the difference of man, and man,]
  To thee a Womans ſeruices are due,
  My Foole vſurpes my body.
    Stew. Madam, here come's my Lord.
          Enter Albany.
   Gon. I haue beene worth the whiſtle.
   Alb. Oh Gonerill,
  You are not worth the duſt which the rude winde

Gonerill's added line appears to be part of extensive Folio correction and revision in this scene (see above, p. 271, and Commentary). In Q, Gonerill's line is unnecessary, since she apparently addresses Edmond (whose exit is missing); but in F, Edmond leaves, and Gonerill comments to herself. Compare Stone, p. 245; Taylor, 'Date and authorship', p. 379.

(xlviii) 4.5.157–62:

rough tatter'd cloathes great Vices do appeare: Robes,
and Furr'd gownes hide all. [Place ſinnes with Gold, and
the ſtrong Lance of Iuſtice, hurtleſſe breakes: Arme it in
ragges, a Pigmies ſtraw do's pierce it. None do's offend,
none, I ſay none, Ile able 'em; take that of me my Friend,
who haue the power to ſeale th'accuſers lips,] Get thee
glaſſe-eyes, and like a ſcuruy Politician, ſeeme to ſee the
things thou doſt not. Now, now, now, now. Pull off my

Stone, pp. 68, 122, and Doran, p. 68, agree that the F-only lines are an interpolation, since 'Get thee glasse eyes' naturally follows from 'hide all'. Chambers, I, 467, believes the lines were cut from Q because of censorship, but censorship would hardly affect foul papers. Roger Warren, p. 52, cites these lines as complementing the omission of the mock trial in 3.6. The passage shows other signs of correction and revision (see collation). Stone, pp. 123–5, sees an allusion in the lines to the Overbury affair (1613–16), but Taylor rejects the allusion on grounds that the lines are too general and commonplace; he compares *Ham.* 3.3.57–60 ('Date and authorship', p. 403).

(xlix) 4.6.59:

Q: *Lear.* Pray doe not mocke,
 I am a very foolifh fond old man,
 Fourefcore and vpward, and to deale plainly
 I feare I am not in my perfect mind,
 Met thinks I fhould know you, and know this man;

F: *Lear.* Pray do not mocke me:
 I am a very foolifh fond old man,
 Fourefcore and vpward,
 [Not an houre more, nor leffe:]
 And to deale plainely,
 I feare I am not in my perfect mind.
 Me thinkes i fhould know you, and know this man,

Lear's nonsense line seems more like an interpolation than an accidental omission from Q. Compare the later augmentation at 68, Cordelia's 'I am: I am'.

(l) 5.2.11:

Glo. No further Sir, a man may rot euen heere.
Edg. What in ill thoughts againe ?
Men muft endure
Their going hence, euen as their comming hither,
Ripeneffe is all come on.
 [*Glo.* And that's true too.]   *Exeunt.*

Gloucester's final half-line may have been dropped by the Q compositor, whose page (K4^r) shows signs of crowding; or it may have been added in F by a reviser concerned to fill out the line (Stone, p. 247) and/or intent upon augmenting the play's 'complementarity': see Commentary.

(li) 5.3.70:

Rega. Lady I am not well, elfe I fhould anfwere
From a full flowing ftomack. Generall,
Take thou my Souldiers, prifoners, patrimony,
[Difpofe of them, of me, the walls is thine:]
Witneffe the world, that I create thee heere
My Lord, and Mafter.

'Very possibly an accidental omission from Q' (Stone, p. 246).

(lii) 5.3.83–4:

Q: And I her husband contradict the banes,
     If you will mary, make your loue to me,
     My Lady is befpoke, thou art arm'd Glofter,
     If none appeare to proue vpon thy head,
     Thy hainous,manifeft,and many treafons,
     There is my pledge, ile proue it on thy heart

F: And I her husband contradict your Banes.
     If you will marry,make your loues to me,
     My Lady is befpoke.
        Gon. An enterlude.]
      Alb. Thou art armed Glefter,
     [Let the Trmpet found :]
     If none appeare to proue vpon thy perfon,
     Thy heynous,manifeft, and many Treafons,
     There is my pledge : Ile ma ke it on thy heart

F's additions are obviously interpolated. Gonerill's half-line provides 'dramatic punctuation' (compare xxx, p. 279 above, 1.4.217; and Stone, p. 246). The addition to
Albany's speech underscores the duke's eagerness for confrontation with Edmond
(compare Urkowitz, pp. 109–11). The passage contains other indications of revision (e.g. F 'person'/Q 'head'; F 'make'/Q 'prove'), which appear throughout the
scene.

(liii) 5.3.134:

Q: Baft. In wifdome I fholud aske thy name,
     But fince thy outfide lookes fo faire and warlike,
     And that thy being fome fay of breeding breathes,
     By right of knighthood,I difdaine and fpurne
     Heere do I toffe thofe treafons to thy head.
     With the hell hatedly, oreturnd thy heart,

F: Baft. In wifedome I fhould aske thy name,
     But fince thy out-fide lookes fo faire and Warlike,
     And that thy tongue(fome fay) of breeding breathes,
     [What fafe,and nicely I might well delay,]
     By rule of Knight-hood,I difdaine and fpurne.
     Backe do I toffe thefe Treafons to thy head,
     With the hell-hated Lye,ore-whelme thy heart,

Stone, pp. 68–9, believes F's additional line and other alterations are the result of
a misprint in Q at the beginning of 135, 'By' for 'My'. Failing to detect the error
(after substituting 'tongue' for 'being' at 133), the reviser recognised that 'disdaine and
spurne' required an object; hence, he added a new line and changed 'right' to 'rule' to
make the phrase more idiomatic. Alterations in other lines also show revision as well as
correction.

(liv) 5.3.256:

Q: *Kent.* If Fortune brag'd of two fhe loued or hated,
One of them we behold.   *Lear.* Are not you *Kent?*
Kent. The fame your feruant *Kent*,where is your feruant *Caius*,
Lear. Hees a good fellow, I can tell that,
Heele ftrike and quickly too, hees dead and rotten.

F: *Kent.* If Fortune brag of two,fhe lou'd and hated,
One of them we behold.
     Lear. [This is a dull fight]are you not *Kent* ?
     Kent. The fame : your Seruant *Kent*,
Where is your Seruant *Caius* ?
     Lear. He's a good fellow,I can tell you that,
He'le ftrike and quickly too,he's dead and rotten.

Lear's added half-line helps improve the metre. The Q compositor, nearing the end of his copy and obviously crowding his text (as the last three pages of Q reveal), may have omitted the speech deliberately. Compare Stone, p. 247.

(lv) 5.3.284–5 (see above, p. 81).

The additions together with other alterations undoubtedly indicate revision, an attempt to improve dramatically the play's final moments (Stone, p. 247). Certainly they change the ending, as Clayton notes, pp. 129, 133–7.

Conclusions

The weight of the evidence clearly indicates that F represents a revised text of *King Lear*, with Q reflecting a version of the original. Only a few, short omissions from Q and F can be attributed to compositor errors. In revising, very likely more than one motive and possibly more than one hand were involved over the period of time (seventeen years) that separates the date of first composition from the date of publication of the Folio text. Several of the largest omissions from the Q text – those after 3.6.13, 3.7.97, 4.6.82, 5.3.195, and a whole scene in Act 4 – may be the result of theatrical shortening, but it is by no means clear that Shakespeare did not have any responsibility for them. The remaining cuts often involve other alterations that point to a reviser's hand at work. Similarly, the F additions are usually, though not always, the result of deliberate interpolation, not accidental omission from Q. On stylistic grounds, Shakespeare remains the leading candidate for the authorship of the additions, which often mesh well with other changes in the Q text. Although Stone has proposed Philip Massinger as the reviser, Foster and Taylor have argued that he was not (his involvement with the King's Men as a reviser of old plays notwithstanding) and that Shakespeare was.

The Folio text, then, presents a version of *King Lear* that was performed in the early seventeenth century, first at the Globe and at court, and afterwards at the Blackfriars and probably again at court in revised form (or forms). The instability not only of Shakespeare's texts, but of any play-text, is notorious. Compare the sample from the script of Tennessee Williams's *The Rose Tattoo* used during its original try-out in

Chicago (illustration 16, overleaf) with the same lines in their final, printed form (illustration 17). Since one aim of this edition (as of the New Cambridge Shakespeare in general) is to emphasise Shakespeare's plays as *plays*, that is, scripts for performance, the choice of F as the copy-text for *King Lear* is both logical and appropriate. But as no definitive, 'final' text of the play does or can exist, what Shakespeare wrote in both Q and F is preserved. Unlike traditionally conflated texts, however, this edition removes Q-only passages from the text proper and presents them in an Appendix. By consulting those passages and taking careful note through the collation of the Folio additions and other alterations, the reader may reconstruct the quarto, whereas the main body of the text presents an acting version of *King Lear* that Shakespeare may have seen performed on one of the stages he was familiar with. The reader should thus not become confused about a text – Q + F – that is neither Shakespeare's nor the King's Men's, but a construct of modern conflating editors in the tradition of Alexander Pope and his contemporaries.

2-2-16

Bessie
Come on, come out! To the depot!

Flora
Just wait, I wanta hear this, it's too good to miss!

Serafina
I count up the nights, and I can tell you how many, each night
for twelve years, Four thousand! Three hundred! And eighty
nights that I had him, all night, all night in my arms! And
I am satisfied with it. I grieve for him - yes, my pillow at
night's never dry - But I'm satisfied to remember. And I
would feel cheap and degraded and not fit to live with my
daughter or under the roof with the urn of his blessed ashes,
those - ashes of a rose - if after that memory, after knowing
that man, I went to some other, some middle-aged man, not
young, not full of young passion, but getting a pot-belly on
him and losing his hair and smelling of sweat and liquor -
and trying to fool myself that that was love-making! I know
what love-making was. And I'm satisfied just to remember...
        (She is panting as though she had
        run upstairs)
Go on, you do it, you go on the streets and let them drop their
sacks of dirty water on you! - I'm satisfied to remember the
love of a man that was mine -

ONLY MINE! Never touched by the hand of nobody! Nobody but
me! - Just me!
        (She gasps and runs out to the porch.
        The sun floods her figure. It seems
        to astonish her. She finds herself
        sobbing. Digs in purse for handker-
        chief)

Flora
        (Crossing to open door)
Never touched by nobody?

Bessie
Let sleeping dogs lie!

Flora
Never nobody, nobody at all but you?

Bessie
Hush, now, Flora! Ignorance is bliss!

Flora
I know somebody that could a tale unfold! And not so far
from here neither. Not no further than the Square is, that
place on Esplanade!

16   A page from the original typescript of *The Rose Tattoo* by Tennessee Williams

THE ROSE TATTOO   ACT ONE

SERAFINA:

I count up the nights I held him all night in my arms, and
I can tell you how many. Each night for twelve years. Four
thousand—three hundred—and eighty. The number of
nights I held him all night in my arms. Sometimes I didn't
sleep, just held him all night in my arms. And I am satisfied with it. I grieve for him. Yes, my pillow at night's
never dry—but I'm satisfied to remember. And I would
feel cheap and degraded and not fit to live with my daughter or under the roof with the urn of his blessed ashes, those
—ashes of a rose—if after that memory, after knowing that
man, I went to some other, some middle-aged man, not
young, not full of young passion, but getting a pot belly on
him and losing his hair and smelling of sweat and liquor—
and trying to fool myself that *that* was love-making! I
know what love-making was. And I'm satisfied just to remember . . . [*She is panting as though she had run up-
stairs.*] Go on, you do it, you go on the streets and let them
drop their sacks of dirty water on you!—I'm satisfied to
remember the love of a man that was mine—*only mine!*
Never touched by the hand of *nobody! Nobody* but *me!*—
Just me! [*She gasps and runs out to the porch. The sun
floods her figure. It seems to astonish her. She finds herself
sobbing. She digs in her purse for her handkerchief.*]

   FLORA [*crossing to the open door*]:
Never touched by nobody?

   SERAFINA [*with fierce pride*]:
Never nobody but me!

   FLORA:
I know somebody that could a tale unfold! And not so far
from here neither. Not no further than the Square Roof is,
that place on Esplanade!

                                                        312

17   The same passage from *The Rose Tattoo* as it appears in the printed text

APPENDIX:
PASSAGES UNIQUE TO THE FIRST QUARTO

(i) After 1.2.85 ('such a monster') Q reads:

EDMOND   Nor is not, sure.
GLOUCESTER   To his father, that so tenderly and entirely loves him. Heaven and earth!

1 EDMOND . . . **sure** Edmond interrupts
Gloucester in mid sentence with an emphatic double negative.

(ii) After 1.2.125–6 ('I promise you, the effects he writes of succeed unhappily') Q reads:

    as of unnaturalness between the child and the parent, death, dearth, dissolutions
    of ancient amities, divisions in state, menaces and maledictions against king and
    nobles, needless diffidences, banishment of friends, dissipation of cohorts, nuptial
    breaches, and I know not what.
EDGAR   How long have you been a sectary astronomical?   5
EDMOND   Come, come,

2 amities] Q; armies Q2

3 **diffidences** distrusts, doubts.
3 **dissipation of cohorts** dispersal of military companies. NS suggests desertion and disease, 'a common fate of military bands' at that
time, but Shakespeare is doubtless anticipating
the dissolution of Lear's hundred knights, just as

'nuptial breaches' anticipates Gonerill's adultery
with Edmond.
5 **sectary astronomical** believer in astrology,
or student of it; 'sectary' appears in Florio's *Montaigne* (Muir).

(iii) After 1.3.16 Q reads (as prose):

    Not to be overruled. Idle old man,
    That still would manage those authorities
    That he hath given away! Now, by my life,
    Old fools are babes again, and must be used
    With checks as flatteries when they are seen abused.

1–5 Not . . . abused] *Theobald's lineation; as prose* Q

1 **Idle** Silly, foolish.
4 **Old . . . again** Compare Tilley M570: 'Old
men are twice children.'
4–5 **used . . . abused** i.e. we must use rebukes

as well as soothing words ('flatteries') with foolish
old men when they are deluded ('abused'; compare
4.6.50).

293

(iv) After 1.3.20 Q reads (as prose):

> I would breed from hence occasions, and I shall,
> That I may speak.

1–2 I . . . speak] *Capell's lineation; as prose* Q

1 **occasions** opportunities.

(v) After 1.4.117 Q reads (with first three lines also in F):

FOOL Dost thou know the difference, my boy, between a bitter fool and a sweet
    one?
LEAR No, lad; teach me.
FOOL   That lord that counselled thee
          To give away thy land,   5
       Come place him here by me,
          Do thou for him stand;
       The sweet and bitter fool
          Will presently appear,
       The one in motley here,   10
       The other found out there.
LEAR Dost thou call me fool, boy?
FOOL All thy other titles thou hast given away; that thou wast born with.
KENT This is not altogether fool, my lord.
FOOL No, faith; lords and great men will not let me. If I had a monopoly out, they   15
    would have part on't; and ladies too – they will not let me have all the fool to
    myself; they'll be snatching.

*1 thou] F; *not in* Q   *2 one] F; fool Q   4–11 That . . . there] *Capell's lineation; four lines ending . . . land, /* . . . stand,
/ . . . appeare, */* . . . there. Q   16 on't; and ladies] *Capell (subst.); an't, and Ladies* Q *corr.; an't, and lodes* Q *uncorr.;*
on't, and lodes Q2   16 all the] Q; all Q2

1–3 **Dost . . . me** These lines appear in F, but were probably intended to be cut along with the rest of this passage, with which they are clearly connected. See Textual Analysis, pp. 84–5 above.

1 **my boy** The Fool's term for Lear that Lear has just used for him (1.4.116).

4 **That lord** In *King Leir*, Skalliger advised the king, but no one advised Lear, who was apparently his own counsel (the implied point of 7).

4 **thee** Wiles, p. 191, says that the Fool here addresses his bauble, or *marotte*, and elsewhere uses his bauble thus to avoid directly addressing the king, as at 1.4.117.

6–7 **Come . . . stand** The Fool is stage-directing, moving characters around and using gestures. He has Lear stand for the counsellor.

10 **The one** i.e. the sweet fool; the Fool indicates himself.

11 **The other** i.e. the bitter fool.

11 **found out** discovered.

11 **there** The Fool points to Lear. Some edi-

tions, e.g. NS, place a dash before 'there' to make the emphasis clearer. 'In early 1606, it would have been hard not to see the Fool's jibe at Lear as a reflection of King James's own royal fool [Archie Armstrong] commenting on the folly of James himself' (Taylor, 'Censorship', p. 105).

13 **that . . . with** either (1) you are a born fool, or (2) folly is a universal human characteristic, i.e. something you can't give away (compare Hunter).

14 **altogether** entirely; but the Fool quibbles on the sense 'only', i.e. having all there is (Kittredge).

15 **out** officially granted. Like the slur implied at 11, this was also a possible cause for censorship: James I was notorious for awarding monopolies to court favourites.

16 **on't** i.e. of it.

16–17 **ladies . . . snatching** The Fool refers to his bauble, used to suggest a phallus. The indecent behaviour of court ladies was another sensitive issue.

(vi) After 1.4.190 Q reads (continuing 'Lear's shadow' as part of Lear's speech: see above, p. 75):

LEAR I would learn that, for by the marks of sovereignty, knowledge, and reason, I
  should be false persuaded I had daughters.
FOOL Which they will make an obedient father.

*1 SH] *Steevens; not in* Q *3 they] Q3; they,* Q, Q2

1 **that** i.e. who I am.
1–2 **for . . . daughters** i.e. every indication – the outward signs of majesty (e.g. my crown), as well as the information I have and my own reason – tells me that I have daughters. But that cannot be,

since no daughters would behave this way towards me.
 3 **Which** Whom. Compare Abbott 265 and 266, and 3.1.16.

(vii) After 2.2.128 ('not to do so') Q reads:

  His fault is much, and the good king, his master,
  Will check him for't. Your purposed low correction
  Is such as basest and contemned'st wretches
  For pilferings and most common trespasses
  Are punished with.   5

3–4 Is . . . trespasses] *Pope's lineation; divided . . .* pilfrings / And Q 3 basest] Q *corr.;* belest Q *uncorr.* *3 contemned'st] *Capell;* contaned Q *uncorr.;* temnest Q *corr.,* Q2

2 **check** rebuke. Compare (iii) above.
3 **contemned'st** most despised. Stone, p. 201, believes 'conte[m]ned' stood in Q copy. Greg thinks the press-corrector crossed out 'taned' in Q uncorr. 'contaned' and wrote 'temnest' in the margin, meaning the compositor to correct that half of the word only. Instead, he altered the entire word to

Q corr. 'temnest' (*Variants*, p. 159). While agreeing that this probably happened, Blayney (pp. 247–8) says that the proofreader's intention may not have been correct and proposes (like Stone) the emendation 'contemned', which Oxford accepts (in *The History of King Lear*).
4 **pilferings** petty thefts.

(viii) After 2.2.133 ('abused, assaulted') Q reads:

  For following her affairs. – Put in his legs.

(ix) After 2.4.17 ('I say, yea.') Q reads:

LEAR No, no, they would not.
KENT Yes, they have.

(x) After 3.1.7 ('That things might change or cease;') Q reads:

       tears his white hair,
  Which the impetuous blasts with eyeless rage

2 **eyeless** blind, undiscriminating.

Catch in their fury and make nothing of;
Strives in his little world of man to outstorm
The to-and-fro-conflicting wind and rain.   5
This night, wherein the cubdrawn bear would couch,
The lion and the belly-pinchèd wolf
Keep their fur dry, unbonneted he runs,
And bids what will take all.

---

*4 outstorm] out-storm *Muir* (*conj. Steevens*); outscorne Q   5 to-and-fro-conflicting] *Hyphenated Capell*   7 belly-pinchèd] *Hyphenated Pope*   8 fur] furre Q *corr.;* surre Q *uncorr.,* Q2

---

3 make nothing of disperse, make it disappear into nothingness.

4 little world of man i.e. the microcosm. Compare *Mac.* 1.3.140.

4 outstorm Steevens first proposed the emendation (an easy *t/c* misreading) and compared *A Lover's Complaint*, 7: 'Storming her world with sorrows wind and rain' (cited by Furness).

5 to-and-fro-conflicting i.e. wildly buffeting.

6 cubdrawn sucked dry by cubs, therefore ravenous. Kittredge compares *Arden of Feversham* 2.2.118–20: 'Such mercy as the staruen Lyones, / When she is dry suckt of her eager young, / Showes to the prey that next encounters her'. The image

of the udder-drawn lioness appears also in *AYLI* 4.3.114.

6 couch lie down (and not be out hunting). Compare the animals in Job's storm, Job 37.8: 'the beasts go into the denne, and remaine in their places' (Colie, p. 130).

8 unbonneted hatless ('a stronger idea then than now: totally abandoning self-respect as well as self-protection': Hunter). Compare xxii below.

9 bids . . . all A cry of desperation: let it all go, the whole world (compare 3.2.1–9). 'Take all!' was the gambler's cry when staking everything on a last throw of the dice; but compare *Ant.* 4.2.8.

(xi) After 3.1.21 ('but furnishings –') Q reads:

But true it is, from France there comes a power
Into this scattered kingdom, who already,
Wise in our negligence, have secret feet
In some of our best ports, and are at point
To show their open banner. Now to you: 5
If on my credit you dare build so far
To make your speed to Dover, you shall find
Some that will thank you making just report

2–6 Into . . . you] *Pope's lineation; lines end* . . . negligēce, [*turned under*] / . . . Ports, / . . . banner, / . . . farre, Q

The consistent though not perfect elimination in F of references to France as the invading power has led critics, e.g. Greg ('Time, place and politics in *King Lear*', *MLR*, 35 (1940), 431–46) and Doran, pp. 73–6, to suspect censorship. Taylor seriously questions that explanation ('Censorship', pp. 80–1). If censorship was not an issue, then motivation on dramatic and/or thematic grounds must explain F's alteration here and elsewhere. Shakespeare de-emphasises invasion by a foreign power in favour of Lear's rescue by his youngest daughter, Cordelia, whom he had rejected and cast out. Love, not politics, thus becomes central. See also Textual Analysis, p. 269 above.

1 power army.

2 scattered divided, broken up.

2 who i.e. the French.

3 Wise in our negligence Informed of our neglect (in making adequate defences).

3 have secret feet i.e. have secretly gained footholds.

4 at point in (armed) readiness. Compare 1.4.278.

6 my credit belief in me.

7 To As to.

8 making i.e. for making.

8 just accurate

Of how unnatural and bemadding sorrow
The king hath cause to plain.   10
I am a gentleman of blood and breeding,
And from some knowledge and assurance offer
This office to you.

12–13 And . . . you] *Jennens's lineation; divided . . . assurance, / Offer* Q

9 **bemadding** maddening.
10 **plain** complain.
13 **office** duty, commission.

(xii) After 3.6.14 ('Come hizzing in upon 'em') Q reads:

EDGAR   The foul fiend bites my back.
FOOL   He's mad that trusts in the tameness of a wolf, a horse's health, a boy's love,
    or a whore's oath.
LEAR   It shall be done; I will arraign them straight.
    [*To Edgar*] Come, sit thou here, most learnèd justicer.   5
    [*To the Fool*] Thou, sapient sir, sit here. – No, you she-foxes –
EDGAR   Look where he stands and glares! Want'st thou eyes at trial, madam?
    [*Sings*] Come o'er the bourn, Bessy, to me.
FOOL   [*Sings*]   Her boat hath a leak
        And she must not speak   10
        Why she dares not come over to thee.

2 health] Q; heels *Singer (conj. Warburton)*   5 SD] *Capell; not in* Q   5 justicer] *Theobald;* Iustice Q   6 SD] *Capell; not in* Q   6 No] Q; now Q2   7 Want'st] wantst Q2; wanst Q   7 eyes at trial, madam?] eies at tri- / all madam, Q2; eyes, at tral madam Q; eyes at troll-madam? *Oxford*   8 SD] *Hunter (conj. Staunton); not in* Q   8 Come . . . me] *As verse, Capell; as prose, continuing from 1* Q   *8 bourn] boorne *Capell;* broome Q   9 SD] *Craig (conj. Cam.); not in* Q   9–10 Her . . . speak] *Capell's lineation; one line* Q

On F's omission of the 'mock trial', see Textual Analysis, p. 270 above.

1 foul . . . back Compare 3.4.144. Tom imagines a lousy devil.

2 tameness of a wolf D. R. Klinck offers evidence that this phrase, like the ones that follow, is proverbial (*N&Q*, n.s. 24 (1977), 113–14).

2 horse's health Horses are notoriously given to disease. Warburton's conjectured emendation, 'heels' for 'health', is supported by the proverb, 'Trust not a horse's heels nor a dog's tooth' (Tilley H711), and by two citations that include analogues to 'whore's oath' (Dent, pp. 31, 140).

2 boy's love Compare 'Love of lads and fire of chats [= small twigs, kindling] is soon in and soon out' (Tilley L526; Dent, p. 161).

4 straight straightaway. Compare 1.3.21.

5 justicer judge. Theobald's emendation is generally accepted as improving the metre and is supported by 36 below, and by 4.2.48.

6 No Duthie accepts Q2 'Now' as 'obviously the required reading' (p. 399). But there is nothing

obvious about it, and many editions, e.g. Hunter, Oxford, retain Q.

7 he i.e. more likely an imagined 'fiend' than Lear. But compare 15 below.

7 Want'st . . . madam i.e. do you lack spectators at (your) trial, madam? Explaining Oxford's emendation, 'eyes at troll-madam', Taylor compares *WT* 4.3.87, 'troll-my-dames', from the French game 'trou-madame' (similar to bagatelle) played by ladies ('Addenda' to *Division*, pp. 486–8).

8 Come . . . me Edgar's fragment, which the Fool picks up, is from an old song recorded in W. Wager's *The Longer Thou Livest, the More Fool Thou Art* (*c.* 1559). Malone (cited by Furness) notes that 'Bessy' and 'poor Tom' may have been vagabond companions.

8 bourn burn, brook.

9–11 Her . . . thee These are not the words of the old song, but the Fool's bawdy improvisation (compare Partridge, pp. 76, 139–40, and *Temp.* 1.1.46–8).

EDGAR The foul fiend haunts poor Tom in the voice of a nightingale. Hoppedance
cries in Tom's belly for two white herring. Croak not, black angel! I have no food
for thee.

KENT How do you, sir? Stand you not so amazed.   15
Will you lie down and rest upon the cushions?

LEAR I'll see their trial first. – Bring in their evidence.
[*To Edgar*] Thou robèd man of justice, take thy place.
[*To the Fool*] And thou, his yoke-fellow of equity,
Bench by his side. [*To Kent*] You are o'th'commission;   20
Sit you too.

EDGAR Let us deal justly.
Sleepest or wakest thou, jolly shepherd?
Thy sheep be in the corn;
And for one blast of thy minikin mouth   25
Thy sheep shall take no harm.
Purr, the cat, is grey.

LEAR Arraign her first; 'tis Gonerill. I here take my oath before this honourable
assembly, she kicked the poor king her father.

FOOL Come hither, mistress. Is your name Gonerill?   30

LEAR She cannot deny it.

15–16 How . . . cushions] *Theobald's lineation; as prose* Q   ***16** cushions] Q2; cushings Q   **17–21** I'll . . . too] *Pope's
lineation; as prose* Q   **18** SD] *Capell; not in* Q   **18** robèd] *Pope;* robbed Q   **19** SD] *Capell; not in* Q   **20** SD] *Capell;
not in* Q   **20** o'th'] o'th Q2; ot'h Q   **22–6** Let . . . harm] *Theobald's lineation; all as prose* Q   ***27** cat,] *This edn;* cat
Q   ***29** she] Q2; *not in* Q

12 The foul . . . nightingale This is Tom's
witty response to the Fool. Rosenberg, p. 233, notes
the growing rivalry between the Fool and Edgar and
suggests a pun, 'foul' – 'fool'; compare 3.4.73 n.

12 Hoppedance 'Hoberdidance' or 'Haberdid-
ance' in Harsnett, pp. 49, 140, 180.

13 white herring fresh, unsmoked herring
(Kittredge).

13 Croak not Poor Tom is hungry, and his belly
rumbles. Exorcists 'would make a wonderful matter' of such 'croaking' (usually caused by fasting),
saying 'it was the deuill . . . that spake with the
voyce of a Toade' (Harsnett, pp. 194–5).

13 black angel i.e. the fiend in his belly.

15 amazed 'A very strong word, indicating a
state of utter confusion' (Kittredge, who compares
Ham. 2.2.565–6). Lear is dumb-founded, or perhaps tranced; compare 5.3.278 n.

16 cushions Duthie, p. 80, suspects that Q
'cushings', like Q 'Aurigular' (1.2.82), may reflect
popular pronunciation.

17 their evidence i.e. witnesses to testify
against them.

18 robèd . . . justice Lear takes Edgar's blanket
for judicial robes, imagining him as the Chief Justice, who presided over the Court of King's Bench
(compare NS).

18 take thy place Lear stage-directs, arranging

Edgar, the Fool, and Kent to sit as a judicial panel,
or 'commission' (20), to hear the trial.

19 yoke-fellow partner; i.e. the Lord Chancel-
lor, who presided over the Courts of Equity (NS).
At exceptional trials, e.g. of Mary Stuart, the Courts
of Justice and of Equity were combined, as Lear
imagines them here (Hunter).

20 Bench Sit on the bench (compare Abbott
290).

22 Let . . . justly Edgar begins sagaciously but
quickly resumes his mad act.

23–6 Sleepest . . . harm This pastoral ditty has
not been traced. Its modern analogue is 'Little Boy
Blue' (Hunter). Whether or not Edgar sings it is
unclear. Does he compete with the Fool in singing,
too? Oxford and Bevington add SD *Sings*, following
Capell, but Hunter does not. Compare 8 n.

25 minikin Either (1) dainty, sprightly (*OED* sv
adj 1a), or (2) shrill (*OED* sv *adj* 2).

27 Purr An apt name for a familiar in the form
of a cat; compare *Mac.* 1.1.8: 'I come, Graymalkin',
and 4.1.1, 'Purre' is the name of a 'fat devil' in
Harsnett, p. 50.

29 she Accidentally omitted by Q compositor
(Duthie, p. 400).

30 Come . . . Gonerill The Fool picks up a
stool and addresses it.

FOOL   Cry you mercy, I took you for a joint-stool.
LEAR   And here's another whose warped looks proclaim
          What store her heart is made on. – Stop her there!
          Arms, arms, sword, fire! Corruption in the place!   35
          False justicer, why hast thou let her 'scape?

---

*32 joint-stool] *Pope; ioyne stoole* Q; *ioynt stoole* Q2   *34 on] *Capell; an* Q

32 I . . . joint-stool A jocose apology for over-looking someone, as in Lyly's *Mother Bombie* 4.2.28 (compare Tilley M897). 'The Fool takes professional delight in this opportunity to give the worn-out phrase a point; for, in this case, the stool is there and Goneril is not' (Kittredge). But the Fool's joke also underscores the reality of the hallucination for Lear. As Granville-Barker suggested, the real and the imagined must carry equal value, so that what Lear feels intensely the audience also feels (Rosenberg, p. 234).

32 joint-stool A stool with fitted legs (as against a carpenter's rougher work). Duthie, p. 400, says Q 'ioyne' for 'ioynt' may be *t/e* misreading (compare Q2 'ioynt stoole'), but 'ioyne-stool' is an accepted seventeenth-century variant spelling (*OED*).

33 here's another Lear points to or grasps another piece of furniture. In the Granada television production, Olivier caught a hen, which then escaped, giving point to his later outcries (Bratton, p. 153). But note the pun on 'warped'.

33 warped (1) (of wood) twisted, (2) (of the face) distorted by evil passions (Kittredge).

34 store material, stuff.

34 Stop her there Mischievously trying to gain attention, the Fool may snatch the object away from Lear and hide it; or perhaps Lear drops it and the Fool takes it away. But the whole episode may be purely Lear's hallucination, evoking Edgar's 'Bless thy five wits' (3.6.15). Compare Rosenberg, pp. 234–5.

(xiii) After 3.6.53 ('Give thee quick conduct') Q reads:

KENT   Oppressed nature sleeps.
          This rest might yet have balmed thy broken sinews
          Which, if convenience will not allow,
          Stand in hard cure. – Come, help to bear thy master;
          Thou must not stay behind.   5

3–5 Which . . . behind] *Theobald's lineation; divided . . . cure,* / *Come* Q   4 cure. –] *This edn; SD To* Fool *Theobald*

2 balmed . . . sinews soothed your shattered nerves. For the analogy of nerves to 'sinews', Muir quotes from 'The Senses' in Sir John Davies's *Nosce Teipsum* (1599): 'Lastly, the feeling power which is life's root, / Through every living power itself doth shed / By sinews, which extend from head to

foot, / And like a net, all o'er the body spread.'

4 Stand in hard cure i.e. will be difficult to heal.

4–5 Come . . . behind Kent addresses the Fool who, exhausted, lags behind and may even be dying, as he does not appear again. See 3.6.41 n.

(xiv) After 3.6.53 ('Come, come away') Q reads:

EDGAR   When we our betters see bearing our woes,
           We scarcely think our miseries our foes.
           Who alone suffers, suffers most i'th'mind,

1–2 When . . . foes] Q2 *lineation; as prose* Q   *3 suffers, suffers most] *Theobald; suffers suffers, most* Q; *suffers, most* Q2

1 our woes i.e. miseries like ours.
3 Who . . . mind i.e. anguish is exacerbated mentally by isolation. NS compares *Lucrece*, 790:

'Fellowship in woe doth woe assuage', and Tilley C571 ('It is good to have company in misery').

Leaving free things and happy shows behind.
But then the mind much sufferance doth o'erskip,   5
When grief hath mates, and bearing, fellowship.
How light and portable my pain seems now,
When that which makes me bend makes the king bow.
He childed as I fathered. Tom, away!
Mark the high noises, and thyself bewray   10
When false opinion, whose wrong thoughts defile thee,
In thy just reproof repeals and reconciles thee.
What will hap more tonight, safe 'scape the king!
Lurk, lurk!

---

4 free i.e. free from trouble or suffering; care-free.

4 happy shows joyous sights.

5 sufferance suffering.

6 bearing suffering, endurance (syllepsis).

7 portable bearable.

9 He . . . fathered His experience of children is the same as mine of my father.

10 high noises rumours or events among the mighty. Compare 'noises' = rumours, *Tro.* 1.2.12; 'high' = mighty, *Ant.* 1.2.189–90.

10 bewray reveal.

12 In . . . reproof i.e. when the charges against you have been justly disproved or refuted; 'reproof' = disproof, refutation (compare *Cor.* 2.2.33).

12 repeals calls back into favour or honour (Onions).

12 reconciles i.e. to your former standing (with your father).

13 What . . . more Whatever else will happen.

13 safe . . . king may the king escape safely.

14 Lurk Lie hidden and in wait (Schmidt).

(xv) After 3.7.97 Q reads:

SECOND SERVANT   I'll never care what wickedness I do,
          If this man come to good.
THIRD SERVANT   If she live long
          And in the end meet the old course of death,
          Women will all turn monsters.
SECOND SERVANT   Let's follow the old earl and get the Bedlam   5
          To lead him where he would; his roguish madness
          Allows itself to anything.
THIRD SERVANT   Go thou. I'll fetch some flax and whites of eggs
          To apply to his bleeding face. Now, heaven help him!

          Exeunt

---

1 SH] *Capell; Seruant* Q   2, 8 SH] *Capell; 2 Ser.* Q   2–4 If she . . . monsters] *Theobald's lineation; as prose* Q   5 SH] *Capell; 1 Ser.* Q   *6 roguish] Q *uncorr.; not in* Q *corr.*   8–9 Go . . . him] *Theobald's lineation; as prose* Q   9 SD *Exeunt*] *Exit* Q; *Exeunt severally / Theobald*

---

1 SH SECOND Capell renumbered the servants to account for the one who died.

2 this man Cornwall.

2 she Regan.

3 meet . . . death i.e. die a natural death.

4 Women . . . monsters i.e. because they will not fear retribution.

5 the Bedlam Poor Tom.

6 roguish characteristic of vagrants (*OED* sv *adj* 1). Q corr.'s omission is probably an accident.

Perhaps the corrector, intending an alteration, crossed the word out and forgot to insert his emendation (Greg, *Variants*, p. 169). Compare Blayney, p. 250, who suggests that a deletion symbol, or what looked like one, somehow got into the Q uncorr. margin, resulting in false correction.

7 Allows . . . anything i.e. lets him do anything.

8 flax . . . eggs Sixteenth- and seventeenth-century medical books recommend this treatment for injured eyes.

(xvi) After 4.1.58 Q reads:

Five fiends have been in poor Tom at once: of lust, as Obidicut; Hobbididence, prince of dumbness; Mahu, of stealing; Modo, of murder; Flibbertigibbet, of mopping and mowing, who since possesses chambermaids and waiting-women. So, bless thee, master!

1–4 Five . . . master] *Pope; as verse, lines ending . . . once,* / *. . . dumbnes,* / *. . . Stiberdigebit of* / *. . . chambermaids* / *. . . maister.* Q *2 Flibbertigibbet] *Pope; Stiberdigebit* Q *3 mopping and mowing] *Theobald;* Mobing, & *Mohing* Q

The passage derives directly from Harsnett and was cut not only to shorten the play, but to remove the allusion to chambermaids, since the joke had probably been forgotten (Johnson).

1 **Five fiends** On multiple possession by devils, compare Harsnett, p. 141, where Maynie recalls the 'Maister-deuils' who were made to depart from him, taking the form of the Seven Deadly Sins.

1 **of lust** i.e. prince of lust (syllepsis). All the devils named are 'princes', not only Hobbididence.

1 **as** namely.

1 **Obidicut** 'The Prince of hel . . . Hoberdicut' (Harsnett, p. 119).

2–3 **Flibbertigibbet . . . mowing** A 'flibbertigibbet' is a flirt or frivolous creature (*OED* sv 1),

hence a good name for a demon that prompts affectations, such as grimacing and making faces ('mopping and mowing') (Kittredge). Harsnett, p. 136, uses the term 'mop and mow like an ape' in context with 'make antike faces, grinne'. The compositor got the spelling of 'Flibbertigibbet' wrong and has taken mowing (Q '*Mohing*') for another devil. Compare NS and Duthie, p. 404, who suspects that Q 'Mobing' may be a misreading for 'moking' (= mocking), which Oxford adopts. Compare also *Temp.* 3.3.82 SD, 4.1.47.

3 **since** i.e. since he left me.

3 **possesses chambermaids** In Harsnett, Sarah and Friswood Williams and Anne Smith, chambermaids, submitted to exorcism.

(xvii) After 4.2.33 ('Blows in your face') Q reads:

I fear your disposition:
That nature which condemns its origin
Cannot be bordered certain in itself.
She that herself will sliver and disbranch
From her material sap, perforce must wither   5
And come to deadly use.
GONERILL   No more, the text is foolish.
ALBANY Wisdom and goodness to the vile seem vile;
Filths savour but themselves. What have you done?

*2 its] Q3; it Q *uncorr.,* Q2; ith Q *corr.*

1 **fear** have fears concerning (Muir).

2 **its** Greg, *Variants*, pp. 172–3, believes that Q uncorr. 'it' is right, and Q corr. 'ith' wrong, but that the corrector's intention is unclear. Stone, p. 213, agrees that Q uncorr. is right and compares the genetive 'it' at 1.4.176. He does not press the comparison; the Fool there, after all, is using baby-talk. Thus it seems best to modernise the genetive.

3 **Cannot . . . itself** Cannot be certain of itself, i.e. know itself and its boundaries (hence, may be uncontrollable).

4–6 **She . . . use** That woman who will detach herself from the nourishing substance of her life and being must necessarily degenerate and die. The

image is of a branch broken off from its trunk that dries up and is used for firewood. Shaheen compares *King Leir* 1242–6, and especially John 15.6: 'If a man abide not in me, he is cast forth as a branche, and withereth: and men gather them, and cast them into the fire, and they burne.'

5 **material** substantial, essential.

6 **come . . . use** Muir, Hunter compare Hebrews 6.8; NS suspects a hint of hell-fire.

6 **text** (1) commentary, (2) passage of scripture; perhaps Gonerill anachronistically recognises the biblical allusion.

8 **savour** relish.

Tigers, not daughters, what have you performed?
A father, and a gracious agèd man,   10
Whose reverence even the head-lugged bear would lick,
Most barbarous, most degenerate, have you madded.
Could my good brother suffer you to do it?
A man, a prince, by him so benefited?
If that the heavens do not their visible spirits   15
Send quickly down to tame these vilde offences,
It will come.
Humanity must perforce prey on itself
Like monsters of the deep.

11 even] Q; *not in* Q2   14 benefited] Q *corr.;* benefflicted Q *uncorr.,* Q2; benefacted *Oxford*   16–17 Send . . . come]
Malone's lineation; one line (come *turned over*) Q   *16 these] *Jennens* (*conj. Heath*); the Q *uncorr.,* Q2; this Q *corr.*   16
vilde] Q2; vild Q; vile *Pope*   18–19 Humanity . . . deep] *Pope's lineation; one line* (the deepe. *turned under*) Q   18
Humanity] Q *corr.;* Humanly Q *uncorr.,* Q2

11 head-lugged i.e. ill-tempered (because tugged along by the head; compare *1H4* 1.2.74).
12 madded maddened.
13 brother i.e. brother-in-law (= Cornwall).
14 benefited Taylor believes Q uncorr. 'beniflicted' is a mistake for 'benefacted', not the more common and obvious 'benefited', which became the correction ('Four new readings in *King Lear*', *N&Q* 29 (1982), 121–2).
15 visible spirits supernatural beings in visible form: Albany speaks apocalyptically of 'lightning and thunderbolt' (NS).
16 these Q corr. 'this' (from 'thes' = these) may have been intended as a correction for Q uncorr. 'the', but as in the false correction 'ith' (2 above) something has gone awry. Compare Greg, *Variants*, p. 173; *Textual Companion*, p. 520.
16 vilde The old spelling of 'vile', adopted here for the sake of the pun on 'wild', playing off 'tame' (Muir).

17 It will come Either 'It' is a pronoun, with divine retribution as an implied antecedent; or an expletive = it will come to this, that (Gres, *Variants*, p. 173). Although the short, elliptical line induces a pause emphasising Albany's conclusion, the words are in an extremely crowded, turned-over line; the orthography, as well as syntax and metrical irregularity, thus suggests possible textual disruption.
18–19 Humanity . . . deep Greg (*Variants*, p. 173) compares Shakespeare's lines in *Sir Thomas More* 84–7: 'For other ruffians . . . / Would shark on you, and men like revenous fishes / Would feed on one another.' Compare also *Tro.* 1.3.121–4: 'And appetite, an universal wolf / (So doubly seconded with will and power), / Must make perforce an universal prey, / And last eat up himself.' The concept was widespread and can be traced back to Hesiod, *Works and Days*, 1.434–7, and Theodoretus; it appeared also in Renaissance iconography (Muir).

(xviii) After 4.2.36 ('from thy suffering') Q reads:

that not know'st
Fools do those villains pity who are punished
Ere they have done their mischief. Where's thy drum?
France spreads his banners in our noiseless land,

1–4 that . . . land] *Theobald's lineation; lines end* . . . pitty / . . . mischiefe, / . . . land, Q   2 those] Q; these Q2   4
noiseless] Q *corr.,* Q2; noystles Q *uncorr.*

2–3 Fools . . . mischief Compare 1.4.282–4. Gonerill condemns soft-hearted fools who do not see the value of preventive punishment. She appar-   ently refers to Lear, not Gloucester, since it is of her father, who has done no 'mischief' yet, that Albany has been speaking.

With plumèd helm thy flaxen biggin threats,   5
Whilst thou, a moral fool, sits still and cries
'Alack, why does he so?'

5 thy] Q; his *Duthie* (*conj. Greg*)   *5 flaxen] *Oxford;* slayer Q *uncorr.;* slaier Q2; state Q *corr., Jennens*   *5 biggin] *Oxford*
(*conj. Stone*); begin Q *uncorr.;* begins Q *corr.,* Q2, *Jennens*   *5 threats] Q *uncorr.;* thereat Q *corr.;* threats Q2; to threat
Jennens   6 Whilst] Q *corr.;* Whil's Q *uncorr.,* Q2; Whiles *Oxford*

5 **flaxen biggin threats** An unsolved crux for many years; no plausible alternative was found to Jennens's universally accepted emendation, 'state begins to threat', which cannot be defended on the evidence (Greg, *Variants*, p. 174). Stone, p. 184, however proposed 'slyre' (= fine linen or lawn) and 'biggin' (= a cap or hood for the head, a nightcap; sometimes spelled 'begin'), but was uncomfortable with 'slyre', a Scottish word. Taylor ('Addenda' to *Division*, p. 488) then proposed 'flaxen' for Q uncorr. 'slayer' instead of 'slyre' or Q corr.'s 'state'. The emendation, which makes sense and is palaeographically sound, alters Q uncorr. minimally. The comparison between the King of France with his plumèd helm and Albany in his nightcap is deliberately ludicrous. Compare *2H4* 4.5.27.
6 **moral** i.e. moralising.

(xix) After 4.2.38 ('O vain fool!') Q reads:

ALBANY   Thou changèd and self-covered thing, for shame
Be-monster not thy feature. Were't my fitness
To let these hands obey my blood,
They are apt enough to dislocate and tear
Thy flesh and bones. Howe'er thou art a fiend,   5
A woman's shape doth shield thee.
GONERILL   Marry, your manhood! Mew!

Enter a GENTLEMAN

ALBANY   What news?

*4 dislocate] Q3; dislecate Q, Q2   *7 manhood! Mew!] *NS;* manhood – Mew! *Cam.* (*conj. Daniel*); manhood mew—Q
corr.; manhood now—Q *uncorr.;* man-hood now—Q3   7 SD] Q (*after 8*); Messenger F

1 **changèd** transformed, i.e. from woman to monster.
1 **self-covered** hidden from one's true form or self, disguised; i.e. the devil in woman's form. Compare 5–6 below.
2 **Be-monster . . . feature** i.e. don't make your appearance hideous (by revealing your true nature). Gonerill's features, distorted with anger and contempt, make her look diabolical.
2 **Were't my fitness** If it were fitting for me (as a man).
3 **blood** emotion, passion.
4 **apt** ready.
4–5 **dislocate . . . bones** An example of chiasmus, the rhetorical figure in which the order of words in one of two parallel elements is inverted in the other. 'Albany maddens at the terrible impulses crowding him' (Rosenberg, p. 255).
5 **Howe'er** However much, although.
7 **Marry . . . Mew** Greg does not doubt the correctness of Q corr.'s 'excellent emendation' (*Variants*, p. 175); Stone does (p. 213). Both Q uncorr. and Q corr. make sense, differing only in the degree of contempt Gonerill expresses. Q corr. is stronger, consistent with Q's version of Gonerill; moreover, why would the corrector alter Q uncorr. if 'mew' were not a bona fide correction from copy?
7 **Marry** An oath, literally 'By the Virgin Mary!'
7 **Mew** Imitating mockingly the sound of a cat. Compare *1H4* 3.1.127.

(xx) After 4.2, Q adds a scene:

Enter KENT *and a* GENTLEMAN

KENT   Why the King of France is so suddenly gone back, know you no reason?
GENTLEMAN   Something he left imperfect in the state which since his coming forth
is thought of, which imports to the kingdom so much fear and danger that his
personal return was most required and necessary.
KENT   Who hath he left behind him general?   5
GENTLEMAN   The Marshal of France, Monsieur La Far.
KENT   Did your letters pierce the queen to any demonstration of grief?
GENTLEMAN   Ay, sir. She took them, read them in my presence,
   And now and then an ample tear trilled down
   Her delicate cheek. It seemed she was a queen   10
   Over her passion, who most rebel-like
   Sought to be king o'er her.
KENT   O, then it moved her?
GENTLEMAN   Not to a rage. Patience and sorrow strove
   Who should express her goodliest. You have seen
   Sunshine and rain at once; her smiles and tears   15
   Were like a better way; those happy smilets
   That played on her ripe lip seemed not to know
   What guests were in her eyes; which parted thence
   As pearls from diamonds dropped. In brief,
   Sorrow would be a rarity most beloved   20
   If all could so become it.

1 no] Q; the Q2   *1 reason?] Q2; reason. Q   *5 him general?] *Theobald;* him, General. Q; him, Generall? Q2   *8 Ay, sir] *Johnson;* I, sir *Theobald;* I say Q   10–12 Her . . . o'er her] *Pope's lineation; lines divided* . . . passion, / Who Q   *13 strove] *Pope;* streme Q   *15 Sunshine] Sun-shine Q2; Sun shine Q   *17 seemed] *Pope;* seeme Q   *18 eyes;] eyes, Q2; eyes Q   *19 dropped.] dropt; Q2; dropt Q

0 SD GENTLEMAN Apparently the same Gentleman that Kent spoke to in 3.1. See 3.1.0 SD n.
   1 gone back Steevens (cited by Furness) aptly
explains why, in view of his different ending, Shakespeare decided to return the king to France rather
than have him present at the battle, as in *King
Leir.* Eliminating references to his arrival in the first
place obviates the need to send him back later.
   3 imports carries with it, involves as a consequence (Onions).
   6 The . . . La Far Pope emended Q 'Marshall' to 'Mareschal', making the word trisyllabic so
that the line scanned as blank verse. Steevens, who
spelled the name 'le Fer', thought Shakespeare had
an impoverished French nomenclature, because the
Marshal bears the same name as the common soldier, 'M. Fer', who was *fer'd, ferreted,* and *ferk'd'*
by Pistol in *H5* 4.4.26–31.
   7 your letters Compare 3.1.10–20.
   9 trilled trickled. Compare Cotgrave,
'*Transcouler,* To glide, slide . . . trill, or trickle'
(Wright, cited by Furness).
   11 who The pronoun personifies 'passion'.

13 rage violent outburst of grief (Kittredge).
   13 strove See collation: *o/e, u/m* misreading.
   15 Sunshine . . . tears Proverbial (Tilley L92a).
Compare *R2* 3.2.9–10 and Sidney's *Arcadia,* Bk III,
ch. 5: 'Her tears came dropping down like rain in
sunshine' (Steevens, cited by Furness).
   16 a better way i.e. of expressing conflicting
attitudes. For various interpretations and emendations, compare Furness, Duthie, pp. 408–9, Hunter.
   16 smilets little smiles.
   18 which i.e. the 'guests' (= tears).
   19 As . . . dropped Shakespeare often refers to
tears as pearls, as in *Lucrece,* 1213 ('And wip'd the
brinish pearl from her bright eyes'; compare *ibid.,*
1548–53) and *TGV* 3.1.226 ('A sea of melting pearl,
which some call tears'); eyes as 'diamonds' is a rarer
image (compare *Wiv.* 3.3.55). The elegant simile is
appropriate to a courtier (Kittredge).
   20 rarity something excellent, precious; compare Sonnet 60.11.
   21 If . . . it i.e. if everyone could make it so
attractive.

KENT Made she no verbal question?
GENTLEMAN Faith, once or twice she heaved the name of father
          Pantingly forth, as if it pressed her heart;
          Cried 'Sisters, sisters! Shame of ladies! Sisters!   25
          Kent! Father! Sisters! What, i'th'storm? i'th'night?
          Let pity not be believed!' There she shook
          The holy water from her heavenly eyes,
          And clamour moistened. Then away she started
          To deal with grief alone.
KENT   It is the stars,   30
          The stars above us, govern our conditions,
          Else one self mate and make could not beget
          Such different issues. You spoke not with her since?
GENTLEMAN No.
KENT Was this before the king returned?
GENTLEMAN   No, since.   35
KENT Well, sir, the poor distressèd Lear's i'th'town,
          Who sometime in his better tune remembers
          What we are come about and by no means
          Will yield to see his daughter.
GENTLEMAN   Why, good sir?
KENT A sovereign shame so elbows him: his own unkindness   40
          That stripped her from his benediction, turned her
          To foreign casualties, gave her dear rights
          To his dog-hearted daughters – these things sting

---

*27 pity . . . believed] pitie . . . beleeft Q; pitty . . . beleeu'd Q2; pity ne'er believe it *Pope;* piety not be believed
Oxford *29 moistened] *Capell;* moystened her Q; mastered *Oxford (conj. Stone)* *30–1 It . . . conditions] *Theobald's
lineation; one line* Q *38–9 What . . . daughter] *Pope's lineation; one line* (daughter *turned under*) Q *43–5 To . . .
Cordelia] *Johnson's lineation; lines divided* . . . mind, / So Q

22 Made . . . question Did she not say anything?
22 question speech.
23 Faith In faith.
27 Let . . . believed Either (1) let (it for) pity not be believed (Harbage), or (2) let pity not be believed (to exist) (Steevens, cited by Furness). See collation. The accidental indentation of the line in Q suggests that a letter has dropped out. Blayney conjectures 'Lest' but recognises that an inkball could not pull out a long *s* from a long *s/t* ligature. Oxford emends 'pity' to 'piety' (*Textual Companion*, p. 521). Perhaps Q 'not beleeft' contains a contraction (= not believe it) and an excrescent 'be' was added in proof (NS: J. D. Wilson).
29 clamour moistened i.e. moistened her outcries with tears ('holy water'), thus silencing them. Compare *2H4* 4.5.138–9: 'my tears, / The moist impediments unto my speech'. Warburton (cited by Furness) proposed hyphenating 'clamour-moistened', putting it in apposition with 'heavenly'. Oxford adopts Stone's conjecture, 'mastered' (= overcame; presumably spelled 'maystered' in

copy). Q's 'her' is metrically superfluous, probably attracted from the line above. (See Duthie, p. 409; Stone, p. 184; *Textual Companion*, p. 521.)
29–30 Then . . . alone Compare Gen. 43.30, Joseph's dealing with grief alone (Theobald, cited by Furness).
30–1 It is . . . conditions Compare Edmond's opposing view (1.2.104–16).
31 conditions dispositions, characters. Compare *MV* 1.2.129.
32 Else . . . and make Otherwise one and the same husband and wife ('make').
37 sometime sometimes.
37 in . . . tune i.e. when his wits are together; compare 4.6.16.
40 sovereign all-powerful.
40 elbows him Either (1) jostles, thrusts him back, or (2) stands beside him remindingly; haunts (compare *R3* 1.4.145).
42 foreign casualties accidents, chances abroad.
43 dog-hearted pitiless; compare *TGV* 2.3.10–11.

His mind so venomously that burning shame
Detains him from Cordelia.   45
GENTLEMAN Alack, poor gentleman!
KENT Of Albany's and Cornwall's powers you heard not?
GENTLEMAN 'Tis so. They are afoot.
KENT Well, sir, I'll bring you to our master, Lear,
And leave you to attend him. Some dear cause   50
Will in concealment wrap me up awhile.
When I am known aright, you shall not grieve
Lending me this acquaintance. I pray you, go
Along with me.

Exeunt

47 not?] Q2; not. Q   *53–4 Lending . . . me] *Jennens's lineation; one line* Q   *54 SD *Exeunt*] *Pope; Exit* Q

47 **powers** armies.
48 **afoot** on the march.
50 **dear cause** important business (we are never
told what, but compare 4.6.9–11).

52–3 **When . . . acquaintance** Compare 3.1.23–
8.
52 **aright** rightly, as myself.

(xxi) After 4.6.25 Q reads:

CORDELIA   Very well.
DOCTOR Please you, draw near. – Louder the music there!

(xxii) After 4.6.32 Q reads:

To stand against the deep dread-bolted thunder?
In the most terrible and nimble stroke
Of quick cross lightning? to watch, poor perdu,
With this thin helm?

1 dread-bolted] *Hyphenated Theobald*   *3 lightning?] *Theobald;* lightning Q; lightning, Q2   *3 watch,] *Warburton;*
watch Q   *4 helm?] Q2; helm Q

1 **deep** Either (1) deeply dreaded, or (2) deep-
toned, bass.
1 **dread-bolted thunder** thunder, armed or
equipped ('bolted') with dread, i.e. thunderbolts
conveying dread.
3 **cross** zigzag.

3 **watch** (1) stand guard, (2) go without sleep.
3 **perdu** (1) a sentry in an advanced and dangerous position, (2) a castaway, lost one.
4 **thin helm** (1) meagre helmet, (2) scant hair,
(3) bare head; probably (3).

(xxiii) After 4.6.78 ('You see is killed in him') Q reads:

and yet it is danger
To make him even o'er the time he has lost.

1–2 and . . . lost] *Theobald's lineation; as prose* Q

2 **even o'er** balance up, fill up and smooth over;
i.e. it is dangerous to make him account for what
he has gone through.

(xxiv) After 4.6.82 Q reads:

GENTLEMAN Holds it true, sir, that the Duke of Cornwall was so slain?
KENT Most certain, sir.
GENTLEMAN Who is conductor of his people?
KENT As 'tis said, the bastard son of Gloucester.
GENTLEMAN They say Edgar, his banished son, is with the Earl of Kent in   5
  Germany.
KENT Report is changeable. 'Tis time to look about. The powers of the kingdom
  approach apace.
GENTLEMAN The arbitrement is like to be bloody. Fare you well, sir.   [*Exit*]
KENT My point and period will be throughly wrought   10
  Or well or ill as this day's battle's fought.   *Exit*

7–8 Report . . . apace] *As prose, Theobald; two verse lines divided . . . about, / The* Q   *9 SD Exit] *After Theobald; not in* Q

1 **Holds it true** Is it confirmed?
7 **Report is changeable** Hence, the Gentle-man's question earlier, 1.
7 **look about** be alert.
9 **arbitrement** decisive action.
10–11 **My point . . . fought** 'The completion

of my lot in life will be worked out, for good or ill, according as this battle results in victory or defeat' (Kittredge).
10 **point** object, purpose; compare *Mac.* 3.1.86.
10 **period** full stop, end.
10 **throughly** thoroughly.

(xxv) After 5.1.11 ('To the forfended place') Q reads:

EDMOND   That thought abuses you.
REGAN I am doubtful that you have been conjunct
  And bosomed with her, as far as we call hers.

2–3 I . . . hers] Q2 *lineation; as prose* Q

1 **abuses** dishonours.
2 **doubtful** suspicious.
2 **conjunct** (1) united, closely joined, (2) con-spiring (King).

3 **bosomed** (1) close, (2) sexually intimate.
3 **as far . . . hers** i.e. to the fullest extent, all the way.

(xxvi) After 5.1.14 SD Q reads:

GONERILL [*Aside*] I had rather lose the battle than that sister
  Should loosen him and me.

1 SD Aside] *Theobald; not in* Q   1–2 I . . . me] *Theobald's lineation; as prose* Q; *two lines divided . . . battell / Then* Q2   *1 lose] *Theobald;* loose Q, Q2

1–2 **lose . . . loosen** Gonerill's word-play heightens the antithesis.

(xxvii) After 5.1.18 ('Forced to cry out') Q reads:

> Where I could not be honest,
> I never yet was valiant. For this business,
> It touches us as France invades our land,
> Not bolds the king with others whom I fear
> Most just and heavy causes make oppose.   5
> EDMOND Sir, you speak nobly.

*4 king] King, Q   *4 fear] *Duthie;* feare, Q; fear. *Oxford*

1 be honest be honourable, act with good conscience (Kittredge).
2 For As for.
3 touches concerns, affects.
3 France i.e. the King of France.
4 bolds emboldens, encourages (compare Abbott 290).
4 with along with.
5 Most . . . oppose i.e. very justified and serious reasons motivate them to fight. Oxford places a period after 'fear', making this line a separate sentence and changing the sense to suggest 'just and heavy causes' on both sides. Muir notes that 'with others whom' occurs also at 5.1.17 and the line restates the earlier point; he suspects the passage may be corrupt.
6 nobly Edmond is sarcastic (NS).

(xxviii) After 5.1.23 ('On our proceeding') Q reads:

> EDMOND I shall attend you presently at your tent.

1 I . . . tent Stone, p. 237, suspects the line was inadvertently dropped from F by a copyist or compositor.

(xxix) After 5.3.35 ('Or thrive by other means.') Q reads:

> CAPTAIN I cannot draw a cart nor eat dried oats;
> If it be man's work, I'll do it.

1 I . . . oats i.e. I'm not a horse (or other animal).

(xxx) After 5.3.53 ('hold your session') Q reads:

> At this time
> We sweat and bleed. The friend hath lost his friend,
> And the best quarrels in the heat are cursed

1–4 At . . . sharpness] *Theobald's lineation; three lines ending . . . bleed, / . . . quarrels / . . . sharpnes,* Q   2 We] Q *corr.,* Q2; *mee* Q *uncorr.*

1–6 At . . . place Edmond's hypocrisy is patent: he pretends to safeguard Lear and Cordelia until they can get a fair trial, but in reality he is stalling to give the Captain time to fulfil his orders. The lines motivate Albany's censure of Edmond's presumptuousness perhaps better than those retained in F, which focus rather on Edmond's authority to deal with the prisoners. (Compare Urkowitz, p. 107; Stone, p. 238.)
3 quarrels causes.
3 in the heat i.e. of passion engendered by battle.

By those that feel their sharpness.
The question of Cordelia and her father
Requires a fitter place.   5

4 sharpness] Q *corr.*, Q2; sharpes Q *uncorr.*

4 **sharpness** severity, harshness (Schmidt). See collation. Q corr. may follow copy; but Stone (p. 213), NS, and Greg (*Variants*, p. 179) suspect that the press-corrector thought an *n* was missing and wrongly altered Q uncorr. 'sharpes' (= sharp edges, points; *OED* Sharp *sb*¹ 2).
6 **fitter place** i.e. not the battlefield.

(xxxi) After 5.3.195 Q reads:

EDGAR   This would have seemed a period
To such as love not sorrow; but another
To amplify too much would make much more
And top extremity.
Whilst I was big in clamour, came there in a man   5
Who, having seen me in my worst estate,
Shunned my abhorred society. But then, finding
Who 'twas that so endured, with his strong arms
He fastened on my neck and bellowed out
As he'd burst heaven; threw him on my father;   10
Told the most piteous tale of Lear and him
That ever ear received; which in recounting
His grief grew puissant and the strings of life
Began to crack. Twice then the trumpets sounded,
And there I left him tranced.
ALBANY   But who was this?   15
EDGAR Kent, sir, the banished Kent, who in disguise
Followed his enemy king and did him service
Improper for a slave.

1–4 This . . . extremity] *Theobald's lineation; three lines ending* . . . such / . . . much, / . . . extreamitie Q   *10 him] *Theobald; me Q   11 Told the most] Q; And told the Q2   *14 crack. Twice] *Theobald; cracke twice, Q

1 **period** (1) climax, (2) full stop.
2–4 **another . . . extremity** To describe in detail another (tale of sorrow) would add a great deal more (to what I have already told) and exceed the furthest limit (of what is bearable). Compare Furness and *Textual Companion*, p. 526. Edgar, nevertheless, proceeds with Kent's story.
5 **big** i.e. loud.
5 **clamour** lamentation; compare xx.29 above.
6 **estate** condition.
10 **As** As if.
10 **him** himself.
13 **puissant** strong, powerful.
13 **strings of life** i.e. his heartstrings; compare *R3* 4.4.365.
15 **tranced** in a faint or trance.
17 **enemy king** Compare 1.1.167–73.
18 **Improper** Unfitting.

READING LIST

This list includes a selection of books and articles referred to in the Introduction or Commentary along with several additional items that may serve as a guide to those who wish to undertake further study of the play.

Berlin, Normand. *The Secret Cause: A Discussion of Tragedy*, 1981
Bevington, David. *Shakespeare*, 2002
Blayney, Peter W. M. *The Texts of 'King Lear' and Their Origins*, 1982
Bloom, Harold. *Shakespeare: The Invention of the Human*, 1998
Booth, Stephen, *'King Lear', 'Macbeth', Indefinition, and Tragedy*, 1983
Bradley, A. C. *Shakespearean Tragedy*, 2nd edn, 1905
Brockbank, Philip. *'Upon Such Sacrifices'*, The British Academy Shakespeare Lecture, 1976
Brown, John Russell. *Shakespeare: The Tragedies*, 2001
Bruce, Susan. *William Shakespeare: 'King Lear'*, 1998
Carlisle, Carol Jones. *Shakespeare from the Greenroom*, 1969
Cavell, Stanley. *Must We Mean What We Say?*, 1969
Clayton, Thomas. 'Old light on the text of *King Lear*', *MP* 78 (1981), 347–67
Cohen, Derek. *Shakespearean Motives*, 1988
Colie, Rosalie L. and F. T. Flahiff (eds.). *Some Facets of 'King Lear': Essays in Prismatic Criticism*, 1974
Colman, E. A. M. *The Dramatic Use of Bawdy in Shakespeare*, 1974
Cox, Brian. *The Lear Diaries*, 1992
Danby, John F. *Shakespeare's Doctrine of Nature*, 1948, reprinted 1961
Davies, Oliver Ford. *Playing Lear*, 2003
Dollimore, Jonathan. *Radical Tragedy: Religion, Ideology and Power in the Drama of Shakespeare and his Contemporaries*, 1984; 2nd edn, 1989
Doran, Madeleine. *Shakespeare's Dramatic Language*, 1976
    The Text of 'King Lear', 1931, reprinted 1967
Elton, William. *'King Lear' and the Gods*, 1966, 2nd edn, 1988
Foakes, R. A. *Hamlet versus Lear: Cultural Politics and Shakespeare's Art*, 1993
Fortin, René. 'Hermeneutical circularity and Christian interpretations of *King Lear*', in *Gaining upon Certainty: Selected Criticism*, 1995, pp. 125–38
Fraser, Russell A. *Shakespeare's Poetics in Relation to 'King Lear'*, 1962
Gardner, Helen. *King Lear*, 1967
Greenblatt, Stephen. 'Shakespeare and the Exorcists', in *Shakespearean Negotiations*, 1988
    Will in the World, 2004

Greg, W. W. *The Editorial Problem in Shakespeare*, 1942
 The Shakespeare First Folio: Its Bibliographical and Textual History, 1955
 The Variants in the First Quarto of 'King Lear', 1940
Halio, Jay L. (ed.). *Critical Essays on Shakespeare's 'King Lear'*, 1996
Hamilton, Donna. 'Some romance sources for *King Lear*: Robert of Sicily and Robert the Devil', *SP* 71 (1966), 345–59
Hawkes, Terence. *William Shakespeare: King Lear*, 1995
Heilman, Robert. *This Great Stage: Image and Structure in 'King Lear'*, 1948, reprinted 1963
Hoeniger, F. D. *Medicine and Shakespeare in the English Renaissance*, 1992
Holland, Norman N. *The Shakespearean Imagination*, 1964
Holland, Peter (ed.). '*King Lear*' and its *Afterlife*, *S.Sur.* 55, 2002
Honigmann, E. A. J. *Myriad-Minded Shakespeare*, 1989
 'Shakespeare's revised plays: *King Lear* and *Othello*', *The Library*, 6th ser., 4 (1982), 142–73
 The Stability of Shakespeare's Text, 1965
Howard-Hill, Trevor. 'The problem of manuscript copy for Folio *King Lear*', *The Library*, 6th ser., 4 (1982), 1–24
Ioppolo, Grace. *Revising Shakespeare*, 1991
Ioppolo, Grace (ed.). *Shakespeare Performed: Essays in Honor of R. A. Foakes*, 2000
James, D. G. *The Dream of Learning: An Essay on 'The Advancement of Learning', 'Hamlet', and 'King Lear'*, 1951
Jorgensen, Paul A. *Lear's Self-Discovery*, 1967
Kinney, Arthur F. 'Some Conjectures on the Composition of *King Lear*', *S.Sur.* 33 (1980), 13–25
Knight, G. Wilson. *The Wheel of Fire*, 4th edn, 1960
Knights, L. C. *Some Shakespearean Themes*, 1960
Kozinstev, Grigori. '*King Lear*': *The Space of Tragedy*, trans. Mary Mackintosh, 1977
Leggatt, Alexander. *King Lear*, Harvester New Critical Introductions, 1988
 Shakespeare in Performance: 'King Lear', 1991
 'Two Lears: notes for an actor', in Lois Potter and Arthur F. Kinney (eds.), *Shakespeare: Text and Theater: Essays in Honor of Jay L. Halio*, 1999, pp. 310–19
Levenson, Jill. 'What the silence said: still points in *King Lear*', in Clifford Leech and J. M. R. Margeson (eds.), *Shakespeare 1971*, 1972, pp. 215–29
Lusardi, James, and June Schlueter. *Reading Shakespeare in Performance: 'King Lear'*, 1991
Mack, Maynard. '*King Lear' in Our Time*, 1965
Maguire, Laurie E. and Thomas L. Berger (eds.). *Textual Formations and Reformations*, 1998
McAlindon, T. *Shakespeare's Tragic Cosmos*, 1991
McElroy, Bernard. *Shakespeare's Mature Tragedies*, 1973
Meagher, John C. 'Vanity, Lear's feather, and the pathology of editorial annotation', in Clifford Leech and J. M. R. Margeson (eds.), *Shakespeare 1971*, 1972, pp. 244–59

Muir, Kenneth. *'King Lear': A Critical Study*, 1986
Nevo, Ruth. *Tragic Form in Shakespeare*, 1972
Noble, Richmond. *Shakespeare's Biblical Knowledge*, 1935
Ogden, James, and Arthur H. Scouten (eds.). *'Lear' from Study to Stage*, 1997
Peat, Derek. "'And that's true too": *King Lear* and the tension of uncertainty', *S.Sur.* 33 (1980), 43–53
Perrett, Wilfrid. *The King Lear Story from Geoffrey of Monmouth to Shakespeare*, Berlin, 1904
Reibetanz, John. *The Lear World*, 1977
Ringler, William A. Jr. 'Shakespeare and his actors: some remarks on *King Lear*', in *Shakespeare's Art from a Comparative Perspective*, ed. Wendell M. Aycock, 1981, pp. 187–93
Rosenberg, Marvin. *The Masks of King Lear*, 1972, reprinted, 1992
Rothwell, Kenneth S. *A History of Shakespeare on Screen: A Century of Film and Television*, 1999
Ryan, Kiernan (ed.). *King Lear*. New Casebooks, 1992
    '*King Lear*: a retrospect, 1980–2000', *S.Sur.* 55 (2002), 1–11
Salingar, Leo. *Dramatic Form in Shakespeare and the Jacobeans*, 1986
Shaheen, Naseeb. *Biblical References in Shakespeare's Tragedies*, 1987
Snyder, Susan. *The Comic Matrix of Shakespeare's Tragedies*, 1979
    Shakespeare: A Wayward Journey, 2000
Speaight, Robert. *Shakespeare on the Stage: An Illustrated History of Shakespearian Performance*, 1973
Spurgeon, Caroline. *Shakespeare's Imagery and What It Tells Us*, 1935
Stampfer, Judah. 'The catharsis of *King Lear*', *S.Sur.* 13 (1960), 1–10
Stockholder, Katherine. 'The multiple genres of *King Lear*: breaking the archetypes', *Bucknell Review* 16 (1968), 40–63
Stone, P. W. K. *The Textual History of 'King Lear'*, 1980
Taylor, Gary 'A new source and an old date for *King Lear*', *RES* 132 (1982), 396–413
    'Revolutions of perspective: *King Lear*', in *Moment by Moment by Shakespeare*, 1985, pp. 162–260
    'The war in *King Lear*', *S.Sur.* 33 (1980), 27–34
Taylor, Gary, and Michael Warren (eds.). *The Division of the Kingdoms: Shakespeare's Two Versions of 'King Lear'*, 1983
Urkowitz, Stephen. *Shakespeare's Revision of 'King Lear'*, 1980
Warren, Michael. 'Quarto and Folio *King Lear* and the interpretation of Albany and Edgar', in David Bevington and Jay L. Halio (eds.), *Shakespeare: Pattern of Excelling Nature*, 1978, pp. 95–107
Warren, Michael (ed.). *The Complete 'King Lear', 1608–1623*, 1989
Wells, Stanley. *Shakespeare: A Life in Drama*, 1995
Wells, Stanley, and Gary Taylor, with John Jowett and William Montgomery. *Shakespeare: A Textual Companion*, 1987
Welsford, Enid. *The Fool: His Social and Literary History*, 1935

Whitaker, Virgil. *The Mirror Up to Nature: The Technique of Shakespeare's Tragedies*, 1965

Wiles, David. *Shakespeare's Clown*, 1987

Wittreich, Joseph. *'Image of that Horror': History, Prophecy, and Apocalypse in 'King Lear'*, 1984

Wood, Michael. *In Search of Shakespeare*, 2003